INTERNATIONAL ACCOUNTING

A Global Perspective

Second Edition

M. Zafar Iqbal

California Polytechnic State University

SOUTH-WESTERN
™
THOMSON LEARNING

Australia · Canada · Mexico · Singapore · Spain · United Kingdom · United States

International Accounting: A Global Perspective, 2e by M. Zafar Iqbal

Acquisitions Editor: Scott Person
Developmental Editor: Carol Bennett
Marketing Manager: Dan Silverburg
Production Editor: Heather Mann
Media Developmental Editor: Sally Nieman
Media Production Editor: Lora Craver
Manufacturing Coordinator: Doug Wilke
Cover Design: Rik Moore
Production House: Cover to Cover Publishing, Inc.
Printer: Quebecor World

Printed in the United States of America
1 2 3 4 5   04 03 02 01

For more information contact South-Western, 5101 Madison Road, Cincinnati, Ohio, 45227 or find us on the Internet at http://www.swcollege.com.
For permission to use material from this text or product, contact us by
- telephone: 1-800-730-2214
- fax: 1-800-730-2215
- web: http://www.thomsonrights.com

Library of Congress Cataloging-in-Publication Data

Iqbal, M. Zafar.
    International accounting : a global perspective / M. Zafar Iqbal.--2nd ed.
        p. cm.
    Includes bibliographical references and index.
    ISBN 0-324-02350-2
        1. Accounting--Standards. 2. Financial statements--Standards.
    3. Comparative accounting. 4. International business enterprises--Accounting.
    I. Title.

HF5626 .I66 2001
657'.96--dc21

                                                                        2001032288

Preface

International Accounting: A Global Perspective focuses on the issues in international accounting in today's global economy. The text offers a unique approach: It has a global perspective, is free from any cultural bias, and has a multinational orientation. This enhances objective discussion of international accounting issues.

This 2nd edition is a current and comprehensive text for an upper-division undergraduate course or a graduate-level course. With its global orientation, it is suitable for adoption worldwide. The second edition is completely rewritten to streamline presentation of the material. Many numerical examples have been added within the chapter texts. End-of-chapter problems and cases have been greatly expanded.

FEATURES OF THE TEXT

The textbook contents are current and include a description of emerging trends in international accounting. Students and faculty should find the text lucid, succinct, and accurate. Some of the special features are outlined below.

Global perspective. The book has a truly global perspective. The author feels that an international accounting textbook should be free from any country, regional, or cultural bias.

Currency of contents. The material is up to date and includes the most recent developments in international accounting. Some examples are:

- World Trade Organization
- Restructuring of the IASC
- Inclusion of Internet-based material
- European Monetary Union
- Technology alliances
- Modern approaches to cost management in global operations
- Expanded discussion of cultural influence

Clear writing style.   Discussion is substantive yet succinct. Presentations are organized to lead the student from basic to advanced levels step by step. Key points are emphasized after the discussion.

Real-life applications of concepts.   Actual events are brought into discussion to reinforce students' understanding of the concepts. Numerous examples and financial statements from actual companies are incorporated in each of the chapters.

Comparative practices in selected countries.   The same five countries, from different regions of the world, are used for comparison of practices. This provides the students an opportunity to learn the important similarities and differences in accounting and auditing practices in those countries.

Impact of advances in technology.   Among the unique features of this book is a discussion of how advancements in information technology affect the development of global information systems, environmental factors, and worldwide accounting practices.

End-of-chapter materials.   These include:

- **Note to Students.** This innovative and unique feature will help the student keep current on the chapter topics by using listed sources of information, including websites.
- **Chapter Summary.**
- **Questions for Discussion.**
- **Exercises/Problems.**
- **Cases.** Most of the chapters have at least one end-of-chapter case and several have more than one.
- **Critical Thinking Problems.**
- **Footnotes and References.** This text includes extensive footnotes and chapter bibliographies. This should be helpful for several reasons:
  - Many undergraduate students are only vaguely aware of international accounting literature. Simply scanning these listings should increase their awareness of the content of international accounting and international business.
  - The text is intended for use in graduate as well as undergraduate courses. The references will help in pursuing the topics in greater depth, especially in graduate courses.
  - Some instructors may not have significant international experience but are interested in teaching the international accounting course. Additional readings will help them feel comfortable in the classroom, and also help them broaden their own knowledge base.

The references include classic materials such as Sweeney's dissertation on general price-level-adjusted accounting, statements by standard-setting bodies such as the International Accounting Standards Committee and the Financial Accounting Standards Board, and current developments from sources such as *Business Week*, *The Wall Street Journal*, and *The Economist*.

CHAPTER DESCRIPTIONS

Chapter 1: Introduction to International Accounting. Chapter 1 lays the foundation of the text by discussing the importance of the global economy. The chapter develops a definition of international accounting.

Chapter 2: Foreign Currency. Chapter 2 discusses foreign currency transactions, forward exchange contracts, and common methods for foreign currency translation. The four common translation methods are analyzed and compared.

Chapter 3: Accounting for Changing Prices. Chapter 3 deals with issues from both accounting and economic standpoints. The chapter contains a discussion and examples of constant monetary unit restatement and current value accounting. Gearing adjustments are explained within the context of current value accounting.

Chapter 4: Cultural Influences on Accounting. Chapter 4 is new to the second edition. It develops a model of cultural influences on accounting.

Chapter 5: Accounting Measurement and Disclosures. Chapter 5 examines the issues related to measurement and disclosure. The chapter includes discussion of reserves disclosures, segment disclosures, and social impact disclosures. Examples of value-added statements from actual companies are provided in the chapter.

Chapter 6: Worldwide Disclosure Diversity and Harmonization. Chapter 6 contains a discussion of the differences between standardization and harmonization. It reviews the harmonization efforts being undertaken at various levels in the world.

Chapter 7: International Financial Statement Analysis. Chapter 7 contains a section dealing with problems in the availability of financial information, such as reliability of data, timeliness, language and terminology, different currencies, and different formats of financial statements. Financial statement analysis is divided into international financial ratio analysis and trend analysis. Limitations of analysis are also discussed.

Chapter 8: Strategic Planning and Control. Chapter 8 is the first of the three chapters on managerial accounting topics. The chapter covers strategic planning with special attention to cultural considerations. Control systems are discussed with added emphasis given to the selection of performance criteria for international subsidiaries. The last section ties in information systems, technological advances, and compatibility with international accounting standards.

Chapter 9: Budgeting, Risk Management, and Cost Management.

Chapter 9 includes discussion of issues encountered by multinational companies in the development of a master budget and a discussion of capital budgeting. Product costing and cost management approaches are described. Cost management approaches discussed include restructuring, activity-based costing, activity-based management, total quality management, just-in-time, kaizen, target costing, worldwide manufacturing locations, and outsourcing. Risk management is discussed within the context of economic risk exposure and political risk exposure.

Chapter 10: Transfer Pricing and International Taxation.

Chapter 10 discusses various approaches for transfer pricing and also examines international taxation issues.

Chapter 11: Auditing Issues for Global Operations.

Chapter 11 deals with auditing in its two dimensions: internal and external. Six models of an internal audit organization structure are presented. The chapter also includes a discussion of the Foreign Corrupt Practices Act. External auditing in the international environment is discussed within the framework of various countries and regions. "True and fair view" is contrasted with "present fairly." The chapter includes a description of the existing independent audit environments in the featured five countries.

Chapter 12: The Emerging World Economies.

Chapter 12 describes both the challenges and the opportunities in developing countries. Special emphasis is placed on the importance of the role of accounting in developing countries, especially due to large expenditures on infrastructure projects.

SUPPLEMENTS

The comprehensive package includes three supplements: a *Solutions Manual* and a combination *Test Bank* and *Instructor's Manual*, all written by the textbook author. The *Instructor's Manual* should be especially helpful to instructors with little or no teaching or practical international experience. It contains many helpful hints and side comments, as well as detailed chapter outlines and teaching transparency masters. The *Test Bank* is available both in hard copy and computerized form.

It is vital that supplements receive as much attention as the text itself. For example, a solutions manual full of errors can greatly reduce the usefulness of a first-rate textbook. Since the author of the textbook has written the supplements, the accuracy and cohesiveness of the package is ensured.

Ignite discussions, augment, and research in lectures with the latest developments in accounting. InfoTrac College Edition (packaged free with this text) gives students four month's free access to an easy-to-use online database of reliable, full-length articles (not abstracts) from hundreds of top academic journals and popular sources, including *The Journal of Accountancy*, *Management Accounting*, *Tax Adviser*, and *National Tax Journal*. This is exclusive to South-Western/Thomson Learning and available to North American college and university students only. Journals are subject to change.

ACKNOWLEDGMENTS

Many individuals provided assistance and feedback throughout the writing and development stages of this text.

Appreciation and gratitude are due to Dave Shaut, Scott Person, and Dick Thiel at South-Western/Thomson Learning. It has been a pleasure working with them. Their assistance and guidance were invaluable in bringing the project to its successful culmination. Their professionalism is exemplary.

My wife Patrice Iqbal played a critical role in the development of this book. Her hard work and long hours made a notable difference in the quality of this book. She deserves special thanks and acknowledgment.

The author would like to recognize the excellent contribution of Charles You, Purdue University, verifier of the Solutions Manual. A special thanks should be given to the production house, Cover to Cover, for their diligent attention to detail.

The author gratefully acknowledges the valuable reviews, critiques, and comments from the following persons.

Ajay Adhikari, *American University*

Charles A. Tritschler, *Purdue University*

Marc Massoud, *Claremont McKenna College*

Thomas M. McGhee, *Savannah State University*

Reza Mazhin, *California State University—Dominguez*

M. Zafar Iqbal

Brief Contents

Contents

part two   INTERNATIONAL FINANCIAL REPORTING TECHNICAL TOPICS   *31*

chapter 2   Foreign Currency   *33*

chapter 5   Accounting Measurement and Disclosures   *141*

chapter 6   Worldwide Disclosures Diversity and Harmonization   *189*

chapter 9 Budgeting, Risk Management, and Cost Management 325

chapter 10   Transfer Pricing and International Taxation   *377*

part six   INTERNATIONAL AUDITING AND EMERGING ISSUES   *421*

chapter 11   Auditing Issues for Global Operations   *423*

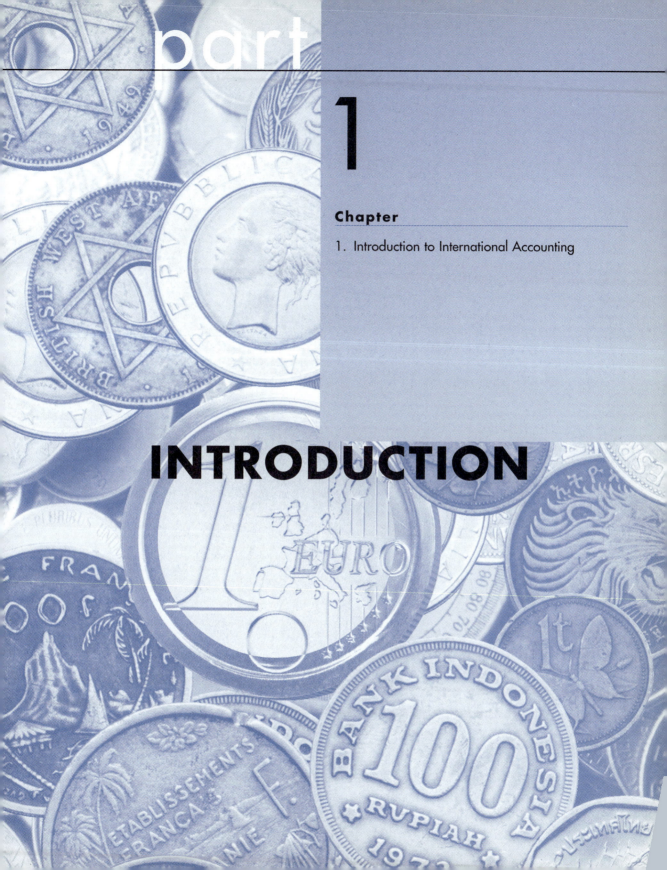

Chapter

1. Introduction to International Accounting

INTRODUCTION

chapter

1

Introduction to International Accounting

learning objectives

After reading this chapter, you should be able to:

1. Discuss the nature of international accounting.

2. Describe globalization, including factors that have accelerated globalization phenomenon.

3. Identify the reasons for a business's involvement in international trade and investment.

4. Compare the types of international involvement.

5. Identify the reasons for economic importance in the Asia-Pacific Rim region.

6. Show how the two developments described in the chapter have created new challenges for international accounting.

7. Compare the philosophy of the World Trade Organization (WTO) with its functions.

8. Identify the major issues facing the WTO.

9. Examine the problem of growing economic disparity within the context of globalization.

Accounting provides information that can be used in making economic decisions. It is a service activity and exists only to serve decision makers. The decision makers use both qualitative and quantitative information from various sources. Accounting provides quantitative information that is primarily financial in nature.[1]

Perhaps the most familiar form of an economic entity is a business organization. In order for the accountant to meet the information needs of decision makers, the information provided should aid in making "reasoned" choices among alternative uses of scarce resources in the conduct of business and economic activities.[2] The linkage between decision makers and accounting is shown in Figure 1.1. It shows the communication of accounting information to the decision makers. This information is provided by the accountant in the form of reports—the final output of an accounting system. The reports are based on the data from economic activities and events of the entity.

Definition of International Accounting

International accounting is defined as *accounting for international transactions, comparisons of accounting principles in different countries, harmonization of diverse accounting standards worldwide, and accounting information for the management and control of global operations.* This definition encompasses financial, managerial, tax, auditing, and other areas of accounting. Additionally, it takes into account broader conceptual issues involving contrasts among different ac-

figure 1.1   **Relationship Between Accounting and Decision Making**

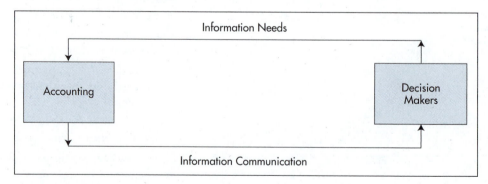

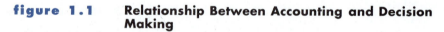

---

1 *Statement of the Accounting Principles Board No. 4.* "Basic Concepts and Accounting Principles Underlying Financial Statements of Business Enterprises." New York: American Institute of Certified Public Accountants, 1970, par. 40.

2 *Statement of Financial Accounting Concepts No. 1.* "Objectives of Financial Reporting by Business Enterprises." Stamford, Conn.: Financial Accounting Standards Board, 1978, par. 9.

counting standards as well as harmonization of diverse accounting principles throughout the world.

Why Study International Accounting?

From a student's perspective, the major reason for studying accounting is to develop competencies in collecting and processing data from economic activities and events, and preparing the financial reports so that useful information may be communicated to the decision makers. Relevance and reliability are the primary qualities that make accounting information useful to decision makers.[3] This leads us to an important conclusion. *Since the environments in which an economic entity operates are dynamic, the accounting profession must be current to remain useful. Only then can it satisfy the information needs of decision makers in ever-changing business environments.* In a global economy, natural, human, and financial resources often can be shifted from one part of the world to another part conveniently, efficiently, and at great speed. International accounting provides pertinent information to decision makers in the global economy, helping them make resource allocation decisions that optimize the benefit to humankind.

For this reason, it is important to study international accounting. Otherwise, in this age of international operations and worldwide markets there would be an information vacuum, resulting in less than optimal economic decisions. The end result would be misallocation of scarce economic resources worldwide.

The Age of Global Economy

We live in a global economy. Some of the evidence includes the **North American Free Trade Agreement (NAFTA)**—a free trade agreement among Canada, Mexico, and the U.S.—the 15-member **European Union (EU)**, and the formation of the World Trade Organization (WTO) at the start of 1995. Another interesting and significant phenomenon is the emergence of the economies of the Asia-Pacific Rim region as active and influential participants in the global economy.

An increase in international trade, facilitating the movement of goods, services, and financial resources worldwide, improves the efficiency of resource allocation and usage. Each country then specializes in producing those goods and services that it can generate efficiently, and it exchanges what it produces for the products and services that are produced more efficiently in other countries. Increased competition in global markets forces firms to be more efficient. This should contribute to the attainment of a higher standard of living in the countries involved in international trade.

---

3 *Statement of Financial Accounting Concepts No. 2.* "Qualitative Characteristics of Accounting Information." Stamford, Conn: Financial Accounting Standards Board, 1980, par. 15.

International Business

International business, or international trade, transcends national boundaries. It includes all commercial transactions resulting in flows of goods, services, or financial resources from country to country. International trade has been steadily growing in importance and size. From 1970 to 1998, international trade grew from $314 billion to $6 trillion, and the trend continues. According to consultants at McKinsey & Company, the value of world output available to consumers through global markets will be $73 trillion by 2027, more than 12 times the 1998 level.[4] Global markets will then comprise 80 percent of the world output, four times the percentage now. A survey of 409 senior executives of U.S.-based business enterprises with revenues of at least $1 billion revealed that by 2005 almost all U.S.-based companies will be competing in a global marketplace. In the same survey, "international competition" and "adapting to rapid changes in markets" were listed as challenging issues in 2005 by 74 and 71 percent of the respondents, respectively.[5] According to Deloitte & Touche, by 2010 more than half of the world's corporate organizations will operate on a seamless, global basis.[6]

Accelerating Factors

Several factors have helped accelerate globalization of economies. Standardization of products and processes, advancements in technology, improvements in infrastructure, economic reforms, and privatization of public sector enterprises are all major contributors.

The privatization process has enabled many previously wholly state-owned enterprises to restructure and become formidable international competitors. In some cases this has resulted in cross-pollination of restructuring efforts that go beyond national boundaries. Renault, for example, had a loss of 5.2 billion francs in 1996 when it was a 100 percent state-owned enterprise. After 55.8 percent of the company was privatized and restructured, it earned a net income of 8.8 billion francs in 1998. In March 1999, Renault acquired 36.8 percent equity in Nissan, Japan's Number 2 automaker. A team of former Renault executives is now behind Nissan's restructuring efforts.[7]

In this age of international markets and global operations, it is sometimes impossible to identify a product's country of origin. Conexant, based in the U.S., sells chips to Sweden-based Ericsson and Finland-based Nokia. The chips are made in Taiwan and inspected in Mexico.

---

4 Lowell Bryan, Jane Fraser, Jeremy Oppenheim, and Wilhelm Rall. *Race for the World: Strategies to Build A Great Global Firm.* Boston: Harvard Business School Press, 1999, pp. 3–4.

5 "What Challenges Will the Business World Face in 2005?" *Deloitte & Touche Review*, 20 July 1998, pp. 1–2.

6 "Deloitte & Touche Analyzes Key Business Issues." *Deloitte & Touche Review*, 2 February 1998, p. 4.

7 David Woodruff. "French Firms Embrace Capitalism In Spite of Government's Meddling." *The Wall Street Journal*, 24 November 1999, p. A15.

"Hey, this says 'Made in Japan.'"

Globalization is not a zero-sum game. According to the CEO of Swiss-Swedish conglomerate Asea Brown Baveri (ABB), a gain in one part of the world does not mean a loss in another. For ABB, which operates in 140 countries through 1,100 subsidiaries and has 180,000 employees, "it is best for good things to happen everywhere."[8]

Dependencies on International Trade

The dependency of many well-known companies on international trade can be determined by reviewing a few facts. Eighty percent of Coca-Cola's and 70 percent of Gillette Co.'s sales are from international trade. In 1998, the revenues realized from international operations by Renault, Bayer, and ICI were 61, 69, and 82 percent, respectively. This dependency on international business is not confined to large corporations. Tens of thousands of small businesses are involved in exporting or importing. In 1999, for example, 97 percent of U.S. exporters were small business organizations.

---

8 Lewis Dolinsky. "For this CEO, All Business is Local." *San Francisco Chronicle*, 10 December 1999, p. A21.

The Reasons for Going International

A survey by Deloitte Touche Tohmatsu International entitled *Why Companies Go International: International Strategy of Middle Market Companies* summarizes information on the international strategy of 400 medium-size companies in 20 developed countries. Frequently stated reasons for engaging in international operations follow.[9]

Reason	Percentage
Growth opportunities	84%
Less dependence on domestic economy	39
Customer demand	34
Lower costs	24

The survey also identified problems most often encountered by companies that had decided to become participants in the global economy. The main problems noted by the U.S. and Canadian companies follow.

Problem	Eastern Europe	Rest of the World
Administrative formalities	25%	34%
Uncertain legislative and business environment	56	26
Obtaining information	33	24
Taxation	11	24
Financing	31	18
Currency restrictions	28	16
Poor ownership rights	19	11

Findings of the survey are consistent with generally recognized reasons for involvement of a company in international business. Those reasons are discussed next.

Theory of Comparative Advantage

According to this classical economic theory, each country should produce only those goods and services that it can produce with relative efficiency. Such goods and services should be exported to other countries. In return, a country should import goods and services that can be produced with relative efficiency in other countries. Taking advantage of the opportunities to sell abroad is one of the major reasons for expansion in international trade. This advantage is realized due to specialization that results from comparative advantage.

Multinational business has generally increased over time. Part of this growth is due to the increasing realization that specialization by coun-

---

9 "Companies Surveyed on Going Global." *Deloitte & Touche Review*, 5 October 1992, pp. 1–2.

tries can increase production efficiency. Some countries, such as Japan and the United States, have a technology advantage, while countries such as Jamaica, Mexico, and South Korea have an advantage in the cost of basic labor. Since these advantages cannot be easily transported, countries tend to use their advantages to specialize in the production of goods that can be produced with relative efficiency. This explains why countries such as Japan and the U.S. are large producers of computer components, while countries such as Jamaica and Mexico are large producers of agricultural and handmade goods.

Specialization in some products may result in no production of other products, so trade between countries is essential. This is the argument made by the classical **theory of comparative advantage**. Due to comparative advantages, it is understandable why firms are able to penetrate foreign markets. Many of the Virgin Islands rely completely on international trade for most products, while they specialize in tourism. While the production of some goods is possible on these islands, there is more efficiency in the specialization of tourism. That is, the islands are better off using some revenues earned from tourism to import products than attempting to produce all the products that they need.[10]

The concept of comparative advantage has come under some criticism in recent years because it explains only the export-import dimension of international business. Multinationals, corporations with global operations, are not merely engaged in large volumes of imports and exports. Their worldwide operations include manufacturing, financing, investment, and many other types of activities. The theory of comparative advantage assumes that factors of production (e.g., labor and capital) are constant for a country. This assumption has been challenged on the basis that due to advancements in technology, factors of production are often quite mobile. A company engaged in international trade may be able to relocate its operations with relative ease by shifting factors of production to the desired location.

Clearly, the theory of comparative advantage has its limitations and it cannot explain all dimensions of international business. This does not necessarily lead to the conclusion that the theory is invalid. The concept of comparative advantage can and does partially explain the expansion of international trade. When coupled with **product cycle theory** (explained next), the theory of comparative advantage also explains why firms enter international markets in the first place.

Product Cycle Theory

According to product cycle theory, a firm starts selling first in the domestic market because it has an important advantage—access to information about its

---

10 Jeff Madura. *International Financial Management*, 4th ed. St. Paul: West Publishing Co., 1995, p. 9.

customers and competition. Later, any demand for the company's product in foreign markets is satisfied first by exporting. *Exporting is typically the entry point in international trade for most firms.* Subsequently, the company may decide to locate parts of its operations abroad.

> As time passes, the firm may feel the only way to retain its advantage over competition in foreign countries is to produce the product in foreign markets, thereby reducing its transportation costs. Over time, the competition in the foreign markets may increase as other producers become more familiar with the firm's product. Thus, the firm may develop strategies to prolong the foreign demand for its product. A common approach is to attempt differentiating the product so that other competitors cannot offer exactly the same product.[11]

According to product cycle theory, there is a progression from home markets to international markets, *with exports being the entry point to international markets.*

Imperfect Market Theory

The third reason for international operations is to gain access to factors of production. The factors of production may include cheap labor, labor with some special skills, availability of raw materials, etc.

> . . . the real world suffers from **imperfect market** conditions where factors of production are somewhat immobile. There are costs and often restrictions related to the transfer of labor and other resources used for production. There may also be restrictions on funds and other resources transferred among countries. Because markets for the various resources used in production are "imperfect," firms often capitalize on a foreign country's resources. Imperfect markets provide an incentive for firms to seek out foreign opportunities.[12]

Many U.S.-based firms have moved their manufacturing operations to Mexico to lower their cost by taking advantage of cheap labor. These companies include Tyson, Delphi Automotive Systems Corp., John Deere, Caterpillar, and IBM. American manufacturing companies hired 600,000 workers in Mexico during the period 1994–1998.[13]

The assertion by some that factors of production are no longer fixed for a country is somewhat exaggerated. There is indeed more mobility but by no means total mobility of factors of production.

---

11 Madura, p. 10.

12 *Ibid.*

13 Nikhil Deogun. "Made in U.S.A.: Deals From Europe Hit Record." *The Wall Street Journal*, 25 October 1999, p. C1.

Technology Transfers

A company may engage in international business because it desires to obtain access to advanced technologies developed in different parts of the world. Conversely, a company may be willing to share its advanced technology with companies or governments in other parts of the world to gain access to their markets. Though not new, this phenomenon has become increasingly important in recent years.

Many technological alliances have been formed and others are being formed to share knowledge for mutual benefit. In global markets, time is often more important than cost. To compete in dynamic global markets, an organization has to be able to swiftly produce and distribute the products to meet demand. This means that the organization must have the necessary flexibility to respond quickly to competitive challenges.

Preserving Strategic Position

When a large corporation has reached the limit to growth, it is necessary for it to become more aggressive to preserve its strategic position. Buying companies in other countries is increasingly becoming the preferred tactic employed to maintain the strategic position. This may provide a "basket" of benefits considered critical to improve competitive ability, including access to new markets, technology, and expertise for enhancing leadership position.

Exhibit 1.1 shows the largest acquisitions of U.S.-based companies by corporations from outside the United States for a recent 12-month period.

exhibit 1.1 **Largest Acquisition of U.S.-based Companies May 1998—April 2000**

Acquirer (Country)	Acquired	Date	Value (in Billions of U.S. Dollars)
Glaxo Wellcome (U.K.)	SmithKline	January 2000	$184.0
Pfizer (U.K.)	Warner-Lambert	*January 2000	74.0
Vodafone (U.K.)	AirTouch Comm.	June 1999	69.0
British Petroleum (U.K.)	Amoco	August 1998	55.0
Daimler-Benz (Germany)	Chrysler	May 1998	40.5
BP Amoco (U.K.)	ARCO	April 1999	33.7
Scottish Power (U.K.)	PacifiCorp	December 1998	12.6
Aegon (Netherlands)	TransAmerica	February 1999	10.8
Deutsche Bank (Germany)	Bankers Trust	November 1998	9.1
Nortel Networks (Canada)	Bay Networks	June 1998	9.0

*Final negotiations in progress.
Sources: Thomson Financial Securities Data, Chronicle New Services, and Associated Press.

Many large companies buy companies in other countries to improve their competitive ability in global markets. The rate of such acquisitions has dramatically increased recently. During the first nine months in 1999, acquisitions of U.S.-based companies by corporations based in other countries amounted to $256 billion—four times 1997's volume. During the same nine-month period, the U.S.-based companies made purchases of companies in other countries totaling $121.9 billion.

In some cases, an acquisition can give the acquiring corporation the dominant position in an industry. Germany-based media company Bertelsmann acquired U.S.-based Random House in 1998. This purchase "instantly made Bertelsmann the biggest publisher of English-language books," thus giving it a dominant position worldwide.[14]

Types of International Involvement

A company can conduct international business by choosing from many different types of activities and levels of involvement. We will next discuss this topic.

International Companies—Exporters

A company that exports its products or services overseas is classified as an international corporation.[15] One of the best-known international corporations is The Boeing Company. It makes airplanes in the U.S., its home base, and sells them throughout the world. A company may be a direct exporter, an indirect exporter, or both. Being a direct exporter requires the company to have its own marketing operations at various locations worldwide. This includes its own sales staff, channels of distribution, collections, etc. A direct exporter assumes greater risks and costs than an indirect exporter, but also has more control over the marketing of its products throughout the world. With successful marketing strategies, the direct exporter may enjoy growth in profits and market share. An indirect exporter sells its product to domestic buyers who subsequently sell it in international markets. Alternately, an indirect exporter may retain an intermediary to identify potential buyers in other countries. Indirect exporting is the less expensive of the two alternatives, at least in the beginning. A company may be a direct exporter to some countries and an indirect exporter to others.

Strategic Alliances

A company may collaborate with companies in other countries to share rights and responsibilities as well as revenues and expenses. These collaborations are called **strategic alliances**. A strategic alliance that results in a network of companies is easy to form and has minimal associated risks. Airlines have been forming such alliances

---

14 Nikhil Deogun. "Made in U.S.A.: Deals From Europe Hit Record." *The Wall Street Journal*, 25 October 1999, p. C1.

15 KPMG. "Blurring Boundaries." *World*, vol. 27, no. 2, 1993, pp. 42–46.

for the last few years. Examples include American Airlines with British Airways and United Airlines with Germany-based Lufthansa. In some countries, alliances may be the answer to prevalent political and cultural biases against "foreign" companies. Exhibit 1.2 shows some of the common types of strategic alliances.

Joint ventures that involve a technology alliance can create a "win-win" situation by providing mutual benefit to all of the collaborators. Organización Mabe, an appliance maker in Mexico, is a good example of a successful joint venture. Mabe is half Mexican-owned and half General Electric-owned. Through this partnership Mabe has access to GE's worldwide purchasing power and its advanced technology, while GE benefits from low-cost labor and Mexico's fast-growing appliance market.[16] Examples of technology alliances formed in 1999 include AT&T with British Telecommunications, and Microsoft with Sweden-based Ericsson.

Multinational Corporations

A corporation becomes multinational because of management's global vision. A company that considers the globe as a single marketplace is a **multinational corporation** (MNC). To capitalize on international business opportunities, an MNC has worldwide product development, purchasing, manufacturing, marketing, and financial operations. Such companies are active players in international trade and international investments. Two other terms commonly used to describe an MNC

exhibit 1.2   **Common Types of Strategic Alliances**

> The terms of a strategic alliance are defined in a written agreement between the parties. Strategic alliances can be formed for a variety of reasons. The following are some of the more common reasons.
>
> **Research collaboration**: Two or more companies participate in a defined research program and benefit from the results. Research costs can be funded entirely by one of the parties, shared equally by the parties, or shared according to some other agreed-upon proportion.
>
> **Licensing program**: Proprietary information, such as patent rights or expertise, is licensed by the owner (licenser) to another party (licensee). Compensation paid to the licenser usually includes license issuance fees, milestone payments, and/or royalties.
>
> **Comarketing agreement**: Two or more companies share risks and rewards of long-term marketing programs.
>
> **Copromotion agreement**: A product is promoted jointly by two companies under the same brand name and marketing plan. Generally the manufacturing company handles receivables, inventory, and so on and pays a commission to the copromotor. Compensation is almost always based on the product sales level.
>
> Other types of strategic alliances include joint venture, production collaborations, equity investments, and outsourcing arrangements.
>
> Source: Greg L. Cellini, *Management Accounting*, June 1993, pp. 56–59 (adapted).

---

16 Geri Smith. "This Venture Is Cooking With Gas." *Business Week*, 8 November 1993, p. 70.

are **multinational enterprise (MNE)**, and **transnational corporation (TNC)**. The latter term is favored by the United Nations.

Perhaps the best-known example of an MNC is Coca-Cola. Many companies often considered as American are in fact multinationals, deriving over half of their revenues from sales outside the United States. Examples include Colgate Palmolive, Dow Chemical, IBM, American Brands, Gillette, and of course Coca-Cola.

MNCs have been a significant driving force in the development of international accounting. Their interest in international accounting extends beyond the esoteric, theoretical issues. The complexity of their operations and the diversity of their transactions demand solutions to many recording and reporting issues not pertinent to purely domestic companies.

The strategies of MNCs increasingly involve more complex forms of worldwide economic integration. This new approach is made possible by advancements in communications and information technologies, which allow MNCs to coordinate a growing number of activities in locations all over the sphere.

The Asia-Pacific Rim Region

A discussion of international business would be incomplete without a discussion of the Asia-Pacific Rim region. It has become an important economic region in the world. Japan and South Korea are the second and thirteenth largest economies in the world, respectively. South Korea's economy is expected to grow 9.5 percent in 1999.

Factors Contributing to Economic Development

Several Asia-Pacific Rim countries have either emerged as economic powers or are making progress toward that goal. According to a forecast by Merrill Lynch & Co. economists, the Asia-Pacific region, excluding Japan, will have economic growth of 5.6 and 6.0 percent in 1999 and 2000, respectively. This is a remarkably quick rebound from the economic crisis that started in July 1997 and continued in 1998. In mid-1998, the World Bank had predicted that this economic recovery may take up to four years.

Focus on Value-Added Activities

Interestingly, countries in the region are not rich in natural resources. Their productivity is primarily attributable to the focus on **value-added activities**. They manufacture and export quality goods that have won approval in global markets because consumers perceive them as a "good value." Many of the management practices and production techniques of successful companies, such as Toyota, have been adopted by their competitors in other parts of the world, including the U.S. and Western Europe. Some of those concepts include product quality, a teamwork approach, cellular manufacturing, just-in-time purchasing, and just-in-time production.

Government Policies

In many Asia-Pacific countries, government policies encourage and foster business growth. The governments play a cooperative, silent-partner role in facilitating all forms of commercial activity—especially international trade. "The intricate arrangement of back-scratching between business and government" is the way a knowledgeable observer described this relationship in Japan.[17]

Asian Values

Some have identified Asian values, based on the culture, as the critical factor for productivity:

> . . . perhaps the most important reason for the cohesiveness and efficiency of these Asian countries is their unique culture, known as Confucius Capitalism, which encompasses 2,500 years of Chinese values now called neo-Confucianism, a mixture of Buddhist and Confucian doctrines. Under the neo-Confucianism philosophy, people should seek their own moral self-development while fulfilling their social duties, thereby emphasizing the importance of education. The disciplined surge of Japan's Meiji modernization owed much to the teachings of Confucianism. Thus, a Confucius code of ethics combined with the Buddhist ideas of divine compassion and sacrifice of earthly desires emerged as Asian culture. Therefore, what makes these economies grow are Confucius-Buddhist values.[18]

The Asian values factor has come under criticism lately. William Schultz, Executive Director of Amnesty International U.S.A., believes that the Western world has used Asian values as an excuse for ignoring social and economic inequities perpetrated by governments in the region. Reacting to the political and economic turmoil in the Asia-Pacific region in 1997 and 1998, he observed:

> The desire for freedom and democracy is just as strong in that part of the world as it is everywhere else. The events of the past year have put to shame those Western apologists for Asian human rights violations . . . The myth of Asian values is dead and it deserves a well-attended funeral . . .
>
> Currencies collapse not just because of bad business decisions. They collapse because of cronyism and corruption, because of a lack of a free press to tell the hard economic truths, because of the lack of a political opposition to challenge a sitting government's policies.[19]

---

17 Rudi Dornbusch. "Japan's Closed Markets: How to Open Them Now." *Business Week*, 19 July 1993, p. 14.

18 Dhia D. AlHashim and Jeffrey S. Arpan. *International Dimensions of Accounting*, 3d. ed. Boston: PWS-Kent Publishing Company, 1992, pp. 3–4. Also see, Louis Kraar. "Asia 2000." *Fortune*, 5 October 1992, p. 113.

19 "Asian Values A Device To Prop Up Tyrants." *Gulf News*, 19 June 1998, p. 18.

The last British Governor of Hong Kong, Chris Patten, approaches it from another perspective. He insists that the region's economic growth was never a miracle performed by Asian values: "This was a consequence of opening up international markets and above all a triumph for free trade." Patten also makes an insightful observation that it is erroneous to believe there is a single set of Asian values because of the region's rich cultural diversity.[20]

The advent of a sizable middle class in many of the Asia-Pacific countries is noteworthy. India has the largest middle class of any single country in the world, estimated to number between 300 and 350 million people. Approximately half of the people in Singapore, Taiwan, and South Korea can be classified as an upwardly mobile middle class, while 20 percent of the population in Thailand, Indonesia, and Malaysia approach this economic status. The new buying power of the Asia-Pacific consumers, with its creation of huge new markets, has not gone unnoticed in other parts of the world.

South Korea, Taiwan, and Singapore, as well as other Asia-Pacific nations, are developing high-technology industries through technology transfers from industrialized countries. Multinational companies are playing a critical role in this phenomenon.

Many countries within the region are collaborating with each other for mutual trade benefits. Indonesia, Malaysia, Singapore, the Philippines, Thailand, and Brunei have formed the Association of Southeast Asian Nations. In January 1992, the six countries agreed to remove tariff barriers over the next 15 years.

Open Regionalism

In September 1992 representatives from 20 Pacific Rim nations held a conference in San Francisco. The meeting resulted in the signing of the San Francisco Declaration. Five key goals of the declaration are:

- Removal of barriers to trade, investment, and the flow of technology.
- Nondiscriminatory commercial access for outside economies.
- Strengthening efforts to keep the Asia-Pacific Rim region and the global economic system open.
- Adherence to the principles of the General Agreement on Tariffs and Trade.
- Accommodation of sub-regional trade pacts.

Unlike a treaty that binds the parties, a declaration lacks an enforcement provision. It can, however, be influential by getting commitment from the signatories. The declaration is unique because it combines an informal regional trading and investment strategy with a commitment to global openness. This concept of trade and investment is called **open regionalism.**

20 Louis Kaar. "Chris Patten: Asia's Bad Boy." *Fortune*, 25 May 1998, pp. 27–28.

Asia-Pacific Economic Cooperation (APEC)

The **Asia-Pacific Economic Cooperation (APEC)** is a new organization committed to the trade and investment concept of open regionalism. The following 20 countries are members of the organization.

Australia	Korea	Russia
Brunei	Malaysia	Singapore
Canada	Mexico	Chinese Taipei
Chile	New Zealand	Thailand
China*	Papua New Guinea	U.S.A.
Indonesia	Peru	Vietnam
Japan	Philippines	

*includes Hong Kong

http://

In November 1994, leaders of the APEC countries reached consensus that the developed economies among their members should remove trade and investment barriers by the year 2010, and that the remaining members would do the same by the year 2020. APEC's future priorities can be found at the Web site **http://www1.apecsec.org.sg/**.

International Accounting—Conceptual and Operational Issues

Earlier in this chapter we briefly discussed the reasons why international accounting is an important subject. We also defined international accounting in a manner that takes into account the issues arising from a global economy.

Challenges Facing International Accounting

International business has progressed beyond the import-export type of activities. Because of the nature of the global economy, more economic interdependencies exist between countries now than ever before in history. Two developments are especially noteworthy.

- Global operations of MNCs cover a wide spectrum and include product development, manufacturing, marketing, and distribution. Technology alliances are an increasingly important factor in global operations.

- Global capital markets are providing opportunities for investors and borrowers to engage in financing activities worldwide. Technological advancements and deregulation now enable investors and borrowers to engage in financial transactions on a real-time basis in international capital markets. The trend continues in this direction.

In June 1999, the National Association of Securities Dealers Inc. formed a joint venture with Softbank Corp. to develop a version of its electronic U.S. NASDAQ Stock Market in Japan. The market, to be known as NASDAQ-Japan, is expected to open in the latter part of 2000. Eventually, the U.S. NASDAQ market and the planned market together will provide investors with the ability to trade up to 21 hours a day. Stocks listed on the U.S. NASDAQ Stock Market include Intel Corp. and Microsoft.

The two previously described developments have widened the scope of international accounting beyond the following traditional topics.

- Foreign currency transactions
- Foreign currency translations
- Foreign exchange risk management
- Taxation of international operations
- Consolidation of financial statements of foreign subsidiaries and affiliates
- General purchasing power adjustments of financial statements
- Multinational transfer pricing
- Comparative disclosure requirements

This is not to imply that the traditional topics are no longer important. In fact, due to the magnitude of international trade and international investments, they have gained increased significance. However, many new and broader issues are at the very core of international accounting, i.e., provision of relevant and reliable information to decision makers worldwide. We discuss some of those next.

Cultural Dimension

Globalization has heightened the importance, and broadened the scope of "people skills" for modern professional accountants. An understanding of different cultures, cultural sensitivity, and an appreciation of cultural diversity is now required to be a successful professional. New professionals must possess a global perspective and ideally should have exposure to multicultural experiences.

Understanding the Cross-Functional Linkages

It is no longer enough to be proficient merely in accounting techniques, procedures, and applications of standards. Today's accountants need to develop competencies that enable them to view a global business in terms of integrated functions. The real value of accounting is in providing information that deals with how various courses of actions affect all parts of a business that are interdependent and increasingly in different parts of the world. Product quality, manufacturing flexibility, and the ability to produce, market, and distribute swiftly before the competitors seize a lion's share of the market are the considerations with which a modern-day accountant must be concerned. This is beyond the traditional role of accountants and involves many "soft" areas where judgment has as much of a role to play as the numbers. The number and variety of these judgmental factors are far greater now than in the past—and they continue to increase.

Financial Analysis and Comparability

Another major challenge facing international accounting is that the financial statements of various countries are prepared in accordance with differing accounting standards. This causes many problems in performing financial analysis. At least three factors contribute to the problem.

- Accounting transactions are measured and reported differently in different countries. Financial ratios using numbers from such reports are inherently incomparable.

- Business culture and business practices vary from country to country. In some countries, such as Japan, financing is mostly through debt, while in other countries, such as the U.K., the major source of financing is from equity holders. How can a comparison of the debt to equity ratio of a Japanese operation with a British operation be made to gain useful insights?

- Terminology is a problem for accounting throughout the world. In some languages, no terms exist to describe certain items. There may not even be a term for accounting. Even among the countries that speak the same language, the same term may carry different meanings. For example, "turnover" has an entirely different meaning in the U.S. than in the U.K., while both are English-speaking countries.

Global Information System Development

Worldwide operations require a global information system. The system should be able to meet management's needs for strategic planning, short-term planning, organizing, controlling, decision making, and financial reporting. This is one of the major challenges facing international accounting. The development of such a system to serve the multiple and varied needs of management in managing global operations and for financial reporting is a complex undertaking. In addition to the usual complications encountered in the development of an information system, factors such as national differences in accounting standards, monetary units, tax laws, restrictions on currency movements, and general price level changes need to be taken into account. Perhaps the most difficult of all factors is the varying level of uncertainty across the globe.

World Trade Organization

http://

The World Trade Organization (WTO)—**http://www.wto.org/**—was established on January 1, 1995. Headquartered in Geneva, Switzerland, it is the governing body of international trade. As of November 2000, it had 140 member countries. The member countries account for 90 percent of international trade. Over 30 countries, including Russia and China, have applied to join the organization. Among big countries, Russia and China are the only non-member countries.

Philosophy

The WTO was founded on the philosophy that free trade among countries, without import tariffs or other protectionist measures (to protect domestic companies or domestic industries from competition), contributes to growth of world economy and benefits everyone. Standards of living rise since costs of imported goods go down, which helps control inflation, and each country does what it does most efficiently and effectively. Thus regardless of geographical and political boundaries, free international trade makes everyone economically more prosperous.

Functions

The World Trade Organization has several functions and it carries enforcement powers to perform those functions. Some of its major functions are:

- Administering WTO trade agreements;
- Serving as a forum for trade negotiations;
- Handling trade disputes;
- Monitoring national trade policies;
- Providing technical assistance and training to developing countries;
- Cooperating with other international organizations.[21]

Being a regulatory body, the WTO has an enforceable commercial code. It sets and enforces the rules for international trade in goods and services and intellectual property. Any disputes between or among member countries are settled by the WTO. The number of disputes brought to the WTO by November 1999 was 183.[22] After a nation files a complaint with the WTO, it sets up a panel of three experts, usually business lawyers, to handle the case. The panel makes the decision. If a defendant country is found in violation of the WTO rules, it must end the offending practice or face heavy trade sanctions imposed by the WTO. Of the 183 cases filed with the WTO, only 24 had been completed by the end of November 1999. This indicates that the decision-making process is rather slow.

Critical Issues

Recently the WTO has come under severe and open criticism. This was highlighted by December 1999 demonstrations in Seattle, Washington, U.S.A., which prevented the WTO from holding its summit conference. *Among the major issues are environment, labor rights, and human rights.*

The WTO's push for free trade is viewed by the critics as encouragement of worker exploitation in developing countries. They say that most workers in those countries accept sweatshop working conditions due to their economic depriva-

---

21 Bhushan Bahree. "WTO's Job Will Get Tougher With China's Entry." *The Wall Street Journal*, 17 November 1999, p. A2.

22 *Ibid.*

tion and their inability to exercise any significant influence on their socio-economic environment. Human rights advocates reject the notion that basic rights, including workers' rights, differ among different cultures. They assert that human rights are universal.

Southeast Asian countries challenged a U.S. law requiring turtle-excluding devices on shrimp boats selling shrimp to the United States. A WTO trade dispute panel ruled in favor of the Asian countries. The WTO ruling consequently nullified the U.S. law for protection of the environment. Ralph Nader has stated that WTO is a threat to democracy because it can revoke U.S. laws that protect the environment and consumers. "It's becoming a global government that undermines federal laws," he said.[23] It is fair to state that few were aware of the fact that the WTO has the authority to nullify laws of a member nation. In the countries with mature and well-established democratic systems, many have difficulty accepting this WTO power in the interest of free trade. Their feeling is expressed by Representative George Miller, a member of the U.S. House of Representatives, "The rules don't reflect the values of this country. It limits the countries' rights to legislate against labor and environmental abuse, so it basically ratifies the right to use sweatshops, prison labor or child labor, or kill dolphins or use asbestos."[24]

Many knowledgeable commentators have, however, expressed the view that the real reason for criticism against the WTO is global anxiety over the growing gap between the haves and the have-nots.

A Challenge for the Millennium— The Gap Between the Haves and the Have-Nots

The demonstrations in Seattle put the issue of growing economic disparity in the world in the limelight. Since 1995, when the WTO was created, international trade has increased by 37 percent and 1.5 million new jobs have been created worldwide. However, free trade has left many workers, industries, and nations behind in the race toward growth and progress. There is a growing awareness that free trade and global markets pose new problems. The most troubling: "The benefits of trade have not been shared equally across countries and within countries," according to Charles Bean, an economist at London School of Economics. A labor union economist, Thea Lee, states "Globalization isn't delivering good jobs across the board." In the U.S., which has experienced unprecedented economic prosperity in recent years, 400,000 manufacturing jobs disappeared in just two years and agricultural exports are down sharply.[25]

In the developing countries there is a growing concern that globalization will widen the economic gap within their populations. It has impoverished millions of

---

23 "WTO: Selfish Cabal Or Beneficial Global Trade." *The Tribune*, 3 December 1999, p. A10.

24 Robert Collier. "Next Week's WTO Summit Will Spotlight Division, Dissent." *San Francisco Chronicle*, 24 November 1999, p. A1.

25 Michael J. Mandel and Paul Magnusson. "Global Growing Pains." *Business Week*, 13 December 1999, pp. 41–42.

people because they do not fit in the export-oriented New Economy. The governments in developing countries are also suspicious of the WTO because many of its decisions are made in closed-door meetings. These meetings are open only to a few economically powerful member countries. They view the organization as a rich countries' club.

Mexico provides a good case study. In 1999, Mexico's exports were estimated to be $135 billion, twice the amount five years earlier. Currently, Mexico has 3,000 manufacturing plants for production of export goods. These plants employ 1 million Mexicans. The jobs in these plants pay 20 percent higher wages than the jobs in non-export plants. Mexicans whose livelihoods depend on domestic economy are not doing well. Wages and job markets in labor-intensive industries, such as restaurants, hotels, banking, retail, and construction, are depressed. More than 3 million Mexicans lost their jobs in the 1995 recession. Most have become a part of the underground economy:[26]

> Antonia Menezes, a 38-year-old mother of three, is a typical underground economy worker. She lost her job as a shop clerk in 1995. Nowadays, she sells Christmas decorations from a sidewalk stand in downtown Mexico City. She earns just 300 pesos—a little over $32—in a 60-hour week. Her husband, a construction worker, is unemployed.[27]

According to the World Bank, about 1 million people in Thailand were pushed below the poverty line between 1996 and 1998. The greatest increase in poverty was in the Northeast, traditionally Thailand's poorest region.[28]

Most thoughtful observers agree that the growing problems of economic disparity and anxiety brought upon by globalization need to be addressed. Social unrest more often than not can be traced directly to economic disparity. In sum, the relative economic disparity exists and is growing at two levels:

1. Between developing countries and developed countries.
2. Within populations of both developing and developed countries.

The editors of *Business Week* summed up the situation and related issues succinctly in a recent editorial:

> Perhaps the most important lesson to be taken from the debacle in Seattle is that beneath the overall prosperity globalization is generating throughout the world, there is pent-up anxiety, fear, and anger. Globalization itself is a process of such rapid change that it is causing uncertainties as well as opportunities, downward mobility as well as upward advancement, and economic losers as well as winners . . .
>
> Take the U.S. A dual economy exists in America. By most measures, the New Economy is creating enormous wealth—but not for everyone.

---

26 Geri Smith. "Breaking the Curse." *Business Week*, 20 December 1999, p. 62.

27 *Ibid.*

28 Peter Eng. "Thai Workers Fear Foreign 'Takeover' of Economy." *San Francisco Chronicle*, 9 July 1999, p. A14.

The growth rate for wages, average hourly earnings, the employment cost index, and compensation per manhour are actually falling.

. . . A dual economy exists in China and most other developing countries as well . . . For people anywhere whose industries are under siege in dual economies, globalization is a problem, not a promise; a threat, not an opportunity . . . Before a backlash curbs the enormous benefits that trade and economic growth bring to the world, attention should be paid to those being left behind.[29]

The solution proposed by knowledgeable observers is not to turn the clock back on globalization and resume protectionist policies. The solution instead lies in education and retraining of displaced workers. Highly respected Chairman of the U.S. Federal Reserve Board Alan Greenspan has stated that protectionism almost always fails to halt technological progress, meaning that jobs in uncompetitive industries will eventually be lost anyway. Greenspan's insightful observation delineates a noteworthy point: *Globalization is influenced by international trade policies of nations as well as by technological progress.* He further stated, "It would be a great tragedy were we to stop the wheels of progress because of an incapacity to assist the victims of progress." Rather than erecting protectionist barriers to benefit particular industries, Greenspan believes that the better course is for governments to supply retraining programs to more workers.[30]

Accounting provides information to decision makers on economic activities and events. Accounting information and analysis are used in policy formulation and in resource allocation decisions. It is important for accounting professionals to be aware of the existing and emerging economic issues and challenges. This makes the challenge discussed in this section doubly important to accountants. World economy and domestic economy have a direct impact on them professionally as well as personally.

Note to Students

First, congratulations for studying this relatively new and exciting area of accounting. As you already know from reading this chapter, it is a dynamic area filling an important need in a global economy. One of the best ways to become an active participant is to gain international professional experience yourself. Multinational companies consider such experience essential, always listing it among the top items of required qualifications for key management positions. Presidents and CEOs of many companies have been selected primarily due to their international experience. A recent example is the selection of a new CEO at Coca-Cola.

---

29 "The Anxiety Behind Globalization." *Business Week*, 20 December 1999, p. 118.
30 "Greenspan Concerned About Trade Barriers." *The Tribune*, 17 April 1999, p. D5.

It is critical to develop greater understanding and appreciation of the local cultures. If possible, take an internship abroad. After you graduate, take advantage of available international training programs in your firm. Seek an overseas assignment when possible.

International trade is not a new phenomenon. It goes as far back as the recorded human history. Its benefits extend beyond the direct economic gains. The concept of zero was discovered by Hindu mathematicians in India. Arab traders transmitted the notion of zero along with the modern Arabic symbols for counting numbers (1, 2, 3, . . .) to Europe during the Middle Ages. Until then the Europeans had no concept of zero and used Roman numerals that were awkward and inefficient for calculations. Scholars attribute the invention of calculus by Newton to this transmission of the concept of zero. Calculus became the driving force behind the Scientific Revolution. Thus international trade started the momentum for sweeping new discoveries benefiting humankind.

http://

To keep abreast of new developments, regularly read at least one international business periodical such as the *Asian Wall Street Journal* (**http://www.dowjones.com/awsjweekly/**), the *Financial Times* (**http://www.ft.com**), the *Economist*, the *Far Eastern Economic Review* (**http://www.feer.com/**), or *Business Week* (**http://www.businessweek.com**). Most large accounting firms and all of the "Big Five" have publications dealing with specific countries and specific international topics.

Chapter Summary

1. The study of international accounting is important since it provides relevant and reliable information to decision makers in the global economy.

2. Increase in international trade ultimately results in efficient resource allocation.

3. Several factors have helped accelerate globalization.

4. International trade is now a source of over one-half of the revenues of many multinational corporations.

5. The reasons for international business can be explained by the theory of comparative advantage, the product cycle theory, the imperfect market theory, technology transfers, and preserving strategic position.

6. The types of international involvement by companies include exports, strategic alliances, and multinational operations.

7. The Asia-Pacific Rim region has become an important economic region in the world.

8. The Asia-Pacific Economic Cooperation (APEC) is an organization committed to open regionalism. It has 20 member countries.

9. International accounting faces many new challenges, and modern-day accountants need to possess new skills not previously required for success in the profession.

10. Soft skills are now as important for the accountants as technical competency and analytical skills.
11. The World Trade Organization is empowered to regulate international trade. Its rulings are binding on member countries.
12. The WTO was founded on the philosophy of free trade and investments among countries without any barriers.
13. The WTO has come under attack for various reasons including environmental concerns, labor rights, and human rights.
14. The challenge facing globalization is the widening economic disparity among and within countries throughout the world.

Questions for Discussion

1. Define international accounting.
2. Why is the study of international accounting important?
3. Why is the development of a global economy beneficial?
4. Describe the trends toward a global economy.
5. What important factors have accelerated the globalization process?
6. "Removing barriers to foreign trade will cost our country jobs." Give arguments on both sides of this statement.
7. What type of difficulties might arise in identifying "foreign-made" goods?
8. Why might a company choose to engage in international operations?
9. What is the perceived weakness of the theory of comparative advantage?
10. Is there a link between the theory of comparative advantage and the product cycle theory?
11. What theory would explain a company's action to move its operations to another country to take advantage of cheap labor?
12. Explain the difference between a direct and an indirect exporter. Can one company be both?
13. In terms of international trade, what is a strategic alliance?
14. Can you identify any differences among the terms multinational corporation, multinational enterprise, and transnational corporation?
15. Discuss Asian values and Confucius Capitalism.
16. What is APEC? What are its main objectives?
17. Discuss two of the challenges facing international accounting.
18. Why is it important for modern accountants to have a cultural dimension?
19. Describe the philosophy of the WTO. What are its functions?
20. What are the major issues facing the WTO?

21. Are basic human rights universal or do they differ from culture to culture?

22. Describe the problem of widening economic disparity. Do you think it is linked to globalization? If so, how?

23. What is the solution suggested by Alan Greenspan to bridge the gap between the haves and the have-nots?

Case 1

Comparative Advantage

The following statement was made by Sir James Goldsmith before the U.S. Senate Commerce Committee on November 15, 1994:

> The principal theoretician of free trade was David Ricardo, a British economist of the early nineteenth century. He believed in two interrelated concepts: specialization and comparative advantage . . . But these ideas are not valid in today's world. Why?
>
> During the past few years, 4 billion people have suddenly entered the world economy. They include the populations of China, India, Vietnam, Bangladesh, and the countries that were part of the Soviet empire, among others. These populations are growing fast; in 35 years, that 4 billion is forecast to expand to over 6.5 billion. These nations have very high levels of unemployment and those people who do find jobs offer their labor for a tiny fraction of the pay earned by workers in the developed world . . .
>
> Until recently, these 4 billion people were separated from our economy by their political systems, primarily communist or socialist, and because of a lack of technology and of capital. Today all that has changed. Their political systems have been transformed, technology can be transferred instantaneously anywhere in the world on a microchip, and capital is free to be invested wherever the anticipated yields are highest.
>
> The principle of global free trade is that anything can be manufactured anywhere in the world to be sold anywhere also. That means that these new entrants into the world economy are in direct competition with the workforce of developed countries. They have become part of the same global labor market. Our economies, therefore, will be subjected to a completely new type of competition.
>
> It must surely be a mistake to adopt an economic policy which makes you rich if you eliminate your national workforce and transfer production abroad, and which bankrupts you if you continue to employ your own people.

Required: Critique the previous statement. Among others, address the following issues:

(1) Do you think that population growth in these countries will continue at the rate indicated by the forecasts? Discuss.

(2) Discuss the points mentioned in the statements contained in the third paragraph. Do you agree?

(3) Based on recent developments, is the theory of comparative advantage obsolete? Discuss.

(4) What policy recommendations would you offer to address the concerns raised in the last paragraph?

Present pros and cons when an issue has no clear solution. Otherwise, be specific in your answer.

Case 2

Economic Disparity—Is It a Problem?

The following statement deals with the issue of growing economic disparity within the United States:

> In 1992 the Congressional Budget Office of the United States, a scrupulously non-partisan body, revealed that personal income in the U.S. increased by $740 billion between 1977 and 1989 after adjustment for inflation. Of this total almost two-thirds went to just 660,000 families, the wealthiest 1 percent. For that fortunate group, average income rose from $315,000 to $560,000, or by 77 percent. The middle classes gained a miserly 4 percent over this period while 40 percent of all families actually ended up worse off in real terms at the end of this decade of affluence. The incentives, which may have been the fertilizers to grow more wealth, ended up consuming all the wealth which they created.[31]

Required: Discuss the ethical, societal, and economic ramifications of the situation described in the case.

Case 3

Is the Glass Half Full or Half Empty?

A day after America's Independence Day an editorial appeared in an American newspaper that contained the following statements:

---

31 Charles Handy. *The Empty Raincoat.* London: Arrow Business Books, 1995, p. 12.

. . . The nation is enjoying one of its most prosperous eras ever. It is not a perfect picture. The good life is still beyond the reach of too many Americans. But for the vast majority of us, the final Independence Day celebration of this millennium is the best ever. According to the indexes, more of us are working, more of us own our own homes, more of us are confident of the future. It's a proud America that counts its blessings and prepares to carry the cornucopia of plenty into the year 2000 . . .[32]

On the same page was an article by the Chairman of the Made in the USA Foundation, Joel D. Joseph. The following statements are taken from the article:

While our economy superficially appears to be flying high, it is actually undergoing the most serious hollowing-out of manufacturing companies in our history. Entire industries, like clothing, toys and even steel are disappearing. Our balance of payments is the true measure of how our economy is doing, and it is dangerously out of whack. We are now running an annual trade deficit of more than $200 billion, about $1,000 for every American. Where do these dollars go? They go overseas and then are lent back to the U.S. government and American corporations. The deficit has made the United States the largest debtor nation in the world . . .

When you purchase an American-made product, you are also paying for the American way of life. American products may be more expensive for very good reasons. Their prices include the costs of: strong consumer protection laws; the toughest environmental laws in the world; safe, humane working conditions; no child labor; no slave labor; and decent wages and working conditions. All things considered, when you buy a quality American-made product, you are purchasing a piece of a society with the most freedom and highest standard of living of any nation in the entire world. To help retain this way of life that we all enjoy, we must continually invest in it. Buying American is one very important way to do so.[33]

At the end of 1999, investors from other countries owned almost $1.3 trillion of the U.S. government's debt securities. This was 40 percent of the U.S. government's $3.2 trillion marketable debt. Five years earlier, the U.S. government's debt securities held by investors from other countries amounted to $641 billion, just 20 percent of the total at that time. According to the chief economist of Merrill Lynch & Co., "Americans don't seem so interested in the Treasury market these days."[34]

---

32 "Celebrate Two Days and More." *The Tribune*, 5 July 1999, p. B6.

33 Joel D. Joseph. "For An American Fourth of July, Buy American." *The Tribune*, 5 July 1999, p. B6.

34 Michael M. Phillips. "Foreigners' Share of Treasury Is Growing." *The Wall Street Journal*, 20 December 1999, p. A2.

Required: Discuss the following issues:

(1) How can two parties form such different perceptions of the same state of affairs in a country?

(2) Is balance of payments of a country the true measure of the state of its economy?

(3) Are there any potential undesirable consequences to the U.S. if investors from other countries continue to increase their share of the U.S. government debt?

(4) Should consumers be expected to pay a higher purchase price for a product if it is made in their own country and thus embodies a way of life?

(5) Do you agree with Joseph that the price of a product made in the consumer's own country includes many indirect and intangible benefits related to societal values?

(6) Would there be any ramifications affecting Americans if citizens of other countries took the same position as Joseph regarding "foreign-made" goods?

References

AlHashim, Dhia D., and Jeffrey S. Arpan. *International Dimensions of Accounting*, 3d ed. Boston: PWS-Kent Publishing Company, 1992.

American Accounting Association. *Accounting and Culture*. Sarasota, Fla.: American Accounting Association, 1987.

"Asian Values A Device To Prop Up Tyrants." *Gulf News*, 19 June 1998, p. 18.

Bahree, Bhushan. "WTO's Job Will Get Tougher With China's Entry." *The Wall Street Journal*, 17 November 1999, p. A2.

Bryan, Lowell, Jane Fraser, Jeremy Oppenheim, and Willhelm Rall. *Race for the World: Strategies to Build A Great Global Firm*. Boston: Harvard Business School Press, 1999.

Cellini, Greg L. "Strategic Alliances in the '90s." *Management Accounting*, June 1993, pp. 56–59.

Deloitte & Touche. "Companies Surveyed on Going International." *Deloitte & Touche Review*, 5 October 1992, pp. 1–2.

_____. "Deloitte & Touche Analyzes Key Business Issues." *Deloitte & Touche Review*, 2 February 1998, p. 4.

Deogun, Nikhil. "Made In U.S.A.: Deals From Europe Hit Record." *The Wall Street Journal*, 25 October 1999, p. C1.

Dolinsky, Lewis. "For This CEO, All Business Is Local." *San Francisco Chronicle*, 10 December 1999, p. A21.

Dornbusch, Rudi. "Japan's Closed Markets: How to Open Them Now." *Business Week*, 19 July 1993, p. 14.

Iqbal, M. Zafar. "Market Expansion Challenges Smaller Practice Units." *The Ohio CPA Journal*, April 1994, pp. 41–42.

Israeloff, Robert L. "Positioning a Firm for International Opportunities." *Journal of Accountancy*, February 1993, pp. 46–48, 50.

KPMG Peat Marwick. "Blurring Boundaries." *World*, vol. 27, no. 2 (1993), pp. 44–46.

Kraar, Louis. "Chris Patten: Asia's Bad Boy." *Fortune*, 25 May 1998, pp. 27–28.

Madura, Jeff. *International Financial Management*, 4th ed. St. Paul: West Publishing Co., 1995.

Mandel, Michael J., and Paul Magnusson. "Global Growing Pains." *Business Week*, 13 December 1999, pp. 40–43.

Murray, Mark F. *International Business*. New York: American Institute of Certified Public Accountants, 1992, pp. 131–133.

Rosenzweig, Philip. "Why is Managing in the United States So Difficult for European Firms?" *European Management Journal*, March 1994, pp. 31–38.

Sack, Robert J., James R. Boatsman, Robert S. Fell, Jack L. Krogstad, Spencer J. Martin, and Marcia S. Niles. "Mountaintop Issues: From the Perspective of the SEC." *Accounting Horizons*, March 1995, pp. 79–86.

Smith, Geri. "This Venture Is Cooking with Gas." *Business Week*, 8 November 1993, p. 70.

_____. "Breaking the Curse." *Business Week*, 20 December 1999, pp. 60–62.

"What Challenges Will the Business World Face in 2005?" *Deloitte & Touche Review*, 20 July 1998, pp. 1–2.

Why Companies Go International. Brussels, Belgium: Deloitte Touche Tohmatsu International, 1992.

Wills, Stefan, and Kevin Barham. "Being an International Manager." *European Management Journal*, March 1994, pp. 49–58.

Woodruff, David. "French Firms Embrace Capitalism In Spite of Government's Meddling." *The Wall Street Journal*, 24 November 1999, p. A15.

Zahra, Shaker, and Galal Elhagrasey. "Strategic Management of International Joint Ventures." *European Management Journal*, March 1994, pp. 83–93.

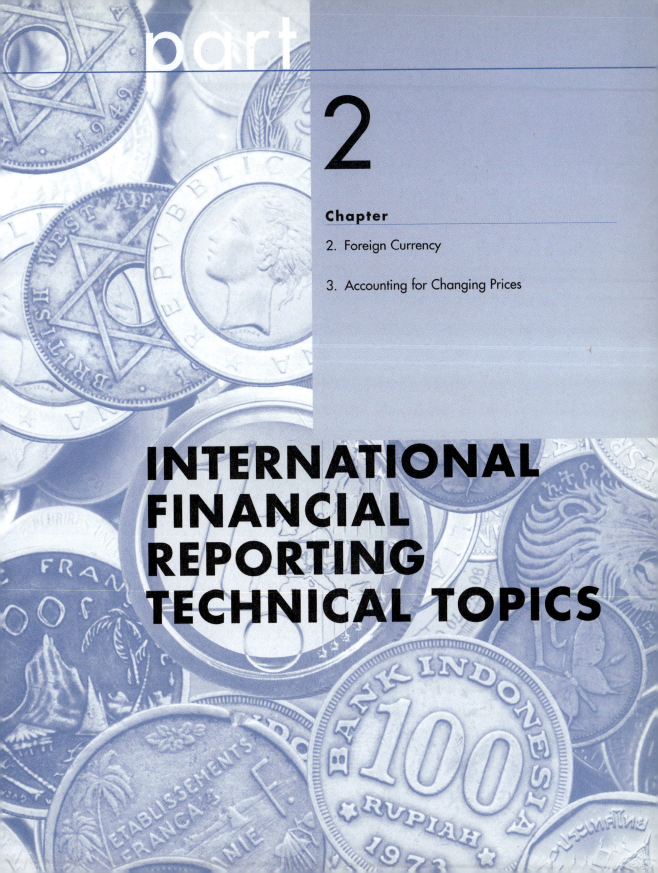

part

2

INTERNATIONAL
FINANCIAL
REPORTING
TECHNICAL TOPICS

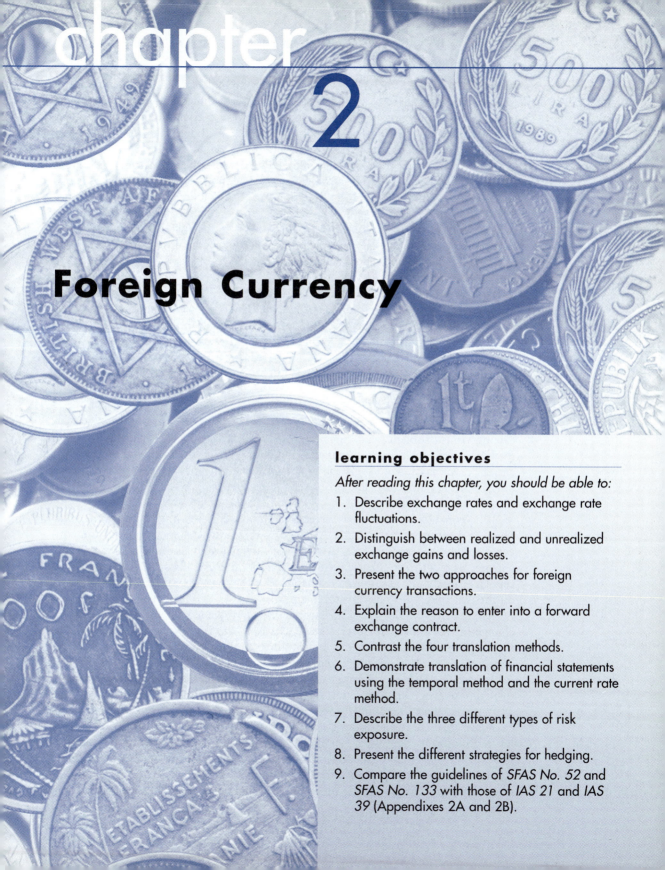

chapter

2

Foreign Currency

learning objectives

After reading this chapter, you should be able to:

1. Describe exchange rates and exchange rate fluctuations.

2. Distinguish between realized and unrealized exchange gains and losses.

3. Present the two approaches for foreign currency transactions.

4. Explain the reason to enter into a forward exchange contract.

5. Contrast the four translation methods.

6. Demonstrate translation of financial statements using the temporal method and the current rate method.

7. Describe the three different types of risk exposure.

8. Present the different strategies for hedging.

9. Compare the guidelines of *SFAS No. 52* and *SFAS No. 133* with those of *IAS 21* and *IAS 39* (Appendixes 2A and 2B).

A company doing business is involved in international activities: international operations and international investments. This increases the complexity of its transactions. Consequently, the financial reporting system of a company involved in international activities is inherently more complex. It should be able to satisfy information needs of multiple users in different parts of the world.

One of the major factors contributing to the complexity of financial reporting is having to deal with different currencies to carry on international activities. Each country has its own currency, currency laws, and regulations. All transactions are recorded by the subsidiaries in the currency of the country in which they are located. The question is: How may the total amounts for a multinational company be determined either for a period or at a date when multiple currencies are involved? This requires that different currencies be converted to one currency. Let us assume that a multinational company's headquarters are in the Netherlands, and it has subsidiaries in the U.S., Spain, Thailand, and South Africa. This requires that before the consolidated statements can be prepared, all the account balances in the local currency of the U.S. (dollar), Spain (peseta), Thailand (baht), and South Africa (rand) will have to be converted to guilders, the currency of the Netherlands where the parent company is based.

Exchange Rates

The previous problem may appear to have an easy solution: Convert amounts in the local currency of each country to guilders by using the exchange rate for the currency. An **exchange rate** is the amount of one currency needed to obtain one unit of another currency. The problem is more complex, however, since exchange rates are seldom stable.

The **conversion value** of a currency is the equivalent amount of another currency at a given exchange rate. As the exchange rate changes, so does the conversion value of an amount in a foreign currency. Therefore, exchange rate changes have a direct effect on the conversion value in the consolidated financial reports. Clearly, the greater the exchange rate fluctuations, the greater the impact on the consolidated financial statements.

Changes in values of different currencies, reflected by the changes in exchange rates, result from several factors. One of the important factors is a country's *rate of inflation*. Currency of a country with a high inflation rate will depreciate in value when compared with the currency of a country with a low inflation rate. With a high inflation rate, a country's currency has declining power to purchase everything—including another country's currency.

Interest rates in a country play an important role in the exchange rate of its currency. Investors from other countries purchase the currency of a country that has high interest rates. They use the currency purchased to invest in debt securities that have high interest rates. This increases the demand for the currency, resulting in appreciation of its value. Generally speaking, countries with high interest rates are able to attract more capital than can countries with low interest rates.

Another important reason for exchange rate fluctuations is a country's *balance of payments*. A country whose cumulative exports exceed its cumulative imports will run a balance of payments surplus. This surplus appreciates the value of its currency. Of course, a country with a deficit in its balance of payments will experience a decline in the value of its currency.

Many of the environmental influences that are discussed in Chapter 4 also have a direct impact on the exchange rate changes of a country. Especially important are the *economic system*, *political system*, and *political stability*.

Exchange Gains and Losses

Changes in exchange rates result in exchange gains and losses. Exchange gains or losses may be realized or unrealized. **Realized gains or losses** are the gains or losses actually incurred. These result from the *exchange* of one currency for another. These gains and losses are from foreign currency *transactions*. **Foreign currency transactions** are transactions denominated in a currency other than the reporting currency of the economic entity.

In the case of **unrealized gains or losses**, no exchange of currency takes place. These unrealized gains or losses result from a **foreign currency translation**, a conversion of the amounts in accounts of international subsidiaries (recorded in foreign currencies) to the currency used for preparation of consolidated financial statements.

Foreign Currency Transactions

As noted earlier, realized exchange gains and losses result from foreign currency transactions. Such transactions require future settlements in a foreign currency.[1] Since exchange rates fluctuate, the result of exchange rate change from the transaction date to the settlement date results in transaction gains or losses. A **settlement date** is the date when payment of funds is made on the maturity of a foreign exchange contract.

Example

Let us assume that a Pakistani firm buys equipment from a U.S. firm for $1 million when the exchange rate is $1.00 = 50.00 rupees (Rs). The transaction is recorded:

Equipment	50,000,000	
Accounts Payable		50,000,000

The Pakistani firm settles the account after 6 months when the exchange rate is $1.00 = Rs52.00. To pay off the liability, Rs52 million will be required to obtain $1 million. This results in a transaction loss to the Pakistani firm in the amount of Rs2 million:

---

1 *Statement of Financial Accounting Standards No. 52.* "Foreign Currency Translation." Stamford, Conn.: Financial Accounting Standards Board, 1981, par. 15.

$$\text{Transaction Loss} = 1{,}000{,}000 \times (52 - 50) = \textbf{Rs2,000,000}$$

The previous equation can be summarized in the following manner:

Transaction Gain or Loss = (Amount owed in foreign currency units) × (Difference between exchange rates on the transaction date and the settlement date)

How should the transaction loss be recorded by the Pakistani firm on the settlement date? There are two methods—the *one-transaction approach* and the *two-transaction approach*.

One-Transaction Approach

Under the **one-transaction approach**, the final settlement would be shown as an adjustment to the equipment account:

Accounts Payable	50,000,000	
Equipment	2,000,000	
Cash		52,000,000

Under the one-transaction approach, the transaction is considered not completed until the final settlement. Any transaction gain or loss will be reflected on the settlement date in an adjustment to the recorded value of the resource acquired. In the previous example, the foreign exchange rate change required Rs2 million more than originally recorded. The cost of the equipment is, therefore, increased by the amount of this loss. In sum, a foreign exchange loss would be reflected in higher recorded cost for the resource acquired, through an upward adjustment made on the settlement date. Had the situation been reversed, the foreign exchange loss would have been reflected in a downward adjustment of the equipment, since it would not have cost as many rupees to obtain $1 million on the settlement date as originally recorded.

In the previous example, we assumed that the buyer had to satisfy the seller's claim in a foreign currency on the settlement date. Now let us assume that, instead, the American seller agrees at the date of transaction to accept payment in a foreign currency on the date of settlement.

Example

Using the same data we used in the previous example, the U.S. seller makes the following entry to record the sale on the transaction date:

Accounts Receivable	1,000,000	
Sales		1,000,000

The entry to record receipt of the Rs50 million on the settlement date is recorded by the American seller as follows:

Cash	961,538	
Sales	38,462	
Accounts Receivable		1,000,000

The dollar amount equivalent to Rs50 million is $961,538, since the exchange rate now is Rs52 = $1.

Note: *No exchange gain or loss is recorded in the one-transaction approach.*

Two-Transaction Approach

Under the **two-transaction approach,** there are two separate and distinct transactions. Purchase of the equipment is recorded in the same manner as shown previously:

Equipment	50,000,000	
Accounts Payable		50,000,000

Under the two-transaction approach, no adjustment to the equipment account is made at the settlement date. Instead, any gain or loss is separately recorded as a gain or loss on foreign exchange. The following entry records the cash settlement and the foreign exchange loss of Rs2,000,000:

Accounts Payable	50,000,000	
Loss on Foreign Exchange	2,000,000	
Cash		52,000,000

Example

Let us now assume that the American seller had, instead, agreed on the transaction date to accept payment in Pakistani rupees (Rs50 million) on the settlement date. The American seller's entry on the transaction date will be the same as in the previous example:

Accounts Receivable	1,000,000	
Sales		1,000,000

The entry made by the American seller to record receipt of payment on the settlement date would be:

Cash	961,538	
Loss on Foreign Exchange	38,462	
Accounts Receivable		1,000,000

Which of the two approaches is preferable? There is no consensus on this issue. Both approaches are practiced in different parts of the world. In some countries one of the approaches is specifically required. In other countries, it is left to the managers to choose. In the U.S., any gains or losses from foreign exchange transactions must be recorded in accordance with the two-transaction approach and shown immediately in the income statement as normal operating items.[2]

---

2 *Statement of Financial Accounting Standards No. 52.* Stamford, Conn.: Financial Accounting Standards Board, 1981.

Rationale

Supporters of the two-transaction approach point out that there are two separate decisions made by management and recording for each decision should be kept separate from the other: The decision to import or export, and the decision to select a settlement method. *Exchange gains and losses result from the decision on the settlement method.* The assumption of foreign currency exchange risk by selecting settlement in the future should not affect the recording on the decision to import or export. Therefore, the cost of imported assets or the sales revenue from exported assets should be based solely on the exchange rate on the transaction date. There is merit to the argument and for this reason popularity of the two-transaction approach is increasing worldwide.

Note: No adjustment to the payables or receivables is made in the two-transaction approach on the settlement date.

Forward Exchange Contracts

A firm may plan to protect itself from potential losses from exchange rate changes. This can be done by entering into a forward exchange contract. A **forward exchange contract** is an agreement to exchange a given amount of one currency for another currency on an agreed date at a specified exchange rate. The specified exchange rate in a forward exchange contract is called **forward rate**. Efficient and well-established foreign exchange markets exist for all major currencies. Forward exchange contracts usually cover 1-month, 3-month, or 6-month periods (see Exhibit 2.1). In our example, the Pakistani firm could have avoided the Rs2 million loss from the exchange rate change by entering into a 6-month forward exchange contract.

While a forward exchange contract enables a firm to avoid a potential future loss, it may also result in foregoing a potential future gain. For example, if the Pakistani firm had entered into a forward exchange contract at the rate of $1.00 = Rs51.00 and the actual rate on the settlement date was $1.00 = Rs49.00, the Pakistani firm would miss the opportunity to make a gain of Rs2,000,000. Had the Pakistani firm purchased one million dollars at the spot rate on the settlement date, it would have spent only Rs49,000,000. A **spot rate** is the *current* rate of exchange between two currencies.

With reference to Exhibit 2.1, the following two points are noteworthy:

- The loss or gain in the value of a country's currency is not across the board. The currency may lose value against one currency and simultaneously gain value against another currency. The value of the U.S. dollar increased against the Australian dollar from Tuesday to Wednesday. On the other hand, the U.S. dollar dropped against the German mark during the same two-day period.

- The forward rates can be higher or lower for longer periods in a given situation. The forward rates of the British pound to the U.S. dollar are increasingly smaller from a 1-month to a 6-month period. The opposite is true for the forward rates for Canada.

exhibit 2.1   Sample Exchange Rates

Wednesday, December 15, 1999
EXCHANGE RATES

The New York foreign exchange mid-range rates below apply to trading among banks in amounts of $1 million and more as quoted at 4 p.m. Eastern time by Reuters and other sources. Retail transactions provide fewer units of foreign currency per dollar. Rates for the 11 Euro currency countries are derived from the latest dollar-euro rate using the exchange ratios set 1/1/99.

Country	U.S. $ equiv. Wed	U.S. $ equiv. Tue	Currency per U.S. $ Wed	Currency per U.S. $ Tue	Country	U.S. $ equiv. Wed	U.S. $ equiv. Tue	Currency per U.S. $ Wed	Currency per U.S. $ Tue
Argentina (Peso)	1.0002	1.0002	.9998	.9998	Japan (Yen)	.009641	.009658	103.72	103.54
Australia (Dollar)	.6361	.6363	1.5722	1.5715	1-month forward	.009691	.009712	103.19	102.97
Austria (Schilling)	.07314	.07299	13.672	13.701	3-months forward	.009783	.009801	102.21	102.03
Bahrain (Dinar)	2.6525	2.6525	.3770	.3770	6-months forward	.009931	.009948	100.70	100.53
Belgium (Franc)	.0249	.0249	40.0810	40.1650	Jordan (Dinar)	1.4075	1.4075	.7105	.7105
Brazil (Real)	.5413	.5397	1.8475	1.8530	Kuwait (Dinar)	3.2819	3.2873	.3047	.3042
Britain (Pound)	1.6052	1.6115	.6230	.6205	Lebanon (Pound)	.0006634	.0006634	1507.50	1507.50
1-month forward	1.6063	1.6127	.6225	.6201	Malaysia (Ringgit)	.2632	.2632	3.8000	3.8000
3-months forward	1.6062	1.6126	.6226	.6201	Malta (Lira)	2.4272	2.4295	.4120	.4116
6-months forward	1.6056	1.6121	.6228	.6203	Mexico (Peso)				
Canada (Dollar)	.6743	.6755	1.4830	1.4803	Floating rate	.1070	.1064	9.3475	9.3950
1-month forward	.6751	.6765	1.4812	1.4783	Netherland (Guilder)	.4567	.4557	2.1896	2.1942
3-months forward	.6759	.6773	1.4794	1.4764	New Zealand (Dollar)	.4951	.4944	2.0198	2.0227
6-months forward	.6769	.6784	1.4774	1.4741	Norway (Krone)	.1242	.1240	8.0530	8.0614
Chile (Peso) (d)	.001863	.001861	536.75	537.45	Pakistan (Rupee)	.01926	.01926	51.925	51.925
China (Renminbi)	.1208	.1208	8.2794	8.2794	Peru (new Sol)	.2886	.2886	3.4650	3.4650
Colombia (Peso)	.0005314	.0005308	1882.00	1884.00	Philippines (Peso)	.02460	.02458	40.650	40.680
Czech. Rep. (Koruna)					Poland (Zloty)	.2381	.2380	4.2000	4.2025
Commercial rate	.02803	.02805	35.677	35.656	Portugal (Escudo)	.005020	.005010	199.20	199.61
Denmark (Krone)	.1353	.1350	7.3908	7.4066	Russia (Ruble) (a)	.03720	.03715	26.885	26.915
Ecuador (Sucre)					Saudi Arabia (Riyal)	.2666	.2666	3.7507	3.7507
Floating rate	.00005731	.00005634	17450.00	17750.00	Singapore (Dollar)	.5966	.5951	1.6763	1.6803
Finland (Markka)	.1693	.1689	5.9077	5.9200	Slovak Rep. (Koruna)	.02376	.02373	42.083	42.140
France (Franc)	.1534	.1531	6.5176	6.5312	South Africa (Rand)	.1625	.1631	6.1535	6.1315
1-month forward	.1538	.1535	6.5008	6.5139	South Korea (Won)	.0008815	.0008822	1134.50	1133.50
3-months forward	.1545	.1541	6.4730	6.4872	Spain (Peseta)	.006049	.006036	165.32	165.67
6-months forward	.1555	.1551	6.4304	6.4454	Sweden (Krona)	.1174	.1172	8.5205	8.5303
Germany (Mark)	.5146	.5135	1.9433	1.9474	Switzerland (Franc)	.6291	.6281	1.5895	1.5922
1-month forward	.5159	.5149	1.9383	1.9422	1-month forward	.6316	.6306	1.5833	1.5858
3-months forward	.518	.5170	1.9301	1.9343	3-months forward	.6358	.6347	1.5729	1.5755
6-months forward	.5216	.5203	1.9173	1.9218	6-months forward	.6426	.6412	1.5561	1.5595
Greece (Drachma)	.003048	.003045	328.12	328.41	Taiwan (Dollar)	.03161	.03165	31.640	31.600
Hong Kong (Dollar)	.1286	.1286	7.7748	7.7749	Thailand (Baht)	.02605	.02592	38.385	38.585
Hungary (Forint)	.003963	.003962	252.31	252.40	Turkey (Lira)	.00000189	.00000189	530450.00	529615.00
India (Rupee)	.02299	.02298	43.490	43.525	United Arab				
Indonesia (Rupiah)	.0001417	.0001388	7055.00	7205.00	Emirates (Dirham)	.2723	.2723	3.6729	3.6729
Ireland (Punt)	1.2781	1.2757	.7824	.7839	Uruguay (New Peso)				
Israel (Punt)	.2387	.2389	4.1892	4.1854	Financial	.08623	.08629	11.598	11.590
Italy (Lira)	.0005198	.0005187	1923.97	1927.88	Venezuela (Bolivar)	.001554	.001554	643.45	643.45
SDR	1.3661	1.3687	.7320	.7306					
Euro	1.0065	1.0050	.9935	.9950					

Special Drawing Rights (SDR) are based on exchange rates for the U.S., German, British, French, and Japanese currencies. Source: International Monetary Fund.
a-Russian Central Bank rate. Trading band lowered on 8/17/98. b-Government rate, d-Floating rate; trading band suspended on 9/2/99.

Source: *The Wall Street Journal*, 16 December 1999, p. C21.
Note: Ecuador plans to adopt the U.S. dollar as its national currency in 2001.

Foreign Currency Translation

Unlike foreign currency transactions, **foreign currency translation** does not involve actual currency exchanges. The foreign currency translation gains and losses result from translation of all foreign subsidiary accounts in the currency of the parent company. Translation is necessary to prepare consolidated financial statements that view the parent company and its subsidiaries as one reporting entity. Companies with international operations prepare consolidated financial statements for a variety of uses and users. A total of non-translated amounts in different currencies would be useless for the purpose of preparing consolidated financial statements.

If currency exchange rates were static, the currency translation process would be no more than a simple arithmetical exercise. However, as mentioned earlier, most exchange rates are seldom stable—let alone static. This makes foreign exchange translation a complex technical topic.

Four of the common methods used to convert amounts from different foreign currencies for preparing consolidated financial statements are described next, followed by their comparison and analysis.

Current Rate Method

The **current rate method** is the simplest and the easiest to use of all translation methods. All assets and all liabilities are translated at the **current exchange rate**—the exchange rate on the balance sheet date. Paid-in capital accounts are translated at the applicable historical rates. Dividends are translated at the exchange rate on the *date of declaration* (not the date of payment). Gains or losses from translation are included in the accumulated translation adjustment account in the stockholders' equity. On the income statement, all revenue and expense items are translated at the weighted average exchange rate for the period.

Example

It is assumed for this illustration that:

1. The French franc (F) is the local currency of the subsidiary, and the U.S. dollar is the currency of its parent company.
2. The subsidiary's inventories are stated at cost. The inventory at December 31, 20x2, was acquired when the exchange rate was $0.11. Inventory on hand on December 31, 20x1, was acquired when the exchange rate was $0.16.
3. Property, plant, and equipment items were acquired in prior years when the exchange rate was $0.16, except for equipment costing 300,000 francs that was acquired late in December 20x2 when the exchange rate was $0.11. No depreciation was recorded for 20x2 on this equipment purchased in December 20x2.
4. Sales, purchases, and operating expenses all occurred uniformly throughout the year 20x2.

5. The common stock was issued when the exchange rate was $0.16.
6. The December 31, 20x1, translated retained earnings balance was $217,000.
7. The cumulative translation adjustment at December 31, 20x1, was a negative $22,000.
8. Selected exchange rates follow:

Current rate (C) at December 31, 20x1	$0.15
Average rate (A) for 20x2	0.12
Current rate (C) at December 31, 20x2	0.10

Exhibits 2.2 and 2.3 show the translated income statement and the balance sheet respectively using the current rate method.

The balancing figure of $(179,000) shown in Exhibit 2.3 is the accumulated translation adjustment. This represents all the translation gains and losses of the past periods as well as the current period added together.

Current-Noncurrent Method

Under the **current-noncurrent method,** balance sheet items classified as "current" are translated at the current exchange rate, and items classified as "noncurrent" are translated at appropriate historical rates. Therefore, all current assets and

exhibit 2.2   **Translated Income Statement Using the Current Rate Method**

The French Subsidiary Income Statement For the Year Ended December 31, 20x2			
	Francs	**Rate**	**Dollars**
Sales	F10,000,000	A .12	$1,200,000
Expenses			
Cost of goods sold:			
Beginning inventory	F 1,500,000		
Purchases	6,000,000		
Ending inventory	(2,000,000)		$5,500,000
	F 5,500,000	A .12	660,000
Depreciation expense	200,000	A .12	24,000
Operating expense	3,300,000	A .12	396,000
Income tax expense	400,000	A .12	48,000
Total expenses	F 9,400,000		$1,128,000
Net income	**F 600,000**	To balance sheet	**$ 72,000**

exhibit 2.3　　**Translated Balance Sheet Using the Current Rate Method**

The French Subsidiary Balance Sheet December 31, 20x2			
	Francs	Rate	Dollars
Assets:			
Cash	F　　200,000	C .10	$　　20,000
Accounts receivable, net	1,000,000	C .10	100,000
Inventory	2,000,000	C .10	200,000
Property, plant, and equipment	6,300,000	C .10	630,000
Accumulated depreciation	(500,000)	C .10	(50,000)
Total assets	**F9,000,000**		**$900,000**
Liabilities and owners' equity:			
Accounts payable	F　2,500,000	C .10	$　250,000
Income tax payable	200,000	C .10	20,000
Long-term debt	2,800,000	C .10	280,000
Total liabilities	F　5,500,000		$　550,000
Common stock	F　1,500,000	H .16	$　240,000
Retained earnings:			
Beginning balance	1,400,000	Given	217,000
Net income	600,000	From inc. stmt.	72,000
Cumulative translation adjustment		Balancing	(179,000)
Total owners' equity	F　3,500,000		$　350,000
Total liabilities and owners' equity	**F9,000,000**		**$900,000**

current liabilities are translated at the exchange rate on the balance sheet date. All noncurrent assets/noncurrent liabilities are translated at the historical exchange rates in effect when those items were acquired/incurred.

In the current-noncurrent method, all income statement items (revenues and expenses) except depreciation and amortization of noncurrent assets are translated at a weighted average exchange rate. The depreciation and amortization expenses of noncurrent assets are translated at their appropriate historical rates.

Monetary-Nonmonetary Method

The **monetary-nonmonetary method** emphasizes monetary-nonmonetary classification for the translation. On the balance sheet, monetary items are translated at the current exchange rate on the balance sheet date and nonmonetary items are translated at their historical exchange rates. **Monetary items** include all assets and liabilities expressed in fixed amounts of currency. Examples of monetary assets include cash and receivables (current and noncurrent). Assets such as prepaid insurance, inventory, fixed assets, etc. do not fit the definition of monetary items and are considered nonmonetary. Since liabilities almost always are stated in fixed units of currency, they are considered monetary. However, if the amount of a liability is not fixed, then it would be considered a nonmonetary item. Examples of nonmonetary liabilities include items such as warranties on products sold and advances on sales contracts.[3]

Income statement items with the exception of cost of goods sold and depreciation and amortization of noncurrent assets are translated at a weighted average exchange rate for the period. Cost of goods sold and depreciation and amortization expenses of noncurrent assets are translated at the appropriate historical rates.

Temporal Method

Under the **temporal method,** currency translation is viewed as a restatement of the financial statements. The foreign currency amounts are translated at the exchange rates in effect at the dates when those items were measured in the foreign currency. This results in the following:

- Cash, receivables, and payables are translated at the current rate on the balance sheet date.

- All remaining assets, liabilities, and capital stock are translated at the historical exchange rates that were in effect when those assets were acquired, liabilities were incurred, and capital was contributed.[4] This assumes use of the historical cost basis.

- Most revenues and expenses are translated at a weighted average rate for the period. Cost of goods sold, depreciation expense, and amortization expense are translated at the appropriate historical exchange rates.

- All translation gains and losses are taken directly to the income statement and, therefore, affect income reported for the period.

Example
It is assumed for this illustration that:

- The French franc is the local currency of The French Subsidiary, and the U.S. dollar is the currency of its parent company.

---

3 *Statement of Financial Accounting Standards No. 33.* Stamford, Conn.: Financial Accounting Standards Board, 1979, Appendix D.

4 If current value accounting is used, assets and liabilities are carried at their current value in foreign currency. The temporal method would then require them to be translated at the current exchange rate.

- The subsidiary's inventories are stated at cost. The inventory on hand at December 31, 20x2, was acquired when the exchange rate was $0.11. Inventory on hand on December 31, 20x1, was acquired when the exchange rate was $0.16.

- Property, plant, and equipment were all acquired in prior years when the exchange rate was $0.16, except for equipment costing 300,000 francs that was acquired late in December 20x2 when the exchange rate was $0.11. No depreciation was recorded in 20x2 on this equipment purchased in December 20x2.

- Sales, purchases, and operating expenses all occurred uniformly throughout 20x2.

- The common stock was issued when the exchange rate was $0.16.

- The December 31, 20x1, translated retained earnings balance was $260,000.

- Relevant exchange rates are:

Current rate at December 31, 20x1	$0.15
Average rate for 20x2	0.12
Current rate at December 31, 20x2	0.10

Exhibits 2.4 and 2.5 show the translated income statement and the balance sheet, respectively, using the temporal method.

Comparison and Analysis

The Current Rate Method

The current rate method is the only method of translation among the four discussed that originated outside the U.S. It was proposed by the Institute of Chartered Accountants in England and Wales in 1968.[5] In 1970, The Institute of Chartered Accountants of Scotland declared the current method to be the only acceptable method of translation.[6] This is the easiest of all the methods to apply and is attractive due to its simplicity.

The current rate method merely restates the foreign currency financial statements into the reporting currency. Accounting principles used by the international subsidiary are not changed for translation. This gives recognition to the fact that the international subsidiary operates in an environment different from the operating environment of the parent company. The original income statement ratios in the foreign currency are unaffected by the current rate method translation since the account balances in foreign currency are multiplied by a constant rate. In essence, this method keeps intact the operating relationships of the inter-

---

5 *The Accounting Treatment of Major Changes in the Sterling Parity of Overseas Currencies.* London: Institute of Chartered Accountants in England and Wales, 1968, par. 14.

6 Institute of Chartered Accountants of Scotland. "Treatment in Company Accounts of Changes in the Exchange Rates of International Currencies." *The Accountant's Magazine*, September 1970, pp. 415–423.

exhibit 2.4   **Translated Income Statement Using the Temporal Method**

The French Subsidiary Income Statement For The Year Ended December 31, 20x2			
	Francs	**Rate**	**Dollars**
Sales	F 10,000,000	A .12	$1,200,000
Expenses:			
Cost of goods sold			
Beginning inventory	1,500,000	H .16	240,000
Purchases	6,000,000	A .12	720,000
Ending inventory	(2,000,000)	H .11	(220,000)
	F 5,500,000		$ 740,000
Depreciation expense	200,000	H .16	32,000
Operating expense	3,300,000	A .12	396,000
Income tax expense	400,000	A .12	48,000
Total expenses	F 9,400,000		$1,216,000
Income (loss) before translation gain	F 600,000		$ (16,000)
Translation gain		Balancing	219,000
Net income		From bal. sheet	**$203,000**

national subsidiary. *The current rate method is the most popular translation method in practice worldwide.*

The Current-Noncurrent Method

The current-noncurrent method of foreign currency translation is based on the balance sheet classification of items as current or noncurrent. Shortcomings of the current-noncurrent method are equally applicable to the monetary-nonmonetary method. This classification is not relevant for the purpose of translation.[7] As noted by Professor Samuel Hepworth of the University of Michigan, the lack of association of foreign exchange gains and losses with income from international operations distorts reported earnings.[8] This method can be problematic when long-term assets are disposed or long-term liabilities are settled.

---

7 *Research Report No. 36, Management Accounting Problems in Foreign Operations.* New York: National Association of Accountants, 1960, p. 17.

8 Samuel R. Hepworth. *Reporting Foreign Operations.* Ann Arbor, Mich.: Bureau of Business Research, University of Michigan, 1956.

exhibit 2.5   **Translated Balance Sheet Using the Temporal Method**

The French Subsidiary Balance Sheet December 31, 20x2			
	Francs	**Rate**	**Dollars**
Assets:			
Cash	F 200,000	C .10	$ 20,000
Accounts receivable, net	1,000,000	C .10	100,000
Inventory	2,000,000	H .11	220,000
Property, plant, and equipment	6,000,000	H .16	960,000
Property, plant, and equipment	300,000	H .11	33,000
Accumulated depreciation	(500,000)	H .16	(80,000)
Total assets	**F9,000,000**		**$1,253,000**
Liabilities and owners' equity:			
Accounts payable	F 2,500,000	C .10	$ 250,000
Income tax payable	200,000	C .10	20,000
Long-term debt	2,800,000	C .10	280,000
Total liabilities	F 5,500,000		$ 550,000
Common stock	F 1,500,000	H .16	$ 240,000
Retained earnings:			
Beginning balance	1,400,000	Given	260,000
Net income	600,000	Balancing	203,000
Total owners' equity	F 3,500,000		$ 703,000
Total liabilities and owners' equity	**F9,000,000**		**$1,253,000**

The Monetary-Nonmonetary Method

The monetary-nonmonetary method is also based on the balance sheet classification of the items. The classification is on the basis of the monetary or nonmonetary nature of each item. The reason given earlier for the shortcomings of the current-noncurrent method are equally applicable to the monetary-nonmonetary method: Balance sheet classification of an item is not necessarily a relevant basis for the translation method. A translation method based solely on a monetary-nonmonetary distinction is unsatisfactory for the purpose of translation.[9] An ad-

9 *Statement of Financial Accounting Standards No. 8.* "Accounting for the Translation of Foreign Currency Transactions and Foreign Currency Financial Statements." Stamford, Conn.: Financial Accounting Standards Board, 1975, pp. 58–59.

ditional problem arises when an international subsidiary states its nonmonetary assets on a basis other than historical cost. For example, let us assume that a foreign subsidiary states its fixed assets at replacement cost. Under the monetary-nonmonetary method, the historical exchange rate would be applied to the non-historical (replacement) cost of the fixed assets for translation. The resulting figure from translation would have at best a questionable information value, and probably would be misleading.

The Temporal Method

The temporal method has several attractive features. It retains the original measurement bases of the items in the foreign currency, since it uses the exchange rates in effect at the dates when the measurements in foreign currency were made. The objective is to translate assets and liabilities in a manner that will keep their measurement base at the dates of original transactions.[10] The temporal method is adaptable to any basis of measurement (historical cost, replacement cost, net realizable value, etc). The temporal method merely converts the foreign currency amounts and does not change the accounting standards used by the international subsidiary.

If current value accounting is used, assets and liabilities are carried at their current value in the foreign currency. The temporal method would then require that they be translated at current rates.

Exhibit 2.6 shows the translation exchange rate used in each of the four translation methods for selected balance sheet and income statement items. None of the translation methods is perfect for all situations. Each has its strengths and weaknesses. Unless a country's accounting standards specify the method required, the selection of a translation method is an important decision. Different translation methods applied to the same set of financial statements of a subsidiary would show different results. A subsidiary showing net income in its local currency before translation may show a net loss after the translation due to a translation loss. Conversely, a subsidiary with a net loss in its local currency before translation may show net income after the translation due to a translation gain. Clearly, translation methods also affect amounts in the consolidated balance sheet.

Foreign Exchange Risk Management

Foreign exchange risk management is the management of the risk of loss arising from currency exchange rate movements on foreign currency transactions, translation, or remeasurement. It represents the actions taken by a company's management to protect the company against potential losses arising from future changes in currency exchange rates. Cross-border business transactions such as

---

10 Leonard Lorensen. *Reporting Foreign Operations of U.S. Companies in U.S. Dollars.* New York: American Institute of Certified Public Accountants, 1972.

exhibit 2.6   **Exchange Rates Used in Various Translation Methods for Selected Balance Sheet and Income Statement Items**

	Exchange Rate for Translation			
	Current Rate Method	Current-Noncurrent Method	Monetary-Nonmonetary Method	Temporal Method
Cash	C	C	C	C
Current receivables	C	C	C	C
Inventory—cost basis	C	C	H	H
Long-term receivables	C	H	C	C
Long-term investments—cost basis	C	H	H	H
Long-term investments—market basis	C	H	H	C
Property, plant, and equipment	C	H	H	H
Intangible assets	C	H	H	H
Current liabilities	C	C	C	C
Long-term debt	C	H	C	C
Common stock	H	H	H	H
Retained earnings	B	B	B	B
Revenues	A	A	A	A
Cost of goods sold	A	A	H	H
Depreciation expense	A	H	H	H
Amortization expense	A	H	H	H

A = Weighted average exchange rate for the current period
C = Current exchange rate at the balance sheet date
H = Historical exchange rate
B = Balancing figure

sourcing of raw materials and transfer of income across national boundaries are denominated in more than one currency. This exposes the entities to risks associated with changes in foreign currency exchange rates. Many corporations are taking into account foreign currency risk exposure while making their cross-border sales and sourcing plans. Everything else being equal, it is advantageous to sell in countries with relatively strong currencies, and to purchase and manufacture in countries with relatively weak currencies. This is an effective way to increase revenue and reduce costs.

A distinction can be made between integrated and self-sustaining international operations. An **integrated international operation** is one whose economic activities have a direct impact on the reporting (parent) entity. Such an international subsidiary is financially and/or operationally dependent on its parent company. On the other hand, a **self-sustaining international operation** is one whose activities generally have no direct impact on the reporting entity's operations.

Typically, the funds generated by a self-sustaining foreign operation are adequate to meet its operating and financing needs. Such operations usually have few dealings with the parent company.

International subsidiaries purchase assets, make payments on liabilities, earn revenues, and pay expenses in local currency. The parent company faces the risk of a decline in the value of its equity in the subsidiary every time the value of the local currency depreciates against major currencies such as the U.S. dollar. This applies equally to integrated and self-sustaining international operations.

Fixed Rate Currency Versus Floating Rate Currency

The currency of a country can be either a fixed rate currency or a floating rate currency. A **fixed rate currency** has a fixed rate of exchange *within narrow limits* against a major currency, such as the U.S. dollar or the British pound. The term is slightly inaccurate since the value of the currency may change within a narrow range. The exchange rate of a **floating rate currency** is determined by market forces. One of the market forces may be intervention by the central bank of a country. **Intervention** is an action taken by the central bank of a country to influence the exchange rate of its currency in the market. Japan's central bank, the Bank of Japan, spent over $40 billion in currency interventions during the last six months in 1999.[11] The objective was to weaken the yen by selling it, to boost Japan's exports. A strong yen makes Japanese goods costly for consumers in other countries. A strong yen had caused a sharp drop in Japanese exports, thereby hurting profits of major Japanese exporters. Toyota Motor Corp., Honda Motor Co., and Mazda Motor Co. were among the Japanese exporters who had reported declines in their 1999 profits.[12]

In an extreme case, a sharp drop in the profits of major companies within a country causes stock prices to plummet, effectively eroding their market value. This may result in an exodus of foreign investors, which can lead to a drastic weakening of the country's currency, as shown in Figure 2.1.

"Interestingly, foreign investors were the major contributors to the yen's ascent in 1999. They had been buying Japanese stocks in the belief that Japan's economy was on the verge of recovery. Their demand for the currency needed to purchase those shares strengthened the yen."[13]

A floating rate currency, unlike a fixed rate currency, has no limit to its exchange rate fluctuations against other currencies. Temporary exchange rate discrepancies in different foreign exchange markets for a currency lead to arbitrage. **Arbitrage** is the activity to take advantage of rate discrepancies by buying the currency in the low-cost markets and selling in the high-cost markets. This forces the rates in different markets to be the same eventually.

---

11 Brian Bremner. "Will the Yen's Surge Do Japan In?" *Business Week*, 13 December 1999, p. 56.

12 "Yen's Strength Hurts Toyota Despite Net Rise." *The Wall Street Journal*, 19 November 1999, p. A18.

13 Peter Landers. "Japanese Firms Hope Tokyo Will Brake the Yen." *The Wall Street Journal*, 3 September 1999, p. A6.

figure 2.1   **Possible Consequences of a Sharp Rise in Currency Value**

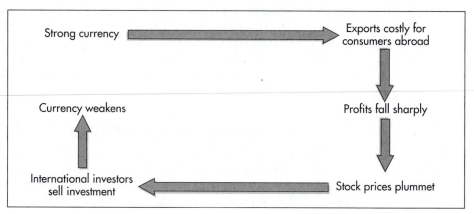

The increased volume of international trade and the expansion of the global capital markets has brought pressure on many countries to let market forces determine the relative value of their currencies against other currencies. This has made frequent changes in exchange rates an almost daily occurrence. The currencies of many countries have appreciated in value relative to other currencies, while others have declined.

Mundell-Fleming Model

The economics theory of monetary and fiscal policy, called the Mundell-Fleming model, has gained increasing importance due to capital mobility that exists worldwide. According to the theory, the capital mobility offsets the impact of either monetary or fiscal policy depending on whether a country has a fixed rate currency or a floating rate currency.

If the country's currency has a fixed exchange rate, the monetary policy measures are ineffective. A central bank's intervention by curtailing the money supply to combat inflation would increase the interest rate, which attracts international investors eager to earn a higher return. This capital inflow increases the value of the currency. To keep the exchange rate fixed, the central bank has to increase money supply, thereby decreasing its value. This monetary expansion leaves the economy of the country where it was before the central bank's intervention.

If the country has a floating rate currency, its exchange rate is determined by the market. In this case monetary policy is effective, but fiscal policy has little impact. When government either decreases its spending or increases taxes, the budget deficit goes down. Consequently, the interest rates go down. International investors react by taking their funds out of the country, which decreases the value of the currency and increases the country's exports by making them more affordable to the consumers abroad. Simultaneously, imports fall because they become more expensive for domestic consumers, which improves the country's balance of payments and offsets any contractive effect of the fiscal policy.

The Mundell-Fleming model was developed in the 1960s, before the advent of a global economy. "Now that funds can be transferred from dollar-to-yen-denominated assets with only a few clicks of a mouse," states Professor Mankiw of Harvard, the theory's "assumption of perfect capital mobility looks downright prescient."[14]

Foreign Currency Risk Exposure

An asset, liability, revenue, or expense account denominated in a foreign currency is exposed to foreign currency risk when that currency's exchange rate changes. In the case of translation, the currency rate changes affect only those accounts that are translated at the current rate; accounts translated at the historical rate are not affected. An international subsidiary has a **positive exposure** when its current assets exceed its current liabilities, and a **negative exposure** when its current liabilities exceed its current assets.

Example

Consider the following position of two international subsidiaries, fully owned by a U.S. parent company. The British subsidiary has a positive exposure because its current assets exceed its current liabilities. The French subsidiary has a negative exposure because it is in the reverse situation.

	British Subsidiary	French Subsidiary
Current assets	£8,000,000	F16,000,000
Current liabilities	5,500,000	20,000,000

The U.S. parent company will experience a translation gain when the value of the British pound appreciates relative to the U.S. dollar or when the value of the French franc declines relative to the U.S. dollar. The U.S. parent company will experience a translation loss when the value of the British pound depreciates relative to the U.S. dollar. The same will happen when the value of the French franc appreciates relative to the U.S. dollar.

Foreign Currency Rate Movement	Positive Exposure (CA>CL)	Negative Exposure (CA<CL)
Foreign currency appreciates	Translation gain	Translation loss
Foreign currency depreciates	Translation loss	Translation gain

The exposure to foreign currency risk is not limited to translation of financial statements. An appreciation in the value of the Japanese yen relative to the U.S. dollar adversely affects the value of a Japanese parent's investment in a U.S.

14 N. Gregory Mankiw. "A Theory for an Open World." *Fortune*, 20 December 1999, p. 58.

subsidiary. It also reduces the value of its profits and cash flows. Any cash flows from the U.S. subsidiary to the Japanese parent company would buy fewer yen at the new exchange rate.

Buyers and sellers of foreign goods and services are also exposed to foreign currency risk when the exchange rate changes between the transaction date and the settlement date. The following two sections discuss the transaction risk exposure and translation risk exposure in greater detail.

Transaction Risk Exposure

Foreign currency transactions require settlement in a foreign currency. This has implications for future cash flows. The **transaction risk exposure** is caused by the changes in the exchange rate between the transaction date and the settlement date. Only one of the two parties to the transaction is exposed.

Assume that an Egyptian company buys goods from a Dutch supplier and is required to pay at a later date in Dutch guilders. The Egyptian buyer faces transaction risk exposure while the Dutch supplier does not. If the contract requires payment in Egyptian pounds, then the Dutch supplier is the party facing a transaction risk exposure.

Example

Exhibit 2.7 shows business transactions entered into by a Japanese multinational company's Austrian subsidiary.

Note: Transaction risk exposure exists only when a transaction is denominated in a foreign currency and the settlement date is different from the transaction date.

Hedging Strategies

A company that faces transaction risk exposure may choose to do nothing to protect itself against possible future loss. In such a situation, if the foreign currency exchange rate is different at the settlement date, the company will experience a *realized* gain or loss depending on whether the rate change is favorable or unfavorable. To protect against the risks associated with foreign exchange fluctuations, managers may decide to take certain measures referred to as **hedging**. There are numerous financial instruments available for implementation of hedging strategies. Forward exchange contracts, discussed earlier in the chapter, are one of the commonly used instruments in hedging strategies.

Financial markets offer many ways to protect (hedge) against transaction risk exposure, and new ones are being developed. Some of the methods used to hedge against unacceptable levels of transaction risk exposure include:

- *Transaction denomination.* Either the buyer or the seller requires that the transaction be denominated in its currency. Accordingly, the foreign exchange risk exposure shifts to the other party.

- *Risk sharing.* The buyer and seller agree on a base transaction price at a specified exchange rate. The base price remains fixed if the exchange rate

exhibit 2.7   **Transaction Risk Exposure—Austrian Subsidiary of a Japanese Multinational Corporation**

Transaction	Transaction Date	Settlement Date	Transaction Denomination	Transaction Exposure	Exposed Currency
Purchase of raw material from Switzerland	February 1	April 1	Swiss franc	Yes	Swiss franc
Purchase of parts from a Korean supplier	February 1	March 1	Austrian schilling	No	—
Purchase of parts from Germany	February 10	April 10	German mark	Yes	German mark
Payment to a Brazilian company for use of its patent	March 1	March 1	Brazilian real	No	—
Service contract with a local trucking company	March 1	May 1, July 1	Austrian schilling	No	—
Sale of equipment to a Turkish company	June 1	September 1	Austrian schilling	No	—
Sale of parts to a U.S. company	June 1	August 1	U.S. dollar	Yes	U.S. dollar
Sale of equipment to a French company	June 15	September 15	French franc	Yes	French franc

changes within the range. The two parties share equally the effect of a change in the exchange rate outside the range.

- *Price adjustment.* The parties agree in advance to adjust the transaction price to offset any adverse impact to the exposed party from changes in the exchange rate.

- *Foreign currency forward contract.* A foreign currency forward contract with a currency dealer, e.g., a bank, to deliver in the future a certain amount of a foreign currency at an agreed-upon exchange rate.

- *Currency options contract.* A **currency options contract** gives one of the parties involved in the contract the right to decide in the future whether an exchange will actually take place at a certain price.

- *Cross-currency swap.* In a **cross-currency swap** two parties agree to exchange their liabilities or assets in different currencies.

- *Currency swaps.* A **currency swap** is an agreement to exchange two different currencies at an agreed exchange rate.

Companies account for transaction risk exposure currency by currency. Multinational corporations must decide whether to centralize or decentralize management of transaction risk exposure.

Accounting for Forward Exchange Contracts

Assume that General Motors (GM) sells trucks to a Saudi Arabian buyer on January 15, 20x3. The transaction price is 20 million Saudi riyals (SR) payable on April 15, 20x3. The spot rate on January 15 is SR1 = $0.30. GM faces a transaction risk exposure because any change in the exchange rate will affect the equivalent dollar amount GM receives on April 15.

GM chooses to hedge against this transaction risk exposure by entering into a forward exchange contract at the forward rate of SR1 = $0.28. GM is then assured of receiving $5,600,000 by delivering the 20 million Saudi riyals it receives on April 15 to the currency dealer.

GM records would show the following journal entries and ledger account amounts (in U.S. dollars).

January 15	1. Accounts Receivable	6,000,000	
	Sales Revenue		6,000,000
	Records sales transaction at the spot rate.		
	2. Deferred Foreign Exchange Expense	400,000	
	Deferred Credit		400,000
	Records the discount based on 20 million × ($0.30 – $0.28).		
April 15	3. Foreign Exchange Expense	400,000	
	Deferred Foreign Exchange Expense		400,000
	Records foreign exchange expense due to difference between the spot rate ($0.30) and the forward rate ($0.28).		
	4. Cash	5,600,000	
	Deferred Credit	400,000	
	Accounts Receivable		6,000,000
	Records execution of the forward exchange contract.		

Accounts Receivable					Sales Revenue		
(1)	6,000,000	6,000,000	(4)			6,000,000	(1)

Deferred Foreign Exchange Expense					Deferred Credit		
(2)	400,000	400,000	(3)	(4)	400,000	400,000	(2)

Cash			Foreign Exchange Expense		
(4)	5,600,000		(3)	400,000	

While a company protects itself against unacceptable changes in the exchange rate, it also gives up the opportunity for any potential gain in case the rate changes in its favor. This *opportunity gain or loss*, based on the forecast of future movements in the exchange rates, is one of the factors considered by financial managers when they contemplate entering into a forward exchange contract.

Example

Aalborg ApS, a Danish company, sold equipment to Falun AB, a Swedish company, on August 1. Falun will pay 1 million Swedish krona (Sk) to Aalborg on October 1. Exhibit 2.8 presents a forward exchange contract opportunity gain or loss based on assumed future spot rates of the Danish krone (Dkr) of .80, .82, .85, and .86 for one Swedish krona. Aalborg has entered into a forward exchange contract at the rate of Sk1 = Dkr.84.

Euro

Twelve members of the 15-member European Union have formed the European Monetary Union (EMU). The EMU introduced a common currency called the Euro on January 1, 1999. The Euro should provide at least two benefits to the EMU countries: Removal of the exchange rate risk among the 12 EMU countries, and reduction in intra-EMU transaction costs. Disappearance of the exchange rate risk, since all 12 countries have a common currency, is especially important to small businesses. Many of them previously did not export to other EMU countries due to foreign exchange risks. The benefit should be especially significant to small businesses in countries like Spain and Italy whose currencies have had a history of volatility. The companies in core EMU countries, such as Germany and France, might have stayed away from doing business with them due to unacceptable levels of exchange rate risks.

A common currency lowers transaction costs among the EMU member countries since the complexities of transacting business in different currencies disappear. It also benefits the consumers in those countries directly. A consumer in one member country can easily compare the cost of a product throughout the EMU. Such cost comparison enables the consumers to make purchases where they find the price to be most favorable.[15] Such a comparison is becoming increasingly easier, especially due to e-commerce.[16]

exhibit 2.8   Forward Contract Opportunity Gain or Loss

Spot Rate October 1	Accounts Receivable October 1		Aalborg ApS	
	Sk	Dkr	Cash Inflow	Opportunity Gain (Loss)
Sk1 = Dkr.80	1 million	800,000	840,000	40,000
Sk1 = Dkr.82	1 million	820,000	840,000	20,000
Sk1 = Dkr.85	1 million	850,000	840,000	(10,000)
Sk1 = Dkr.86	1 million	860,000	840,000	(20,000)

15 "Euro Set to Become Major International Trading Currency." *Gulf News*, 14 May 1998, p. 32.

16 *Statement on International Management Accounting Practice 3.* "Currency Exposure and Risk Management." New York: International Federation of Accountants, 1996, par. 30.

Translation Risk Exposure

Multinational corporations prepare consolidated financial statements reflecting worldwide results of operations, financial position, and cash flows. *Only the accounts translated at the current exchange rate are subject to translation risk exposure. Accounts translated at the historical exchange rate continue to appear at their constant value in the parent company's currency.* Earlier parts of this chapter presented four methods for translating the accounts of international subsidiaries into the parent company's currency. The amount of translation risk exposure depends on the method used to translate an international subsidiary's financial statements, its net asset or net liability position, the direction of the change in the foreign exchange rates, and the magnitude of such change. The combined effect of these four factors results in a change in the value of an international subsidiary's assets and liabilities measured in the parent company's currency.

We earlier presented four financial statement translation methods: the current rate method, the current-noncurrent method, the monetary-nonmonetary method, and the temporal method. We will use the example of the U.S. subsidiary in France, presented earlier in the chapter, to illustrate the accounting measurement of translation risk exposure on the subsidiary's balance sheet under each of the four translation methods. The following is The French Subsidiary's balance sheet on December 31, 20x2 in French francs (F):

The French Subsidiary
Balance Sheet
December 31, 20x2

Assets:			Liabilities and stockholders' equity:		
Cash	F	200,000	Accounts payable	F	2,500,000
Accounts receivable		1,000,000	Income tax payable		200,000
Inventories		2,000,000	Long-term debt		2,800,000
Property, plant, and			Total liabilities	F	5,500,000
equipment (net)		5,800,000	Stockholders' equity	F	3,500,000
			Total liabilities and		
Total assets		**F9,000,000**	stockholders' equity		**F9,000,000**

We will use an exchange rate of F1 = $0.15 to translate The French Subsidiary's accounts into U.S. dollars. As discussed earlier, a translation gain or loss occurs when the exchange rate changes. We will assume a decline in the value of the French franc to F1 = $0.10.

Exhibits 2.9 through 2.12 show the measurement of the balance sheet translation exposure under each of the four translation methods. Each translation method shows a different translation exposure amount measured in French francs, and a different translation gain (loss) amount measured in U.S. dollars.

Under the current rate translation method shown in Exhibit 2.9, the subsidiary net assets (equal to the stockholders' equity) in the amount of F3,500,000

exhibit 2.9 Translation Risk Exposure—Current Rate Method

	Balance Sheet in Francs	Translation before Devaluation of Franc (F1=$0.15)	Translation after Devaluation of Franc (F1=$0.10)
Assets:			
Cash	F 200,000	$ 30,000	$ 20,000
Accounts receivable	1,000,000	150,000	100,000
Inventories	2,000,000	300,000	200,000
Net property, plant, and equipment	5,800,000	870,000	580,000
Total assets	**F9,000,000**	**$1,350,000**	**$ 900,000**
Liabilities and stockholders' equity:			
Accounts payable	F 2,500,000	$ 375,000	$ 250,000
Income tax payable	200,000	30,000	20,000
Long-term debt	2,800,000	420,000	280,000
Stockholders' equity	3,500,000	525,000	350,000
Total liabilities and stockholders' equity	**F9,000,000**	**$1,350,000**	**$ 900,000**
Translation exposure	**F3,500,000**		
Translation loss			**$(175,000)**

is exposed. The devaluation of the French franc causes a translation loss of F3,500,000 × $0.05 = $175,000. Translation loss can also be computed as the difference between the balances of stockholders' equity before and after devaluation.

Stockholders' equity balance before devaluation	$525,000
Stockholders' equity balance after devaluation	350,000
Translation loss	$175,000

Under the current-noncurrent translation method shown in Exhibit 2.10, only the net working capital of F500,000 is exposed. The decline in the value of the French franc causes a translation loss to the U.S. parent company of F500,000 × $0.05 = $25,000.

Under the monetary-nonmonetary translation method shown in Exhibit 2.11, only the monetary assets and liabilities are exposed accounts. The French Subsidiary has a negative risk exposure because its monetary liabilities

exhibit 2.10 Translation Risk Exposure—Current-Noncurrent Method

	Balance Sheet in Francs	Translation before Devaluation of Franc (F1=$0.15)	Translation after Devaluation of Franc (F1=$0.10)
Assets:			
Cash	F 200,000	$ 30,000	$ 20,000
Accounts receivable	1,000,000	150,000	100,000
Inventories	2,000,000	300,000	200,000
Net property, plant, and equipment	5,800,000	870,000	870,000
Total assets	**F9,000,000**	**$1,350,000**	**$1,190,000**
Liabilities and stockholders' equity:			
Accounts payable	F 2,500,000	$ 375,000	$ 250,000
Income tax payable	200,000	30,000	20,000
Long-term debt	2,800,000	420,000	420,000
Stockholders' equity	3,500,000	525,000	500,000
Total liabilities and stockholders' equity	**F9,000,000**	**$1,350,000**	**$1,190,000**
Translation exposure	**F 500,000**		
Translation loss			$ (25,000)

(F5,500,000) exceed its monetary assets (F1,200,000). The negative risk exposure of F4,300,000 causes a translation gain of F4,300,000 × $0.05 = $215,000.

Under the temporal translation method shown in Exhibit 2.12, cash, accounts receivable, and total liabilities are exposed, the reason being that the total liabilities consist of payables only. Total liabilities of F5,500,000 exceed the exposed current assets of F1,200,000 by F4,300,000. This negative risk exposure results in a translation gain of F4,300,000 × $0.05 = $215,000.

The translation risk exposure measured previously represents a risk that results from consolidation of The French Subsidiary's foreign currency balance sheet into the parent company accounts measured in U.S. dollars. A decline in the value of the French franc with a negative exposure resulted in a translation gain. If a decline in the value of the French franc were accompanied by a positive exposure, a translation loss would have been incurred.

Multinational corporations can manage their translation exposure presented by entering into forward exchange contracts. Alternatively, they can adjust the international subsidiary fund flows. For example, a positive exposure and a decline

exhibit 2.11 Translation Risk Exposure—Monetary-Nonmonetary Method

	Balance Sheet in Francs	Translation before Devaluation of Franc (F1=$0.15)	Translation after Devaluation of Franc (F1=$0.10)
Assets:			
Cash*	F 200,000	$ 30,000	$ 20,000
Accounts receivable*	1,000,000	150,000	100,000
Inventories	2,000,000	300,000	300,000
Net property, plant, and equipment	5,800,000	870,000	870,000
Total assets	**F9,000,000**	**$1,350,000**	**$1,290,000**
Liabilities and stockholders' equity:			
Accounts payable*	F 2,500,000	$ 375,000	$ 250,000
Income tax payable*	200,000	30,000	20,000
Long-term debt*	2,800,000	420,000	280,000
Stockholders' equity	3,500,000	525,000	740,000
Total liabilities and stockholders' equity	**F9,000,000**	**$1,350,000**	**$1,290,000**
Translation exposure	**F4,300,000**		
Translation gain			**$ 215,000**

*Monetary items

in the value of the foreign currency would mean that the parent company should attempt to reduce the foreign currency assets and increase the foreign currency liabilities. The following summarizes the adjustment of fund flows between a parent company and its international subsidiary.

Foreign Currency Rate Movement	Net Assets Exposure	Net Liabilities Exposure
Foreign currency appreciates	Increase	Decrease
Foreign currency depreciates	Decrease	Increase

The transaction risk exposure and the translation risk exposure are known as **accounting exposures**. Transaction exposure focuses on the outstanding future foreign currency receipts and payments. Translation exposure focuses on the classification of financial statement items in two categories: those affected by changes in the foreign currency rates and those that are unaffected. Neither exposure

exhibit 2.12 Translation Risk Exposure—Temporal Method

	Balance Sheet in Francs	Translation before Devaluation of Franc (F1=$0.15)	Translation after Devaluation of Franc (F1=$0.10)
Assets:			
Cash	F 200,000	$ 30,000	$ 20,000
Accounts receivable	1,000,000	150,000	100,000
Inventories	2,000,000	300,000	300,000
Net property, plant, and equipment	5,800,000	870,000	870,000
Total assets	**F9,000,000**	**$1,350,000**	**$1,290,000**
Liabilities and stockholders' equity:			
Accounts payable	F 2,500,000	$ 375,000	$ 250,000
Income tax payable	200,000	30,000	20,000
Long-term debt	2,800,000	420,000	280,000
Stockholders' equity	3,500,000	525,000	740,000
Total liabilities and stockholders' equity	**F9,000,000**	**$1,350,000**	**$1,290,000**
Translation exposure	**F2,300,000**		
Translation gain			**$ 215,000**

addresses the impact of changes in the exchange rates on future cash flows resulting from operating decisions.

Economic Exposure

Changes in foreign exchange rates affect the competitive position of the company in international markets. **Economic exposure** results from the impact of changes in exchange rates on future cash flows.

A change in exchange rates affects prices of a subsidiary's inputs and outputs in the market, thus affecting its profitability and its future cash flow.

Economic exposure will almost certainly be many times more significant than either transaction or translation exposure for the long-term well-being of the enterprise. By its very nature, it is subjective and variable, due *in part* to the need to estimate future cash flows in foreign currencies. The enterprise needs to plan its strategy, and to make operational decisions in the best way possible, to optimize its position in anticipation of changes in economic conditions.[17]

An international subsidiary that obtains its raw material and labor from its local market will not have its costs affected by changes in the exchange rates. However, if it acquires raw materials from another country, the cost of raw material will increase every time the subsidiary's local currency depreciates relative to the currency of the country from which it acquires raw material. Sales revenues are affected as well when the subsidiary sells its output in a foreign market. Sales revenues will increase every time the currency of that market appreciates relative to the subsidiary's local currency.

Economic exposure is caused by actual changes in exchange rates between currencies of countries in which the subsidiary operates.

To measure the economic exposure of a U.S. multinational corporation having two subsidiaries in Great Britain, we will assume a change in the British pound exchange rate from £1 = $2.00 to £1 = $1.50.

Exhibit 2.13 shows an example of the results of operations for each subsidiary measured in British pounds and U.S. dollars before a decrease in the value of the pound relative to the dollar. Each subsidiary sells its outputs in, and acquires its inputs from, both countries. Each subsidiary is allocated parent company overhead of $250,000. Each subsidiary shows an operating income of $750,000 and cash flow from operations of $1,000,000.

Exhibit 2.14 shows the effect of a decline in the exchange rate of £1.00 from $2.00 to $1.50. This affects the competitive position, the reported operating income, and the cash flows of the two subsidiaries. Subsidiary A, which sells more in the U.S. and sources more inputs in Britain, gained from the change in the

exhibit 2.13 **Results of Operations with Exchange Rate of £1 = $2.00**

	Subsidiary A			Subsidiary B		
	$	£	Total $	$	£	Total $
Sales (a)	$4,000,000	£ 500,000	$ 5,000,000	$1,000,000	£2,000,000	$ 5,000,000
Operating expenses (b)	1,000,000	1,500,000	4,000,000	3,000,000	500,000	4,000,000
Allocated corporate overhead	250,000	—	250,000	250,000	—	250,000
Operating income			$ 750,000			$ 750,000
Cash flow (a – b)			$1,000,000			$1,000,000

17 *Statement on International Management Accounting Practice 3.* "Currency Exposure and Risk Management." New York: International Federation of Accountants, 1996, par. 30.

exhibit 2.14   **Results of Operations with Exchange Rate of £1 = $1.50**

	Subsidiary A			Subsidiary B		
	$	£	Total $	$	£	Total $
Sales (a)	$4,000,000	£ 500,000	$ 4,750,000	$1,000,000	£2,000,000	$ 4,000,000
Operating expenses (b)	1,000,000	1,500,000	3,250,000	3,000,000	500,000	3,750,000
Allocated corporate overhead	250,000	—	250,000	250,000	—	250,000
Operating income			**$1,250,000**			**$ 0**
Cash flow (a − b)			**$1,500,000**			**$ 250,000**

exchange rate. Its operating income and cash flow have increased to $1,250,000 and $1,500,000, respectively. Subsidiary B, which sells relatively more in Britain and sources less inputs in Britain, finds that its operating income disappears as a result of the change in the exchange rate. Its cash flow also drops from $1,000,000 to $250,000.

Note: Cash flows from the subsidiaries are not affected by the allocated corporate overhead.

The following table summarizes the effects of a change in the foreign currency exchange rate on a subsidiary's competitive position, operating profit, and cash flows resulting from the depreciation or appreciation of the value of its currency relative to other currencies. It assumes that the outside selling price is expressed in the currency of the country where sales are made and it does not change.

Foreign Currency Rate Movement	Selling More Output to Outside and Sourcing More at Home	Selling Less Output to Outside and Sourcing Less at Home
Subsidiary currency appreciates	Worse	Improved
Subsidiary currency depreciates	Improved	Worse

Managing economic exposure is a complex task for corporations that do business in countries with volatile foreign exchange rates. Methods of managing economic exposure include:

- Taking into account economic exposure in the decision-making process involving the location of manufacturing facilities.
- Using the portfolio approach. In the **portfolio approach**, the parent company balances negative economic exposure in one country with positive economic exposure in other countries.
- Flexible planning to take advantage of favorable changes in foreign currency exchange rates and avoiding or minimizing the impact of unfavorable movement in foreign currency exchange rates.

- Pricing and promotion planning to adjust to changing competitive position in weak currency countries.

Prediction of Foreign Currency Exchange Rate Changes

The measurement of transaction, translation, and economic risk exposures, and the management of foreign currency exchange risk require the ability to accurately predict changes in exchange rates. Multinational corporations must develop an effective information system that will enable them to track, assess, and predict changes in foreign exchange rates. The system must account for all major relevant factors that will most likely cause changes in exchange rates. Some of the important factors that affect the exchange rate between two currencies include:

- *The political and social environments of the countries.* Stable environments have lower risks. A country with social unrest and/or political instability carries a higher risk level, with adverse effect on the value of its currency.
- *Political risk.* Government policies toward multinationals' economic activities and investments. If the government of a country nationalizes or expropriates assets of multinationals, other multinationals and investors would be motivated to divest in that country. This depreciates the value of a country's currency.
- *Economic growth.* Rates of economic growth and changes in productivity have a direct relationship to the value of a country's currency.
- *Inflation.* Typically, the inflation rate of a country has an inverse relationship to the exchange rate of its currency relative to the currency of other countries with lower inflation rates.
- *Balance of payments.* A country experiencing a balance of payments problem may devalue its currency in an attempt to improve its balance of trade and payments.
- *Interest rates.* Higher interest rates generate more demand on that country's currency. This results in a higher exchange rate with respect to countries with lower interest rates.

These factors should be considered in the design of a multinational company's information system.

Important: *Collective*, and not individual, impact of the previous factors should be considered. Weight assigned to each factor would vary from country to country.

Appendix 2A

Statements of Financial Accounting Standards No. 52: Foreign Currency and No. 133: Accounting for Derivative Instruments and Hedging Activities

Translation and Remeasurement

In the U.S., the Financial Accounting Standards Board's *Statement of Financial Accounting Standards No. 52*, "Foreign Currency Translation," is the current authoritative pronouncement on foreign currency. *SFAS No. 52* recognizes a local company perspective. The method of conversion depends on the functional currency of the foreign operation. **Functional currency** is the currency of the primary economic environment in which the international subsidiary operates. Generally, it means that the international entity generates and expends cash in the functional currency.[18] The following summarizes other guidelines provided by the Financial Accounting Standards Board to determine a firm's functional currency in addition to cash flows.

- If the sales price of the international subsidiary's products is determined by worldwide competition rather than the local market, then the functional currency may be the parent's currency.

- If costs for the subsidiary's product are primarily local costs, then the functional currency may be the international subsidiary's local currency.

- If the sales market is mostly in the parent's country or sales are denominated in the parent's currency, then the functional currency may be the parent's currency.

- If financing is denominated in the international subsidiary's local currency, then the functional currency may be the subsidiary's local currency.[19]

The *SFAS No. 52* requirements are designed to reflect in the consolidated financial statements the financial results and relationships of individual consolidated entities as measured in their primary, that is, functional currency.[20]

The previous discussion may be summarized in the following manner:

- If the international subsidiary is self-sustaining, that is, its operations are confined to the country in which it is located, the local currency would be the functional currency. For example, if the subsidiary of a U.S. pharmaceutical firm manufactures, markets, and distributes its products in Thailand, the functional currency of the subsidiary will be the local currency, the Thai baht.

---

18 *Statement of Financial Accounting Standards No. 52.* "Foreign Currency Translation." Stamford, Conn.: Financial Accounting Standards Board, 1981, Appendix A.

19 Jay M. Smith and K. Fred Skousen. *Intermediate Accounting*, 11th ed. Cincinnati, Ohio: South-Western Publishing Co., 1992, p. 1022.

20 *SFAS No. 52*, par. 70.

- If operations of a foreign subsidiary are integrated with the parent company, the functional currency would be the parent company's currency. For example, an Indonesian operation assembles the parts received from its U.S. parent company and returns the product to the U.S. parent for marketing and distribution. The functional currency of the Indonesian subsidiary is the U.S. dollar.

In a highly inflationary economy, *SFAS No. 52* requires the use of the reporting currency as the functional currency. A highly inflationary economy is defined as one that has cumulative inflation of approximately 100 percent or more over a three-year period.

If the international subsidiary's functional currency is judged to be the foreign currency (self-sustaining operation), its financial statements are *translated* to U.S. dollars using the current rate method. Translation gains and losses are disclosed separately in the stockholder's equity section of the consolidated balance sheet.

If the U.S. dollar is deemed to be the functional currency (integrated operation), the international subsidiary's financial statements are *remeasured* using the temporal method. Translation gains and losses are included in the current period's consolidated income statement.[21]

Note the terminology *translated* and *remeasured* as used in *SFAS No. 52*.

Foreign Currency Transactions

SFAS No. 52 defines a foreign currency transaction as a transaction requiring settlement in a foreign currency.

The rules for foreign currency transactions in *SFAS No. 52* are:

- At the date of transaction, each asset, liability, revenue, expense, gain, or loss arising from the transaction are measured and recorded in the functional currency of the recording entity by use of the exchange rate in effect at that date.
- At each balance sheet date, recorded balances that are denominated in a currency other than the functional currency of the recording entity are adjusted to reflect the current exchange rate.[22]

For foreign currency transactions, the two-transaction approach is used. There are two exceptions to this requirement: when the exchange adjustments relate to certain intercompany transactions that are of a long-term nature, and when foreign currency transactions are intended to offset other exchange gains or losses that would normally be reported in the income statement.

Required financial statement disclosures include:

- A total transaction gain or loss included in determining income for the current period.

---

21 *Ibid.*, par. 15.
22 *Ibid.*, par. 16.

- An analysis of changes during the period in shareholders' equity arising from translation adjustments.
- Any material rate changes that occur after the balance sheet date.

Summary of SFAS No. 52

According to *SFAS No. 52*, the method of conversion depends on the international subsidiary's functional currency. If the functional currency is the U.S. dollar, its financial statements are *remeasured* using the temporal method. If the functional currency is the local currency, the financial statements are *translated* using the current rate method.

SFAS No. 52 requires the two-transaction approach for foreign currency transactions.

Hedge Accounting

Statement of Financial Accounting Standards No. 133, "Accounting for Derivative Instruments and Hedging Activities," provides standards for hedge accounting:

- All derivative financial statements must be measured and reported at their fair value in the balance sheet.
- No method used for hedge accounting should result in the reporting of deferred gains or losses in the balance sheet.
- Any gain or loss from remeasuring hedging instruments at fair value is recognized in the income statement immediately.[23]

Appendix 2B

International Accounting Standards 21 (Revised) and 39: The Effects of Changes in Foreign Exchange Rates Financial Instruments: Recognition and Measurement

The International Accounting Standards Committee's *IAS 21* deals with foreign currency.[24] For integrated international operations, *IAS 21* requires that the financial statements be translated using the temporal method. Translation gains or losses are included in the current period's consolidated income statement.

The standard requires the use of the current rate method for translation of self-sustaining international operations. The translation gains or losses are transferred to reserves and reported in the shareholders' equity section of the consolidated balance sheet.

---

23 *Statement of Financial Accounting Standards No. 133.* "Accounting for Derivative Instruments and Hedging Activities." Stamford, Conn.: Financial Accounting Standards Board, 1998.

24 *International Accounting Standard 21.* "The Effects of Changes in Foreign Exchange Rates." London: International Accounting Standards Committee, 1983 and the revisions approved in 1993.

The disclosure requirements include:

- An analysis of the impact of the translation adjustment on related parts of the stockholders' equity and the income statement.
- Methods used for translation.

In general, *IAS 21* recommends the two-transaction approach for foreign currency transactions. The revised *IAS 21* requires that the financial statements of international subsidiaries operating in hyperinflationary economies must be restated in accordance with *IAS 29*, prior to translation.

IAS 39 went into effect on January 1, 2001. Its guidelines and U.S. guidelines in *SFAS No. 133* (discussed earlier in Appendix 2A) are similar. Both *IAS 39* and *SFAS No. 133* require that any gain or loss from remeasuring hedging instruments at fair value is recognized in the income statement immediately. However, there are a few differences between *IAS 39* and *SFAS No. 133* relating to the type of transactions that qualify for hedge accounting, and in the application of some hedge accounting methods.[25]

Appendix 2C

Currencies of Selected Countries Not Included in Exhibit 2.1

Angola	Kwanza	Jamaica	Dollar
Azerbaijan	Manat	Kenya	Shilling
Bahamas	Dollar	Luxembourg	Franc
Bangladesh	Taka	Morocco	Dirham
Bermuda	Dollar	Nigeria	Naira
Bolivia	Boliviano	Oman	Rial
Botswana	Pula	Papua New Guinea	Kina
Brunei Darussalam	Dollar	Paraguay	Guaraní
Cambodia	Riel	Qatar	Riyal
Costa Rica	Colon	Swaziland	Lilangeni
Cyprus	Pound	Tanzania	Shilling
Egypt	Pound	Tunisia	Dinar
El Salvador	Colon	Uganda	Shilling
Fiji	Dollar	Vietnam	Dong
Ghana	Cedi	Western Samoa	Tala
Iceland	Krona	Yemen	Riyal
Iran	Rial	Zimbabwe	Dollar

25 *International Accounting Standard 39*. "Financial Instruments: Recognition and Measurement." London: International Accounting Standards Committee, 1998.

Note to Students

To get an in-depth understanding of the accounting treatment of foreign currency in generally accepted accounting principles of a specific country, study the authoritative pronouncements. It is also helpful to review annual reports of actual companies showing the application of the foreign currency standards. The foreign currency topic is extremely important: The greater the degree of globalization, the greater the cross-border mobility of funds in different currencies.

One of the important lessons you should learn from this chapter is that drastic downward changes in the value of a country's currency often have important ramifications on its economy. These include the balance of payments, rate of inflation, and interest rate. Their ripple effect sometimes can lead to political tremors. Why? Because in a free market system it is virtually impossible to separate economics from politics. You have probably heard the often made comment during political elections, "It is the economy, stupid!" Crude as it may sound, there is a lot of truth in it. Political turmoil in Thailand, Indonesia, South Korea, and other countries that followed the 1997 Asian currency crisis attests to this fact. The crisis started with the rapid outflow of foreign investment funds from the region, which drastically and adversely affected currency values in this region.

In this age of global economy, it is important to understand that numbers often act as catalysts for changes in social, economic, and political environments.

Chapter Summary

1. One of the complexities in the financial reporting of companies involved in international activities (operations and investment) is caused by different currencies.

2. Accounting for foreign currency transactions and foreign currency translation requires the application of prescribed standards.

3. For foreign currency transactions, two approaches exist: the one-transaction approach or the two-transaction approach. The latter is more popular in practice worldwide.

4. The four basic methods for translating financial statements in a foreign currency are the current rate method, the current-noncurrent method, the monetary-nonmonetary method, and the temporal method.

5. Assets, liabilities, revenues, and expenses denominated in a foreign currency are exposed to foreign exchange risk.

6. Transaction, translation, and economic exposures are related to the payment and receipt of cash, amount of exposed resources, and future cash flows, respectively.

7. Introduction of the Euro as a common currency in the EMU provides several benefits to the member countries.

8. The concept of economic exposure relates to the impact of volatile exchange rates on a company's competitive position.

9. Forecasting foreign exchange rates depends on multiple factors.

10. Requirements for financial statement translation and hedge accounting are similar, though not identical in *SFASs* and *IASs* (Appendices 2A and 2B).

Questions for Discussion

1. Define foreign currency transactions.

2. What are the two approaches for recording foreign currency transactions?

3. What is the underlying logic for using the two-transaction approach as opposed to the one-transaction approach?

4. What are the advantages and disadvantages of using the one-transaction approach versus the two-transaction approach in accounting for foreign exchange gains and losses?

5. Do you prefer the one-transaction approach or the two-transaction approach to foreign currency transactions? Give reasons for your preference.

6. Can a firm take measures to eliminate the risks associated with foreign currency transactions due to exchange rate fluctuations? Explain.

7. What is a forward exchange contract?

8. What are the key features of a forward exchange contract?

9. Refer to Exhibit 2.1 in the chapter. Did the market expect the Swiss franc to steadily increase, decrease, or stay the same relative to the U.S. dollar over the next few months?

10. Regarding a transaction gain or loss and a translation gain or loss, which one is realized?

11. What is meant by an integrated operation? a self-sustaining operation?

12. Discuss the current rate method of foreign currency translation.

13. Explain and evaluate the current-noncurrent method of foreign currency translation.

14. Explain and evaluate the monetary-nonmonetary method of foreign currency translation.

15. Discuss the temporal method of foreign currency translation.

16. Which of the four translation methods discussed in the chapter recognizes the different operating environment of a foreign operation?

17. Since foreign currency translation merely involves conversion of a foreign currency balance to another currency by using the appropriate exchange rate, why is it such a complex topic?

18. Define, compare, and contrast the following:
    a. Transaction exposure.
    b. Translation exposure.
    c. Economic exposure.

19. A multinational corporation is considering a large sale to a Jordanian company and is considering whether to agree to accept sales proceeds in Jordanian dinars. You are the business consultant to the multinational company. Write a memorandum to the management of the company discussing the relevant issues before entering into a sales agreement.

20. What is meant by foreign exchange risk management?

21. According to the Mundell-Fleming Model, either monetary or fiscal policy is effective depending on whether the country has a fixed rate currency or a floating rate currency. Explain.

22. What are the expected benefits to the EMU countries from the euro?

23. (Appendix 2A) Explain the concept of functional currency as used in *SFAS No. 52*.

24. (Appendix 2A) Identify the primary factor in determining a firm's functional currency. What other factors can influence the determination of the firm's functional currency?

25. (Appendix 2A) Explain the terms *translation* and *remeasurement* as used in *SFAS No. 52*, "Foreign Currency Translation."

26. (Appendix 2A) Describe the requirements of *SFAS No. 52* of the methods for conversion of financial statements of an international subsidiary.

27. (Appendix 2A) What is the required approach for foreign currency transactions by *SFAS No. 52*?

28. (Appendix 2B) What is the approach of *IAS 21* (revised) for translation of financial statements of an international subsidiary?

29. (Appendix 2B) What method should be used for foreign currency transactions according to *IAS 21* (revised)?

30. (Appendices 2A and 2B) Compare the hedging guidelines of *SFAS No. 133* with *IAS 39*.

Exercises/Problems

2-1 Shaukat Imports, a German corporation, purchased merchandise on May 1 on a 30-day open account in the sum of 60,000 Dutch guilders from Netherlands Exports. On May 1, the rate of exchange was 1 Dutch guilder = 0.90 German mark.

On May 31, Shaukat Imports purchased a draft in the sum of 60,000 Dutch guilders for payment to Netherlands Exports at the cost of 50,000 German marks.

Required:

(1) Using the one-transaction approach, what entries are to be recorded on the books of Shaukat Imports:

    a. on May 1.
    b. on May 31.
    Show computations.

(2) Do requirement (1) using the two-transaction approach. Show computations.

2-2 Nabila Surfboards, a U.S. corporation, sold merchandise on March 1 on a 30-day open account in the sum of 100,000 Argentine pesos to Juan Importers. The rate for the Argentine peso on March 1 was 1 U.S. dollar = 1.05 Argentine pesos. On April 1, Juan Importers paid its account by remitting 100,000 Argentine pesos to Nabila Surfboards. The rate on April 1 was 1 U.S. dollar = 1.10 Argentine peso.

Required:

(1) Using the one-transaction approach, what entries are to be recorded by Nabila Surfboards:

    a. on March 1.
    b. on April 1.
    Show computations.

(2) Complete requirement (1) using the two-transaction approach. Show computations.

2-3 On July 15, Robison Los Osos Enterprises, a calendar-year U.S. manufacturer, purchased 100 million yen worth of parts from Yokoyama Company paying 20 percent down, with the balance to be paid in three months. Interest at the annual rate of 10 percent is payable on the unpaid foreign currency balance. The exchange rate on July 15 was $1.00 = ¥125. On October 15, the exchange rate was $1.00 = ¥110.

Required:

Prepare journal entries for Robison to record the incurrence and settlement of this foreign currency transaction using the:

(1) one-transaction approach.

(2) two-transaction approach.

2-4 Li Corporation is the Taiwanese subsidiary of Armstrong International, a Canadian manufacturer. The current exchange rate is Can$.05 = NT$1 (20 Taiwanese dollars to the Canadian dollar). The historical exchange rate is Can$.04 = NT$1 (25 Taiwanese dollars to the Canadian dollar). Li's balance sheet follows.

Li Corporation
Balance Sheet
June 30, 20x1
(Amounts in 000,000)

Assets:			Liabilities and stockholders' equity:		
Cash	NT $	10,000	Accounts payable	NT $	20,000
Accounts receivable		20,000	Long-term liabilities		30,000
Inventories (cost $30,000)		25,000	Total liabilities	NT $	50,000
Fixed assets (net)		50,000	Shareholders' equity	NT $	55,000
Total	**NT$105,000**		Total	**NT$105,000**	

Inventories are carried at the lower of cost or market.

Required:

Translate the Taiwanese dollar balance sheet of Li Corporation into Canadian dollars using the current rate method.

2-5 Based on the information in Problem 2-4, translate Li Corporation's balance sheet using the current-noncurrent method.

2-6 Based on the information in Problem 2-4, translate Li Corporation's balance sheet using the monetary-nonmonetary method.

2-7 Based on the information in Problem 2-4, translate Li Corporation's balance sheet using the temporal method.

2-8 Waheed, SA is a Switzerland-based multinational company. The financial statements of its Malaysian subsidiary, Waheed Malaysian Bhd., follow in Malaysian currency, ringgit (RM).

Waheed Malaysian Bhd.
Balance Sheet
December 31, 20x1
(in 000,000)

Assets:	
Cash	RM 150,000
Accounts receivable	225,000
Merchandise inventory	60,000
Fixed assets (net)	400,000
Total assets	**RM835,000**

Liabilities and stockholders' equity:	
Current liabilities	RM 200,000
Long-term debt	250,000
Common stock	310,000
Retained earnings	75,000
Total liabilities and stockholders' equity	**RM835,000**

Waheed Malaysian Bhd.
Statement of Income and Retained Earnings
for the Year Ended December 31, 20x1
(in 000,000)

Sales	RM 600,000
Cost of goods sold	(250,000)
Gross profit	RM 350,000
Depreciation expense	RM (55,000)
Other expense	(105,000)
Total operating expenses	RM (160,000)
Income before tax	RM 190,000
Income tax	(90,000)
Net income	RM 100,000
Retained earnings January 1, 20x1	20,000
Dividends	(45,000)
Retained earnings December 31, 20x1	**RM 75,000**

The following exchange rates are per unit of RM for Swiss Franc (SFr):

At December 31, 20x1	SFr.40
When fixed assets acquired, long-term	
debt incurred, and capital stock sold	.60
Weighted average for 20x1	.48
At July 1, 20x1	.47
At October 1, 20x1	.53
At December 31, 20x1	.55
For 20x1 beginning inventory	.42
For 20x1 ending inventory	.54

Additional information:

- Revenues were earned, expenses were incurred, and inventory purchases were made uniformly during the year.
- Dividends were declared in equal amounts on July 1 and October 1 in 20x1.
- The balance in the retained earnings account on January 1, 20x1 was SFr15,000,000,000.
- Beginning and ending inventory balances were RM50,000,000,000 and RM60,000,000,000, respectively.

Required:

(1) Translate the financial statements using the current rate method.

(2) Translate the financial statements using the temporal method.

2-9 Identify the exchange rates for the items below under each of the four foreign currency translation methods discussed in this chapter by using the appropriate letter. If the item happens to be a balancing figure, use the letter B.

H—Historical rate
C—Current rate
A—Weighted average rate
B—Balancing figure

a. Cash
b. Accounts receivable
c. Inventory (at cost)
d. Long-term receivables
e. Long-term investments
f. Property, plant, and equipment
g. Long-term intangible assets
h. Accounts payable
i. Long-term debt
j. Paid-in capital
k. Retained earnings
l. Sales revenue
m. Cost of goods sold
n. Depreciation expense
o. Amortization expense

2-10 Asma & Co., an Egyptian subsidiary of Parvin Industries PLC, had the following balance sheet on March 31, 20x3:

Asma & Co.
Balance Sheet
March 31, 20x3
(in 000)

Assets:			Liabilities and stockholders' equity:		
Cash	£E	1,998	Taxes payable—current	£E	2,502
Short-term investments,			Other current liabilities		23,502
equity securities		1,500	Long-term notes payable		25,500
Accounts receivable		39,000	Bonds payable		45,000
Inventories		26,004	Total liabilities	£E	96,504
Net long-term assets		91,998	Stockholders' equity	£E	63,996
Total		£E160,500	Total		£E160,500

The exchange rate on March 31 was 6 Egyptian pounds (£E) for one British pound (£UK).

Required:

Compute Asma's translation exposure under the current-noncurrent translation method.

2-11 Refer to the balance sheet of Asma & Co. in Problem 2-10.

Required:

Compute Asma's translation exposure under the monetary-nonmonetary translation method. Assume all long-term assets are nonmonetary and other current liabilities are monetary.

2-12 Gopal Canadian, Inc. entered into the following business transactions during 20x3:

a. Purchased raw material from a Mexican supplier for 8,000,000 pesos on February 1. The purchase agreement calls for payment within 45 days in pesos. The exchange rate on February 1 was Canadian dollar (Can$)1 = 6.3 pesos (Ps).

b. Purchased parts and components from a U.S. supplier. Delivery of goods and payments occurred on March 1 and June 1. Each shipment had a price of Can$250,000. Exchange rates on March 1 and June 1 were Can$1 = US$0.63 and US$0.69, respectively.

c. Sold equipment to a French company for 6,500,000 francs (F) on March 20. Collection of receivables in francs is scheduled for June 20. The exchange rate on March 20 was F4.1 = Can$1.

d. Granted a loan on March 1 to a newly starting company in the Philippines with the option to convert the loan to equity capital within four months. Otherwise, the loan amount of Can$3,200,000 is to be paid back in Philippine pesos (P) on August 1. The exchange rate on March 1 was Can$1 = P27.

e. On May 10 paid Can$800,000 to an American software vendor for a new computer system.

f. Borrowed 12,000,000 yen (¥) on April 1 from a Japanese bank. The loan and interest are to be paid back after six months. The annual interest rate is 12 percent.

g. Agreed to send 20 middle managers to attend a summer session at Harvard Business School. Total cost of the program is estimated to be U.S.$11,500 per person. The session begins on July 15. A deposit of 20 percent of the cost is required two months in advance. The remainder is due on the first day of the session. The exchange rate on May 15 was Can$1 = U.S.$0.68.

h. Entered into a contract to purchase components from another Canadian company. The contract calls for six shipments beginning May

1 at a cost of Can$120,000 per shipment. Each payment is due one month after delivery.

Required:

For each of the previous transactions, indicate whether Gopal Canadian, Inc. faces a transaction risk exposure. For each risk exposure, indicate the currency and the amount exposed.

2-13 Refer to transaction c in Problem 2-12. Gopal Canadian, Inc. decided to hedge against future changes in the exchange rate and entered into a forward exchange contract with Banque de France. The forward rate was F4.2 = Can$1.

Required:

Record the entries on March 20 and June 20 relating to the sales transaction and the forward contract agreement.

2-14 Soenen A/S is a fully owned Norwegian subsidiary of Mehta Montana Co. (MM), a U.S.-based corporation. The budgeted income statement of Soenen A/S for 20x3 follows. Soenen is expected to transfer its net cash flow to MM annually on December 31. Budget variances were immaterial. The exchange rate at the time of budget preparation was Norwegian krone (NKr)7.6 = $1. At the end of the year, the exchange rate was NKr8.0 = $1.

Soenen A/S
Budgeted Income Statement
For the Year ending December 31, 20x3

Sales revenue	NKr 24,000,000
Cost of sales	(13,200,000)
Gross margin	10,800,000
Operating expenses*	(4,400,000)
Income before taxes	6,400,000
Income tax	(1,600,000)
Net income	**NKr 4,800,000**

*Includes NKr940,000 depreciation expense.

Required:

(1) Compute the net cash flow in the Norwegian krone and in the U.S. dollar.

(2) Explain the economic impact of the exchange rate change.

(3) What can Soenen A/S do in the future to manage its risk exposure?

2-15 A sale for 200,000 francs was made by a French company to a Canadian company when the exchange rate was F4.0 = Can$1.00. The rate changed to F4.5 = Can$1.00 on the date payment was due. The transaction is denominated in francs.

Required:

(1) Did the seller face any transaction exposure? If the answer is yes, what was the amount?

(2) Did the buyer have any transaction gain or loss? If the answer is yes, was it a gain or loss, and what was the amount?

2-16 U.S.-based Anderson Company engages in a number of foreign currency transactions that have resulted in the following balances:

Cash: British pounds	800,000
Cash: Swiss francs	500,000
Accounts receivable: Swiss francs	3,200,000
Accounts receivable: British pounds	1,050,000
Accounts payable: Swiss francs	700,000
Accounts payable: Swedish krona	800,000
Notes payable: Swedish krona	200,000

Management forecasts the following exchange rate changes for the near future:

- The Swiss franc will weaken against the dollar by 5 percent.
- The British pound will strengthen relative to the dollar by 10 percent.
- The Swedish krona will strengthen against the dollar by 15 percent.

Required:

Develop a strategy for Anderson's foreign currency. The strategy should maximize Anderson's gain or minimize its loss, whatever the case.

2-17 (Appendix 2A) The functional currency of an international operation is the South African rand (R). The following items are denominated in rand.

  a. Cash
  b. Merchandise inventories
  c. Accounts receivable
  d. Corporate headquarters building
  e. Accounts payable
  f. Long-term debt
  g. Revenue from sales
  h. Long-term notes receivable
  i. Prepaid rent
  j. Copyrights
  k. Depreciation expense
  l   Amortization expense
  m. Accounts payable for copyrights
  n. Short-term notes payable

Required:

For each previous item indicate whether a current (C), a weighted average (A), or an historical (H) exchange rate would be used to translate its foreign currency amount into U.S. dollars under *SFAS No. 52*.

2-18 (Appendix 2A) Assume that the U.S. dollar is the functional currency of a subsidiary in Portugal. The following items are denominated in the Portugese escudo (Esc).

- a. Sales revenue
- b. Depreciation expense
- c. Accounts receivable
- d. Long-term notes receivable
- e. Long-term bonds payable
- f. Prepaid insurance
- g. Goodwill
- h. Salaries expense
- i. Property, plant, and equipment
- j. Cash
- k. Accounts payable
- l. Income taxes expense
- m. Merchandise inventories

Required:

For each item, indicate what exchange rate under *SFAS No. 52* should be used to remeasure its foreign currency amounts into the U.S. dollar. Use (H) for the historical rate, (C) for the current rate, and (A) for the weighted average rate.

2-19 (Appendix 2A) Holt Corporation's subsidiary in Poland has fixed assets valued at 10,000,000 zloty (zl). Of these, one-quarter was acquired four years ago when the exchange rate was zl3.50 = $1.00. The balance was acquired two years ago when the exchange rate was zl3.80 = $1.00. Fixed assets are being depreciated using the straight-line method with an estimated useful life of 10 years and assuming no salvage value. The following exchange rates are for the current year:

Year-end rate:	zl4.20 = $1.00
Weighted average rate:	zl4.00 = $1.00

Required:

(1) Conforming to *SFAS No. 52*, calculate the Polish subsidiary's depreciation expense for the current year assuming the zloty is the functional currency.

(2) Repeat requirement (1) assuming the U.S. dollar is the functional currency.

Case

Translation of Foreign Currency Financial Statements

You have just graduated from a reputable university and started your first professional job with Canadian International, a multinational corporation.

On your third day at the job, the controller walked into your office and said, "We just received the financial statements of our new operation in France, The French Subsidiary. I am still undecided as to what translation method we should use. Could you please translate the balance sheet and the income statement from French francs to Canadian dollars using the current rate method and the temporal method. Then we will discuss which of the two methods would be appropriate for us to use." He handed you the following information and left.

You were delighted to receive this assignment since you had taken the international accounting course in your senior year at the university.

The French Subsidiary
Balance Sheet
December 31, 20x1
Assets

Cash		F 500,000
Accounts receivable		2,000,000
Inventory		1,500,000
Land		2,000,000
Buildings and equipment	F10,000,000	
Accumulated depreciation	(1,000,000)	9,000,000
Total assets		**F15,000,000**

Liabilities and stockholders' equity

Accounts payable		F 2,500,000
Other current liabilities		1,000,000
Long-term debt		5,500,000
Total liabilities		F 9,000,000
Paid-in capital		5,000,000
Retained earnings, January 1, 20x1	F 0	
Net income	1,500,000	
Dividends	(500,000)	
Retained earnings, December 31, 20x1		1,000,000
Total liabilities and stockholders' equity		**F15,000,000**

The French Subsidiary
Income Statement
For the Year Ended December 31, 20x1

Sales		F 12,000,000
Cost of sales:		
Inventory, January 1, 20x1	F 0	
Purchases	8,500,000	
Inventory, December 31, 20x1	(1,500,000)	(7,000,000)
Gross margin		F 5,000,000
Depreciation expense		(1,000,000)
Other operating expenses		(2,000,000)
Income tax expense		(500,000)
Total expenses		F (3,500,000)
Net income		**F1,500,000**

Other information:

1. The French Subsidiary started its operations at the beginning of January 20x1.
2. The exchange rate on December 31, 20x1 was Can$1.00 = F4.50.
3. The ending inventory was purchased when the exchange rate was Can$1.00 = F4.65.
4. The land and equipment were purchased when the exchange rate was Can$1.00 = F4.45.
5. The common stock was issued when the exchange rate was Can$1.00 = F4.45.
6. The dividends were declared when the exchange rate was Can$1.00 = F4.60.
7. The weighted average exchange rate for the year 20x1 was Can$1.00 = F4.55.

Required:

(1) Translate The French Subsidiary's balance sheet and income statement from French francs into Canadian dollars using the current rate method.

(2) Complete requirement (1) using the temporal method.

(3) Compare the two foreign currency methods. Which of the two methods do you prefer? Give your reasons.

References

American Institute of Certified Public Accountants. *Derivatives—Current Accounting and Auditing Literature*. New York: American Institute of Certified Public Accountants, 1994.

Bremner, Brian. "Will the Yen's Surge Do Japan In?" *Business Week*, 13 December 1999, pp. 56–57.

Coopers & Lybrand. *Guide to Financial Instruments*, 3d ed. New York: Coopers & Lybrand, 1994.

_____. *Foreign Currency Translation and Hedging*. New York: Coopers & Lybrand, 1994.

Deloitte & Touche. *A Survey and Analysis of Standards and Practices on Accounting for Foreign Currency*. Wilton, Connecticut: Deloitte & Touche, 1991.

Dubina, Daniel E., and David L. Unger. "Derivatives: How to Monitor the Risk." *Outlook*, Spring 1995, pp. 24–30.

Financial Accounting Standards Board. *Statement of Financial Accounting Standards No. 52*. "Foreign Currency Translation." Stamford, Connecticut: Financial Accounting Standards Board, 1981.

_____. *Statement of Financial Accounting Standards No. 133*. "Accounting for Derivative Instruments and Hedging Activities." Norwalk, Connecticut: Financial Accounting Standards Board, 1998.

_____. *The IASC-U.S. Comparison Project: A Report on the Similarities and Differences between IASC Standards and U.S. GAAP*, 2d ed. Norwalk, Connecticut: Financial Accounting Standards Board, 1999.

Glasgall, William, and Greg Burns. "Hedging Commandments." *Business Week*, 31 October 1994, pp. 98–99.

Halsey, G.B., R.C. Wilkins, and C.C. Woods, III. "The Fundamental Financial Instrument Approach." *Journal of Accountancy*, November 1989, pp. 71–78.

Haskins, Mark, Kenneth Ferris, and Thomas Selling. *International Financial Reporting and Analysis*, 2d ed. New York: Irwin McGraw-Hill, 2000.

Hepworth, Samuel. *Reporting Foreign Operations*. Ann Arbor, Mich.: Bureau of Business Research, University of Michigan, 1956.

International Accounting Standards Committee. *International Accounting Standard 21*. "The Effects of Changes in Foreign Exchange Rates." London: International Accounting Standards Committee, 1983. Revised in 1993.

_____. *International Accounting Standard 32*. "Financial Instruments: Disclosure and Presentation." London: International Accounting Standards Committee, 1998.

_____. *International Accounting Standard 39*. "Financial Instruments: Recognition and Measurement." London: International Accounting Standards Committee, 1998.

International Federation of Accountants. *Statement on International Management Accounting Practice 3*. "Currency Exposure and Risk Management." New York: International Federation of Accountants, 1996.

Landers, Peter. "Japanese Firms Hope Tokyo Will Brake the Yen." *The Wall Street Journal*, 3 September 1999, p. A6.

Lorenson, Leonard. *Accounting Research Study No. 12.* "Reporting Foreign Operations of U.S. Companies in U.S. Dollars." New York: American Institute of Certified Public Accountants, 1972.

Lueshman, T.A. "The Exchange Rate Exposure of a Global Competitor." *Journal of International Business Studies*, 2d quarter 1990, pp. 225–242.

Molvar, Roger H.D., and James F. Green. "The Question of Derivatives." *Journal of Accountancy*, March 1995, pp. 55–61.

Shapiro, Alan C. *Multinational Financial Management*, 5th ed. Upper Saddle River, N.J.: Prentice-Hall, Inc., 1996.

Steward, J.E. "The Challenges of Hedge Accounting." *Journal of Accountancy*, November 1989, pp. 48–60.

Veazey, Richard E., and Suk H. Kim. "Translation of Foreign Currency Operations: SFAS No. 52." *Journal of World Business*, Winter 1982, pp. 17–22.

"Yen's Strength Hurts Toyota Despite Net Rise." *The Wall Street Journal*, 19 November 1999, p. A18.

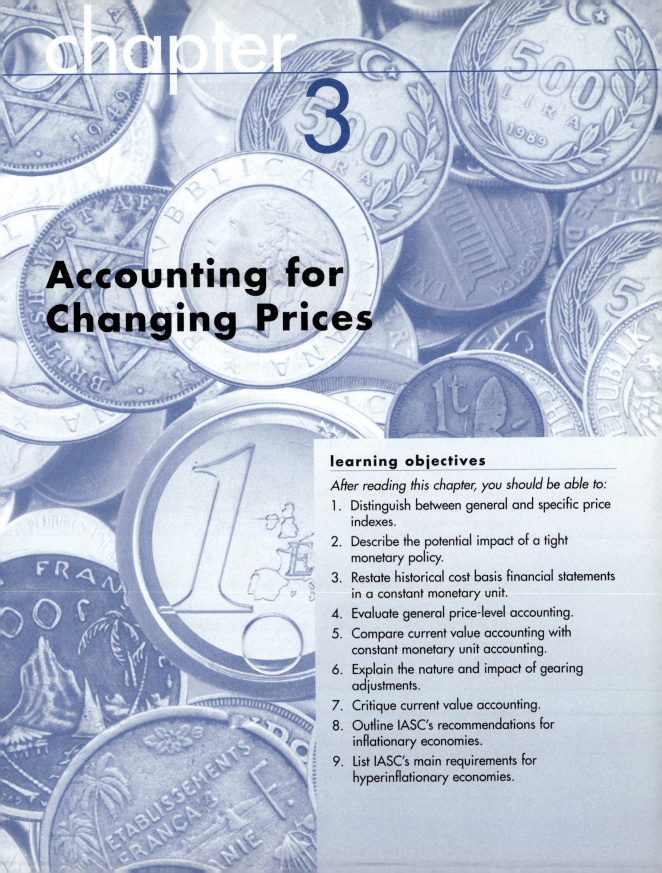

chapter

3

Accounting for Changing Prices

learning objectives

After reading this chapter, you should be able to:

1. Distinguish between general and specific price indexes.

2. Describe the potential impact of a tight monetary policy.

3. Restate historical cost basis financial statements in a constant monetary unit.

4. Evaluate general price-level accounting.

5. Compare current value accounting with constant monetary unit accounting.

6. Explain the nature and impact of gearing adjustments.

7. Critique current value accounting.

8. Outline IASC's recommendations for inflationary economies.

9. List IASC's main requirements for hyperinflationary economies.

In accounting theory, we assume that the monetary unit is stable over time, inflation does not exist, and a dollar, a yen, or a guilder is worth the same today as it was many years ago. This assumption is important for the historical cost model. Of course, in reality this is not the case, especially in many developing countries. In 1996, Bulgaria's inflation rate was 400 percent while its gross domestic product declined by 11 percent.

The historical cost model has been criticized for failing to take into account the economic realities. Critics assert that failure to consider general or specific price changes makes comparability among financial statements difficult.

General Versus Specific Price Indexes

General Price Index

A **general price index** is developed by taking the prices of a "basket" of goods and averaging them at a certain point in time. This average is then compared with the average price of those same goods at some base period. We can thus estimate the amount of inflation or deflation. In the United States, a widely used index is the Consumer Price Index for all Urban Consumers.

Example

Exhibit 3.1 illustrates the construction of a general price index. To keep it simple, the basket consists of only five goods and their respective prices in the years 1995 and 2000. Prices for this group of consumer goods increased an average of 13 percent. However, while prices of four of the items increased, the price of plastic wrap actually decreased by 8 percent. A general price index incorporates the *collective* change in prices of a group of items rather than the change in price of a *specific* item.

exhibit 3.1   Development of a General Price Index

Item	2000	1995	Change ($)	Change (%)
Margarine (16 oz.)	$1.13	$0.95	$+0.18	+19
Aluminum foil (25 ft. roll)	1.70	1.85	−0.15	−08
Milk (half gallon)	1.80	1.50	+0.30	+20
Chicken (I lb.)	0.90	0.70	+0.20	+29
Bread (loaf)	1.25	1.00	+0.25	+25
	$6.78	$6.00	$ 0.78	
Price index (1995 base year)	113*	100		

*100 × ($6.78 ÷ $6.00) = 113

Specific Price Index

The price of a specific good may or may not be affected by changes in general price levels. It may depend mostly on its supply and demand. While prices of most goods have risen in recent years, prices of many other products have declined due to technological advances. Prices of personal computers, printers, and electronic calculators are good examples. A **specific price index** shows the price changes for a specific good or service over time. One way to determine the specific price of a product is to ascertain the current cost of that item, that is, what it would cost to replace. For example, the cost of a building may require the use of a construction index. Many specific indexes are published by industry groups. Alternately, a specific index may be for the net realizable value of a good, that is, the net amount that would be received if an item were sold.

Valuation Problems with Changing Prices

As mentioned in the introduction to this chapter, prices are assumed to be stable under the historical cost model. The central flaw in this model, however, is that it combines together monetary units of different purchasing power. Since monetary units have different purchasing power at different points in time, when combined in financial statements, they cause distortion.

Example

Assume Machine A was purchased five years ago and Machine B is purchased today, each for 100,000 deutsche marks (DM). The machinery account balance would be DM200,000. However, since one deutsche mark buys less today than it did five years ago, the DM200,000 balance in the machinery account is misleading.

Now suppose that the machinery is depreciated by applying a 10 percent annual rate to the DM200,000 cost. The annual depreciation is DM20,000. Of this amount, DM10,000 applies to Machine A and DM10,000 to Machine B. However, these are deutsche marks of different purchasing power. Though easy to compute, the amount is meaningless. We are referring to two pieces of equipment that were purchased when the deutsche mark had different values. When we try to match the period's revenues with expenses, the problem arises again—the DM10,000 depreciation expense in each case relates to a different purchasing power.

The accounting profession has been struggling with the problem of changing prices for many decades. The German economy had extremely high inflation rates in the 1920s. After World War II, increasing prices caused financial reporting problems in the U.S. In recent years, inflation rates have been moderate in most industrialized economies, while high inflation rates are still common in many of the developing nations. Exhibit 3.2 contains the percentage changes in the consumer price index for selected countries. The actual percentages are shown for 1998 and 1999, while those for 2000 are forecasted.

exhibit 3.2   **Consumer Price Index (CPI) Percent Changes**

Country	Actual 1998	Actual 1999	Forecast 2000
Brazil	−1.8%	8.9%	6.5%
Canada	0.9	1.8	2.4
Euro Zone*	1.1	1.1	1.6
Japan	−0.9	−0.6	0.8
Mexico	15.0	12.9	10.9
South Korea	7.5	0.8	3.2
United Kingdom	3.4	1.5	2.9
United States	1.6	2.7	1.9

*Includes these 12 countries: Austria, Belgium, Finland, France, Germany, Greece, Ireland, Italy, Luxembourg, Netherlands, Portugal, and Spain.
Source: *Business Week*, 27 December 1999, p. 86, U.S. Bureau of Labor Statistics, and Merrill Lynch.

It is noteworthy that a significant change has occurred in Brazil since the early 1990s. From the data in Exhibit 3.2, it would be hard to imagine that Brazil's inflation rate in 1991 was 1,800 percent.

Central banks in industrialized countries have used monetary policy to curb inflation by limiting money-supply growth. The major concern of central banks in most developing countries, however, is to finance economic development projects or provide operating resources for public sector enterprises.[1]

Not all developing countries have high inflation. Over the past decade many fast-developing countries such as Malaysia, Taiwan, and Thailand managed to achieve economic development with low inflation and high savings rates.

Tight monetary policy, resulting in high interest rates, is effective in controlling inflation. At the same time, it fuels consumer demand for goods and services. This has two potential consequences. First, rising consumer demand may increase imports. Second, the strong currency (due to the low inflation rate) puts the country at a relative disadvantage in exporting its goods since they become more expensive for consumers in other countries. The combined effect of the two can create a trade deficit for the country. This dilemma is currently being faced by countries such as Taiwan and Israel. Figure 3.1 depicts the potential consequences of a tight monetary policy.

The constant challenge is to find a balance between acceptable levels of inflation while maintaining economic growth and competitiveness in world markets. Mexico has done an impressive job of using its monetary policy to manage the economy and to achieve an annual inflation objective known as "corto." The strategy has enabled its central bank, the Bank of Mexico, to control infla-

---

1 Christopher Farrell. "Inflation's Uneven Spread." *Business Week*, 8 May 1995, p. 28.

figure 3.1   **Potential Impact of Tight Monetary Policy**

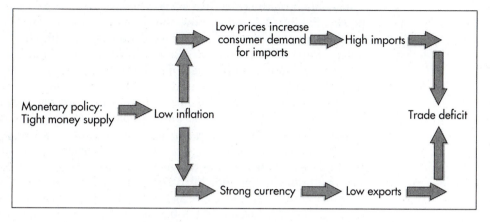

tion by reducing the annual rate from 51.7 percent in 1995 to 12.9 percent in 1999.[2]

Monetary Items

A **monetary item** is either cash or another asset or liability that will be received or paid out in a fixed number of monetary units. Examples of monetary assets include accounts receivable and notes receivable, and examples of monetary liabilities are accounts payable and salaries payable. In a balance sheet that has been restated for changes in the general purchasing power of the monetary unit, monetary items are shown at their current (nominal) amounts.

During an inflationary period, a holder of monetary assets experiences a holding loss because such assets, representing a fixed number of monetary units, will have less purchasing power in the future. On the other hand, a person holding monetary liabilities will have a holding gain from paying off the liabilities in a fixed number of monetary units in the future that have lesser purchasing power. Such gains or losses (from holding monetary items) appear as monetary gains or losses in the income statement that has been adjusted for general price-level changes.

Nonmonetary Items

A **nonmonetary item** does not represent either a claim to or a claim for a specified number of monetary units. Examples of nonmonetary items include inventory, equipment, land, liability for warranties, liability for future pension costs,

2 Guillermo Ortiz. "Reducing Inflation is Mexico's Monetary Policy Goal." *The Wall Street Journal*, 10 December 1999, p. A19.

capital stock, and retained earnings. In general price-level adjusted financial statements, nonmonetary items are adjusted for changes in *general* purchasing power. Exhibit 3.3 shows how the historical cost of land in nominal dollars would be restated in constant dollars, denoted C$ in this chapter. *These constant-dollar amounts are restated historical costs.* The C$525,000 amount in the 12/31/02 column is simply the original $500,000 cost at 12/31/00 adjusted to reflect the general price level over the two-year period since the land was acquired.

Note: *General price-level adjusted financial statements are restated historical cost statements.* For students, an example on salary levels is closer to home. Assume that starting salaries for accounting graduates five years ago averaged $33,000 per year. The average salary for current-year graduates is $40,000. At first, this sounds like an improvement. But is it? Not if there was 25 percent inflation during this period. In today's purchasing power terms, $33,000 would mean $33,000 × (125 ÷ 100) = $41,250. Therefore, in terms of purchasing power of the dollar, the current $40,000 salary is $1,250 *less* than the salary five years ago.[3] For simplicity in Exhibit 3.3, the base period index has been assumed to be 100, making it easy to see that the adjustment ratio at 12/31/02 is (105 ÷ 100). More typically, the indexes are less convenient; a current index of 180.39 and a base index of 171.80 also reflects the same 5 percent inflation during the period. The adjustment ratio is the current index divided by the base index. Multiplying the historical amount by this ratio yields the historical cost expressed in constant monetary units.

Constant Monetary Unit Restatement

Constant monetary unit restatement is a general term for restating financial statements for changes in purchasing power of the monetary unit. In the United Kingdom, accountants use the term **current purchasing power accounting**. In the

exhibit 3.3   Land Account in Constant Dollars (C$)

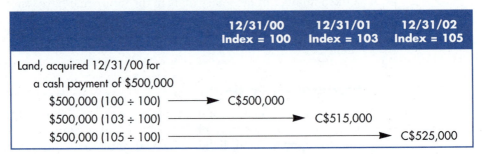

	12/31/00 Index = 100	12/31/01 Index = 103	12/31/02 Index = 105
Land, acquired 12/31/00 for a cash payment of $500,000			
$500,000 (100 ÷ 100)	→ C$500,000		
$500,000 (103 ÷ 100)		→ C$515,000	
$500,000 (105 ÷ 100)			→ C$525,000

3 Adjustments for inflation are made so that amounts are expressed in current dollars. Restatement in terms of purchasing power at some prior date *could* be done, but we all tend to think in terms of today's purchasing power, and rarely is there a basis for selecting a particular prior date.

United States, accountants refer to **constant dollar accounting** or **general price-level accounting**.

Regardless of the terminology, we should remember that restatement to a constant monetary unit does not change the basis of the financial statement. *They remain historical cost basis statements, albeit restated.* The rest of this section contains a brief summary of the steps involved in constant monetary unit restatement. The subsequent section provides a comprehensive example.[4]

Balance Sheet

The starting point for the restatement process is usually the balance sheet. The basic steps are as follows:

- Identify assets and liabilities as either monetary or nonmonetary.
- Extend monetary items at their face (nominal) amounts.
- Adjust for the changes in purchasing power of nonmonetary assets and non-monetary liabilities from the date of their acquisition and incurrence respectively.
- Roll-forward previous year balances. If general price-level adjusted statements were prepared for the previous year, all balances to be used for comparison with the current year must be rolled forward, that is, expressed in terms of current-year price levels. If there was 10 percent inflation, all balances in the previous year's statements would be multiplied by 110 percent.

Income Statement

The income statement is normally restated after the balance sheet, since cost of goods sold uses the adjusted inventory balances and depreciation is based on adjusted property, plant, and equipment amounts. The basic idea is that the amounts are adjusted from the price levels in effect at the time the events occurred to the current year's year-end levels.

- Identify and adjust items using the price indexes in effect at the date applicable to each item when it occurred.
- Compute depreciation expense based on the adjusted historical cost of the depreciable assets.
- Adjust items that can be assumed to occur evenly throughout the year, such as sales and purchases, using a weighted average index.

---

4 This summary of steps and the following comprehensive example assume that the unadjusted financial statements are expressed in the parent company currency, and that the price indexes used are drawn from the parent company's country. There are significant issues as to whether adjustments for inflation should be made in subsidiary statements *before* translation (using the foreign country's price-level index) or *after* translation (using the parent country's price-level index). Discussion of these issues is beyond the scope of this text.

- Compute cost of goods sold, using the price-level adjusted amounts for beginning and ending inventories calculated when adjusting the balance sheet, and the adjusted purchases amount from the preceding step.
- Calculate the purchasing power gain or loss from holding monetary items.

Illustration of Constant Monetary Unit Restatement

Exhibit 3.4 shows comparative balance sheets for December 31, 2001, and December 31, 2000, for Osaka Corporation. The income statement for the year ended December 31, 2001, is shown in Exhibit 3.5. *Both statements are in nominal dollars.* In the following illustration we will be preparing a price-level adjusted balance sheet as of December 31, 2001, and a price-level adjusted income statement for the year 2001. The assumed indexes for consumer prices at pertinent dates are in Exhibit 3.6.

Restatement of Balance Sheet

Exhibit 3.7 (page 93) shows the restated balance sheet for Osaka Corporation at December 31, 2001.

Monetary Items

Cash, accounts receivable, accounts payable, salaries payable, and *bonds payable* are monetary items. Thus they are extended to the constant-dollar balance sheet at the face amount because Osaka Corporation will receive or pay out those amounts in the future.

Nonmonetary Items

Inventories have to be adjusted to reflect the change in purchasing power. To do this requires knowing the inventory method (cost flow assumption) being used and the date for each purchase. Osaka uses the first-in, first-out method, and ending inventories are assumed to have been acquired evenly throughout the last quarter of the year.

The *property, plant, and equipment* category requires reviewing the accounts to find out the acquisition date of each item.

Common stock and *paid-in capital in excess of par or stated value* are adjusted using the index when shares were sold.

Retained earnings are the difference between the total of restated assets and the total of restated liabilities and all other restated stockholders' equity. In restating, it is the balancing figure.

Restatement of Income Statement

Exhibit 3.8 (page 94) shows the 2001 income statement of Osaka Corporation restated to constant dollars.

exhibit 3.4   **Comparative Balance Sheets (Nominal Dollars)**

Osaka Corporation Comparative Balance Sheets December 31, 2001 and 2000	2001	2000
Assets		
Current:		
Cash	$ 30,000	$ 10,000
Accounts receivable (net of allowance for		
doubtful accounts)	100,000	90,000
Inventories (FIFO)	120,000	100,000
Total current assets	$ 250,000	$200,000
Property, plant, and equipment:		
Land	$ 100,000	$100,000
Building (net of accumulated depreciation)	200,000	220,000
Equipment (net of accumulated depreciation)	130,000	120,000
Total property, plant, and equipment	$ 430,000	$440,000
Total assets	$ 680,000	$640,000
Liabilities and stockholders' equity		
Liabilities:		
Current		
Accounts payable	$ 100,000	$ 50,000
Salaries payable	50,000	70,000
Total current liabilities	$ 150,000	$120,000
Bonds payable	300,000	300,000
Total liabilities	$ 450,000	$420,000
Stockholders' equity:		
Common stock ($1 par value, 100,000 shares		
issued and outstanding)	$ 100,000	$100,000
Paid-in capital in excess of par	20,000	20,000
Retained earnings	110,000	100,000
Total stockholders' equity	$ 230,000	$220,000
Total liabilities and stockholders' equity	$ 680,000	$640,000

exhibit 3.5   Income Statement (Nominal Dollars)

Osaka Corporation Income Statement for the Year Ended December 31, 2001		
Revenues		$530,000
Expenses:		
Cost of goods sold	$360,000	
Selling and administrative	60,000	
Depreciation	30,000	
Interest	30,000	
Loss on sale of equipment	5,000	
Income taxes	15,000	500,000
Net income		$ 30,000

exhibit 3.6   Index of Consumer Prices at Various Dates

Date	Index	Date	Index
January 1991 (corporation		January 2001	130
formed and land purchased)	100	February 2001	132
Average for the year 1992		March 2001	134
(building constructed)	105	April 2001	135
April 1995 (equipment purchased)	107	May 2001 (equipment purchased)	136
November 1998 (equipment purchased)	115	June 2001 (equipment sold)	138
October 2000	120	July 2001	139
November 2000	122	August 2001	141
December 2000	125	September 2001	144
		October 2001	146
		November 2001	148
		December 2001	150
		Weighted average for 2001	148
Weighted average for 4th quarter 2000		Weighted average for 4th quarter 2001	
(beginning inventory acquired)	122.3	(ending inventory acquired)	139.4

Items with Specific Dates

Equipment purchased in 1995 with an original cost of $15,000 and accumulated depreciation (at date of sale) of $5,000 was sold in June 2001 for $5,000. The loss on sale of equipment was restated as follows:

exhibit 3.7   **Restatement of Balance Sheet to Constant Dollars**

	Nominal Dollars	Ratio	Constant Dollars
Osaka Corporation **Restatement of Balance Sheet from Nominal to Constant Dollars** **December 31, 2001**			
Assets			
Current:			
Cash	$ 30,000	150/150	C$ 30,000
Accounts receivable (net of allowance for doubtful accounts)	100,000	150/150	100,000
Inventories	120,000	Exhibit 3.9	121,622
Total current assets	$250,000		C$251,622
Property, plant, and equipment:			
Land	$100,000	150/100	C$150,000
Building (net of accumulated depreciation)	200,000	150/105	285,714
Equipment (net of accumulated depreciation)			
1995 purchase	76,000	150/107	106,542
1998 purchase	25,000	150/115	32,609
2001 purchase	29,000	150/136	31,985
Total property, plant, and equipment	$430,000		C$606,850
Total assets	$680,000		C$858,472
Liabilities and stockholders' equity			
Liabilities:			
Current			
Accounts payable	$100,000	150/150	C$100,000
Salaries payable	50,000	150/150	50,000
Total current liabilities	$150,000		C$150,000
Bonds payable	300,000	150/150	300,000
Total liabilities	$450,000		C$450,000
Stockholders' equity:			
Common stock ($1 par value, 100,000 shares issued and outstanding)	$100,000	150/100	C$150,000
Paid-in capital in excess of par	20,000	150/100	30,000
Retained earnings	100,000	Balancing	228,472
Total stockholders' equity	$230,000		C$408,472
Total liabilities and stockholders' equity	$680,000		C$858,472

exhibit 3.8   Restatement of Income Statement to Constant Dollars

Osaka Corporation
Restatement of Income Statement from Nominal to Constant Dollars
for the Year Ended December 31, 2001

	Nominal Dollars	Ratio	Constant Dollars
Revenues	$530,000	150/139.4	C$570,301
Expenses:			
Cost of goods sold	$360,000	Exhibit 3.9	C$409,922
Selling and administrative	60,000	150/139.4	64,562
Depreciation:			
1992 building acquisition	20,000	150/105	28,571
1995 acquisition	4,000	150/107	5,607
1997 acquisition	5,000	150/115	6,522
2000 acquisition	1,000	150/136	1,103
Interest	30,000	150/139.4	32,281
Loss on sale of equipment	5,000	See text	8,584
Income taxes	15,000	150/139.4	16,141
Total expenses	$500,000		C$573,293
Income (loss) before purchasing power gain or loss			C$ (2,992)
Purchasing power gain on net monetary position		Exhibit 3.10	63,231
Net income	$ 30,000		C$ 60,239

Selling price: $5,000 × (150 ÷ 138)	C$ 5,435
Less book value ($15,000 − 5,000) × (150 ÷ 107)	14,019
Constant dollar loss on sale	C$ 8,584

Depreciation

Details of the depreciation restatement appear in Exhibit 3.8. Note that the $28,571 adjusted depreciation on the building is based on the original cost restated in current purchasing power that is allocated to the current year.

Items Spread Uniformly During the Year

Revenues, selling and administrative expenses, interest expense, and income tax expense are assumed to have occurred evenly throughout the year. Accordingly, these items are adjusted to year-end dollars using the weighted average price index for the year.

Cost of Goods Sold

The calculation of the constant dollar cost of goods sold, shown in Exhibit 3.9, is based on the assumptions that beginning and ending inventories were acquired at the weighted average price levels in effect during the last quarters of 2000 and 2001, respectively. Purchases are assumed to have been acquired at the average price level in effect throughout the year 2001.

Purchasing Power Gain or Loss

Purchasing power gains or losses arise from holding monetary items during times when the general purchasing power of the monetary unit changes. Exhibit 3.10 displays the computation of, in this case, a purchasing power gain. Osaka Corporation paid $20,000 in dividends at the end of 2001.

Osaka Corporation had a purchasing power gain for 2001 because the company owed more to others than others owed to it during a time of rising prices. *This means paying net debt with cheaper dollars.* Gain is computed as follows:

- Determine the net monetary position at the beginning of the year.

- Analyze all transactions that affect monetary items and restate each of those using the appropriate index. For example, when sales increase, it results in an increase of cash and accounts receivables, which thereby increase monetary assets.

- Add or subtract the adjusted amounts to arrive at the constant dollar net monetary position.

- The difference between the year-end net monetary positions in nominal and constant dollars is the purchasing power gain or loss.

exhibit 3.9   Restatement of Cost of Goods Sold to Constant Dollars

Osaka Corporation Restatement of Cost of Goods Sold from Nominal to Constant Dollars For the Year Ended December 31, 2001			
	Nominal Dollars	Ratio	Constant Dollars
Beginning inventories	$ 100,000	150/122.3	C$ 122,649
Purchases	380,000	150/139.4	408,895
Goods available for sale	$ 480,000		C$ 531,544
Ending inventories	(120,000)	150/148.0	(121,622)
Cost of goods sold	$ 360,000		C$ 409,922

exhibit 3.10 Purchasing Power Gain or Loss

Osaka Corporation Calculation of Purchasing Power Gain or Loss for the Year Ended December 31, 2001	Nominal Dollars	Ratio	Constant Dollars
Net monetary position, January 1, 2001	$(320,000)*	150/125	C$(384,000)
Increases in net monetary assets from:			
Sales	$530,000	150/139.4	C$ 570,301
Sale of equipment	5,000	See text	5,435
	$ 535,000		C$ 575,736
Decreases in net monetary assets from:			
Purchases of inventories	$ 380,000	150/139.4	C$ 408,895
Selling and administrative expenses	60,000	150/139.4	64,562
Interest expense	30,000	150/139.4	32,281
Income taxes	15,000	150/139.4	16,141
Dividend payments	20,000	150/150.0	20,000
Equipment purchase	30,000	150/136.0	33,088
	$ 535,000		C$ 574,967
Net monetary position, December 31, 2001	$(320,000)		C$(383,231)
Less: *nominal-dollar* net monetary position, December 31, 2001			
Purchasing power gain			(320,000)
			C$ 63,231

* Monetary assets:

Cash and accounts receivable (net)	$ 100,000
Monetary liabilities:	
Accounts payable, salaries payable, and bonds payable	(420,000)
Net monetary position	$ (320,000)

Evaluation of Constant Monetary Unit Accounting

Constant monetary unit accounting provides comparative information on the effect of inflation across firms. However, inflation affects different firms differently. The impact of inflation on a firm is a function of the composition of its assets and liabilities. Highly leveraged firms experience monetary gains during inflationary times.

Constant monetary unit financial statements are not designed to provide information on current prices of specific goods and services. This type of information is provided by current value accounting.

Constant monetary unit accounting has been used commonly in South America for many years. The current trend, however, appears to be toward adoption of a current value approach. For example, Argentina used to require general price-level adjustment. A resolution now requires use of current value accounting since the periods beginning on or after January 1, 1993.

Exhibit 3.11 contains the note from the 1997 annual report of Teléfonos de México SA de C.V. dealing with inflation adjustments.

Current Value Accounting

The synonymous terms **current value accounting** and **current cost accounting** include all valuation systems designed to express specific prices. Current value financial statements show the effects of changes in prices of individual items. Cash and accounts receivable are generally stated at their cash or cash equivalent value. Other assets are adjusted, as necessary, to reflect their current value. In some cases, especially for property, plant, and equipment items, a specific price

exhibit 3.11 **Teléfonos de México Inflation Adjustments**

Recognition of the effects of inflation on financial information

The Company recognizes the effects of inflation on financial information as required by Mexican Accounting Principles Bulletin B-10 ("Accounting Recognition of the Effects of Inflation on Financial Information"), as amended, issued by the Mexican Institute of Public Accountants (MIPA). Consequently, the amounts shown in the accompanying financial statements and in these notes are expressed in thousands of Mexican pesos with purchasing power at December 31, 1997. The December 31, 1997 restatement factor applied to the financial statements at December 31, 1996 was 15.72% (corresponding to inflation for 1997).

Plant, property and equipment, and construction in progress are restated as described in Note 3. Depreciation is calculated on the restated investment using the retirement and replacement method, based on the estimated useful lives of the assets.

Inventories are valued at average cost and are restated on the basis of specific costs. The stated value of inventories is not in excess of market.

Capital accounts, the premium on the sale of shares, and retained earnings are restated using adjustment factors obtained from the Mexican National Consumer Price Index (NCPI).

The deficit from restatement of stockholders' equity consists of the accumulated monetary position loss at the time the provisions of Bulletin B-10 were first applied (Ps. 7,514,075 at December 31, 1997) and of the result from holding nonmonetary assets, which represents the net difference between restatement by the specific-cost method through 1996 and the alternate method (see Note 3) effective January 1, 1997, compared to restatement based on the NCPI.

The monetary effect represents the impact of inflation on monetary assets and liabilities. The net monetary effect of each year is included in the statements of income as a part of the comprehensive financing income.

Source: Teléfonos de México S.A. de C.V., *Annual Report 1997*, p. 34.

index to approximate the current value of the item may be employed. Alternately, independent market appraisals or an assignment of current value by the board of directors may be used. Most current liabilities are shown at the face amount. Long-term debt requires a present value calculation. The excess of current value of assets over current value of liabilities equals stockholders' equity. Amounts in the income statement are restated to approximate their current value.

Input Price Measurement Versus Output Price Measurement

There are two different approaches to the measurement of current value: Input price measurement or output price measurement. The **input price measurement** assigns current value to an item on the basis of its replacement cost. **Replacement cost** is the total cost to acquire another item that would perform the functions identical to those performed by an existing item. The **output price measurement** considers the current value of an item to be equal to its net realizable value. **Net realizable value** is the disposal value of an item less the related disposal costs. **Exit measurement** has the same meaning as the output price measurement.

Example

Patrice Ltd. acquired a building five years ago at a cost of £500,000. The following is pertinent information in case Patrice Ltd. decides to sell the building:

Selling price	£610,000
Property company's sales commission	39,650
Legal fees	10,000
Taxes and other costs	30,350

The net realizable value of the building is: £610,000 − (£39,650 + £10,000 + £30,350) = £530,000.

Example

Referring to the previous example, let us now assume that if Patrice Ltd. were to purchase a building that would provide functionality identical to the existing building, the following costs would be required:

Purchase price	£650,000
Title search, title insurance,	
registration, etc.	5,000
Legal fees	6,000
Other costs	3,000

The replacement cost of the building is: £650,000 + £5,000 + £6,000 + £3,000 = £664,000.

Realized and Unrealized (Holding) Gains and Losses

An **unrealized, or holding, gain or loss** arises from holding an asset. It is the difference between the change in the current value of an item during the period. Current value, as mentioned earlier, may be based on either input price measurement or output price measurement. A **realized gain or loss** occurs when an item is disposed at an amount different from its recorded net value on the disposal date.

Example

A building was purchased by Armstrong Company on January 1, 2000, the beginning of its fiscal period, for $1,000,000. During the year, the construction cost index increased by 8 percent. Armstrong Company uses current value accounting. Using the construction cost index, the current value of the building is adjusted to $1,080,000 on December 31, 2000. This results in a holding, or unrealized, gain of $80,000 for Armstrong during 2000.

There is no universal consensus on whether unrealized gains or losses should be shown in the income statement or whether they should be taken directly to the balance sheet. Most current value accounting models include them in the income statement. We will follow this approach.

Example

Referring to the previous example, let us assume that Armstrong Company sells the building on October 17, 2001, for net proceeds of $1,120,000. There is a realized gain of $40,000 on the sale of the building ($1,120,000 – $1,080,000).

Note: An unrealized gain or loss results from holding a nonmonetary asset when it is revalued to reflect its current value (either replacement cost or net realizable value). A realized gain or loss arises only when an asset is disposed. It is the difference between the net disposal value and the recorded current value of the asset.

Another example of current value accounting's impact on the income statement is in the following example.

Example

Hasham Plc. has sales revenue of $50,000,000. The cost of goods sold is $30,000,000 on an historical cost basis, and $40,000,000 according to current cost. Under current value accounting, Hasham's gross profit would be:

Sales $50,000,000 – Current cost of goods sold $40,000,000 = $10,000,000

The gross profit according to an historical cost basis would be:

Sales $50,000,000 – Historical cost of goods sold $30,000,000 = $20,000,000

Let us assume that Hasham's ending inventory is as follows:

Historical cost	$5,000,000
Current cost	7,000,000

This would result in a $2,000,000 unrealized gain on inventory.

The combined effect of the previous on Hasham's income is:

Cost of goods sold (decrease in gross profit using current value)	$10,000,000 realized loss
Ending inventory	2,000,000 unrealized gain
Combined effect	$ 8,000,000 current value loss

Gearing Adjustments

Many current value accounting models incorporate a gearing adjustment. The gearing adjustment is made in the income statement and it relates to the effect of inflation. Though different current value accounting models have their own version of the gearing adjustment, the basic idea is the same as described next.

The **gearing adjustment** is made to recognize that it is unnecessary to make the current cost adjustments for the operating assets that are financed by creditors. In an inflationary economy, when average borrowings are greater than average monetary assets, the stockholders are in a favorable position. Expressed differently, the loss of an entity's creditors, due to eroding purchasing power of the monetary unit, is a gain to the stockholders. Therefore, income is increased by making a gearing credit. In situations where the amount of average monetary assets is greater than average borrowing, a gearing charge is made to the income statement, thereby reducing the income amount. In a deflationary economy, the gearing adjustment has the opposite effect on the reported income.

The amount of gearing adjustment is computed by multiplying the ratio of average borrowing to average operating assets with the current value adjustments for items such as cost of goods sold and depreciation expense:

$$\text{Gearing adjustment} = \frac{\text{Average borrowing}}{\text{Average operating assets}} \times \begin{array}{l}\text{Total current value adjustments} \\ \text{made (for cost of goods sold,} \\ \text{depreciation, etc.)}\end{array}$$

A gearing adjustment thus takes into account the effect of inflation while applying a current value accounting model.[5]

Example

The following information is from Avila Company's records for 2001:

---

5 M. Zafar Iqbal. *Comparison of the Alternatives Proposed in Selected Countries to Cope with the Impact of Changing Prices on Published Financial Statements*, Ph.D. dissertation, Lincoln, Nebr.: University of Nebraska, 1979, pp. 78–92.

Current cost profit excluding interest and income tax expenses	$ 300,000
Interest expense	45,000
Average borrowings	500,000
Average operating assets	2,000,000

Current value adjustments in expenses:

Description	Historical amount	Current value	Adjustment
Cost of goods sold	$1,160,000	$1,200,000	$40,000
Depreciation	170,000	190,000	20,000
Total	$1,330,000	$1,390,000	$60,000

$$\text{Gearing adjustment} = \frac{\$500,000}{\$2,000,000} \times \$60,000 = \$15,000$$

Avila Company is operating under inflationary economic conditions. Its average borrowing exceeds its average monetary assets. The impact of gearing adjustment on Avila Company's income is as follows:

Current cost profit before interest expense	$300,000
Less interest expense	45,000
	$255,000
Add gearing adjustment	15,000
Profit attributable to stockholders before income tax expense	$270,000

Evaluation of Current Value Accounting

Although current value accounting can provide relevant information for coping with changing prices, critics have made several arguments against its use:

- Current cost determination is inherently subjective.
- Current costs are difficult or impossible to obtain in cases involving the products that are not commonly sold. It is especially applicable in situations where special-purpose, customized products are manufactured.
- Purchasing power gains or losses often are not recognized in current value models.
- How should the holding gains or losses be treated? Should they appear in the income statement or should they be entered directly into stockholders' equity in the balance sheet? The treatment selected may have a significant effect on the reported earnings of the company. There is no consensus on the treatment of holding gains or losses.

Many countries allow historical cost with optional current value revaluation. Very few countries require exclusive use of current cost accounting.

Exhibit 3.12 shows an example of current value accounting disclosures for Norway-based Dyno.

IASC and Inflation Accounting

http://

The IASC (**http://www.iasc.org.uk/frame/cen0.htm**) accepted the reality that there were different schools of thought on accounting for inflation. In 1981, it issued *IAS 15*, which *recommends* that the following information should be disclosed by large public companies:[6]

- The amounts of the adjustment to or the adjusted amount of depreciation of property, plant, and equipment.
- The amount of the adjustment to or the adjusted amount of cost of sales.
- The adjustments to monetary items.
- The overall effect on income.
- The current cost of property, plant, and equipment and inventories if the current cost method is used.

exhibit 3.12 Dyno Current Value Revaluations

PROPERTY, PLANT, AND EQUIPMENT

Property, plant, and equipment are reported on the balance sheet at original purchase cost, plus revaluation, and less straight-line depreciation. The rates for calculating straight-line depreciation have been determined on the basis of an evaluation of the individual asset's economic lifetime. Property, plant, and equipment under construction are not depreciated. Profits from the sale of tangible assets are reported as operating revenue, and losses as operating expenses.

NOK million	Buildings	Land
Parent Company		
Cost and revaluation		
Cost as of Jan. 1, 1998	403	28
Revaluations as of Jan. 1, 1998	22	125
Investments 1998	20	—
Disposals in 1998	(125)	(5)
Transfers in 1998	3	—
Balance as of Dec. 31, 1998	323	148

Source: Dyno, *Annual Report 1998*, pp. 50 and 56.

---

6 *International Accounting Standard 15*. "Inflation Reflecting the Effects of Changing Prices." London: International Accounting Standards Committee, 1981.

- The methods used to calculate the preceding information as well as the type of indexes used.

The IASC issued *IAS 29*, "Financial Reporting in Hyperinflationary Economies," in 1989. It *requires* that financial statements of a company reporting in a currency of a hyperinflationary economy be restated at the balance sheet date for general purchasing power changes.[7] This applies whether statements were based on historical cost or current value.

Although *IAS 29* does not indicate a specific rate characterizing a hyperinflationary economy, it does give some guidelines:

- The population prefers nonmonetary assets or a relatively stable foreign currency over local currency.
- Sales and purchases on credit incorporate amounts for expected losses in purchasing power even for relatively short credit periods.
- Interest rates, prices, and wages are tied to a price index.
- The cumulative inflation rate for three years is approaching or exceeds 100 percent.

IAS 29 applies to *primary* financial statements. The gain or loss on the net monetary position should be included in net income and separately disclosed.

Concluding Observations

Two observations can be made regarding accounting for changing prices.

First, accounting for changing prices becomes a hotly debated topic in industrialized countries when they experience high rates of inflation. When inflation rates are low, interest in the topic disappears.

Second, the question of how to deal with inflation has been studied for a long time but has not been resolved. Some of the references listed at the end of this chapter make interesting reading, not only because of their incisiveness but also because they present strong but diverse arguments both for and against the proposed solutions.

Note to Students

To further your knowledge in this topic, develop a conceptual foundation of inflation accounting. This can be accomplished by reading some of the references at the end of the chapter. I especially recommend Henry Sweeney's *Stabilized Accounting*, an accounting classic on general price-level adjustments. For current cost (value) adjustments, *Guidance Manual on Current Cost Accounting*,

---

7 *International Accounting Standard 29.* "Financial Reporting in Hyperinflationary Economies." London: International Accounting Standards Committee, 1989.

published by the Institute of Chartered Accountants in England and Wales, is suggested.

To keep current on worldwide inflation rates, there is no better way than regularly reading popular business periodicals. They provide a barometer for inflation rates throughout the world.

Debates about inflation accounting have apparently come to a standstill in the industrialized countries. Many requirements for supplementary financial statements disclosures for inflation have been rescinded.

Most developing countries continue to have high inflation rates. Their dilemma is to find a balance between acceptable rates of inflation and the desired levels of economic growth. It is a daunting challenge—expending on economic development projects while simultaneously keeping inflation under control.

Chapter Summary

1. In accounting theory, we assume that purchasing power of a monetary unit is stable.

2. Much research has been done on the subject of changing prices—both specific and general price changes.

3. Inflation rates in industrialized countries have been relatively low in recent years.

4. High inflation rates still abound in most developing countries.

5. Broadly speaking, the price-level change adjustments have been made using two approaches: the *constant monetary* unit approach and the *current value* approach.

6. The constant monetary unit approach merely restates historical cost basis financial statements using a general price index.

7. Current value accounting adjusts the historical amounts of specific items for specific price changes.

8. Common approaches for specific price change adjustments include replacement cost and net realizable value.

9. The gearing adjustment is incorporated in many current value accounting models.

10. The gearing adjustment recognizes that in an inflationary economy it is not necessary to make current cost adjustments for the portion of operating assets financed by creditors.

11. *IAS 15* recommendations deal with information disclosures related to changing prices.

12. *IAS 29* provides disclosure standards for companies reporting in currencies of hyperinflationary economies.

Questions for Discussion

1. What is inflation?

2. What are the merits of restating financial statements by using general price-level indexes?

3. What is a monetary item? a nonmonetary item? Give two examples of each.

4. What are the perceived deficiencies of the historical cost basis financial statements of a company operating in a country with a high inflation rate?

5. How is a fixed asset restated for changes in general price levels? How about the related depreciation expense and accumulated depreciation?

6. What is a net monetary gain or loss?

7. In what financial statement does a monetary gain or loss appear?

8. Indicate for each of the following whether it is a monetary or nonmonetary item:

   a. Shares of common stock held as an investment.
   b. Bonds held as investments.
   c. Merchandise inventory.
   d. Liability for warranties on products.
   e. Accounts payable.

9. If prices are steadily rising, indicate whether the following produces a purchasing power gain, purchasing power loss, or neither:

   a. Maintaining a balance in a checking account.
   b. Depreciating an asset.
   c. Additional paid-in capital on preferred stock.

10. What is a specific price index?

11. What is an input price? an output price?

12. When and why are countries likely to require inflation adjustments in financial statements?

13. What is the purpose for making the gearing adjustment? How is it accomplished?

14. Discuss *IAS 15* guidelines.

15. What is the criterion for an economy to be considered hyperinflationary according to *IAS 29*?

16. What are the major requirements of *IAS 29*?

Exercises/Problems

3-1 Select the best available answer:

1. The inherent flaw of the historical cost basis is that it:
   a. Misstates monetary items.
   b. Fails to match revenue with expenses.
   c. Combines monetary units of different purchasing power.
   d. Shows equipment at the same book value as a number of years ago.
   e. b and c.

2. Purchasing power gains or losses arise from:
   a. Fluctuations in the currency exchange rate.
   b. Changes in the stock market.
   c. Holding monetary items during a period when the general purchasing power of the monetary unit changes.
   d. Holding nonmonetary items during a period when the general purchasing power of the monetary unit changes.
   e. None of the above.

3. Monetary items include all of the following except:
   a. Cash.
   b. Accounts receivable.
   c. Inventories.
   d. Accounts payable.
   e. Notes payable.

4. Accounting approaches for changing prices include:
   a. The current value approach.
   b. The historical cost approach.
   c. The general price-level adjustments approach.
   d. a and b.
   e. a and c.

5. Nonmonetary items include:
   a. Inventory.
   b. Equipment.
   c. Investment in common stock.
   d. All of the above.
   e. None of the above.

6. A change in a general price index from 120 to 180 during a period shows that purchasing power has declined by:
   a. 60 percent.
   b. 50 percent.
   c. 33 1/3 percent.
   d. 180 percent.
   e. None of the above.

7. Which of the following is a nonmonetary item?
   a. Goodwill
   b. Notes payable
   c. Notes receivable
   d. Prepaid expense
   e. None of the above

8. During a period of inflation, a purchasing power loss results from holding:
   a. Nonmonetary assets.
   b. Nonmonetary liabilities.
   c. Monetary assets.
   d. Monetary liabilities.
   e. None of the above.

3-2 Kumar Co. purchased a new machine on January 1, 2001, for 500,000 francs. The machine is depreciated using the straight-line method and a 10-year life. Assume the estimated salvage value is zero. The general price-level index was 200.0 on January 1, 2001, and 225 on December 31, 2001. The weighted average index for 2001 was 215.

Required:

Calculate the depreciation expense for 2001 and the book value of the machine on December 31, 2001 using historical costs restated for the general price-level changes.

3-3 Lindberg Company's monetary liabilities exceeded its monetary assets by $10,000 on January 1, 2002. The following transactions and events occurred during 2002:

1. Made cash sales of $300,000 uniformly during the year.
2. Paid salaries of $90,000 uniformly during the year.
3. Sold investment in Farhan, Iman & Laraib shares of common stock for $50,000 at the end of September.
4. Issued 2,000 shares of common stock at $20 per share at the end of June.
5. At the end of 2002: Purchased equipment for $120,000 cash, paid income taxes of $40,000, and paid dividends of $10,000.

The general price index for 2002 was as follows:

Beginning of year	120	End of 3rd quarter	128
End of 1st quarter	122	End of 4th quarter	132
End of 2nd quarter	124	Weighted average for year	126

Required:

Compute Lindberg Company's purchasing power gain or loss for 2002.

3-4 Sattar N.V. is preparing a constant guilder (Fl) balance sheet. The average general price index for the year was 150, and at the year-end it was 155.

Historical cost basis amounts in selected accounts, and the corresponding index when the amount was recorded, follow.

	Amount	Index
Accounts receivable (net of allowance for doubtful accounts)	Fl 20,000	155
Machinery	100,000	125
Accumulated depreciation on machinery	30,000	125
Patent	10,000	130
Accounts payable	25,000	155
Bonds payable	75,000	120
Common stock	80,000	100

Required:

Restate the historical cost basis amounts for preparing the constant guilder balance sheet for Sattar N.V.

3-5 Z.H. Mudh Company is preparing a constant monetary unit income statement for the year ended December 31, 2002. The average general price index for the year was 150. The general price index at the year-end was 160. Amounts in selected accounts with corresponding indexes follow.

	Amount	Index
Sales revenue	$200,000	150
Cost of goods sold	90,000	140
Depreciation expense	30,000	?
Salaries expense	40,000	150
Interest expense	15,000	?

The depreciation expense is on the equipment that was purchased when the index was 130. Interest expense is on bonds payable, issued at par when the index was 120. Mudh's tax rate is 30 percent. Taxes and interest are paid evenly throughout the year. The purchasing power gain on net monetary position for 2002 was $5,000.

Required:

Prepare a constant dollar income statement.

3-6 Selected information in deutsche marks from Lieber AG's financial statements follows.

	2001	2002
Building (acquired in 1998)	DM300,000	DM300,000
Accumulated depreciation	60,000	80,000
Land (acquired in 1998)	100,000	100,000

Price index information:

Weighted average for 1998	90
December 31, 2001	135
December 31, 2002	150
Weighted average for 2002	140

Required:

(1) Calculate depreciation expense in constant deutsche marks for 2002.

(2) Calculate the book value of the building at December 31, 2002, in constant deutsche marks.

(3) Determine the amount for land in constant deutsche marks in the December 2002 balance sheet.

3-7 Peterson Company began business in 1990 when the general price index was 80. At that time, the company acquired all of its plant assets. Sales, purchases, and operating expenses occur evenly throughout a year. Peterson's comparative balance sheets included the following information in Swiss francs:

	31 December	
	2001	**2002**
Monetary assets	SFr 300,000	SFr 280,000
Monetary liabilities	320,000	315,000
Nonmonetary assets	240,000	300,000
Nonmonetary liabilities	80,000	115,000
Other data for 2002:		
Sales		SFr 270,000
Beginning inventory (FIFO basis)		70,000
Purchases of merchandise		170,000
Ending inventory (FIFO basis)		95,000
Depreciation expense		20,000
Other operating expenses and taxes		70,000
Dividends paid at the end of 2002		45,000
General price index information:		
Beginning of operations	80	
Beginning of 2002	120	
Average index during 2002	122	
End of 2002	124	

Required:

(1) Calculate Peterson's purchasing power gain or loss for 2002.

(2) Prepare Peterson's income statement on a constant franc basis.

3-8 The income statement for 2002 and the balance sheet on December 31, 2002 for Shahruz Co. follow.

Shahruz Co.
Income Statement
For the Year Ended December 31, 2002

Sales	$400,000
Cost of goods sold	250,000
Gross profit	$150,000
Operating expenses	50,000
Net income	$100,000

Shahruz Co.
Balance Sheet
December 31, 2002

Assets		Liabilities and stockholders' equity	
Cash	$ 70,000	Notes payable	$ 30,000
Accounts receivable (net)	50,000	Accounts payable	60,000
Inventory	80,000	Paid-in capital	410,000
Land	500,000	Retained earnings	200,000
		Total liabilities and	
Total assets	$700,000	stockholders' equity	$700,000

Additional information:

1. The general price indexes for selected dates follow.

January 1, 1999	105
June 30, 2001	120
December 31, 2002	140
Weighted average for 2002	130

2. The company was founded on January 1, 1999. All shares of capital stock were issued on that date.

3. One-half of the land was acquired on January 1, 1999. The other one-half was acquired on June 30, 2001.

4. The purchasing power loss for 2002 is $10,000.

5. Ending inventory consists of units purchased uniformly in 2002.

6. There was no beginning inventory for 2002. Cost of goods sold consists of the units purchased uniformly throughout 2002.

Required:

(1) Prepare a constant dollar income statement for Shahruz Co. for the year ended December 31, 2002.

(2) Prepare a constant dollar balance sheet for Shahruz Co. on December 31, 2002.

3-9 Zaki and Safi Inc.'s condensed financial statements for its first year of operations follow.

Zaki and Safi Inc.
Income Statement
For the Year Ended December 31, 2002

Sales	$350,000
Cost of goods sold	200,000
Gross margin	$150,000
Operating expenses	70,000
Net income	$ 80,000

Zaki and Safi Inc.
Balance Sheet
December 31, 2002

Assets		Liabilities and stockholders' equity	
Cash	$ 50,000	Liabilities	$100,000
Inventory	100,000	Stockholders' equity	300,000
Fixed assets (net)	250,000	Total liabilities and	
Total assets	$400,000	stockholders' equity	$400,000

Current cost information for 2002 is as follows:

Sales	$350,000	Cash	$ 50,000
Cost of goods sold	230,000	Inventory	120,000
Operating expenses	70,000	Fixed assets	275,000

Required:

Compute Zaki and Safi Inc.'s net income on a current cost basis. Assume that holding gain or loss appears in the current cost basis income statement.

3-10 Anderson Company uses historical cost basis. It uses the periodic system and the first-in, first-out inventory method. On January 1, 2001, Anderson's inventory consisted of 20,000 units at $2 per unit. During the first quarter of 2001, the following purchases were made:

Date	Units purchased	Actual Cost
January 17	25,000	$55,000
February 13	30,000	67,500
March 20	20,000	47,000

A total of 80,000 units were sold during the first quarter. The current cost per unit was $2.10 on December 31, 2000 and $2.40 on March 31, 2001.

Required:

Using the current cost basis, compute for the first quarter of 2001:

(1)   Ending inventory.

(2)   Cost of goods sold.

3-11 Rodriguez S.A.'s machinery and equipment account balance on an historical cost basis is 102 million pesos. The balance in the accumulated depreciation account is 34 million pesos. The estimated current (replacement) cost of the machinery and equipment, if purchased new, would be 127.5 million pesos.

Required:

Compute the current cost of Rodriguez's machinery and equipment, net of accumulated depreciation.

3-12 The following information is from Aysha N.V.'s accounting records:

Average borrowings		Fl 3,000,000
Average total assets		10,000,000
Current cost adjustments:		
Depreciation expense	Fl 750,000	
Cost of goods sold	1,250,000	2,000,000

Required:

(1)   Compute Aysha's gearing adjustment.

(2)   Discuss the rationale for making the gearing adjustment.

3-13 Miller Company reported an historical cost operating income of $7,000,000. Current cost adjustments (increases) are as follows:

Cost of goods sold	$ 500,000
Depreciation expense	1,500,000
Unrealized gains	2,500,000
Other information:	
Interest income	600,000
Interest expense	750,000
Income taxes	2,200,000

Required:

Treat each of the following situations independent of each other.

(1)   Miller operates in inflationary economic conditions. Its monetary liabilities exceed its monetary assets. The amount of gearing adjustment is $580,000. Determine the current value net income.

(2)   Refer to requirement 1 but assume that Miller operates in a deflationary economy. Compute Miller's current value net income.

Case

Accounting for Changing Prices

Carols Rodriguez S.A. started manufacturing operations in 1965. The company has been continuously experiencing growth in its sales and manufacturing activities. Recently, a new controller, Ms. Shiza, was hired. She feels that historical cost financial statements do not provide adequate information to the users for informed decisions. After consideration of various proposals for supplementary financial information to be included in the 2002 annual report, she has decided to present a balance sheet as of December 31, 2002, and the income statement for 2002, both restated for general price-level changes.

Required:

(1)   Contrast between financial statements restated for general price-level changes and current value financial statements.

(2)   Distinguish between monetary and nonmonetary items.

(3)   Describe the steps Ms. Shiza should follow in preparing the supplementary constant monetary unit statements.

(4)   Identify the similarities and differences between the unadjusted historical cost financial statements and constant monetary unit financial statements.

(5)   Can the 2002 supplementary statements be presented for comparative purposes in 2003 without adjustments? Explain.

References

Accounting Principles Board. *APB Statement No. 3.* "Financial Statements Restated for General Price-Level Changes." New York: American Institute of Certified Public Accountants, 1969.

Accounting Standards Committee. *Statement of Accounting Practice No. 16.* "Current Cost Accounting." London: Institute of Chartered Accountants in England and Wales, 1980.

Cooper, Helene. "U.S. Current Account Deficit Widens to Record." *The Wall Street Journal*, 15 December 1999, p. A2.

Cooper, James C., and Kathleen Madigan. "Steering Clear of the Limits—But Where Are They?" *Business Week*, 31 January 2000, pp. 35–36.

_____. "Another Hike Done—How Many More to Go?" *Business Week*, 14 February 2000, pp. 35–36.

Dyno Industrier A.S. *Annual Report 1998*. Oslo, Norway: Dyno, 1999.

Epstein, Barry J., and Abbas Ali Mirza. *IAS 2000: Interpretation and Application of International Accounting Standards 2000*. New York: John Wiley & Sons, Inc., 2000.

Financial Accounting Standards Board. *Statement of Financial Accounting Standard No. 115*. "Accounting for Certain Investments in Debt and Equity Securities." Norwalk, Conn.: Financial Accounting Standards Board, 1993.

Forest, Stephanie Anderson, Wendy Zellner, and Laura Cohn. "Inflation: The Storm Ahead?" *Business Week*, 14 February 2000, pp. 42–43.

Gibson, R.W. "Accounting for Monetary Items Under CCA." *Accounting and Business Research*, Fall 1981, pp. 281–290.

Hale, David. "A Second Chance." *Fortune*, 22 November 1999, pp. 189–190.

"Hong Kong's CPI Falls; Deflation May Be Ending." *The Wall Street Journal*, 24 January 2000, p. A23.

Inflation Accounting Steering Group. *Guidance Manual on Current Cost Accounting*. London: Institute of Chartered Accountants in England and Wales, 1976.

International Accounting Standards Committee. *International Accounting Standard 15*. "Information Reflecting the Effects of Changing Prices." London: International Accounting Standards Committee, 1981.

_____. *International Accounting Standard 29*. "Financial Reporting in Hyperinflationary Economies." London: International Accounting Standards Committee, 1989.

Iqbal, M. Zafar. "Comparison of the Alternatives Proposed in Selected Countries to Cope with the Impact of Changing Prices on Published Financial Statements," Ph.D. dissertation, University of Nebraska, 1979.

_____. "Development of Inflation Accounting Standards in the United States." *Industrial Accountant*, October–December 1981, pp. 31–33.

_____. "Reporting the Impact of Changing Prices in Great Britain." *Accounting for Inflation*. Englewood Cliffs, N.J.: Prentice-Hall, 1981, pp. 153–163.

_____. "Reporting the Impact of Changing Prices in New Zealand." *Accounting for Inflation*. Englewood Cliffs, N.J.: Prentice-Hall, 1981, pp. 174–181.

"Japan Bank Woes May Foil Flight Against Deflation." *Gulf News*, 27 June 1998, p. 24.

Lueck, Sarah, and John Simons. "Consumer Inflation Hits a 4-Month Low." *The Wall Street Journal*, 18 November 1999, p. A2.

Madigan, Kathleen. "Greenspan for Greenhorns." *Business Week*, 7 February 2000, pp. 124 and 126.

Ortiz, Guillermo. "Reducing Inflation is Mexico's Monetary Policy Goal." *The Wall Street Journal*, 10 December 1999, p. A19.

PricewaterhouseCoopers. *Understanding IAS: Analysis and Interpretation of International Accounting Standards*, 2d ed. London: PricewaterhouseCoopers (United Kingdom), 1998.

Raymond, Robert H., M. Zafar Iqbal, and Eldon L. Schafer. "The Gearing (Leverage) Adjustment: A Historical and Comparative Analysis." *The International Journal of Accounting*, vol. 17 (Fall 1982), pp. 139–157.

Rosenfield, Paul. "The Confusion Between General Price-Level Restatement and Current Value Accounting." *Journal of Accountancy*, October 1972, pp. 63–68.

Shriver, Keith A. "An Empirical Examination of the Potential Measurement Error in Current Cost Data." *Accounting Review*, January 1987, pp. 79–96.

"Stagflation Threatens Malaysia Economy." *Gulf News*, 28 May 1998, p. 35.

"Submission on the Report of the Committee of Inquiry into Inflation Accounting." *Accountants Journal* (New Zealand), May 1977, pp. 153–156.

Sweeney, Henry W. *Stabilized Accounting*. New York: Holt, Reinhart & Winston, 1964. Originally published by Harper in 1936.

Teléfonos de México S.A. de C.V. Annual Report 1997. Cuauhtémoc, Mexico: TELMEX, 1998.

Westwick, C.A. "The Lesson to be Learned from the Development of Inflation Accounting in the U.K." *Accounting and Business Research*, Autumn 1980, p. 356–364.

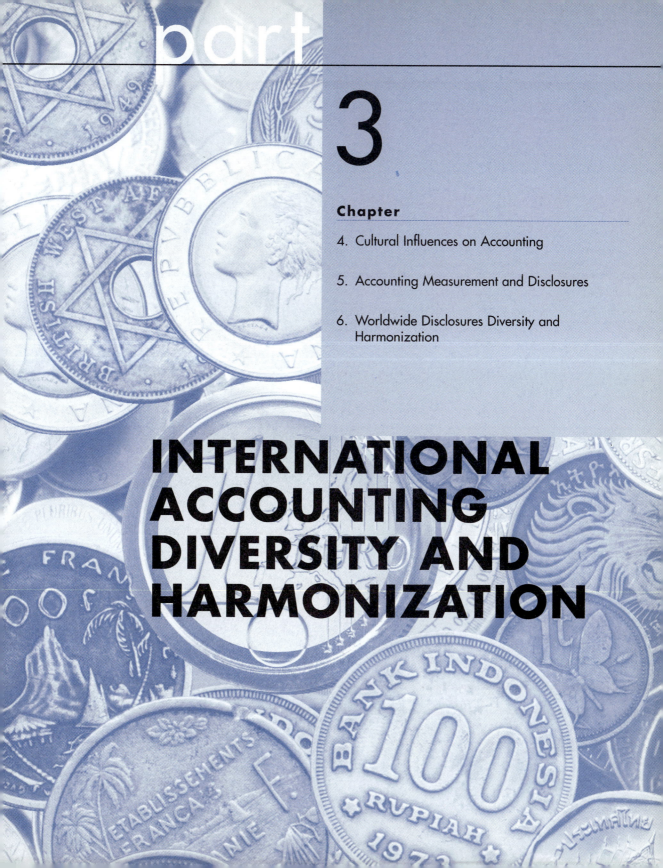

part

3

INTERNATIONAL ACCOUNTING DIVERSITY AND HARMONIZATION

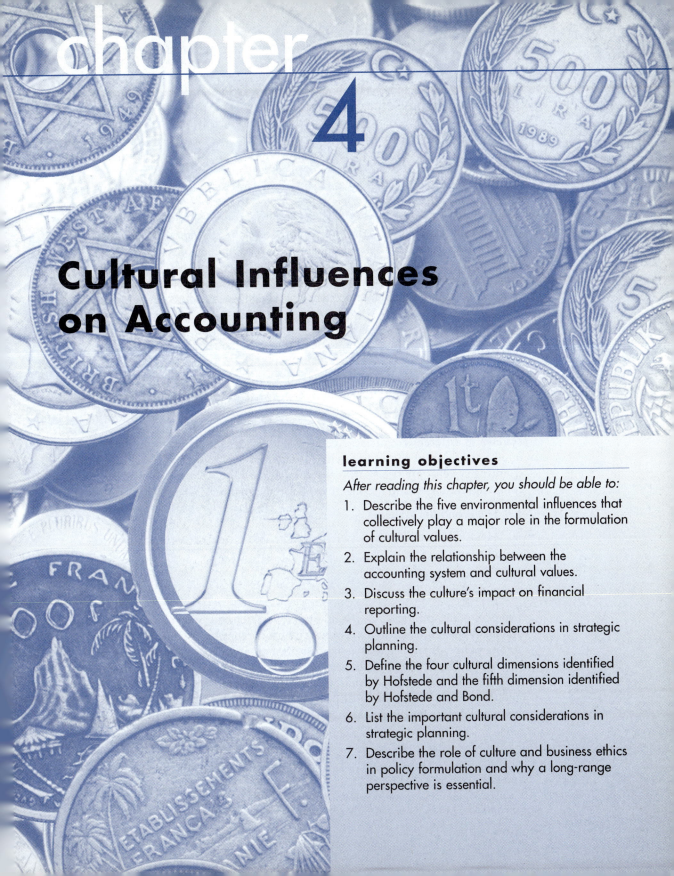

chapter

4

Cultural Influences on Accounting

learning objectives

After reading this chapter, you should be able to:

1. Describe the five environmental influences that collectively play a major role in the formulation of cultural values.

2. Explain the relationship between the accounting system and cultural values.

3. Discuss the culture's impact on financial reporting.

4. Outline the cultural considerations in strategic planning.

5. Define the four cultural dimensions identified by Hofstede and the fifth dimension identified by Hofstede and Bond.

6. List the important cultural considerations in strategic planning.

7. Describe the role of culture and business ethics in policy formulation and why a long-range perspective is essential.

By the year 2010, more than half of the world's corporations will operate on a seamless, global basis. The companies that become multicultural entities will be rewarded.[1] The globalization of the economy requires many new skills in professional accountants that were previously not critical or even necessary. They include an appreciation of cultural diversity and cultural sensitivity. To be professionally successful, accountants must possess a global perspective.[2]

Cultures vary from country to country and exercise heavy influence on business practices. In some countries, such as Japan, the source of financing is mostly debt, while in other countries, such as the U.K., it is from investment by equity holders. How may the debt to equity ratio of a Japanese operation be compared with a British operation? Would such a comparison provide any useful insights to the analyst? This example gives some idea of the challenges faced by accounting in the international arena. The decision-making process for resolution of operational and conceptual issues must, therefore, take into account cultural influences on accounting.

Culture and Environmental Influences

One of the major objectives of financial reporting is to provide information to users for making economic decisions. Since environments differ from country to country, the types of decisions that need to be made and their information requirements are also different. This explains why there are different accounting systems in different countries: Accounting provides information for making economic decisions in the *unique* environment of each country, therefore, the accounting systems are necessarily *environment-specific*. There are five major environmental influences that collectively formulate cultural or societal values:

1. The economic system
2. The political system
3. The legal system
4. The educational system
5. Religion

The economic, political, and legal systems are closely intertwined. The educational system can be a force to counter, reinforce, or modify influences of the economic, political, and legal systems. Since religion is a matter of faith, it is shown separately. The degree of influence of religion, as an environmental factor, varies from country to country. In many parts of the world, especially in some Muslim countries, it is perhaps the most powerful of the environmental influences. These major environmental influences collectively play a key role in the formation of

---

1 Deloitte & Touche. "Deloitte & Touche Analyses Key Business Issues." *Deloitte & Touche Review*, 2 February 1998, p. 4.

2 American Institute of Certified Public Accountants. "CPA Vision Project Identifies Top Five Issues for Profession." *The CPA Letter*, April 1998, pp. 1 and 12.

cultural values. The cultural values affect, among others, the accounting profession's values. The shared values of the accounting professionals influence the accounting system of a country. In turn, information from the accounting system affects the economic, political, legal, and educational systems. These relationships are illustrated in Figure 4.1.

We will now take a closer look at these environmental influences, and also discuss some major issues related to each of them.

The Economic System

The *degree of economic development and the level of technology* in a country determine, to a great extent, the level of complexity of its accounting system. The accounting system of an economically developed country with a high-technology economy would be different from the accounting system of a country with primarily an agrarian economy. Intangibles (e.g., patents and copyrights) have significantly greater importance in a country that has a high-technology economy than one that has a subsistence-level economy.

figure 4.1 **Environmental Influences on Accounting**

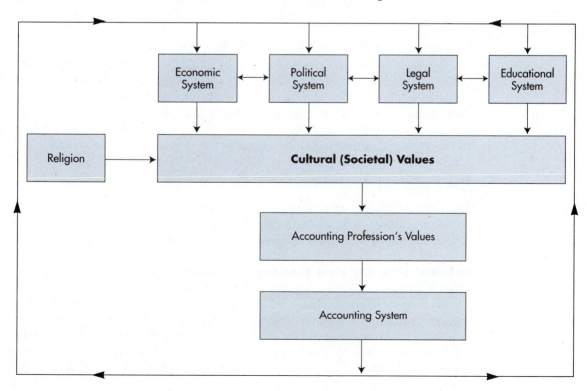

The degree of the *concentration of ownership* of business in a society influences the need for and extent of disclosures. If business ownerships are dispersed in a country, there would likely be greater and varied disclosures to meet the needs of the many investors.

The *source of business financing* is an important consideration for the orientation of accounting reports and disclosures. If debt is the major source of financing, then much of the information can be furnished directly to the lenders, instead of being disclosed to the public at large. Financial reports, as a result, would be creditor-oriented, and their content would primarily address the information needs of the lenders. In case equity capital is the major source of financing, the financial reports would be mainly geared toward equity holders.

To varying degrees, the *tax laws* of a country have an impact on income measurement. In many countries, e.g., Japan, Germany, and France, income for taxation is the same as for financial reporting. In such cases the accounting system is synchronized with the tax laws. In other countries, e.g., the U.S. and the U.K., income for taxation is computed differently from the income for financial reporting. The accounting systems in such countries are hence relatively independent of the provisions of the tax laws.

If a country has a *highly inflationary economy*, the accounting system would require restatement of the historical-cost-based financial statements to reflect the impact of inflation. In extreme cases, there may be a departure to a non-historical-cost-based, i.e., current value-based measurement, especially if the price-level volatility is either a combination of general and specific or is mainly specific.

Economic Stability and Economic Risk Exposure

The degree of economic risk exposure to the investors and creditors in a country is directly related to the degree of economic instability of the country. A highly unstable economy makes it very difficult to formulate reasonably reliable forecasts. It also necessitates a frequent, and sometimes drastic, changing of plans.

Economic stability of a country, among others, facilitates the development and continuous improvement of a conceptually sound accounting system.

The Political System

The political system of a country, its philosophy, and its objectives determine broad economic policies such as centrally planned versus market-driven economies, and private ownership versus public ownership of property.

Political Stability and Economic Stability

There is a close link between political stability and economic stability. They usually go hand in hand. As discussed in the previous section, economic stability is necessary for the development and continuous improvement of a cogent and responsive accounting system. Due to the relationship between economic stability and political stability, it can be inferred that the development of an accounting system is facilitated when the country has political stability. An Ernst & Young survey of the Global 1000 companies identified political instability to be *the major barrier* to investment in a country. Fifty-three percent of the respondents cited political instability as a major barrier while 36 percent stated it is somewhat of a barrier. Next in line are financial risk, legal infrastructure, bureaucracy, exchange controls, and commercial infrastructure.[3]

The concern of the Global 1000 companies regarding political instability as the major barrier to investment is understandable. Evidence exists that a successive government may not honor a contract entered into by the previous government. In 1997, the new Pakistani government refused to accept terms of a $1.6 billion contract that the previous government had entered into with The Hub Power Company. Interestingly, this was the biggest direct investment project in the country made by a foreign investor.[4] An editorial in one of the major Pakistani newspapers summed up the impact of the 3-year-old dispute as follows:

> Since efforts are underway to encourage investment inflows, the country can ill-afford such image-denting issues. . .
>
> The controversy has attracted much international attention and important world capitals have asked Pakistan to settle it quickly. . .
>
> Pakistan's efforts to attract new investment cannot bring the desired results without burying this hatchet. Fresh capital inflows are critical for economic recovery and revival of its growth momentum. The government should know which side of its economy's bread needs to be buttered.[5]

During the same year, 1997, South Korea's LG Electronics Inc. canceled a plan to build a consumer electronics plant in Russia due to "political instability."[6] Political instability of a country scares off foreign investors because it is generally due to the mismanagement of the economy, corruption, lack of accountability, lengthy delays in decision making, and political interference in economic and business affairs. *In sum, political instability of a country is often a result of the deterioration of economic conditions. The development of a comprehensive and sophisticated accounting system is difficult under such a set of circumstances.*

Bureaucratic Hurdles

A political system that is supported by a complex bureaucracy often leads to long delays due to indecisions or untimely decisions. Sometimes the delays are too long for the investors, resulting in the termination of the projects. In December 1999, U.S.-based Cogentrix Energy Inc. decided to stop development of a $1.3 billion power plant in India. In 1992, India had invited Cogentrix to make the investment, and designated the project "fast-track." Cogentrix lost patience and decided to terminate the project in 1999 due to lengthy delays in obtaining government

3 "What's Ahead with Global Investors?" *Management Accounting*, January 1995, p. 21.

4 Scott McDonald. "Power Feud Casts Harsh Spotlight on Pak Woes." *India-West*, 10 September 1999, p. B25.

5 "The Power-tariff Row." *The News International*, 25 March 2000, p. 7.

6 "LG Drops Russia Plant." *Gulf News*, 4 January 1997, p. 20.

approvals. After seven years, the so-called "fast track" project had not even broken ground.[7] Often the delays result from complex rules, procedures, and obligations developed by the bureaucracy, a byproduct of the political system.

Political Corruption

A corrupt political system contributes to the economic deterioration of a country because the policy formulation and the decisions of those in power leads to inefficient allocation of scarce economic resources. Their objective is to amass personal wealth, create family fiefdoms, and practice cronyism. The *modus operandi* is political favors and financial kickbacks, rather than adhering to laws and principles and allocating resources for the common good.

It is encouraging to note that recently societal pressure in some countries is successful in curtailing widespread corruption. In March 2000, Thailand's politically powerful interior minister resigned after an anti-corruption organization, formed in 1997, accused him of concealing his assets by falsely claiming that he had borrowed $1.21 million from a private company. The National Counter-Corruption Commission, an independent body, thus toppled one of the most influential figures in Thailand politics. It is a sign that the "landscape of the nation's deeply corrupt political system has begun to shift."[8] The corruption case against the interior minister next goes before a special Constitutional Court.

In Indonesia, also during March 2000, state prosecutors for the first time arrested a key member of former President Suharto's inner circle, Mohamad "Bob" Hasan, after a corruption investigation. Hasan had served as the minister of trade and industry in Suharto's last government. He also looked after business interests of the Suharto family. The arrest raised hopes "the new government is getting serious about probing the financial dealings of the onetime ruler."[9]

The Legal System

In many countries, including some Western European countries, the legal system has a direct impact on accounting. Laws contain detailed accounting regulations specifying comprehensive accounting rules and procedures. In such countries, accounting rules are based on legislative requirements. The government, therefore, determines and enforces these requirements through accounting rules.

The comprehensive body of statute and case law was a concept that the Romans borrowed from the Greeks. Romans put the idea into practice and many countries in the world have adopted the ideal of written law to protect individuals from other individuals and from the power of the state.

---

7 Jonathan Karp. "Cogentrix, CLP Halt Development of India Power Plant." *The Wall Street Journal*, 10 December 1999, p. A12.

8 Seth Mydans. "A Top Thai Official Resigns in Scandal." *San Francisco Chronicle*, 30 March 2000, p. A18.

9 Jay Solomon and Puspa Madni. "Indonesia Arrests Big Crony of Suharto, Raising Hopes for Full Corruption Probe." *The Wall Street Journal*, 29 March 2000, p. A19.

The rule of law is so central to Western civilization that most of us take it for granted. Of course we are governed by laws, we say—it's natural. In fact, though, the rule of law is not a necessary aspect of the human condition. Another great ancient empire, China, arranged things precisely the opposite of the Roman way. Confucius and his disciples down through the centuries distrusted written laws. A dusty statute book was too inflexible to handle the infinite variety of human experience, the Chinese sages felt. They chose to trust people, not laws—to rely on innate human goodness as the best guarantee of a civil society. Even today the concept of written law and written contract is fairly weak in China and other East Asian nations within its cultural ambit.[10]

Legal systems of most non-Western countries are quite different from the legal systems common in Western countries. The sanctity of contract is fundamental to business dealings in the West. However, in many countries, including China, the concept of written contract is literally foreign. Since global economy involves cross-border transactions, it is essential that a common commitment to the sanctity of contract and rule of law by all parties to the transaction be understood and accepted. In 1999, the Chinese government sent 35 lawyers, judges, government officials, and law professors to a program on U.S. law at Temple University. In China it is common for a court to try a criminal suspect who does not have legal counsel. One of the participants in the Temple University program stated, "It is true, our legal system is still developing. We can learn from the American legal system how to move forward our own Chinese legal system."[11]

Besides the underdevelopment of a legal system that can handle transactions in a global economy, there are two other issues that are noteworthy: Lengthy trials and judicial corruption.

Lengthy Trials

In some countries a civil litigation may last for several decades. For example, in India a legal case may take 30 years. The same is true of India's neighboring country Pakistan. A case that had been pending in the Supreme Court of Pakistan for 26 years was finally settled out of court by descendants of the parties involved:

> Interestingly, the majority of the characters in the case have died. Lal Din, the petitioner, and Haji Abdul Waheed, the respondent, died during the pendency of the case in the Supreme Court. Two out of three members of the Supreme Court bench, which had decided the case, have died. Both the counsels for the appellant, and Shaikh Saeed Akhtar, have died. Advocate Gul Mohammad was later made a judge of the Lahore High Court. Subsequently, he became the chief justice of the Federal Shariat Court. He is also no more in this world.[12]

---

10 T.R. Reid. "The World According to Rome." *National Geographic*, August 1997, pp. 63–64.

11 Jennifer Lin. "Chinese Lawyers, Judges Studying Law, American-Style." *The Tribune*, 25 September 1999, p. C8.

12 "Case Settled After 26 Years." *Dawn*, 13 June 1997, p. 3.

There are some encouraging signs that the situation could possibly improve in the future. Several countries are considering different options to alleviate the problem of long delays. India had a backlog of more than three million cases in 1997, and the options considered included adopting the U.S.-style plea bargaining system. The Federal Law and Justice Minister of India stated that the ultimate objective is to limit the duration of a trial to possibly less than one year.[13] In Pakistan the Chief Justice of Pakistan has directed that cases pending since 1990 be declared "old cases" and scheduled for daily hearing. He also directed the chief justices of provincial high courts to monitor progress in the speedy disposal of long-pending cases and compile the data relating to their disposal.[14] The lengthy delays can be attributed to the Asian legal framework that is completely different from that of Western countries.[15]

Judicial Corruption

In some countries judicial corruption is rampant. The majority or a sizeable minority of judges willingly accept and sometimes even solicit bribes. In cases when a party to a case pays a bribe to the presiding judge, it clearly makes the judge unfit for rendering an impartial verdict. In 1999, a constitutional assembly in Venezuela declared a judicial emergency because of an accusation of corruption and other irregularities against nearly half of Venezuela's 4,700 judges.[16]

The Educational System

The educational system and the level of literacy in a country impact the country's accounting system in two ways:

- Well-educated users of accounting information can understand sophisticated accounting information.
- The accountants in a country that has high educational standards are usually better trained and possess the necessary competencies and skills to satisfactorily complete their professional assignments.

In sum, educational backgrounds of both users and preparers of accounting information strongly affect the degree of development and level of sophistication of a country's accounting system.

Sometimes changes in the environment of a country make the country's accounting system obsolete. Some local authorities in Russia still require use of the accounting system that was developed and practiced during the era of the Soviet-planned economy. Obviously, the old accounting system is unable to meet the requirements of the current economy that is no longer centrally planned. Conse-

---

13 "India Seeks to Clear Court Backlog." *Gulf News*, 3 July 1997, p. 20.

14 "CJ Satisfied With Court's Disposal of Cases." *The Nation*, 25 March 2000, p. 14.

15 Alan Gersten. "Eastern Exposure." *Journal of Accountancy*, August 1999, p. 53.

16 "Judicial Emergency Declared in Venezuela." *San Francisco Chronicle*, 20 August 1999, p. D3.

quently, some Western firms keep two sets of accounting books: one to meet the local authorities' requirements and the other to meet their own information needs.

Religion

Religion, in the broad sense of the term, affects basic accounting concepts. In many Muslim countries, e.g., Pakistan, the idea of interest on loans is contrary to widely held religious beliefs. In December 1999, Pakistan's Supreme Court declared that both paying and receiving interest are unacceptable in Islam. The court ordered the government to introduce an interest-free economic system by 2001.[17] The likely result is to find different ways of presenting and communicating accounting information related to credit transactions.

It should be understood that some religious requirements might be interpreted differently in different countries. Take the separation of sexes, for example. Laws in Saudi Arabia prohibit mixing of the sexes. This requires that Saudi businesswomen must have a male sponsor to represent them in dealings with the governmental departments and business organizations. The female owner of a business cannot deal directly even with her own male employees. Not surprisingly, a survey of Saudi Arabian businesswomen showed that the difficulty of dealing directly with other parties was the most common complaint among them.[18] In contrast, businesswomen and female workers in many other Muslim countries such as Indonesia, Egypt, and Oman can deal directly with their male employees, co-workers, and the government employees.

Culture's Impact on Financial Reporting

Culture's deep imprint on financial reporting can be illustrated by the secondary statement approach. The **secondary statement approach** uses the accounting principles of another country for the preparation of financial statements. Secondary financial statements are also audited according to auditing standards of the same country. The objective is to enhance the understandability and usefulness of the financial statements for the target audience, i.e., the users in that country.

The approach, however, cannot compensate for the differences in cultural environments. The interpretation of secondary financial statements is difficult because business customs based on local culture differ from country to country. *National business customs leave an imprint on the primary financial statements that cannot be duplicated in the secondary financial statements.* Howard Lowe has eloquently stated this in discussing Japanese consolidated financial statements using U.S. accounting principles.

---

17 Raja Asghar. "Pakistan Top Court Rules Bank Interest is Un-Islamic." *India-West*, 31 December 1999, p. A44.

18 "Businesswomen Try to Overcome Obstacles in Saudi Arabia." *Gulf News*, 3 July 1998, p. 18.

The notion of control through direct or indirect majority share ownership and the presence of a holding company or a dominant parent company are foreign concepts to the typical Japanese executive. Share ownership is generally regarded as of major significance in the forming and maintaining of corporate groups. Consequently, American practices of consolidation tend to group Japanese corporations in a manner contrary to their normal functioning. Such practices tend to break up the complex and dynamic reality of the natural groups into American-type corporate groups attempting to portray an American perspective to something uniquely Japanese.

Japanese consolidated statements patterned after American standards have survived only because foreign users have been largely unaware of their inappropriate focus and innocent misrepresentation.

Many of the most important firms affecting the future fortunes of the group are not even represented in these statements.

Consequently, its [Japan's] unique business organizational environment often makes its consolidated financial reports less rather than more useful to readers.[19]

This reminds us again that the global economy is making it increasingly important to be knowledgeable in other cultures to do our jobs effectively.

Cultural Considerations in Strategic Planning

Most of the information for strategic planning is external in nature. The stability and complexity of environments vary from country to country. The economies of Sweden and Germany are relatively stable, and they remain strong free market economies. The environments of some countries are quite dynamic. France's policies on socialism versus private enterprise are noticeably affected by each election. The greater the degree of environmental instability in a country, the more difficult it is to predict environmental conditions.[20]

Cultural Diversity

Cultural diversity can be a source of synergy in a multinational organization. By adopting a multinational strategy, an organization can become more than a sum of its parts. Japanese and Indian managers, for example, are subject to norms and values that are far more complex than are U.S. managers.[21] Operations in one

---

19 Howard D. Lowe. "Shortcomings of Japanese Consolidated Financial Statements." *Accounting Horizons*, September 1990, pp. 8–9.

20 Warren J. Keegan. *Global Marketing Management*, 4th ed. Englewood Cliffs, N.J.: Prentice Hall, 1989, p. 682.

21 Gregory Moorhead and Ricky W. Griffin. *Organizational Behavior*, 2d ed. Boston, Mass.: Houghton Mifflin Company, 1989, p. 682.

cultural setting can benefit from operations in another cultural setting by gaining a better understanding of how the world works.[22]

U.S. Federal Reserve Board Chairman Alan Greenspan has repeatedly spoken about the contributions made by the immigrants to America's extraordinary prosperity. He advocates that the U.S. Congress should liberalize all categories of immigration to sustain America's economic prosperity.

Recent studies by the Rand Corporation and the U.S. Bureau of Economic Research have found that legal immigrants to the U.S. have higher educational levels and more skills than the native born.[23]

National Boundaries and Cultural Boundaries

At this stage, an important point needs to be noted: *National boundaries and cultural boundaries often do not coincide.*[24] Cultural patterns in California are much different from those in Alabama. The culture in the northern part of Italy is more similar to Switzerland than it is to the southern part of Italy. Quebec's culture is different than that of any other province in Canada. In other words, in each country there are many subcultures.

Culture and Individual Behavior

Individual behavior varies across cultures. A large-scale study by Hofstede, based on 116,000 responses from workers in 40 countries, identified cultural differences that could be grouped in four dimensions.[25] Later Hofstede collaborated with Bond on a subsequent research project. The outcome of their joint effort was the identification of a fifth cultural dimension.

Large Power Distance Versus Small Power Distance

Power distance reflects the tolerance of inequality between superiors and subordinates. In a **large power distance culture**, a person at a higher position in the organizational hierarchy makes the decisions, and the employees at the lower levels simply follow the instructions. In a **small power distance culture**, employees perceive few power differences and follow a superior's instructions only when they either agree or feel threatened.

The following excerpt from a column by a Pakistani satirist illustrates the contrast between large power distance (Pakistan) and small power distance (Germany) quite effectively:

---

22 Tamotsu Yamaguchi. "The Challenge of Internationalization." *Academy of Management Executive*, February 1988, pp. 33–36.

23 Frank Sharry. "Immigrants' Contribution to America." *Business Week*, 3 April 2000, p. 16.

24 Nancy J. Adler, Robert Doctor, and S. Gordon Redding. "From the Atlantic to the Pacific Century: Cross Cultural Management Review." *Journal of Management*, Summer 1986, pp. 295–318.

25 Geert H. Hofstede. *Culture's Consequences: International Differences in Work-Related Values.* Beverly Hills, Calif: Sage Publications, 1980.

How unfortunate are some of the highly developed nations of Europe, and even the USA itself, that they have no VIPs in the sense that we know the breed! What does the common man in those countries look up to become? From Germany came the news some time ago that the foreign minister of that country was fined for parking his car in the wrong place, and he paid the fine. Obviously he did not think of himself as a VIP.

Obviously again, the people of Germany—or any other European country for that matter—do not know how to pay proper respect to their government leaders, despite claims of having advanced so much in the field of public service and practical democracy.

It is one thing to raise the level to which ordinary people must be honoured in a democracy and quite another to drag leaders down to the plebeian level. This is something we don't do in Pakistan in spite of our backward ways. We neither promote the people nor do we demote the leaders, however dismal the record of the latter may be in respect of character and performance. We believe in the status quo.

One thing is certain. Had the German foreign minister been a Pakistani and our foreign minister, he would have been a distinguished citizen, a VIP, and wouldn't have had to submit to the indignity of a traffic challan*. Had he chosen to park his car in the middle of Islamabad's Constitution Avenue or Karachi's Bunder Road, and blocked the traffic, the police would have smiled indulgently and invited him to do it again.[26]

*citation; ticket.

Among the large power distance countries are Pakistan, Spain, France, Japan, Singapore, Mexico, Brazil, and Indonesia. The examples of cultures with a small power distance include Germany, the U.S., Israel, Austria, Denmark, Ireland, Norway, and New Zealand.

Individualism Versus Collectivism

Individualism is the trait in which the employee attaches higher importance to personal and family interests than to the organization. **Collectivism** is the cultural characteristic in which interests of the organization should have top priority.

The employees in a culture that values individualism usually assess situations in terms of how decisions will affect them personally and professionally. The people in cultures characterized by collectivism put the needs of the organization uppermost. Therefore, organizational interests take higher priority than do personal and family interests.

The most individualistic cultures include the U.S., Australia, the U.K., the Netherlands, Canada, and New Zealand. Cultures characterized by a very high

---

26 Hafizur Rahman. "The Pampered Lot." *The News International*, 25 March 2000, p. 6.

degree of collectivism include Columbia, Pakistan, Taiwan, Peru, Singapore, Japan, Mexico, Greece, Hong Kong, and South Korea.

Uncertainty Avoidance Versus Uncertainty Acceptance

Uncertainty avoidance is the extent to which uncertainty is avoided in a culture. A society with a high level of uncertainty avoidance gives importance to employment stability and a low level of stress. **Uncertainty acceptance** characterizes accepting uncertainty as a normal part of life, and feeling comfortable with ambiguity and unfamiliar risks.

Employees in Denmark, the U.S., Canada, Norway, Singapore, Hong Kong, and Australia tolerate a high level of uncertainty. Uncertainty avoidance is high among employees in Japan, South Korea, Mexico, Israel, Austria, Italy, Argentina, Peru, France, and Belgium.

Masculinity Versus Femininity

Masculinity is the relative importance of the qualities such as assertiveness and materialism. **Femininity** is characterized by quality of life, nurturing, and relationships. Masculine societies define male-female roles more rigidly than do the societies with a high degree of femininity.

Two points need to be emphasized regarding this cultural dimension: First, this dimension deals with the relative importance attached to the aforementioned qualities in a culture, and it should not be confused with sexual orientation. Secondly, this dimension may, at first, appear not to be relevant for accounting. In fact, it is very relevant. This can be illustrated by focusing on employee incentives. Everything else being equal, the employees in a culture with a relatively high degree of masculinity are likely to be more motivated by overtime premium pay and monetary bonus than a longer vacation time. The employees in a society with a relatively high degree of femininity would most probably prefer more time with the family, i.e., foregoing overtime premium pay and monetary bonuses in lieu of a longer vacation time. The compensation package and fringe benefits can, therefore, be made consistent with the cultural needs.

Finland's culture is highly feminine. The wife of the Finnish Prime Minister gave birth to their first daughter in 1998, and to the second daughter in March 2000. Both times the Prime Minister took parental leave. This shared parenting is consistent with the nurturing quality, a characteristic of the femininity dimension.

Highly masculine cultures include Japan and Austria, while the highly feminine societies include Sweden, Norway, Denmark, and Finland.

Long-Term Orientation Versus Short-Term Orientation

This cultural dimension is also called Confucian Dynamism. The values comprising this dimension can be attributed to the philosophy of Confucius, a Chinese scholar who lived during the sixth century B.C. The **long-term orientation** emphasizes the adaptation of traditions to meet current needs. It values perseverance, efficiency and economy in using resources, and willingness to make sacrifices to achieve objectives. The **short-term orientation** values respect for tradition, personal stability, quick results from the efforts made, and concern with appearances.[27] Japan, Taiwan, Singapore, South Korea, and Hong Kong have long-term orientation. Germany, the U.K., the U.S., and Sweden have short-term orientation.

Cross-cultural considerations are important in the strategic planning process as well as in the design of control systems (discussed in the next section). To cope with the challenges posed by cultural environments in different parts of the world, it is necessary that a multinational company adapt to different cultures where it conducts business. *Cultural variations have a direct impact on how managers and employees in different parts of the world make and accept decisions, how they view their professional careers in comparison with personal and family interests, and, most importantly, what motivates them.*

Business managers of multinationals are increasingly becoming aware of cultural implications. A survey of 150 senior executives of Fortune 1000 companies by Deloitte & Touche indicated that the executives feel, "Globalization is more than international business—it is a complete, conceptual evolution."[28] The executives stated that as companies expand globally, the primary challenge they face is the cultural barrier, followed by economic barriers and trade and political barriers. They also stated that when management makes the decision to expand overseas, the keys to success are:[29]

- Building a local presence.
- Modifying products and services to suit local cultures.
- Using technology effectively.
- Employing local staff to run foreign operations.

Immigrants to the base country of a multinational company are often valuable resources for bridging cultural gaps and fostering cultural understanding. The following example illustrates the important role played by the immigrants from India to the U.S. in helping U.S.-based multinationals establish business operations in India.

> . . . U.S. émigrés often return to head operations for such companies as GE Capital, McKinsey, and AT&T. They often end up explaining Indians and Americans to each other. "My role is to provide a cultural interpretation," says Kartar Singh, senior vice-president of Cogentrix Inc. in Charlotte, N.C.[30]

---

27 G. Hofstede and M. Bond. "The Confucius Connection: From Cultural Roots to Economic Growth." *Organizational Dynamics*, 1988.

28 "Global Expansion Not Deterred by Falling Dollar." *Deloitte & Touche Review*, 10 July 1995, p. 3.

29 *Ibid.*, p. 4.

30 Joyce Barnathan, Sharon Moshavi, Heidi Dawley, Sunity Wadekar Bhargava, and Helen Chang. "Passage Back to India: Expatriates Seek a Motherlode in the Motherland." *Business Week*, 17 July 1995, p. 45.

Local presence often makes it easier to receive acceptance from local culture. Texas Instruments has effectively used the strategy of local presence. Before its global strategy, Texas Instruments was almost forced out of the market by competition. Now Texas Instruments has fabrication plants in more countries than any other chip manufacturer, and other chip makers are following Texas Instrument's example. Local presence enables a company to tap market growth wherever it occurs.[31]

Cultural Considerations in Control Systems

The previous section discussed culture's role in strategic planning. This section presents control concepts and considerations for designing an effective control system in multinational operations.

A **control system** compares the actual performance (results) with the planned performance (goals) so that management may take appropriate action when necessary. A control system includes information that is internal, external, financial, and nonfinancial.

In addition to formal control systems, informal control methods play an important role in multinational companies. The main informal control method is to transfer an executive from one international operation to another with explicit or implicit understanding about expected performance. Another informal control method is to hold meetings between parent company executives and subsidiary executives, usually at a subsidiary's location. Annual meetings of executives from international operations also provide an opportunity to informally assess performance and to exchange information.

Cultural differences necessitate adaptation of control measures to each country's cultural environment. Different languages and communication styles are but a couple of the issues facing multinational corporations while designing and implementing control measures across national boundaries.

A subsidiary organized in a new country might mean another language in which strategic plans, budgets, and reports are written. In many countries, there are different languages and each has many dialects. Some technical words may be difficult or impossible to translate into the local language.

Cultural Considerations for Motivation

An information system provides control measures that attempt to motivate—and motivation has to do with human behavior. Since companies in a global economy operate in multiple societies, each with its own culture, designing a system that will influence human behavior in the desired manner requires cultural awareness.

---

31 Peter Burrows, Linda Bernier, and Pete Engardio. "Texas Instruments' Global Chip Payoff: The Company Is Ready to Cash in on the Biggest Bonanza in High-tech History." *Business Week*, 7 August 1995, p. 64.

This is a prerequisite for a successful system. Otherwise, there may be undesirable consequences.

> If the damage to cultural values is substantial, the members of the culture will find ways to retaliate. They withhold their cooperation, resort to foot-dragging, and use other subtle ways to make the changes not worth having. The resulting lowered morale is one of the prices paid by managers who choose to ignore the social consequences of the intended changes.[32]

Policy Formulation in Different Cultures

Cultural realities must be confronted and issues resolved to ensure that corporate policies are well thought out and well articulated. This requires taking into account not only organizational goals but also cultural differences, different business practices, and business ethics. Some issues are easy to resolve. In a company function, pork should not be served in Israel or in Muslim countries. Other issues are more complex. They can be addressed only after first thoroughly analyzing them and then articulating a clear corporate policy. It is important to always remember that MNC operations are not confined to one part of the world. *MNCs are inherently corporate citizens of the base country as well as of the world.*

Business Ethics

Some assert that cultural differences preclude applying one set of ethical standards worldwide. Research findings, however, indicate that despite cultural differences, standards of moral judgment do not vary significantly among countries.[33] Therefore, ethical considerations become critically important variables in the long-run decision process.

There are also side benefits. Instituting formal ethical policies in a company leads to lower internal control costs for the company.[34] In 1999, a Conference Board survey of 124 companies in 22 countries found that 78 percent of boards of directors are setting ethics standards, up from 41 percent in 1991 and 21 percent in 1987. Business leaders see the self-regulation as a way to avoid legislative or judicial intrusions into their operations. Ethics codes also help promote tolerance of diverse practices and customs while doing business abroad.[35]

The previous discussion is not to imply that all ethical issues are easily resolved and the situations involving ethical dilemmas do not exist. However,

---

32 Joseph M. Juran. *Juran on Quality by Design: The New Steps for Planning Quality into Goods and Services.* New York: The Free Press, 1992, p. 433.

33 Robert B. Sweeney. "Ethics in an International Environment." *Management Accounting,* February 1991, p. 27.

34 "Ethics Policies Help Reduce Internal Control Costs." *Journal of Accountancy,* April 1994, p. 14.

35 "Global Ethics Codes." *The Wall Street Journal,* 19 August 1999, p. A1.

proper focus does help. *Formulation of corporate policy should focus on long-run results rather than short-term expediency.* The leadership and attitude of top management coupled with a proactive management style can go a long way toward cultivation of a corporate culture in which all constructive ideas are accepted, nourished, and given a chance to flourish. A performance evaluation system that takes into account performance in the areas of cultural sensitivity and long-run perspective provides incentives that motivate managers and employees to behave in an ethical manner consistent with corporate policies.

Because of familiarity with local culture and business customs, a local staff can be invaluable during the corporate policy formulation process to ensure that the policies are consistently local-culture-sensitive as well as motivators for ethical behavior.

Note to Students

To prepare for an international assignment in the future, take courses to develop greater cultural understanding and appreciation. If possible, spend time as an exchange student or take an internship abroad. It is also helpful to learn other languages. When you start your career after graduation, take advantage of international training programs, if they are available in your company.

Before seeking an international assignment, ask yourself how it will fit in your career plan. When seeking an overseas assignment, make sure you discuss with your manager the objectives of the assignment. The outcome of the discussion should be a clear understanding of what is expected from you when you are overseas. This expectation should be articulated in clear, well-defined goals that you are to accomplish. Equally important are two considerations: The time frame for achieving the goals and the level of resource support necessary to achieve the goals.

According to Deloitte & Touche, a successful candidate for an international assignment should have the following characteristics and skills:

- Genuine interest in other cultures and points-of-view.
- Ability to interact comfortably with people at different levels in an organization, as well as with people from different cultural backgrounds.
- Leadership skills that can be channeled to promote cross-functional and cross-cultural interaction and learning.
- Global business and marketing knowledge/perspective.
- Solid verbal and written communication skills.[36]

While overseas, communicate regularly with the office in the base country. This not only keeps you in the loop, but also makes the transition far smoother after you return from the international assignment.

---

36 Deloitte & Touche. "Considering an International Assignment?" *The Review,* 25 October 1999, p. 7.

Chapter Summary

1. A study of cultural influences is the necessary first step in explaining the accounting system of a nation. The important environmental influences include the economic system, the political system, the legal system, the educational system, and religion.

2. Environmental factors affect the development of global business strategy.

3. International operations pose unique and complex challenges in the design of a control system.

4. Problems encountered in the design of a global control system include diversity among nations with respect to culture and languages.

5. The same control system may work well in one country but not in another due to cultural differences.

6. Policy formulation in different countries should take into account organizational goals, cultural differences, business practices, and business ethics.

7. A local staff can provide valuable input during the policy formulation process due to their knowledge of local culture.

8. Top management's attitude and its leadership are critical factors in the cultivation of an ethical corporate culture that is essential for the long-term survival of an organization.

Questions for Discussion

1. The text identifies five major environmental influences on accounting. How does each affect accounting?

2. List the types of environmental factors that are considered important while designing a control system for international operations.

3. "One would expect multinational corporations to prefer to design one uniform control system for domestic and international operations." Do you agree or disagree? Why?

4. In your opinion, are people from diverse cultures more alike or more different? Explain.

5. Contrast cultural dimensions of:
   a. Masculinity versus Femininity.
   b. Individualism versus Collectivism.

6. Describe, in your own words, the cultural dimension of:
   a. Uncertainty avoidance.
   b. Uncertainty acceptance.

7. Use examples to illustrate the cultural dimension of:
   a. Large power distance.
   b. Small power distance.

8. Compare long-term orientation with short-term orientation.
9. Discuss the role of ethics in policy formulation.
10. Can company management help set the "right tone" for corporate culture? Explain.

Case 1

Saving Souls Is His Priority No. 1!

Former U.S. Ambassador James Sasser, who left China in mid-1999 after $3\frac{1}{2}$ years, told Henry Chu of the *Los Angeles Times*: "When I first got here, there was a delightful old French ambassador who was retiring. I was trying to learn the Chinese language. He told me, 'Young man (Sasser is in his 60s), your time would be better spent learning China than learning Chinese.'"

Sasser, who arrived as a novice, has been a proponent of engagement in order to encourage China to act responsibly. Washington Post correspondent Michael Laris said Sasser "understood intrinsically the Chinese concept of Guanxi—the trusting, give-and-take relationships"—that are helpful in a crisis.

After a bad stretch, Sasser shepherded more than 100 members of the U.S. Congress to a dinner in Beijing hosted by a Chinese deputy foreign minister, who spoke and then took questions. A great chance for rapprochement. One congressman said, "I just want to know if you've accepted Jesus Christ as your personal savior." Sasser said the Chinese official, looking stunned, said, "No." Other Americans nearly fell on the floor.[37]

Required:

(1) What did the retiring French Ambassador mean by his statement that it is more important to learn China than Chinese?
(2) What, in your opinion, was the motive behind the statement made by one congressman to the Chinese deputy foreign minister?
(3) Was the statement referred to in (2) appropriate for the occasion?
(4) Is cultural sensitivity important while dealing with people from different cultures?

Case 2

When Is a Bribe Not a Bribe?

In September 1997, the Iranian Central bank governor, while addressing a joint meeting of the World Bank and the International Monetary Fund, called for an international agreement to determine what constitutes bribery.

---

37 "Priorities." *San Francisco Chronicle*, 9 July 1999, p. A12.

He welcomed the efforts by the World Bank and the International Monetary Fund to root out corruption. But he warned that anti-corruption efforts by the two organizations could be abused, becoming "a tool to impinge on national sovereignty." He claimed that interpretations of corruptions could differ. "What in one case may be counted as bribery in another case is treated as the legal payment of commissions to intermediaries."

He called for a general agreement on bribery at the international level to ensure that "legal and constitutional definitions of corruptions adopted by different governments are compatible."[38]

Required:

(1) Do you agree that what may be viewed as bribery in one situation, may be a legitimate payment in a different situation? Give your reasons.

(2) Do you think it would be desirable to have an international agreement on what constitutes bribery?

(3) Do you think it is possible to have an international agreement on bribery? Give your reasons.

Case 3

No Motorcade? Good Heavens!

The Prime Minister of an East Asian country went to Sweden on a state visit. At that time, late Olaf Palme was Prime Minister of Sweden. Among the scheduled events was a customary state banquet for the visiting dignitary.

The visiting Prime Minister gave a return banquet at the national embassy for Palme. He stood at the porch of the embassy for quite a while, waiting for the arrival of the motorcade, to receive Prime Minister Palme.

No motorcade was in sight, but suddenly Palme appeared. He was hurriedly walking to the porch with a topcoat on his shoulder. He apologized for the delay and explained that he had gone to park his car in the parking lot of the embassy.

Required:

Identify which of the five cultural dimensions identified by Hofstede is most applicable in this case. Provide your reasons.

References

AlHashim, Dhia D., and Jeffrey S. Arpan. *International Dimensions of Accounting*, 3d ed. Boston: PWS-Kent Publishing Company, 1992.

38 "Iran Calls For Global Rule on Corruption." *Gulf News*, 25 September 1997, p. 36.

American Accounting Association. *Accounting and Culture*. Sarasota, Fla.: American Accounting Association, 1987.

Chow, Chee W., Michael D. Shields, and Anne Wu. "The Importance of National Culture in the Design of and Preference for Management Controls for Multinational Operations." *Accounting, Organizations and Society*, Vol. 24 No. 5/6 1999, pp. 441–461.

Franke, R., G. Hofstede, and M. Bond. "Cultural Roots of Economic Performance: A Research Note." *Strategic Management Journal*, Vol. 12, 1991, pp. 165–173.

Gersten, Alan. "Eastern Exposure." *Journal of Accountancy*, August 1999, pp. 3–55, 57–58.

Harrison, Graeme L., and Jill L. McKinnon. "Cross-cultural Research in Management Control Systems Design: A Review of the Current State." *Accounting, Organizations and Society*, Vol. 24 No. 5/6, 1999, pp. 483–506.

Hofstede, G. *Culture's Consequences: International Differences in Work-Related Values*. Beverly Hills: Sage Publications, 1980.

_____. *Cultures and Organizations: Software of Mind*. Berkshire, England: McGraw-Hill, 1991.

_____, and M. Bond. "Hofstede's Culture Dimensions: An Independent Validation Using Rokeach's Survey." *Journal of Cross-Cultural Psychology 15*, December 1984, pp. 417–433.

_____. "The Confucius Connection from Cultural Roots to Economic Growth." *Organizational Dynamics*, Spring 1988, pp. 4–21.

Ihlwan, Moon, Pete Engardio, Irene Kunii, and Roger Crockett. "Samsung: The Making of A Superstar." *Business Week*, 20 December 1999, pp. 137–138, 140.

Iqbal, M. Zafar. "Market Expansion Challenges Smaller Practice Units." *The Ohio CPA Journal*, April 1994, pp. 41–42.

_____. "The Global Arena: A Guide for Small and Medium-Sized Firms." *Outlook: The Professional Publication for California CPAs*, Spring 2000, pp. 10–12, 14, 16, 25, 29.

Kraar, Louis. "China's Car Guy." *Fortune*, 11 October 1999, pp. 238–240, 244, 246.

Mandel, Michael J., and Paul Magnusson. "Global Growing Pains." *Business Week*, 13 December 1999, pp. 40–43.

Palmer, Brian. "The View From China." *Fortune*, 8 November 1999, pp. 121, 211, 214, 216.

Tarumizu, Kimimasa. "Global Perspectives." *Journal of Accountancy*, January 1993, p. 66.

Thornton, Emily. "Carload of Troubles." *Business Week*, 27 March 2000, pp. 56–57.

chapter

5

Accounting Measurement and Disclosures

learning objectives

After reading this chapter, you should be able to:

1. Distinguish between accounting measurement and disclosure.

2. Define financial reporting disclosures.

3. Explain the reasons for providing information to stakeholders.

4. Describe the reasons for making disclosures.

5. Describe the difficulties encountered in applying the costs versus benefits criterion to disclosure decisions.

6. Contrast the expense liability reserves, the legal reserves, the general reserves, and the revaluation reserves.

7. Outline and critique the six reporting approaches used by multinational companies.

8. Discuss the social impact of disclosures on employees, value-added statements, and environmental performance.

9. Demonstrate the diversity in practice involving consolidations, goodwill, and leases.

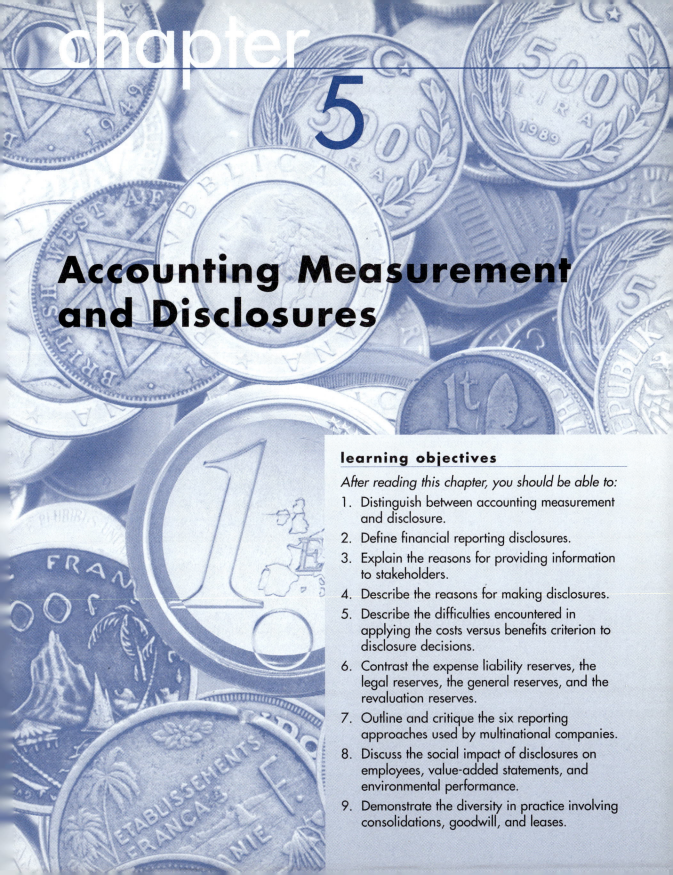

In this chapter, we will discuss a variety of issues relating to financial reporting disclosures and current disclosure practices and trends. Recording economic transactions and events in the accounting system (**measurement**) precedes preparation of the financial statements (**disclosure**). At the time of recording, monetary values are assigned to economic transactions and events. The accounting standards of a country provide the rules for assigning those monetary values. Since accounting standards differ from country to country, consequently recording (measurement) of the same type of economic transactions and events differs. Thus financial reports (disclosures) are directly affected by accounting measurement. *Note: Accounting measurement and disclosure are interconnected.*

The term **financial reporting disclosures** includes the disclosures from the accounting system as well as outside the accounting system. For example, a contingent loss that is probable but cannot be estimated reasonably is disclosed even though it cannot be recorded in the accounting system. Different types of financial reporting disclosures include:

- Disclosures within the financial statements.
- Disclosures supplementary to the financial statements.
- Required disclosures.
- Voluntary disclosures.
- Disclosures in monetary terms.
- Disclosures in nonmonetary terms.
- Quantitative disclosures.
- Nonquantitative (narrative) disclosures.

Both the scope and the extent of financial reporting disclosures have widened considerably in recent years. The trend is expected to continue because of the rapid pace of globalization. Varied international environments in which a multinational company operates contribute to varied disclosures. For example, intense environmental concerns or powerful labor unions have a direct impact on the scope and the extent of disclosures made by a company about its performance in those areas.

The Evolving Disclosure Process

It is widely acknowledged that a corporations accountability extends beyond its investors and creditors, which is due to two reasons. First, a society entrusts a corporation with the management of its scarce resources, which makes the corporation accountable to the society. A corporation needs to provide information to members of the society so that they can assess whether scarce resources are used efficiently and effectively. Second, the corporation's activities affect quality of life and standard of living of the individuals who may be neither its investors nor its creditors. Such individuals need information to be able to form an opinion about corporate performance in their areas of concern. Depending on their perceptions, they may wish to take some appropriate actions to influence activities of the corporation. This wider concept of corporate disclosure responsibility has been recognized and accepted for decades. It is evidenced by the statement, "We maximize shareholder value over the long term by harmonizing the interests of *all* our stakeholders: customers, suppliers, employees, and members of the community at large, as well as shareholders."[1] The users of financial reports include various groups of people collectively known as **stakeholders**.

The area of accounting disclosures is still evolving. At least two issues remain unresolved. First, no commonly accepted framework exists for providing information to the users who are neither investors nor creditors. Such users are hard to identify and their number and demands for disclosures are apparently increasing. The second issue is that the benefits of disclosures, unlike most of their costs, are often difficult or impossible to trace. The diversity of user groups and how each user group benefits from the disclosures pose monumental problems in identifying the relationship between cause (costs) and effect (benefits).

Reasons for Financial Reporting Disclosures

Conceptually, there are two major socio-economic reasons for disclosures:

- To reduce uncertainty to capital providers (investors and creditors) so that they can use the information to weigh the predicted returns of each alternative against the associated risk level.

- To provide relevant information to the individuals and groups who are affected by the operating activities of corporations in their quality of life and standard of living.

Broadly, disclosures are made to provide information so that decision makers can make informed decisions, to satisfy externally imposed requirements, and to meet certain self-interest objectives.

Internationalization of Financial Markets

Global financial markets are a reality. Corporations can now raise capital from sources in different parts of the world. Global financial markets have become such powerful sources of capital that many companies are now listing on security exchanges of other countries.

A country's regulatory agency sets the minimum disclosure requirements for listing on its security markets. Globalization of financial markets has created an acute awareness among the securities regulators in many countries that their regulatory disclosure requirements need to be strengthened.

Statutory and Legal Requirements

In some countries, e.g., Germany and Japan, statutory and legal requirements prescribe the accounting treatment of transactions. In such countries, company

---

1 Toyota. "To Our Fellow Toyota Stakeholders." *Toyota Annual Report 1998*, p. 1.

law and taxation systems are the most important influences on accounting practice and financial reporting.

Significant impact of multinational enterprises on a nation's social, economic, and ecological environments has resulted in the enactment of many new statutes and laws requiring additional disclosures in recent years.

Accounting Profession

In many countries where the accounting profession has advanced to a mature state, e.g. the U.S., and the U.K., financial reporting disclosure requirements are determined by the profession. The accounting profession in such countries is typically quite influential. The standard-setting process includes open deliberations. Diverse interest groups are given opportunities to provide their input before a standard is promulgated. Internationalization has compelled the accounting profession in such countries to address the issues related to those topics that have become significantly more important. Segment reporting, consolidation, foreign currency transactions, and foreign currency translation are just a few examples.

Additional disclosures are also being required to enhance the comparability of financial statements that are prepared using accounting standards of different countries. This topic is discussed in Chapter 6.

Influential Special Interest Groups

Some groups are so influential that a corporation makes special disclosures directed to their information needs. For example, a labor union may successfully negotiate special disclosures on matters such as safe working conditions, number of work-related injuries, and classification of employees by age, sex, etc. The nature and emphasis of special interest disclosures varies across nations.

Voluntary Disclosures

Corporations make voluntary disclosures for a variety of reasons:

- *Educating the users of financial reports.*   This may be on a variety of topics such as operating conditions, future prospects, reasons for certain corporate actions, etc.

- *Image building.*   Disclosure about socially responsible actions generate goodwill for future economic benefits. Examples include disclosures of the expenditures made for environmental protection, safe working conditions, scholarship funds for college students, and training programs for underrepresented segments of the population.

- *Avoidance of potential governmental regulation or control.*   A corporation may make voluntary disclosures if there is a risk that non-disclosures may result in governmental regulations or control. The objective is to forestall any potential governmental action that would have adverse effects. The timing, nature, and extent of such disclosures require managerial judgment.

- *Lower cost of capital.*   Voluntary disclosures are inherently above and beyond what is required by regulators. A corporation competing with other enterprises in global capital markets may find it advantageous to voluntarily provide additional disclosures. Everything else being equal, capital providers would choose Company A over Company B if they perceive Company A to carry lower risk. Disclosures remove or reduce uncertainties about the future, thus reducing the perceived level of risk.

Firms participating in global capital markets generally tend to voluntarily disclose more information than is required by regulators. The competition for investment funds is propelling this practice. *A number of the disclosures made in annual reports are, therefore, driven by market rather than regulatory requirements.* While formulating their disclosure policies companies may find it in their best interest to go beyond the minimum requirements.[2]

Costs Versus Benefits Criterion

As mentioned earlier, identifying the users and their information needs are necessary for deciding on the types of disclosure to be made and the extent of detail provided. We have noted earlier that the identity of user groups is not always clear. Due to the existence of multiple users with varied information needs for a variety of decisions, there is always a question regarding the "right balance" for providing information. Due to multiplicity of the variables in a given situation, it is not surprising that no consensus on what constitutes the right balance exists.

Accounting information is not free; accounting systems cost money. Using the cost versus benefits criterion while choosing an accounting system requires that the expected benefits exceed the expected costs of the system.[3] The difficulty, or impossibility, of establishing cause (costs of disclosures) and effect (benefits to the users of information) relationship in the situations involving non-investors and non-creditors poses a daunting challenge in attempting to use the costs versus benefits criterion.

The costs of financial reporting disclosures, however, are not limited to the monetary amounts for installing and maintaining an accounting system. They also include other costs that are difficult, if not impossible, to quantify. *The common thread among this group of costs is that the information obtained through disclosures may be used for purposes that are against the best interest of the company providing the information.* For example:

- Competitors may obtain competitive advantage.
- Workers' unions may make costly demands.

2 C.A. Frost, and K.P. Ramin. "Corporate Financial Disclosure: A Global Assessment." in F. Choi (ed.), *International Accounting and Finance Handbook*, 2nd ed. New York: John Wiley & Sons, Inc., 1997, p. 18.31.

3 Charles T. Horngren, George Foster, and Srikant M. Datar. *Cost Accounting: A Managerial Emphasis*, 10th ed. Upper Saddle River, N.J.: Prentice Hall, 2000, p. 11.

- Regulatory agencies may increase regulation.
- Plaintiffs may find the information helpful in their legal claims against the corporation.

Competitive Advantage

One of the costs of disclosures listed previously merits discussion. It is often claimed by corporate executives that extensive disclosures erode their ability to compete. Interestingly, there is no evidence to support this assertion. Efficient flow of information is a prerequisite to a free market economy. It is difficult to visualize the existence of an efficient, free market economy in the absence of extensive information flow.

Disclosures stimulate and encourage competition, which leads to streamlining operations. Without streamlining, it would be impossible to survive, let alone grow, in an intense competitive environment. Internationalization of trade and investments has increased competition as well as the need for information. The ultimate beneficiaries are the consumers.

Worldwide Diversity in Measurement and Reporting

Now we will look at some examples of worldwide diversity in measurement and reporting. Our objective is to develop an appreciation of how the same type of economic transaction or event may be recorded differently because of different accounting principles worldwide.

The accounting standards of a country provide guidelines for recording economic transactions and events. Within the framework, they provide an answer to the question: What accounts are to be debited and credited, and for what amounts? We will illustrate the diversity by focusing on certain accounting aspects of inventories. The information for selected countries is shown in Exhibit 5.1.

We will use two examples to illustrate how the measurement of information affects disclosures in financial reports.

Example

Foster Company, based in Australia, uses the first-in, first-out (FIFO) cost flow assumption. The following information is pertinent regarding Foster's inventory.

	(000) Units	Unit Cost	(000) Total Cost
Beginning inventory	100	$10	$ 1,000
Purchases	1,000	12	12,000
Goods available for sale	1,100		$13,000
Ending inventory, 50 units:			
Net realizable value		$550	
Replacement cost		$650	

exhibit 5.1   **Accounting Differences—Inventories**

Country	"Market" in Lower of Cost or Market	LIFO Allowed	LIFO Common In Usage
Australia	Net realizable value	No	N/A*
Austria	Replacement cost or net realizable value	Yes	No
Brazil	Replacement cost or net realizable value, whichever is lower.	Yes	No
Canada	Replacement cost or net realizable value	Yes	No
Czech Republic	N/A	No	N/A
Denmark	Net realizable value	No	N/A
Finland	Replacement cost or net realizable value	Yes	No
France	Net realizable value	No	N/A
Germany	Replacement cost or net realizable value minus normal profit	Yes	No
India	Net realizable value	Yes	No
Japan	Replacement cost	Yes	Yes
Mexico	Realizable value	Yes	Yes
Netherlands	Net realizable value	Yes	Yes
New Zealand	Net realizable value	No	N/A
Spain	Net realizable value	Yes	No
Sweden	Net realizable value	No	N/A
Switzerland	Net realizable value	Yes	No
United Kingdom	Net realizable value	Yes	No
United States	Middle amount from replacement cost, net realizable value, and net realizable value minus normal profit	Yes	Yes

*N/A: Not applicable

Using the Australian accounting principles, as shown in Exhibit 5.1, "market" is generally considered to be net realizable value while applying the lower of cost or market.

The cost basis of ending inventory for financial reporting is determined as follows:

Historical cost using FIFO (50 × $12)	$600
Net realizable value (given)	$550

The ending inventory in the balance sheet will be shown in the amount of $550, the lower of historical cost using FIFO ($600) and net realizable value ($550). The income statement will reflect an additional $50 expense resulting from writing down inventory from $600 to $550.

Example

Using the same information as in the previous example, except assuming that the accounting standards define "market" as replacement cost, the value of ending inventory would be:

Historical cost basis using FIFO (50 × $12)	$600
Replacement cost (given)	$650

The ending inventory in the balance sheet will be shown at $600, which is the lower of the two amounts. In this case, application of the lower of cost or market principle will have no impact on the income statement.

Exhibit 5.2 shows the differences in the capitalization of research and development costs among selected countries.

exhibit 5.2   Accounting Differences—Capitalization of Research and Development Costs

Country	Research Costs	Development Costs
Australia	No	No
Austria	No	No
Brazil	Yes	Yes
Canada	No	Yes
Czech Republic	Yes	Yes
Denmark	No	Yes
Finland	No	Yes
France	No	Yes
Germany	No	No
India	No	No
Italy	No	Yes
Japan	No	No
Mexico	No	No
Netherlands	Yes	Yes
New Zealand	No	Yes
Spain	Allowed	Allowed
South Korea	Yes	Yes
Sweden	No	Yes
Switzerland	No	Yes
United Kingdom	No	Yes
United States	No	No

Notes: "Allowed" indicates under specified set of circumstances.

Role of Reserves

Reserves are commonly used in many countries for a variety of reasons. In many countries, e.g., Japan, France, and Italy, financial reports are creditor-oriented. Banks are the primary users of financial reports since they are the major source of funds for enterprises—rather than the stockholders. Naturally, accounting standards in those countries were established to ensure that creditors' interests would be protected. This has resulted in a conservative accounting practice called the **prudence concept.** Laws in many countries permit undervaluation of assets and overstatement of expenses and liabilities. For example, in Germany, if a loss is *reasonably possible*, it must be recorded. This contrasts with the U.S. practice of recognizing a contingent loss only if it is *probable* (likely to occur) and reasonably estimable.

We now discuss the role of reserves in accomplishing various objectives. All of the reserves in the following discussion are **equity reserves.** They appear in the stockholders' equity section of the balance sheet.

Expense Liability Reserve

One of the many purposes for using reserves is to achieve income smoothing, i.e., to show a steady growth in income from one year to the next. Reserves used for this purpose are generally called **expense liability reserves.** In a highly profitable year, the company transfers a portion of its actual income into an expense liability reserve, thus understanding reported income for that year. The firm moves an amount from the reserve to the reported income in a later year when actual income is low, thereby overstating reported income for the year. This phenomenon has been called **income smoothing, income leveling,** and **managed earnings.** The use of reserves to transfer income between periods is done by a majority of firms in Austria, Spain, South Korea, Australia, and Switzerland.[4]

Clearly, in countries where income smoothing is practiced to a significant degree, the income statements of the firm are less meaningful for financial analysis, particularly when the movement of funds into and out of reserves is not disclosed. In fact, in a number of countries the actual existence of reserves is not even disclosed. These undisclosed reserves are called "hidden" or "silent" reserves.[5] In 1993, when Daimler-Benz applied for listing on the New York Stock Exchange, it disclosed 4 billion Deutsche marks ($2.45 billion) in hidden reserves.[6]

Example

In 2001 the actual income of Hommen N.V. was 56 million Dutch guilders, showing an above average increase from the previous year. The reported income for 2000 was 50 million guilders. Hommen N.V. prefers to show an 8 percent annual growth in reported income.

---

4 Dhia D. AlHashim, and J.S. Arpan. *International Dimensions of Accounting*, 3d ed. Boston: PWS-Kent Company, 1992, pp. 86–87.

5 *Ibid.*, p. 87.

6 *Annual Report 1993* (Stuttgart, Germany: Daimler-Benz, 1994), p. 73.

The actual income is 6 million guilders greater than the previous year's income. If the company is to report an annual 8 percent increase in income, the reported income should be 50 million × 108% = 54 million guilders. The amount to be credited to the expense liability reserve is 2 million guilders (56 million guilders actual income less 54 million guilders income for reporting). The following shows the entry to accomplish this.

Current Period Expenses	2,000,000	
Reserve for Future Liability		2,000,000

In a year when the reverse is true, the entry for transferring the amount out of the reserve would involve debiting the reserve account and crediting an expense account, as shown in the next example.

Example
In 2002 the actual income of Hommen N.V. was 57.32 million guilders. Since the reported income in 2001 was 54 million guilders, the company would like to report 58.32 million guilders (108% × 54 million) income in 2002. This requires transferring 1 million guilders from the reserve to reported income.

Reserve for Future Liability	1,000,000	
Current Period Expenses		1,000,000

The expense liability reserve is only one of the many types of reserves. Next we discuss some other commonly used reserves.

Legal (Statutory) Reserve
Several countries legally require that companies maintain legal (statutory) reserves. The purpose is to provide additional protection to creditors. The amounts transferred to the legal reserve are not available for dividends. Usually, the legal requirements specify that a certain percentage of income (sometimes dividends) be credited to a legal reserve. For example, in Oman 10 percent of the annual net profit is transferred to the legal reserve until the reserve balance equals one third of share capital. In France the requirement calls for an annual transfer of 5 percent of the net income to the legal reserve until the reserve equals 10 percent of legal capital.

Example
Strenger AG's income for the current year is 100 million Deutsche marks. The legal requirement is to transfer 5 percent of the annual income into a legal reserve. The following entry shows the transfer.

Income Summary	100,000,000	
Legal Reserve		5,000,000
Retained Earnings		95,000,000

General Reserve

Another commonly used reserve is called a general reserve. This reserve normally serves the same purpose as an appropriation of retained earning, i.e., it restricts the maximum amount that can be declared for dividends.

Example

The directors of Miller Manufacturing Ltd. vote to transfer $5 million from retained earnings to a general reserve. The purpose is to make the amount unavailable for dividends. The entry to record this transaction follows.

Retained Earnings	5,000,000	
General Reserve		5,000,000

In some countries a general reserve is also used for income soothing. Accounting procedures to accomplish this are similar to those discussed earlier for the expense liability reserve.

Revaluation Reserve

In some countries, notably Denmark, Portugal, Sweden, the Netherlands, and the U.K., valuing fixed assets at a higher current value is acceptable. This is accomplished by recording an upward adjustment of the asset and correspondingly crediting the revaluation reserve for an equal amount. In subsequent periods, the asset is depreciated at the adjusted value, thus resulting in a higher depreciation expense. The incremental depreciation may be charged either directly to the revaluation reserve or to income, depending on accounting standards and tax laws of the country.

Example

Andersens A/S, a Denmark-based company, marks up depreciable assets by Dkr100,000. The company uses the straight-line method of depreciation assuming no salvage value and a 10-year remaining useful life. Incremental depreciation resulting from the write-up is charged directly to the revaluation reserve. The following entry records the revaluation.

Equipment—Value Adjustment	100,000	
Revaluation Reserve		100,000

Annual depreciation on the revaluation part only is recorded as follows.

Revaluation Reserve	10,000	
Accumulated Depreciation—Value Adjustment		10,000

Example

This example is based on the same facts as the preceding Andersens A/S example, except we assume that the incremental depreciation is charged against income.

The entry to record revaluation will be identical to the first entry in the preceding example. The entry for recording depreciation on the revaluation part only will be as follows.

Depreciation Expense—Value Adjustment	10,000	
Accumulated Depreciation—Value Adjustment		10,000

Note: In the previous example, the amount of depreciation expense charged against the revenue of the period was based on the historical cost of the asset, and was not affected by upward revaluation. In the current example, the amount of depreciation expense charged against income is based on the marked-up value of the asset. Therefore, the income statement reflects incremental depreciation expense from revaluation.

An additional entry is required under this method to adjust the revaluation reserve as follows.

Revaluation Reserve	10,000	
Retained Earnings		10,000

Note 1: The previous entry makes the ending balances in the revaluation reserve account and retained earnings account the same as in the previous example. From a financial reporting perspective, the only difference between the two alternatives is in the reported income. It is reduced by the amount of incremental depreciation expense on the upward adjustment in the previous example, while it is unaffected in the current example.

Note 2: The effect of upward adjustment on the asset and the ending balances of the revaluation reserve account and retained earnings accounts will be identical under both alternatives after the previous entries are posted.

Perceptions Based on the Method of Disclosure

Research suggests that different disclosure methods result in different user perceptions. A study compared the effects of two methods of disclosing an obligation: **balance sheet recognition** versus **footnote disclosure**. Commercial lenders were surveyed to determine whether the disclosure method affected their perceptions of the item. It was discovered that the commercial lenders were more likely to perceive the obligation as a form of debt when it was recognized as a balance sheet liability than when disclosed in the footnotes accompanying the financial statements. The researchers concluded that the method of disclosing is an important issue that must be considered in formulation of accounting standards.[7]

It is erroneous to conclude that uniform accounting standards lead to uniform disclosures. Accounting standards normally provide a range of acceptabil-

---

7 R.M. Harper Jr., W.G. Mister, and J.R. Strawser. "The Effect of Recognition versus Disclosure of Unfunded Postretirement Benefits on Lenders' Perceptions of Debt." *Accounting Horizons,* September 1991, pp. 50–56.

ity, as opposed to prescribing one "right" disclosure method. Empirical evidence suggests that while using accounting standards of the same country, there can be a variety of ways companies make disclosures. A study comparing goodwill disclosures by 621 publicly traded firms in the U.S. demonstrated that the firms varied substantially in their goodwill-related asset and expense disclosures. The authors of the study concluded that due to this reason investors cannot easily identify the financial statement effects of existing goodwill accounting rules for a substantial number of firms with material goodwill.[8]

Reporting Approaches of Multinational Companies

A multinational company (MNC) has to decide on its disclosure mode for reporting in different countries. Since no required international reporting standards exist that provide the guidance, MNCs have tried a variety of approaches to communicate information to the target audiences abroad. We will discuss six of these approaches.

1. **Compliance with base country's requirements.** Most countries in the world (the U.S. being a notable exception) accept financial reports prepared according to accounting principles of a reporting entity's base country. This is the most convenient and the least costly way for MNCs to fulfill their legal reporting requirements. No special effort is made to assist the users in other countries in understanding and interpreting the financial reports.

2. **Translation into the local language.** A slight improvement over the first approach is to translate the text part of financial reports into the local language. It is common for many MNCs to publish their reports in several languages in addition to the languages of their base countries. Bayer publishes its complete annual report in English and German and a shorter version in English, German, French, Italian, Japanese, and Spanish.

3. **Translations into the local language and currency.** Besides translating the text portion of the financial reports into the local language, many companies also translate the monetary amounts into the local currency. Commonly the exchange rate on the balance sheet date is used to translate all of the monetary amounts. For example, Toyota uses this approach for its U.S. audience using the Tokyo Foreign Exchange market's exchange rate for yen to the U.S. dollar on the balance sheet date.

4. **Provision of information on the base country's accounting standards used.** A few multinational companies provide information on the accounting principles of their base country used in preparation of the financial reports. This approach recognizes the reality of different accounting standards in the world and attempts to help the users by providing an explanation of the accounting standards on which financial reports are based.

---

8 L. Duvall, R. Jennings, J. Robinson, and R. Thompson II. "Can Investors Unravel the Effects of Goodwill Accounting?" *Accounting Horizons*, June 1992, pp. 1–14.

Philips N.V., based in the Netherlands, lists all the relevant differences between U.S. GAAP and Dutch GAAP in the annual report targeted to the U.S. audience. It provides an item-by-item narrative explanation of the differences between the two sets of GAAP as well as the resulting monetary differences in its annual report. Exhibit 5.3 contains the narrative information from the Philips 1998 annual report.

5. **Selective restatements.** A few companies provide partial restatements of their financial statements using the GAAP of the target audience country. For example, a Sweden-based multinational may restate its income amount according to Australian accounting principles. The Australian users can correctly assume that the restated income amount is comparable to income amounts of other companies using Australian accounting standards.

   Selective restatements partially solve the problems created by worldwide diversity in accounting standards.

   Philips and BP Amoco restate their net income from their base country GAAP to U.S. GAAP as shown in Exhibits 5.4 and 5.5, respectively (pages 156 and 157).

6. **Secondary statements.** Secondary statements are a complete set of financial statements (including accompanying notes) prepared according to accounting standards of another country. In addition, the independent auditors express an opinion on the secondary statements using auditing standards of the other country. These statements, prepared specifically for users in another country, attempt to enhance their understanding and usefulness to the target audience. Honda, Sony, and DaimlerChrysler issue secondary statements for U.S. users.

Analysis of the Six Approaches

As we move from the first approach to the last one, it becomes clear that each succeeding approach indicates a higher level of effort on the part of an MNC to reach out to its financial statement users in another country.

exhibit 5.3   **Philips: Differences Between Dutch GAAP and U.S. GAAP in Narrative Form**

The accounting policies followed in the preparation of the consolidated financial statements differ in some respects from those generally accepted in the United States of America.

To determine net income and stockholders' equity in accordance with generally accepted accounting principles in the United States of America (U.S. GAAP), Philips has applied the following accounting principles:

- Under Dutch GAAP, goodwill arising from acquisitions prior to 1992 was charged directly to stockholders' equity. According to U.S. GAAP, goodwill arising from acquisitions, including those prior to 1992, is capitalized and amortized over its useful life up to a maximum period of 40 years. As a result of the sale of PolyGram, goodwill has been fully amortized and charged to the gain on disposal in 1998 income under U.S. GAAP.

exhibit 5.3   *(continued)*

- Philips reported a charge to income from operations of NLG 726 million for restructurings in its 1998 financial statements. A portion of this restructuring, NLG 89 million (NLG 51 million net of taxes), was not communicated to employees until early 1999 and, accordingly, will be recorded under U.S. GAAP as a charge in 1999.

An identical restructuring charge for Grundig was recorded in 1995 under Dutch GAAP for an amount of NLG 262 million, which under U.S. GAAP was reflected in the 1996 accounts.

Until 1997 the Company had an obligation under certain put options given to other shareholders in Grundig. For the purposes of U.S. GAAP this liability was recorded in 1995, whereas under Dutch GAAP it was accrued in 1996. Philips settled this obligation.

- In 1998, Philips reported a charge to net income of NLG 74 million (1997: NLG 139 million) relating to a higher accumulated benefit obligation compared to the market value of the plan assets or the existing level of the pension provision in two of the Company's pension plans. For U.S. GAAP purposes, this amount is capitalized as an intangible asset for this additional minimum liability, or directly charged to comprehensive income.

- In July 1995, Philips contributed its net assets of cable networks, with a book value of approximately NLG 200 million, to UPC, a newly established joint venture in which Philips had acquired a 50% interest. Under Dutch GAAP, this transfer resulted in a gain of NLG 127 million relating to the partial disposal of its interest in these assets to the other joint venture party (UIH). For U.S. GAAP purposes, this gain was not considered realized because the consideration received by Philips principally consisted of equity and notes issued by UPC and equity in UIH, instead of cash. In 1997, Philips sold its 50% interest in this joint venture, the gain of NLG 127 million on this transaction was recognized under U.S. GAAP in 1997.

- Under Dutch GAAP's historical cost convention, Philips generally considers the functional currency of entities in a highly inflationary economy to be the U.S. dollar. Under U.S. GAAP, the functional currency would be the reporting currency. The difference between the use of the U.S. dollar as the functional currency instead of the reporting currency is not material.

- Under Dutch GAAP, securities available for sale are valued at the lower of cost or net realizable value. Under U.S. GAAP they are valued at market price, unless such shares are restricted by contract for a period of one year or more. Under U.S. GAAP, unrealized holding gains or losses will be credited or charged to stockholders' equity.

- Under U.S. GAAP, it is not appropriate to record a liability for dividends/distribution to shareholders subject to approval of the annual General meeting of Shareholders.

- Under Dutch GAAP, majority-owned entities are consolidated. Under U.S. GAAP, consolidation of majority-owned entities is not permitted if minority interest holders have the right to participate in operating decisions of the entity. Although Philips owned 60% of Philips Consumer Communications under U.S. GAAP, the venture with Lucent Technologies could not be consolidated but should have been accounted for under the equity method. For the effect of the consolidation, reference is made to note I.

- Under Dutch GAAP, catalogues of recorded music, music publishing rights, film rights, and theatrical rights belonging to PolyGram, which company was sold in 1998, were written down if and to the extent that the present value of the expected income generated by the acquired catalogues falls below their book value. Under U.S. GAAP they were initially amortized over a maximum period of 30 years. As a result of the sale of PolyGram, the cumulative amortization has been credited to the gain on disposal in 1998 income under U.S. GAAP.

- According to U.S. GAAP, divestments which cannot be regarded as discontinued segments of business must be included in income from continuing operations. Under Dutch GAAP, certain material transactions such as disposals of lines of activities, including closures of substantial production facilities, have been accounted for as extraordinary items, which under U.S. GAAP would be recorded in income from operations.

- Under Dutch GAAP, funding of NavTech activities is accounted for as results relating to unconsolidated companies (1998: NLG 134 million, 1997: NLG 210 million, 1996: NLG 66 million), whereas under U.S. GAAP these amounts have to be included in income from operations as research and development costs.

Source: Philips, *Annual Report 1998*, pp. 115–116.

exhibit 5.4   **Philips: Restatement of Net Income From Dutch GAAP to U.S. GAAP**

	(In Millions of Dutch guilders)	
	1998	**1997**
Income from continuing operations as per the consolidated statement of income	**1,192**	2,712
Reclassification of extraordinary items under Dutch GAAP	**1,044**	2,538
Adjustments to U.S. GAAP:		
— amortization of goodwill from acquisitions prior to 1992	—	(21)
— reversal of provisions for restructuring (net)	**51**	—
— additional minimum liabilities under SFAS No. 87 (net)	**74**	139
— reversal of gain on UPC transaction	—	127
— pension cost relating to the acquisition of PENAC	—	(16)
— other items	**(15)**	(15)
Income from continuing operations in accordance with U.S. GAAP	**2,346**	5,464
Income from discontinued operations	**462**	513
Gain on disposal of discontinued operations	**10,316**	—
Extraordinary items	**(34)**	(96)
Net income in accordance with U.S. GAAP	**13,090**	5,881

Source: Philips, *Annual Report 1998*, p. 117. (adapted)

The first approach, compliance with base country requirements, does not create any extra disclosure burden for the MNC. No special efforts are made to help users abroad.

Translating either the text part of financial reports into the local language or both the text and the monetary amounts may provide limited assistance to some users. It is questionable, however, if these approaches are noteworthy in terms of the user's ability to understand and interpret the reports. Granted that, for example, a British user who cannot read the Dutch language would not be able to read the financial reports of a Netherlands-based multinational in the Dutch language and currency. But is the usefulness of the financial reports improved when the text is translated into the English language? Is the usefulness further enhanced if the currency amounts are translated from guilders into British pounds using the year-end exchange rate? These types of translations fail to reflect the differences in accounting standards, terminology, currency exchange rate fluctuations, and business customs. Particularly troublesome is the **convenience translation** currency amounts using the year-end exchange rate. The amounts from convenience translation could be misleading.

The next approach entails providing information on the accounting standards used for preparation of the financial statements. This information may be useful if *both* of the following criteria are satisfied:

exhibit 5.5   **BP Amoco: Restatement of Net Income from U.K. GAAP to U.S. GAAP**

The following is a summary of adjustments to profit for the year and to BP Amoco shareholders' interest, which would be required if generally accepted accounting principles in the U.S. (U.S. GAAP) had been applied instead of those generally accepted in the United Kingdom (U.K. GAAP).

	$ million	
	1999	**1998**
Profit for the year	**5,008**	3,220
Adjustments:		
Depreciation charge[a]	**(81)**	(76)
Decommissioning and environmental expense	**(165)**	(131)
Onerous property leases	**133**	—
Interest expense	**110**	124
Sale and leaseback of fixed assets	**(37)**	(211)
Deferred taxation[a]	**(378)**	(72)
Other	**6**	(28)
Profit for the year as adjusted	**4,596**	2,826

a Under U.K. GAAP, provision for deferred taxation is made where timing differences are expected to reverse in the foreseeable future. Under U.S. GAAP, deferred taxation is provided on a full liability basis on all temporary differences as defined in U.S. Statement of Financial Accounting Standard No. 109. As required by this standard, assets and liabilities of acquired businesses have been adjusted from a net-of-tax to a pre-tax basis.
Source: BP Amoco, *Annual Report and Accounts*, 1999, p. 73. (adapted)

- The company thoroughly describes and clearly explains its accounting policies and the accounting standards and methods used.
- The users have the technical knowledge to reconcile differences in amounts resulting from two sets of accounting principles.

Based on the previous criteria, it is safe to say that this approach has limited usefulness if it is left to the users to develop the requisite expertise to reconcile the differences in amounts. The usefulness of this approach is enhanced in cases when the company provides the reconciling amounts, as shown in Exhibits 5.4 and 5.5.

Selective restatements are an improvement over any of the approaches analyzed so far. Selected amounts, restated using accounting principles of the country of the target audience, are comparable to corresponding items in other companies. The main limitation of this approach is that it can give misleading results if financial ratios are computed by erroneously using a combination of restated and non-restated amounts.

Example

A Netherlands-based multinational restates its sales ($1,000,000) and income ($120,000) for U.S. users. However, no balance sheet items are restated. The non-restated total of assets on the balance sheet is $15,000,000. If a U.S. user is interested in computing the profit margin, it is possible since both income and sales amounts are restated.

$$\text{Profit margin} = \$120,000 \div \$1,000,000 = 12\%$$

However, if the user is interested in computing return on investment (income ÷ total assets), it would not be possible because total assets are not restated. *Restated and non-restated amounts should not be combined to perform ratio analysis.*

The secondary statements approach uses the accounting principles of another country for the preparation of financial statements with the objective that it will enhance the understandability and usefulness for the target audience. This approach, though clearly preferable to any of the first five approaches, has two drawbacks. The obvious one is the cost. The costs include the cost of preparing the financial statements using generally accepted accounting principles of another country plus the cost of an independent audit performed according to generally accepted auditing standards of the same country. Secondly, *the approach cannot compensate for the cultural differences in the operating environments of a different country.* The interpretation of secondary financial reports may be difficult because business customs differ from country to country. As stated in Chapter 4, *national business customs, based on culture, leave an imprint on the primary financial statements that cannot be duplicated in secondary statements.*[9] The problem can be alleviated by providing, along with secondary statements, a discussion of important and unique cultural traits affecting business customs of the country. This reinforces the point that it is essential to be knowledgeable about other cultures to do our jobs effectively in a global economy.

Disclosure Issues for Multinationals

In the absence of required worldwide disclosure standards, the type and quality of disclosures made by companies vary from country to country and from company to company. To appreciate the complexity of the problem faced by an MNC in deciding the nature and extent of disclosure, let us note these issues:

- There are multiple users with varied information needs.
- Users in different countries have varying levels of education. It directly affects their ability to comprehend and interpret sophisticated financial information. Conscious efforts need to be made so that the information is interpreted correctly by the users.

---

9 Howard D. Lowe. "Shortcomings of Japanese Consolidated Financial Statements." *Accounting Horizons*, September 1990, pp. 8–9.

- The sheer size of a typical MNC generates information of mind-boggling volume. A decision must be made regarding what and how much should be disclosed from the great mass of data.

- Information originates from different parts of the world with different cultures that result in different operating environments. Some types of disclosures may embarrass or even anger the local government or general population, leading to adverse effects on the MNC. Balancing of local sensitivities against the need for adequate disclosures is necessary.

- A balance must be struck between legitimate information needs of users for decision-making against the possibility that disclosures may be misused by others to harm the company.

- Cost effectiveness of disclosure when many user groups cannot be identified and benefits to the user groups cannot be traced requires exercise of a high degree of professional judgment.

It should be clear from the previous issues that deciding on what to disclose, how much to disclose, and how to disclose it are complex questions. Responses require weighing and balancing many opposing factors. In the end, the manager can only hope that the final mix will serve the appropriate needs of users in a cost-effective manner.

Selected Social Impact Disclosure Practices

Social impact disclosures are of many different types. They may be *required* disclosures, to hold the management accountable for effective and efficient use of scarce economic resources. On the other hand, many companies make *voluntary* disclosures for the reasons already discussed. The orientation of social impact disclosures is heavily influenced by specific societal concerns in a country. We will focus on disclosures in three categories: employees, value-added statements, and environmental protection.

Employees

Human resource disclosure requirements have received the greatest attention in the social impact reporting area. Annual reports of companies from most countries routinely contain information on employees. The level of specificity and detail, however, varies considerably. As mentioned earlier, this is explained by the societal conditions and environmental pressures in a country. For example, in the U.S., the disclosures may include equal employment opportunities for underrepresented groups, while in Germany the disclosures may emphasize working conditions and employee training. Even though this area has received more attention than any other area of social impact reporting, the disclosure requirements are still quite limited.

At the international level, perhaps the United Nations (U.N.) has been in the forefront in recommending extensive disclosures in this area. The U.N. recommends disclosures of the number of employees for the company and by segments (geographic and line of business). It also recommends that corporate policies regarding the recognition of labor unions and labor relations be disclosed.[10] The European Union's Fourth Directive and Seventh Directive require information on the average number of employees, a breakdown of the number of employees by category, and a breakdown of employee costs. Interestingly, the Directives do not define what constitutes a "category."

At the national level, perhaps the most extensive disclosures are required in France. **Bilan Social** (social report) contains mainly employee-related information covering topics such as pay structure, hiring policies, health and safety conditions, training, and industrial relations. The most common disclosure to be found in practice at the national level is the number of employees. Reporting in this area is still at an early stage of development as evidenced by the existing diversity in practice.

Value-Added Statements

The purpose of a company's value-added statement is to show, in financial terms, the contributions made by all participating groups in the creation of wealth. Value-added statements show the value added to acquired materials and services by a company, and the beneficiaries to whom the created value was distributed.

$$\text{Value added} = \text{Total revenue} - \text{Cost of goods, materials, and services purchased externally}$$

Value-added statements of Bayer and ICI are shown in Exhibits 5.6 and 5.7, respectively.

Value-added statements are prepared primarily in Western European countries, especially Germany, the U.K., France (where they are required as part of *Bilan Social*), the Netherlands, and Sweden. They are also found in South Africa, Australia, and New Zealand.

At the international level, there are no formal requirements regarding value-added statements. In the absence of any requirements at the international or national level (except in France), there is a lack of uniformity in value-added disclosures.

Environmental Performance

Environmental concerns have been receiving considerable attention for many reasons, including heightened public awareness, tougher governmental laws and regulations, and well-publicized major environmental disasters in the recent past.

---

10 United Nations Center on Transnational Corporations. *Conclusions on Accounting and Reporting by Transnational Corporations.* New York: United Nations, 1988.

exhibit 5.6   **Value-Added Statement—Bayer**

Value added

In 1998, the value added of the Bayer Group was DM22.9 billion, an increase of 3 percent compared with the previous year.

Our employees again received the largest share of this, namely 69 percent or DM15.9 billion. Governments received DM2.5 billion or 11 percent. As in the previous year, interest expense accounted for 6 percent of the value added. Stockholders will receive DM1.5 billion. The remaining DM1.7 billion will be retained to strengthen the company's growth potential.

Value-Added Statement

Source			Distribution		
(DM million)	1998	Change in %	(DM million)	1998	Share in %
Net sales	**54,884**	−0.2	Stockholders and		
Other income	**2,159**	+19.7	minority interests	**1,463**	6.4
Total operating performance	**57,043**	**+0.4**	Employees	**15,854**	69.4
Cost of materials	**(18,653)**	−0.8	Governments	**2,527**	11.0
Depreciation	**(2,974)**	+2.8	Lenders	**1,330**	5.8
Other expenses	**(12,546)**	−2.9	Earnings retention	**1,696**	7.4
Value added	**22,870**	**+3.1**	**Value added distributed**	**22,870**	**100.0**

Source: Bayer, *Annual Report 1998*, p. 16. (adapted)

For example, Union Carbide's chemical leak in Bhopal (India) in 1984 caused approximately 4,000 deaths and 200,000 injuries. The investors are especially interested in this disclosure area because the costs for environmental cleanup, legal claims paid for damages, and fines imposed on a company for non-compliance with environmental laws and regulations have an adverse effect on current and future corporate earnings.

In spite of the acknowledged importance of this disclosure area, only a few requirements exist worldwide. When disclosures are made, they generally tend to be narrative in form. At the international level, the U.N. recommends disclosure of the measures undertaken by a company to promote a cleaner environment and to reduce risks of harm to the environment. Interestingly, the U.N. guidelines also recommend environmental audits and risk assessments by companies.[11]

At the regional level, the European Union has a policy for environmental protection. The policy includes setting up requirements in the future on corporate disclosures on environmental impacts. The North American Free Trade Agreement among the U.S., Canada, and Mexico includes side agreements for environmental protection.

---

11 United Nations Commission on Transnational Corporations. *Information Disclosure Relating to Environmental Measures.* New York: United Nations, 1990, p. 6.

exhibit 5.7   **Value-Added Statement—ICI**

Sources and disposal of value added (unaudited) for the year ended 31 December 1998	1998 (£m)
Sources of income	
Turnover	9,286
Royalties and other trading income	91
Less materials and services	(6,663)
Value added by manufacturing and trading activities	2,714
Share of profits less losses of associated undertakings	3
Value added related to exceptional items taken below trading profit	159
Total value added	2,876
Disposal of total value added:	
Employees	
Employee costs charged in arriving at profit before tax	1,867
Governments	
Corporate taxes	112
Less grants	(2)
	110
Providers of capital	
Interest cost of net borrowings	332
Dividends to shareholders	232
Minority shareholders in subsidiary undertakings	(12)
	552
Re-investment in the business	
Depreciation and amortisation of goodwill	386
Profit/(loss) retained	(39)
	347
Total disposal	2,876

This table is based on the audited accounts; it shows the total value added to the cost of materials and services purchased from outside the Group and indicates the ways in which this increase in value has been disposed.

Source: ICI, *Annual Report and Accounts and Form 20-F*, 1998, p. 100.

The countries requiring environmental disclosures include Norway, the U.S., and France. Norway requires that the board of directors report to include information on emission levels and the measures taken or planned to clean up the environment. The Securities and Exchange Commission (SEC) of the U.S. requires disclosure of contingent environmental liabilities. The SEC staff has been looking closely over the past several years at the adequacy of environmental disclosures. The SEC regularly receives information from the U.S. Environmental Protection Agency on companies that have past, present, or potential problems in compliance with environmental laws.[12] France's revised penal code, effective March 1, 1994, makes corporations accountable for endangering others. The code includes provisions dealing with "environmental terrorism," including willful pollution.

President Vicente Fox of Mexico has repeatedly expressed his commitment to include ecological considerations at every stage of his government. He has adopted the following environmental stance:

- A sharp reduction in commercial logging.
- Inclusion of pollution as an offsetting cost (negative factor) when calculating economic growth.
- Special tax breaks to industry for installing environmental controls.
- A substantial funding increase and added policing authority for the governmental agency that enforces pollution laws and investigates their violations.

Soon after his election, Fox stated, "We will make Mexico's environment, its water and forests, a national-security issue." He added, "We will turn around the concept of development to include the environment as a factor in economic and social decisions—not as a separate sector, but as an essential element in creating sustainable economic and social progress."[13]

In order to strengthen compliance with environmental laws and to instill sensitivity to the protection of the environment among corporate personnel, top management can take the following steps:

- The mission statement includes a firm commitment to environmentally responsible operations and activities.
- A detailed policy document developed for employees on how to prevent, detect, and correct environmental problems.
- Environmental audits performed periodically to ensure compliance with corporate policies.
- Performance in the environmental area included among the criteria used to evaluate managers. This can be a powerful incentive to managers.
- Corporate support to the organizations engaged in environmental cleanup, renewal of natural resources, and development of cleaner technologies.

A growing number of corporations such as General Motors and Imperial Chemical Industries are making extensive voluntary environmental disclosures. The disclosures in this area are becoming increasingly detailed.

---

12 "Environmental Disclosure: Recent Developments." *Deloitte & Touche Review*, 13 July 1992, pp. 1–2.

13 Robert Collier. "Helping Fox Paint a Greener Mexico." *San Francisco Chronicle*, 6 July 2000, pp. A1 and A15.

Specific Technical Issues

The theory and practice of international accounting contains a number of important technical issues. Chapters 2 and 3 dealt with the topics of foreign currency and accounting for price changes, respectively. Since it is not feasible to cover every technical issue affecting international accounting, we will limit our discussion to three major reporting issues:

- Business Combinations and Consolidations.
- Goodwill.
- Leases.

Each of these topics will be discussed in a separate section.

Business Combinations and Consolidations

The fundamental reason for business combinations is to control. This is accomplished either by acquiring net assets or acquiring over 50 percent of the voting stock of another entity. A **statutory merger** is a business combination in which net assets of a company are acquired by another company. A combination where control is achieved by acquisition of more than 50 percent of another company's voting stock is considered a **parent/subsidiary relationship**. The company acquiring the stock is called the **parent**; the company whose stock is acquired is the **subsidiary**. In this type of business combination both the parent and the subsidiary continue to exist as separate legal entities and maintain their respective financial records and financial reporting system. For external reporting, consolidated financial statements are issued.

The two methods used for consolidating financial statements of a parent and its subsidiaries are the **purchase method** and the **pooling of interests method**. The main characteristics of purchase and pooling are as follows:

- *Purchase method.* The acquired entity's assets and equities are consolidated at their fair market values. Goodwill is created to the extent that the acquisition cost exceeds the fair market value of the identifiable assets of the subsidiary.
- *Pooling of interests method.* The acquired entity's assets and equities are consolidated at their book value. No goodwill is created in a pooling of interests.

In either case, the parent company's own assets and equities are included in the consolidated financial statements at their book value.

International Perspectives

The pooling of interests method is relatively rare. Australia prohibits its use. France lists its assets and liabilities at agreed-upon prices according to the purchase agreement. Brazil and Canada use the pooling of interests method only when the acquiring company cannot be identified. In Japan, the purchase method is the norm for preparing consolidated financial statements. Germany and the U.K. consider pooling acceptable only if certain criteria are met. In the Netherlands, the purchase method is commonly used though the pooling of interests method is allowed in certain types of business combinations.

In the U.S., currently both the pooling of interests and the purchase methods are generally accepted accounting principles. However, the U.S.'s Financial Accounting Standards Board has a proposed standard that will eliminate the pooling of interests method.

Purchase Method

In the purchase method, the acquiring company records the transaction at its cost. Cost must be allocated to the identifiable assets. Any excess of cost over the sum of the identifiable assets (including intangibles) less liabilities is recorded as goodwill. To illustrate, suppose that on January 1, 2002, Paz Company, a Mexican company, acquired the assets and assumed the liabilities of Solis Company in a merger by giving one of its 15 peso par value common shares to the former stockholders of Solis Company for every five shares of the 5 peso par value common shares they held. Assume further that this combination is to be accounted for as a purchase. Paz Company stock has a fair value of 45 pesos. Balance sheets for Paz Company and Solis Company (along with pertinent fair values) on January 1, 2002 are as shown in Exhibit 5.8.

exhibit 5.8   **Pre-Merger Balance Sheet Data**

	January 1, 2002 (Pesos)	Solis Company	
	Paz Company Book Value	Book Value	Fair Value
Cash and receivables	Ps 50,000	Ps 10,000	Ps 10,000
Inventories	100,000	50,000	50,000
Other assets	450,000	170,000	210,000
Total assets	Ps 600,000	Ps 230,000	
Current liabilities	Ps 25,000	Ps 40,000	40,000
Common stock (15 par value)	375,000		
Common stock (5 par value)		150,000	
Retained earnings	200,000	40,000	
Total liabilities and stockholders' equity	Ps 600,000	Ps 230,000	

To record the exchange of stock for the net assets of Solis Company, Paz Company would make the following entry:

Cash and Receivables	10,000	
Inventories	50,000	
Other Assets	210,000	
Goodwill	40,000	
Current Liabilities		40,000
Common Stock (6,000 × 15)		90,000
Paid-in Capital in Excess of Par Value		180,000

Solis Company ceases to exist as a legal entity. Under the purchase method, the cost of the net assets of Solis is equal to the fair value (6,000 shares × 45 pesos or 270,000 pesos) of the shares given in exchange. Common stock is credited for 6,000 shares multiplied with the par value of 15 pesos, and the remainder is credited to paid-in capital in excess of par value. Individual assets acquired and liabilities assumed are recorded at their fair values. After all identifiable assets and liabilities are recorded, an excess over fair value of 40,000 pesos results and is recorded as goodwill.

Exhibit 5.9 represents the balance sheet of Paz Company immediately after the acquisition of the net assets of Solis Company, which has ceased to exist.

Consolidated Financial Statements

Consolidated financial statements essentially portray the financial position and results of operations of the parent and its subsidiaries as though they are one economic entity. We know that the parent and its subsidiaries are distinct legal entities and keep their individual books and records. However, it is important to give the stockholders a "single-company" view of the parent and its subsidiaries. Since the parent company and its subsidiaries are considered a single entity from a consolidation standpoint, transactions within the affiliated group must be elim-

exhibit 5.9 Paz Company Balance Sheet after Acquisition of Solis Net Assets

Paz Company Balance Sheet January 1, 2002 (pesos)			
Cash and receivables	Ps 60,000	Current liabilities	Ps 65,000
Inventories	150,000	Common stock (15 par value)	465,000
Other assets	660,000	Excess over par value	180,000
Goodwill	40,000	Retained earnings	200,000
		Total liabilities and	
Total assets	Ps 910,000	stockholders' equity	Ps 910,000

inated. For example, intercompany receivables and payables are eliminated to avoid double counting of assets and liabilities. Similarly, intercompany profits on assets sold from one member of the affiliated group to another are eliminated since an entity cannot profit from transactions with itself.

Basic to the preparation of consolidated statements is the elimination of the investment account and the subsidiary's equity. The investment account represents the parent's investment in the net assets of the subsidiary. Thus, the investment account and the subsidiary's equity account are reciprocal. Since the subsidiary's assets and liabilities are combined with the parent's assets and liabilities, the investment account must be eliminated so that there is no double counting. In other words, the subsidiary's net assets are in fact substituted for the investment account. It is important to emphasize that the elimination entries are made on the workpapers and not in journals. The individual sets of journals, ledgers, and records of the parent and its subsidiaries remain intact.

We can illustrate the process of creating a consolidated balance sheet with three different examples where P Company has acquired stock of S Company. The illustrations are based on the balance sheets for P Company and S Company at December 31, 2001, shown in Exhibit 5.10.

exhibit 5.10 Balance Sheets for P Company and S Company

P Company
Balance Sheet (unconsolidated)
December 31, 2001

Assets		Liabilities and Equity	
Cash	$140,000	Accounts payable	$ 30,000
Accounts receivable	50,000	Long-term debt	200,000
Other assets	545,000	Total liabilities	230,000
		Common stock (no par value)	400,000
		Retained earnings	105,000
		Total stockholders' equity	505,000
		Total liabilities and	
Total assets	$735,000	stockholders' equity	$735,000

S Company
Balance Sheet
December 31, 2001

Assets		Equity	
Cash	$ 30,000	Common stock	$100,000
Other assets	70,000		
Total assets	$100,000	Total equity	$100,000

Example

The cost of the parent company's investment is equal to the book value of the subsidiary's stock acquired. One hundred percent of the subsidiary's stock is acquired.

Assume that on January 1, 2002, S Company had 10,000 shares of $10 par value stock. P Company acquires all of the shares of S Company stock for $100,000 in cash. After this transaction, P Company has $40,000 remaining in Cash and an Investment in S Company of $100,000.

Exhibit 5.11 illustrates a workpaper for the preparation of a consolidated balance sheet for P Company on January 1, 2002.

The workpaper entry to eliminate the investment account against S Company's stockholders' equity is as follows:

Common Stock—S Company	100,000	
Investment in S Company		100,000

Note that the assets of the subsidiary were substituted for the $100,000 investment in S Company and the $100,000 common stock of S Company has been eliminated. This leaves the consolidated stockholders' equity the same as the parent company stockholders' equity. The elimination entries are made only on the workpaper; the individual records of P Company and S Company are not changed.

exhibit 5.11   Consolidated Balance Sheet Workpaper 100%-Owned Subsidiary

	P Company and Subsidiary Consolidated Balance Sheet Workpaper January 1, 2002				
	P Company	**S Company**	**Eliminations Debit**	**Eliminations Credit**	**Consolidated Balance Sheet**
Cash	$ 40,000	$ 30,000			$ 70,000
Accounts receivable	50,000				50,000
Other assets	545,000	70,000			615,000
Investment in S	100,000			(A)$100,000	0
	$735,000	$100,000			$735,000
Accounts payable	$ 30,000				$ 30,000
Long-term debt	200,000				200,000
Common stock	400,000	$100,000	(A)$100,000		400,000
Retained earnings	105,000				105,000
	$735,000	$100,000	$100,000	$100,000	$735,000

Example

The cost of the parent company's investment is equal to the book value of the subsidiary's stock acquired. Less than 100 percent of subsidiary's stock is acquired.

Assume that on January 1, 2002, S Company had 10,000 shares of $10 par value stock. P Company acquires 7,000 shares of stock in S Company for $70,000 in cash. After this transaction, P Company has $70,000 remaining in Cash and an Investment in S Company of $70,000. The workpaper appears in Exhibit 5.12.

The workpaper entry is:

Common Stock—S Company	70,000	
Investment in S Company		70,000

Note that again the assets of the subsidiary were substituted for the investment on the parent company's books. Also note that the consolidated stockholders' equity is still the same as the parent stockholders' equity. The minority interest appears at $30,000 because the parent's share of $70,000 (70% of $100,000, the stockholders' equity of S Company) has been eliminated.

exhibit 5.12 **Consolidated Balance Sheet Workpaper Minority Interest, No Goodwill**

P Company and Subsidiary
Consolidated Balance Sheet Workpaper
January 1, 2002

	P Company	S Company	Eliminations Debit	Eliminations Credit	Consolidated Balance Sheet
Cash	$ 70,000	$ 30,000			$100,000
Accounts receivable	50,000				50,000
Other assets	545,000	70,000			615,000
Investment in S	70,000			(A)$70,000	0
	$735,000	$100,000			$765,000
Accounts payable	$ 30,000				$ 30,000
Long-term debt	200,000				200,000
Common stock, P	400,000				400,000
Common stock, S		$100,000	(A)$70,000		30,000M
Retained earnings	105,000				105,000
	$735,000	$100,000	$70,000	$70,000	$765,000

M = Minority interest

Again remember that elimination entries are made only on the workpaper. The individual records of P Company and S Company remain intact.

Example

The cost of the parent company's investment exceeds the book value of the subsidiary's stock acquired. Less than 100 percent of the subsidiary's stock is acquired.

Assume that on January 1, 2002, P Company acquired 70 percent of the shares of S Company for $75,000. P Company then has $65,000 remaining in Cash and an Investment in S Company of $75,000. Note that the $75,000 represents $5,000 more than 70 percent of the $100,000 S Company stockholders' equity. If the excess is not attributable to any identifiable assets, P Company has paid $5,000 for goodwill. A workpaper for a consolidated balance sheet on January 1, 2002, appears in Exhibit 5.13.

The workpaper entry is:

Common Stock—S Company	70,000	
Goodwill	5,000	
Investment in S Company		75,000

exhibit 5.13 **Consolidated Balance Sheet Workpaper Minority Interest and Goodwill**

P Company and Subsidiary
Consolidated Balance Sheet Workpaper
January 1, 2002

	P Company	S Company	Eliminations Debit	Eliminations Credit	Consolidated Balance Sheet
Cash	$ 65,000	$ 30,000			$ 95,000
Accounts receivable	50,000				50,000
Other assets	545,000	70,000			615,000
Investment in S	75,000			(A)$75,000	0
Goodwill			(A)$ 5,000		5,000
	$735,000	$100,000			$765,000
Accounts payable	$ 30,000				$ 30,000
Long-term debt	200,000				200,000
Common stock, P	400,000				400,000
Common stock, S		$100,000	(A)70,000		30,000M
Retained earnings	$105,000				105,000
	$735,000	$100,000	$75,000	$75,000	$765,000

M = Minority interest

Note the differences between Exhibit 5.12 and Exhibit 5.13. In the first exhibit, cash is greater because it took less cash to acquire S Company stock. In Exhibit 5.13, goodwill appears in the consolidated balance sheet column.

Goodwill

Goodwill arises in a purchase type of transaction where the acquiring company pays more than the fair value of the net identifiable assets or more than the fair value of the common stock of the subsidiary. In effect, it is the consideration given for above-normal earning power of the company being acquired.

A difference of opinion exists on what periods the cost of the goodwill benefits the acquiring company. Should goodwill be written off against stockholders' equity immediately or should it be amortized over some stated period? The underlying rationale for permanently keeping goodwill as an asset is that in a successful business, goodwill will continue because the economic benefits will accrue to the entity over its life—assumed to be indefinite. Those of the opinion that goodwill should be amortized argue that purchased goodwill has a limited life, and that its cost should be written off over some period of time, in conformity with the matching concept.

Another school of thought argues that goodwill should be written off immediately against stockholders' equity. Goodwill is not separate from the business as a whole. In other words, it is not separately realizable and thus should be immediately written off against stockholders' equity. Another argument is that the expense arising from amortization of goodwill hinders comparability and thus should be omitted from the income statement.

Accounting for goodwill is diverse among the countries of the world. Exhibit 5.14 shows how a selected group of countries accounts for goodwill.

If the cost of a business combination is less than the sum of the fair values of its identifiable assets, the difference can be viewed as negative goodwill. Practices to account for negative goodwill are diverse. In Australia, Canada, and the U.S. this requires a reduction in certain acquired assets. Negative goodwill is credited to equity in the Netherlands and the U.K.

Leases

A **lease** is a contract between a lessor and a lessee that gives the lessee the right to use specific property owned by the lessor, for a given time period, in exchange for cash or other consideration—typically a commitment to make future cash payments. Leases are important means to finance the acquisition of property or of rights to use property in both domestic and international operations. In some cases, it is taken for granted that the property will be returned to the lessor at the end of the lease term. In other cases, the property is expected to remain with the lessee. In still other cases, eventual disposition of the property may be subject to option, or may be negotiated during or at the end of the lease term.

exhibit 5.14 Accounting for Goodwill

	Immediate Expensing	Immediate Write-off Against Equity Reserve	Maximum Years For Amortization
Austria	No	No	E*
Australia	No	No	20
Brazil	No	No	E
Canada	No	No	40
Czech Republic	Yes	No	5
Denmark	No	Yes	20
Finland	Yes	No	20
France	No	No	40
Germany	No	Yes	40
India	No	No	E
Italy	No	Yes	E
Japan	Yes	No	5
Mexico	No	No	20
Netherlands	Yes	Yes	E
South Korea	No	No	5
Spain	No	No	20
Sweden	No	Yes	E
United Kingdom	No	Yes	20
United States	No	No	40

*E: Estimated life

Operating Leases

Leases commonly referred to as rentals are called **operating leases**. While the application of accounting treatments differs widely in different countries, the following possible treatments and their associated terminology are adequate to form a useful classification scheme. In the examples in this section, we use broad terms such as liability, revenue, and expense rather than the specific terminology of any one country. In the interest of simplicity, we ignore recurring items such as maintenance and taxes, which can be paid by either the lessor or the lessee.

Example

Lessor Company purchases a bulldozer from Bilal Tractor on January 1, 1994, at a price of $80,000. Lessor leases (rents) the machine to Lessee Company for $3,000 per month, and depreciates it over an 8-year term with no estimated residual value. On January 1, 2002, Lessor sells the used bulldozer for $5,000. Lessor Company entries for 1994 follow:

January 1, 1994	Asset (equipment held for lease)	80,000	
	Cash		80,000
	To record the acquisition of bulldozer.		

January 31, 1994	Cash	3,000	
	Rent Revenue		3,000
	To record rent for a typical month.		

December 31, 1994	Depreciation Expense	10,000	
	Accumulated Depreciation, Asset		10,000
	To record depreciation for a year.		

Lessor's entry for sale of the bulldozer is:

January 1, 2002	Cash	5,000	
	Accumulated Depreciation, Asset	80,000	
	Asset (equipment held for lease)		80,000
	Gain on Sale of Asset		5,000
	To record the sale of bulldozer.		

With an operating lease, the lessor's profit, if any, emerges gradually over time as the excess of revenues and gain over expenses. The Lessee Company entry to record rent expense for January follows:

January 31, 1994	Rent Expense	3,000	
	Cash		3,000
	To record rent for a month.		

The lessee will make a similar entry at the end of each month. Under an operating lease, the lessee shows rent expense, but no asset and liability, and no depreciation expense or interest expense.

Finance (Capital) Leases

A lease treated as a sale by the lessor to the lessee is commonly known as a **finance** or **capital lease**. For the lessor, a finance lease is further broken down as either a **sales-type lease**, where a dealer's profit or loss is a basic part of the transaction, or a **direct-financing lease**, where the lessor provides financing and earns interest revenue but has no profit or loss on the sale.

Example

Lessor Company purchases a bulldozer from Bilal Tractor on December 31, 1995, at a price of $80,000. Lessor leases the bulldozer to Lessee Company for a downpayment of $2,000, plus $1,586 due at the end of each month for a fixed term of 100 months, based on a price of $102,000 and an implicit interest rate of 12 percent. The title to the bulldozer passes to Lessee at the end of the lease term. Lessee depreciates the machine over a 10-year term with no estimated residual value. On December 31, 2005, Lessee sells the used bulldozer for $5,000.

This is a finance lease for both parties. Since Lessor is earning a dealer's profit, the lease will be classified as a sales-type lease by the lessor.

The lessor's entries for recording the acquisition and lease of the bulldozer under the sales-type finance lease follow:

Lessor Company, sales-type lease

December 31, 1995	Asset (inventory)	80,000	
	Cash		80,000
	To record acquisition of a bulldozer.		

December 31, 1995	Cash	2,000	
	Receivable	158,600	
	Cost of Goods Sold	80,000	
	Discount on Receivable		58,600
	Sales		102,000
	Asset (inventory)		80,000
	To record lease of a bulldozer as a sales-type lease.		

The lessor will make monthly entries as follows:

January 31, 1996	Cash	1,586	
	Receivable		1,586
	To record receipt of monthly payment.		

January 31, 1996	Discount on Receivable	1,000	
	Interest Revenue		1,000
	To record interest for first month.		
	(12% ÷ 12) × $100,000 = $1,000		

Note that Lessor Company, acting as a dealer, is recording a sale on December 31, 1995. Lessor also recognizes the dealer's profit immediately, and records a long-term receivable.

In a lease treated as a finance lease, the lessee is in roughly the same position as an outright purchaser. Lessee Company's entry is:

December 31, 1995	Asset (bulldozer)	102,000	
	Cash		2,000
	Payable (obligation under lease)		100,000
	To record leased asset and related obligation.		

For each monthly payment, the lessee will make an entry similar to the one made at the end of January 1996:

January 31, 1996	Interest Expense	1,000	
	Payable (obligation under lease)	586	
	Cash		1,586
	To record January payment and interest.		

The lessee records annual depreciation for 1996 as follows:

December 31, 1996	Depreciation Expense	10,200	
	Accumulated Depreciation (bulldozer)		10,200
	To record depreciation for 1996.		

The entry for the sale of the bulldozer follows:

December 31, 2005	Cash	5,000	
	Asset (bulldozer)	100,000	
	Accumulated Depreciation (bulldozer)		100,000
	Gain on Sale of Asset		5,000
	To record the sale of bulldozer.		

Direct-financing lease.   In a direct-financing lease, the sale is recorded by the dealer since the lessor provides financing only. The lessor records the receivable at the lease date. Subsequently, the lessor records, on a monthly basis, the cash receipts from the lessee, and interest revenue. The lessee's accounting is identical to the sales-type capital lease as shown.

The accounting differences for the capitalization of finance leases among selected countries are shown in Exhibit 5.15. The complexities of lease accounting arise from the determination as to *when* a particular method is applicable. Once this is decided, the *how* problem is less difficult.

Note to Students

We live in exciting times. It will be even more exciting for those who are studying accounting presently because they will see how indispensable accounting is in international business. Accounting does not function in a vacuum; it is a useful tool that will help the countries of the world in their efforts to make efficient and effective utilization of resources.

It is a common misconception that financial reports contain only required disclosures. As we discussed in this chapter, corporations often develop and present new types of voluntary disclosures. Value-added statements are one example of such disclosures. As a professional, you should always keep the main purpose of accounting—providing information to meet legitimate needs of users of financial statements—foremost. Accounting standards set the minimum disclosure requirements. You can make disclosures beyond the minimum requirements.

Accounting is dynamic by its very nature since it is always attempting to meet the *current* information needs of users. Often members of the profession identify the need and take the initiative to develop new methods to communicate requisite information.

Exhibit 5.15 **Accounting Differences— Capitalization of Finance Leases**

Country	Allowed	Common in Practice
Australia	Yes	Yes
Austria	Yes	Yes
Brazil	Yes	No
Canada	Yes	Yes
Czech Republic	No	N/A*
Denmark	No	N/A
Finland	No	N/A
France	No	N/A
Germany	Yes	No
India	No	N/A
Italy	No	N/A
Japan	Yes	No
Mexico	Yes	Yes
Netherlands	Yes	Yes
New Zealand	Yes	Yes
Spain	Yes	Yes
South Korea	Yes	Yes
Sweden	Yes	Yes
Switzerland	Yes	No
United Kingdom	Yes	Yes
United States	Yes	Yes

*N/A: Not applicable
Note: In France, capitalization of finance leases is not allowed for statutory financial statements but is allowed for consolidated statements.

Environmental accounting is an emerging area of specialization in accounting. According to Robert Half International Inc., public accounting clients are increasingly asking for environmental accounting specialists. Accountants have an important role to play in the protection of our environment, as they do in solving many other problems confronting our global community.

Chapter Summary

1. Financial reporting disclosures include many types of disclosures and the trend is toward more disclosures.

2. A corporation is held accountable to investors and creditors as well as society at large. The latter accountability arises from a corporation using scarce resources, and its ability to influence lifestyles and quality of life of parties other than capital providers.

3. Several factors prompt corporations to make financial reporting disclosures. Corporations make required as well as voluntary disclosures.

4. Total costs of disclosures include both monetary costs as well as non-monetary costs.

5. Disclosures in financial reports are directly affected by how economic transactions are recorded (measured).

6. There is a diversity in the measurement process worldwide.

7. Reserves are used for multiple purposes, including additional protection to creditors.

8. The method of disclosure affects perceptions of users of financial reports.

9. Lack of disclosure uniformity exists even when companies are using the same accounting standards.

10. Different multinationals use different disclosure approaches ranging from compliance with base country requirements to preparation of secondary statements.

11. Social impact disclosures are heavily influenced by societal concerns in a country, with human resource disclosures receiving the most attention.

12. The discussion of selected technical topics provides evidence of diversity among the countries.

Questions for Discussion

1. Give at least four types of disclosures included in financial statements.

2. What are some of the reasons for the trend toward more disclosures?

3. What are the two issues that remain unresolved in the area of disclosures for users other than capital providers?

4. "Corporations disclose only what they are required to disclose." Do you agree? Explain.

5. List at least three reasons why corporations make financial reporting disclosures.

6. Why do many firms operating in global capital markets tend to exceed minimum financial disclosure requirements?

7. "Extensive disclosure hurts our company's competitive position." Do you agree? Discuss.

8. How are financial reports affected by the measurement process?

9. What is meant by the prudence concept?

10. Describe how income smoothing is accomplished by using an expense liability reserve.

11. "Uniform accounting standards would lead to uniform disclosures." Do you agree? Discuss.

12. There are six multinational disclosure approaches discussed in the chapter. Can you name four of those?

13. Distinguish between selective restatements and secondary statements.

14. Discuss the pros and cons of selective restatements.

15. What are the two drawbacks of the secondary statements approach?

16. In discussion of social impact disclosures, three types of disclosures were mentioned: employees, value-added statements, and environmental protection. Which type of the three disclosures has received the most attention?

17. "Value added = Total revenues − Cost of goods sold." Do you agree? Explain.

18. "Because of its importance, the environmental disclosures area is at an advanced state of development." Do you agree? Explain.

19. Which three countries require environmental disclosures?

20. Contrast and compare the pooling of interests method with the purchase method.

21. How does goodwill arise in a business combination?

22. Relative to the purchase method, how prevalent is the use of the pooling of interests method in the world?

23. What is the purpose for preparing consolidated financial statements?

24. What is the difference between a capital lease and an operating lease?

25. Can you think of situations where it would make economic sense *not* to amortize goodwill?

26. In a high-technology environment, intangible assets become increasingly more important. Do you agree? Explain.

Exercises/Problems

5-1 James Anderson Company is a major company based in Sydney, Australia. The company uses FIFO. The following information is available regarding Anderson's inventory.

	Units	Unit Cost
Beginning inventory	500	$A15
Purchases	10,000	$A17

Ending inventory has 700 units, which can be sold for $A10,000. However, if sold, Anderson will have to pay the freight expenses in the amount of $A200. The replacement cost of ending inventory is $A11,200.

Required:

Determine the value of ending inventory using Australian GAAP.

5-2   Refer to the information in Problem 5-1, but assume that Australian accounting standards for inventory valuation now define "market" as replacement cost in the application of lower of cost or market method.

5-3   In 2002, the actual income of Kim Company in Korea was 75 million won. Kim Company likes to show an annual growth of 10 percent in earnings. The reported income in 2001, the previous year, was 60 million won. Kim Company uses an expense liability reserve.

Required:

Make an appropriate entry for the transfer into or out of the expense liability reserve to achieve the desired income amount for reporting.

5-4   Refer to Problem 5-3. The actual income of Kim Company was only 70 million won in 2003.

Required:

Make an appropriate entry for the transfer into or out of the expense liability reserve to achieve the desired income amount for reporting.

5-5   Pierre Company has share capital in the amount of F80 million. The income for 2001 is in the amount of F6 million. Pierre is subject to the legal reserve requirements in France, which mandate that 5 percent of the income must be transferred to the legal reserve until its balance is 10 percent of the share capital.

Required:

Make the entry to close out the income summary account assuming:

(1)   The balance in the legal reserve is F8.0 million.

(2)   The balance in the legal reserve is F7.0 million.

(3)   The balance in the legal reserve is F7.9 million.

5-6   The directors of Foster Company in Australia vote to transfer $A3 million to the general reserve to make this amount unavailable for dividends.

Required:

Make the appropriate entry to record the previous transaction.

5-7   Thompson Company, a U.K.-based multinational, has decided to make an upward adjustment of equipment in the amount of £500,000. The company uses the straight-line depreciation method and assumes no salvage value and that the remaining useful life of the equipment is five years.

Required:

Make entries for:

(1)   Upward adjustment of assets.

(2) Annual depreciation assuming:

  (a) incremental depreciation is charged to the revaluation reserve.
  (b) incremental depreciation is charged against income.

(3) Refer to Requirement (2). In which case, (a) or (b), is the depreciation expense in the income statement based on historical cost?

(4) Make the appropriate entry to adjust the revaluation reserve when the incremental depreciation is charged against income.

5-8 Prepare a succinct analysis of the six disclosure approaches of multinationals. Limit your analysis to approximately 200 words.

5-9 The author has made five suggestions regarding corporate responsibility for environmental protection.

Required:

Discuss those suggestions. Can you think of other ideas that might be helpful in this area?

5-10 The traditional income statement of Sharif International follows in rupees.

Sharif International
Income Statement
For the Year Ended March 31, 2002

		Rs000s
Sales		Rs90,000
Cost of goods sold (all purchased from outside companies)		60,000
Gross profit		Rs30,000
Salaries and retirement benefits	15,000	
Rent expense	3,000	
Auditing and legal services	1,000	
Interest expense	2,000	21,000
Income before taxes		9,000
Provision for income taxes		4,000
Net income		Rs 5,000

Dividends declared and paid during the year amounted to Rs1,500,000.

Required:

Transform Sharif International's traditional income statement into a value added statement.

5-11 Patrice Inc.'s income statement appears on the following page.

Notes:

1. All goods sold were purchased from outside suppliers.

2. Dividends declared and paid during 2001 amounted to $100,000.

Required:

Prepare a value-added statement for Patrice, Inc.

Patrice, Inc.
Statement of Income
For the Year Ended December 31, 2001

	$000s	
Sales	$3,975	
Cost of goods sold	2,830	
Gross profit		$1,145
Salaries, wages, and employment-related expenses	650	
Rent expense	47	
Outside consulting fees	53	
Interest expense	17	767
Income before taxes		378
Provision for income taxes		179
Net income		$ 199

5-12 The value-added statement for Waheed International for 2002 follows:

Waheed International Ltd.
Value-Added Statement
For the Period Ended June 30, 2000

Turnover (sales revenues)		£14,800
Other income (non-operating income)		600
		15,400
Acquired resources (cost of sales 60%; depreciation 20%; other service expenses 20%)		8,800
Value added		£ 6,600
Distribution of value added:		
Employees: Wages and salaries	£3,200	
Creditors: Interest expense	1,200	
Government: Income tax	800	
Shareholders: Dividends	400	5,600
Retained for future investment		1,000
Distribution of value added		£ 6,600

Required:

(1) Prepare a traditional income statement based on the previous information.

(2) Comment on the differences between the two statements.

(3) What are the benefits of the value-added statement?

5-13 On January 1, 2002, Wakamatsu Corporation purchased 100 percent of the common stock of Shigao by issuing 40,000 shares of its ¥40 common stock with a market value of ¥60. The equity sections of the two companies' balance sheets on December 31, 2001, were:

	Wakamatsu	Shigao
Common stock	¥ 700,000	¥600,000
Additional paid-in capital	280,000	90,000
Retained earnings	320,000	210,000
Total	¥1,300,000	¥900,000

Required:

(1)   Prepare the journal entry on Wakamatsu Corporation's books to record the purchase of Shigao Company.

(2)   Prepare the elimination entry required for the consolidated balance sheet.

5-14 On January 1, 2002, Aamer Company purchased a 70 percent interest in Wong Company for $650,000, at which time Wong Company had retained earnings of $250,000 and capital stock of $300,000. Any difference between the cost and book value was attributable to goodwill with a remaining useful life of 20 years. Aamer and Wong reported net incomes from their independent operations of $300,000 and $200,000, respectively.

Required:

Prepare an analysis to determine consolidated net income for the year ended December 31, 2002.

5-15 On January 1, 2001, Swazy Company purchased a 75 percent interest in Shaukat Company for 300,000 French francs. On this date, Shaukat Company had common stock of F75,000 and retained earnings of F200,000. Shaukat Company's equipment on the date of Swazy Company's purchase had a book value of F200,000 and a fair value of F300,000.

Required:

Prepare the December 31 consolidated financial statements workpaper entries for 2001.

5-16 The balance sheets of Penman Company and Saen Company as of January 1, 2003, are as follows in Dutch guilders.

	Penman	Saen
Building and equipment (net)	f4,800,000	f1,000,000
Inventories	2,500,000	250,000
Receivables	800,000	300,000
Cash	600,000	250,000
Total assets	f8,700,000	f1,800,000

Share capital	f4,500,000	f1,000,000
Share premium	500,000	0
Reserves	2,200,000	400,000
Liabilities	1,500,000	400,000
Total liabilities and stockholders' equity	f8,700,000	f1,800,000

On that date, the two companies agreed to merge. To effect the merger, Penman Company agreed to exchange 10,000 unissued shares of its common stock for all of the outstanding shares of Saen Company. The total par value of 10,000 shares of Penman common stock is f1,500,000 and their total market value is f1,700,000. The fair market values of Saen Company's assets and liabilities are equal to their book values with the exception of buildings and equipment, which have an estimated fair market value of 1,200,000 guilders.

Required:

Prepare a balance sheet for Penman Company immediately after the merger under the assumptions that the merger is treated as a purchase.

5-17 The balance sheets of two Canadian companies, P Company and S Company, as of January 1, 2003, follow.

	P	S
Cash	$ 1,200,000	$ 500,000
Receivables	1,600,000	500,000
Inventories	5,000,000	400,000
Buildings and equipment (net)	9,600,000	2,000,000
Total assets	$17,400,000	$3,400,000
Payables	$ 3,000,000	$1,000,000
Paid-in capital	9,000,000	2,000,000
Retained earnings	5,400,000	400,000
Total liabilities and stockholders' equity	$17,400,000	$3,400,000

The two companies effect a merger whereby P Company exchanged its capital stock for all the outstanding shares of S Company. Shares of S Company were exchanged at a ratio of one share of P for every two shares of S. Market values per share were $100 and $200 for P and S, respectively. The fair values of S Company's assets and liabilities are equal to their book values except buildings and equipment, which have an estimated fair value of $2,500,000.

Required:

Prepare a balance sheet immediately after the merger using the pooling of interests method.

5-18 Hasham Company leases a large specialized machine to Salman Company at a total rental of 1,800,000 French francs, payable in five annual installments in the following declining pattern: 25 percent for each of the first two years, 20 percent in the third year, and 15 percent in each of the last two years. The lease begins January 1, 2000. In addition to the rent, Hasham is required to pay annual costs of F15,000 to cover repairs, maintenance, and insurance. The lease qualifies as an operating lease for reporting purposes. Hasham incurred initial direct costs of F15,000 in obtaining the lease. The machine cost Hasham F3,100,000 to build and has an estimated life of 10 years with an estimated residual value of F100,000. Hasham uses the straight-line method of depreciation. Both companies report on a calendar-year basis.

Required:

(1) Prepare appropriate journal entries on Hasham's books for the years 2000 and 2004 related to the lease.

(2) Prepare appropriate journal entries on Salman's books for the years 2000 and 2004 related to the lease.

5-19 In 2001 Fatima Sharif, Inc., a U.S.-based company, entered into a lease for a new oil press. The lease states that annual payments will be made for five years. The payments are to be made in advance on January 1 of each year. At the end of the five-year period, Fatima Sharif may purchase the oil press. The estimated economic life of the equipment is 12 years. Fatima Sharif uses the calendar year for reporting purposes and uses straight-line depreciation for the equipment. The following additional information about the lease is available:

Annual lease payments	$110,000
Purchase option price	$40,000
Estimated fair market value of oil press after 5 years	$100,000
Incremental borrowing rate	10 percent
Date of first lease payment	January 1, 2001
Lease type	capital lease

Required:

(1) Compute the amount to be capitalized as an asset for lease of the oil press.

(2) Prepare a schedule showing computation of the interest expense for each period.

(3) Provide the journal entries that would be made on Fatima Sharif's books for each of the first two years of the lease.

(4) Assume that the purchase option is exercised at the end of the lease. Make the journal entry to record the exercise of the option by Fatima Sharif.

Case

Management Control Systems and the Environment[14]

ICI, a multinational chemical company with its head office in London, publishes a supplement to its annual report titled, *Group Safety Health and Environment Performance Report*, generally referred to as the *SHE Report*. It is sent to its shareholders. The following information is taken from this report.

(1) Details of environment-related expenditures. For instance, at ICI's Huddersfield plant, a new boiler plant was constructed using "novel technology for capturing sulfur dioxide. The result has been a halving of sulphur dioxide emissions in the flue gases." ICI stated that all major new projects it undertakes now are assessed for their impact on the environment at all stages in their development. Environmental expenditures, total revenues, and net earnings of ICI were reported to be:

Environmental expenditures (billions)	Year 1	Year 2	Year 3
Capital equipment related	0.081	0.132	0.164
Operating related	0.194	0.187	0.197
Revenues (billions)	12.906	12.488	12.061
Net earnings (billions)	0.919	0.789	0.565

(2) Number of fines and prosecutions for noncompliance with environmental laws and regulations:

	Year 1	Year 2	Year 3
	36	26	21

(3) Total waste emissions to land, air, and water (in millions of tons):

	Year 1	Year 2	Year 3
Nonhazardous	5.334	5.205	4.817
Hazardous	0.678	0.475	0.350
	6.012	5.680	5.167

(4) Number of reportable accidents per 100,000 working hours:

	Year 1	Year 2	Year 3
	0.28	0.23	0.18

---

14 Charles T. Horngren, George Foster, and Srikant M. Datar. *Cost Accounting: A Managerial Emphasis*. 8th ed. Englewood Cliffs, N.J.: Prentice Hall, 1994, pp. 490–491. Adapted. Reprinted by permission of Prentice-Hall.

Required:

(1)   Why might ICI send its *SHE Report* to its shareholders in addition to sending its *Annual Report*?

(2)   One commentator argued that ICI's *SHE Report* should not have been sent to shareholders with its *Annual Report*. His argument was: "The financial information in the Annual Report is objective and audited by KPMG Peat Marwick. Information about safety, health, and the environment is subjective and nonaudited. I object to this pandering to the greenies. We should not waste ICI money responding to every social pressure group." How would you respond to this commentator?

(3)   Should the data in items 2 (fines), 3 (emissions), and 4 (accidents) be included in a management control system, or should a management control system focus only on financial/internal information? Explain.

(4)   What problems might arise in ICI determining what amount of its expenditures is related to "safety, health, or the environment"?

(5)   Comment on trends in ICI's data reported in this question: Does an increase in environment-related expenditures mean an improvement in environmental performance?

Critical Thinking Problem

Goodwill Forever?

The following item summarizes a proposal by the U.K.'s Accounting Standards Board:[15]

> The Accounting Standards Board's proposals on accounting for goodwill are a triumph of diplomacy as well as intellectual ingenuity. The ASB's style has hitherto been somewhat confrontational, but the new rules are designed to please those who prepare accounts—namely companies— and those who use them, chiefly investors.
>
> Amazingly, given the passions which goodwill accounting provokes, the proposals are likely to meet with widespread approval. This is despite the fact that [the] companies' favoured way of dealing with the substance—writing it off against reserves—is set to be outlawed. The reason is that companies will not be obliged to write goodwill off against earnings over an arbitrary number of years. They may do this if they want, but in practice big companies will opt to leave the goodwill on the balance sheet, testing it from year to year to see whether there has been any diminution in its value. Sensibly, companies will be able to keep brands and other intangibles on the balance sheet, subject to similar tests.

---

15 "Goodwill." *Financial Times*, 15 June 1995, p. 14.

If the proposals are adopted, the quality of accounts will be doubly improved. Goodwill will be visible in the accounts, not written off and forgotten. Furthermore, the tests on the value of goodwill seem rigorous and yet not unduly complicated, and will prove a useful discipline for managers. They will however add to the pressures on auditors, who will be forced to exercise judgment where they may have preferred clear-cut guidelines.

Required:

(1)   Discuss reasons supporting amortization of goodwill.

(2)   Discuss reasons against amortization of goodwill.

(3)   What alternative do you prefer based on the points made in (1) and (2)? Explain.

(4)   Can the arguments supporting or against goodwill amortization be extended to other intangibles? Explain. Include examples in your analysis.

References

Alexander, D., and S. Archer, eds. *European Accounting Guide*, 3rd ed. San Diego: Harcourt Brace Professional Publishing, 1998.

Beets, S.D., and C.C. Souther. "Corporate Environmental Reports: The Need for Standards and an Environmental Assurance Service." *Accounting Horizons*, June 1999, pp. 129–145.

Deloitte Touche Tohmatsu. *Austria: International Tax and Business Guide*. New York: Deloitte Touche Tohmatsu, 1999.

_____. *Denmark: International Tax and Business Guide*. New York: Deloitte Touche Tohmatsu, 1999.

_____. *Finland: International Tax and Business Guide*. New York: Deloitte Touche Tohmatsu, 1999.

_____. *India: International Tax and Business Guide*. New York: Deloitte Touche Tohmatsu, 2000.

_____. *Japan: International Tax and Business Guide*. New York: Deloitte Touche Tohmatsu, 1997.

_____. *Netherlands: International Tax and Business Guide*. New York: Deloitte Touche Tohmatsu, 1998.

_____. *New Zealand: International Tax and Business Guide*. New York: Deloitte Touche Tohmatsu, 1998.

_____. *Spain: International Tax and Business Guide*. New York: Deloitte Touche Tohmatsu, 2000.

_____. *Sweden: International Tax and Business Guide*. New York: Deloitte Touche Tohmatsu, 2000.

Duvall, L., R. Jennings, J. Robinson, and R. Thomson II. "Can Investors Unravel the Effects of Goodwill Accounting?" *Accounting Horizons*, June 1992, pp. 1–14.

Frost, C.A., and M.H. Lang. "Foreign Companies and U.S. Securities Markets: Financial Reporting Policy Issues and Suggestions for Research." *Accounting Horizons*, March 1996, pp. 95–109.

_____, and G. Pownall. "Accounting Disclosure Practices in the United States and the United Kingdom." *Journal of Accounting Research*, Spring 1994, pp. 75–102.

Garrod, Neil, and Isabel Sieringhaus. "European Union Accounting Harmonization: The Case of Leased Assets in the United Kingdom and Germany." *The European Accounting Review*, vol. 4, no. 1 (1995), pp. 155–164.

Harper, R.M. Jr., W.G. Mister, and J.R. Strawser. "The Effect of Recognition Versus Disclosure of Unfunded Postretirement Benefits on Lenders' Perceptions of Debt." *Accounting Horizons*, September 1991, pp. 50–56.

Horngren, Charles T., George Foster, and Srikant M. Datar. *Cost Accounting: A Managerial Emphasis*, 10th ed. Upper Saddle River, N.J.: Prentice Hall, 2000.

Iqbal, M. Zafar. "A Critique of Value Added Reporting—Lessons for the United States." *The International Journal of Accounting*, Fall 1996, pp. 399–401.

Lawrence, S. *International Accounting*. London: International Thomson Business Press, 1996.

Lowe, Howard D. "Shortcomings of Japanese Consolidated Financial Statements." *Accounting Horizons*, September 1990, pp. 1–9.

Meek, G.K., ed. *Country Studies in International Accounting—Americas and the Far East*. Cheltenham, U.K.: Edward Elger Publishing, 1996.

Nobes, C., and R.H. Parker. *Comparative International Accounting*, 5th ed. Upper Saddle River, N.J.: Prentice Hall, 1998.

Piet, J. "Guarding the Globe." *Accountancy International*, August 1999, pp. 62–63.

PricewaterhouseCoopers. *Doing Business and Investing in the Czech Republic*. Jersey City, N.J.: PricewaterhouseCoopers, 1999.

Riahi-Belkaoui, Ahmed. *Value Added Reporting—Lessons for the United States*. New York: Quorum Books, 1992.

United Nations Center on Transnational Corporations. *Conclusions on Accounting and Reporting by Transnational Corporations*. New York: United Nations, 1988.

_____. *Information Disclosure Relating to Environmental Measures*. New York: United Nations, 1990.

Walton, P., ed. *Country Studies in International Accounting—Europe*. Cheltenham, U.K.: Edward Elger Publishing, 1996.

Zeff, Stephen A., and Bala G. Dharan. *Readings and Notes on Financial Accounting*. New York: McGraw-Hill, Inc., 1994.

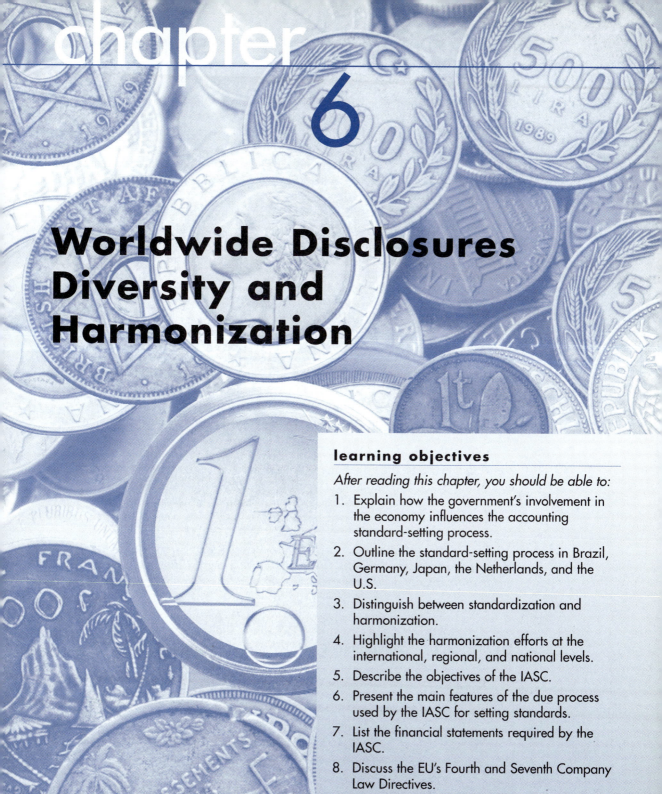

chapter

6

Worldwide Disclosures Diversity and Harmonization

learning objectives

After reading this chapter, you should be able to:

1. Explain how the government's involvement in the economy influences the accounting standard-setting process.

2. Outline the standard-setting process in Brazil, Germany, Japan, the Netherlands, and the U.S.

3. Distinguish between standardization and harmonization.

4. Highlight the harmonization efforts at the international, regional, and national levels.

5. Describe the objectives of the IASC.

6. Present the main features of the due process used by the IASC for setting standards.

7. List the financial statements required by the IASC.

8. Discuss the EU's Fourth and Seventh Company Law Directives.

9. Describe the EMU and the euro.

Though accounting is called the language of business, its meaning varies from country to country. Accounting standards reflect its role in a nation's culture, especially its economy. Whereas a public accountant in Mexico City considers the stockholders the primary users of financial statements, an accountant in Frankfurt gears financial statements toward tax authorities. How are accounting standards developed in different countries? What are the implications of different accounting standards? What efforts are being made to achieve harmonization? These are some of the topics discussed in this chapter.

The global economy is making nations increasingly interdependent. Businesses that aspire to profit from international trade and investments must understand the impact of varying accounting standards on financial statements. Today's international accountants have the expertise for assisting businesses in becoming active participants in the global economy.

Disclosure Diversity

As discussed in Chapter 4, accounting standards are heavily influenced by a nation's culture. An important cultural factor is the degree of government involvement in the economy. All economies lie somewhere between the two extremes of total state control and a completely free-market system as illustrated in Figure 6.1.

In countries with relatively few publicly owned enterprises and mostly state-controlled markets, the government usually takes a decisive role in promulgating accounting standards. In contrast, in the countries with large corporations that have widely dispersed ownership, the responsibility for accounting standard setting is often assumed by the profession itself. Chapter 5 presented some examples of the resulting diversity.

Since different approaches to standard setting arise from different perceptions of what constitutes useful financial information, the diversity of approaches yields dramatically different accounting standards worldwide.

figure 6.1   Government Involvement in Economy

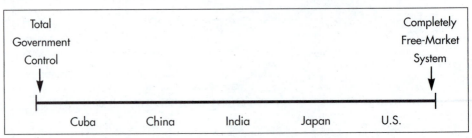

The Balance Sheet Emphasis Versus the Income Statement Emphasis

Accounting standards tend to be oriented toward users of financial reports. From among all the users, capital providers exercise the greatest influence over their orientation. If banks are the main capital providers, then standards typically emphasize the balance sheet. Bank authorities focus on the information that helps them evaluate the short-term and long-term liquidity position of a borrower. An entity's financial position helps the lending bank to assess its ability to pay back its debts.

In contrast, where stockholders are the main source of funds, a corporation's earnings are perceived as an important predictor of its future success. Therefore, the income statement receives greater attention from the standard setters. Any change in accounting principles affecting reported income often generates tremendous interest and sometimes great controversy. Some years ago, the U.S. Financial Accounting Standards Board (FASB) attempted to promulgate a financial accounting standard that would have required companies to show employee stock options as an expense in the income statement. The reaction from large, powerful corporations against the proposed standard was so strong that, according to many observers, the FASB was left with little choice but to drop the idea.

Accounting Standard Setting and Financial Reporting in Selected Countries

In this section we will take a close look at the accounting standard-setting process and financial reporting practices of five countries: Brazil, Germany, Japan, the Netherlands, and the United States. We will review the accounting and reporting differences among the five countries and the cultural influences contributing to those differences. As we noted in Chapter 4, cultural values of a country and its accounting system influence each other. The natural outcome is the worldwide diversity of accounting and reporting differences. In Chapter 5, through comparative analyses, we obtained an overview of the diversity among many countries in the areas selected. In this section, a closer look at each of the five countries will enhance our appreciation of the relationship between accounting and its environments.

Brazil

Brazil is a Latin country. The government, Corporation Law, and tax regulations have a strong influence on accounting and financial reporting practices. Though the government has adopted liberal trade policies and privatization of some government-controlled industries in recent years, Brazilian stock markets are relatively small when compared with those of industrialized countries of Western Europe, North America, and the Asia-Pacific region. Financial statements disclosures in Brazil are oriented mostly toward creditors, who are the major source of funds, and tax authorities. The disclosures geared toward equity investors are relatively minor.

Standard Setting

The Corporation Law of 1976, amended in 1997, is the primary source of accounting principles and practices applicable to Brazilian corporations. The Brazilian Institute of Accountants, *Instituto Brasileiro de Contadores—IBRACON*, and the Federal Council of Accounting, Conselho Federal de Contabilidade, are accounting professional organizations. They also provide guidance on accounting principles, preparation of financial statements, and auditing standards. The Securities Exchange Commission, *Commissao de Valores Mobiliarios—CVM*, is responsible for accounting standards for the companies that are publicly traded. If IBRACON standards are approved by the CVM, they are binding on all publicly traded companies.

Financial Statements

Comparative financial statements must be prepared annually. They include:

- Balance sheet.
- Income statement.
- Statement of changes in stockholders' equity.
- Statement of changes in financial position.
- Notes to the financial statements.

Financial statements are accompanied by a report by the board of directors. The basis for measurement is historical cost. Financial statements are prepared on the accrual basis. The principles of conservatism, materiality, and consistency are considered important in the preparation of financial statements.

Revaluation of Assets

Corporation Law permits the upward revaluation of assets, but tax regulations permit the revaluation of long-term assets only. In practice only property, plant, and equipment are revalued for both accounting and tax purposes.

Finance Leases

Finance leases are not capitalized in practice, even though their capitalization is allowed.

Capitalization of Interest

Normally all interest costs must be expensed. An exception exists for enterprises at the developmental stage.

Inventory Valuation

Inventories are valued at the lower of cost or market. Market value is considered to be the lower of replacement cost and net realizable value. The first-in, first-out

(FIFO) and average cost are commonly used methods for determining inventory cost. The last-in, first-out (LIFO) method is not commonly used since it is unacceptable for tax purposes.

Research and Development Costs

Research and development costs that are expected to benefit future years may be capitalized and amortized over their useful life. For tax purposes, the minimum amortization period is five years.

Segment Reporting

Segment reporting is not required.

Consolidation

Normally the purchase method is required. The pooling of interests method is allowed only under rare circumstances.

Netherlands

Standard Setting

Title 9 of the Civil Code, updated in 1997, sets the accounting and financial reporting requirements. Title 9 also provides flexibility to comply with the European Union's Fourth Company Law Directive and Seventh Company Law Directive dealing with financial statement contents and consolidation, respectively.

Financial Statements

Required financial statements are:

- Balance sheet.
- Income statement.
- Notes to the financial statements.

The annual report includes a report by the supervisory board. Civil Code requires an accrual basis. The required concepts include matching, going concern, and prudence concepts. The historical cost basis is allowed for valuation purposes. However, for inventories, tangible, financial, and fixed assets, current value is also allowed. Financial reporting and tax reporting are independent of each other.

Revaluation of Assets

The law permits the upward revaluation of assets using a current cost convention with the exception of intangible assets. Depreciation expense for tax purposes is on an historical-cost basis only. For financial reporting, depreciation can be on a current value basis.

Finance Leases

The lessee holding assets on a finance lease is required to capitalize such assets, and the related lease commitment is included in liabilities.

Capitalization of Interest

Interest costs on the borrowings that are directly attributable to manufacturing or construction of assets can be capitalized as part of the total cost of the asset during the manufacturing or construction period.

Inventory Valuation

Inventories are valued at the lower of cost or net realizable value. The cost in this context is actual historical cost or current cost. To arrive at cost, weighted average, FIFO, and LIFO are commonly used methods.

Research and Development Costs

Costs for research and development are commonly written off as an expense during the period when incurred in practice. They may, however, be capitalized. If capitalized, they should be disclosed separately as an intangible asset.

Segment Reporting

Segment disclosures are required if sales of a business or a geographical segment exceed 10 percent of the total net sales.

Consolidation

Title 9 requires that all group companies and the parent company should be consolidated. Group companies are defined as subsidiaries plus other entities. The other entities include partnerships and entities with 50 percent or less ownership, provided they are controlled. Subsidiaries not operated by the parent company and economically independent are excluded from consolidation. Normally, only the purchase method is allowed for consolidation. The pooling of interests method is allowed only if neither entity can be identified as the acquirer. As a result, the pooling of interests method is not used in practice.

Germany

Standard Setting

The Commercial Code, as amended in 1994, is the primary source of standards for financial reporting. The strongest influence on generally accepted accounting principles in Germany is the German Stock Corporation Law of 1965, as amended in 1993, and the Limited Liability Companies Law of 1892, which contain accounting standards specific to those entities. Generally, tax benefits can be claimed only if the items are treated in the same manner for financial reporting and tax reporting. Consequently, German companies tend to understate assets and overstate liability, to the extent possible, for minimizing their tax liability.

Financial Statements

Companies are required to present:

- Balance sheet.
- Income statement.

- Statement of cash flows.
- Notes to the financial statements.

Relatively very few companies are listed on stock exchanges. Debt financing is considered preferable to equity financing due to tax regulations. The Commercial Code requires corporations to supplement financial statements with a management report. Banks are the major source of business financing.

Basic accounting concepts include going concern, matching, the historical-cost basis, and the accrual basis. In addition, the prudence concept must also be followed. The prudence concept provides for the recognition of all anticipated risks and losses up to the balance sheet date. Recognition of unrealized profits is prohibited. Netting of assets against liabilities or income against expenses is not allowed. Accounting principles must be applied consistently across periods.

Revaluation of Assets
The historical-cost basis is strictly followed. The Commercial Code does not permit the revaluation of an individual asset above its historical acquisition cost.

Finance Leases
Finance leases are required to be capitalized by the lessor and the lessee.

Capitalization of Interest
The interest cost on a loan used to finance the production of an asset may be capitalized and included in its costs. The interest to be capitalized in this manner is limited to the amount incurred during the production period. In case of interest capitalization, disclosure is required in the notes to the financial statements.

Inventory Valuation
Inventories are valued at the lower of cost or market. For cost determination, specific identification, average cost, FIFO, and LIFO inventory methods are acceptable. For the application of the lower of cost or market concept to inventories, market value can be either replacement cost or net realizable value. When both replacement cost and net realizable value are available, the lower of the two is considered to be market value. If replacement cost information is not available, then net realizable value is considered market value. Since the tax laws allow the deduction of normal profit to arrive at the net realizable value amount, the same practice is followed for financial reporting. The net realizable value, as a result, often means net realizable value minus normal profit.

Research and Development Costs
Expenditures related to research and development must be expensed as incurred.

Segment Reporting
The Commercial Code requires disclosures of sales by industry and by geographically defined markets in the notes to the financial statements.

Consolidation

A company is required to prepare consolidated financial statements and a group management report. The entities included in the consolidated financial statements are subsidiaries as well as the companies that are under control even though a majority of the voting shares are not owned. Consolidated statements are generally prepared according to the purchase method. The pooling of interests method is allowed only in certain circumstances.

Japan

Standard Setting

The primary source of standards for financial reporting is the Commercial Code of Japan. In addition, the Income Tax Law and the Securities and Exchange Law are important influences on financial reporting practices of major Japanese companies. The Income Tax Law is very influential because financial reporting and taxation reporting in Japan are the same. In essence, the Income Tax Law prescribes what revenues and expenses can be recognized. Interestingly, the Commercial Code has creditor (balance sheet) orientation, while the Securities and Exchange Law has investor (income statement) orientation.

Financial Statements

The Commercial Code requires the preparation of four financial statements:

- Balance sheet.
- Income statement.
- Notes to the financial statements.
- Business report.
- Proposal for retained earnings appropriations.

The Securities and Exchange Law also requires cash flow statements for publicly traded companies.

The objective of financial statements in Japan is to protect the interest of both the creditors and the investors. Thus, disclosures dealing with dividend availability, creditworthiness, and earnings per share are of paramount importance. The accrual basis of accounting is employed.

The **business report** covers many of the matters typically found in the Management Discussion and Analysis part of companies' annual reports in North America. An example of the topics include a description of the business; financial summary data for the year and the past three years; and disclosures relating to capital, employees, names of major shareholders, names of major creditors, and names of directors and statutory auditors. It also includes significant events after the balance sheet date.

The **proposal for appropriation of retained earnings** is prepared for approval at the stockholders' meeting for dividend payments and bonus payments to members of the board of directors and statutory auditors.

Revaluation of Assets
Revaluation of assets is not permitted.

Finance Leases
Tax regulations stipulate conditions under which a lease can be capitalized. Financial statements follow the tax treatment for leases. Capitalization of leases is rare in practice.

Capitalization of Interest
A corporation has the option to capitalize interest costs during the construction period for the assets constructed for its own use.

Inventory Valuation
The tax regulation allows a corporation to value inventory at the lower of cost or market value. Market value is defined as the replacement cost. The cost determination may be made by using specific identification, FIFO, LIFO, average, most recent purchase, or retail inventory methods. A change in inventory method can be made only after obtaining approval from the tax office. The method of inventory valuation adopted for tax purposes must be used for financial reporting purposes.

Research and Development Costs
Expenditures for research and development are expensed as incurred.

Segment Reporting
Listed companies that file consolidated financial statements must provide segment information on their industry segments and geographic segments. The disclosures required are sales and operating profit by segment. The criterion for an industry segment is that its sales or its operating profit exceeds 10 percent of total sales or 10 percent of total operating profit. The criterion for a geographic segment is that its sales exceed 20 percent of total sales.

Consolidation
Only listed companies are required to prepare consolidated financial statements. The parent company must own, directly or indirectly, majority ownership in the other entities for consolidation purposes. Consolidated financial statements are prepared according to the purchase method. The pooling of interests method is allowed but rarely used.

United States

Standard Setting
The U.S. Congress has given the Securities and Exchange Commission (SEC) responsibility for establishing generally accepted accounting principles (GAAP) for companies whose stock is publicly traded. The SEC has, in turn, largely delegated this responsibility to the accounting profession.

1. The Financial Accounting Standards Board (FASB)—**http://www.fasb.org**—is the main body responsible for promulgating accounting standards in the U.S. Established in 1973, the FASB is composed of seven members. The Financial Accounting Foundation oversees the FASB's operations and provides its funding. The FASB follows due process procedures in establishing accounting principles.

   Pronouncements of the FASB include:

   • *Statements of Financial Accounting Concepts*. These are fundamental concepts on which accounting and reporting standards are based.

   • *Statements of Financial Accounting Standards*. These are the major pronouncements issued by the FASB, and are the primary basis for GAAP.

2. The Governmental Accounting Standards Board (GASB) was created in 1984. GASB's responsibility is to establish accounting principles for municipal and state government bodies, hospitals, universities, and other not-for-profit entities. The Financial Accounting Foundation oversees the operations and financing of the GASB.

3. The American Institute of Certified Public Accountants (AICPA) is an organization of certified public accountants. It is influential in the development of accounting principles and practices. The AICPA has formed the Accounting Standards Executive Committee (AcSEC) which issues *Statements of Position* on accounting issues not covered by the FASB.

Financial Statements

The required set of financial statements consists of:

• Balance sheet.
• Statement of comprehensive income.
• Statement of cash flows.
• Statement of changes in stockholders' equity.
• Notes to the statements.

The concepts used in financial statements include going concern, matching, consistency in the application of accounting principles across periods, and accrual basis.

Revaluation of Assets

The historical-cost basis is used for the valuation of most assets. Certain types of investments and all derivatives are required to be revalued at their fair (market) value.

Finance Leases

Finance leases are required to be capitalized.

Capitalization of Interest

Interest costs must be capitalized for self-constructed property or equipment. The amount to be capitalized is the interest costs that could have been avoided if construction costs for the asset had not been incurred.

Inventory Valuation

The application of the lower of cost or market principle is required. Cost may be determined by using FIFO, LIFO, average cost, and specific identification. If LIFO is used for taxation, it must also be used for financial reporting. In the application of lower of cost or market, market is the middle amount from among replacement cost, net realizable value, and net realizable value minus normal profit.

Research and Development Costs

Research and development costs are expensed immediately.

Segment Information

Segment reporting is required of all companies whose securities are publicly traded. A segment is reportable if it meets any one of the following three criteria:

- *Revenue.* A segment's total revenue is 10 percent or more of the total revenue of the company.
- *Profit or loss.* The operating profit is greater than 10 percent of the total operating profit of all segments that reported operating profits (or greater than 10 percent of the total operating loss of all segments that reported operating losses).
- *Assets.* The assets are 10 percent or more of the combined assets of all operating segments.

The following information is required to be disclosed for a reportable segment:

- Operating profit or loss.
- Specified income statement items such as operating revenues, depreciation, and noncash expenses.
- Total assets.
- Total capital expenditures.
- Reconciliation of the sum of segment totals to the company total for each of the following three items:
  1. Revenues.
  2. Operating profit.
  3. Assets.

The company is required to disclose how reportable segments are identified. The criteria for the identification of segments for external reports should be the same as those used by the management to distinguish business segments for internal reporting purposes.

Consolidation

Consolidated financial statements are required when a parent has a controlling interest in the voting stock of other entities. Exceptions to the requirement for consolidated statements occur when control is temporary or when restrictions cast doubt on the parent's ability to control a subsidiary, e.g., the subsidiary is in bankruptcy. Currently, either the purchase method or the pooling of interests method is required to be used based on the application of the criteria in a given business combination situation. The FASB has published a proposed statement of financial accounting standards. If adopted, only the purchase method will be acceptable.

Exhibits 6.1, 6.2, and 6.3 summarize the elements of financial statements, the segment disclosure requirements, and the basic accounting concepts and conventions, respectively, for the five countries we have discussed previously.

Standardization Versus Harmonization

The efficient flow of goods, capital, and resources across national boundaries and the location of financial and business operations in more than one country re-

exhibit 6.1   Elements of Financial Statements

Country	Balance Sheet	Income Statement	Statement of Funds/Cash Flow
Brazil	R	R	R
Germany	R	R	O
Japan	R	R	P
Netherlands	R	R	O
United States	R	R	R

R = Required
P = Required for publicly traded companies
O = Optional

exhibit 6.2   Basic Accounting Concepts and Conventions

Country	Cost Basis	Accrual Basis	Going Concern	Legal Form vs. Substance
Brazil	HP, HR	Required	Required	Legal
Germany	HC	Required	Required	Legal
Japan	HC	Required	Required	Legal
Netherlands	CC, HC, HR	Required	Required	Substance
United States	MA	Required	Required	Substance

CC = Current cost
HC = Historical cost
HP = Historical cost with price-level adjustments
HR = Historical cost with revaluation option
MA = Mixed attributes (a blend of historical cost and current cost)

exhibit 6.3   **Segment Disclosure Requirements**

Country	Required Segment Disclosures	
	Geographical	Industrial
Brazil	O	O
Germany	R	R
Japan	R	R
Netherlands	R	R
United States	I	I

R = Required
O = Optional
I = Segments identified by using the same criteria that were used for internal reporting purposes

quire that accounting standards not be country-specific. Many factors, e.g., foreign currencies, different inflation rates, and the need for consolidated financial statements are promoting internationalization of accounting standards.

One of the early calls to internationalize accounting standards came from a prominent European executive, the president of Royal Dutch Petroleum Company, in 1979:

> Financial information is a form of a language. And if the language of financial information is to be put to use, so that investment and credit decisions can more readily be taken, it should not only be intelligible, it should also be comparable. International differences in accounting standards should be narrowed. Although this may seem to be an impossible chasm, it can be achieved—if enough countries are willing.[1]

Different accounting treatment of the same type of transactions and events makes it difficult to analyze and compare financial statements. This explains why there is growing support for international accounting standards.

> An international set of accounting standards would allow a more level playing field because income statements and balance sheet ratios would become more consistent between competing companies.[2]

According to Wyatt, "The linkage of worldwide capital markets is one of the driving forces behind the movement toward a single set of accounting rules."[3]

---

1 D. De Bryjne. "Global Standards: A Tower of Babel?" *Financial Executive*, February 1980, pp. 30–39.

2 Nancy Anderson. "The Globalization of GAAP." *Management Accounting*, August 1993, pp. 52–54.

3 Arthur R. Wyatt and Joseph F. Yospe. "Wake-up Call to American Business: International Accounting Standards Are on the Way." *Journal of Accountancy*, July 1993, pp. 80–85.

Comparability of accounting information is vital to international trade and investment. The question is how to achieve comparability. **Standardization** means requiring the same accounting standards worldwide. Standardization would ensure full comparability.

Many, however, doubt the feasibility of complete standardization of accounting rules. Specific needs linked with national cultural needs make national accounting standards necessary. As a solution, the concept of *harmonization* has gained widespread popularity. **Harmonization** means that the differences among national accounting standards should be kept to the minimum. Harmonization accommodates the existence of alternative accounting rules or practices in different countries as long as they are *in harmony* with each other and can be reconciled.

The remainder of this chapter addresses the efforts to harmonize accounting standards among nations. Harmonization efforts will be discussed at the regional and international levels, along with recent developments.

International Level Efforts

To be successful, efforts to harmonize accounting standards need an international base to ensure wide acceptance and implementation. Such efforts would require taking into consideration the views of national standard-setting bodies. Given the diversity existing among different national standards, the task of harmonization is obviously challenging.

International harmonization efforts are divided between bodies that represent governments and bodies that represent the accounting profession or other interested groups. In this section, we discuss the harmonization efforts of the following:

- The International Accounting Standards Committee (IASC)—representing the accounting profession.
- The Organization for Economic Cooperation and Development (OECD)—representing governments of member nations.
- Other international efforts.

There is another active international group representing the accounting profession—the International Federation of Accountants (IFAC)—that has actively encouraged harmonization for many years. The IFAC however, focuses its attention on establishing international auditing standards and dealing with issues in education, ethics, and management accounting. The work of the IFAC will be discussed in Chapter 11.

International Accounting Standards Committee

The IASC (**http://www.iasc.org.uk/**) is the most active and prominent international body with the responsibility to promulgate international accounting

standards. These standards are meant to apply to all business environments regardless of the size or type of business activity. The IASC is the only setter of international accounting standards with a clearly stated due process to propose, study, and ultimately issue such standards.

The IASC was established in 1973 as a result of an agreement between the professional accounting organizations of 10 countries.[4] The IASC membership consists of 138 professional accounting organizations from 112 countries. The member organizations include 2 million accountants worldwide.

The stated objectives of the IASC are:

- To formulate and publish accounting standards for use in the presentation of financial statements and to promote their worldwide acceptance.

- To work for the improvement and harmonization of accounting standards and procedures relating to the presentation of financial statements.

IASC activities are funded by contributions from member professional accounting organizations, multinational companies, financial institutions, accounting firms, other organizations, and the sale of IASC publications. There is no funding from governments or intergovernmental organizations.

The IASC is currently being restructured. The restructured committee will have 14 members, 12 of which will be full time. Moreover, a Board of Trustees will have the governance, fundraising, and public awareness responsibilities for the restructured IASC. The restructured IASC will be supported by a technical director and technical staff.

IASC Consultative Group

To expand the representation of organizations interested in financial reporting, the IASC has established an international consultative group. The group includes representatives of users and preparers of financial statements, standard-setting bodies, and observers from intergovernmental organizations. This group meets regularly with the Board to discuss policies, principles, and issues relevant to IASC work. The following are some of the member organizations of the consultative group:

- International Association of Financial Executives Institutes
- International Chamber of Commerce (ICC)
- International Organization of Securities Commission (IOSCO)
- International Banking Association
- The World Bank

---

4 These charter organizations were from Australia, Canada, France, Germany, Ireland, Japan, Mexico, the Netherlands, the U.K., and the U.S.

- U.S. Financial Accounting Standards Board (FASB) (observer)
- European Commission (observer)
- Organisation for Economic Co-operation and Development (observer)

The IASC steering committees include representatives from the consultative group.

Development of International Accounting Standards

Any member of the IASC or any other interested party may submit suggestions for new accounting standard topics. If accepted by the Board, that topic is put on the agenda for review.

The IASC has established the following procedures, or due process, to develop international standards.

- After consideration of the issues involved, a *point outline* is prepared.
- A *draft statement of principles* is prepared after the Board comments on the point outline.
- A *final statement of principles* is prepared after review of the comments on the draft statement.
- After Board approval, the final statement of principles serves as the basis for the preparation of an *exposure draft*.
- A *draft international accounting standard* is prepared after review of the comments on the exposure draft by interested parties.
- The draft international accounting standard is reviewed by the Board and is finally published as an *international accounting standard* (IAS), after any revisions.

Figure 6.2 summarizes the previous process and its major outcomes.

Current and Future IASC Projects

The IASC Board is attempting to gain greater support from national and international preparers and users of financial statements. It has already gained support from the International Organization of Securities Commissions. Many countries either adopt *IASs* as national standards or use them as the basis for developing national requirements. In developing countries, the tendency is to adopt or adapt *IASs*. It is especially true of the countries that are or have been members of the British Commonwealth.[5] In addition, many European, London, and other, e.g., Hong Kong, stock exchanges allow foreign issuers to comply with their listing requirements by presenting financial statements prepared using *IASs*.

---

5 S.E.C. Purvis, H. Gernon, and M.A. Diamond. "The IASC and its Comparability Project: Prerequisites for Success." *Accounting Horizons*, June 1991, pp. 28–29.

figure 6.2   **Development of IASC International Accounting Standards**

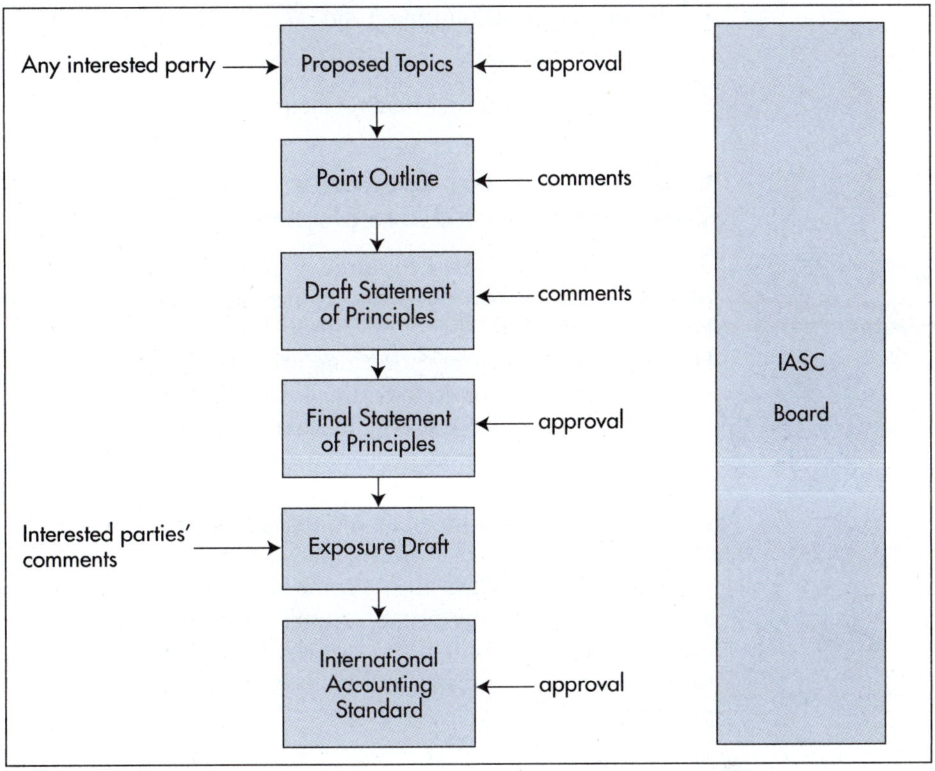

Increased competition in international capital markets may force other countries to follow the lead of these two stock exchanges.

IAS 1: Presentation of Financial Statements

IAS 1 deals with the disclosure of all significant accounting policies used in the preparation of financial statements.[6] It provides guidance on going concern, assumption, consistency, accrual, and materiality. Accounting policies should lead to relevant and reliable information. Financial statements prepared in accordance with *IAS 1* should include:

- Balance sheet.
- Income statement.

6 *IAS 1*. "Presentation of Financial Statements" (London: International Accounting Standards Committee, 1997).

- Statement of changes in equity.
- Cash flow statement.
- Summary of accounting policies.
- Explanatory notes.

IAS 1 does not require a management report.

Organisation for Economic Co-operation and Development

The Organisation for Economic Co-operation and Development (OECD)—**http://www.oecd.org**—was formed in 1961 and has 30 government members. Though the OECD has limited international membership, the world's largest multinational corporations are based in OECD member countries. The OECD countries produce two-thirds of the world's economic output.

The objectives of the OECD are to enhance economic growth and development in member nations, to promote international trade among members, and to serve as an information clearinghouse for its members. The organization serves as a forum for member countries to share vital economic information, discuss issues of mutual concern, and attempt to provide solutions to common problems. The OECD's efforts to harmonize international accounting standards are only a part of the organization's focus on economic growth and development. A valuable contribution of the OECD is its surveys of accounting practices in member countries and its assessment of diversity or conformity of such practices.

Other International Efforts

Many other international organizations and entities are also involved in the process of harmonizing accounting standards. Among these are:

- *International Organization of Securities Commissions* (IOSCO). IOSCO (**http://www2.iosco.org**) is interested in listing foreign stocks on national stock exchanges. Its endorsement of the efforts to harmonize accounting and auditing standards carries much weight in global capital markets. In July 1995, the IOSCO and the IASC reached an agreement to work together to achieve harmonization of accounting standards. The IASC revised its standards to the satisfaction of the IOSCO. Companies in those IOSCO member countries that adopt the *IASs* will be able to list their securities on the world's capital markets.

- *G4+1*. The G4+1 originally included the accounting standard-setting organizations from four countries: Australia, Canada, the U.K., and the U.S. The International Accounting Standards Committee was invited to participate in their discussions. This is how it came to be known as the Group of four plus one, commonly referred to as G4+1. Though New Zealand joined the Group later, it is still called G4+1. G4+1 is perhaps one of the most influential groups working toward harmonization of accounting standards. The five countries in the Group have been supportive of the IASC efforts in the past, but more recently urged the IASC to work in cooperation with national standard setters.

Regional Efforts

This section presents the leading regional efforts to harmonize accounting standards and covers the:

- European Union.
- North American Free Trade Agreement.
- Other regional efforts.

Their impact on the standardization of major laws and regulations is expected to increase as business activities among countries within various regions increase.

European Union

http://

The European Community became the European Union (EU) on January 1, 1994 (**http://www.europa.eu.int**). It is a trading bloc of 15 nations. EU countries felt that business activities should not be confined to their national borders. Stakeholders would benefit from the harmonization of laws and regulations governing the free flow of goods, services, capital, and resources within the member countries. This process involved:

- The elimination of national custom duties and other barriers to the free movement of goods and services.
- The standardization of tariffs and trade restrictions with non-member nations.
- The unification of economic policies by creating a uniform economic environment in the EU. This includes the harmonization of fiscal, monetary, tax, and corporate laws. *It also includes the harmonization of accounting standards.*

Development of EU Standards

The European Union functions through the activities of the European Commission. The Commission establishes the standardization and harmonization of corporate and accounting rules through the issuance of Directives and Regulations. *EU Directives must be incorporated into the laws of member nations. Regulations are laws applicable to all members without the need for national legislation by the member countries.* Exhibit 6.4 lists selected EU Directives and Regulations relative to EU accounting standards and corporate law. The Fourth and Seventh Directives deal exclusively with accounting issues and standards, and are discussed in detail in this chapter.

exhibit 6.4   **EU Directives and Regulations Relevant to Corporate Accounting**

Directives		
Directive	**Topic**	**Adoption Date**
First	Publication of accounts	1968
Second	Separation of private from public companies, minimum capital, limitation on distribution	1976
Fourth	Annual accounts format and rules and presentation rules	1978
Seventh	Consolidated accounts, including associated companies	1983
Eighth	Qualification and work of auditors	1984
Eleventh	Branch disclosures	1989

Regulation			
Item	**Topic**	**Draft Date**	**Adoption Date**
European Economic Interests Grouping	Business form for multinational joint ventures	1973, 1978	1985

The process of setting EU Directives is somewhat similar to the process used by other standard-setting bodies such as the International Accounting Standards Committee presented earlier in this chapter. *Adoption of a proposed directive or regulation requires a unanimous vote of the European Union Council of Ministers.* As stated earlier, member nations must then incorporate the Directive into their laws and regulations.

The EU is working with other standard-setting bodies to coordinate its harmonization efforts, and the European Commission is a member of the IASC consultative group. The Accounting Advisory Forum, composed of preparers and users of financial information, serve as a consultative group to the EU Commission on its standard harmonization efforts.

The Fourth Company Law Directive

The EU Fourth Directive contains comprehensive accounting rules. It covers financial statements, their contents, methods of presentation, valuation methods, and disclosure of information. The Directive was adopted in 1978 and implemented in national accounting regulations by EU members in 1991. EU member countries have some flexibility in implementing and incorporating the Directive in their national accounting regulations. As such, the Directive serves as a model for all member nations. Member countries may require more information than what is required under the Directive. They may require different reporting disclosures and measurement rules based on size or other corporate characteristics. Thus, implementation of the Directive may differ among member countries.

The Directive provides a broadly defined structure of financial information classification and presentation. It requires a balance sheet, an income statement, and notes to financial statements. Financial statements are to present a "true and fair view" (discussed in a later section) of the company's results of operations and its financial position.

The Directive allows either a horizontal or vertical presentation of the balance sheet and income statement. The horizontal balance sheet is similar to the format used in the U.S. However, items are presented in reverse order of liquidity. Fixed assets are listed, and the category includes intangible assets, tangible assets, and long-term investments ahead of current assets. The vertical format displays two grand totals: (1) Total assets less current liabilities and (2) Long-term liabilities, and capital and reserves. Exhibits 6.5 and 6.6 show abbreviated horizontal and vertical balance sheet formats, respectively. Appendix 6C shows detailed contents of the horizontal balance sheet.

The income statement offers choices among horizontal or vertical formats as well as classification of expenses by function or nature. The horizontal format shows turnover (sales revenue) added to all other sources of income on the left side, while ordinary and extraordinary charges (expenses) are presented on the right side of the statement. The vertical format shows the profit or loss on ordinary activities after subtracting all charges (expenses) from turnover. Extraordinary profit or loss is shown after offsetting extraordinary charges against extraordinary income. The statement concludes with profit or loss for the fiscal year. Exhibits 6.7 and 6.8 (pages 211 and 212) show abbreviated horizontal and

exhibit 6.5   **EU Fourth Directive Horizontal Balance Sheet**

XYZ Company
Balance Sheet
December 31, 20XX

Stockholders' Equity and Liabilities	Assets
Capital and reserves called:	Called-up share capital not paid
Called-up share capital	[stock subscriptions receivable]
Share premium account	Fixed assets:
Revaluation reserve	Intangible assets
Other reserves	Tangible assets
Profit and loss account (retained earnings)	Investments [long-term]
Provisions for liabilities and charges	Current assets:
	Stocks [inventories]
Creditors [payables]	Debtors [receivables]
	Investments [short-term]
	Cash
Accruals and deferred income	Prepayments and accrued income
Total stockholders' equity and liabilities	Total assets

exhibit 6.6   **EU Fourth Directive Vertical Balance Sheet**

XYZ Company
Balance Sheet
December 31, 20XX

Called-up share capital not paid (Stock subscriptions receivable)

Fixed assets:
   Intangible assets
   Tangible assets
   Investments (long-term)

A. Current assets:
   Stocks (inventories)
   Debtors (receivables)
   Investments (short-term)
   Cash

B. Prepayments and accrued income

C. Creditors due within one year (current liabilities)
   Net current assets (liabilities) A + B − C

Total assets less current liabilities

Creditors due after more than one year
Provisions for liabilities and charges
Accruals and deferred income
Capital and reserves
Long-term liabilities and stockholders' equity

vertical income statement formats, respectively. Appendix 6C shows the detailed horizontal and vertical format of the income statement. As stated earlier, *the Fourth Directive allows four income statement formats: horizontal or vertical, and natural or functional classification of expenses.*

True and Fair View

An important feature of the Fourth Directive is the adoption of the *true and fair view* concept. It is a British concept of what financial statements ought to convey. The concept was not widely applied in continental Europe prior to its inclusion in the Fourth Directive. The implementation of the true and fair view concept means that companies may be required to disclose additional or different information. Each country, based on its own circumstances, determines how its corporations should comply with the true and fair view concept.

exhibit 6.7   **EU Fourth Directive Horizontal Profit and Loss Account**

XYZ Company
Income Statement
For 20XX

Charges

  Cost of sales

  Distribution costs

  Administrative expenses

  Investment write-off

  Interest payable and similar charges

  Tax on profit or loss on ordinary activities

Profit or loss on ordinary activities

Extraordinary charges

Tax on extraordinary profit or loss

Other taxes not shown under above items

Profit or loss for the financial year

Income

  Turnover (sales)

  Other operating income

  Income from shares in group companies

  Income from other fixed asset investments

  Other interest receivable and similar income

Profit or loss on ordinary activities

  Extraordinary income

Profit or loss for the financial year

The Seventh Company Law Directive

The Seventh Directive was adopted by the EU commission in 1983. The Directive addresses consolidated financial statement issues. Member nations are given many choices as to how to incorporate its provisions into their company laws.

The key element of this Directive is the definition of the "group" for which consolidation is required. The German view focuses on effective management control and share ownership. The British view focuses on share ownership and legal control. The Seventh Directive adopted the British view, but also allows other control criteria to be applied on an optional basis by member countries. Legal control exists when the parent company has:

- A majority of voting rights or control over a majority of voting rights based on an agreement with other shareholders.

- A control contract agreement giving it the right of dominant influence over another entity.

- The right to appoint the majority of the entity's board of directors.

The Directive provides these guidelines for the preparation of consolidated accounts (financial statements):[7]

---

7 Section 2, Article 16.

exhibit 6.8   **EU Fourth Directive Vertical Profit and Loss Account**

XYZ Company **Income Statement** **For 20XX**
Turnover (sales)
Cost of sales
Gross profit or loss
Distribution cost
Administrative expenses
Other operating income
Income from shares in group companies
Income from shares in related companies
Income from other fixed asset investments
Other interest receivable and similar income
Investment write-off
Interest payable and similar charges
Tax on profit or loss on ordinary activities
Profit or loss on ordinary activities
Extraordinary income
Extraordinary charges
Tax on extraordinary profit or loss
Other taxes not shown under above items
Profit or loss for the financial year

- Consolidated accounts include the consolidated balance sheet, the consolidated profit and loss account (income statement), and the notes on the accounts (financial statements).

- Clear preparation of the consolidated accounts should be in accordance with the Directive.

- Additional information is required if the application of the Directive is not sufficient to give a true and fair view.

- If the application of specified provisions, in exceptional cases, is incompatible with the true and fair view, departure from that provision is allowed in order to give a true and fair view.

- Member countries may require or permit other information disclosures in the consolidated accounts, in addition to required disclosure under this Directive.

The Seventh Directive is a major development toward the harmonization of accounting practices in the EU countries. Previously, many European countries did not have any legal requirement for consolidated statements. Prior to the Directive, Germany required the consolidation of domestic subsidiaries only. France did not have any requirement for consolidated statements. The Seventh Directive requires worldwide consolidation regardless of where the parent company is located. It also requires that assets purchased through acquisition be measured at fair value. The segment disclosure requirement includes sales by line of business and geographical location.

European Monetary Union

On January 1, 1999, the European Union launched a new currency, the euro. Currently, 12 EU member countries are in the European Monetary Union (EMU): Austria, Belgium, Finland, France, Germany, Greece, Ireland, Italy, Luxembourg, the Netherlands, Portugal, and Spain. The EMU countries are collectively referred to as Euroland or Eurozone. The euro is essentially a virtual currency until December 31, 2001. During this transition phase, the EMU countries continue with their national currencies. However, their respective values are based on the euro. For example, one euro equals approximately 40.34 Belgian francs and 1.96 deutsche marks (these values fluctuate). During the transition phase, the euro is being used for non-cash transactions.[8] The euro will be available in real form on January 1, 2002, when euro coins and bank notes will be introduced. At that time national currencies of Euroland will be withdrawn from circulation. Effective June 30, 2002, the national currencies of EMU countries will cease to be legal tender for any transactions. All of them will have the euro as common currency.

A common currency among the EMU countries means cheaper transaction costs and no foreign exchange transaction risk when they deal among themselves. This should further facilitate commerce among the Eurozone countries.

North American Free Trade Agreement—and Beyond

The previous section presented the EU efforts to harmonize accounting standards in member states. The North American Free Trade Agreement (NAFTA) was signed in 1992 among Canada, Mexico, and the U.S. to create a common market. Will NAFTA follow the footsteps of the EU and achieve the same progress to unify the economies of its member countries? It is too early to tell. However, NAFTA has the potential to achieve what the EU countries were able to achieve.

Many economic, political, social, and historical factors have contributed to increased trade and economic cooperation among the three nations. The initial proposal to negotiate a free trade agreement came from the U.S. in 1989. In late 1992, the NAFTA document and two accompanying agreements were signed by government representatives and were ready for legislative approval. By the end of 1993, NAFTA had won legislative approval in Canada, Mexico, and the U.S.

---

8 Clar Rosso. "The Euro: Revolutionizing a Continent's Economy." *Outlook: The Professional Publication for California CPAs*, Spring 2000, p. 19.

NAFTA calls for phasing out duties on most goods and services produced in the three countries. It also calls for free movement of professionals—accountants included—within the three countries. A licensed U.S. CPA would eventually be allowed to practice in Canada and Mexico. NAFTA objectives include:

- Eliminate barriers to trade and facilitate cross-border movement of goods and services among the member nations.
- Promote conditions of fair competition in the free trade area.
- Increase investment opportunities in the three countries.
- Provide adequate and effective protection and enforcement of intellectual property rights in each member country.
- Establish a framework for further cooperation to expand and enhance the benefits of the agreement.

NAFTA would improve access to the market for goods produced in the three countries. All tariffs are to be eliminated on goods originating in Canada, Mexico, and the U.S. either immediately (effective January 1, 1994) or in 5 or 10 equal annual stages. Goods are grouped into four categories, each with a specified date for the elimination of tariffs. NAFTA is administered by a commission, similar to the EU. Committees are established for each area. For example, there is a Committee for Financial Services.

The agreement provided that within two years from the signing date citizenship or permanent residency requirements for licensing or certification of professional service providers would be eliminated, however, it hasn't happened yet. When it does happen, it will be an important step toward the harmonization of accounting and auditing practices in the three countries, and will also have a significant impact on accounting education.

At the Summit of the Americas meeting held in December 1994, leaders of 34 North and South American countries agreed to work toward a free trade agreement. This would create the largest free trade area in the world, with more than 850 million people and a gross domestic product of $13 trillion. If an agreement is reached, it is expected to go into effect by the year 2005.[9]

Other Regional Efforts

There are several other regional economic efforts, some of which are new while others are long-standing. As these agreements move toward economic integration, the need to harmonize accounting standards will become inevitable. Exhibit 6.9 includes examples of some other trade and economic agreements. Some of these efforts have transcended their regional focus and have begun to focus on increased international trade.

---

9 "A Free Trade Agreement for the Americas." *Deloitte & Touche Review*, 26 December 1994, p. 4.

exhibit 6.9   **Selected Regional Economic Blocs**

- *Association of South East Asian Nations.* Brunei, Indonesia, Laos, Malaysia, Myanmar, the Philippines, Singapore, Thailand, and Vietnam.
- *Central American Common Market.* Guatemala, Honduras, El Salvador, Nicaragua, and Costa Rica.
- *Andean Pact.* Bolivia, Colombia, Ecuador, Peru, and Venezuela.
- *Mercosur.* Argentina, Brazil, Paraguay, and Uruguay.
- *Gulf Cooperation Council.* Saudi Arabia, Kuwait, United Arab Emirates, Oman, Bahrain, and Qatar.

Recent Developments

National efforts to harmonize accounting standards across national boundaries are as important as regional and international efforts. In many cases, national standard-setting bodies are key players in harmonizing their national standards with international standards, e.g., the International Accounting Standards promulgated by the IASC. The IASC has no power to enforce its standards. It relies on member organizations to implement its harmonization efforts at the national level.

National efforts to harmonize accounting standards include the following:

- In many countries, national accounting standard setters have adopted the International Accounting Standards and published them as their own national standards. Examples include Singapore, Kuwait, Thailand, and Mexico.
- In many cases, the national standards have been formulated by using the International Accounting Standards. Examples include Brazil, India, Portugal, and Taiwan.

When professional accounting organizations have the primary responsibility for setting national accounting standards, the result should be sharing ideas, discussing issues, and working on joint projects to find solutions to common problems. This should lead to a reconciling mechanism that achieves the harmonization of accounting standards between and among countries.

Appendix 6A

International Accounting Standards Committee Publications

Standards

IAS 1   Presentation of Financial Statements
IAS 2   Inventories

Standards *(continued)*

IAS 3	No longer effective
IAS 4	Depreciation Accounting
IAS 5	No longer effective
IAS 6	No longer effective
IAS 7	Cash Flow Statements
IAS 8	Profit or Loss for the Period, Fundamental Errors and Changes in Accounting Policies
IAS 9	No longer effective
IAS 10	Events After the Balance Sheet Date
IAS 11	Construction Contracts
IAS 12	Income Taxes
IAS 13	No longer effective
IAS 14	Segment Reporting
IAS 15	Information Reflecting the Effects of Changing Prices
IAS 16	Property, Plant, and Equipment
IAS 17	Leases
IAS 18	Revenue
IAS 19	Employee Benefits
IAS 20	Accounting for Government Grants and Disclosure of Government Assistance
IAS 21	The Effects of Changes in Foreign Exchange Rates
IAS 22	Business Combinations
IAS 23	Borrowing Costs
IAS 24	Related Party Disclosures
IAS 25	Accounting for Investments
IAS 26	Accounting and Reporting by Retirement Benefits Plans
IAS 27	Consolidated Financial Statements and Accounting for Investments in Subsidiaries
IAS 28	Accounting for Investments in Associates
IAS 29	Financial Reporting in Hyperinflationary Economies
IAS 30	Disclosures in the Financial Statements of Banks and Similar Financial Institutions
IAS 31	Financial Reporting of Interests in Joint Ventures
IAS 32	Financial Instruments: Disclosures and Presentation
IAS 33	Earnings per Share
IAS 34	Interim Financial Reporting
IAS 35	Discontinuing Operations
IAS 36	Impairment of Assets
IAS 37	Provisions, Contingent Liabilities and Contingent Assets
IAS 38	Intangible Assets
IAS 39	Financial Instruments: Recognition and Measurement
IAS 40	Investment Property
IAS 41	Agriculture

Framework

Framework for the Preparation and Presentation of Financial Statements

Appendix 6B
IASC Constitution

Name and Objectives

1. The name of the organization shall be the International Accounting Standards Committee (IASC).

2. The objectives of IASC are:

    (a) to formulate and publish in the public interest accounting standards to be observed in the presentation of financial statements and to promote their worldwide acceptance and observance.

    (b) To work generally for the improvement and harmonization of regulations, accounting standards and procedures relating to the presentation of financial statements.

Membership

3. As from 1 January 1984 membership of the International Accounting Standards Committee shall consist of all professional accountancy bodies that are members of the International Federation of Accountants (IFAC). Until 1 January 1984 membership shall be as laid down in the previous Constitution.

The Board

4. The business of the Committee shall be conducted by a Board of up to 17 members consisting of:

    (a) up to thirteen countries as nominated and appointed by the Council of IFAC that shall be represented by representatives from the professional accountancy bodies that are members of IFAC in these countries (in this Constitution the term 'country' shall include two or more countries that may be nominated to accept jointly a single seat on the Board), and

    (b) up to four organizations co-opted under clause 12(a).

5. (a) The term of appointment to the Board of a Member selected under clause 4(a) shall be no more than five years. A retiring Board Member shall be eligible for reappointment. The first appointments under clause 4(a) shall be as of 1 January 1983.

    (b) The term of appointment to the Board of a Member selected under clause 4(b) shall be determined by the Board at the time of appointment.

6. The professional accountancy bodies referred to in clause 4(a) and the organizations co-opted under clause 12(a) may nominate not more than two representatives from their Board Member country or their organization to serve on the Board. The nominated representatives from each country or organization may be accompanied at meetings of the Board by a staff observer.

7. The representatives on the Board and the persons nominated to carry out particular assignments or to join steering committees/working parties/groups shall not regard themselves as representing sectional interests but shall be guided by the need to act in the public interest.

8. The President of IFAC, or his designate, accompanied by not more than one technical adviser, shall be entitled to attend meetings of the Board of IASC, be entitled to the privilege of the floor, but shall not be entitled to vote.

9. A report on its work shall be prepared by the Board each year and sent to the professional accountancy bodies and organizations which are represented on the Board and to the Council of IFAC for dissemination to member bodies.

Chairman

10. The Board shall be presided over by a Chairman elected for a term of two-and-a-half years by the Members of the Board from among their number. The Chairman shall not be eligible for re-election. The member country providing the Chairman shall be entitled to a further representative.

Voting

11. Each country represented on the Board and each organization co-opted under clause 12(a) shall have one vote which may be taken by a show of hands or by written ballot. Except where otherwise provided either in this Constitution or in the Operating Procedures, decisions shall be taken on a simple majority of the Board.

Responsibilities and Powers

12. The Board shall have the power to:

    (a) invite up to four organizations having an interest in financial reporting to be represented on the Board;

(b) remove from membership of the Board any country or any organization co-opted under clause 12(a) whose contribution is more than one year in arrears or which fails to be represented at two successive Board meetings;

(c) publish documents relating to international accounting issues for discussion and comment provided a majority of the Board votes in favor of publication;

(d) issue documents in the form of exposure drafts for comment (including amendments to existing Standards) in the name of the International Accounting Standards Committee provided at least two-thirds of the Board votes in favor of publication;

(e) issue International Accounting Standards provided that at least three-quarters of the Board votes in favor of publication;

(f) establish operating procedures so long as they are not inconsistent with the provisions of this Constitution;

(g) enter into discussions, negotiations or associations with outside bodies and generally promote the worldwide improvement and harmonization of accounting standards.

Issue of Discussion Documents, Exposure Drafts, and Standards

13. (a) Discussion documents and exposure drafts shall be distributed by the Board to all Member Bodies. A suitable period shall be allowed for respondents to submit comments.

(b) Dissenting opinions will not be included in any exposure drafts or standards promulgated by the Board.

(c) Exposure drafts and standards may be distributed to such governments, standard-setting bodies, stock exchanges, regulatory and other agencies, and individuals as the Board may determine.

(d) The approved text of any exposure draft or standard shall be that published by IASC in the English language. The Board shall give authority to the individual participating bodies to prepare translations of the approved text of exposure drafts and standards. These translations should indicate the name of the accountancy body that prepared the translation and that it is a translation of the approved text. The responsibility for and cost of translating, publishing, and distributing copies in any country shall be borne by the professional body(ies) of the country concerned.

Financial Arrangements

14. (a) An annual budget for the ensuing calendar year shall be prepared by the Board each year and sent to the accountancy bodies and organizations which are represented on the Board, and to the Council of IFAC.

(b) IFAC shall contribute 5% of the budget of IASC in January and 5% in July of each year to defray the costs of participation in Steering Committees by member bodies not represented on the Board of IASC. The remainder of the budget of IASC shall be borne by the members of the Board, except that the Council of IFAC may decide to reimburse wholly or in part the share of the budget charged to one or more Board members.

(c) The countries or organizations represented on the Boards shall contribute on 1st January and 1st July each year a sum in such proportions as shall be decided by a three-quarters vote of the Board. Unless otherwise agreed, members of the board shall contribute equally to the annual budget. Members who are represented on the Board for part only of a calendar year shall contribute a pro rata proportion calculated by reference to the period of their representation on the Board in that year. All Board member contributions shall be billed and collected by IASC.

(d) The Committee shall reimburse the traveling, hotel, and incidental expenses of attendance at Board meetings by one representative from each country or organization represented on the Board. In addition, the Chairman shall be reimbursed for expenses incurred in attending Board meetings and otherwise on behalf of IASC.

(e) The Board shall determine in its operating procedures what other expenses shall be a charge against the revenues of the Committee.

(f) The Board shall annually prepare financial statements and submit them for audit and send copies thereof to the professional accountancy bodies and organizations which are represented on the Board and to the Council of IFAC for dissemination to the member bodies.

Meetings

15. Meetings of the board shall be held at such times and in such places as the members of the Board may mutually agree.

16. In conjunction with the General Assembly of IFAC a meeting of the members of IASC shall be held during or immediately prior to each International Congress of Accountants at the location chosen for the congress.

Administrative Office

17. The location of the administrative office of the International Accounting Standards Committee shall be London, England.

Amendments to Constitution

18. Amendments to this Constitution shall be discussed with the Council of IFAC and shall require a three-quarters majority of the Board and approval by the membership as expressed by a simple majority of those voting.

Source: International Accounting Standards Committee.

Appendix 6C

Balance Sheet and Income Statement Format: EU 4th Directive

Section 3
Layout of the Balance Sheet
Article 8

For the presentation of the balance sheet, the Member States shall prescribe one or both of the layouts prescribed by Articles 9 and 10. If a Member State prescribes both, it may allow companies to choose between them.

Article 9
Assets

A. **Subscribed capital unpaid of which there has been called** (unless national law provides that called-up capital be shown under 'Liabilities.' In that case, the part of the capital called but not yet paid must appear as an asset either under A or under D(II)(5)).

B. **Formation expenses** as defined by national law, and in so far as national law permits their being shown as an asset. National law may also provide for formation expenses to be shown as the first item under 'intangible assets.'

C. **Fixed Assets**

   I. Intangible assets

     1. Costs of research and development, in so far as national law permits their being shown as assets.

     2. Concessions, patents, licenses, trade marks, and similar rights and assets, if they were:

       (a) acquired for valuable consideration and need not be shown under C(I)(3); or

       (b) created by the undertaking itself, in so far as national law permits their being shown as assets.

     3. Goodwill, to the extent that it was acquired for valuable consideration.

     4. Payments on account.

   II. Tangible assets

     1. Land and buildings.

     2. Plant and machinery.

     3. Other fixtures and fittings, tools, and equipment.

     4. Payments on account and tangible assets in course of construction.

   III. Financial assets

     1. Shares in affiliated undertakings.

     2. Loans to affiliated undertakings.

     3. Participating interests.

     4. Loans to undertakings with which the company is linked by virtue of participating interests.

     5. Investments held as fixed assets.

     6. Other loans.

     7. Own shares (with an indication of their nominal value or, in the absence of a nominal value, their accounting par value) to the extent that national law permits their being shown in the balance sheet.

D. **Current assets**

   I. Stocks

     1. Raw materials and consumables.

     2. Work in progress.

     3. Finished goods and goods for resale.

     4. Payments on account.

   II. Debtors (amounts becoming due and payable after more than one year must be shown separately for each item).

     1. Trade debtors.

     2. Amounts owed by affiliated undertakings.

3. Amounts owed by undertakings with which the company is linked by virtue of participating interests.

4. Other debtors.

5. Subscribed capital called but not paid (unless national law provides that called-up capital be shown as an asset under A).

6. Prepayments and accrued income (unless national law provides for such items to be shown as an asset under E).

III. Investments

1. Shares in affiliated undertakings.

2. Own shares (with an indication of their nominal value or, in the absence of a nominal value, their accounting par value) to the extent that national law permits their being shown in the balance sheet.

3. Other investments.

IV. Cash at bank and in hand.

E. **Prepayments and accrued income** (unless national law provides for such items to be shown as an asset under D(II)(6)).

F. **Loss for the financial year** (unless national law provides for it to be shown under A(VI) under liabilities).

Liabilities

A. **Capital and reserves**

I. Subscribed capital (unless national law provides for called-up capital to be shown under this item. In that case the amounts of subscribed capital and paid-up capital must be shown separately).

II. Share premium account.

III. Revaluation reserve.

IV. Reserves.

1. Legal reserve, in so far as national law requires such a reserve.

2. Reserve for own shares, in so far as national law requires such a reserve, without prejudice to Article 11(1)(b) of Directive 77/91/EEC.

3. Reserves provided for by the articles of association.

4. Other reserves.

V. Profit or loss brought forward.

VI. Profit or loss for the financial year (unless national law requires that this item be shown under F under 'assets' or under E under "liabilities').

B. **Provisions for liabilities and charges**

1. Provisions for pensions and similar obligations.

2. Provisions for taxation.

3. Other provisions.

C. **Creditors** (amounts becoming due and payable within one year and amounts becoming due and payable after more than one year must be shown separately for each item and for the aggregate of these items).

1. Debenture loans, showing convertible loans separately.

2. Amounts owed to credit institutions.

3. Payments received on account of orders in so far as they are not shown separately as deductions from stocks.

4. Trade creditors.

5. Bills of exchange payable.

6. Amounts owed to affiliated undertakings.

7. Amounts owed to undertakings with which the company is linked by virtue of participating interests.

8. Other creditors including tax and social security.

9. Accruals and deferred income (unless national law provides for such items to be shown under D under 'liabilities').

D. **Accruals and deferred income** (unless national law provides for such items to be shown under C(9) under 'Liabilities').

E. **Profit for the financial year** (unless national law provides for it to be shown under A(VI) under 'Liabilities').

Section 5
Layout of the Profit and Loss Account
Article 22

For the presentation of the profit and loss account, the Member States shall prescribe one or more of the layouts provided for in Articles 23 to 26. If a Member State prescribes more than one layout, it may allow companies to choose from among them.

Article 23

1. Net turnover.

2. Variation.

3. Work performed by the undertaking for its own purposes and capitalized.

4. Other operating income.

5. (a) Raw materials and consumables.

   (b) Other external charges.

6. Staff costs:

   (a) Wages and salaries.

   (b) Social security costs with a separate indication of those relating to pensions.

7. (a) Value adjustments in respect of formation expenses and tangible and intangible fixed assets.

(b) Value adjustments in respect of current assets, to the extent that they exceed the amount of value adjustments which are normal in the undertaking concerned.

8. Other operating charges.

9. Income from participating interests, with a separate indication of that derived from affiliated undertakings.

10. Income from other investments and loans forming part of the fixed assets, with a separate indication of that derived from affiliated undertakings.

11. Other interest receivable and similar income, with a separate indication of that derived from affiliated undertakings.

12. Value adjustments in respect of financial assets and of investments held as current assets.

13. Interest payable and similar charges, with a separate indication of those concerning affiliated undertakings.

14. Tax on profit or loss on ordinary activities.

15. Profit or loss on ordinary activities after taxation.

16. Extraordinary income.

17. Extraordinary charges.

18. Extraordinary profit or loss.

19. Tax on extraordinary profit or loss.

20. Other taxes not shown under the above items.

21. Profit or loss for the financial year.

Article 24

A. **Charges**

1. Reduction in stocks of finished goods and in work in progress.

2. (a) Raw materials and consumables.

    (b) Other current charges.

3. Staff costs:

    (a) Wages and salaries.

    (b) Social security costs, with a separate indication of those relating to pensions.

4. (a) Value adjustments in respect of formation expenses and of tangible and intangible fiscal assets.

    (b) Value adjustments in respect of current assets, to the extent that they exceed the amount of value adjustments which are normal in the undertaking concerned.

5. Other operating charges.

6. Value adjustments in respect of financial assets and of investments held as current assets.

7. Interest payable and similar charges, with a separate indication of those concerning affiliated undertakings.

8. Tax on profit or loss on ordinary activities.

9. Profit or loss on ordinary activities after taxation.

10. Extraordinary charges.

11. Tax on extraordinary profit or loss.

12. Other taxes not shown under the above items.

13. Profit or loss for the financial year.

B. **Income**

1. Net turnover.

2. Increase in stocks of finished goods and in work in progress.

3. Work performed by the undertaking for its own purposes and capitalized.

4. Other operating income.

5. Income from participating interests, with a separate indication of that derived from affiliated undertakings.

6. Income from other investments and loans forming part of the fixed assets, with a separate indication of that derived from affiliated undertakings.

7. Other interest receivable and similar income with a separate indication of that derived from affiliated undertakings.

8. Profit or loss on ordinary activities after taxation.

9. Extraordinary income.

10. Profit or loss for the financial year.

Article 25

1. Net turnover.

2. Cost of sales (including value adjustments).

3. Gross profit or loss.

4. Distribution costs (including value adjustments).

5. Administrative expenses (including value adjustments).

6. Other operating income.

7. Income from participating interests, with a separate indication of that derived from affiliated undertakings.

8. Income from other investments and loans forming part of the fixed assets, with a separate indication of that derived from affiliated undertakings.

9. Other interest receivable and similar income, with a separate indication of that derived from affiliated undertakings.

10. Value adjustments in respect of financial assets and of investments held as current assets.

11. Interest payable and similar charges with a separate indication of those concerning affiliated undertakings.

12. Tax on profit or loss on ordinary activities.

13. Profit or loss on ordinary activities after taxation.

14. Extraordinary charges.

15. Extraordinary income.

16. Extraordinary profit or loss.

17. Tax on extraordinary profit or loss.

18. Other taxes not shown under the above items.

19. Profit or loss for the financial year.

Article 26

A. **Charges**

1. Cost of sales (including value adjustment).

2. Distribution costs (including value adjustments).

3. Administrative expenses (including value adjustments).

4. Value adjustments in respect of financial assets and of investments held as current assets.

5. Interest payable and similar charges, with a separate indication of those concerning affiliated undertakings.

6. Tax on profit or loss on ordinary activities.

7. Profit or loss on ordinary activities after taxation.

8. Extraordinary charges.

9. Tax on extraordinary profit or loss.

10. Profit or loss, for the financial year.

Source: EU Secretariat, Fourth Directive, EU, Brussels.

B. **Income**

1. Net turnover.

2. Other operating income.

3. Income from participating interests, with a separate indication of that derived from affiliated undertakings.

4. Income from other investments and loans forming part of the fixed assets, with a separate indication of that derived from affiliated undertakings.

5. Other interest receivable and similar income, with a separate indication of that derived from affiliated undertakings.

6. Profit or loss on ordinary activities after taxation.

7. Extraordinary income

8. Profit or loss for the financial year.

Note to Students

The appendices at the end of the chapter provide you with valuable information. You may wish to do the following:

- Compare the standard-setting process of the IASC with any of the national accounting standard setters you are familiar with.

- Assess the information content of vertical versus horizontal income statements and balance sheets. Refer to Appendix 6C for detailed information.

Many professional and governmental organizations provide valuable information on their Web sites on topics such as national accounting standards, harmonization, the European Union, and Eurocurrency. You would find that each of the following Web site addresses offers a wealth of information.

http://

Organization	Web Site Address
American Institute of Certified Public Accountants	http://www.aicpa.org
European Union (EU)	http://europa.eu.int
European Commission	http://www.europa.eu.int/euro/
Federation of European Accountants	http://www.euro.fee.be
Financial Accounting Standards Board	http://www.fasb.org
International Accounting Standards Committee (IASC)	http://www.iasc.org.uk
International Federation of Accountants	http://www.ifac.org
International Organization of Securities Commissions (IOSCO)	http://www2.iosco.org

http://

Organisation for Economic Co-operation and
  Development (OECD)   **http://www.oecd.org**

United Nations Conference on Trade
  and Development   **http://www.unicc.org**

To keep abreast of accounting standard setting and related developments around the world, it is also necessary to read professional journals. Some of the popular periodicals like *Financial Times* and *The Wall Street Journal* carry news items on the changes in accounting standards. Professional journals carry feature articles as well as news items dealing with accounting standards. Major public accounting firms publish information guides dealing with accounting standards and business environments in various countries. They also publish newsletters to provide timely information on new developments in accounting standards.

Chapter Summary

1. Facilitation of international trade and investment requires accounting standards that are not country-specific.

2. Harmonization of accounting standards improves the comparability of financial statements.

3. Worldwide harmonization efforts consist of three levels: international, regional, and national.

4. The International Accounting Standards Committee is the leading organization in the efforts to harmonize accounting standards.

5. The IASC standards cover measurement, recording, and disclosure issues dealing with the preparation of financial reports.

6. The European Union is the leading trading bloc in the efforts to harmonize accounting standards among its member countries.

7. The Fourth and Seventh EU Company Law Directives address the preparation and consolidation of financial statements, respectively.

8. The European Monetary Union will introduce euro bank notes and coins on January 1, 2002, thus making the national currencies of Euroland countries obsolete.

9. Canada, Mexico, and the U.S. are members of the North American Free Trade Agreement.

10. National efforts to harmonize accounting standards should be encouraged. The ultimate success of worldwide harmonization efforts will depend on their acceptance by the setters of national accounting standards.

11. The five countries selected for comparative analysis have different environments. As a result, diversity in standard setting is a natural outcome.

12. All of the five countries selected require the balance sheet and the income statement. The same is not true for the statement of funds/cash flow.

13. The five countries examined have generally reached similar understandings on issues of going concern, accrual basis, and consistency in the application of accounting principles from one period to the next.

14. Many countries have adopted International Accounting Standards as their national standards. Others have used *IASs* to develop the national standards.

Questions for Discussion

1. What is the impact of diversity of national accounting standards on the providers and users of financial information?

2. Compare standardization with harmonization of accounting standards. Should accounting standards be standardized or harmonized worldwide? Discuss.

3. What international organizations are involved in harmonization efforts?

4. Describe the International Accounting Standards Committee's efforts to harmonize accounting standards to date. Be specific.

5. Describe and assess the standard-setting process used by the IASC.

6. The accounting standard setters in the U.S. and U.K. have gone through major organizational changes in the last 40 years. Do you think that the IASC may have to go through similar changes?

7. What is the main role of the OECD in harmonizing worldwide accounting standards?

8. What is the main thrust of EU efforts to harmonize accounting standards?

9. Examine and evaluate the objectives of the EU Fourth Directive.

10. Examine and evaluate the objectives of the EU Seventh Directive.

11. Compare and evaluate EU versus IASC harmonization efforts.

12. Describe the likely impact of the North American Free Trade Agreement on accounting standards.

13. Critically examine the impact of regional economic and trade agreements on the efforts toward harmonization of accounting standards.

14. Japan is not currently a member of any regional trading bloc. Does this affect the development of accounting standards in Japan? If yes, how?

15. "National efforts to harmonize accounting standards across national boundaries are as important as international and regional efforts." Comment on this statement.

16. Why is there a need for accounting standards?

17. How does the extent of the government's involvement in the economy influence a nation's accounting standards?

18. Who are generally the primary users of financial statements in countries where a private entity issues accounting standards?

19. Why is it useful to understand the standard-setting process in different countries?

20. The terms "taxable income" and "financial reporting income" are used in the U.S. Is there such a difference in Japan? Germany? Explain.

21. What is the scope of GASB responsibility in the United States?

22. "If goodwill was a person, she/he would probably stand trial around the world on numerous counts of complicity in undesirable or criminal acts."[10] Discuss the possible meanings of this statement.

Exercises/Problems

6-1 Prepare a matrix showing the financial statements required by GAAP in the five countries selected for discussion in the chapter.

6-2 Prepare a comparative analysis of the five countries, selected for discussion in the chapter, showing their accounting treatment of the following:

a. Revaluation of assets (upward).

b. Finance leases (capitalization).

c. Capitalization of interest.

d. Inventory valuation (application of the lower of cost or market principle).

e. Research and development costs (capitalization).

f. Segment reporting.

g. Consolidation.

6-3 Taimur Company in the U.S. has four industry segments, A, B, C, and D. The revenue from the segments for the past year amounted to:

Segment	Revenue
A	$4,000,000
B	3,000,000
C	500,000
D	2,500,000

Required:

Identify the segments that qualify as reportable segments, using the revenue criterion.

6-4 Faisal Company, a U.S. entity, has four industry segments, Aneeka, Bronislava, Catalina, and Daska. During the year, the sales revenue of each segment was as follows (in millions of U.S. dollars):

---

10 L. Kirkham and J. Arnold. "Goodwill Accounting in the UK." *The European Accounting Review*, vol. 1, no. 2, p. 421.

Segment	Revenue
Aneeka	150
Bronislava	980
Catalina	590
Daska	100

Required:

Identify the reportable industry segments according to U.S. GAAP, using only the sales revenue criterion. State the basis for your selections.

6-5   Daimler-Benz became the first Germany-based company to be listed on a U.S. securities market. This occurred after a long stalemate between Daimler-Benz and the U.S. Securities and Exchange Commission over compliance with U.S. accounting standards. The two parties finally struck a compromise in which Daimler-Benz agreed to conform in substance to U.S. accounting standards. Critics of the SEC maintain that U.S. accounting rules deter companies based in other countries from listing their shares in the U.S. Defenders of the SEC argue that the U.S. has the best accounting rules in the world and that U.S. standards should not be lowered.

Required:

(1)   Present arguments supporting the SEC position.

(2)   Present arguments opposing the SEC position.

6-6   Select the best available answer:

1.   The European Union accounting standards are called:
   a.   Guidelines.
   b.   Regulations.
   c.   Directives.
   d.   EU International Standards.

2.   The International Accounting Standards Committee pronouncements are called:
   a.   Company Law Directives.
   b.   International Accounting Pronouncements.
   c.   International Accounting Standards.
   d.   International Accounting Statements.

3.   The policy-making body of the International Accounting Standards Committee is called the:
   a.   Commission.
   b.   Council of Ministers.
   c.   Board.
   d.   Steering Committee.

4.   The Organisation for Economic Co-operation and Development efforts are mainly to:
   a.   Issue International Accounting Standards.

      b. Advise member governments on auditing standards.

      c. Prepare guidelines for financial disclosure by MNCs.

      d. Require environmental disclosures.

6-7 Werner Schneider GmbH(WS) has provided you with the following financial information for 2001 (amounts in thousands):

Stocks	DM 16,100	Creditors due within one year	DM 14,300
Long-term investments	8,100	Other liabilities (short-term)	2,800
Intangible assets	6,200	Property, plant, and equipment	43,500
Long-term creditors	12,600	Debtors	8,400
Share capital	8,600	Other receivables (short-term)	500
General reserve	?	Short-term investments	200
Dividends	2,000	Prepayments	700
Turnover	109,000	Cost of goods and expenses	98,200
Bank deposits	6,800	Bonds payable	30,000
Profit and loss account (beginning balance)	5,000		

Required:

Prepare a horizontal balance sheet for WS.

6-8 Refer to Problem 6-7.

Required:

Prepare a vertical balance sheet for WS.

6-9 Refer to Problem 6-8. WS expects that next year's sales will increase, costs will decrease, and overall worldwide operations will show a major improvement. WS also expects dividends to triple, and stockholders' equity to increase by 50 percent.

Required:

What is the estimated income (ignore taxes) for 2002?

Case

Tanaguchi Corporation—Identifying Differences Between U.S. and Japanese GAAP

ABSTRACT: This case examines the effects of differences in accounting principles between the United States and Japan on financial statements and financial statement ratios. It also illustrates the impact of different economic, strategic, institutional, and cultural factors on interpretations of profitability and risk. It places particular emphasis on the relation between financial and tax reporting, and the importance in Japan of operating through corporate groups, or keiretsu.[11]

Dave Ando and Yoshi Yashima, recent business school graduates, work as research security analysts for a mutual fund specializing in international equity investments. Based on several strategy meetings, senior managers of the fund decided to invest in the machine tool industry. One international company under consideration is Tanaguchi Corporation, a Japanese manufacturer of machine tools. As staff analysts assigned to perform fundamental analysis on all new investment options, Ando and Yashima obtain a copy of Tanaguchi Corporation's unconsolidated financial statements and set out to calculate their usual spreadsheet of financial statement ratios. Exhibit 6.10 presents the results of their efforts. As a basis for comparison, Exhibit 6.10 also presents the median ratios for U.S. machine tool companies for a comparable year. The following conversation ensues.

Dave: Tanaguchi Corporation does not appear to be as profitable as comparable U.S. firms. Its operating margin and rate of return on assets are significantly less than the median ratios for U.S. machine tool operators. Its rate of return on common equity is only slightly less than its U.S. counterparts, but this is at the expense of assuming much more financial leverage and therefore risk. Most of this leverage is in the form of short-term borrowing. You can see this in its higher total liabilities to total assets ratio combined with its lower long-term debt ratio. This short-term borrowing and higher risk are also evidenced by the lower current and quick ratios. Finally, Tanaguchi Corporation's shares are selling at a higher multiple of net income and stockholders' equity than are those of U.S. machine tool companies. I can't see how we can justify paying more for a company that is less profitable and more risky than comparable U.S. companies. It doesn't seem to me that it is worth exploring this investment possibility further.

Yoshi: You may be right, Dave. However, I wonder if we are not comparing apples and oranges. As a Japanese company, Tanaguchi Corporation operates in an entirely different institutional and cultural environment than U.S. machine tool companies. Furthermore, it prepares its financial statements in accordance with Japanese generally accepted accounting principles (GAAP), which differ from those in the U.S.

Dave: Well, I think we need to explore this further. I recall seeing a report on an associate's desk comparing U.S. and Japanese accounting principles. I will get a copy for us (Exhibit 6.14).

Required:

Using the report comparing U.S. and Japanese accounting principles (Exhibit 6.14) and Tanaguchi Corporation's financial statements and notes (Exhibits 6.11 through 6.13), identify the most important differences between U.S. and Japanese GAAP. Consider both the differences in acceptable methods and in the methods

---

11 Paul R. Brown and Clyde P. Stickney. "Instructional Case: Tanaguchi Corporation." *Issues in Accounting Education*, vol. 7, no. 1, Spring 1992, pp. 57–68 (abridged).

exhibit 6.10 Comparative Financial Ratio Analysis for Tanaguchi
Corporation and U.S. Machine Tool Companies

	Tanaguchi Corporation	Median ratio for U.S. Machine Tool Companies[a]
Profitability ratios		
Operating margin after taxes (before interest expense and related tax effects)	2.8%	3.3%
Total assets turnover	1.5	1.8
= Return on assets	4.2%	5.9%
Common's share of operating earnings[b]	.83	.91
Capital structure leverage[c]	3.8	2.6
= Return on common equity[d]	133.0%	139.0%
Operating margin analysis		
Sales	100.0%	100.0%
Other revenue/sales	.4	—
Cost of goods sold/sales	(73.2)	(69.3)
Selling and administrative/sales	(21.0)	(25.8)
Income taxes/sales	(3.4)	(1.6)
Operating margin (excluding interest and related tax effects)	2.8%	3.3%
Asset turnover analysis		
Receivable turnover	5.1	6.9
Inventory turnover	6.3	5.2
Fixed asset turnover	7.5	7.0
Risk analysis		
Current ratio	1.1	1.6
Quick ratio	.7	.9
Total liabilities/total assets	73.8%	61.1%
Long-term debt/total assets	4.7%	16.1%
Long-term debt/stockholders' equity	17.9%	43.2%
Times interest covered	5.8	3.1
Market price ratios (per common share)		
Market price/net income	45.0	5.7
Market price/stockholders' equity	5.7	1.2

a Source: Robert Morris Associates, *Annual Statement Studies* (except price-earnings ratio).
b Common's share of operating earnings net income to common/operating income after taxes (before interest expense and related tax effects).
c Capital structure leverage = average total assets/average common stockholders' equity.
d The amounts for return on common equity may not be precisely equal to the product of return on assets, common's share of operating earnings, and capital structure leverage due to rounding.

exhibit 6.11 Unconsolidated Balance Sheet—
Tanaguchi Corporation

	(in billions of yen) March 31	
	Year 4	**Year 5**
Assets		
Current assets		
Cash	¥ 30	¥ 27
Marketable securities (Note 1)	20	25
Notes and accounts receivable (Note 2):		
Trade notes and accounts	200	210
Affiliated company	30	45
Allowance for doubtful accounts	(5)	(7)
Inventories (Note 3)	130	150
Other current assets	25	30
Total current assets	¥ 430	¥ 480
Investments		
Investment in and loans to affiliated companies (Note 4)	¥ 110	¥ 140
Investments in other companies (Note 5)	60	60
Total investments	¥ 170	¥ 200
Property, plant, and equipment (Note 6)		
Land	¥ 25	¥ 25
Buildings	110	130
Machinery and equipment	155	180
Less: Depreciation to date	(140)	(165)
Total property, plant, and equipment	¥ 150	¥ 170
Total assets	¥ 750	¥ 850
Liabilities and Stockholders' Equity		
Current liabilities		
Short-term bank loans	¥ 185	¥ 200
Notes and accounts payable:		
Trade notes and accounts	140	164
Affiliated company	25	20
Other current liabilities	40	50
Total current liabilities	¥ 390	¥ 434
Long-term liabilities		
Bonds payable (Note 7)	¥ 20	¥ 20
Convertible debt	20	20
Retirement and severance allowance (Note 8)	122	153
Total long-term liabilities	¥ 162	¥ 193

(continued)

exhibit 6.11 (continued)

Stockholders' equity		
Common stock, ¥10 par value	¥ 15	¥ 15
Capital surplus	40	40
Legal reserve (Note 9)	16	17
Retained earnings (Note 9)	127	151
Total stockholders' equity	¥ 198	¥ 223
Total liabilities and stockholders' equity	¥ 750	¥ 850

exhibit 6.12 **Unconsolidated Statement of Income and Retained Earnings—Tanaguchi Corporation**

	(in billions of yen) Fiscal Year 5
Revenues	
Sales (Note 10)	¥1,200
Interest and dividends (Note 11)	5
Total revenues	¥1,205
Expenses	
Cost of goods sold	¥ 878
Selling and administrative	252
Interest	13
Total expenses	¥1,143
Income before income taxes	¥ 62
Income taxes (Note 12)	(34)
Net income	¥ 28
Retained earnings	
Balance, beginning of fiscal year 5	¥ 127
Net income	28
Deductions:	
Cash dividends	(3)
Transfer to legal reserve (Note 9)	(1)
Balance, end of fiscal year 5	¥ 151

commonly used. For each major difference, indicate the likely effect (increase, decrease, or no effect) on:

(1) net income,

(2) total assets, and

(3) the ratio of liabilities divided by stockholders' equity resulting from converting Tanaguchi's financial statements to U.S. GAAP.

exhibit 6.13 Notes to Financial Statements

Note 1: Marketable securities. Marketable securities appear on the balance sheet at acquisition cost.

Note 2: Accounts receivable. Accounts and notes receivable are non-interest-bearing. Within 15 days of sales on open account, customers typically sign non-interest-bearing, single-payment notes. Customers usually pay these notes within 60 to 180 days after signing. When Tanaguchi Corporation needs cash, it discounts these notes with Menji Bank. Tanaguchi Corporation remains contingently liable in the event customers do not pay these notes at maturity. Receivables from (and payable to) affiliated company are with Takahashi Corporation (see Note 4) and are non-interest-bearing.

Note 3: Inventories. Inventories appear on the balance sheet at the lower of cost or market. The measurement of acquisition cost uses a weighted average cost flow assumption.

Note 4: Investments and loans to affiliated companies. Intercorporate investments appear on the balance sheet at acquisition cost. The balances in this account at the end of Year 4 and Year 5 comprise the following:

	Year 4	Year 5
Investments in Tanaka Corporation (25%)	¥ 15	¥ 15
Investment in Takahashi Corporation (80%)	70	70
Loans to Takahashi Corporation	25	55
	¥110	¥140

Note 5: Investments in other companies. Other investments represent ownership shares of less than 20 percent and appear at acquisition cost.

Note 6: Property, plant, and equipment. Fixed assets appear on the balance sheet at acquisition cost. The firm capitalizes expenditures that increase the service lives of fixed assets, while it expenses immediately expenditures that maintain the originally expected useful lives. It computes depreciation using the declining balance method. Depreciable lives for buildings are 30 to 40 years and for machinery and equipment, 6 to 10 years.

Note 7: Bonds payable. Bonds payable comprises two bond issues as follows:

	Year 4	Year 5
12% semi-annual, ¥10 billion face value bonds, with interest payable on March 31 and September 30 and the principal payable at maturity on March 31, Year 20; the bonds were initially priced on the market to yield 10%, compounded semi-annually	¥11.50	¥11.45
8% semi-annual, ¥10 billion face value bonds, with interest payable on March 31 and September 30 and the principal payable at maturity on March 31, Year 22; the bonds were initially priced on the market to yield 10%, compounded semi-annually	¥20.00	¥20.00

Note 8: Retirement and severance allowance. The firm provides amounts as a charge against income each year for estimated retirement and severance benefits but does not fund these amounts until it makes actual payments to former employees.

Note 9: Legal reserve and retained earnings. The firm reduces retained earnings and increases the legal reserve account for a specified percentage of dividends paid during the year. The following plan for appropriation of retained earnings was approved by shareholders at the annual meeting held on June 29, Year 5:

(continued)

exhibit 6.13 *(continued)*

Transfer to legal reserve	¥(1)
Cash dividend	(3)
Directors' and statutory auditors' bonuses	(1)
Elimination of special tax reserve relating to sale of equipment	1

Note 10: Sales revenue. The firm recognizes revenues from sales of machine tools at the time of delivery. Reported sales for Year 5 are net of a provision for doubtful accounts of ¥50 billion.

Note 11: Interest and dividend revenue. Interest and dividend revenue includes ¥1.5 billion from loans to Takahashi Corporation, an unconsolidated subsidiary.

Note 12: Income tax expenses. The firm computes income taxes based on a statutory tax rate of 55 percent for Year 5.

exhibit 6.14 Comparison of U.S. and Japanese GAAP

1. Standard-setting process

U.S. The U.S. Congress has the legal authority to prescribe acceptable accounting principles, but it has delegated that authority to the Securities and Exchange Commission (SEC). The SEC has stated that it will recognize pronouncements of the Financial Accounting Standards Board (FASB), a private-sector entity, as the primary vehicle for specifying generally accepted accounting standards.

Japan The Japanese Diet has the legal authority to prescribe acceptable accounting principles. All Japanese corporations (both publicly and privately held) must periodically issue financial statements to their stockholders following provisions of the Japanese Commercial Code. This Code is promulgated by the Diet. The financial statements follow strict legal entity concepts.

   Publicly listed corporations in Japan must also file financial statements with the Securities Division of the Ministry of Finance following accounting principles promulgated by the Diet in the Securities and Exchange Law. The Diet, through the Ministry of Finance, obtains advice on accounting principles from the Business Advisory Deliberations Council (BADC), a body composed of representatives from business, the accounting profession, and personnel from the Ministry of Finance. The BADC has no authority on its own to set acceptable accounting principles. The financial statements filed with the Securities Division of the Ministry of Finance tend to follow economic entity concepts, with intercorporate investments either accounted for using the equity method or consolidated.

   All Japanese corporations file income tax returns with the Taxation Division of the Ministry of Finance. The accounting principles followed in preparing tax returns mirror closely those used in preparing financial statements for stockholders under the Japanese Commercial Code. The Minister of Finance will sometimes need to reconcile conflicting preferences of the Securities Division (desiring financial information better reflecting economic reality) and the Taxation Division (desiring to raise adequate tax revenues to run the government).

2. Principal financial statements

U.S. Balance sheet, income statement, statement of cash flows.

Japan Balance sheet, income statement, proposal for appropriation of profit or disposition of loss. The financial statements filed with the Ministry of Finance contain some supplemental information on cash flows.

3. Income statement

U.S. Accrual basis.

Japan Accrual basis.

(continued)

exhibit 6.14 *(continued)*

---

4.   **Revenue recognition**

U.S.   Generally at time of sale; percentage-of-completion method usually required on long-term contracts; installment and cost-recovery-first methods permitted when there is high uncertainty regarding cash collectibility.

Japan   Generally at time of sale; percentage-of-completion method permitted on long-term contracts; installment method common when collection period exceeds two years regardless of degree of uncertainty of cash collectibility.

5.   **Uncollectible accounts**

U.S.   Allowance method.

Japan   Allowance method.

6.   **Inventories and cost of goods sold**

U.S.   Inventories valued at lower of cost or market. Cost determined by FIFO, LIFO, weighted average, or standard cost. Most firms use FIFO, LIFO, or a combination of the two.

Japan   Inventories valued at lower of cost or market. Cost determined by specific identification, FIFO, LIFO, weighted average, or standard cost. Most firms use weighted average or specific identification.

7.   **Fixed assets and depreciation expense**

U.S.   Fixed assets valued at acquisition cost. Depreciation computed using straight line, declining balance, and sum-of-the-years'-digits methods. Permanent declines in value are recognized. Most firms use straight line for financial reporting and an accelerated method for tax reporting.

Japan   Fixed assets valued at acquisition cost. Depreciation computed using straight line, declining balance, and sum-of-the-years'-digits methods. Permanent declines in value are recognized. Most firms use a declining method for financial and tax reporting.

8.   **Intangible assets and amortization expense**

U.S.   Internally developed intangibles expensed when expenditures are made. Externally purchased intangibles capitalized as assets and amortized over expected useful life (not to exceed 40 years). Goodwill cannot be amortized for tax purposes.

Japan   The cost of intangibles (both internally developed and externally purchased) can be expensed when incurred or capitalized and amortized over the period allowed for tax purposes (generally 5 to 20 years). Goodwill is amortized over 5 years. Some intangibles (e.g., property rights) are not amortized.

9.   **Liabilities related to estimated expenses (warranties, vacation pay, employee bonuses)**

U.S.   Estimated amount recognized as an expense and as a liability. Actual expenditures are charged against the liability.

Japan   Estimated amount recognized as an expense and as a liability. Actual expenditures are charged against the liability. Annual bonuses paid to members of the Board of Directors and to the Commercial Code auditors are not considered expenses, but a distribution of profits. Consequently, such bonuses are charged against retained earnings.

10.   **Liabilities related to employee retirement and severance benefits**

U.S.   Liability recognized for unfunded accumulated benefits.

Japan   Severance benefits more common than pension benefits. An estimated amount is recognized each period as an expense and as a liability for financial reporting. The maximum liability recognized equals 40 percent of the amount payable if all eligible employees were terminated currently. There is wide variability in the amount recognized. Benefits are deducted for tax purposes only when actual payments are made to severed employees. Such benefits are seldom funded beforehand.

(continued)

exhibit 6.14 *(continued)*

11. Liabilities related to income taxes

U.S. Income tax expense based on book income amounts. Deferred tax expense and deferred tax liability recognized for temporary (timing) differences between book and taxable income.

Japan Income tax expense based on taxable income amounts. Deferred tax accounting not practiced. In consolidated statements submitted to the Ministry of Finance by listed companies (see No. 18), deferred tax accounting is permitted.

12. Non-interest-bearing notes

U.S. Notes stated at present value of future cash flows and interest recognized over term of the note.

Japan Notes stated at face amount and no interest recognized over term of the note. Commonly used as a substitute for Accounts Payable.

13. Bond discount or premium

U.S. Subtracted from or added to the face value of the bond and reported among liabilities on the balance sheet. Amortized over the life of the bond as an adjustment to interest expense.

Japan Bond discount usually included among intangible assets and amortized over the life of the bonds. Bond discount and premium may also be subtracted from or added to face value of bonds on the balance sheet and amortized as an adjustment of interest expense over the life of the bonds.

14. Leases

U.S. Distinction made between operating leases (not capitalized) and capital leases (capitalized).

Japan All leases treated as operating leases.

15. Legal reserve (part of shareholders' equity)

U.S. Not applicable.

Japan When dividends are declared and paid, unappropriated retained earnings and cash are reduced by the amount of the dividend. In addition, unappropriated retained earnings are reduced and the legal reserve account is increased by a percentage of this dividend, usually 10 percent, until such time as the legal reserve equals 25 percent of stated capital. The effect of the latter entry is to capitalize a portion of retained earnings to make it part of permanent capital.

16. Appropriations of retained earnings

U.S. Not a common practice in the U.S. Appropriations have no legal status when they do appear.

Japan Stockholders must approve, each year, the proposal for appropriation of profit or disposition of loss. Four items commonly appear: dividend declarations, annual bonuses for directors and Commercial Code auditors, transfers to legal reserves, and changes in reserves.

The income tax law permits certain costs to be deducted earlier for tax than for financial reporting and permits certain gains to be recognized later for tax than for financial reporting. To obtain these tax benefits, the tax law requires that these items be reflected on the company's books. The pretax effect of these timing differences do not appear on the income statement. Instead, an entry is made decreasing unappropriated retained earnings and increasing special retained earnings reserves (a form of appropriated retained earnings). When the timing difference reverses, the previous entry is reversed. The tax effects of these timing differences do appear on the income statement, however. In the year that the timing difference originates, income tax expense and income tax payable are reduced by the tax effect of the timing difference. When the timing difference reverses, income tax expense and income tax payable are increased by a corresponding amount.

(continued)

exhibit 6.14 (continued)

---

17.   **Treasury stock**

U.S.   Shown at acquisition cost as a subtraction from total shareholders' equity. No income recognized from treasury stock transactions.

Japan   Re-acquired shares are either cancelled immediately or shown as a current asset on the balance sheet. Dividends "received" on treasury shares are included in income.

18.   **Investments in securities**

A.   **Marketable securities (current asset)**

U.S.   Lower of cost or market method.

Japan   Reported at acquisition cost, unless price declines are considered permanent, in which case lower of cost or market.

B.   **Investments (noncurrent asset)**

U.S.   Accounting depends on ownership: less than 20%, lower of cost or market; 20% to 50%, equity method; greater than 50%, consolidated.

Japan   The principal financial statements are those of the parent company only (that is, unconsolidated statements). Intercorporate investments are carried at acquisition cost. Listed companies must provide consolidated financial statements as supplements to the principal statements in filings to the Ministry of Finance. The accounting for investments in securities in these supplementary statements is essentially the same as in the U.S.

19.   **Corporate acquisitions**

U.S.   Purchase method or pooling of interests method.

Japan   Purchase method.

20.   **Foreign currency translation**

U.S.   The translation method depends on whether the foreign unit operates as a self-contained entity (all-current method) or as an extension of the U.S. parent (monetary/nonmonetary method).

Japan   For branches, the monetary/nonmonetary translation method is used, with any translation adjustment flowing through income. For subsidiaries, current monetary items are translated using the current rate, other balance sheet items use the historical rate, and the translation adjustment is part of shareholders' equity.

21.   **Segment reporting**

U.S.   Segment information (sales, operating income, assets) disclosed by industry segment, geographical location, and type of customer.

Japan   Beginning in 1990, sales data by segment (industry, geographical location) are required. No disclosure by type of customer.

Sources: The Japanese Institute of Certified Public Accountants. *Corporate Disclosure in Japan* (July 1987); KPMG Peat Marwick. *Comparison of Japanese and U.S. Reporting and Financial Practices* (1989).

Critical Thinking Problem

Why Don't We All Speak Japanese or English?

The following statement was made by a participant at the International Financial Reporting Forum to debate the IASC's Comparability Project:

I am a user but not a sophisticated user. It seems to me that like things ought to look alike and different things should look different, no matter where they exist. There was an article a little over a year ago in *Management Accounting*, where professors from Rider College took a set of identical circumstances and prepared financial statements as they would appear in four countries. The lowest net income number was 10 and that was in Germany. You can add as many zeros as makes you feel comfortable. The highest was 260 and that was in the U.K. Twenty-six times bigger. Now how can financial statements be useful when they show those differences? The U.S. and Australia were in-between, with the U.S. closer to Germany and Australia closer to the U.K. There must be a better way. When you go to a foreign country and do not speak the language, you can get an interpreter and you can analyze, you can spend a lot of money and a lot of time. It would be a great deal easier if we all spoke the same language.

Mr. Cairns and I were in Japan a few weeks ago making presentations to the Ministries of Finance and Justice. We had to use interpreters and it took about three times as long to convey our message to them and their reactions back to us. Why don't we all speak Japanese or English? What we are shooting for here is a common language to make international financial traffic more efficient. We have erected trade barriers in each of our countries through non-comparable financial reporting. It is as clearly a trade barrier as other trade barriers you see. It is a matter of culture and habit rather than a matter of reason. Reason says we ought to be accounting in the same way.[12]

Required:

(1) Discuss the issues raised in the previous statement. What are the pros or cons of the suggested approach?

(2) Discuss other relevant issues besides the ones raised in the previous statement.

(3) Aside from any merits, do you think the suggested approach is a practical one? Discuss.

References

Agami, Abdel M. "NAFTA and Harmonization of Accounting." *Multinational Business Review*, Spring 1995, pp. 1–7.

Alexand, D., and S. Archer, eds. *European Accounting Guide*, 3rd ed. San Diego: Harcourt Brace Professional Publishing, 1998.

---

12 School of Accounting, University of Southern California. *An Analysis of the Implications of the IASC's Comparability Project.* Los Angeles: University of Southern California, 1990, pp. 42–43.

Anderson, Nancy. "The Globalization GAAP." *Management Accounting*, August 1993, pp. 52–54.

Beresford, D. "Internationalization of Accounting Standards." *Accounting Horizons*, December 1990, pp. 99–107.

Bremmer, B. "Japan's Real Crisis." *Business Week*, 18 May 1998, pp. 136–142.

Chandler, Roy A. "The International Harmonization of Accounting: In Search of Influence." *The International Journal of Accounting*, vol. 27, no. 3 (1992), pp. 222–233.

Coopers & Lybrand. *International Accounting Summaries*, 2d. ed. New York: John Wiley & Sons, Inc., 1993.

Corbridge, Curtis L., Walter W. Austin, and David J. Lemak. "Germany's Accrual Accounting Practices." *Management Accounting*, August 1993, pp. 45–47.

Cushing, Robert G., et al. (eds.). *The Challenge of NAFTA*. Austin: The University of Texas, 1993.

Deloitte Touche Tohmatsu. *An International Accounting Comparison—Focus on Asia Pacific*, 2nd ed. Hong Kong: Deloitte Touche Tohmatsu, 1999.

_____. *Brazil: International Tax and Business Guide*. New York: Deloitte Touche Tohmatsu International, 1993.

_____. *Brazil: International Tax and Business Guide*. New York: Deloitte Touche Tohmatsu, 1997.

_____. *Germany: International Tax and Business Guide*. New York: Deloitte Touche Tohmatsu, 1995.

_____. *Japan: International Tax and Business Guide*. New York: Deloitte Touche Tohmatsu, 1997.

_____. *Netherlands: International Tax and Business Guide*. New York: Deloitte Touche Tohmatsu, 1998.

EC Commission. *Fourth Council Directive for Coordination of National Legislation Regarding the Annual Accounts for Limited Liability Companies*. Brussels: EC, 1978.

_____. *Seventh Council Directive on Consolidated Accounts*. Brussels: EC, 1983.

Epstein, B., and A. Mirza. *IAS 2000: Interpretation and Application of International Accounting Standards*. New York: John Wiley & Sons, Inc., 2000.

Financial Accounting Standards Board. *The IASC-U.S. Comparison Project: A Report on the Similarities and Differences Between IASC Standards and U.S. GAAP*, 2nd ed. Norwalk, Conn.: Financial Accounting Standards Board, 1999.

Forker, John, and Margaret Greenwood. "European Harmonization and the True and Fair View: The Case of Long-Term Contracts in the U.K." *The European Accounting Review*, vol. 4, no. 1, (1995), pp. 1–31.

Grove, Hugh D., and John D. Bazley. "Disclosure Strategies for Harmonization of International Accounting Standards." *The International Journal of Accounting*, vol. 28, no. 2 (1993), pp. 116–128.

Gumbel, Peter, and Greg Steinmetz. "German Firms Shift to More-Open Accounting." *The Wall Street Journal*, 15 March 1995, pp. C1, C10.

Haller, Axel. "The Relationship of Financial and Tax Accounting in Germany: A Major Reason for Accounting Disharmony in Europe." *The International Journal of Accounting*, vol. 27, no. 4 (1992), pp. 310–323.

Harney, A., and P. Abrahams. "Death of a Salaryman?" *Financial Times*, 12 November 1998, p. 15.

Harris, Trevor S. *International Accounting Standards versus US-GAAP Reporting*. Cincinnati, Ohio: South-Western Publishing Company, 1995.

International Accounting Standards Committee. *International Accounting Standards*. London: International Accounting Standards Committee, 1995.

Iqbal, M. Zafar. "The Global Arena: A Guide for Small & Medium-Sized Firms." *Outlook: The Professional Publication for California CPAs*, Spring 2000, pp. 10–16 and 25–39.

Price Waterhouse. *Doing Business in Germany*. New York: Price Waterhouse, 1996.

PricewaterhouseCoopers. *Understanding IAS: Analysis and Interpretation of International Accounting Standards*, 2nd ed. U.K.: PricewaterhouseCoopers, 1998.

_____. *International Accounting Standards: Similarities and Differences IAS, US GAAP and UK GAAP*. UK: PricewaterhouseCoopers, 2000.

Rohwer, J. "Japan's Quiet Revolution." *Fortune*, 30 March 1998, pp. 82–88.

Rosso, Clar. "The Euro: Revolutionizing a Continent's Economy." *Outlook: The Professional Publication for California CPAs*, Spring 2000, pp. 19–24.

Saudagaran, S., and M. Solomon. "Worldwide Regulatory Disclosure Requirements," in F. Choi (ed.), *Handbook of International Accounting*. New York: John Wiley & Sons, Inc., 1991.

Skousen, F., E. Stice, and J. Stice. *Intermediate Accounting*, 14th ed. Cincinnati, Ohio: South-Western College Publishing, 2000.

Statement of Financial Accounting Concepts No. 1. "Objectives of Financial Reporting by Business Enterprises." Stamford, Conn.: Financial Accounting Standards Board, 1978.

Statement of Financial Accounting Concepts No. 6. "Elements of Financial Statements." Stamford, Conn.: Financial Accounting Standards Board, December 1985, pp. ix–x.

Tett, G. "Japan's Banks to Tighten Bad Debt Rules." *Financial Times*, 25 March 1998, p. 8.

_____. "Bank of Japan Turns to Overseas Consultant." *Financial Times*, 21 January 1999, p. 1.

Theunisse, Hilda. "Financial Reporting in EC Countries." *The European Accounting Review*, vol. 3, no. 1 (1994), pp. 143–162.

Thorell, Per, and Geoffrey Whittington. "The Harmonization of Accounting Within the EU: Problems, Perspectives and Strategies." *The European Accounting Review*, vol. 3, no. 2 (1994) pp. 215–239.

Wallace, R.S. Olusegun. "Survival Strategies of a Global Organization: The Case of the International Accounting Standards Committee." *Accounting Horizons*, June 1990, pp. 1–22.

Wyatt, Arthur R. "An Era of Harmonization." *Journal of International Financial Management and Accounting*, Spring 1992, pp. 63–68.

_____. "Seeking Credibility in a Global Economy." *New Accountant*, September 1992, pp. 4–6, 51–52.

Zeff, Stephen A. "International Accounting Principles and Auditing Standards." *The European Accounting Review*, vol. 2, no. 2 (1993), pp. 403–410.

part

4

Chapter

7. International Financial Statement Analysis

INTERNATIONAL
FINANCIAL
ANALYSIS

chapter

7

International Financial Statement Analysis

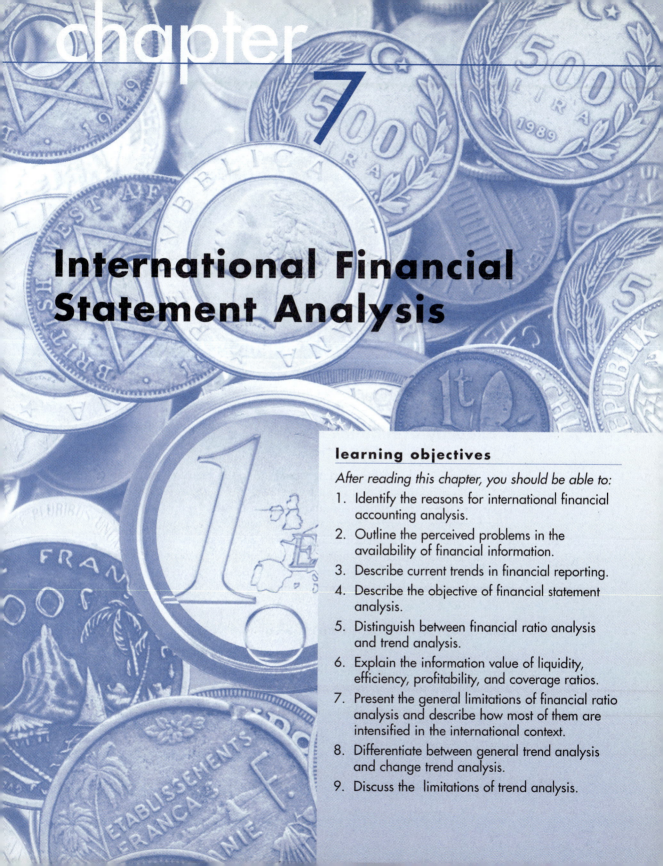

learning objectives

After reading this chapter, you should be able to:

1. Identify the reasons for international financial accounting analysis.

2. Outline the perceived problems in the availability of financial information.

3. Describe current trends in financial reporting.

4. Describe the objective of financial statement analysis.

5. Distinguish between financial ratio analysis and trend analysis.

6. Explain the information value of liquidity, efficiency, profitability, and coverage ratios.

7. Present the general limitations of financial ratio analysis and describe how most of them are intensified in the international context.

8. Differentiate between general trend analysis and change trend analysis.

9. Discuss the limitations of trend analysis.

Financial statement analysis is the conversion of the data in financial statements into useful information. Current trends are making financial statement analysis increasingly important for several reasons. There has been a worldwide movement toward the privatization of public enterprises and the liberalization of trade, investment, and currency policies. This has resulted in a substantial increase in international trade and cross-border investments. Advances in information technology have made it feasible to make financial and nonfinancial information available in different parts of the world—on an online basis if necessary.

The availability and communication of information is vital for the global market's efficiency. Parties doing business with each other now often live in different countries. They must be able to both access and understand financial information for making decisions. Parties making direct or indirect investments, or buying or selling products and services in other countries need financial information to transact their business.

Reasons for International Financial Statement Analysis

Activity in international markets has increased dramatically, which has necessitated financial statement analysis for the reasons discussed next.

Availability of High-Investment Returns in Other Countries

Investors, especially institutional investors, are often attracted by the high returns they can earn in many developing countries in Asia, Latin America, and Africa. The high rates often cannot be matched by investment opportunities in economically developed countries. Opportunities in developing countries extend beyond the investments in the securities of business corporations. They also include securities issued by the governments to meet their capital needs for planned expenditures on development programs, especially those involving infrastructure projects, and for plans to meet maturing debt obligations.

Risk Diversification in Emerging Markets

Fund managers are also interested in risk diversification. While some emerging markets may be volatile, others are not. The reason being that their business cycles aren't tied to one another's, nor do they move in unison with the industrial world's.[1] Knowledgeable sources agree that it is important to diversify while investing in emerging markets.

---

1 John Pearson, Joyce Barnathan, Bill Hinchberger, and George Wehrfritz. "Many Third World Players Are Going World-Class," *Business Week*, 12 July 1993, p. 56.

Positioning for Competitive Reasons

Many companies are making direct investments abroad to have a geographic base that will position them to target certain markets competitively. Quite a few developing countries already have a sizable population with disposal income available for spending on consumer goods. Estimates show that at least half of the populations in South Korea, Taiwan, Hong Kong, and Singapore are middle class. The percentage for Thailand, Indonesia, Malaysia, and India is approximately 25–35 percent. This new addition to the global middle class is a rich potential market for large companies such as General Electric, Philips, Asea Brown Boveri, as well as for small business organizations. It is not surprising that many corporations have selected specific countries as their target markets. For example, General Electric has selected India, China, and Mexico as its target markets for the future expansion. The consumer demand in these countries as well as many others is projected to grow dramatically in the coming years.

Another competitive reason is provided by the imperfect market theory. According to the theory, one of the main reasons for having international operations is to gain access to factors of production. Cheap labor, availability of raw materials, technological knowledge, and managerial expertise are important factors of production for companies to become competitive.

Simultaneous Appreciation of Investment with Currency

When the currency of a country becomes stronger and more valuable relative to other countries, the value of investments made in that country also appreciates. Let us assume that a German citizen makes an investment in South Korea. If the South Korean won appreciates relative to the German mark, it increases the value of the investment. This appreciation in the investment's value is attributable to the appreciation in the value of the Korean currency and is independent of the investment's own performance.

Relaxation of Equity Ownership Restrictions

Many countries have implemented economic reforms. These include the relaxation or removal of the limits on equity ownership for foreigners. For example, Brazil used to allow foreigners to acquire only up to 40 percent of any Brazilian enterprise. In October 1993, the Brazilian government amended its law to permit foreign investors to own 100 percent of any company. Multinational companies are now able to acquire subsidiaries in such countries, and are in a position to exercise the desired degree of operating and financial control over them. Even a highly decentralized multinational may prefer to have majority ownership in a company by establishing a parent-subsidiary relationship. Such a relationship ensures that the parent company can count on the subsidiary as an integral component of its strategic plan. It gives direction to the subsidiary to align its plans with its parent's worldwide strategy.

Industry and Competitor Analysis

The companies engaged in global trade and investments often need to analyze financial statements of their competitors and other leading companies in the industry. This allows them to note important trends and to gain knowledge of their own relative strengths and weaknesses. This is crucial in situations when there are a small number of key players in the market. Many decisions, such as the pricing of products and services, are heavily influenced by the competitors' strategies, plans, capacity, product innovation, and product development.

Decisions Involving Business Transactions

Financial information is needed to make many operating and financing decisions. Before extending credit, the suppliers need financial information to assess the creditworthiness of the customer. Financial information is also often helpful in negotiating a mutually agreeable price between a seller and the buyer.

Perceived Problems in the Availability of Financial Information

There are several factors that make it difficult to obtain or use financial information about economic entities located in other countries. Some of these problems are simply minor inconveniences. Others are more serious and require attention from the accounting profession, security market regulators, multinationals, and others.

Before we start discussing these problems, it should be noted that the current trend is clearly toward greater availability of financial information. Many financial services exist that provide financial and other types of information specific to countries and companies. Such information is available in print as well as electronically, the latter sometimes on an online basis. Next we will focus on some of the issues concerning the availability of financial information in global markets.

Reliability of Data

Many developing countries do not have reliable systems to accumulate data.[2] In other cases the data may be deliberately changed to show a better than actual performance.[3] The unreliability of data is a common problem in many countries. The problem, however, seems to be diminishing.

> Still, statistical shenanigans are becoming much less pervasive than before. In much of the world, there are genuinely impressive efforts under way to improve the quality of economic statistics, often with the advice

2 M.I. Lashkar. "Miscalculations in CPI Make Inflation Rate Doubtful." *The News International*, 11 June 1997, p. 13.
3 "U.K. Unemployment: Neat Figures Hide Flaws." *Gulf News*, 6 March 1997, p. 32.

of outside consultants and international agencies. And for good reason. It takes accurate numbers to institute free-market reforms. "When rigid command economies crumble and highly decentralized markets take over, governments suddenly need sound data to run their fiscal and monetary policies," said Jan Svejnar, economist at the University of Pittsburgh, and economic adviser to Czech President Vaclav Havel.

And as foreign investors and multinational corporations expand their presence in developing countries, they require better guideposts on wages, prices, and other critical variables, before committing millions in equity investments or in new factories. "Countries which develop a reputation for not having reliable statistics may pay a price in the international capital markets," said William Sterling, international economist at Merrill Lynch & Co. Carlos Jarque, president of Mexico's National Institute of Statistics, Geography & Informatics (INEGI) added: In today's world, "we think a country without statistics cannot develop."[4]

The previous item further states that when free market technocrats gain power in an emerging capitalist country, one of the first things they do is overhaul the data collection system.

Adequacy of Disclosures

As discussed in Chapters 5 and 6, the disclosures made in annual reports vary from country to country. The U.S. generally accepted accounting principles unquestionably have the most comprehensive disclosure requirements. In many other countries, including some industrialized nations, disclosures are usually limited to the legal requirements. Some of the financial statements that are required in most countries are commonly not published in other countries. As noted in Chapter 6, a statement of cash flows or a statement of changes in financial position are not required in Germany and the Netherlands. The same is the case in many other countries. Exhibit 7.1 displays information regarding EU countries involving the funds flow statement and other selected topics.

The situation, however, is improving. The global capital markets are motivating the companies that desire to raise capital from cross-border sources to make disclosures that would satisfy the information needs of sophisticated users—security market regulators, financial analysts, and mutual fund managers. The current trend is to make the financial statements contain the information that would be needed by investors, potential investors, creditors, and other stakeholders.

Timeliness of Information

To be useful, the information should be adequate, relevant, accurate, and also *timely*. It is necessary for the users to receive information early enough so that it

---

4 Christopher Farrell, Joyce Barnathan, and Elisabeth Malkin. "Statistics Can't be Damn Lies any Longer." *Business Week*, 7 November 1994, p. 118.

exhibit 7.1   EU Countries' Accounting Treatments

Country	Funds flow statement required	Upward revaluation allowed	Reserve accounts used	
			Statutory	Other
Austria	No	No	Yes	Yes
Belgium	No	Yes	Yes	Yes
Denmark	No	Yes	Yes	Yes
Finland	No	Yes	No	Yes
France	No	Yes	Yes	Yes
Germany	Yes	No	Yes	Yes
Greece	No	Yes	Yes	Yes
Ireland	Yes	Yes	No	Yes
Italy	No	Yes	Yes	Yes
Luxembourg	No	No	Yes	Yes
Netherlands	No	Yes	Yes	Yes
Portugal	No	Yes	Yes	Yes
Spain	No	Yes	Yes	Yes
Sweden	Yes	Yes	Yes	Yes
United Kingdom	Yes	Yes	No	Yes

is still relevant. The time lags between the year-ends and the availability of financial statements typically run into months. In many countries, the financial statements are commonly published four months or longer after the end of the fiscal year. The delay between the dates of the year-end and the auditor's report is shown in Exhibit 7.2 for selected companies. Time lags increase the likelihood that financial statements will be obsolete by the time they are published. With continuing advances in data collection and information technology, one would expect that the time lags would shorten. Surprisingly, there appears to be no noticeable change.

Language and Terminology

Much has been written about the worldwide communication problems posed by different languages. For several reasons, this perceived problem appears to have created no major hurdle in the global economy. English has been widely accepted by the business world for cross-national transactions. Given the current trend, it is conceivable that the English language will be the language of choice for business communications worldwide.

Terminology differences, even when the same language is used, create varying levels of difficulty. In many cases, terminology differences are no more than a minor inconvenience. Financial analysts and sophisticated investors tend to adapt

exhibit 7.2 Delay Between Year-End and Date of Auditor's Report

Company	Country Base	Date of Year-End	Date of Auditor's Report
Bayer	Germany	12-31-98	02-26-99
BP Amoco	United Kingdom	12-31-99	02-15-00
Daimler Chrysler	Germany	12-31-98	03-15-99
Danone Group	France	12-31-98	03-17-99
Dyno	Norway	12-31-98	03-03-99
General Motors	United States	12-31-98	01-20-99
ICI	United Kingdom	12-31-98	01-10-99
Nycomed Amersham	United Kingdom	12-31-98	03-12-99
Orkla	Norway	12-31-98	03-10-99
Philips	Netherlands	12-31-98	02-09-99
Renault	Norway	12-31-98	03-16-99
Schering	Germany	12-31-98	03-02-99
Sherwin Williams	United States	12-31-99	01-25-00
Sony	Japan	03-31-99	04-26-99
Teléfonos de México	Mexico	12-31-97	03-05-98
Toyota	Japan	03-31-98	06-25-98
Unisys	United States	12-31-99	01-18-00
Volkswagen	Germany	12-31-98	02-26-99

quickly to terminology differences *when there are no differences in their definition.* To facilitate the understanding, computer software is now available that helps one cope with differences between "British English" and "American English." Many U.K.-based companies include a glossary of terms in both types of English (British and American) in their annual reports as shown in Exhibit 7.3.

When the same term has different definitions in different countries, it poses a greater challenge to the analyst. One would expect that *cash and cash equivalents* would have a fairly uniform meaning worldwide. This, however, is not the case.[5] The same is true of the terms *income* and *fixed assets.*

Different Currencies

Working with unfamiliar currencies requires some experience to get used to them. However, once users become familiar with a foreign currency (in terms of its

---

5 R.S. Olusegun Wallace and Paul A. Collier. "The 'Cash' in Cash Flow Statements: A Multi-Country Comparison." *Accounting Horizons*, December 1991, p. 48.

exhibit 7.3   Terminology Differences Between the U.S. and the U.K.

U.K. terminology	U.S. equivalent terminology or brief description
Accounts	Financial statements
Acquisition accounting	Purchase accounting
Advance corporation tax	No direct U.S. equivalent. Tax paid on company distribution recoverable from U.K. taxes due on income
Allotted	Issued
Associated undertaking	20%–50% owned investee
Called-up share capital	Ordinary shares, issued and fully paid
Capital allowances	Tax term equivalent to U.S. tax depreciation allowances
Capital redemption reserve	Other additional capital
Cash at bank	Cash
Class of business	Industry segment
Closing rate method	Current rate method
Creditors	Accounts payable/payables
Creditors: Amounts falling due after more than one year	Long-term debt liabilities
Creditors: Amounts falling due within one year	Current liabilities
Debtors	Accounts receivable/receivables
Debtors: Amounts falling due after more than one year	Other noncurrent assets
Decommissioning	Dismantlement, restoration, and abandonment
Depreciation	Amortization
Employment costs	Payroll costs
Employee share schemes	Employee stock benefit plans
Finance lease	Capital lease
Financial year	Fiscal year
Fixed asset investment	Ownership with absolute rights in perpetuity
Fixed tangible assets/Tangible fixed assets	Property, plant, and equipment
Freehold	Ownership with absolute rights in perpetuity
Freehold land	Land owned
Gearing	Leverage
Group, or consolidated accounts	Consolidated financial statements
Hire charges	Rent
Interest receivable	Interest income
Interest payable	Interest expense
Loan capital	Long-term debt
Merger accounting	Pooling of interests accounting
Net asset value	Book value

exhibit 7.3   *(continued)*

U.K. terminology	U.S. equivalent terminology or brief description
Nominal value	Par value
Other debtors	Other current assets
Own shares	Treasury stock
Pension scheme	Pension plan
Profit	Income (or earnings)
Profit and loss account	Retained earnings
Profit and loss account	Income statement
Profit attributable to ordinary shareholders	Net income
Profit for year	Net income
Profit on sale of fixed assets or business	Gain on disposal of properties or long-term investments
Provision for doubtful debts	Allowance for doubtful accounts
Provisions	Noncurrent liabilities other than debt and specific accounts payable
Reconciliation of movements in shareholders' funds	Statement of changes in stockholders' equity
Redundancy charges	Severance costs
Reserves	Stockholders' equity other than capital stock and profit and loss account
Scrip dividend	Stock dividend
Share capital	Ordinary shares, capital stock or common stock issued and fully paid
Share premium account	Additional paid-in capital relating to proceeds of sale of stock in excess of par value or paid-in surplus (not distributable)
Shares in issue	Shares outstanding
Shareholders' funds	Stockholders' equity
Stocks	Inventories
Trade debtors	Accounts receivable (net)
Turnover	Sales and other operating revenue

Sources: 1. ICI. *Annual Report and Accounts and Form 20-F 1998*, p. 106.
2. BP Amoco. *Annual Report and Accounts 1999*, p. 74.

relative value to the domestic currency), adaptation comes quickly. Most investors and other users of financial statements deal with a limited number of financial statements that are denominated in a foreign currency at a given time. This makes the currency differences manageable. It would be difficult, and perhaps confusing, for experienced investors and financial analysts if they had to simultaneously use the information in financial statements of, say, 30 unfamiliar currencies.

Differences in Format of Financial Statements

Financial statement formats are not uniform worldwide. There are many variations involving the order of presentation, the individual items that are grouped in each classification, the extent of netting of different accounts, and the length of the period used for the distinction between current and noncurrent items.

In Germany, for example, the order of presentation in the balance sheet is to list fixed assets first and then current assets. The German fixed asset classification includes intangible assets, tangible assets (property, plant, and equipment), and long-term investments. In the U.S., the fixed assets classification is limited to property, plant, and equipment only. Current assets are presented before noncurrent assets in the U.S. The German balance sheet shows the stockholders' equity section first, followed by liabilities. The reverse order is used in the U.S. Exhibits 7.4 and 7.5 (pages 253 and 254–255) present examples of balance sheets of Schering AG (Germany) and The Quaker Oats Company (U.S.).

The presentation in the U.K. balance sheet has a unique feature. After the presentation of fixed asset classification (which includes intangible assets, tangible assets, and long-term investments) the next listing includes current assets, followed by current liabilities. Then a subtotal is shown for total assets less current liabilities. This, of course, precludes the presentation of current liabilities with noncurrent liabilities. Exhibit 7.6 (pages 256–257) illustrates the balance sheet of ICI, a U.K.-based multinational company.

The classification of irregular items, such as "extraordinary," in the income statement varies across countries. Even when the criteria for identifying extraordinary items may appear to be similar, they are interpreted and applied differently. Thus, an item considered extraordinary in one country may not necessarily be identified as such in another country.

Format-related differences in financial statements such as the order of presentation, classification differences, and offsetting practices may or may not be a major impediment to the use of financial statements, depending on whether they are reconcilable.

Current Trends in Financial Reporting

As mentioned earlier, the current trends favor more disclosures in financial reporting. Many external forces are influencing this trend. The major sources of institutional pressure include the IASC, the IFAC, the EU, and the IOSCO. The IOSCO especially has had a major and notable impact because of capital markets' globalization and its support of harmonization efforts of the IASC and the IFAC. EU directives have a force of law for the member countries. All EU member countries, within the range of flexibility allowed, must adhere to the directives. The standards issued by the IASC are having increasingly more influence. Many countries have adopted the IASC standards as national accounting standards. Other countries are using IASC standards as national standards with the

exhibit 7.4   **Schering AG Consolidated Balance Sheet**

Assets	Thousands of DM			
	Dec. 31, 1998		Dec. 31, 1997	
Intangible assets		744,629		807,567
Tangible assets		2,114,213		2,073,091
Investments in associates	756,382		706,923	
Other financial assets	116,605		192,875	
Financial assets		872,987		899,798
Fixed assets		3,731,829		3,780,456
Stocks		1,161,275		1,072,047
Trade debtors	1,276,178		1,246,729	
Other debtors	813,831		528,767	
Trade and other debtors		2,090,009		1,775,496
Liquid funds		1,953,271		1,964,020
Current assets		5,204,555		4,811,563
		8,936,384		8,592,019

Equity and liabilities	Dec. 31, 1998		Dec. 31, 1997	
Issued capital	338,290		341,710	
Share premium account	689,611		686,191	
Paid-up capital of Schering AG		1,027,901		1,027,901
Retained earnings of the Group		2,903,056		2,795,421
Capital and reserves of the Group		3,930,957		3,823,322
Minority interests		94,413		88,161
Capital and reserves		4,025,370		3,911,483
Provisions for pensions and similar obligations	2,218,227		2,094,087	
Other provisions	1,575,536		1,413,802	
Provisions		3,793,763		3,507,889
Liabilities to banks	345,722		420,570	
Other liabilities	771,529		752,077	
Liabilities		1,117,251		1,172,647
		8,936,384		8,592,019

Source: Schering. *Annual Report 1998*, p. 54.

exhibit 7.5   The Quaker Oats Company and
Subsidiaries Consolidated Balance Sheets

Consolidated Balance Sheets December 31	Dollars in Millions	
	1999	1998
Assets		
Current Assets		
Cash and cash equivalents	$ 282.9	$ 326.6
Marketable securities	0.3	27.5
Trade accounts receivable—net of allowances	254.3	283.4
Inventories		
Finished goods	186.6	189.1
Grains and raw materials	50.0	48.4
Packaging materials and supplies	29.6	23.9
Total inventories	266.2	261.4
Other current assets	193.0	216.1
Total Current Assets	996.7	1,115.0
Property, Plant, and Equipment		
Land	28.2	24.1
Buildings and improvements	407.6	390.2
Machinery and equipment	1,416.1	1,404.5
Property, plant, and equipment	1,851.9	1,818.8
Less: Accumulated depreciation	745.2	748.6
Property—Net	1,106.7	1,070.2
Intangible Assets—Net of Amortization	236.9	245.7
Other Assets	55.9	79.4
Total Assets	$ 2,396.2	$ 2,510.3

(continued)

modifications made for local environments. Most stock exchanges allow or require the use of IASC standards from the companies based in other countries that list securities in those countries. Some European stock exchanges give the domestic companies the options to use national GAAP or IASC standards for consolidated financial statements.

Perhaps the most important factor providing momentum toward greater disclosure is the self-interest motive. The participants in international markets are motivated to provide voluntary disclosures to achieve their investment and busi-

exhibit 7.5   *(continued)*

Consolidated Balance Sheets December 31	Dollars in Millions	
	1999	**1998**
Liabilities and Shareholders' Equity		
Current Liabilities		
Short-term debt	$ 73.3	$ 41.3
Current portion of long-term debt	81.2	95.2
Trade accounts payable	213.6	168.4
Accrued payroll, benefits, and bonus	139.1	131.4
Accrued advertising and merchandising	138.7	125.6
Income taxes payable	40.1	63.7
Other accrued liabilities	252.3	383.5
Total Current Liabilities	938.3	1,009.1
Long-term Debt	715.0	795.1
Other Liabilities	523.1	533.4
Preferred Stock, Series B, no par value, authorized 1,750,000 shares; issued 1,282,051 of $5.46 cumulative convertible shares (liquidating preference of $78 per share)	100.0	100.0
Deferred Compensation	(38.5)	(48.4)
Treasury Preferred Stock, at cost, 366,079 and 302,969 shares, respectively	(39.0)	(29.9)
Common Shareholders' Equity		
Common stock, $5 par value, authorized 400 million shares	840.0	840.0
Additional paid-in capital	100.7	78.9
Reinvested earnings	854.6	555.8
Accumulated other comprehensive income	(95.1)	(80.1)
Deferred compensation	(45.5)	(67.6)
Treasury common stock, at cost	(1,457.4)	(1,176.0)
Total Common Shareholders' Equity	197.3	151.0
Total Liabilities and Shareholders' Equity	$ 2,396.2	$ 2,510.3

Source: The Quaker Oats Company. *Annual Report 1999*, pp. 36 and 37.

ness goals. They do so regardless of the disclosure requirements. *The globalization of markets may thus turn out to be the primary factor for greater disclosure and harmonization of accounting and auditing principles worldwide.*

exhibit 7.6   ICI Balance Sheets

Balance sheets at December 31, 1998	Group £m		Company £m	
	1998	1997	1998	1997
Assets employed				
Fixed assets				
Intangible assets—goodwill	652	—	—	—
Tangible assets	3,816	3,956	320	431
Investments				
Subsidiary undertakings			10,025	10,093
Participating and other interests	170	254	24	68
	4,638	4,210	10,369	10,592
Current assets				
Stocks	1,213	1,319	62	75
Debtors	2,360	2,457	2,834	3,065
Investments and short-term deposits	455	935	—	1
Cash at bank	367	340	25	22
	4,395	5,051	2,921	3,163
Total assets	9,033	9,261	13,290	13,755
Creditors due within one year				
Short-term borrowings	(1,445)	(1,105)	—	(1)
Current installments of loans	(585)	(950)	(493)	(807)
Other creditors	(2,356)	(2,583)	(7,421)	(6,683)
	(4,386)	(4,638)	(7,914)	(7,491)
Net current assets (liabilities)	9	413	(4,993)	(4,328)
Total assets less current liabilities	4,647	4,623	5,376	6,264

(continued)

Diversity of Accounting Principles and Business Practices

Notwithstanding the trend toward greater disclosure, the lack of harmonization of accounting principles remains a major obstacle for financial statements users outside the country where the issuing company is based. *Since financial measurement is heavily influenced by accounting principles, different accounting principles often result in reported differences while there are no differences, in fact.* According to a study by Schieneman, the differences in accounting principles had a significant impact on the financial statements of most of the compa-

exhibit 7.6   *(continued)*

Balance sheets at December 31, 1998	Group £m		Company o £m	
	1998	**1997**	**1998**	**1997**
Financed by				
Creditors due after more than one year				
Loans	**2,954**	2,975	**360**	694
Other creditors	**55**	67	**2,784**	3,262
	3,009	3,042	**3,144**	3,956
Provisions for liabilities and charges	**1,429**	1,342	**210**	218
Deferred income: Grants not yet credited to profit	**11**	14	—	—
Minority interests—equity	**49**	79	—	—
Shareholders' funds—equity				
Called-up share capital	**728**	727	**728**	727
Reserves				
Share premium account	**587**	581	**587**	581
Associated undertakings' reserves	**15**	26		
Profit and loss account	**(1,181)**	(1,188)	**707**	782
Total reserves	**(579)**	(581)	**1,294**	1,363
Total shareholders' funds	**149**	146	**2,022**	2,090
	4,647	4,623	**5,376**	6,264

Source: ICI. *Annual Report and Accounts and Form 20-F 1998*, p. 52.

nies included in the study. When adjusted to U.S. GAAP, net income of one U.K.-based company *dropped* by 27.1 percent, while the net income of a Germany-based company *increased* by 40.1 percent. The restatement had an even more dramatic change on the shareholders' equity, which was in the range of −32.5 to +60.1 percent.[6]

Practices in some countries include income smoothing through the use of reserves, or entering irregular items (such as income or loss from discontinued operations) directly into retained earning. As mentioned in Chapter 5, the complete restatement from one accounting framework to another can be helpful in overcoming such problems.

6 Gary S. Schieneman. "The Effect of Accounting Differences on Cross-Border Comparisons." *International Accounting and Investment Review*, 29 April 1988, pp. 1–14.

An alternative to complete restatements is developing the capability to understand and interpret the local generally accepted accounting principles used. While it may not be a viable alternative for most investors for their decision making, it may be feasible for institutional and corporate investors. The latter groups may find it cost-effective to develop such expertise.

Some investment managers consciously decide not to invest their resources in complete restatement of financial statements or on acquiring knowledge of the local GAAP. They feel that they can achieve satisfactory results by diversifying the portfolios in a manner that provides them desired returns at risk levels that are acceptable. This approach, admittedly, may not provide the optimal returns but may be satisfactory if neither of the two analytical approaches previously discussed are considered cost-effective under the circumstances.

Different Business Practices

Let us recall an important point made from Chapter 5. Different accounting principles are not *the* major problem. As previously discussed, they can be managed to varying levels of satisfaction. *The major problem in financial statement analysis is the influence of different business operating environments in different cultures.* An example is the debt ratio of Japanese and German companies. Companies in those two countries are typically heavily leveraged. They tend to rely significantly on debt, rather than equity, as the major source of capital.

It is of the utmost importance to understand cultural differences to correctly interpret financial statement analysis. The presence of significant cultural differences in which businesses operate makes this understanding critical.

Financial Statement Analysis

The objective of financial statement analysis is to extract useful information for decision making. For decision making, a variety of approaches can be used. One approach is to review the annual report that includes financial statements, schedules, the notes accompanying the statements, the independent auditor's report, management's discussion and analysis, and other important information, such as product development and product innovation, market conditions, and the company's plans. A careful review of the annual report may provide an understanding of the company's operating performance, its financial position, and its future potential. Since no comparison is made with another firm in this approach, the complexities associated with international comparisons are avoided.

If a comparison between, or among, firms is desired, then two financial analysis alternatives are available. **Financial ratio analysis** enables comparability across firms, i.e., interfirm comparisons. **Trend analysis**, the second alternative, provides intrafirm as well as interfirm comparisons for two or more periods or dates. In the subsequent sections we will discuss these two techniques of financial statement analysis.

Financial Ratio Analysis

Financial ratio analysis is done for the evaluation of operating performance and financial position. It helps assess factors such as the level of credit risk and earnings potential. If the financial statements of the company are not restated, this fact needs to be taken into account while performing financial ratio analysis. The analyst should understand the accounting framework according to which the accounting statements have been prepared, and also should understand the foreign business practices based on the local culture. *Simply restating the statements is not enough by itself to avoid drawing misleading conclusions from financial statement analysis.*

Ratio analysis is the starting point in developing information desired by the analyst. Ratio analysis is generally classified as follows.[7]

Liquidity ratios. Measures of the enterprise's short-run ability to pay its maturing obligations. Also called *solvency ratios*.

Efficiency ratios. Measures of how effectively the enterprise is using the assets employed. Also called *turnover ratios* or *activity ratios*.

Profitability ratios. Measures of the degree of success or failure of the entity for a given period of time.

Coverage ratios. Measures of the degree of protection for long-term creditors and investors. Also called *leverage ratios* or *capital structure ratios*.

Some of the commonly used financial statement ratios are shown in Exhibit 7.7 under each category.

It is unnecessary to convert amounts expressed in different currencies to a single currency. Doing so would not change the ratios. Ratios based on the same amounts will be the same regardless of the currency.

Example

A French company's current assets are F2.5 million and current liabilities amount to F2.0 million. The convenience translation (year-end exchange) rate is $1.00 = F5.2.

$$\text{Current ratio using amounts in F} \quad \frac{2,500,000}{2,000,000} = 1.25 \text{ to } 1$$

$$\text{Current ratio using amounts in \$} \quad \frac{2,500,000 \div 5.2}{2,000,000 \div 5.2} = 1.25 \text{ to } 1$$

This example illustrates that financial ratio analysis can be performed without converting the amounts expressed in different currencies to a single currency.

General Limitations of Financial Ratio Analysis

Ratio analysis has several *general limitations*, besides the complexity introduced by different accounting frameworks and business practices worldwide.

---

7 Donald E. Kieso and Jerry J. Weygandt. *Intermediate Accounting,* 9th ed. New York: John Wiley & Sons, Inc., 1998, pp. 1383–1384.

exhibit 7.7   Common Financial Ratios

Classification	Ratio	Computation
Liquidity	Current ratio *To determine the ability to meet short-term debt.*	$\dfrac{\text{Current assets}}{\text{Current liabilities}}$
Efficiency	Inventory turnover *To measure how quickly inventory is sold.*	$\dfrac{\text{Cost of goods sold}}{\text{Average inventory}}$
	Accounts receivable turnover *To determine the efficiency of collections from accounts receivable.*	$\dfrac{\text{Credit sales}}{\text{Average accounts receivable}}$
	Asset turnover *To measure reserve generated from the assets used.*	$\dfrac{\text{Net sales}}{\text{Average total assets}}$
Profitability	Profit margin *To compare margin to competitors' margins.*	$\dfrac{\text{Net income}}{\text{Net sales}}$
	Return on assets *To measure competitive profit efficiency of assets.*	$\dfrac{\text{Net income}}{\text{Average total assets}}$
	Return on equity *To measure profit efficiency of stockholders' investment.*	$\dfrac{\text{Net income}}{\text{Average stockholders' equity}}$
Coverage	Debt ratio *To analyze the ability to meet debt obligations.*	$\dfrac{\text{Total liabilities}}{\text{Total assets}}$
	Debt-to-equity ratio *To compare the financing from borrowing with the equity investment.*	$\dfrac{\text{Total liabilities}}{\text{Stockholders' equity}}$

- *Valuation basis.* Financial ratios are based on historical cost in most countries. The users may make the erroneous assumption that the costs reflect current prices. Consequently, poor decisions may be made.

- *Estimates.* In situations involving substantial estimated amounts—such as depreciation and amortization—the ratios lose their effectiveness for intercompany comparisons.

- *Omissions.* Many important informational items are not included in financial statements. Examples include intellectual capital, product innovation, labor relations, and competitors' actions. Though important to a company's future, such items do not enter the accounting system. Their omission limits the usefulness of ratios.

- *Alternatives allowed by GAAP.* Different companies use different alternatives allowed by accounting standards. Examples include:

- Inventory valuation: LIFO, FIFO.
- Depreciation methods: straight-line, double-declining balance.

Use of different alternatives allowed within the same accounting framework makes intercompany comparisons difficult.

International Financial Ratio Analysis

Most of the *general limitations* of financial ratio analysis are *intensified* in the international context.

- *Valuation basis.* Though many countries use historical cost basis, other countries' financial statements are prepared using hybrid historical-current cost basis, or historical costs basis adjusted for general price-level changes. The U.K. has a hybrid of historical-current cost basis. In Mexico, historical-cost-based statements are adjusted for general price-level changes.
- *Estimates.* The varying levels of flexibility for estimating specific items allowed in different countries makes the ratio comparisons more difficult. For example, a maximum of 40 years is allowed for amortization of goodwill in the U.S. In Finland, the amortization period for goodwill is normally 5 years with a maximum of 20 years.
- *Omissions.* As discussed earlier, ratio analysis suffers in general from omission of some important information. The problem is exacerbated by the fact that some information that is required to be disclosed in the financial reports in some countries is altogether omitted in other countries. For example, in Sweden, no contingent losses are accrued. In the U.S., contingent gains are not recorded, and contingent losses are recorded if they are probable and a reasonable estimate can be made. In Germany, contingent losses are recorded if they are possible.

The previous discussion focused on the *intensifying effect* of internationalization on the *general limitations* of financial ratio analysis. We will next discuss financial statement analysis in the international context.

Different Accounting Frameworks

Accounting frameworks differ from country to country. In the absence of restated financial statements, the comparison of financial ratios of different companies' financial statements prepared using different accounting frameworks is a futile exercise.

The acceptable accounting treatment of certain irregular items varies among countries. For example, there is little comparability internationally in the accounting treatment of prior-year adjustments. In the U.S., prior-year adjustments do not appear in the current period's income statement. In Germany and Denmark, they do. In the U.S., the events and transactions considered to be both unusual and infrequent in occurrence are considered extraordinary items, shown separately in the income statement. In South Korea, prior-period adjustments may be reported as extraordinary items in the income statement. Mexico's GAAP is silent on the type of items that should be reported as extraordinary. In practice, however, non-operational items such as gains or losses on sales of fixed assets are reported as extraordinary items on the income statement.

In some countries it is acceptable to arbitrarily make charges against income to achieve income smoothing. This practice is not allowed in other countries. *Such differences directly affect reported profitability and other ratios, not because of the real income differences, but because of the diversity in income reporting practices.*

Different Business Customs

Business practices are not uniform throughout the world. If the user of financial analysis is not knowledgeable about the differences, it is likely that wrong conclusions will be drawn. The restatement of financial statements alone is not enough to overcome this problem. As mentioned earlier, Japanese companies typically have relatively higher debt to equity ratios than comparable U.S. companies. Knowledgeable analysts would correctly interpret this as a direct result of Japanese business customs.

The orientation of financial statements poses another challenge. In many countries, financial statements are oriented toward investors; in other countries, the orientation is toward creditors. This influences the information content of the financial statements and the extent to which detailed disclosures are made on individual items. This, again, highlights the importance of understanding business practices in the countries whose financial statements are being analyzed.

Influence of Tax Laws

In order to reduce taxes, it is common practice in some countries to prepare financial statements that purposely minimize reported income. In Italy, the tax law generally applies to any profit presented in financial statements, even if such profit is not required to be recognized according to tax regulations. In Germany, there are many areas where an accounting method selected for income tax purposes is required for financial reporting. Consequently, there are few differences in Germany between income for taxation and income for financial reporting.

Data Accuracy

It was mentioned in an earlier section of this chapter that in some cases the data may be deliberately changed to show a better-than-actual performance. Ratios based on inaccurate data would obviously be inaccurate and unreliable for comparison.

Financial Ratios and GAAP Diversity—Case Studies

In this section, we will review the impact of different accounting standards on two financial ratios earnings per share and rate of return on equity. As we discussed in Chapter 5, the impact of financial measurements, prescribed by different GAAP, affects disclosures in the financial statements. Consequently, the financial ratios using amounts from the financial statements are directly affected.

From a review of Exhibits 7.8 through 7.12, it becomes obvious that:

- Financial ratios of a firm can be drastically different under different accounting standards. Exhibits 7.11 and 7.12 provide clear evidence in support of this point.

- The magnitude of differences (in the ratios) depends to a great extent on the types of transactions an enterprise enters into. Exhibits 7.10 through 7.12 compare the ratios under the U.S. and the U.K. GAAP for three companies. In the case of BP Amoco (Exhibit 7.10) the differences are relatively small. The opposite is true in the cases of Nycomed Amersham plc (Exhibit 7.11) and ICI (Exhibit 7.12). In both of the latter cases, not only are the differences significant in magnitude, they are also in opposite direction: Positive ratios under the U.K. GAAP and negative ratios computed using the U.S. GAAP.

The previous discussion should help us avoid the pitfalls of relying exclusively on ratio analysis. *The impact of the measurement process under GAAPs of different countries may result in drastic differences in the financial ratios of the same company for the same period.*

Trend Analysis

Ratio analysis is for one date or one period. *Trend analysis compares the information for an item for two or more different dates or periods.* Trend analysis shows the change taking place in an item and the rate of the change. It is common for companies to present 5- or 10-year summaries of selected items in their annual reports. Examples are shown in Exhibit 7.13 (page 266) for Sony Corporation and Exhibit 7.14 (page 267) for Dyno (a Norway-based company). Companies also normally present comparative financial statements for the past one or two years alongside the current year's financial statements (Exhibits 7.4 through 7.6).

While performing trend analysis for comparison with other companies, it is desirable to convert the amounts to a common base. This enables the analyst to

exhibit 7.8   **Case 1: Teléfonos de México—1997**

	U.S. GAAP	Mexican GAAP
Net income	Ps. 12,241,801,000	Ps. 12,850,613,000
Stockholders' equity	78,679,648,000	88,230,958,000
Ratios		
Earnings per share (in Mexican Pesos)	1.456	1.529
Rate of return on equity	15.559%	14.565%

Source: Teléfonos de México. *Annual Report 1997*, p. 40.

exhibit 7.9   Case 2: Philips—1997

	U.S. GAAP	Dutch GAAP
Net income	f. 13,090,000,000	f. 13,339,000,000
Stockholders' equity	32,362,000,000	31,292,000,000
Ratios		
Earnings per share (in Dutch guilders):		
Basic	36.36	37.05
Diluted	36.06	36.75
Rate of return on equity	40.449%	42.628%

Source: Philips. *Annual Report 1998*, pp. 78, 79, 81, 117, and 118.

exhibit 7.10   Case 3: BP Amoco—1999

	U.S. GAAP	U.K. GAAP
Profit for the year	$ 4,596,000,000	$ 5,008,000,000
Stockholders' interest	37,838,000,000	43,281,000,000
Ratios		
Earnings per ordinary share (in U.S. cents):		
Basic	23.70	25.82
Diluted	23.56	25.68
Rate of return on equity	12.147%	11.571%

Source: BP Amoco. *Annual Report and Accounts 1999*, pp. 46 and 73.

exhibit 7.11   Case 4: Nycomed Amersham plc—1998

	U.S. GAAP	U.K. GAAP
Net income (loss)	£ (2,600,000)	£ 122,200,000
Stockholders' equity	1,618,400,000	207,100,000
Ratios		
Earnings (loss) per ordinary share (in U.K. pences):	(0.4)	19.5
Rate of return on equity	(0.161)%	59.005%

Source: Nycomed Amersham plc. *Annual Report and Accounts 1998*, pp. 33 and 63.

exhibit 7.12 Case 5: ICI—1998

	U.S. GAAP	U.K. GAAP
Net income (loss)	£ (44,000,000)	£ 193,000,000
Stockholders' equity	3,557,000,000	149,000,000
Ratios		
Earnings (loss) per ordinary share (in U.K. pences):		
Basic	(0.4)	19.5
Diluted	(6.1)	26.5
Rate of return on equity	(1.237)%	129.5%

Source: ICI. *Annual Report and Accounts and Form 20-F 1998*, pp. 51, 97, and 98.

evaluate the rate of growth or decline across time more readily. A common approach is to select the earliest year as the base year. The amount of each succeeding year is then divided by the amount of the base year. When comparing two or more firms, the same base year should be used for all of the firms included in the analysis.

The trends can be significantly influenced by the base year. For this reason, the base year chosen should be a representative year. This precludes selecting as a base any year with a negative amount. Trend analysis is illustrated in Exhibit 7.15 (page 268), using Volkswagen AG and General Motors sales data for the period 1994–1998.

When this analytical technique is used for comparison, no complexity is added by different currencies—the German mark and the U.S. dollar in our example. The growth trend is expressed in percentages and not in the currency amounts.

Change Trend Analysis

A variation of trend analysis is to compute the changes from one period to the next. Using the information from Exhibit 7.15 for Volkswagen AG, the percent change in sales revenue from 1994 to 1995 is computed as follows:

$$\frac{(88,119 - 80,041)}{80,041} \times 100 = 10.1\% \text{ (approximately)}$$

Annual sale change trends for Volkswagen AG and General Motors from 1994 to 1998 are shown in Exhibit 7.16 (page 268). A review of Exhibit 7.16 indicates far more volatility in sales from year to year for General Motors than was apparent from the sale trends shown in Exhibit 7.15.

exhibit 7.13 Sony Five-Year Summary of Selected Financial Data

	Sony Corporation and Consolidated Subsidiaries Year Ended March 31					Dollars in thousands except per share amounts
	Yen in millions except per share amounts					
	1995	1996	1997	1998	1999	1999
FOR THE YEAR						
Sales and operating revenue	¥3,990,583	¥4,592,565	¥5,663,134	¥6,755,490	**¥6,794,619**	**$56,621,825**
Operating income (loss)	(166,640)	235,324	370,330	520,210	**338,649**	**2,822,075**
Income (loss) before income						
taxes	(220,948)	138,159	312,429	453,749	**368,128**	**3,067,733**
Income taxes	65,173	77,158	163,570	214,868	**176,973**	**1,474,775**
Net income (loss)	(293,356)	54,252	139,460	222,068	**179,004**	**1,491,700**
Per share data:						
Net income (loss)						
—Basic	¥(784.7)	¥145.1	¥367.7	¥557.7	**¥436.9**	**$3.64**
—Diluted	(784.7)	134.0	309.2	483.4	**391.0**	**3.26**
Cash dividends	50.0	50.0	55.0	60.0	**50.0**	**0.42**
Depreciation and amortization	¥ 226,984	¥ 227,316	¥ 266,532	¥ 301,665	**¥ 307,173**	**$ 2,559,775**
Capital expenditures						
(additions to fixed assets)	250,678	251,197	298,078	387,955	**353,730**	**2,947,750**
R&D expenses	239,164	257,326	282,569	318,044	**375,314**	**3,127,617**
AT YEAR-END						
Net working capital	¥ 537,733	¥ 816,361	¥ 843,500	¥1,151,152	**¥1,126,848**	**$ 9,390,400**
Stockholders' equity	1,007,802	1,169,147	1,459,332	1,815,555	**1,823,665**	**$15,197,208**
Stockholders' equity						
per share	¥ 2,695.31	¥ 3,125.53	¥ 3,798.62	¥ 4,461.39	**¥ 4,448.69**	**$37.07**
Total assets	¥4,223,914	¥5,045,699	¥5,680,246	¥6,403,043	**¥6,299,053**	**$52,492,108**
Number of shares issued at						
year-end (thousands of shares)	373,911	374,068	384,185	407,195	**410,439**	

Source: Sony Corporation. *Annual Report 1999*, p. 44.

Limitations of Trend Analysis

Though trend analysis is informative, it should be used with caution for forecasting. It compares only growth (or decline) from period to period.

There are two major limitations of trend analysis. First, the base year has a significant impact on the long-term trend. For this reason, *the representativeness of the base year selected cannot be overemphasized.* Presence of irregular items in the base year, e.g., extraordinary items, would distort the long-term trend figures.

exhibit 7.14 Dyno—Key Financial Figures

	NOK Million				
	1998	1997	1996	1995	1994
Income					
Operating revenue	**11,868**	11,329	9,714	10,411	9,698
Revenue outside Norway (percent)	**90**	89	88	89	88
Profit					
Operating profit	**529**	575	460	602	860
Profit before extraordinary items	**661**	450	373	435	693
Consolidated net profit/loss (−)	**156**	−62	211	343	418
Profitability					
Net operating margin (percent)	**4.5**	5.1	4.7	5.8	8.9
Return on capital employed (percent)	**9.2**	10.1	9.5	12.1	16.6
Return on equity (percent)	**6.7**	−1.6	8.4	14.0	18.5
Capital Structure as of December 31					
Cash flow from operating activities	**399**	561	665	778	786
Gross investments	**886**	1,083	1,162	727	646
Capital employed	**6,136**	5,860	5,238	4,914	5,345
Equity as % of total assets	**32.3**	31.0	36.4	38.2	32.2
Net interestbearing debt	**2,325**	2,362	1,839	1,474	2,084
Personnel					
Employees as of December 31	**8,839**	8,707	7,706	7,316	7,569
Shares					
Number of shares as of Dec. 31 (1,000)	**25,598**	25,583	25,525	25,421	25,102
Average number of shares (1,000)	**25,591**	25,569	25,502	25,341	25,033
Dividend per share	**3.00**	3.00	4.00	4.00	4.00
Earnings per share before net extraordinary items	**13.96**	10.09	8.26	9.63	16.69
Earnings per share	**6.10**	−2.41	8.26	13.53	16.69
Payout ratio (average last 3 years) (percent)	**83.7**	56.8	31.2	27.5	32.2
Marked price Dec. 31	**113**	142	162	148	198
Marked price capitalization at Dec. 31	**2,893**	3,633	4,135	3,762	4,970
Price/earnings at Dec. 31	**18.5**	—	19.6	10.9	11.9
No. of shareholders	**5,122**	4,995	5,044	5,441	5,186

Source: Dyno. *Annual Report 1998*, pp. 38–39.

exhibit 7.15 Annual Sales Trends—
Volkswagen AG and General Motors

	1994	1995	1996	1997	1998
Volkswagen AG					
Sales (DM millions)	80,041	88,119	100,123	113,245	134,243
Base year trend (%)	100	110	125	141	168
General Motors					
Sales ($ millions)	148,261	160,001	163,885	178,252	161,315
Base year trend (%)	100	108	111	120	109

Sources: 1. Volkswagen AG. *Annual Report 1998*, p. 97.
2. General Motors Corporation. *1998 Annual Report*, p. 89.

exhibit 7.16 Annual Sales Change Trends—
Volkswagen AG and General Motors

	1994	1995	1996	1997	1998
Volkswagen AG (%)	—	10.1	13.6	13.11	18.5
General Motors (%)	—	7.9	2.4	8.8	−9.5

Second, *the base year cannot be a negative number for change trend analysis.* A change trend cannot be developed from using a negative number. For this reason, there may be gaps in the series when a year-to-year change trend is being developed. This is illustrated in Exhibit 7.17 for Philips.

The gap in the series for 1997 is because the base year 1996 has a negative number (loss in the amount of f.590 million). When such gaps develop, no comparisons with other companies can be made for the affected years in the series.

exhibit 7.17 Annual Net Income Change Trends
(in Millions of Dutch Guilders)—The Philips Group

	1994	1995	1996	1997	1998
Net income (loss)	2,125	2,518	(590)	5,733	13,339
Annual net income change trend (%)	—	18.5	−123.4	—	132.7

Source: Philips. *Annual Report 1998*, p. 142.

Foreign Currency Considerations

In an earlier section of this chapter, it was stated that financial ratios are identical regardless of the currency denomination of the account balances. For that reason, it is unnecessary to convert the amounts denominated in a foreign, i.e., local, currency to the domestic currency for ratio analysis.

For the purpose of performing comparative trend analysis, it is not only desirable but necessary to use the amounts expressed in the local (foreign) currency; the reason for this being that the trend data based on amounts translated from a foreign currency to the domestic currency distort the underlying financial relationships. This is true whether the year-end exchange rates are used for translation, or one of the currency translation methods discussed in Chapter 2 is employed.

If the year-end exchange rates are used, a base year must be chosen for the years that are included in the trend analysis. The decision as to which one of the years should be selected as the base year depends on personal preference. Perhaps the only situation for which a base year guideline exists is when foreign currency balances have been adjusted for changes in the general purchasing power of the currency. In such a case, the year-end exchange rates of the year used as the base year for inflation adjustments should be used.

Example

Sales revenue data of a U.K.-based company for four years follow.

Year	Sales (£ millions)	Year-End Exchange Rates, £ to $
1	600	0.50
2	680	0.45
3	800	0.60
4	980	0.70

(a) Four years cumulative sales change trend using the domestic currency:

$$\frac{980 - 600}{600} = 63\%$$

(b) Year 1 as the base year:

$$\frac{(980 \div 0.5) - (600 \div 0.5)}{(600 \div 0.5)} = 63\%$$

(c) Year 4 as the base year:

$$\frac{(980 \div 0.7) - (600 \div 0.7)}{(600 \div 0.7)} = 63\%$$

(d) Change trend using the applicable convenience translation rates at the end of year 1 and year 4:

$$\frac{(980 \div 0.7) - (600 \div 0.5)}{(600 \div 0.5)} = \frac{1{,}400 - 1{,}200}{1{,}200} = 17\%$$

As can be seen from (a), (b), and (c), when a base-year's exchange rate is used the change trend analysis results are unaffected from translating the local currency by using convenience rates. It does not matter which year's year-end convenience rate is used or if the amounts are not translated at all. However, when we use the year-end convenience rates applicable to the sales amounts of specific years, we get a distortion. This is demonstrated in part (d).

For translation purposes if one of the currency translation methods is employed, distortion may be caused by the translation process itself. Using the same amounts that are denominated in a foreign currency, each one of the translation methods discussed in Chapter 2 results in different translated amounts in many instances. Unless an effort is made to isolate exchange rate influences, the trend analysis may be distorted and could lead to misleading conclusions.

Note to Students

Many financial services provide information about companies and countries. Most of the big public accounting firms publish country guides that include helpful information about different countries. The following Web site addresses are quite useful for getting information on countries and companies:

Federation of European Stock Exchanges	**http://www.fese.be**
International Federation of Stock Exchanges	**http://www.fibv.com**
Political and Economic Risk Consultancy	**http://www.asiarisk.com**
U.S. Securities and Exchange Commission (a free service offering access to U.S.-based companies' reports filed with the Securities and Exchange Commission)	**http://www.sec.gov/edgarhp.htm**

Comprehensive databases are also available to compare companies in an industry or across industries. They contain data on thousands of companies in major financial centers of the world.

Five databases that have extensive coverage of international companies are:

Laser D II
Datastream
FIS Online
Global Access
World Scope

For obtaining free information on hundreds of non-U.S.-based companies, you might find **http://www.hoovers.com** very useful.

Chapter Summary

1. Several current developments are making financial statement analysis increasingly important.

2. Information is vital for the global market's efficiency.

3. There are multiple reasons for international financial statement analysis including high returns availability, risk diversification, effect of foreign currency appreciation on investment, and cross-border business transactions.

4. Perceived problems in the availability of financial information include reliability of data, adequacy of disclosures, timeliness of information, language and terminology differences, different currencies, and financial statements format differences.

5. The globalization of markets appears to be the motivating factor contributing to voluntary disclosures and greater harmonization of accounting and auditing principles.

6. Different accounting standards may result in different reported amounts for the same transactions or events.

7. For a financial analyst, the diversity of business practices worldwide is a greater challenge than the diversity of accounting principles worldwide.

8. Two of the techniques for financial analysis are financial ratio analysis and trend analysis.

9. There are several general limitations of financial ratio analysis. The effect of these limitations is compounded when financial ratio analysis is done in the international context.

10. It is important to select a representative year as the base year for doing trend analysis since the trends can be significantly influenced by the base year selected.

11. The presence of different currencies does not add complexity to trend analysis since trends are expressed in percentages.

12. It is desirable to use amounts expressed in local (foreign) currency for change trend analysis for several reasons. Translation is not advisable since the translated amounts can distort the results.

Questions for Discussion

1. Define financial statement analysis.

2. Discuss at least two reasons for the increasing importance of financial statement analysis.

3. Does an appreciation in a country's currency affect the value of an existing investment in the country?

4. Discuss at least three perceived problems on the access and quality of financial information in different countries.

5. Name the organizations that are significantly affecting financial reporting practices of the companies engaged in international business and investment.

6. Identify the most important factor contributing toward voluntary disclosure and toward the harmonization of accounting and auditing principles.

7. Discuss the two alternatives for coping with diversity of accounting principles worldwide.

8. What is the objective of financial statement analysis?

9. Describe and contrast financial ratio analysis and trend analysis.

10. Describe what these types of ratios measure: Liquidity, activity, profitability, and coverage.

11. Give one example for each of the four types of ratios in Question 10.

12. Discuss at least two general limitations of financial ratio analysis.

13. "The general limitations of financial ratio analysis pose relatively more serious problems when financial ratio analysis is done in the international context." Explain.

14. Why is it important to choose a representative year as the base year in trend analysis?

15. Discuss the two limitations of trend analysis.

16. Why is it desirable to use the amounts denominated in local (foreign) currency for trend analysis?

17. State the base-year guideline for trend analysis when foreign currency balances have been adjusted for general price-level changes.

18. "Amounts denominated in a foreign currency that are translated using one of the translation methods may cause distortion due to the translation process." Explain.

Exercises/Problems

7-1 You have completed a financial statement analysis of a successful Japanese company. While comparing results of the analysis to a comparable U.S.

company, you made the observation that the Japanese company had a relatively high debt to equity ratio compared with the U.S. company, as follows.

	(In millions)		Debt to Equity Ratio
	Debt	**Equity**	
Japanese	¥40,000	¥20,000	2.0
U.S.	$200	$400	0.5

You are curious to know why there is such a difference in the leverage position of the two supposedly comparable companies.

Required:

Explain the factor(s) causing the difference between the two companies. What can you do so as not to draw erroneous conclusions in such comparisons?

7-2   Imperial Chemical Industries (ICI) is the U.K.'s largest manufacturing company. ICI is listed in the U.S. and therefore is required by the U.S. Securities and Exchange Commission to provide data reconciling U.K. GAAP with U.S. GAAP.

The following are selected data for the year 1998.

	£ (in millions)	
	U.K. GAAP	**U.S. GAAP**
Sales	8,430	8,430
Net income (loss)	193	(44)

Required:

(1)   Compute the profit margin using U.K. GAAP.

(2)   Complete requirement (1) using U.S. GAAP.

(3)   Comment on the difference between your solutions in the two requirements.

7-3   Refer to Exhibits 7.5 and 7.6, which contain The Quaker Oats Company and ICI balance sheets, respectively, to complete the following.

Required:

(1)   Identify some of the major differences in the two balance sheets in terminology and format.

(2)   Prepare a balance sheet for the ICI Group at December 31, 1998, using U.S. terminology and format.

(3)   Prepare a balance sheet for The Quaker Oats Company and subsidiaries at December 31, 1998, using U.K. terminology and format.

7-4   Review and analyze the annual report of a foreign company to complete the following. Also, research the culture of the country that affects its business practices.

Required:

Prepare a 400–500 word report, discussing the following:

(1) The culture's effect on business and financial reporting practices.

(2) Selected ratio and trend analysis (you choose the ratios and trends).

(3) Your opinion of the company's operating performance and financial position.

7-5 Write a 150–200 word report on:

(1) General limitations of financial ratio analysis.

(2) Limitations of financial ratio analysis in the international context.

7-6 In a report of 150–200 words, describe limitations of trend analysis, including the foreign currency aspect.

7-7 Refer to Exhibits 7.5 and 7.6 in the chapter to complete the following.

Required:

(1) Prepare these ratios for The Quaker Oats Company and the ICI Group for 1998 only:

  a. Current ratio.

  b. Debt ratio.

(2) Explain what the previous ratios measure.

(3) Refer to Exhibit 7.4. Is it possible to compute the current ratio for Volkswagen? Explain.

7-8 Refer to Exhibit 7.13 to complete the following.

(1) Using yen amounts, compute the year 1999 ratios listed here for Sony. Use the year-end amounts in cases where average amount for the year is needed but not available.

  a. Asset turnover;

  b. Profit margin;

  c. Return on assets;

  d. Return on equity;

  e. Debt ratio;

  f. Debt to equity ratio.

(2) Classify each of the previous ratios using liquidity, efficiency, profitability, and coverage classifications.

7-9 Refer to Exhibit 7.13 in the chapter to complete the following.

Required:

Prepare the annual sales and operating revenue trends for Sony for the period 1995–1999. Use the amounts in yen for your analysis.

7-10 Refer to Exhibit 7.13 in the chapter to complete the following.

Required:

Prepare the annual sales and operating revenue change trends for Sony for the period 1995–1999. Use the amounts in yen for your analysis.

7-11 The following is the annual net income (loss) in millions of French francs for a France-based company.

	Year 1	Year 2	Year 3	Year 4	Year 5
Net income (loss)	6,932	1,123	2,467	3,251	(5,225)

Required:

(1) Prepare annual income (loss) trends using Year 1 as the base year.

(2) Prepare annual income (loss) change trends.

7-12 The following are the net income (loss) data for Hasham and Salman for years 1 through 6 in millions of U.S. dollars.

	Year 1	Year 2	Year 3	Year 4	Year 5	Year 6
Salman	4,856	4,224	(1,986)	(4,453)	(23,498)	2,466
Hasham	(1,230)	3,109	3,104	522	3,807	(3,794)

Required:

Compute the annual net income (loss) change trends for the two companies for the years indicated.

7-13 A Japanese company's current assets are ¥100 million and current liabilities amount to ¥300 million. The convenience translation rate is $1.00 = ¥99.

Required:

(1) Compute the current ratio using amounts in yen.

(2) Compute the current ratio using amounts in dollars.

(3) Compare your answers in requirements (1) and (2) and comment.

7-14 Sales revenue data of a Norwegian company for four years follow in Norwegian krone.

Year	Sales (NKr Millions)	Year-End Exchange Rates NKr to $
1	750	0.17
2	890	0.14

Required:

(1) Perform change trend analysis using the Norwegian krone.

(2) Perform change trend analysis using the Year 1 exchange rate at year-end.

(3) Perform change trend analysis using the Year 2 exchange rate at year-end.

(4) Perform change trend analysis using the applicable exchange rates at the end of Year 1 and Year 2.

(5) Comment on your results in the previous four requirements.

7-15 Using the Internet to download the annual report of a company based in a country other than your own, complete the following.

Required:

(1) Write a two- to three-page report on how the annual report differs from a typical annual report in your country. Some of the following items may be relevant:

    a. Convenience translation.

    b. Significant accounting policies.

    c. Valuation principle.

    d. Required financial statements and disclosures.

    e. Format of financial statements.

    f. Depreciation policy (e.g., in Japan and Germany, financial reporting is consistent with tax treatment).

    g. Culture.

    h. Auditor's report.

(2) Perform the ratio analysis using as many of the ratios contained in Exhibit 7.7 as possible. You may wish to supplement the analysis by using other ratios of your choice.

(3) Perform trend analysis to determine its annual sales trends, annual sales change trends, and annual net income change trends for the last five years.

7-16 Using the Internet, download the annual report of a company based in a country other than your own.

Required:

Write answers to the following questions, and also be prepared to discuss your responses in class.

(1) Company name.

(2) Base country.

(3) Statements prepared in:

    a. language.

    b. currency.

(4) Auditor's report: How is it similar to or different from your country's auditor's report? What are its contents? What is your understanding of the extent of responsibility assumed by the auditors for the discovery of any inaccuracies, lack of transparency, detection of fraud, etc.?

(5) Is there any reference to the GAAP used in the auditor's report or the notes accompanying financial statements? If yes, what GAAP is used?

(6) Is a reconciliation to another country's GAAP provided? If so, what country? What are the most significant reconciliation items?

(7) How are the formats of the financial statements similar to or different from your country's formats?

(8) Are segment disclosures presented? If yes, what type of segments?

(9) Are reserves used? If yes, what type?

(10) Is foreign currency translated? If yes, what translation method is used?

(11) Are any inflation restatements or current cost adjustments made? If yes, what approach is used?

(12) Are there any unusual or unique disclosures?

(13) Did any of the disclosures provide insights into the culture of the base country (e.g., legal system, religion, etc.)?

(14) Are there any significant terminology differences?

Case

Lustra S.p.A. (B)
(Copyright © by the President and Fellows of Harvard College.)[8]

In February 1990, Peter Scala decided not to issue and list Lustra S.p.A.'s common stock in the United States of America. The principal reason was a reluctance to go into the U.S. market with a declining earnings per share trend that, in Peter Scala's mind, was simply the result of *Opinion No. 15's* "arbitrary and unrealistic" rules for computing earnings per share. Instead, he decided to explore the possibility of listing the company's stock on the London Exchange as a preliminary step to raising equity capital in the United Kingdom at some future date.

Based on his experience with *Opinion No. 15*, Peter Scala decided to check quickly on the United Kingdom's earnings per share calculation and disclosure rules. Based on his research, he concluded:

1. Statements of Standard Accounting Practice (SSAP) 3 required listed companies to show earnings per share on the face of the income statement.

2. Earnings per share was defined as the period's after-tax consolidated profit, deducting minority interest and preferred dividends but before taking into account extraordinary items based on the weighted-average share capital eligible for dividends. This figure was known as *basic earnings per share*.

3. A second fully diluted earnings per share figure reflecting potential earnings per share dilution from warrants, opinions, or conversion rights should be disclosed, if applicable.

Peter Scala believed this last requirement would not be a problem, since he believed he could limit the potential dilution to an immaterial amount by the calculation methodology he elected to employ. Also, Peter Scala believed that U.K. investors did not use fully diluted earnings per share figures in their investment decisions.

During 1991 and 1992, the demand for fashion eyewear was hurt by the global recession. And despite a significant increase in new store openings,

---

8 Professor David F. Hawkins prepared this case as the basis for class discussion rather than to illustrate either effective or ineffective handling of an administrative situation.

Lustra's sales and profits reflected this adverse development. The company's poor financial results and the significant operating demands on Peter Scala's time led him to conclude that any listing decision should be postponed.

Early in the fourth quarter of 1992, Peter Scala decided to restructure the company by closing a number of unprofitable stores, discontinuing a recently started small chain of specialty stores, and disposing of some excess and slow-moving inventories. The after-tax losses associated with these three actions were:

	(Millions of British pounds equivalent at year-end pound-lira exchange rate)
Unprofitable store closings	£0.50
Discontinuance of specialty store business	.35
Inventory disposal	.60
Total loss	£1.45

Lustra's chief financial officer told Peter Scala that the £1.45 million after-tax loss associated with these actions could be treated as an extraordinary item and as such excluded from the company's 1992 earnings per share calculation, as shown in Exhibit 7.18.[9]

In early January 1993, encouraged by the 1992 improvement in earnings per share, Peter Scala decided the time had come to get a London listing for the company's stock. The first step was to communicate his decision to Harold Denning,

exhibit 7.18 Lustra S.p.A.—Financial Information (millions, except earnings per share)[a]

	1990	1991	1992
Net sales	£86.00	£92.00	£81.00
Profit on ordinary activities and attributable to ordinary shareholders	1.05	0.70	0.85
Extraordinary items	—	—	(1.45)
Profit for the financial year	£ 1.05	£ 0.70	£ (0.60)
Earnings per share[b]	£ 1.05	£ 0.70	£ 0.85

a Converted to British pounds at the year-end pound-lira exchange rate.
b Computation for Italian reporting purposes. Profit on ordinary activities and attributable to ordinary shareholders divided by average number of common shares outstanding.

9 There are no requirements covering extraordinary items or earnings per share computation and disclosure in the Italian civil code or in the accounting standards issued by the representative body of the Italian accounting profession.

the senior partner of the London office of Peat, Waterhouse & Company, the company's auditors. At this time, the 1992 audit was still in progress. Lustra's 1992 financial statements were due to be released in mid-March.

Peter Scala was surprised to learn from Harold Denning that under a new U.K. accounting standard (*FRS3*) Lustra would not show an improving earnings per share trend in 1992. Instead, 1992 earnings per share would not only be lower than the 1991 figure, they would be negative.

The day after his conversation with Harold Denning, Peter Scala received a letter from Denning explaining the new standard (Exhibit 7.19). Immediately after reading the letter, Scala met with his chief financial officer to reassess his London listing decision.

Required:

(1)   Determine Lustra's 1992 basic earnings per share presentation using *FRS3*.

(2)   If Lustra proceeds with a London listing application, what adjusted earnings per share figure, if any, should the company include in its 1992 financial report? Why should the company present an adjusted 1992 earnings per share figure? Explain the justification for your adjustment.

(3)   Does *FRS3* represent a significant improvement over SSAP3? Discuss.

(4)   How might *FRS3* influence Lustra's decision to list on the London Exchange?

exhibit 7.19 **Letter to Peter Scala from Harold Denning**

January 10, 1993

Mr. Peter Scala
President
Lustra S.p.A.
Lustra Building, Via Saicar 551
Naples, Italy

Dear Peter:

This letter is written to clarify my comments made to you yesterday regarding the format of your 1992 financial statements and earnings per share calculation should you decide to seek a London listing.

Since its formation in 1991, the Accounting Standards Board has undertaken a far-reaching review of U.K. generally accepted accounting principles. This has resulted in major changes to the way companies present their accounts. In line with the recommendations of the Accounting Standards Board, we urge you to adopt *Financial Reporting Standard No. 3* (*FRS3*) at the earliest opportunity. This standard replaces SSAP3.

The objective of *FRS3* is to highlight a range of important components of financial performance to aid users in their understanding of accounts and to assist them in forming a basis for their assessment of future results and cash flows. The format laid down in *FRS3* for the profit and loss account will be demanded by investors to analyze your financial statements.

(continued)

exhibit 7.19 *(continued)*

The basic *FRS3* format we recommend for Lustra's 1992 profit and loss account in any listing submission is:

	Continuing Operations	Discontinued Operations	Total
Turnover	£XXX	£XXX	£XXX
Cost of sales	XXX	XXX	XXX
Trading profit (loss)	£XXX	£XXX	£XXX
Exceptional items	XXX	XXX	XXX
Operating profit (loss) on ordinary activities	£XXX	£XXX	£XXX
Minority interest	XXX	XXX	XXX
Profit (loss) for the financial year	£XXX	£XXX	£XXX
Profit (loss) per ordinary share	£XXX	£XXX	£XXX

As I explained to you during our phone conversation, *FRS3* limits extraordinary items to very rare occurrences. As the illustrations in *FRS3* clearly indicate, the extraordinary items shown in your Italian-GAAP-based reports no longer qualify as extraordinary items in U.K. GAAP presentations.

Under *FRS3*, a business is classified as a discontinued operation if it is clearly distinguishable; has a material effect on the nature and focus of the Group's activities; represents a material reduction in the Group's operating facilities; and either its sale is completed, or if a termination, its former activities have ceased before the earlier of three months after the commencement of the subsequent period and the date on which the financial statements are approved. In line with these new requirements, we believe the charge associated with the discontinuance of your small specialty store business should be reported as a discontinued operation. To conform to *FRS3*, any prior periods presented will have to be restated to show the specialty stores as a discontinued business.

The store closing and inventory disposal losses are business activities that relate to your continuing business. As such, *FRS3* requires that these losses be included in the calculation of continuing-operations-related operating profit on ordinary activities.

FRS3 also deals with the calculation and disclosure of earnings per share data. It requires basic earnings per share to be calculated on the basis of profit for the financial year less preferred dividends, if any. Therefore, the basic earnings per share you would show under U.K. GAAP would be a negative amount rather than a positive amount as reported on your Italian GAAP statements.

When the *FRS3* earnings per share calculation was proposed, it was bitterly opposed by the business and financial analysts communities. They believed it would lead to more volatile earnings and did not reflect the way investors view and use earnings per share data. As a compromise, the Accounting Standards Board agreed to permit companies to disclose an alternative earnings per share figure that the reporting company believed was a more useful one for investors. The requirements are that this alternative figure be presented with the official one, not be displayed in a more prominent way, and the method used to calculate it be fully disclosed.

We believe that you should consider reporting an alternative earnings per share figure on the face of your 1992 profit and loss account and in the accompanying notes. The presentation of the adjusted earnings per share figure would be accompanied by the following statement: "In the opinion of the directors, the adjustments give a better underlying picture of the Group's performance than the basic earnings per share figure."

Should you decide to proceed with a London Listing, we will be delighted to assist you in the preparation of your listing materials. Please let me know your plans as soon as possible so that we can incorporate this matter into our current year-end audit programme.

Sincerely,

Harold Denning
Managing Partner
Peat, Waterhouse & Company

References

Auerbach, J. "IBM's Accounting Method Faces Scrutiny." *The Wall Street Journal*, 24 November 1999, pp. C1–C2.

Blasch, Doris M., Jerome Kelliher, and William J. Read. "The FASB and the IASC Redeliberate EPS." *Journal of Accountancy*, February 1996, pp. 43–47.

Choi, Frederick D.S., and Richard M. Levich. "Behavioral Effects of International Accounting Diversity." *Accounting Horizons*, June 1991, pp. 1–13.

Diga, J.G. "Financial Reporting in Emerging Capital Markets: Characteristics and Policy Issues." *Accounting Horizons*, June 1997, pp. 41–64.

Hofsteder, G.H. Culture's Consequences. *International Differences in Work-Related Values*. Beverly Hills, CA: Sage Publications, 1980.

Lowe, Howard D. "Shortcomings of Japanese Consolidated Financial Statements." *Accounting Horizons*, September 1990, pp. 1–9.

Palepu, K.G., V. Bernard, and P. Healy. *Business Analysis and Valuation Using Financial Statements*. Cincinnati, OH: South-Western College Publishing, 1996.

Perera, M.H.B. "Towards a Framework to Analyze the Impact of Culture on Accounting." *The International Journal of Accounting*, vol. 24, no. 1 (1989), pp. 42–56.

Pulliam, S. "Analysts Twist Their Yardsticks to Justify P/E of Cisco and Co." *The Wall Street Journal*, 12 April 2000, pp. C1 and C4.

Samuels, J.M., R.E. Brayshaw, and J.M. Craner. *Financial Statement Analysis in Europe*. London: Chapman & Hall, 1995.

Special Committee on Financial Reporting. *Improving Business Reporting—A Customer Focus*. New York: American Institute of Certified Public Accountants, 1994.

Stickney, C., and P. Brown. *Financial Reporting and Statement Analysis: A Strategic Perspective*, 4th ed. Fort Worth, TX: Harcourt, Brace & Company, 1998.

Tondkar, Rasoul H., Ajay Adhikari, and Edward N. Coffman. "Adding an International Dimension to Upper-level Financial Accounting Courses by Utilizing Foreign Annual Reports." *Issues in Accounting Education*, Fall 1994, pp. 271–281.

Wallace, R.S. Olusegun, and Paul A. Collier. "The 'Cash' in Cash Flow Statements: A Multi-Country Comparison." *Accounting Horizons*, December 1991, pp. 44–52.

Weetman P., and S.J. Gray. "International Financial Analysis and Comparative Corporate Performance: The Impact of U.K. versus U.S. Accounting Principles on Earnings." *Journal of International Financial Management and Accounting*, Summer/Autumn 1990, pp. 111–130.

White, G., A. Sondhi, and D. Fried. *The Analysis and Use of Financial Statements*, 2nd ed. New York: John Wiley & Sons, 1998.

Working Group on External Financial Reporting of the Schmalenbach-Gesellschaft-Deutsche Gesellschaft für Betriebswirtschaft. "German Accounting Principles: An Institutionalized Framework." *Accounting Horizons*, September 1995, pp. 92–99.

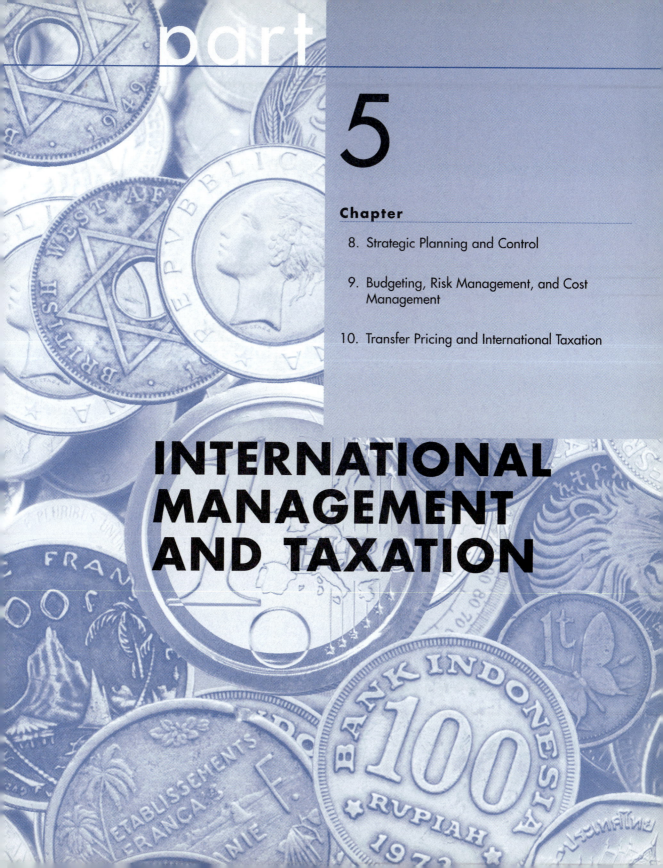

part

5

INTERNATIONAL MANAGEMENT AND TAXATION

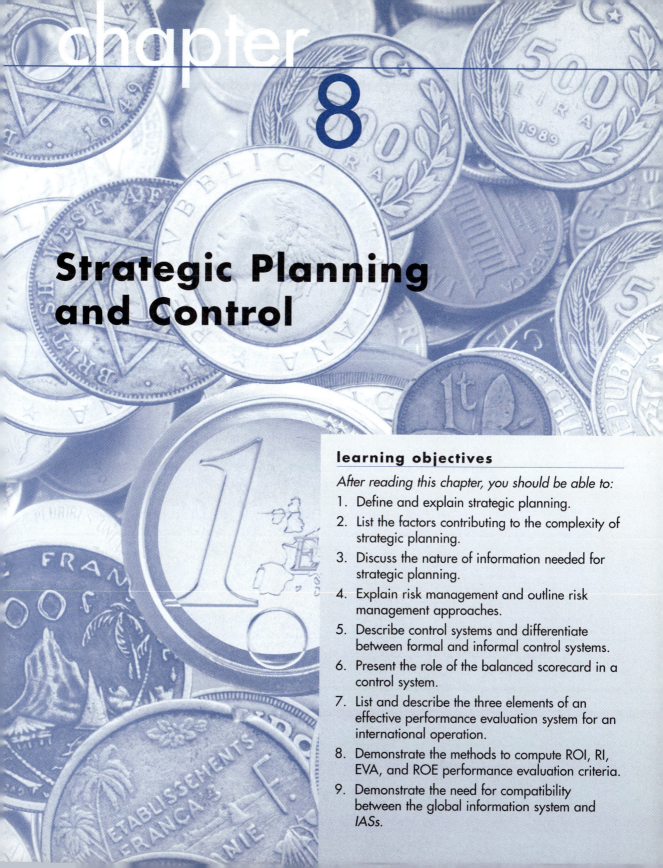

chapter

8

Strategic Planning and Control

learning objectives

After reading this chapter, you should be able to:

1. Define and explain strategic planning.

2. List the factors contributing to the complexity of strategic planning.

3. Discuss the nature of information needed for strategic planning.

4. Explain risk management and outline risk management approaches.

5. Describe control systems and differentiate between formal and informal control systems.

6. Present the role of the balanced scorecard in a control system.

7. List and describe the three elements of an effective performance evaluation system for an international operation.

8. Demonstrate the methods to compute ROI, RI, EVA, and ROE performance evaluation criteria.

9. Demonstrate the need for compatibility between the global information system and IASs.

The focus of this chapter is on strategic planning and control of international operations. The accounting system of an organization may be viewed as consisting of financial accounting and managerial accounting. The distinction between the two is based on the primary users of information. **Managerial accounting** provides the information for users within the organization to help them *plan* and *control* activities of the organization and to *make decisions*. **Financial accounting** furnishes the information primarily for users outside the organization.

Managerial Accounting

Managerial accounting information is for two broad purposes:

- *Policy formulation, strategic planning, and operational planning.* **Special reports** are prepared for providing information to managers for formulating policies, preparing strategic plans, and preparing operational plans. **Operational plans** are designed to implement strategic plans. Typically, an operational plan is for a part of the organization, covers a time period shorter than the strategic plan, and is implemented by middle- and lower-level managers. The trend is toward inclusion of more nonfinancial and nonquantitative information to enhance the usefulness of operational plans.

- *Planning activities and controlling operations.* **Regular reports** assist managers in planning activities and controlling operations. A **performance report** makes a comparison of actual performance with budgetary goals. It is an example of a regular report. The trend is toward preparing more frequent and more nonfinancial regular reports. For example, a shift manager may receive a daily report containing data on the total number of units produced, tons of raw materials used, number of labor hours used, and the number of defective units produced.

The complexity of international operations places additional demands on managerial accounting as discussed in subsequent sections of this chapter.

International Strategic Planning

According to W. Edwards Deming, acknowledged by many to be the father of the quality movement, there must be a clear goal or long-range plan to stay in business. **Strategic planning** is the process of deciding on the goals of the organization, and the strategies for attaining these goals.[1] A **strategic plan** integrates an organization's major goals, policies, and action sequences into a cohesive whole.[2]

---

1 Robert N. Anthony. *The Management Control Function.* Boston: The Harvard Business School Press, 1988, p. 30.

2 James Brian Quinn. *Strategies for Change.* Homewood, Ill.: Richard D. Irwin, Inc., 1980, p. 7.

Strategic planning helps an organization allocate its resources optimally to capitalize on its strengths, take advantage of new opportunities, and become and stay competitive. The strategic planning process is not new on the corporate scene. Many domestic corporations in industrialized countries have prepared strategic plans for several decades. However, strategic planning for international operations is still a recent phenomenon.

Multinational corporations make choices while formulating their international business strategies. For example:

- In which countries should the company expend or curtail its operations?
- What should be the scope of operations in a new country? Should it be a marketing operation? A manufacturing operation? Both?
- What should be the form of the business entity in a new country? A joint venture? A wholly owned subsidiary? A partially owned subsidiary?

The strategic planning process of a multinational corporation takes into account the internal as well as external environmental factors of a company. Predicting external environmental factors is difficult enough within the boundaries of one nation. The task poses a more daunting challenge when many countries are involved. This explains the reluctance exhibited by many multinational corporations to enter into business ventures in the former Soviet republics and some of the East European countries. The legal, political, and economic conditions in those countries plus conflicts among religious beliefs make the external environments often too unstable to forecast.

Factors Contributing to Complexity

Multinational corporations must deal with numerous variables while developing a global business strategy.

Communication of Strategies and Attitude Toward Planning

Language and cultural differences may create problems in communicating strategies and plans. Some cultures make the acceptance of planning difficult due to a cultural sense of fatalism regarding the future. A strong belief that every occurrence is pre-destined results in rejecting the very idea of planning, let alone strategic planning.

Economic and Legal Environments

Each country has its own framework for business regulation, tax system, financial reporting requirements, inflation rates, and currency. Additionally, each country has its own customs and traditions for regulating. It is imperative that a multinational company be knowledgeable about the way things are done in a country. Otherwise, costly mistakes may be made. Coca-Cola was fined over $16 million by Italy's antitrust authority in December 1999. Knowledgeable sources criticized Coke for inflexibility in dealing with Italian antitrust officials.

According to them the company "has had a deaf ear to local politics."[3] This changed after Douglas Daft was appointed the CEO. He changed Coke's approach to "think locally and act locally."[4]

Political System

The political system of a country has a direct impact on the business operations. Governments in some countries do not allow foreign-based companies to form certain types of business organizations or engage in certain types of business activities. Some countries require that a local citizen must be a partner in any business venture of a foreign-based company. Many countries prohibit foreign-based companies from owning a controlling ownership interest in a business organization.

Political Stability

Lack of political stability in a country increases the political risk for foreign-based enterprises. Often a change in government in a country experiencing political instability results in abrupt and frequent change in governmental policies toward business enterprises. This is especially true in countries that do not have a long-standing tradition of a free market economy. Lack of stability in a region and regional political conflicts impede free movement of goods and services.

Labor Considerations

Labor considerations are different for each country. In some countries labor unions are quite powerful. German and Swedish labor laws grant workers' unions many powers including the right of representation on the board. Labor laws may impose severe restrictions on the ability of a multinational company to hire or terminate workers. Egypt and India have strict laws that make it extremely difficult to dismiss an employee. Egyptian laws make it equally difficult to lay off employees for any reason including general economic conditions, a company's declining sales volume, or availability of new technology that makes some jobs obsolete.

Other labor considerations including labor productivity and the availability of a skilled workforce vary in different parts of the world.

Nature of Information

The formulation of a strategic plan is a time-consuming process. According to Robert Anthony, "In the classroom, strategic problems can be analyzed by assuming cause/effect relationships, but in the real world, knowledge of these relationships is likely to be so uncertain that use of sophisticated analytical tools is

---

3 Betsy McKay and Deborah Ball. "Italy Finds Coke Guilty of Anticompetitive Move." *The Wall Street Journal*, 20 December 1999, p. B2.

4 Dean Foust, David Rocks, and Manjeet Kripalani. "Doug Daft Isn't Sugarcoating Things." *Business Week*, 7 February 2000, p. 37.

often not worth the effort."[5] In strategic planning, the information reflects future predictions and therefore, is inherently imprecise.

The sources of information for strategic planning are mostly from the external environment. The nature of strategic planning makes it impossible to foresee all the information needed. Therefore, it is not possible to design an information system that can provide all of the information useful for strategic planning. This explains why strategic planning is such a time-consuming process: Information, mostly about the external environment, has to be collected and analyzed *during* the strategic planning process. Strategic planners may be able to make some use of the data available in the information system. However, due to the unique information requirements of strategic planning, the data must be manipulated to be useful.[6]

Stability and complexity of environments vary from country to country. The economies of Sweden and Germany are relatively stable. They remain strong free market economies. The environments of some countries are quite dynamic. France's policies on socialism versus private enterprise are noticeably affected by each election. The greater the degree of environmental instability in a country, the more difficult it is to predict environmental conditions.[7]

Relationship with the Budget

A budget is a formal plan that is usually expressed in monetary terms for a one-year period. The budget, therefore, is a short-range plan. When an organization has a strategic plan, the role of the budget is to essentially make detailed plans to implement the strategy during the budgetary period. It is critical that the goals in the budget be consistent with the strategic plan.

Risk Management

Risk management is the identification of threats and the design of an approach to their containment. It is a major concern of strategic planners. Economic and business information is vital to the preparation of strategic plans. Such information includes economic development indicators, information about banking and credit availability, employment data, and demographical statistics. Such information may either not be available, or if available may not be reliable. Conditions where requisite information is either unavailable or inaccurate enhance the importance of strategic planning. *The lack of reliable information should not derail the strategic planning process. Planning becomes even more important when the level of risk is high.*

---

5 Robert N. Anthony. *The Management Control Function*. Boston, Mass.: The Harvard Business School Press, 1988, p. 46.

6 *Ibid.*, pp. 50–52.

7 Warren J. Keegan. *Global Marketing Management*, 4th ed. Englewood Cliffs, N.J.: Prentice-Hall, 1989, p. 682.

An enterprise with a well-articulated strategic plan should:[8]

- Set a clear direction.
- Know its strengths and weaknesses compared with its competitors.
- Devote its resources to projects that employ its set of core competencies—the primary skills within the organization.
- Identify factors in the environments that require careful monitoring.
- Recognize which competitor actions need critical attention.

Each strategic choice presents its own set of opportunities and associated risks. A strategist might steer a company away from starting operations in a country because of inherent political risks. An integral part of strategic planning is to determine the level of risk the company is willing to take in making a strategic choice. The degree of risk inherent in a strategic choice may be a function of many variables, some of which are:[9]

- *Risk of value loss.* In evaluating a strategic choice, the planners must take into account that the value of the resources invested in the implementation of its strategic plan creates the risk that those resources may lose their value partially or fully. The potential loss may occur because of internal events such as a chronic shortage of qualified personnel in a country of operations. The loss of value may also result from changes in the external environment. For example, there may be a downward shift in the consumer demand for tobacco products because of the government's concerted effort to educate their population about the health hazards.

- *Risk and length of time.* The longer the time period, the higher the probability of exposure to risk involving value loss. Moreover, with a very long time horizon, there is a possibility that the rate of return demanded by the investors may be so high that it may make it difficult, if not impossible, to attract investment funds necessary for growth.

- *Risk and the proportion of resources committed.* This risk is a function of the proportion of the value of resources being committed to the implementation of a strategic plan. The success or failure of a plan involving an investment of a substantial portion of the total resources available to an enterprise can have drastic and far-reaching consequences for the enterprise and its stakeholders.

Risk Management Approaches

A firm may adopt various risk management approaches. These include forming *joint ventures or alliances* to share the risk. An extreme case is the formation of

---

8 Samuel C. Certo and J. Paul Peter. *Strategic Management—Concepts and Applications*. Burr Ridge, Ill.: Richard D. Irwin, Inc., 1995, p. 6.

9 Tony Morden. *Business Strategy and Planning: Text and Cases*. Berkshire, England: McGraw-Hill Book Company Europe, 1993, pp. 214–216.

a virtual organization. In a virtual organization, various enterprises join forces to take advantage of their respective strengths to work collectively on a project. As soon as the project is completed, the participants go their separate ways. Virtual organizations have been the norm in the movie production industry since its inception.

Another risk reduction mechanism is establishing *geographically dispersed international operations*. Chevron was forced to abandon its operations in Sudan some years ago due to anarchy. The company had already invested nearly $1 billion in the country. Now Chevron has a policy in place requiring that no single country should account for more than 25 percent of its annual investments abroad.

A third risk reduction mechanism is to *avoid insurmountable competitors*. Head-on competition with companies, whose immensity of resources makes them almost invincible, is bound to result in an enormous resource loss. Such competitors may be willing to outspend others for as long a time period as necessary to keep or increase their own market share. "If you don't have a competitive advantage, don't compete," advises one of the most respected CEOs in the United States, Jack Welch, CEO and chairman of General Electric Company.[10]

Role of Accounting

Strategic planning deals with the vision for the future direction of an organization.[11] The role of information is central to the strategic planning process. Accountants are important participants in this process for at least four reasons.

- Accountants have the expertise to perform a variety of *essential analyses*. The analyses of costs, customers, markets, and competitors are necessary during the strategic planning process. By analyzing the competitors' financial statements, accountants provide important insights about competitors' relative strengths and weaknesses. This is a significant contribution to the process.
- Modern accountants are well trained to synthesize. *Synthesis* is critical for formulating strategic plans into financial terms.
- Accountants ensure that there is *integration* of annual operational plans and strategic plans.
- Strategic plans become the blueprint for resource allocation. Accountants provide tools to measure achievement of goals including the goals for effective and efficient resource management, after implementing plans. By a *comparative analysis* of actual results against the plans, accountants provide information on the degree of success in achieving budgetary goals.

According to findings of a recent research project of the Institute of Management Accountants, accounting professionals report a shift in their work activities from

---

10 Greg Foldin. "A Hardhead's 'Soft Values': John F. Welch Jr." *Worldbusiness*, Spring 1995, p. 40.

11 Michael D. Akers and Grover L. Porter. "Strategic Planning At Five World-Class Companies." *Management Accounting*, July 1995, p. 24.

traditional accounting to new activities.[12] According to the research report published in 1999, compared to five years ago, accountants are spending more time on long-term strategic planning. Management accountants think that their work activity most critical to their company's success in three years will be strategic planning. The report included the following observations, "Internal consulting, long-term strategic planning, and process improvement were introduced relatively recently to the profession. Indeed, these work activities that management accountants perform today were not part of the accounting vocabulary 10 years ago."[13] Major findings of the study are shown in Exhibit 8.1.

exhibit 8.1   Transformation in the Management Accounting Profession

Important Work Activities

Management accountants spend more time performing the following work activities.

- Internal consulting;
- Long-term strategic planning;
- Computer systems and operations;
- Process improvement; and
- Financial and economic analysis.

Looking ahead three years, they expect to spend more time on these same work activities.

Most Critical Work Activities

An indicator of coming change is that management accountants think that the following work activities will be most critical to their company's success in three years.

- Long-term strategic planning;
- Financial and economic analyses;
- Customer and product profitability;
- Computer systems and operations; and
- Process improvement.

Outlook for the Next Three Years

Management accountants believe that the trend toward business partnering will continue. They expect the following changes over the next three years:

- Less reporting of information, more planning and analysis;
- More partnering and consulting;
- More involvement with operations; and
- More involvement in decision making.

Source: Institute of Management Accounting. *Counting More, Counting Less: Transformation in the Management Accounting Profession*, 1999, p. 17.

---

12 Institute of Management Accountants. *Counting More, Counting Less: Transformations in the Management Accounting Profession*. Montvale, N.J.: The Institute of Management Accountants, 1999, p. 16.

13 *Ibid.*, p. 17.

Competitiveness and Quality

The intensity of global competition is an influential factor in strategic planning for global operations. According to a survey of U.S. senior executives of Fortune 1000 companies, global competition has moved to the top of the list of the issues considered to be most important.[14]

The impact of competition on strategic planning can be illustrated by using Chevron Corporation's example. Chevron shifted its focus from domestic to global operations in order to become competitive. Watching "big playing fields opening up all around the world" finally persuaded Chevron that it couldn't rely on the "very restrictive set of opportunities here in the U.S.," stated David O'Reilly, Chevron vice president of strategic planning. Chevron's strategic shift is explained by its chairman Kenneth Derr, "Growth opportunities for international oil companies have never been greater."[15]

The strategic plan must consider the competitive forces as an especially important variable in international markets if the competitors are well established and resourceful. To be competitive, a business must have *customer focus*. A comprehensive global study, covering 900 executives in 35 countries, was conducted recently by Deloitte Research. According to the research report:

> Customer demands are on the rise and are more unpredictable than ever. Customers are deciding what, when, how, and where they will purchase goods and services. They want them in zero time and often exert their bargaining power to influence price. . . . Customers expect high-quality tailored goods, services, and solutions delivered rapidly and inexpensively. What are the implications for manufacturers? In an era when the traditional approaches to planning, forecasting, and execution are fast becoming obsolete, the ability to anticipate and quickly adapt to changing customer demands is imperative for sustained success. . . . The new game is about shifting from a product-centric to a customer-centric focus.[16]

The report further states, "While product quality is no longer enough to attract and keep customers, it is an ante to compete."[17]

Quality is the most important of the competitive weapons. Market share leadership requires, above all, quality.

> Businesses know that to survive and build long-term competitive advantage they must focus on fundamentals. This begins with a strategic look at customer needs: What does the customer want? What is the value of

14 Deloitte & Touche LLP. "Global Expansion Not Deterred by Falling Dollar." *Deloitte & Touche Review*, 10 July 1995, p. 3.

15 Andy Pasztor. "Global Search: Chevron Is Plunging Into Foreign Projects to Build Oil Reserves." *The Wall Street Journal*, 24 February 1994, p. 1.

16 Deloitte Research. *Making Customer Loyalty Real: Lesson from Leading Manufacturers*. New York: Deloitte Research, 1999, p. 1.

17 *Ibid.*, p. 11.

the business's products or services? How well do they meet these needs, compared with the competition? Answering these questions, the business can uncover its potential sources of competitive advantage and develop a plan to tap them.

To implement this plan, the business must then conduct a strategic review and where necessary re-engineer its core business processes, re-design its products, and renovate its production methods. In each area, the business must assess its ability to satisfy customers.[18]

Quality Awards

In recognition of the importance of quality, there are several well-known international and national quality awards. The Malcolm Baldrige National Quality Award has been presented annually since 1988 to the companies in the U.S. that have excelled in quality. The award is personally presented by the President of the United States.

The Deming Prize, established by the Japanese Union of Scientists and Engineers, is the most honored quality award in Japan. Requirements for the Deming Prize include perhaps the most demanding auditing process.

Other quality awards include the British Quality Award and the European Quality Award. The European Quality Award was established by the European Foundation for Quality Management. The award emphasizes customer satisfaction, employee satisfaction, and impact on society.[19]

Control Systems

This section presents important control concepts for consideration during the design phase of an effective control system. A **control system** compares the actual performance (results) with planned performance (goals). It enables management to assess whether goals are being achieved. After the review, management may consider taking appropriate actions when necessary. An effective control system should include both internal and external information.

In addition to formal control systems, informal control methods play an important role in controlling global operations. The main informal control method is to transfer an executive from one international operation to another with explicit or implicit understanding about the expected performance. Another informal control method is to hold meetings between the parent company executives and the executives in an international operation, usually at the site of international operation. Annual meetings of executives from international operations also provide an opportunity to informally assess performance and to exchange

18 Coopers & Lybrand. *International Review*. New York: Coopers & Lybrand, 1994, p. 21.

19 John S. Oakland. *Total Quality Management: The Route to Improving Performance*, 2d ed. Oxford, England: Butterworth Heinemann Ltd., 1993, pp. 148–151.

information. Advances in information technology have increased the modes and speed of informal control methods.

Cultural differences necessitate the adaptation of control measures to each country's cultural environment. Different languages, communication styles, and levels of technological development are but a few of the issues facing multinational corporations while designing and implementing control measures across national boundaries.

Languages and national currencies need special mention. A subsidiary in a new country might mean another language in which strategic plans, budgets, and reports are prepared. In some countries, India for example, there are many different languages and each has many dialects. Some technical words may be difficult or impossible to translate into the local language. Different national currencies and their fluctuating exchange rates affect the control aspect of a multinational corporation. A significant change in the exchange rate may render the business plan unrealistic. The problem is compounded when a multinational company has operations in many countries and each of those enterprises, in turn, is involved in business transactions in many countries. Unexpected and sudden restrictions on the transfer of funds by the local governments may also constrain the subsidiary's ability to implement its plans.

Centralization Versus Decentralization

Different multinational companies have different philosophies regarding the extent to which they delegate decision-making authority to the managements of international operations. Highly decentralized multinational organizations give managements of the international operations considerable freedom of action. Centralized multinational organizations retain, to a great extent, the authority to make decisions at the parent company headquarters. Centralization and decentralization are a matter of degree. No organization can possibly be fully centralized or fully decentralized.

The extent of centralization or decentralization is an important consideration during the design phase of a multinational company's control system. All other things being equal, the greater the physical distance between the multinational company headquarters and an international operation, the more autonomous the international operation is likely to be. Physical distance in international operations often makes travel and face-to-face communications costly and time-consuming. This often necessitates greater delegation of authority to local management. But perhaps another important reason is that local managers possess more knowledge about their local environments and conditions. They are in a position to make quick decisions to take timely actions. It becomes especially important if the local environment is highly unstable or the nature of a situation demands immediate response.

The current trend is clearly toward greater decentralization. Most of the well-known multinational companies are highly decentralized, with each operation enjoying a high degree of autonomy. The examples include Unilever, Imperial Chemical Industries, Royal Dutch Shell, and Bestfoods. Still, a few multinationals maintain a high degree of centralization. They include Nikon, Sony, and Matsushita.

Performance Evaluation

A key step in the control process is performance evaluation. *It is important not to limit the information used in performance evaluation to either formal reports or to financial results:*[20]

> Information about what has actually happened comes to the manager's attention both from formal reports and also from informal sources. The informal sources include conversations, memoranda, meetings, and personal observations. Since informal information is not governed by the disciplines that are built into a formal reporting system, its validity varies. Thus, the bias of the originator or other sources of inaccuracy needs to be taken into account. When this is done, informal information can be extremely important. Formal reports alone are an inadequate basis for control.
>
> An important control principle is that the formal performance reports should contain no surprises. Important news should be conveyed to interested parties informally, as soon as feasible, and in any event prior to submission of formal reports.
>
> Since a management control system is built around a financial budget, there is a natural tendency to structure performance reports so that they correspond to the budget and to emphasize the correspondence between actual and budget in evaluating performance. This may result in an overemphasis on the financial results. Because measures to nonfinancial, and especially nonquantitative, performance may be difficult to make, these aspects of performance may be given less weight than they should be. Overemphasis or misuse of these measures can have dysfunctional consequences.

A research report issued by The Conference Board explored the use of new performance measures to better manage business. The study found that purely financial, traditional accounting-based performance measures lack predictive behavior, reward the wrong behavior, and give inadequate consideration to hard-to-quantify resources such as intellectual capital.

The study concluded that nonfinancial *key* performance measures should be used to capture not only the value of existing assets, but also the potential for future performance. Typical key measures include:

- Quality of output.
- Customer satisfaction/retention.
- Employee training.

---

20 Robert N. Anthony. *The Management Control Function.* Boston, Mass.: The Harvard Business School Press, 1988, p. 95.

- Research and development investment and productivity.
- New product development.
- Market growth/success.
- Environmental competitiveness.

The key measures are intended to augment (not replace) traditional performance measures. The study recommended that three critical factors be observed while choosing performance measures:

- Do not mistake data for information.
- You are what you measure.
- What gets measured gets managed.

By tying key measures to the strategic vision of the company, there is assurance that as the vision changes, so do the performance measures.[21]

Balanced Scorecard

The balanced scorecard is a useful tool to integrate financial and nonfinancial performance measures. The Institute of Management Accountants has predicted that by the end of year 2001, 40 percent of U.S.-based companies will be using the balanced scorecard. The balanced scorecard helps management communicate the company's strategic plans and link performance measures to the company's strategy. In essence, the balanced scorecard approach helps a company develop performance measures that are in harmony with its strategic plans.

When designing the balanced scorecard, it is important to focus on the *key* performance measures. Fewer measures provide greater impact. To motivate employees, key performance measures should be the link to their compensation.[22]

Measures of Performance for Workers

Business and accounting literature has very little comparative information on the measures of performance used in different cultures to assess an individual's contributions. Most often we have little choice but to resort to inferences such as: Workers in a culture that puts a premium on individualism would tend to have performance measures that evaluate the individual's own contributions, while a culture dominated by collectivism would use performance measures to assess an individual's performance in terms of what he/she contributes to the group effort.

Performance Evaluation of an International Subsidiary

Performance evaluation of an international subsidiary is an assessment of how the subsidiary carries out corporate strategy. The subsidiary performance reports

21 Deloitte & Touche LLP. "Challenging Traditional Measures of Performance." *Deloitte & Touche Review*, 7 August 1995, pp. 1–2.

22 Mark L. Frigo and Kip R. Krumwiede. "The Balanced Scorecard." *Strategic Finance*, January 2000, pp. 51–53.

compare actual performance with planned performance. This comparison may result either in a corrective action or a revision of the plans.[23] Conceptually, performance evaluation of international subsidiaries is similar to that of domestic operations. The international setting, however, makes it necessary to include additional factors not present in domestic operations. Examples of such factors are different inflation rates and foreign currency exchange rates. Information from the evaluation process directs management's attention to the areas in need of improvement. An effective performance evaluation system should have the following elements:

- Performance evaluation criteria.
- Measurement of actual performance.
- Performance evaluation reports.

We will discuss each of the previous elements in the following sections.

Performance Evaluation Criteria

As discussed earlier, performance evaluation criteria should include both financial and nonfinancial measurements. Each performance evaluation criterion poses its unique measurement and information-gathering problems. Criteria to evaluate performance should be specific to the subsidiary. A cost center is evaluated differently from a profit center. A new subsidiary may be exempted from meeting certain performance standards until it is fully established. Some criteria may not be appropriate for some operating environments. For example, cash flow from a subsidiary to the parent company is not a useful criterion for measuring performance of a subsidiary located in a country with currency movement controls. Employee benefits and employee satisfaction are important components of the evaluation system in some countries, while they are less important elsewhere.

Exhibits 8.2 and 8.3 list examples of financial and nonfinancial performance evaluation criteria, respectively. While selecting the evaluation criteria, it is important to keep in mind that future performance will be judged against the chosen criteria. Different evaluation criteria motivate managers differently. A good guideline is to use multiple criteria so that managers are motivated to improve performance in all areas considered important by top management. As stated earlier, *what gets measured gets managed*.

Issues Relevant to Criteria Selection

Three important issues must be considered while choosing performance criteria for international subsidiaries:

1. Goals and objectives differ for different international subsidiaries. Consequently, uniform performance criteria for all subsidiaries would be inap-

---

23 Robert N. Anthony. *The Management Control Function*. Boston, Mass.: The Harvard School Press, 1988, p. 125.

exhibit 8.2   Performance Evaluation Criteria—Financial

Profitability ratios relative to resources or revenues

- Return on investment
- Return on stockholders' equity
- Return on sales
- Gross profit ratio

Target amount relative to key performance area

- Sales revenues
- Operating income
- Net income
- Residual income
- Economic value added
- Total production costs
- Labor costs
- Research and development costs
- Technology investment costs
- Quality costs

Cash flow from subsidiaries

- Cash flow in local currency
- Cash flow in parent company's currency
- Changes in cash flow over time

Budget comparisons

- Budgeted vs. actual sales
- Budgeted vs. actual costs
- Budgeted vs. actual profit
- Cost, revenue, and volume variances

propriate. An international subsidiary may be established to manufacture parts and components primarily for other subsidiaries. Another subsidiary may be formed to take advantage of advanced technology in the host country. Yet a third subsidiary may be established to benefit from the tax incentives. Exhibit 8.4 (page 301) shows examples of different corporate objectives and some possible performance evaluation criteria.

2. Different international subsidiaries operate in different environments. The evaluation criteria should take into account these environmental differences. A multinational corporation may find it easier to produce and sell a product in one country than in another, depending on policies of local governments.

In the same country, operating environments often change over a period of time. Most developing countries used to levy high tariffs on consumer

exhibit 8.3   Performance Evaluation Criteria—Nonfinancial

- Percent growth in sales
- Market share
- Asset turnover
- Inventory turnover
- New plants and plant expansions (capacity)
- New product development
- Product innovation
- Customer service
- Employee benefits and relations
- Community and social service
- Relations with government and local constituents
- Environmental responsibility
- Labor productivity
- New manufacturing processes
- Manufacturing cycle efficiency
- Throughput time
- Delivery cycle time

goods to discourage their importation. Many of those countries have since relaxed policies for importation of consumer goods. The evaluation standards should be reviewed periodically and, if necessary, adjusted for changes in the operating environments.

3. Many international subsidiaries have very limited or no control over certain local conditions and situations. This should be taken into account while selecting performance evaluation criteria. For example:

    - Price controls may be imposed by local governments, requiring advance governmental approval of all price increases.

    - Employment laws may require that compensation to workers be based solely on seniority regardless of merit.

    - Foreign-based multinational corporations may be prohibited from owning land, thus having no choice but to lease facilities at high rents.

    - The parent company policies or the government in the parent's base country may impose some controls. For example, there may be restrictions on the transfer of technology, capital spending, and certain types of payments made to local government officials.

Subsidiary management should participate in setting the performance criteria. Many multinational corporations express performance standards as a range rather than as a fixed number. This is especially desirable for a newly formed sub-

exhibit 8.4 **Examples of Corporate Goals and Related Evaluation Criteria**

Corporate Goals	Related Performance Evaluation Criteria
Marketing objectives:	
Open new markets	Market share and penetration
Presence in market	Sales volume
Manufacturing objectives:	
Productivity and efficiency	Cost reduction and cost savings
Production of components	Components volume produced
Raw material sourcing	Cost of raw material
Capacity management	Indirect manufacturing cost per unit of output
Advanced manufacturing technology	New manufacturing processes used
Financial objectives:	
Profitable investment	Return on investment; residual income; economic value added
Short-term investment recovery	Cash flows to parent company
Customer service objectives:	
Customer service	Number of customer complaints
Product quality	Warranty costs

sidiary. The amounts should preferably be expressed in the local currency. If translated amounts are to be used for performance evaluation, either the exchange rate to be used for translation should be specified or the manner it will be determined should be clearly stated.

Three well-known financial performance evaluation criteria are return on investment, return on equity, and residual income. Another financial criterion that has received considerable attention in recent years is economic value added.

Return on Investment

Return on investment (ROI) incorporates the investment base, revenue, and profits to assess performance. The higher the ROI, the higher the perceived performance.

$$\text{Return on investment} = \text{Investment turnover} \times \text{Profit margin}$$

$$\frac{\text{Revenue}}{\text{Total assets}} \times \frac{\text{Net income}}{\text{Revenue}} = \frac{\text{Net income}}{\text{Total assets}}$$

As previously shown, ROI has two components: Investment turnover and profit margin. Investment turnover expresses the subsidiary's ability to turn over invested capital, i.e., total assets into revenue. Profit margin is a ratio of profit to revenue. The two components delineate that ROI can be improved by higher revenue, lower costs, or lower invested capital. The management can decide on the "best mix" to improve ROI by examining available options. For example, revenues could be improved by increasing selling prices, increasing sales volume, or increasing both. These courses of action direct management's attention to available alternatives.

According to W. Edwards Deming, concentrating only on short-term profitability is one of the "deadly diseases" for businesses.[24] It undermines quality and productivity. Using ROI as the sole criterion to measure performance may motivate managers to emphasize the short run at the cost of long-run profitability. It is especially true when the investment base used in ROI computations is historical cost of assets net of accumulated depreciation. The older the depreciable assets, the higher the ROI. In fact, it is possible to show higher ROI, when the current period's income has actually declined from the previous period. This is illustrated in the following example.

	Year 1	Year 2
Revenues	DM10,000	DM 9,900
Depreciation expense	1,000	1,000
Other expenses	6,018	6,000
Profit	DM 2,982	DM 2,900
Gross investment	DM30,000	DM30,000
Less: Accumulated depreciation	9,000	10,000
Net investment	DM21,000	DM20,000
Return on investment:	$\dfrac{DM\ 2,982}{DM21,000} = 14.2\%$	$\dfrac{DM\ 2,900}{DM20,000} = 14.5\%$

When ROI is used as a performance measure, the investment base should preferably be either gross amount (historical cost) or current replacement cost.

ROI should be used in combination with other performance evaluation criteria. Otherwise, the managers may be motivated to make no investments in modern assets to replace technologically obsolete and inadequate assets. Why? Doing so would result in a higher investment base that would likely lower ROI. The manager, for self-interest reasons, may decide to keep on using the obsolete assets while fully realizing that investments in new assets is essential for producing quality products. Only quality products can withstand competitive pressures of global markets.

A factor contributing to this type of dysfunctional decision making is the executive mobility prevalent in many Western countries. Without investment in assets that can produce high quality and state of the art products, the declining revenues and profits will eventually drop the ROI. Since it may take several years

---

24 W. Edwards Deming. *Out of the Crisis*. Cambridge, Mass.: MIT Press, 1986.

for this to happen, the manager who was responsible for making the decision purely on a self-interest basis may have already moved on to greener pastures. Ironically, the superiors may have helped the person by giving a glowing recommendation to prospective employers. The reason for favorable recommendation can be explained easily: The performance of the individual while at that company kept on getting better and better according to ROI measure.

Residual Income

Residual income (RI) expresses performance as the amount of profit left after the imputed cost of invested capital has been subtracted.

Residual income: Income – Imputed interest on invested capital

The goal is to maximize residual income while meeting other performance criteria. Senior management must decide in advance on the imputed interest rate to be used for computing the cost of invested capital. It is conceptually desirable to use different rates for different operations to reflect their respective level of risk.

An inherent advantage of the residual income approach is that it focuses on maximizing a monetary amount rather than a percentage, as is the case with ROI. Managers are motivated to make any investment that will increase the residual income amount, even if their ROI drops from its present level. This is illustrated in the following example.

	Without Additional Investment	With Additional Investment
Revenues	DM 6,000,000	DM 6,500,000
Expenses	4,000,000	4,220,000
Profit	DM 2,000,000	DM 2,280,000
Subtract cost of capital:		
10% of DM10,000,000	1,000,000	
10% of DM12,000,000 (after DM2,000,000 additional investment)		1,200,000
Residual income	DM21,000,000	DM21,080,000
Return on investment:	$\frac{2,000,000}{10,000,000} = 20.0\%$	$\frac{2,280,000}{12,000,000} = 19.0\%$

As shown in the previous example, when the performance criterion is residual income the manager is likely to decide in favor of making the additional investment of DM2,000,000. Why? This will result in an increase in the residual income by DM80,000. *Any investment whose return is higher than the imputed cost of capital will increase residual income.* The manager is not likely to make the additional investment if the performance criterion is return on investment. Making the additional investment will drop the ROI from 20 percent to 19 percent.

In spite of the conceptual appeal of the residual income approach, it is not as commonly used as ROI.

Economic Value Added

Economic value added (EVA) has received a great deal of attention in recent years. It is a modification of the residual income approach. Economic value added is after-tax operating income minus weighted average cost of capital. The EVA approach takes into account the cost of long-term debt as well as the implicit cost of equity capital. Similar to residual income, EVA is an amount. If EVA is positive, the entity's return on assets is higher than the cost of long-term debt plus implicit cost of equity capital. The net effect is that there is an increase in stockholder value.

$$\begin{array}{c} \text{Economic} \\ \text{value added} \end{array} = \begin{array}{c} \text{After-tax} \\ \text{operating} \\ \text{income} \end{array} - \left[\begin{array}{c} \text{After-tax} \\ \text{weighted average} \\ \text{cost of capital} \end{array} \times (\text{Total assets} - \text{Current liabilities}) \right]$$

To determine EVA, weighted average cost of capital needs to be computed first as illustrated in the following example.

The following information pertains to Henrique Nacional Companhia SA, a Brazilian subsidiary of a multinational company. All amounts are in thousands of reais.

Total assets	R$27,000
Current liabilities	1,000
Operating income before tax	7,800
Long-term debt:	
Book value	20,000
Market value	21,000
Stockholders' equity:	
Book value	6,000
Market value	9,000
Interest rate on long-term debt	10%
Corporate income tax rate	40%

Since interest costs are tax-deductible, the after-tax cost of debt is:

$$0.10 \, (1 - \text{tax rate}) = 0.10 \, (1 - 0.4) = 0.06 \text{ or } 6\%$$

The implicit cost of equity capital is 12 percent. It is the opportunity cost to stockholders of not investing their capital in some other investment. The weighted average cost of capital computations use market values for both long-term debt and equity.

$$\text{After-tax weighted average cost of capital} = \frac{\left(6\% \times \text{market value of long-term debt}\right) + \left(12\% \times \text{market value of equity}\right)}{\text{Market value of long-term debt} + \text{Market value of equity}}$$

$$= \frac{(6\% \times R\$21{,}000{,}000) + (12\% \times R\$9{,}000{,}000)}{R\$21{,}000{,}000 + R\$9{,}000{,}000}$$

$$= \frac{R\$1{,}260{,}000 + R\$1{,}080{,}000}{R\$30{,}000{,}000}$$

$$= \frac{R\$2{,}340{,}000}{R\$30{,}000{,}000} = 0.078 \text{ or } 7.8\%$$

$$\text{EVA} = \text{After-tax operating income} - \left[\text{After-tax weighted average cost of capital} \times (\text{Total assets} - \text{Current liabilities})\right]$$

$$= R\$7{,}800{,}000 \times 0.6 - [7.8\% \times (R\$27{,}000{,}000 - R\$1{,}000{,}000)]$$

$$= R\$4{,}680{,}000 - R\$2{,}028{,}000$$

$$= R\$2{,}652{,}000$$

Since the economic value added is a positive amount, stockholder value increased by R\$2,652,000 during the period.

Comparing the actual economic value added by an international subsidiary with the estimated EVA amount is useful for evaluating performance.

Return on Equity

Return on equity (ROE) is the ratio of profit of a period to the stockholders' investment. It measures the percentage return on the investment made by stockholders. The return on equity ratio has three components. The analytical framework that focuses on the components provides much more information than simply dividing net income by stockholders' equity.

$$\text{Return on equity} = \text{Investment turnover} \times \text{Profit margin} \times \text{Assets-to-equity ratio}$$

$$\frac{\text{Net income}}{\text{Stockholders' equity}} = \frac{\text{Revenue}}{\text{Total assets}} \times \frac{\text{Net income}}{\text{Revenue}} \times \frac{\text{Total assets}}{\text{Stockholders' equity}}$$

The information values of investment turnover and profit margin were discussed earlier within the context of return on investment ratio. Assets-to-equity ratio is interpreted as the units of assets that have been acquired for one unit of investment by stockholders. Return on equity can be improved by higher revenue, lower costs, or lower investment by the stockholders.

ROE analysis is illustrated in the following example.

	Amounts in millions of francs	
	Year 1	**Year 2**
Revenues	F 3,200	F 3,500
Expenses	(2,400)	(2,500)
Profit	F 800	F 1,000
Liabilities	F 6,600	F 6,800
Stockholders' equity	2,400	3,200
Total assets	F 9,000	F10,000
Profit margin	$\dfrac{F\ 800}{F\ 3,200}$ = 25.00%	$\dfrac{F\ 1,000}{F\ 3,500}$ = 28.57%
Investment turnover	$\dfrac{F\ 3,200}{F\ 9,000}$ = 0.3556	$\dfrac{F\ 3,500}{F10,000}$ = 0.3500
Assets-to-equity ratio	$\dfrac{F\ 9,000}{F\ 2,400}$ = 3.750	$\dfrac{F10,000}{F\ 3,200}$ = 3.125
ROE	33.33%	31.25%

The ROE declined from 33.33% in Year 1 to 31.25% in Year 2. This was primarily due to a lower assets-to-equity ratio in Year 2 compared with Year 1. In other words, the assets were financed relatively more by stockholders in Year 2 than in Year 1.

Performance Criteria Commonly Used in Practice

For market performance, the principal measure used is share of market. It provides a comparison with the competitors in the same markets. Share of market information in larger markets is usually obtained from independent commercial marketing audit services.

The most common measure of financial performance in international operations is return on investment.[25] Application of the ROI concept is complicated in worldwide operations. Different currencies, different inflation rates, and different tax laws contribute to the complexity. In the final analysis, evaluating performance in different countries through financial ratios requires careful interpretation by managers. They should be knowledgeable about the local operating environments.

Exhibit 8.5 contains performance criteria adopted by four multinational enterprises.

Measurement of Actual Performance

International subsidiary investment may be defined variously as total assets available, operating assets, total assets less current liabilities, or parent company's eq-

---

25 Samuel C. Certo and J. Paul Peter. *Strategic Management: Concepts and Applications*, 3d ed. Burr Ridge, Ill.: Richard D. Irwin, Inc., 1995, pp. 184 and 186.

exhibit 8.5   Performance Criteria of Selected Multinationals

Multinational	Financial Criteria	Nonfinancial Criteria
Johnson Controls, Inc.	Cost management	Market share
		Quality
		Product development and innovation
Coors Brewing Company	Return on equity	Growth in international markets
	Price/value rating	Quality
	Sales volume	Product innovation
	Growth/profitability	Employee relations
Xerox Corporation	Return on investment	Market share
		Quality
		Employee motivation
3M Company	Return on investment	Market share
	Earnings per share	Quality
	Cost management	Employee relations

Source: Adapted from Michael D. Akers and Grover L. Porter. "Strategic Planning at Five World-Class Companies." *Management Accounting*, July 1995, pp. 24–31.

uity in the subsidiary. Income may also be defined in different ways such as operating income, income before interest and taxes, income before taxes, or net income. Valuation of individual assets (assigning a monetary value to an asset) may be based on historical cost, current replacement cost, or net realizable value. A depreciable asset has a gross value or a net value after deducting accumulated depreciation. *A decision should be made as to how the terms* investment *and* income *are to be defined, and what basis is to be used for asset valuation.*

International subsidiaries pose additional measurement challenges: foreign currency exchange rates fluctuation, inflation rates, tax laws, and cross-border transfer pricing.

- *Fluctuation in exchange rates affects the computation for performance measurement.* ROI based on the subsidiary's local currency would differ from ROI based on the parent company's currency. A change in the exchange rate affects the ROI computation. For example, let us assume that there is an unfavorable change in the exchange rate of an international operation's local currency against the parent company's currency. If current assets are translated using the current exchange rate, they will be at a lower value in the parent company's currency. A decision should be made regarding what exchange rate is to be used if foreign currency amounts are to be translated. As mentioned in an earlier section, it is desirable to use the amounts expressed in local currency to avoid the complexities related to exchange rate fluctuations.

- *Unless adjusted, subsidiaries in countries with hyperinflation or high infla-tion rates will show more favorable ROIs than those in countries with lower inflation rates.* It is recommended that the computations of ROIs be adjusted for inflation to reflect the relative performance accurately. Concepts and methodology for restating historical costs for inflation by using a general price index were discussed in Chapter 3.

- *Different tax laws have a direct effect on the reported net income of inter-national subsidiaries.* It is conceivable that a subsidiary located in a coun-try with high taxation reports lower net income than a subsidiary in a coun-try with low tax rates *solely* due to different tax rates. For this reason, the management may decide to use income before taxes while measuring actual performance.

- *Different transfer-pricing systems affect reported performance.* A transfer-price system affects reported performance of both the buying subsidiary and the selling subsidiary. Transfer pricing is discussed in Chapter 10.

Performance Evaluation Reports

A **variance** is the difference between actual performance and planned perfor-mance. Managerial and cost accounting textbooks discuss price, efficiency, pro-duction volume, sales, and other types of variances. According to Robert N. Anthony:[26]

> Although textbooks have described the calculations of these variances for years, few formal reporting systems identify any but the most obvi-ous ones, and many systems do not identify any. With the computation power of computers, calculations for most variances can be made rou-tinely and quickly.

Anthony further states, "I do not understand why managers do not require the identification of many textbook variances that seem to me to be impor-tant."[27] A performance report should contain the variances in the key areas at the minimum.

Subsidiary's Performance Versus Subsidiary Management's Performance

It is important to separate a subsidiary's performance from its management's per-formance. The key is to distinguish between the factors under the subsidiary management's control and the factors beyond subsidiary management control. Both local environments as well as policies of the parent company determine the extent of control that can be exercised by the management of an international subsidiary. Though conceptually attractive, such a distinction is often hard to

---

26 Robert N. Anthony. *The Management Control Function.* Boston, Mass.: The Harvard School Press, 1988, p. 133.

27 *Ibid.*

make in practice. For example, a subsidiary manager may not control an item directly but may have significant indirect control over it through his or her actions. The effects of uncontrollable factors should be isolated.

An international subsidiary's performance report should reflect its contributions as an economic entity toward achieving the parent company's goals and objectives.

The objective of performance evaluation is to motivate people toward improving their performance over time, so that they exert the maximum effort to achieve organizational goals. It is, therefore, imperative that managers of international subsidiaries should have a clear understanding of the parent company's goals, and are given the appropriate level of autonomy. Only then can they make the decisions that reflect their true performance within the constraints of local operating environments.

Global Information Systems

Accounting has undoubtedly acquired greater significance because of multinational operations and a global economy. The following statement delineates the importance of information storage and the retrieval aspect of an accounting system:[28]

> Accounting comes into its own with the rise of the corporate economy and large-scale business enterprise—the rapid spread of joint stock companies which began in the nineteenth century. . . . At the same time, in larger-scale business firms, the information storage and retrieval aspect of accounting became even more important than it had been before.

In accounting literature, the emphasis is often placed on financial statements only, without giving due recognition to accounting records. The value of accounting records is made forcefully by Professor Yuji Ijiri.[29]

> The economy may suffer somewhat without financial statements, but should there be a blackout on accounting records, the whole economy will collapse in a matter of weeks, if not days. . . . Lack of records will also let irresponsible behavior proliferate, quickly destroying the fabric of the economy.

Though it is important that accountants be active participants in the design of the information system, the extent of their actual involvement varies from country to country and company to company. For several decades, Scandinavian countries have been using the participatory design approach. In the **participatory design approach**, all users must be actively involved in the development of the information system.

---

28 Basil Yamey. "Accounting in History." *The European Accounting Review*, vol. 3, no. 2 (1994), p. 380.
29 As quoted by Yamey, *Ibid.*, p. 375.

Accountants' participation during the design phase of a global information system ensures that the system will be better suited to their needs, thus enabling them to serve the organization effectively and efficiently. Also, by being involved in the information system design they can provide valuable advice to the system experts in areas such as internal controls, costing, and data communication.[30] According to a Conference Board report, a detached finance function (including accounting) does not respond to the new imperative to execute flexible, worldwide product and customer strategies. Global competition forces chief financial officers (CFOs) to focus on:

- *Reducing the cost of finance function.* Planned actions to reduce costs include centralization and automation of accounting, developing shared financial services by consolidating transactions to attain economies of scale, and reducing costly errors by improving the quality of input.

- *Reorienting their staff to serving and sharing control with line managers.* Global competition has caused many CFOs to encourage finance and accounting personnel to learn more about the business in order to deliver value-added services to line managers.

- *Taking a lead role in formulating and implementing global strategy.* Interestingly, 80 percent of the respondents reported that their companies are centralizing global strategy, and a majority indicated that the finance function (including accounting) is leading the process.[31]

According to the findings of another survey, globalization's effect on information systems is on a wide scale. Eighty-four percent of the companies with international operations planned to further integrate their international systems.[32]

Impact of Technological Advances

The advances in information technology have been phenomenal during the last few years. The problem faced by accountants and business executives in multinational companies today is not the lack of technology. Rather, the problem is choosing the technology that will best meet their needs. An often-encountered impediment to adoption of advanced technology is long-standing business practices:[33]

Does your legal department let you accept a contract that has been sent by electronic mail? Can your employees fill out their expense forms on PCs, then get them approved and filed electronically? Does information

---

30 William M. Baker. "Shedding the Bean Counter Image: Become An Active Participant in Information System Design." *Management Accounting*, October 1994, p. 30.

31 Deloitte & Touche. "Role of Finance Function is Changing in Global Firms." *Deloitte & Touche Review*, 17 October 1994, pp. 1–2.

32 Deloitte Touche Tohmatsu International. *Leading Trends in Information Services.* Wilton, Conn.: Deloitte Touche Tohmatsu International, 1995, p. 29.

33 Catherine Arnst. "The Networked Corporation: Linking Up Is Hard To Do—But It's A Necessity." *Business Week*, 26 June 1995, p. 86.

flow freely throughout your organization to wherever it's needed, rather than up and down the hierarchy? Can customers dial into your computers to check the status of orders—instead of playing phone tag with somebody in your sales department? Is your company saving money by electronically linking up with a dozen suppliers in a just-in-time inventory network?

The answer is probably: Not yet. And it isn't because the telecommunications world hasn't dreamed up enough products and services.

"The technology is here," observes an expert. "The problem is not with the technology, but with the corporate processes. Companies must fundamentally change the way they do business and that's hard."[34] Hard though it may be, the fact is that more and more companies are using technology to improve internal processes and to transact business.

The impact of technological advances on globalization and their dramatic effect on a multinational's operations are expressed succinctly by Jack Smith, Chairman and Chief Executive Officer of General Motors:[35]

> The major driver of change for General Motors today is the same as for most companies: it's globalization. Advances in technology and communication are making the "small world" a reality, and the world will only get smaller and smaller in coming years. The real growth markets of the twenty-first century are outside North America and Western Europe, and it is easier than ever for global companies to manufacture virtually any product in virtually any region. This trend toward global integration should be viewed as an opportunity—not a problem.

Management of the company must be willing to share information with others to put technology to its optimum use.

Software Considerations

To be effective in their jobs, accountants in a multinational corporation must be aware of international accounting issues such as reporting requirements, value-added taxes, and intercompany transactions. Properly configured accounting software can be very helpful because it eliminates costly unreconciled differences and can handle multicurrency and intercompany transactions:[36]

> In multinational companies, resolving issues associated with intercompany processing, fluctuating exchange rates, transfer pricing, and tax laws make the balancing problem a true balancing act without the right software.
>
> A more cost-effective, accurate, and responsible alternative is to implement at each company and division standardized accounting proce-

---

34 *Ibid.*, p. 87.

35 *1994 Annual Report*. Detroit, Mich.: General Motors Corporation, 1995, p. 1.

36 Michael O'Brien. "Going Global: What to Look for in Financial Software." *Management Accounting*, April 1995, p. 59.

dures that are based on a single accounting software system. The key to making this solution work is in selecting software designed with multinational, multicurrency, multilingual applications in mind.

A comprehensive accounting manual that contains charts of accounts and standard practices and procedures can be very helpful for the ease of consolidation, auditing, and communication. Exhibit 8.6 contains important considerations for selecting a multinational accounting software system.

It is important that all operating units of the multinational company have adequate access to the information system. This is necessary to achieve uniformity, integrity, and accuracy of the accounting information.

Enterprise Resource Planning

Enterprise resource planning (ERP) is a software system that allows a company to:

- Integrate its business processes.
- Share data throughout the company.
- Produce and access the information on a real-time basis.

exhibit 8.6   Key Features for Multinational Accounting Software

1. Choose a single system designed and developed for multinational use.

2. Look for an international, single-version system that supports a single set of books in multiple languages. This enables each user to access the system by using a preferred language.

3. Users in a multinational operation should be able to post intercompany entries effortlessly across different charts of accounts, different closing calendars, and different currencies.

4. The system should have the ability to process the foreign currency transactions in its own value, and also have the capability to perform the conversion to the "base" currency in accordance with GAAP while retaining the foreign value dimension.

5. The software system should provide tables that enable users to define average, month-end, spot, and forward currency exchange rates. These defined rates should be available at a transaction level.

6. The system should incorporate international banking procedures. It should allow for payment output methods such as drafts, electronic data interchange, and checks. The system should support various address formats for check and accounts receivable processing.

7. Tax handling in the system should be tax table driven. As tax laws and tax rates change, the user should be able to make the needed changes without having to modify the software.

8. The software vendor should be using industry standard tools to support languages, graphic user interface, and hardware.

9. The system should have treasury management features. A user should be able to view a cash account in its native currency. For example, an account in British pounds should be available to view in British pounds even if the user accesses the account in German marks. Currency forecasting is enhanced when a user can forecast currency position by netting out the activity in accounts receivable and accounts payable based on anticipated due dates.

10. The vendor's support organization should be familiar with multinational accounting issues. More importantly, the same level of support should be available worldwide.

Source: Adapted from Michael O'Brien. "Going Global: What to Look for in Financial Software." *Management Accounting*, April 1995, p. 60.

There are five dominant ERP vendors: SAP, Oracle, PeopleSoft, J.D. Edwards, and Baan. Companies use ERP software to share and exchange information throughout the organization. Global companies with geographically dispersed operations find ERP especially attractive. Deloitte Consulting and Benchmarking Partners, Inc., recently conducted a joint study based on interviews with 230 individuals at 85 global firms. All of the firms had implemented or were in the process of implementing ERP. The benefits cited by the companies included personnel reductions, inventory reductions, and productivity improvement, among others.[37]

Education

The development and installation of a workable information system is no small endeavor. The time and resources required are substantial for a multinational organization. A total and integrated system provides not only the summary information on key elements that will be used by top management, but it also provides information that is detailed enough to meet specific needs of individual responsibility centers.

To ensure that operating managers use the system to its fullest capability, a comprehensive education program is imperative. "The preparation of manuals, explanations, sample reports, and other written material is a necessary part of the education process, but it is not the most important part. The important part is to explain to managers how the new system can help them do a better job."[38]

Global Information System Compatibility with *International Accounting Standards*

The primary focus of this chapter is on managerial functions of strategic planning and control. However, an integrated global information system not only serves the information needs of internal users but also provides the data necessary for external reporting.

Trends and recent developments clearly indicate that the International Accounting Standard Committee's standards are gaining wider acceptance. Many countries, especially developing countries, have already adopted *IASs* as their national accounting principles. The World Bank has strongly endorsed the use of *IASs* for the projects financed by the organization.[39] Specifically, it has directed the Big Five auditing firms to limit their audit opinions in the Asian economies to financial statements that are prepared according to *International Accounting Standards*.[40] Some countries, for example China, use the *IASs* for regulation of

---

37 Deloitte & Touche. "Maximizing the Value of Enterprise Applications." *The Review*, 6 December 1999, p. 3.

38 Robert N. Anthony. *The Management Control Function*. Boston, Mass.: The Harvard School Press, 1988, p. 140.

39 Anne J. Rich. "Understanding Global Standards." *Management Accounting*, April 1995, p. 51.

40 Jim Kelly. "World Bank Warns Big Five Over Global Audit Standards." *Financial Times*, 19 October 1998, p. 1.

their joint ventures. Multinational companies are also increasingly adopting *IASs*. Renault (France-based), Ciba-Geigy Limited Group (Switzerland-based), Shanghai Petrochemical (China-based), and Anglo American Corporation (South Africa-based) are just a few examples. A number of stock exchanges, including the London Stock Exchange and Hong Kong Stock Exchange, accept the *International Accounting Standards* for listing.

The International Organization of Securities Commissions (IOSCO) has endorsed the *IASs* for listing on capital markets. The next step is for each IOSCO member country to adopt the *IASs* for listing purposes in the country. The implications of these developments for the accounting system of a multinational company are profound. It would be highly desirable, and probably necessary, to ensure that the global information system generates information for preparing financial statements in conformity with the *IASs*.

Note to Students

In this chapter, you have been presented with important managerial accounting issues related to strategic planning, control, and information systems. Articles on multinational corporations' strategies, plans, and performance regularly appear in *The Wall Street Journal*, *Financial Times*, *Business Week*, *Forbes*, *Fortune*, and *The Economist*. Now many Web sites are available to help you keep up with new developments. The following are especially useful:

http://

The Wall Street Journal Interactive Edition   **http://www.wsj.com**
International Herald Tribune   **http://www.iht.com**
Business Week Online (Global Business)
http://www.businessweek.com/globalbiz/
Library of Congress Country Studies   **http://lcweb2.loc.gov/**
Intercultural Press   **http://www.interculturalpress.com**
World Bank Group   **http://www.worldbank.com**
Balanced Scorecard Institute   **http://www.balancedscorecard.org**

An important but often overlooked source of information is the management discussion and analysis section of a company's annual report. This section often contains a wealth of information on a company's strategies, plans, policies, markets, products, and customs. For example, Toyota's 1998 annual report has an extensive discussion about Toyota's management strategies for globalization. The following statement from the annual report expresses Toyota's approach:

> We are changing our approach to management to become a more truly global company. We are developing a management hybrid. We are trying to incorporate the best elements of the Japanese and Western traditions while avoiding some of the short-comings of both.
>
> In North America, we have integrated our production and purchasing locally under the umbrella of Cincinnati-based Toyota Motor Manufacturing North America, Inc. We also are strengthening our local

management structure in Europe to integrate our manufacturing and marketing operations more thoroughly there.

Our International Advisory Board furnishes valuable guidance in shaping management strategy, especially in regard to globalization. That board, which we set up in 1996, comprises 10 distinguished leaders from government and industry in nations of Asia, Europe, and the Americas. They meet twice a year with Toyota executives to discuss global and regional issues and policy initiatives.[41]

Many multinational companies have discovered that local managers are typically much more effective, than someone from the corporate headquarters, to run an international operation. Local managers bring the cultural knowledge and experience with them, which is invaluable for the decision-making process.

Chapter Summary

1. Strategic planning focuses on the development of the multinational corporation's overall objectives.

2. Diverse operating environments worldwide affect the development of global business strategy.

3. Each strategy has implications for a multinational's stakeholders as well as for the managerial accounting function.

4. Multinational corporations have to handle complex issues while designing their control systems.

5. Problems encountered in the design of a global control system include diversity among nations with respect to operating environments including languages and national currencies, among others.

6. A control system should be adopted after careful consideration of the unique operating environments of each international subsidiary.

7. The backbone of a control system is reporting on performance. It provides feedback.

8. Performance evaluation of international operations is similar in concept to the performance evaluation of domestic operations, except it must also take local operating environments into account.

9. Performance evaluation criteria include both financial and nonfinancial measurements.

10. A multicriteria evaluation system helps avoid dysfunctional decision making. The balanced scorecard is a valuable tool to ensure a multicriteria system is in place.

---

41 Toyota Motor Corporation. *Annual Report 1998.* Toyota City, Japan: Toyota Motor Corporation, 1998, p. 19.

11. Return on investment and market share are commonly used criteria in practice to evaluate the performance of international subsidiaries.

12. Different goals require different performance evaluation criteria.

13. Four common financial performance evaluation criteria are ROI, RI, ROE, and EVA.

14. It is important to distinguish between the performance of an international subsidiary and the performance of its management.

15. Technological advances are having a profound impact on multinational corporations.

16. Accountants should be actively involved in the design of a global information system.

17. ERP software makes it possible to share and exchange information on a real-time basis.

18. The IASC's International Accounting Standards (*IASs*) are receiving wider acceptance.

19. The information system of a multinational company should be compatible with the *IASs*. It should have the capability to provide data for preparing financial statements according to the *IASs*.

Questions for Discussion

1. Compare financial accounting with managerial accounting.

2. Give examples of unique information requirement features of multinational corporations that increase demands on the managerial accounting function.

3. Define strategic planning.

4. Give some examples of external and internal conditions that need to be addressed during the strategic planning process.

5. What are the reasons for the management accountants to be involved in the strategic planning process of multinational corporations?

6. What is meant by a control system and how does it differ from strategic planning?

7. What are the major considerations while designing a control system?

8. What are some of the information system issues that need to be addressed when designing a multinational control system?

9. Give three examples each of financial and nonfinancial performance evaluation criteria.

10. Describe the benefits of the balanced scorecard.

11. Compare return on investment with return on equity.

12. Compare residual income with economic value added.

13. What are the issues facing multinational corporations in computing ROI and RI for their international subsidiaries?

14. Discuss some of the issues that should be addressed while selecting performance evaluation criteria for international subsidiaries.

15. Why is it important to distinguish between the performance of an international subsidiary and the performance of its management?

16. The chapter included the following statement by Professor Robert N. Anthony: "I do not understand why managers do not require the identification of many textbook variances that seem to me to be important." Comment on the statement.

17. Compare centralization and decentralization.

18. Describe the impact of technology on the development of a global information system.

19. Does ERP have any special implications for international operations?

Exercises/Problems

8-1 A multinational corporation is exploring the feasibility of establishing a business operation in South Korea. You, as a management consultant, are asked to prepare a report that includes information on the following areas.

a. Economy
b. Foreign investment and trade controls
c. Business regulation

d. Employment laws
e. Accounting standards and reporting requirements
f. Taxation

Required:

Prepare a 2–3 page report.

8-2 Toyota Corporation's entry into the U.S. market began with the sale of a few cars and trucks in 1957. Toyota Sales, U.S.A. was established that year to market its products in North America. Since then the company has adopted a new strategy for the U.S. market, which has included establishing Toyota Motor Manufacturing North America, Inc., in 1996. The subsidiary, located in the U.S., coordinates manufacturing and purchasing at Toyota plants in the U.S. and Canada. It also serves as the holding company for Toyota's wholly owned U.S. manufacturing companies.

Required:

Research Toyota's current strategy with regard to the U.S. market relative to each of the following factors:

(1) Location of manufacturing plants.

(2) Sourcing of raw materials and components.

(3) Financing.

(4) Middle-management personnel.

(5) Labor force.

8-3 Refer to the information provided in Problem 8-2. Explain the implications of the current strategy for each of the following constituents:

a. U.S. labor unions.

b. Other Japanese auto manufacturers.

c. U.S. auto buyers.

d. U.S. manufacturers of auto parts and components.

8-4 Refer to the information given in Problems 8-2 and 8-3. Explain the major differences between the control systems under the old strategy and the current strategy.

8-5 Khalid, Inc., a subsidiary of a Pakistani multinational corporation operating in the U.S., provides you with the following performance information for 2003. The information is denominated both in U.S. dollars and in Pakistani rupees (Rs). The dollar-denominated information was translated using appropriate exchange rates for items being reported (e.g., depreciation expense and investment amounts were translated using historical exchange rates).

Khalid, Inc.
Selected Data for 2003
(In Thousands)

Sales revenues	$10,000	Rs622,500
Costs and expenses	8,500	580,500
Operating income	$ 1,500	Rs 42,000
Investment	$ 6,000	Rs264,000

Required:

(1) Compute return on investment using dollar- and rupee-denominated information.

(2) Compute residual income using dollar- and rupee-denominated information. Assume the imputed cost of capital is 8 percent.

(3) Comment on the performance of Khalid, Inc. based on the analysis in (1) and (2).

8-6 The following information is for two subsidiaries of a U.S.-based multinational corporation. The imputed cost of capital for the U.S. corporation is 12 percent.

	Canadian Subsidiary	Swedish Subsidiary
Currency	Canadian dollar (Can$)	Swedish krona (Sk)
Net assets in the operation	Can$62 million	Sk17.5 million
Operating income	Can$15 million	Sk 1.5 million

Required:

(1)   Compute residual income (RI) for each subsidiary, using imputed cost of capital for the parent company.

(2)   Discuss and comment on the use of RI as a performance evaluation criterion for the two subsidiaries.

8-7   The following are the summary balance sheet and income statement of Lyonnaise SA, a French subsidiary of Aneeka International.

Lyonnaise SA Balance Sheet (thousands) March 31, 2002		Lyonnaise SA Income Statement (thousands) For the Year Ended March 31, 2002	
Long-term assets	F16,000	Sales	F 36,000
Current assets	10,500	Cost of goods sold	(18,000)
Other long-term assets	8,500	Gross margin	F 18,000
Total assets	F35,000	Operating expenses	(8,500)
		Non-operating expenses	(3,000)
Stockholders' equity	F18,000	Income before taxes	F 6,500
Long-term liabilities	2,500	Income tax expense	(2,500)
Current liabilities	14,500	Net income	F 4,000
Total liabilities, and stockholders' equity	F35,000		

Required:

(1)   Calculate the return on investment (ROI) for the French subsidiary. What are the two components of ROI?

(2)   Compute the residual income assuming the imputed cost of capital is 10 percent for Aneeka International.

8-8   Aysha Development Company has three divisions. Selected financial information (in millions of rials) for 2003 and 2004 follows:

	Net Income		Revenues		Total Assets	
Division	2003	2004	2003	2004	2003	2004
A	SRls1,000	SRls1,200	SRls5,000	SRls5,400	SRls4,500	SRls4,800
B	150	175	7,500	8,000	3,500	4,000
C	250	300	2,000	2,200	3,000	3,500

Required:

(1)   Calculate the 2003 ROI for each division.

(2)   Calculate the 2004 ROI for each division.

(3)   Rashid, manager of Division A, is considering a proposal to invest SRls250 million in modern equipment. The estimated increment to 2005 net income from the proposed investment is expected to be SRls40 million. Aysha has a 12 percent imputed cost of capital requirement for each division. Would

Rashid be motivated to invest in the equipment if the measure of performance is:

a. residual income? Explain.

b. return on investment? Explain.

8-9 The following data are for Katsushima KK, a Japanese corporation:

Total assets	¥25,000,000
Current liabilities	1,500,000
Operating income before tax	7,500,000
Long-term debt:	
Market value	20,000,000
Book value	17,500,000
Stockholders' equity:	
Market value	10,000,000
Book value	6,000,000
Interest rate on long-term debt	2%
Income tax rate	40%
Implicit cost of equity capital	5%

Required:

Determine the economic value added.

8-10 G.M. Jullundry Co. has the following information available for 2002 (all amounts are in Pakistani rupees):

Sales	Rs 20,000,000
Net income	3,000,000
Total assets	100,000,000
Total liabilities	40,000,000

Required:

Compute the following:

(1) Assets-to-equity ratio.

(2) Profit margin.

(3) Investment turnover.

(4) Return on investment.

(5) Return on equity.

8-11 Kwazulu Trading Company, a South Africa-based multinational, has the following data:

Return on investment	18%
Profit margin	12%
Revenue	R600,000,000*
Total liabilities	R100,000,000

*South African rand

Required:

Compute Kwazulu's

(1)   Net income.

(2)   Total assets.

(3)   Return on equity.

References

Aguayo, Rafael. *Dr. Deming: The Man Who Taught the Japanese About Quality.* London: Mercury Books, 1991.

Akers, Michael D., and Grover L. Porter. "Strategic Planning At Five World-Class Companies." *Management Accounting*, July 1995, pp. 24–31.

Ansoff, H. Igor, and E. McDonnell. *Implanting Strategic Management.* Englewood Cliffs, N.J.: Prentice-Hall, 1990.

Anthony, Robert N. *The Management Control Function.* Boston, MA: The Harvard Business School Press, 1988.

Arnst, Catherine. "The Networked Corporation." *Business Week*, 26 June 1995, pp. 86–89.

Barney, Jay. *Gaining and Sustaining Competitive Advantage.* Reading, MA: Addison-Wesley Publishing Company, 1997.

Bryan, Lowell, J. Fraser, J. Oppenheim, and W. Rall. *Race for the World: Strategies to Build A Great Global Firm.* Boston, MA: Harvard Business School Press, 1999.

Burns, William (ed.). *Performance Measurements, Evaluation, and Incentives.* Boston, MA: Harvard Business School Press, 1992.

Bylinsky, Gene. "Challengers Are Moving In On ERP." *Fortune*, 6 December 1999, pp. 250[B]–250[D].

Certo, Samuel C., and J. Paul Peter. *Strategic Management: Concepts and Applications*, 3d ed. Burr Ridge, Ill: Richard D. Irwin, Inc., 1995.

Clinton, B., and S. Chen. "Do New Performance Measures Measure Up?" *Management Accounting*, October 1998, pp. 38–43.

Deloitte Research. *Making Customer Loyalty Real: Lessons from Leading Manufacturers.* New York: Deloitte Research, 1999.

Deloitte Touche Tohmatsu International. *Leading Trends in Information Services*. Chicago: Deloitte Touche Tohmatsu International, 1995.

Deming, W. Edwards. *Japanese Methods for Productivity and Quality*. Washington, D.C.: George Washington University, 1981.

Dierks, P., and A. Patel. "What Is EVA, and How Can It Help Your Company?" *Management Accounting*, November 1997, pp. 52–58.

_____. *Out of the Crisis*. Cambridge, MA: MIT Press, 1986.

_____. *Quality, Productivity and Competitive Position*. Cambridge, MA: MIT Press, 1982.

Donaldson, Thomas, and Thomas Dunfee. *Ties That Bind*. Boston, MA: The Harvard Business School Press, 1999.

Drucker, Peter F. "The Coming of the New Organization." *Harvard Business Review*, January–February 1988, pp. 45–53.

Frigo, Mark L., and Kip R. Krumwiede. "The Balanced Scorecard." *Strategic Finance*, January 2000, pp. 50–54.

Horngren, Charles T., George Foster, and Srikant M. Datar. *Cost Accounting: A Managerial Emphasis*, 10th ed. Upper Saddle River, N.J.: Prentice Hall, 2000.

Hunger, David, and Thomas Wheelen. *Essentials of Strategic Management*. Reading, MA: Addison-Wesley, 1997.

Institute of Management Accountants. *Counting More, Counting Less: Transformations in the Management Accounting Profession*. Montvale, N.J.: The Institute of Management Accountants, 1999.

International Federation of Accountants. *Preparing Organizations to Manage the Future: An International View*. New York: International Federation of Accountants, 1997.

Iqbal, M. Zafar. "Historical Overview of Developments in Cost and Managerial Accounting." *The Academy of Accounting Historians Working Paper Series*, vol. 2, Richmond, VA: The Academy of Accounting Historians, 1979, pp. 303–317.

_____. "International Dimension in Managerial Accounting." *Management Accounting Campus Report*, Spring 1993, p. 3.

_____. "ISO 9000: Fact and Fiction." *Journal of Accountancy*, February 1994, p. 67.

Ittner, C., D. Larcker, and M. Rajan. "The Choice of Performance Measures in Annual Bonus Contracts." *The Accounting Review*, April 1997, pp. 231–255.

Juran, Joseph M. *Juran on Quality by Design: The New Steps for Planning Quality into Goods and Services*. New York: The Free Press, 1992.

Kaplan, Robert (ed.). *Measures of Manufacturing Excellence*. Boston, MA: Harvard Business School Press, 1990.

_____ and D.P. Norton. *Translating Strategy Into Action: The Balanced Scorecard*. Boston, MA: Harvard Business School Press, 1996.

O'Brien, Michael. "Going Global: What to Look For in Financial Software." *Management Accounting*, April 1995, pp. 59–60.

Ohno, Taiichi. *Toyota Production System: Beyond Large Scale Production*. Cambridge, MA: Productivity Press, 1978.

Ozawa, M. *Total Quality Control and Management*. Tokyo: Japanese Union of Scientists and Engineers, 1988.

Porter, Michael E. *Competitive Strategy*. New York: The Free Press, 1980.

PricewaterhouseCoopers. *Value Reporting Forecast: 2000*. New York: PricewaterhouseCoopers, 1999.

Rosen, Robert, P. Digh, M. Singer, and C. Phillips. *Global Literacies: Lessons on Business Leadership and National Cultures*. New York: Simon & Schuster, 2000.

Siegel, Gary, C.S. Kulesza, and James Sorensen. "Are You Ready for the New Accounting?" *Journal of Accountancy*, August 1997, pp. 42–48.

Simons, R. *Levers of Control: How Managers Use Innovative Control Systems to Drive Strategic Renewal*. Boston, MA: Harvard Business School Press, 1995.

Srikanth, M.L., and S.A. Robertson. *Measurements for Effective Decision Making*. Guilford, CT: The Spectrum Publishing Company, 1995.

Taguchi, Genichi, and Don Clausing. "Robust Quality." *Harvard Business Review*, January–February 1990, pp. 65–75.

Taylor, Frederick W. *The Principle of Scientific Management*. New York: Harper & Row, 1911.

Toyota Motor Corporation. *Annual Report 1998*. Toyota City, Japan: Toyota Motor Corporation, 1998.

chapter

9

Budgeting, Risk Management, and Cost Management

learning objectives

After reading this chapter, you should be able to:

1. Differentiate between budgeting for operations and capital budgeting.

2. Present the master budget considerations for international operations.

3. Explain the concept of risk management.

4. Outline the six-step process for risk management.

5. Distinguish between economic risk and political risk.

6. Outline the financial reporting disclosure requirements for derivatives.

7. Discuss various cost management approaches.

8. Demonstrate your understanding of the ABC system, JIT system, target costing, and outsourcing.

Chapter 8 dealt with strategic planning and control issues for multinational corporations. The chapter also discussed issues related to the design of a global information system. This chapter presents *operational issues* of the framework discussed in Chapter 8: operating budgets, capital budgeting, risk management, and cost management.

Budgeting is among the most widely used managerial accounting tools. A **budget** translates corporate plans into financial terms. Organizations use budgets for planning, control, and performance evaluation. As pointed out in Chapter 8, a budget is the detailed plan for implementing a part of the strategic plan.

Master Operating Budget Issues for Multinational Companies

The **master operating budget** is a plan for achieving the goals for a period of time (normally one year). A good budgeting system includes a budget for each responsibility center in the multinational organization. There are four common types of responsibility centers:

1. A **cost center** is responsible mainly for incurring and controlling costs. Examples of cost centers are purchasing offices, manufacturing plants, and assembly plants located in different parts of the world.

2. A **revenue center** is primarily responsible for generating revenues, e.g., sales offices or service centers in different countries.

3. A **profit center** is responsible for both costs and revenues. An example is an operation responsible for both purchasing and selling goods.

4. An **investment center** is responsible for costs, revenues, profits, and investment in assets. An example is an international operation with responsibility to manufacture and sell goods and to acquire and dispose of its assets.

Major components of a typical master budget for a manufacturing company are:

- Sales budget.
- Production budget.
- Direct materials budget.
- Direct labor budget.
- Manufacturing overhead budget.
- Cash budget.
- Marketing and administrative expenses budget.
- Budgeted income statement.
- Budgeted balance sheet.

We next discuss issues *multinational corporations* face during budget preparation.

Centralized Versus Decentralized Budgeting Systems

A multinational corporation can possibly maintain a centralized budgeting system when the scope of its international operations is narrow. Otherwise, a decentralized budgeting system is necessary for many reasons, including a thorough understanding of local operating conditions, multiple currencies, and multiple sourcing. Educating and training local managers are prerequisites to effective budgeting systems in such settings.

Sales Forecasts

The sales budget is the foundation on which all other budgets are built. Preparation of the sales budget requires reliable sales forecasts using information from various sources:

- *National demographic and economic statistics.* Information such as population size and characteristics, disposable income, national growth, and economic conditions and trends.
- *Company historical data.* Past data on sales, prices, customer service, and marketing campaigns, among others.
- *Sales force.* An active and knowledgeable sales force with first-hand information about markets, customers, and competitors.
- *Market research.* Information such as consumer behavior, consumer tastes and preferences, market trends, and alternative distribution channels.

In some countries, information about national demographic and economic statistics may be readily available, while in others it may be unavailable or unreliable. For example, a developing nation may not have accurate information on disposable income. Information about competition may also be difficult to obtain especially if competition is either from local companies that are protected by the government or from public sector enterprises.

Translation of Budgets from Foreign Currencies

Budgets are first prepared in the currency of the country where an operation is located, and later translated into the parent company's currency. *While financial accounting rules control the translation of foreign currency for financial reporting purposes, there are no translation rules for budgets.* However, the multinational company's management should decide on the mechanism to be used for translating budgets, and should share this information with the managers of international operations.

Significant Changes in Foreign Currency Exchange Rates

Significant unanticipated changes in foreign currency exchange rates render the budget unrealistic. The multinational company should review the budget to determine the revision warranted under the circumstances. The parent company may also impose local sourcing of funds on a subsidiary to mitigate the impact of unfavorable changes in the exchange rate.

Import Regulations and Flow of Funds Restrictions

Many countries enact regulations to limit imports. A country may also restrict or prohibit the transfer of hard currencies out of the country. In case an international operation's budget includes sourcing of factors of production from other countries, any unexpected restriction on imports or fund transfers may make the plan infeasible for implementation.

Global Sourcing of Factors of Production

Global sourcing of factors of production adds uncertainties and necessitates greater coordination. For example, a manufacturing facility located in South Africa may rely on raw materials from Tanzania, Kenya, and Brazil; workers from India, South Korea, and the Philippines; and technology from the U.S. and Germany. Only with proper coordination and consideration of contingencies can a viable budget be developed.

Combined Effect of Exchange Rate Changes and Global Sourcing

When the acquisition of factors of production involves multiple currencies, significant changes in exchange rates of a few currencies may reduce the reliability of projections. This may require frequent revisions of budgets to regain their usefulness.

Capital Budgeting

Capital budgeting is the process of identifying, evaluating, and planning long-term investments. This section focuses on capital budgeting for international investment decisions. Such decisions involve spending large sums of money, and hence have significant long-range implications for the organization.

When there is a lack of availability of market and economic indicators necessary for predicting cash flows, it tends to increase risks of the international investment. Consequently, multinational corporations find it necessary to consider additional factors that are usually not relevant for domestic investment decisions.

- *Securing capital from a domestic bank for investment projects in other countries may be difficult and costly.* Banks often demand higher interest rates and require costly investment insurance.

- *While making investment analyses, only those cash flows that can be repatriated by the parent company should be considered, unless cash flows are to be used for local reinvestment or dividend payment purposes.*

- *Differing inflation rates, fluctuating currency exchange rates, and potential restrictions on cross-border capital transfers necessitate using the methods that take these factors into account.* Net present value and payback period methods readily incorporate many of these factors.

- *When necessary, the political risk factor should be added to the economic risk factor while evaluating investments to be made abroad.*

Capital Budgeting Methods

Commonly used capital budgeting methods include net present value, payback period, and accounting rate of return. These methods require estimates of initial investment, future cash flows from the project, and project life. Application of these methods to investments requires forecasts of future events to assess associated risk levels.

Net Present Value Method

We define **net present value** (**NPV**) as the difference between the initial investment and the net present value of expected future net cash inflows. The rate used to discount the net future cash inflows is normally equal to the corporation's cost of capital plus a risk factor, or is equal to the corporation's desired rate of return. Acceptable projects have a *minimum* of zero NPV. A positive NPV means that the anticipated return from the project exceeds the discount rate. Projects with a negative NPV fall short of the required rate of return.

Example

Naya, Inc., a U.S.-based multinational corporation, is considering opening a manufacturing plant either in Malaysia or in Singapore. The global investment department of Naya gathered the following information about the two prospective plants, expressed in the Malaysian ringgit (RM) and the Singapore dollar (S$). Estimated residual value at the end of useful life for either plant is negligible.

	Malaysian Plant (000)	Singapore Plant (000)
Required investment	RM27,100	S$20,075
Estimated annual cash inflows	RM14,300	S$10,600
Estimated annual cash outflows	8,580	6,350
Project annual net cash inflows	RM 5,720	S$ 4,250
Discount rate (cost of capital)	8%	8%
Risk factor	6%	4%
Useful life	8 years	8 years

The computation of the net present value for each plant *before* taking the appropriate risk factor into consideration is shown in Exhibit 9.1. Present value factors of an ordinary annuity at selected discount rates are also shown in the exhibit.

exhibit 9.1   NPV Analysis before Consideration of Risk (000)

	Malaysian Plant (000)	Singapore Plant (000)
Annual net cash inflows	RM 5,720	S$ 4,250
Present value factor (see below)	5.747	5.747
Present value of net cash inflows	RM 32,873	S$24,425
Required investment	27,100	20,075
NPV in local currency	RM 5,773	S$ 4,350
Current exchange rate in U.S. dollars	÷ 2.75	÷ 1.95
NPV in U.S. dollars	US$ 2,099	US$ 2,231

Present Value of an Ordinary Annuity of One Monetary Unit

Period (Years)	Discount Rate			
	8%	10%	12%	14%
6	4.623	4.355	4.111	3.889
8	5.747	5.335	4.968	4.639
10	6.710	6.145	5.650	5.216

Both plants show positive net present value. The Singapore plant has a higher net present value than the Malaysian plant. Everything else being equal, the Singapore plant is preferable to the Malaysian plant based on the analysis.

The computation of NPV for each plant *after* considering the risk factor is shown in Exhibit 9.2. The present value factors now take into account the level of risk in each country.

exhibit 9.2   NPV Analysis after Consideration of Risk (000)

	Malaysian Plant (000)	Singapore Plant (000)
Annual net cash inflows	RM 5,720	S$ 4,250
Present value factor (Exhibit 9.1)	4.639	4.968
Present value of net cash inflows	RM 26,535	21,114
Required investment	27,100	20,075
NPV in local currency	RM (565)	S$ 1,039
Current exchange rate in U.S. dollars	÷ 2.75	÷ 1.95
NPV in U.S. dollars	US$ (205)	US$ 533

The analysis indicates that the Malaysian plant is no longer acceptable. It shows a negative net present value of RM565,000 (US$205,000). The Singapore plant remains acceptable showing a positive net present value of S$1,039,000 or US$533,000.

Payback Period Method

The **payback period (PBP) method** is a measure of how quickly the investing entity recovers its invested capital. PBP is the length of time it will take to recover invested funds from the project.

$$PBP = \frac{\text{Initial cash investment}}{\text{Net cash inflows from the project each period}}$$

Example

This example illustrates the application of the payback period method for evaluating Project A against Project B.

	Project A	**Project B**
Initial investment (a)	$420,000	$630,000
Estimated annual net cash inflow (b)	$120,000	$140,000
Payback period (a ÷ b)	3.5 years	4.5 years

Everything else being equal, Project A is preferable to Project B because invested cash is recovered sooner, i.e., 3.5 years versus 4.5 years.

Accrual Accounting Rate of Return Method

The **accrual accounting rate of return (AARR) method** is based on the reported accounting income using accrual basis.

$$AARR = \frac{\text{Annual net cash inflows} - \text{Depreciation and other non-cash expenses}}{\text{Initial capital investment}}$$

Example

The following example demonstrates the accrual accounting rate of return method in comparing Project A and B of the previous example, assuming the straight-line method of depreciation. Both projects have a five-year useful life.

	Project A	**Project B**
Annual net cash inflow	$120,000	$140,000
Depreciation expense	84,000	126,000
Accounting income (a)	$ 36,000	$ 14,000
Initial investment (b)	÷420,000	÷630,000
AARR (a ÷ b)	8.6%	2.2%

Again, Project A appears to be preferable to Project B since it earns a higher accounting rate of return. Note, however, that with a different set of data it is possible that the PBP method and the AARR method would favor different projects. In our examples, both methods favored Project A, but this is not always the case.

Application of any capital budgeting method for making an international investment decision requires taking into account the *unique environments* of each prospective location. Those may include:

- Determining the minimum payback period or the minimum required rate of return according to levels of economic risk and political risk.

- Considering the risk of unfavorable changes in currency exchange rates.

- Computing two payback periods and two accrual accounting rates of return, one reflecting a *project perspective* and the other reflecting a *parent company perspective*. This is necessary when differences exist between a project's projected net cash inflows and reported earnings, and the amounts expected to be remitted to the parent company.

- Using after-tax cash flows and after-tax earnings amounts. This is necessary if the alternative projects being considered are in different countries with significantly different tax rates.

- Adjusting for differences in accounting standards among countries. Such differences affect measurement of revenue, expenses, profit, and investment. The amounts compared must be comparable.

The purpose of the preceding discussion is to highlight key issues in international investment decisions due to *unique environments*. Applying capital budgeting methods involves other practical and theoretical considerations that are *general* in nature.[1]

Risk Management

The **risk management** process includes identifying, assessing, grouping, quantifying, consolidating, and solution-developing steps for the risks of a company. Thomas Kaiser recommends the following six-step approach.[2]

1. *Risk identification* is the necessary first step. The information from this step is a prerequisite in carrying out the subsequent steps.

2. *Risk assessment* involves the nature and seriousness of each risk and the probability of its occurrence.

---

1 See, for example, Charles T. Horngren, George Foster, and Srikant M. Datar. *Cost Accounting: A Managerial Emphasis*, 10th ed. Prentice Hall, 2000, Chapter 21 for an in-depth discussion of capital budgeting methods. See also Alan C. Shapiro. *Multinational Financial Management*. Prentice Hall, 1996, Part IV, and David Eiteman, Arthur Stonehill, and Michael Moffett. *Multinational Business Finance*, 8th ed. Addison Wesley, 1998, Part 5 for a comprehensive discussion of foreign investment analysis and decisions.

2 Thomas G. Kaiser. "Strategic Risk Financing." *Strategic Finance*, July 2000, p. 38.

3. *Risk grouping* is putting all the risks that are identified and assessed into separate pools. Each pool contains risks that have approximately the same chance of occurrence and degree of adverse impact on the organization if the event actually occurs. It is necessary to perform the next three steps efficiently.

4. *Risk quantification* translates the risk into monetary terms by taking into account both the amount of risk involved and the probability of its occurrence. *Note: Steps 1–4 are performed at each international operation.*

5. *Risk consolidating* is combining all the risks identified, assessed, grouped, and quantified at each international operation. The step is performed at the multinational's corporate level.

6. *Risk solution development* is based on risk grouping (step 3). It involves developing a solution to address each key risk facing the multinational:[3]

> This solution can involve simple risk management steps—which include things such as "get out of the business of making widgets" or "install sprinklers in all company warehouses"—through to complex financial solutions including risk securitization; multi-year, multi-peril insurance solutions; and other recently developed techniques for parceling and transferring risk.

The previous approach looks at risk management in an integrated fashion to manage risks faced by a multinational company in its worldwide operations.

Exhibit 9.3 presents Bayer's risk management strategies.

Economic Risk Versus Political Risk

International direct investments often face high economic and political risks because of the lack of knowledge or the lack of available information. **Economic risk** is the uncertainty surrounding key elements of the investment process. These elements include the projections of initial and subsequent investments, revenues, operating expenses, inflation, useful life, market conditions, and foreign exchange rate movements. With the exception of foreign exchange rate movements, all of these elements are similar to what corporations face when making domestic investment decisions. Foreign exchange risk was discussed in Chapter 2.

The International Accounting Standard Committee's *IAS 39* deals with disclosures relating to derivatives and other hedging transactions as well as other financial assets and liabilities.[4]

A **derivative** is a contract whose market value fluctuates in direct proportion to fluctuations in the market value of a commodity or a financial instrument (ownership share) or a foreign currency. The most common purpose of using derivatives is risk management.[5]

---

3 *Ibid.*

4 International Accounting Standards Committee. "Financial Instruments: Recognition and Measurement." *International Accounting Standard No. 39.* London: International Accounting Standards Committee, 1999.

5 Ed McCarthy. "Derivatives Revisited." *Journal of Accountancy*, May 2000, p. 35.

exhibit 9.3   **Bayer's Risk Management**

We aim to take full advantage of global market opportunities. At the same time, we want to avoid risks as far as possible, control them where necessary and take appropriate precautions at all times.

To achieve this, we employ a number of instruments, depending on the particular risk profile. We are constantly upgrading these instruments.

For example, we counter financial and currency risks by financing our business in the local currency or by hedging currency and interest positions with derivative financial instruments. These instruments are employed in accordance with the respective risk appraisal, also observing detailed guidelines and requirements.

To counter possible risks arising from the many different laws and regulations concerning taxes, competition, patents, antitrust issues and the environment, our decisions and the design of our business processes are based on comprehensive legal advice, both from our own experts and from acknowledged external specialists.

To ensure that our employees act responsibly from both a professional and a legal point of view within their respective local environment, we have decided to introduce a worldwide code of behavior, supported by thorough training. This "legal compliance" documents the obligation to observe laws and regulations.

Complying with rules at all times and controlling the way staff handle risks are fundamental requirements for all management staff in the Group.

We combat risks involving products and environmental protection by taking appropriate measures relating to quality assurance. This includes having our activities certified to international standards, consistently upgrading our plants and processes, and developing new and improved products. We are committed to the international Responsible Care initiative of the chemical industry and to our safety and environmental management system, which we report on at regular intervals.

The monitoring and control of economic risks in our everyday business is one of the tasks of our worldwide controlling function, which continually submits reports to the Board of Management and operating units for evaluation. Another of our Group-wide monitoring systems is the regular checks carried out by our corporate auditing department on the efficiency of the hedging instruments being used, and the reliability of the control systems.

To guard against possible claims and liability risks, we have concluded insurance agreements to ensure that the financial consequences of any possible claim are kept within reasonable limits or are excluded entirely. The insurance contracts are continuously reexamined and adjusted where necessary. Even if there can be no guarantee that the insurance cover eliminates all conceivable risks, it is safe to assume that any claims would not affect the Group's liquidity, financial position or earnings situation to the extent of jeopardizing the company's existence.

An analysis of the present risk situation showed that, within the reporting period, there were no risks that were likely to endanger the continuing existence of the company, nor were any such risks recognizable in the future.

Source: Bayer. *Annual Report 1998*, pp. 21–22.

IAS 39 requires that all financial assets, including derivatives, and financial liabilities be recognized on the balance sheet. The standard requires, with some exceptions, that all financial assets be measured at market value. Gains or losses arising from changes in their market value may be shown in the income statement if the financial instruments are held for trading purposes. Derivative instruments held for non-hedging purposes are always considered to be held for trading purposes. Derivative instruments that are held for hedging are not considered to be held for trading purposes. Gains or losses from remeasuring their market values may be shown either in the income statement or in the balance sheet as a separate component of stockholders' equity.

The political risk factor is unique to each country and differs from country to country. *Assessing political risk may be the most challenging aspect of inter-*

national direct investment decisions. **Political risk** refers to actions and activities of host governments directed at multinational corporations. Though becoming rare, extreme measures by host governments may include nationalization, expropriation, or forced acquisition of a multinational corporation's assets. More commonly the host governments impose special restrictions on operations of multinational corporations, such as requiring hiring of local managers and workers or prohibiting them from producing and selling certain products in order to protect domestic companies.

As in the case of economic risk, solutions should be developed to address each key political risk. The solutions should include a plan for managing each of the key political risks. There should be a defined threshold to determine when the political risk level in a country becomes unacceptable and in case that happens, how divestment is to be carried out.

A multinational corporation may develop the internal capability to forecast and manage political risks in the countries where it has operations and the countries where it plans to start operations. Consulting firms specializing in political risk assessment and management also exist. Many countries, especially industrialized nations, offer government-sponsored insurance against foreign political risk. For example, the U.S. government's Overseas Private Investment Corporation insures U.S.-based corporate exporters and investors against political risk in developing countries.

Cost Management

Traditional costing methods generally classify costs of producing and selling goods and services into three categories: Manufacturing, marketing, and administrative. This framework can be adapted to each international operation to take into account factors such as multiple sourcing of goods and services from different countries. Additional issues relevant to the determination of product costs in each country include:

- Worker productivity varies among countries. Corporations should take into account both labor costs *and* labor productivity in each international operation.

- Customers in different countries have different expectations for product quality and customer service. Product quality is a major competitive weapon. It can be used effectively only if local customers' expectations are the driving force in developing quality criteria.

- Some countries enjoy a relatively low cost of some factors of production. This advantage may be offset by other costs such as high regulatory compliance costs, distribution costs, or costly delays. Thus, it is important to consider the *overall* costs of each alternative being considered.

- Government regulations may result in different cost behavior in different countries for a cost item. For example, labor cost is considered variable in the U.S. Salary payment requirements in some countries cause labor cost to be fixed.

- Fluctuations in foreign exchange rates result in overcosting or undercosting materials sourced from outside the country of international operation.

Cost as a Competitive Weapon

Costs of individual factors of production are assigned to different products (and services). Indirect costs are allocated to different products by selecting and using one or more allocation base(s). Choosing an inappropriate allocation base results in overcosting some products and undercosting others. *Selling prices are heavily influenced by costs. Overcosting or undercosting affects the competitive position of each product and may result in the unwarranted elimination or expansion of a particular product line.*

Example

Exhibit 9.4 illustrates the previous point. We assume two products, A and B, are produced by two multinational companies, MNC1 and MNC2.

Assume that the two companies' costs are identical. MNC1's cost allocation base overcosts product B. Based on the data, MNC1 might decide to eliminate product B since it has a unit loss margin. Product B's elimination may be ill advised since it would result in no significant reduction of common fixed costs. If Product B is eliminated, all common fixed costs would be assigned to product A. Product A's overcosting is likely to lead to overpricing, and consequently the loss of its market share.

If MNC2's cost allocation base accurately reflects costs, both products A and B are likely to be appropriately priced and should maintain their competitive position.

Cost and Productivity

As mentioned earlier, both labor costs and labor productivity should be considered. **Labor productivity** measures the relationship between workers' hours and

exhibit 9.4 Multinational Product Costing

	MNC1		MNC2	
	A	B	A	B
Selling price per unit	$150	$ 90	$150	$90
Direct costs (traced)	$ 70	$ 60	$ 70	$60
Indirect costs (allocated)	40	40	60	20
Total cost per unit	$110	$ 100	$130	$80
Unit profit (loss) margin	$ 40	$ (10)	$ 20	$10

the actual output produced. It is a key indicator of an economy's competitiveness. Many factors affect productivity and, therefore, the competitiveness of a corporation and a nation. Examples of these factors are:

- Extent of technology utilization.
- Production process and other internal processes.
- Employees' education and training.
- Employees' motivation and performance.
- Employee empowerment.

High labor costs in a country do not necessarily mean competitive disadvantage. The labor costs and labor productivity in a country should be considered together.

Example

Let us use the following example to show how cost and productivity together provide a better indication of the competitive position. In the example, Country Z, despite its higher hourly labor cost, has a competitive advantage over Countries X and Y.

	Country		
	X	**Y**	**Z**
Average cost per labor hour	$20	$30	$40
Output units per one hour of labor time	1	2	4
Average cost per unit of output	$20	$15	$10

National competitive advantage based on overall labor productivity and specific industry productivity has been the subject of public interest in most industrialized nations. Exhibit 9.5 compares manufacturing productivity of nine countries in 1998.

A study compared labor wages and labor productivity of Korea, Thailand, Malaysia, and the Philippines with that of the U.S. It concluded that labor costs to produce one unit of output in those countries are closer to the U.S. levels when *both* wages and productivity were taken into account.[6] As shown in Figure 9.1,

exhibit 9.5   Manufacturing Productivity and National Output (Annual Rate of Change—1998)

	Belgium	Canada	France	Germany	Japan	Norway	Sweden	United Kingdom	United States
Output per Hour	0.5%	0.7%	3.4%	4.3%	0.3%	2.1%	2.2%	1.0%	4.1%
Output	2.6	3.9	3.9	5.2	−5.5	2.8	4.4	0.3	4.2

Source: U.S. Bureau of Labor Statistics. *International Comparisons of Manufacturing Productivity and Unit Labor Cost Trends—1998.*

---

6 Gene Koretz. "The Equalizer: Productivity." *Business Week*, 11 September 1995, p. 26.

figure 9.1   **Manufacturing Industry Productivity in the U.S., Korea, Thailand, Malaysia, and the Philippines**

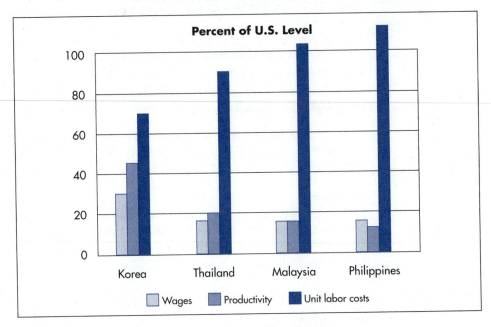

unit labor costs were actually above the U.S. levels in Malaysia and the Philippines due to low productivity despite their low wage rates.

The **New Economy** is characterized by high productivity and low inflation. A recent report on the dynamics of the New Economy concludes that technology and innovation are increasingly important factors in the productivity and growth of firms and countries. Some economies have especially taken advantage of technology to increase productivity. According to the report published by the Organization for Economic Cooperation and Development (OECD), a group of industrialized countries, information technology and communication technology are at the core of innovation in the New Economy. In order to enter the New Economy, the OECD report recommends to the governments to foster competition, encourage entrepreneurship and venture capital, increase spending on research, and revise educational and immigration policies to enhance intellectual capital.[7]

Exhibit 9.6 outlines the critical factors for entering the New Economy.

It is apparent from the previous discussion that technology, productivity, and competitiveness are closely linked together. In order for a firm or a country to

---

7 Organization for Economic Cooperation and Development. *A New Economy? The Changing Role of Innovation and Information Technology in Growth*. Paris: Organization for Economic Cooperation and Development, 2000.

exhibit 9.6 Critical Factors for The New Economy

BOOST INVESTMENT SPENDING on information technology as a share of gross domestic product

RESTRUCTURE CORPORATIONS to cut costs, improve flexibility, and make better use of technology

OPEN FINANCIAL MARKETS to direct capital to the best uses

DEVELOP VENTURE CAPITAL and initial public offering markets to aid innovative companies

ENCOURAGE AN ENTREPRENEURIAL CULTURE and make it easier to start new businesses

INCREASE THE PACE OF DEREGULATION especially in telecommunications and labor markets

ADJUST MONETARY POLICY to the realities of the New Economy by waiting for inflation to appear before raising interest rates.

Source: Michael J. Mandel. "The New Economy." *Business Week*, 31 January 2000, p. 74.

grow, it has to be competitive. International Institute for Management Development (IMD), a Switzerland-based organization, annually publishes countries' rankings by their economic competitiveness using 290 criteria. The ranking for 2000 is shown in Exhibit 9.7.

It reconfirms that a country's economic competitiveness and its adoption of the New Economy depends, to a large extent, on its investment in information and communication technologies. This is evidenced by the rankings of the U.S., Singapore, and Finland, the top three on the list.

Cost Management Approaches

Cost management, along with customer focus, quality, and timely response to market dynamics, is a requisite for success in the current competitive environment. It is impossible to sustain global competitiveness without effective cost management. Some important cost management approaches are described next.

Reengineering

Many multinational corporations have improved their core internal business processes and significantly reduced their workforce during the last decade or so. Examples include Volkswagen, IBM, Daimler-Benz (now DaimlerChrysler), AT&T, and General Motors Corporation.

The **reengineering** approach configures internal processes, products, and employees so that essential operating activities are performed effectively and efficiently. All non-essential activities and tasks are eliminated, thereby reducing costs. Reengineering typically results in eliminating jobs often termed as **downsizing** or **rightsizing**. Understandably, job elimination has an adverse effect on employee morale and the corporate culture. It is important that reengineering be

exhibit 9.7   **Countries' Economic Competitiveness—2000**

Ranking	Country
1	United States
2	Singapore
3	Finland
4	Netherlands
5	Switzerland
6	Luxembourg
7	Ireland
8	Germany
9	Sweden
10	Iceland
11	Canada
12	Denmark
13	Australia
14	Hong Kong
15	United Kingdom
16	Norway
17	Japan
18	Austria
19	France
20	Belgium

Source: International Institute for Management Development, 2000.

consistent with the organization's overall strategy.[8] It is also important that the employee morale problem be addressed, and actions taken to minimize its adverse effects on *both* the company and the employees:

> Bank of America workers reacted with fear and resignation to the news that their company will eliminate 10,000 jobs over the next year in an effort to cut costs.
>
> Company executives hope that the savings will allow the bank to expand customer services and reduce bureaucracy, but they declined to say where the layoffs would hit.
>
> The huge staff reduction is the latest in a series of retrenchments by the former San Francisco-based bank, whose headquarters were moved to Charlotte, N.C., when it was bought in 1998 by NationsBank.

---

8 Charles T. Horngren, George Foster, and Srikant Datar. *Cost Accounting: A Managerial Emphasis,* 10th ed. Upper Saddle River, N.J.: Prentice Hall, 2000, p. 480.

In all, the company has reduced its workforce by firings and attrition from around 171,000 just after the merger to about 140,000 after the latest round of layoffs takes place.

"It's tense," said one Bank of America employee who would only disclose her first name, Jennifer. "People are disheartened and getting pretty caustic about the whole thing. The attitude is, 'What next?'"[9]

If for no other reason, it is in a company's self-interest to treat the terminated employees humanely. Companies with enlightened and experienced management take a variety of actions to alleviate the morale problem while downsizing:

- *A decent severance package.* The package includes generous severance pay, payment for unused vacation time, and continued subsidization of health insurance coverage for several months. In April 2001 when CISCO reduced its workforce, the company announced that it will offer six months of severance pay and benefits to the employees affected by the layoff. In a memorandum, the Chief Financial Officer stated, "Our decision will be based on doing the right thing for our business, and all employees will be treated fairly and with compassion."

- *Accelerated vesting of stock options.* Many companies voluntarily accelerate vesting of stock options for those employees whose jobs are being eliminated. Usually, the employees get full-year credit for the year of downsizing.

- *Helping to find new jobs.* Companies help the terminated employees in finding new jobs. Helpful actions include contacting other companies to inform them about availability, qualifications, and experience of the employees whose jobs are being eliminated. Some companies provide help by either making the professional in-house human resources staff available or engaging an outside placement firm to help the effected individuals during their job search process.

- *Emotional support.* Some companies provide individual or group counseling services to provide emotional support.

Such positive actions serve two purposes. They provide tangible assistance and support to the individuals whose jobs have been eliminated. Additionally, they help retain key employees that the corporation does not want to lose. According to a human resources consultant, "One big way to reassure your remaining employees is to treat the laid off workers fairly. You want to send a message to the survivors: 'If this were to happen to you, you too will be protected.'"[10]

Boeing, the world's biggest aerospace and defense company, is currently undergoing restructuring. It cut 5,000 jobs in the second quarter of 2000, and more job losses are expected in the future.[11]

---

9 Verne Kopytoff. "10,000 More Jobs on Block at B of A." *San Francisco Chronicle*, 29 July 2000, p. A1.

10 Carolyn Said. "Having a Heart Can Make Job Cuts Easier to Handle." *San Francisco Chronicle*, 28 July 2000, p. B3.

11 Mark Odell. "Boeing Growth Is Helped by Restructuring." *Financial Times*, 20 July 2000.

Activity-Based Costing and Activity-Based Management

Activity-based costing (ABC) is a method of measuring the cost of activities. Indirect costs of each activity are grouped in its own separate pool. Activity-based costing recognizes the *causal* relationships of cost drivers to activities. A **cost driver** is any factor that causes a change in the cost of an activity. Costs of an activity are assigned to products, services, or other cost objects according to their use of a cost driver of the activity. A **cost object** is any customer, product, service, project, or other work unit for which a separate cost measurement is desired.

Activity-based costing is a powerful tool for accurately costing products, services, and projects. It allocates indirect costs according to their consumption by cost objects rather than by some arbitrary method. Cost reduction in internal processes is facilitated by activity-based costing because it *identifies* cost drivers. By focusing on the efficient usage of cost drivers, management can achieve cost reductions. This results from the causal relationship between activity cost drivers and activity costs.

Examples of the companies using ABC include Hewlett-Packard, General Motors, Tektronix, Zytec Corporation, Dayton Extruded Plastics, and Northern Telecom Limited.

Activity-based management (ABM) is a discipline that focuses on the management of activities for improving the value received by the customer and the profit achieved by the company providing this value. It is helpful to companies in product strategy, product pricing, and cost management. ABM includes cost driver analysis, activity analysis, and performance measurement. Activity-based management draws on activity-based costing as its major source of information.[12]

In ABM, both cost control and the value received by the customer are important considerations:[13]

> When deciding what to measure, it is helpful to think of process measures as covering two broad categories: the value provided to the customer and the efficiency of the process itself. It is important that an organization have performance data from both categories so it can maintain a balance between the interests of the customer and the business. A company that focuses only on meeting customer needs might find itself losing money as a result of inefficient internal operations, while a company focusing solely on internal efficiency may lose customers whose needs are inadequately met.
>
> Customer "value added" is most easily measured by quantifying the company's ability to meet or exceed key customer needs—measuring such performance attributes as quality, availability, and service. Process efficiency is most easily captured by measuring cycle time.

---

12 James M. Reeve, ed. *Readings & Issues in Cost Management*. Cincinnati, OH.: South-Western College Publishing, 1995, p. 416.

13 Kavasseri V. Ramanathan and Douglas S. Schaffer. "How Am I Doing?" *Journal of Accountancy*, May 1995, p. 82.

The relationship between efficiency and cycle time is apparent from the following logic: If customer needs are being met (that is, providing value-added products or services at competitive cost) in shorter and shorter cycle times, then the processes are by definition becoming increasingly efficient. The following are common examples of measures available in each category:

Measures of customer value added:

- Alignment of product-service performance to customer expectations.
- Cost versus the features-benefit received.
- Quality and reliability.
- Service and support provided.
- Recovery from problems.

Measures of cycle time:

- New product or service development time.
- Time to market.
- Order fulfillment cycle time.
- Performance according to schedule.
- Rework and other nonvalue-added time.

As the previous excerpt demonstrates, cost control has a direct relationship with cycle time: The shorter the cycle time, the greater the efficiency. There are two basic guidelines of activity-based management:[14]

- Deploy resources to activities that yield the maximum strategic benefit.
- Improve what matters to the customer.

Example

Suddarth Corporation manufactures automobile components. The previous job-costing system had a single indirect cost pool and manufacturing overhead, allocated using direct manufacturing labor hours. The manufacturing overhead allocation rate of the previous system for 2002 would have been $200 per direct manufacturing labor hour.

Suddarth decided to replace the single manufacturing overhead cost pool with five indirect cost pools. The cost pools represent five activity areas at the facility, each with its own supervisor and budget responsibility. Pertinent data are shown in the following table.

---

14 Peter B.B. Turney, *Common Cents: The ABC Performance Breakthrough*. Portland, OR.: Cost Technology, 1992, p. 143.

Activity Area	Cost Driver	Activity Rate
Purchasing	Purchase orders	$ 25.00
Material handling	Parts	1.00
Milling	Machine hours	50.00
Lathe work	Turns	2.00
Testing	Units tested	120.00

Data related to two jobs are as follows:

	Job 2071	Job 2072
Direct manufacturing labor hours	30	360
Purchase orders	5	20
Parts	50	250
Turns	250	875
Machine hours	20	700
Units (25% of the units are tested)	20	500

The per unit allocated manufacturing overhead costs of each job under the previous allocation system is computed in the following manner.

	Job 2071	Job 2072
Rate per direct manufacturing labor hour (a)	$200	$200
Direct manufacturing labor hours (b)	30	360
Total manufacturing overhead allocated to the job (a × b)	$6,000	$72,000
Per unit manufacturing overhead costs	$\frac{\$6,000}{20} = \$300$	$\frac{\$72,000}{500} = \$144$

Computation for the per unit allocated manufacturing overhead costs of each job under the activity-based costing system are shown next.

Activity	Job 2071		Job 2072	
Purchasing	$25 × 6 =	$ 150	$25 × 20 =	$ 500
Material handling	$1 × 50 =	50	$1 × 250 =	250
Milling	$50 × 174 =	8,700	$50 × 700 =	35,000
Lathe work	$2 × 250 =	500	$2 × 875 =	1,750
Testing	$120 × (25% of 20) =	600	$120 × (25% of 500) =	15,000
Total manufacturing overhead allocated to the job		$10,000		$52,500
Per unit manufacturing overhead costs allocated	$\frac{\$10,000}{20} =$	$500	$\frac{\$52,500}{500} =$	$105

When activity-based costing is implemented, it is commonly discovered that the low-volume products have higher manufacturing overhead cost than under the traditional manufacturing overhead allocation system. The reverse is true for the high-volume products. The reason being, many costs such as setup costs vary with the number of batches. Other costs such as material ordering and material handling vary with the complexity of the products. In essence, different products and jobs make different use of each activity. The per unit cost comparison from the previous example illustrates the point:

	Job 2071	Job 2072
Number of units	20	500
Per unit manufacturing overhead costs allocated under:		
Traditional system using direct labor hours as allocation base	$300	$144
Activity-based costing	$500	$105

An increasing number of companies have adopted activity-based management. Examples include Siemens, Tektronix, Black & Decker, AT&T, General Motors, and General Electric.

According to a recent survey, product/service costing, process analysis, and performance management are the top three objectives for implementing the ABC and ABM systems. Sixty-four percent of respondents to the survey indicated that ABC and ABM systems must be integrated with the enterprise resource planning (ERP) system. The survey results also revealed that the larger the organization, the greater the expressed need for integration.[15]

Total Quality Management

One of the major outcomes of quality is the elimination of high costs associated with defective units of product. These include the cost of producing defective units, costs of rework, and other costs such as those arising from rescheduling of other work and rush ordering of the materials not in stock. As mentioned in Chapter 8, quality is critical for maintaining competitiveness. Adopting and implementing quality standards and conducting quality audits to ensure that quality standards are being achieved can result in minimizing internal failure costs and external failure costs. **Internal failure costs** are the costs incurred for a defective product that is detected *before* it is shipped to the customer. **External failure costs** are the costs of a defective product *after* it is shipped to the customer. External failure costs include actual costs incurred, for example warranty repairs. In most cases, however, the costs incurred to correct defects are not as detrimental to the organization as the opportunity costs. Loss of customer loyalty may result in the

---

15 Mohan Nair. "Activity-Based Costing: Who's Using It and Why?" *Management Accounting Quarterly*, Spring 2000, p. 30.

loss of potential future sales, the loss of customer goodwill, and the loss of market share due to a bad reputation for poor quality. These factors have a far more harmful effect on a company's competitive ability than the actual external failure costs. *The problem is exacerbated by the fact that opportunity costs associated with poor quality are impossible to measure and can never appear in any financial report.*

According to a recent study, downward pressure on prices is the top marketplace issue and customer loyalty/retention is the most important management challenge for chief executive officers. The study was based on responses of 656 CEOs of companies headquartered in Asia, Europe, North America, and South America.[16] This further confirms the importance of customer focus. Total quality management is critical for survival in today's competitive environment.

Another recent global study concluded that customer-centric companies are "60 percent more profitable and are far more likely to exceed their goals for growth and shareholder value than competitors that do not track customer loyalty or perform poorly in that regard."[17]

Customer-centric companies are companies that set explicit targets for retaining customers and make extraordinary efforts to exceed their customer loyalty goals. The study covered 867 companies in 35 countries. The study further stated, "While product quality is no longer enough to attract and keep customers, it is an ante to compete."[18]

Many successful companies have been able to meet or exceed the six sigma quality target. **Six sigma quality** means 3.4 defects per million units processed. Examples of the organizations achieving six sigma quality include General Electric, Toshiba, Allied Signal, Canon, Motorola, American Express, Sony, and Polaroid, among others. General Electric spent $500 million to put the six sigma into practice and cut costs by billions when it worked.[19]

Just-in-Time and Kaizen

Just-in-time is a system in which materials are purchased and goods are produced only when needed to meet actual customer demand. The just-in-time approach is designed to result in minimum or no inventory and waste during the manufacturing process.[20] Just-in-time has been practiced in Japan for many decades. Through elimination of costly inventory and rework on defective units, companies such as Toyota have been able to reduce costs amounting to billions of U.S. dollars.

---

16 Deloitte & Touche. "Marketplace and Management Challenges for CEOs." *The Review*, 16 August 1999, p. 3.

17 Deloitte Research. *Making Customer Loyalty Real: Lessons From Leading Manufacturers.* New York: Deloitte Research, 1999, p. 1.

18 *Ibid.*, p. 11.

19 Anne Fisher. "Rules for Joining the Cult of Perfectability." *Fortune*, 7 February 2000, p. 206.

20 Callie Berliner and James A. Brimson, eds. *Cost Management for Today's Advanced Manufacturing.* Boston, Mass.: Harvard Business School Press, 1988, p. 241.

Example

Liu Company, based in Hong Kong, has an average inventory costing of 6 million Hong Kong dollar (HK$). Liu's suppliers are willing to deliver materials in smaller lots at additional costs of HK$350,000. The following effects of adopting a JIT system are identified.

- By incurring overtime premiums of HK$600,000 per year, the company would avoid lost sales due to stockouts.

- One warehouse used for inventory storage would no longer be needed. Annual warehouse rent is HK$500,000. Another warehouse is owned by Liu and it could be rented for HK$200,000. Insurance coverage, property tax, security, and clerical costs estimated to be HK$150,000 per year would be eliminated.

Long-term investments by Liu are expected to produce a 15 percent annual rate of return.

The expected savings for Liu Company resulting from the adoption of a JIT inventory control system are:

Savings on carrying cost of average inventory at 20 percent required return on investment:		
20% × HK$6,000,000		HK$ 900,000
Avoidance of warehouse rent per year		500,000
Revenue from renting the warehouse owned by the company		200,000
Savings on insurance coverage, property tax, security, and clerical costs		150,000
Total revenue and savings		1,750,000
Subtract:		
Overtime premium	HK$600,000	
Additional inventory costs	350,000	(950,000)
Net amount in favor of JIT system		HK$7,800,000)

Kaizen is the cornerstone of the just-in-time approach. **Kaizen** is a budgeting approach that incorporates continuous improvement. Kaizen focuses on establishing a cost reduction target for each cost element, product line, organization unit, and manufacturing plant. Cost reduction is achieved through continuous improvement efforts by cross-functional teams.

Exhibit 9.8 shows an annual profit plan based on the kaizen system.

With just-in-time production, Samsung produces goods only after customers place orders and gets them to customers fast, eliminating billions of dollars in inventory costs and accounts receivable.[21] Dell Computer also uses just-in-time

---

21 Moon Ihlwan, Pete Engardio, Irene Kunii, and Roger Crockett. "Samsung: The Making of a Superstar." *Business Week*, 20 December 1999, pp. 138, 140.

exhibit 9.8   **Annual Profit Plan Using Kaizen**

Projected sales revenues	¥ xxx
Less previous year's actual variable costs	xxx
Budgeted contribution margin	xxx
Less cost reduction target	xxx
Adjusted contribution margin	xxx
Less budgeted fixed costs*	xxx
Budgeted operating income	¥ xxx

*No cost reduction targets are established for fixed costs. However, the budgeted amount for each fixed cost element is established after review and analysis of past actual fixed costs.

Source: Yasuhiro Monden and John Lee. "How Japanese Auto Maker Reduces Costs." *Management Accounting*, August 1993, pp. 22–26 (adapted).

production. Customers place their order by calling Dell's toll-free telephone number or logging onto the company's Web site where they can configure their own model. A customer's tailored PC is priced by the features selected, and the price information is instantly made available to the customer. Each PC is made to order, yet the time span from a customer's order placement to its loading it on a delivery truck is just 36 hours. Customer orders are sent to one of the three manufacturing plants, two in the U.S. and one in Ireland. There is no inventory inside any of the three manufacturing plants. According to one of the plant managers, "All our suppliers know that our components must be delivered within an hour."[22] More commonly used components and parts (chips, boards, drives) are kept in trucks backed up in bays 50 feet from the beginning of the production line. As soon as an order is completed, it is immediately shipped to the customer, thus avoiding handling and storing of finished goods inventory.[23]

Target Costing Approach

Target costing is a method to set cost targets for the products whose selling prices are determined by competitive markets. The analysis starts with the estimated (target) selling price that will be acceptable to customers and subtracts desired profit to arrive at target cost:

Target selling price (market-based) = Desired profit + Target cost

Target cost = Target selling price (market-based) − Desired profit

22 Andrew E. Serwer. "Michael Dell Turns the PC World Inside Out." *Fortune*, 8 September 1997, p. 44.

23 *Ibid.*

As previously shown, the target costing approach develops product target cost information by working back from the market-based price and subtracting the desired profit to arrive at an allowable cost for a product. This allowable cost is the target cost. It establishes the cost target for a cross-functional team, motivating it to reduce costs by improving product design, performing value engineering, and perhaps making tradeoffs on functionality.[24]

Example

After market research, the Marketing Department of Sorø A/S determines that there is a market niche for an espresso coffee maker with certain features that would make the product easy to use. The target market is retail buyers who would be using the product at home. It is estimated that 50,000 units of the product could be sold annually at the selling price of 400 Danish krone (Dkr). To develop, design, and produce the new espresso coffee maker, an investment of Dkr10 million would be required. Sorø A/S requires a 16 percent return on investment. The target cost is computed as follows.

Estimated sales (50,000 units × Dkr400)	Dkr20,000,000
Deduct desired profit (16% × Dkr10,000)	1,600,000
Target cost for 50,000 units	Dkr18,400,000
Target cost per unit (Dkr18,400,000 ÷ 50,000)	Dkr368

The Dkr368 target cost would cover product manufacturing, marketing, distribution, and customer support (warranty repairs, etc.) costs.

Target costing has been widely used in Japan since the early 1970s and is gaining popularity worldwide. Among the companies using target costing are Toyota, Texas Instruments, NEC, Compaq Computer Corporation, Isuzu Motors, Epson, Sharp, DaimlerChrysler, Carrier, Nissan, Boeing, IBM, Siemens, and Ford Motor Company.   To bring down the initial estimated cost to the target cost, different companies tend to emphasize different methods. For example, Carrier attempts to achieve target cost by focusing either on design changes or improving the manufacturing processes.[25] IBM and Eastman Kodak examine tradeoffs on functionality, quality, and value engineering. Boeing uses value engineering and kaizen as key components in its target costing approach.[26]

Worldwide Manufacturing Locations

Many multinational corporations are finding that it is economical to geographically disperse manufacturing facilities. All major Japanese automakers

---

24 Robert S. Kaplan, ed. *Measures for Manufacturing Excellence.* Boston, Mass.: Harvard Business School Press, 1990, p. 4.

25 "Target Costing." *Management Accounting*, April 1998, p. 27.

26 "First Annual International Conference on Target Costing." *Management Accounting*, January 1998, p. 63.

have manufacturing plants in the U.S. Toyota and Nissan are planning to expand their U.S. manufacturing facilities because of the popularity of larger trucks in the American market.[27] Interestingly, current Toyota Motor President Fujio Cho previously managed one of the Toyota manufacturing plants in the U.S. Texas Instruments has found it to be advantageous to produce chips at various locations throughout the world. Advances in information technology in recent years make it feasible, while this would not have been the case some years back.

Hiring Local Managers

Many multinational companies have found that using local talent to manage their international operations provides multiple benefits:[28]

> There is a world of differences among the people of Bestfoods and a host of ways in which they connect.
>
> By and large, local men and women manage our businesses around the world, providing the market expertise and experience that are Bestfoods' hallmarks. Mexicans manage our business in Mexico; Pakistanis manage in Pakistan.
>
> But in today's connected world, our local people have the added benefits of global perspective and coordination, which help to maximize our core business strategies, build our product and packaging expertise, increase our purchasing efficiency, and improve our management development and technological capabilities.

The obvious advantage is their knowledge of native culture and language that frequently results in better response to the dynamics of local environments. Additionally, it cuts the costs of sending and keeping the base country executives abroad. Some of those costs are moving families abroad, housing appropriate for maintaining lifestyle, children's education, and cost of living adjustments to the executive's salary to name a few.

Outsourcing

Many companies are outsourcing non-core activities to reduce costs as well as to focus on their core competencies. Non-core activities include payroll processing, real estate property management, and applications processing, among others.

Recently, PricewaterhouseCoopers sponsored a study of 100 companies, based in European countries, with an average annual revenue of $5 billion. Results of the study indicated that 55 percent of the companies have outsourced one or more processes to external service providers. Nine out of ten companies were satisfied with the service they were receiving. The major benefits cited for outsourcing were: Being able to focus on core competencies; increased efficien-

---

27 James R. Healey. "Toyota, Nissan Make Big Plans for U.S. Plants." *USA Today*, 21 October 1999, p. 1B.

28 Bestfoods. *1999 Annual Report*, p. 20.

cies; and greater profitability.[29] In 1999, BP Amoco PLC outsourced most of its U.S. accounting and back-office operations to PricewaterhouseCoopers in a $1.1 billion, 10-year contract. *The Wall Street Journal* reported, "companies have been unloading functions that once were thought inseparable in a multinational corporation. PricewaterhouseCoopers executives credited technology with enabling such outsourcing, making it possible to conceive of a company that concentrates on areas where it has an advantage and leaves non-core functions to others."[30] According to a PricewaterhouseCoopers partner, other companies outsourcing their accounting function received a 10 to 20 percent reduction in their accounting expenses.[31]

Projected Foreign Currency Exchange Rate Considerations

Many multinational corporations are taking into account projected foreign currency exchange rate movements while making their sales and sourcing plans. This can be an effective way to increase revenue and reduce costs. Everything else being equal, it is advantageous to sell in countries with relatively stronger currencies, and to manufacture and purchase in countries with relatively weaker currencies. This cost reduction strategy has been successfully used by Daimler-Chrysler's aerospace division by shifting production and parts purchasing into weaker currency areas.

Note to Students

You have been presented with three additional managerial accounting topics: budgeting, risk management, and cost management.

Software packages are now commonly available and used to minimize the computational burden of budgeting, and to cut down the time consumed by the process. The software packages perform calculations based on the interrelationships between and among operational and financial activities. Many software companies incorporate budgeting modules in their accounting packages. Examples include Great Plains, Computer Associates, and Solomon Software. Some vendors have budgeting software packages by themselves. Hyperion's Pillar is one example of such a budget package.

http://

Risk management of international operations is facilitated by the availability of pertinent information. The International Risk Management Institute provides valuable information on its Web site at **http://www.irmi.com**.

---

29 PricewaterhouseCoopers. *Global Top Decision Makers Study on Business Process Outsourcing: Europe.* New York: PricewaterhouseCoopers, 1999.

30 Steven Liesman. "BP Amoco Is Set to Outsource Accounting in $1.1 Billion Deal." *The Wall Street Journal*, 10 November 1999, p. A4.

31 *Ibid.*

http://

The information includes articles authored by industry specialists on insurance, law, and other aspects of risk management.

Another interesting and informative source for global risk management is a portal that provides access to international news items on business continuity. Its address is **http://www.globalcontinuity.com**.

This site additionally contains back issues of the *Journal of Business Continuity*.

Information about corporate plans for cost reduction, operating strategies, or investment in new plants or locations is reported on a daily basis by major newspapers. Business and news periodicals such as *Fortune, Forbes, Business Week*, and *The Economist* regularly publish detailed articles on multinational corporate investment and production plans.

The U.S. Bureau of Labor Statistics (BLS) publishes reports on topics such as labor costs, productivity, and competitiveness. BLS's Internet address is **http://stat.bls.gov**.

Increased global competition has forced many companies to critically review their internal processes for reducing costs and achieving nimbleness. They find it necessary to maintain or enhance their competitive position.

There is a direct relationship between the competitiveness of business firms in a country and the competitiveness of the country's economy. As mentioned in the chapter, The International Institute for Management Development (IMD) annually publishes countries' competitiveness rankings. IMD's country profiles are at the Web site address **http://www.imd.ch/wcy**.

Profit can be increased by increasing revenues, by managing costs, or by both. Increase in revenues can be achieved in the competitive global markets by fine-tuning selling prices. Ford Motor Company uses a pricing approach that increases its unit sales volume of high-margin vehicles. Ford drops its prices on the most profitable vehicles *just enough* to boost their demand, but not so much that those vehicles are no longer highly profitable. Interestingly, Ford's U.S. market share has fallen from 25.7 percent in 1995 to 23.8 percent in 1999. The market share decline is attributable to a reduction in unit sales of low-margin vehicles. In spite of this loss of market share, Ford's 1999 profit was $7.2 billion. This profit figure was not only a record for Ford but for any automobile company in history.[32]

Pricing to optimize profit by focusing on unit sales of high-margin products requires detailed information about market demand and a company's own capacity to supply for meeting the demand. Yield-management software provides the necessary detailed information to make it possible to use this pricing approach. Talus Solutions Inc. originally developed the yield-management software. Ford uses Talus software, as do many other businesses, especially hotels and airlines.

The design phase of a product has deservedly received a great deal of attention in recent years. For most products, the production, distribution, and cus-

---

32 "The Power of Smart Pricing." *Business Week*, 10 April 2000, pp. 160–161.

tomer service costs are locked in during the design phase. Not much can be done later to reduce the locked-in costs short of a design change. Design is now also emerging as a powerful marketing strategy in the New Economy. Apple is the first large company to recognize its design's great impact in the marketplace, and is using it effectively to boost its earnings.[33]

Chapter Summary

1. The annual budget preparation process begins with a forecast of sales.
2. Capital budgeting is the process of identifying, evaluating, and planning long-term investments.
3. Commonly used capital project evaluation techniques include discounted cash flow, payback period, and accrual accounting rate of return methods.
4. Foreign investment analysis must consider both economic and political risks associated with foreign environments.
5. Political risk refers to possible actions by host governments with potentially negative effects on a multinational company's operations.
6. Issues in determining product costs include labor productivity, product quality, cost management, and changes in foreign currency exchange rates.
7. Accurate costing of goods and services is important for setting prices that are competitive in global markets.
8. Productivity levels influence a company's, as well as a country's, competitive position.
9. Intense global competition has forced multinational corporations to pay more attention to cost management.

Questions for Discussion

1. What are the main purposes of budgeting?
2. How does the budget assist in the coordination of activities among international subsidiaries and between international subsidiaries and the parent company?
3. Why is it more difficult to forecast the sales volumes of a multinational corporation?
4. Define each of the following: Cost center, profit center, revenue center, and investment center.

---

33 "Apple Wins With Design." *Business Week*, 31 July 2000, p. 144.

5. Contrast centralized budgeting systems against decentralized budgeting systems.

6. How do changes in foreign exchange rates affect the budgeting process?

7. Explain how global sourcing of factors of production affects the budgeting process.

8. Explain how currency flow restrictions affect the budgeting process.

9. Define capital budgeting and contrast it with budgeting for operations.

10. List and briefly explain the main methods for capital budgeting.

11. Explain the relationship between the risk and required rate of return for international investment projects. Would you expect the return required from international investment to be *generally* higher than, lower than, or the same as the return required from domestic investments? Why?

12. What is meant by economic risk?

13. What is meant by political risk?

14. Define a derivative.

15. What are the financial reporting disclosure requirements for derivatives according to *IAS39*?

16. Why is activity-based costing considered to be a better system for pricing decisions than traditional costing?

17. What is a target cost for a product unit?

18. Explain how value engineering can be useful in target costing.

19. What are the major characteristics of a JIT production system?

20. What are the advantages of using local managers?

Exercises/Problems

9-1 Rakhshanda SpA is an Italian multinational corporation with plants in 4 countries and sales operations in 21. The company wants to open a new plant to serve the Americas' spare auto parts market. Management has narrowed the new location to three countries: Brazil, Canada, and Mexico. The International Division of Rakhshanda SpA has provided you with the following information about the three proposed plants in each country's respective currency. Rakhshanda SpA's cost of capital is 8 percent.

	Brazil (reals 000,000)	**Canada** (dollars 000)	**Mexico** (pesos 000,000)
Required investment	R$28,200	Can$5,100	Ps.18,600
Annual net cash inflow	R$9,215	Can$1,075	Ps.5,640
Plant useful life	6 years	10 years	8 years
Current exchange rates:			
1 Italian Lira	R$4.3	Can$0.0011	Ps.2.8

Required:

(1) Compute the net present value for each plant according to the cost of capital only. Rank the three plants in their order of preference.

(2) Based on your knowledge of the three countries, you assess the political environment in each. This results in the assignment of the following political risk factors: 8 percent to Mexico, 6 percent to Brazil, and 4 percent to Canada. Compute the net present value for each plant, taking into consideration the assigned risk factor.

(3) Compare and comment on your answers to Parts (1) and (2).

9-2 You have been asked to prepare a capital budgeting analysis for a proposed new plant. Your company, Can Super, Inc. (CSI) has its head office in Hamilton, Canada. CSI is considering opening an assembly plant in North America or Central America. The final four locations being considered are: Austin (U.S.), Mexico City (Mexico), Sacramento (U.S.), and Panama City (Panama). The Financial Forecast Group has provided the following information (all amounts in Canadian dollar):

	Austin	Sacramento	Mexico City	Panama City
Required investment	$16,500	$18,100	$12,400	$11,500
Annual cash inflow	6,800	7,200	5,100	5,200
Annual cash outflow	4,100	4,300	3,900	3,800
Useful life	10 years	10 years	8 years	8 years

Use the straight-line method of depreciation and assume no salvage value.

Required:

(1) Rank the four proposed plants according to the payback period method.

(2) Rank the four proposed plants according to the accrual accounting rate of return method.

9-3 Sonya Inc., a French multinational, is trying to decide whether to open a manufacturing plant in Malaysia or Singapore. The cost of capital for Sonya is 6 percent and the added risk factor, because of the location, is 4 percent for Malaysia and 2 percent for Singapore. The following table shows the expected cash flows related to the project.

Required:

(1) Compute the net present value of each project.

(2) What is your recommendation based on this analysis?

	Malaysia (ringgits 000)	Singapore (dollars 000)
Required initial investment	RM19,000	S$16,000
Expected annual cash inflow	14,300	10,600
Expected annual cash outflow	10,500	7,200
Useful life of manufacturing plant	8 years	8 years

Present Value of an Ordinary Annuity of One Monetary Unit

Years	6%	8%	10%	12%	14%
6	4.917	4.623	4.355	4.111	3.889
8	6.210	5.747	5.335	4.968	4.639
10	7.360	6.710	6.145	5.650	5.216

9-4 The controller of Numair Telecommunications interviewed managers of the Design, Engineering, and Production Departments to determine the cost driver of variable manufacturing overhead costs at their respective departments. The following data were collected for 2002:

Activity Area	Budgeted Variable Manufacturing Overhead in 2002	Cost Driver	Usage
Design	$ 80,000	Design hours	800
Engineering	50,000	Engineering hours	250
Manufacturing	470,000	Machine hours	4,000
	$600,000		

Required:

What is the budgeted activity rate for each activity in 2002?

9-5 Raymond Food Processing PLC decides to apply ABC to three product lines—canned foods, frozen foods, and fruit juices. Raymond identifies four activities. The budgeted activity rates for 2003 are as follows:

Ordering	£50 per purchase order
Delivery of merchandise	£400 per delivery
Power	£200 per machine hour
Customer support	£10 per carton

Pertinent budgeted data for the three product lines for 2003 are as follows (in 000):

	Canned Foods	Frozen Foods	Fruit Juices
Revenues	£75,000	£100,000	£50,000
Cost of goods sold	40,000	65,000	30,000
Other expenses	15,000	18,000	7,000
Indirect costs activity usage			
Ordering: purchase orders	40	35	15
Delivery: deliveries	125	150	30
Power: machine hours	2,000	1,800	500
Customer support: cartons sold	17,500	22,500	7,500

Under the traditional costing system, Raymond allocated indirect costs to the product lines at the rate of £340 per machine hour.

Required:

(1) Use the ABC system to prepare a profitability report for each product line.

(2) What insights does the ABC system provide to Raymond regarding each product line's profitability?

9-6 Younker International manufactures cellular telephones. It uses an activity-based costing approach. Younker's costing system has only one direct cost category, direct materials, and four activity cost pools:

Activity Cost Pool	Cost Driver	Activity Rate
1. Material handling	Number of parts	40 per part
2. Machining	Machine hours	200 per machine hour
3. Assembly	Labor hours	50 per labor hour
4. Quality inspection	Inspection hours	75 per inspection hour

Schwartz AG recently purchased 100 units of Model 2XL from Younker. Each unit has direct materials costs of 1,000, requires 20 parts, 1 machine hour, 0.75 assembly hour, and 0.50 inspection hour.

Required:

Using the ABC system, compute the total manufacturing cost of the Schwartz AG job, and the unit manufacturing cost of Model 2XL.

9-7 Plum Computer Company manufactures and sells personal computers and printers. Susan Peach is the manager of the printer division.

The production of each printer is calculated using an activity-based costing system. Plum has only one direct manufacturing cost category, direct materials, and four activity cost pools for indirect manufacturing costs:

Activity Cost Pool	Cost Driver	Budgeted Activity Rate
1. Materials handling	Number of parts	$1.00 per part
2. Assembly	Machine hours	$30.00 per machine hour
3. Insertion of parts	Number of inserted parts	$1.00 per inserted part
4. Quality testing	Hours of quality testing time	$25.00 per testing hour

Product requirements of the two printers, PT 100 and PT 200, are as follows:

	PT 100	PT 200
Direct materials costs	$200	$150
Number of parts	70 parts	40 parts
Machine hours for assembly	2.2 machine hours	1.5 machine hours
Number of inserted parts	40 parts	25 parts
Hours of quality testing	1.5 hours	1.2 hours

Required:

Compute the unit production cost of:

(1) PT 100.

(2) PT 200.

9-8 Nuzhat AB, a Sweden-based company, manufactures and sells digital camera NB 20. In response to competitive pressures, Nuzhat must reduce the price of NB 20 to 250 Swedish krona (Sk) in 2002 to achieve sales of 100,000 units. Nuzhat's investment is Sk4,000,000. If the company wants a 25 percent return on investment, what is the target cost per unit?

9-9 SLO Corporation manufactures electronic notepads. SLO plans to implement a JIT system, which requires annual costs of $350,000. SLO expects the following annual benefits from the JIT system:

a. Average inventory will decline by $1,500,000.

b. Insurance, materials handling, setup costs, and storage costs would decline by $75,000.

c. The emphasis on quality in JIT systems would reduce rework costs by $100,000.

d. Improved quality would enable SLO to raise the selling prices of its products by $5 per unit. SLO sells 50,000 units annually.

SLO's required rate of return on inventory investment is 12 percent per year.

Required:

Compute the net benefit (or cost) to the SLO Corporation from implementing a JIT system.

Case 1

Global Petroleum Company

Nooristan was one of the world's fastest growing countries during the 1990s and early 2000s. It had a remarkable 12 percent growth rate measured in terms of gross domestic product. Its democratically elected government—though quite corrupt and often slow to respond because of its bureaucracy—implemented policies that were generally considered business-friendly. As a result, hundreds of foreign-based companies made investments and established production and marketing operations in Nooristan. These firms manufactured wide-ranging consumer goods, provided insurance and banking services, and worked on big government developmental projects. They employed hundreds of thousands of Nooristan citizens. Nooristan also became an important trading partner of many developed countries, exporting to them with its natural resources, especially oil, as well as manufactured goods.

In spite of the country's notable economic growth, Nooristan's government faced criticism from a broad spectrum of its population. Intellectuals felt that governmental policies were liberal in the business area, but quite oppressive on individual liberties such as freedoms of speech, association, and political affiliation. The intellectuals had a sizable following among the university students. The students often went on strike—which usually resulted in violent confrontations with the police. Another source of strong opposition was the religious right. Religious fundamentalists claimed that economic and material advancements were often at the cost of traditional values loss. They also felt that multinationals had brought Western influence with them to Nooristan. In their opinion, Western influence had resulted in the erosion of fundamental spiritual beliefs in the country. In 2001, there were widespread strikes and demonstrations that crippled, and at times halted, almost all business and commercial activities. This fostered additional discontent among the population fueled by a shut-down of all means of public transportation, banks, and a shortage of good supplies and gasoline. In September, a military coup overthrew the government. The coup was applauded by a majority of the population, especially by the religious right.

The general who led the coup was installed as the new president. Soon after he took office, he declared that one of his top priorities would be to review all business contracts entered into by the former government with "foreign companies." He stated that most of the contracts had been awarded to those companies on unfavorable terms to Nooristan by corrupt officials in the former government. He asserted that most of those companies were in Nooristan solely to exploit the human and material resources. To support his assertion, he said that those companies applied low safety, health, and environmental standards to their operations in Nooristan, while upholding much higher standards for operations in their own countries. This, he stated, was evidence of their exploitive attitude and disregard for the welfare of the local population.

Soon afterwards, the new government took numerous steps that drastically affected multinational companies. It started to cancel contracts that were deemed to be not in the best interest of Nooristan. Payments to all multinational companies for the government projects completed or in progress were frozen until it was determined that the amounts billed to the government were "reasonable" and "fair."

Next came the nationalization of key industries. These included telecommunication, petrochemical, construction, and hydroelectric industries. The government also expropriated the assets of Nooristan's 100 largest companies, as measured by their net worth. Almost all of these were wholly owned subsidiaries of multinationals. The industry takeovers were estimated to be worth tens of billions of British pound sterling, and involved companies employing approximately 2,000,000 workers.

One of the most costly expropriation losses reported in the U.K. was by Global Petroleum Company. Global had diversified operations in Nooristan, which included oil drilling, oil refining, pipeline construction, and petrochemicals. These operations were conducted through a wholly owned subsidiary called NoorGlo. By the end of 2001, all of NoorGlo's operations had been taken over by the new government. Global provided detailed information in a note in its 2001 annual report. The note stated that the company intends to recover the loss resulting from its expropriated assets (valued at 1.1 billion pound sterling) by aggressively seeking a remedy from the Nooristan government, both in Nooristan and in the U.K. The company also would continue to demand payments (amounting to 50 million pound sterling) from the Nooristan government for work already completed on projects in accordance with contractual agreements. The company acknowledged that substantial future losses may result from the situation in Nooristan.

Required:

(1) What methods can Global use to analyze the risks associated with the political environment of a country such as Nooristan?

(2) What actions should Global take to minimize its risks after the investment is made?

(3) Discuss the implications of the political situation in Nooristan on its economic growth.

(4) Discuss the likely actions to be taken by the current and potential future investors regarding investments in Nooristan.

(5) What would you do, as a investor from the outside, if you have investments in Nooristan? Provide reasons for your actions.

Case 2

Downsizing by Bullying! What Next?

In general, Japanese business traditions prize seniority and experience. Japanese employees assume they will have life-time employment with their employer. Pay raises are based on seniority and age, rather than on merit. However, a dramatic change is taking place in some Japanese companies. Those companies are attempting not only to downsize, but do so by using methods that are not generally considered conventional.

In 1997, 57 employees of Sasebo Heavy Industries Co., a major shipbuilder based in the port city of Nagasaki Prefecture, were transferred to an affiliate of the company. They were ordered to report to work at the cafeteria of a Sasebo Heavy Industries factory every day and write a report on "new business opportunities" for their company. They were also "interviewed" repeatedly by the executives.

In reality, they had very little work to do since they were "transferred to the cafeteria." The company had selected the 57 employees for their new "assignments" because they were no longer needed. The head of the employees union protested by stating that what the company was doing could only be described as bullying to force them out.

Another episode involved about 200 employees of a chemical company in Yoyama Prefecture that had a total workforce of 2,200. The company ordered the 200 staff members to take turns in "retraining" at a mountain cottage. Upon arrival at the cottage, they were confronted by a Tokyo business consultant who ordered them to write essays on what they had done for the company since being recruited. The consultant then "analyzed" these self-criticisms and repeatedly told them to rewrite their essays. Some employees felt so humiliated that they fled the room in tears. But a member of the personnel department was waiting for them outside the room with blank resignation forms.

Ijime or bullying cases are fundamentally the same. Companies try to cut jobs by bullying employees into quitting "voluntarily," a method which does not cost the company any money.

A 29-year-old employee of an information processing company said he had attempted to kill himself after suffering from severe depression due to maltreatment by his boss. Months ago, his boss suddenly stopped giving him any work assignments, and even stopped speaking to him. In addition to feeling suicidal, he stated that he had lost 19 kilos in weight.[34]

Required:

(1) Do you think it is ethical to practice *ijime* to pressure employees to resign?

(2) What could be the possible reason or reasons for not informing the employees directly that their services were no longer needed?

(3) Imagine you are a Japanese executive. How would you handle the situation to achieve the desired cutbacks in your responsibility area?

(4) As an outside consultant, what would be your recommendations to the company management to achieve downsizing?

Case 3

Ameripill Company

The purpose of this case is to illustrate numerous issues involved in evaluating international subsidiary performance using accounting information. In particular, the case demonstrates how performance evaluation impacts decision making at the subsidiary level. Case facts are based on an extensive set of interviews both at the parent and international subsidiary levels. The importance of considering global implications when designing and using accounting-based international subsidiary performance evaluation systems is highlighted. The case can also be used to integrate tax and regulatory issues into the performance evaluation setting and to make links between organizational design and performance evaluation.[35]

---

34 Adapted from Toshio Jo. "Corporate Bullying on the Rise." *Gulf News*, 14 April 1997, p. 2A.

35 Susan F. Haka, Barbara A. Lamberton, and Harold M. Sollenberger. "International Subsidiary Performance Evaluation: The Case of the Ameripill Company." *Issues in Accounting Education*, Spring 1994, pp. 168–179.

Overview of Ameripill Company's International Organization

Located in Bartow, Alabama, the Pharmaceutical Division of Ameripill Company ranks among the top 15 drug companies in the world. The Pharmaceutical Division is divided into three worldwide operating units with a vice president in charge of each: North America, Europe, and the rest of the world including South America, Africa, and Asia. The European vice president, Gene Roget, views Europe and one strategic unit with many markets. He thinks strategically about market share, product innovation, acquisitions, and financial success. Organizationally, he works closely with Collen Stein, Pharmaceutical Vice President of Finance. Stein has recently combined the international and U.S. domestic finance groups. The international subsidiary financial analysis activities are concentrated in one unit under Stein called International and Domestic Financial Services. An abbreviated organization chart for the company is shown in Figure 9.2. Except for the international general managers and the Puerto Rico and The Hague manufacturing managers, all executives are based in Bartow.

Important and explicit responsibilities of Stein are to develop financial policies, make measurement decisions, and monitor results to optimize Ameripill's pharmaceutical profit levels. On an international level, this becomes an extraordinarily complex task. Included are direct and indirect responsibilities to:

- Design a financial performance evaluation system to encourage general managers in specific countries to maximize their contribution to corporate earnings.

- Help maximize the companywide gross margin from pharmaceutical sales through effective marketing, product strategies, and increased market shares.

- Minimize the companywide tax liability through international transfer pricing.

- Coordinate country-by-country pricing strategies to maximize total sales dollars and global gross margin. This includes decisions to market or not market a specific drug in a specific country.

- Obtain approvals for marketing drugs and for prices in each country, since most non-U.S. countries control pharmaceutical prices, as well as access to their markets.

- Minimize production cost by selecting optimal manufacturing locations, while balancing in-country requirements and production loading.

- Maximize cash flows to Bartow and minimize nontransferable cash balances, exposure risk due to currency exchange fluctuations, and transfer penalties.

- Develop financing strategies to help acquire other companies and to create inter-corporate relationships that will contribute to company sales, to market share, and directly to profits.

- Create capital and legal structures to optimize financial, operating, legal, and political needs; avoid operating losses; and protect company investments in non-U.S. countries.

figure 9.2   **Ameripill Company and Pharmaceutical Division Organization**

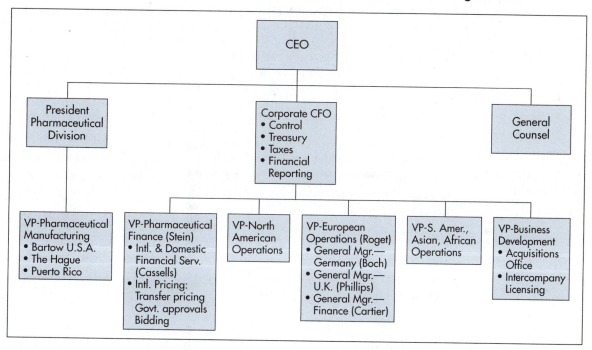

The staffs to accomplish these responsibilities are divided among Stein, the corporate CFO's office, and certain other units reporting to Stein. Coordination occurs through a working group called the International Profitability Group (IPG) chaired by Olivia Cassells, Director of International and Domestic Financial Services. Group membership includes Cassells; the Corporate Director of Taxes Treasury, and Financial Reporting; the Pharmaceutical Division Managers for International Pricing and Manufacturing Accounting; and representatives from the Vice President of Business Development and the General Counsel offices. This group meets regularly to review problem areas, to recommend courses of action within the finance area, and to communicate possible financial impacts to the executive group. Stein believes many of the goals and responsibilities listed previously are inevitably linked to the international incentive evaluation system created and operated by the staff of International and Domestic Financial Services. Over the past two or three years, several complaints have been lodged with Roget and Stein by the international subsidiaries' general managers (GMs) regarding their incentive scheme. Stein has decided to use the coming year's results to evaluate the effectiveness of the international incentive scheme.

The Profit Measurement System

Ameripill domestic units are evaluated on growth in market share, sales volume, and revenue. Because of the complexities of international markets, the international profit measurement system has three reporting levels—legal entity earnings, responsibility earnings, and global earnings. Legal entity earnings are used for required reporting needs such as for tax and regulatory purposes within each country. Responsibility earnings include import and export sales that country managers can influence, given what is known to them about prices, costs, and transfer prices. Global earnings are a broader corporate view of sales and costs and represent an economic earnings view of each subunit. The global earnings figure is calculated only for the Bartow financial and operations executives. For international subsidiaries, the general managers are evaluated in two ways:

1. Actual results compared to budget focusing on gross margin, ROA, cash flow, and inventory and receivables levels. The evaluation looks at the entire operation using "responsibility earnings" and "earnings before taxes" and is the basis for evaluating and comparing the performances of all international general managers.

2. A management incentive system administered through the International Financial Performance System (IFPS). The IFPS is the bonus system and focuses on a subsidiary's contribution to "global earnings," "earnings before taxes," "responsibility earnings" growth over last year, return on managed assets, inventory levels, and market share performance. IFPS bonuses are based 60 percent on the local unit's results and 40 percent on the region's contribution to "global earnings."

Exhibits 9.9, 9.10, and 9.11 (pages 365, 366, and 367) present preliminary results for 1992 and a forecast for 1993 for the United Kingdom, France, and Germany in the format sent to Bartow for early analysis of 1992 performance.

Comments from the Wednesday Meeting

A meeting of the International Profitability Group is planned for Friday, December 11, 1992. It is Wednesday, and Olivia Cassells and Collen Stein are meeting in Bartow to review the agenda and supporting discussion documents that will be sent to each attending member. Cassells has materials from Vice President Roget's office, the directors in the Pharmaceutical Division, and the corporate offices. Cassells is sure that several controversial issues will be raised. Selected items from the agenda include the following:

1. Final financial staff approval of the acquisition of Koblenz Chemie Company.
2. Problems using cash balances in the U.K. and possible production changes at the U.K. subsidiary.
3. Problems with the IFPS.
4. Price increase for a product in the French market.

After a quick review of the tentative 1992 international subsidiary results, attention turns to the agenda.

exhibit 9.9 Financial Results—United Kingdom

International Pharmaceutical Subsidiaries Financial Summary (000s omitted)		
Country: United Kingdom	Budget '93	Actual '92
Sales	$ 49,960	$ 48,080
Cost of sales	(21,982)	(21,155)
Direct expenses	(14,658)	(14,512)
Other income (expense)	(1,499)	(1,155)
Responsibility earnings	$ 11,821	$ 11,258
Interest income (expense)[1]	(358)	(241)
Exchange gain (loss)[2]	(142)	(338)
Division charges[3]	(1,629)	(1,640)
Earnings before tax	$ 9,692	$ 9,039
Managed assets	$ 84,500	$ 88,860
IFPS goals:		
EBT = 18%	19.4%	18.8%
ROA = 15%	11.5%	10.2%
Responsibility earnings growth = 5%	5.0%	4.8%
Inventory (month's supply) = 1.0 months	2.5 months	3.2 months

1 Based on locally incurred debt.
2 Based on average 1992 exchange rate ($1.4 per U.K. pound).
3 Fixed charge negotiated annually between Bartow and the subsidiary.

Acquisition of Koblenz Chemie Company

Olivia Cassells begins the Wednesday meeting by discussing a recommendation from the business development office and Roget that the board of directors acquire Koblenz Chemie Company for DM25,000,000 ($15.5 million), about eight times earnings. The Koblenz Chemie Co. management has forecast 1993 sales to be DM12,000,000 ($7.4 million).[36] Cassells notes that the acquisition has several advantages. First, it gives Ameripill access to a key German generic drug market. Koblenz has an 8 percent market share in Germany in its product lines. Second, it provides Ameripill with the opportunity to have a stronger market

---

36 Assume that the acquisition of the Koblenz business in 1993 will cause the German subsidiary's Sales, Cost of Sales, and Direct Expenses to increase by the same percentage. Other subsidiary income and expenses are not expected to change.

exhibit 9.10 Financial Results—Germany

International Pharmaceutical Subsidiaries Financial Summary (000s omitted)		
Country: Germany	**Budget '93**	**Actual '92**
Sales	$156,840	$137,440
Cost of sales	(65,872)	(57,995)
Direct expenses	(50,286)	(46,603)
Other income (expense)	(300)	(210)
Responsibility earnings	40,382	32,632
Interest income (expense)[1]	(1,312)	(939)
Exchange gain (loss)[2]	(150)	(210)
Division charges[3]	(4,700)	(4,123)
Earnings before tax	$ 34,220	$ 27,360
Managed assets	$ 73,760	$ 72,900
IFPS goals:		
EBT = 18%	21.8%	19.9%
ROA = 15%	46.4%	37.5%
Responsibility earnings growth = 5%	23.7%	15.6%
Inventory (month's supply) = 1.0 months	1.2 months	1.5 months

1 Based on locally incurred debt.
2 Based on average 1992 exchange rate ($.62 per German DM).
3 Fixed charge negotiated annually between Bartow and the subsidiary.

position in Germany, particularly in the newly opened former East German market. In recent years, Ameripill's German market share has remained at about 2 percent of the total pharmaceutical market. Third, Ameripill can offer Koblenz access to international markets.

Stein inquires about inputs from Hans Drossel, controller of the German subsidiary, about the acquisition. Cassells replies, "I'm not sure Drossel knows about it. Our acquisition guys researched this one. They think that the integration of Koblenz into our German organization shouldn't be a problem since they're located within 50 kilometers of each other." Both Stein and Cassells agree that even though the price seems high given Koblenz's earnings since 1989, Koblenz appears to be a quality operation in all respects. Stein notes, "The Koblenz acquisition seems to be a sure thing. I hear the accounting records are a mess. That's not surprising given that it was a privately owned firm. We'll have some work to do to get it into Ameripill's reporting and cash management systems." Cassells

exhibit 9.11 **Financial Results—France**

International Pharmaceutical Subsidiaries Financial Summary (000s omitted)		
Country: France	Budget '93	Actual '92
Sales	$108,720	$102,560
Cost of sales	(53,414)	(50,254)
Direct expenses	(31,529)	(29,742)
Other income (expense)	(946)	(1,026)
Responsibility earnings	22,831	21,538
Interest income (expense)[1]	(1,033)	(1,047)
Exchange gain (loss)[2]	(272)	(286)
Division charges[3]	(3,262)	(3,077)
Earnings before tax	$ 18,264	$ 17,128
Managed assets	$ 74,220	$ 73,460
IFPS goals:		
EBT = 18%	16.8%	16.7%
ROA = 15%	24.6%	23.3%
Responsibility earnings growth = 5%	6.0%	5.2%
Inventory (month's supply) = 1.0 months	0.9 months	1.1 months

1 Based on locally incurred debt.
2 Based on average 1992 exchange rate ($.16 per French franc).
3 Fixed charge negotiated annually between Bartow and the subsidiary.

agrees that system compatibility problems exist but goes on to suggest that no problems with final financial approval of the deal are likely to occur.

Cassells reminds Stein that another German issue might be impacted by this acquisition. Due to the rapid changes in the former East Bloc, business development has been studying the situation and recommends expanding the sales force and entering the former East German market. Business development projects this potential market to be $300 million and conservatively estimates that Ameripill could capture 10 percent of this market by the year 2000. Preliminary contacts have been made with former government officials with whom Ameripill has had previous business relationships. Ameripill sales in the entire Eastern Bloc have been very low.

A request, now nearly eight months old, from the German GM to create a sales force in eastern Germany, has been reviewed by business development. Cassells says, "Business development thinks the near-term financial feasibility looks dim but the question of having an Ameripill presence must be discussed. Roget is pressing all of us for a positive response. I hear he has given the okay to the German GM and controller to create a temporary eastern Germany sales force. Roget says it's now or never." Cassells believes these unilateral steps may be premature and may have adverse effects on the German subsidiary's bottom line for 1992 and 1993.

Cash Balances in the U.K. and Production Changes at the U.K. Subsidiary

Item B on the agenda generates more concern. Stein begins by discussing the historical tax problems associated with moving cash between international locations and the U.S. Stein notes that the U.K. subsidiary has generated a sizable cash position. Stein points out that strategies must be created to move cash to the U.S. or other locations where it can be invested profitably. Cassells suggests expanding manufacturing in the U.K. as a way to move the cash surplus without incurring costly penalties. Stein comments, "I thought that the tax law limited our options about transferring cash from the U.K. to the States." Cassells agrees, but suggests, "We could expand manufacturing and export to other countries, such as Germany, at cost. We may need the cash in Germany to pay for other acquisitions and expansion we see in eastern Germany. Also, we may have more flexibility in transferring cash to the United States."

Cassells and Stein then have a long discussion about implementing the export strategy of moving cash from the U.K. to Germany. Cassells suggests that Smoothkare, a product currently manufactured at The Hague for export to Germany, could be manufactured in the U.K. Cassells remarks, "I'm sure we could easily replace the lost Smoothkare manufacturing volume at The Hague with an equally profitable product." However, a sizable investment would be required to expand manufacturing capacity in the U.K.

Stein reminds Cassells that the cash problem was becoming worse each day, and a two- to three-year wait would only compound the problem. Stein suggests that perhaps current manufacturing capacity could be converted to produce Smoothkare, which could be transferred to Germany at cost. Stein asks Cassells if she had considered these options.

Cassells responds, "Yes, the U.K. general manager won't be too keen on this idea. He has written a detailed memo to Roget outlining the problems associated with expanding manufacturing in the U.K. (see Exhibit 9.12). First, producing Smoothkare will require us to increase the U.K.'s managed assets to approximately $90 million. Also the U.K. GM complained that, at the current volume, nearly half of his time is spent on production problems. Yet his performance is measured by responsibility earnings and ROA numbers—all sales-based. Also, the pressure to keep working capital low backfires in two ways. Low inventories mean that short, frequent, and expensive batches cause per-unit costs to be well above The Hague's and Puerto Rico's manufacturing unit costs. And since cash can't be moved out without significant tax penalties, large near-cash balances cause total working capital to balloon. I'll bet the U.K. GM will think that expanding manufacturing will divert attention away from marketing and that U.K.

exhibit 9.12 **Memo to Roget: U.K. Problems with IFPS**

Date:	March 20, 1992
To:	Gene Roget
	Vice President, European Operations
From:	John Phillips
	General Manager, United Kingdom
Subject:	Difficulties with the IFPS in the U.K.

As you and I have discussed on several occasions, the performance evaluation system for international subsidiaries has a number of negative impacts on our operations here in the U.K. The heavy emphasis on sales, profit margins, and rates of return overlooks the significant management effort put into our manufacturing operations here. Comparing us with a pure sales subsidiary is like comparing Yorkshire pudding and apple strudel. The changes made in the IFPS in 1991 have made the problem all the more severe for us since it focuses more on U.K.'s results.

Manufacturing means investing large amounts in plant and equipment, managing production planning and operations, maintaining inventories of materials, and often billing products at a price just above cost—certainly below normal markups. We are also a satellite plant and therefore often produce overflow from The Hague plant. To keep our inventories down for working capital purposes, we are forced to make frequent runs that inflate our per-unit costs.

While we are working in a very competitive sales market in the U.K., I estimate that my managers and I spend nearly half our time on production issues. I strongly urge a quick review of the performance evaluation system and the IFPS.

If I might, I would like to offer the following suggestions:

- Vice President Stein could be asked to separate the evaluation of U.K. production and sales operations—particularly the investment base and the prices of U.K.-manufactured products.

- If no separate evaluation is possible, U.K. manufactured products could be priced out of our plant at a worldwide wholesale price—either as a real transfer price or as a pseudo-transfer price set in Bartow.

- A revision of the working capital and investment base definitions for country sales subsidiaries could give consideration to nonsales activities.

I am very willing to discuss these and other operating, evaluation, and reporting issues to improve Ameripill's results and the U.K. performance—both real and as reported.

profits will tumble. The U.K. GM will see both of these as bad news for evaluating the U.K. subsidiary's responsibility earnings results and for his IFPS evaluation."

Problems with the International Financial Performance System (IFPS)

Stein notes the problems associated with moving cash out of the U.K. are related to the incentive scheme—an item next on the agenda. Cassells and Stein begin discussing the IFPS and its impact on international decisions. Cassells points out that several previous complaints had been forwarded from the U.K. GM. The regional vice president (under Roget) and one of the financial analysts visit each subsidiary three times a year. During the last visit to the U.K., the GM raised several questions about the IFPS and the annual performance review. Cassells relays the essence of these complaints to Stein: "The GM is not clear how the IFPS measurements are calculated. He sees only reports that show his U.K. responsibility earnings in pounds as they come from the U.K. accounting records. He says the ratios used in the budget and the IFPS are seriously distorted by manufacturing operations in the U.K."

Stein asks, "Is the U.K. GM the only subsidiary that is concerned?" Cassells says, "Not really. None of them seems to understand the incentive system or how their bonus is determined. The U.K. GM's complaint is one that we have heard over and over again from GMs. They want to know what 'global earnings' is and how it's calculated."

Stein recalls, "Yes, now that I think about it, Roget has complained to me about the IFPS scheme and even threatened to send each GM the details of how each subsidiary compares to one another. I assumed that the changes we made in '91—which shifted the scheme away from companywide uniformity to more emphasis on individual subsidiary goals—solved these concerns. Maybe the IPG needs to look at this issue and suggest some improvements."

Product Pricing in the French Market

Cassells and Stein move to the last item on the agenda, the price increase for Saincoeur in France. Saincoeur is a highly successful treatment for heart attack victims and is sold under other names in all of Ameripill's markets. Stein begins by telling Cassells that he understands that the International Pricing office will recommend raising the price of Saincoeur in France. Its low price in France is causing problems for the rest of the European markets. Cassells suggests two options. First, Ameripill could push hard to get approval for a price increase; second, it could withdraw Saincoeur from the French market to protect prices of the same product in other countries. Roget had reported pricing inquiries and pressure from Italy, the Swiss, and even Germany to reduce the price for the equivalent drug in their markets. The International Pricing office also suggested that, without a quick resolution of the pricing issue, Saincoeur should be withdrawn from the French market.

Stein asks, "Olivia, what kind of price concession would that mean for the other European markets? What's the financial impact?" Cassells notes that Saincoeur is barely profitable at the French price. "If Ameripill isn't careful, our margins for the equivalent products will decline all over the European market." Cassells and Stein decide to review the financial summaries for the product at a later date. However, Cassells concludes by stating, "Clearly, withdrawing from the French market is better than cutting our margin for the rest of Europe. Based on our preliminary reading of the data, the potential damage to Ameripill's total global earnings is as much as 10 times the French's Saincoeur earnings loss."

Meanwhile, Back at the International Subsidiaries

Managers in each subsidiary meet on a regular weekly basis to assess operations, trouble-shoot, and review operating plans. During these weekly meetings, information is exchanged among each subsidiary's management group members. In particular, communications from the parent are typically announced and discussed in these weekly meetings. The following meetings took place within 10 days of Cassells' and Stein's Wednesday meeting.

France

In France, the general manager Jacques Cartier, his director of marketing, and his controller are discussing operations and strategies in their weekly meeting. The controller mentions a rumor she heard from the Bartow Financial Analyst who had just been in France for his quarterly visit. The controller comments, "I heard a rumor that the Bartow pricing group is recommending withdrawing Saincoeur from our market. Italy and the Swiss are pressuring Ameripill to match the French price. Bartow is concerned that their margins will suffer all over Europe."

Cartier expresses immediate concern since Saincoeur is 10 percent of France's 1993 sales forecast. Cartier commented, "The French subsidiary currently has problems attaining the corporate goal of 18 percent earnings before tax (EBT). Loss of Saincoeur will make meeting that goal more difficult and reduce our return on assets (ROA) since we lose sales volume without any impact on our investment base. Sales and cost of sales will decrease proportionally, but direct expenses will decrease by only 10 million francs. Other financial accounts will be unaffected. As a result, French bonuses from the IFPS scheme will be reduced." The director of marketing comments, "Americans! I bet that the real financial impact is not that big. What do they care as long as the company overall is making a little more money?"

The controller replies, "I've heard that they are looking at the impact on global earnings. I wish I knew how that was calculated. I have no idea how that is going to impact our bonuses."

United Kingdom

It's Monday in the United Kingdom subsidiary headquarters in Maidenhead near London, and the weekly meeting between the general manager, John Phillips, and the controller, Lee Grant, is about to start. Phillips brings in a fax received late Friday from corporate about expanding manufacturing in Great Britain. The memo requested input from the U.K. general manager about the possibility of producing Smoothkare and then shipping Smoothkare at a little above cost to Germany. Smoothkare is a prescription drug used to treat skin problems in elderly persons and has been produced solely at The Hague plant for worldwide distribution. He points out that corporate is thinking about expanding the U.K. subsidiary's manufacturing capacity.

Phillips wants to persuade corporate to adopt the desired U.K. strategy, whether it is to expand and produce Smoothkare or not. He wonders whether the person who wrote the memo has read any of his reports and memos about IFPS. Grant points out that the U.K. subsidiary already produces several products transferred at close to cost and that those products provide no positive weight in the evaluation process. Phillips wonders if expanding the manufacturing operation would improve the IFPS bonus numbers.

Phillips says, "I don't know; corporate hasn't said too much about timing, but they could implement the expansion fairly quickly. For example, Ameripill could buy that old Worsley manufacturing facility next door and have it operational in less than a year." He adds, still thinking about his communications with Bartow, "You know, I've never seen a report on what our combined sales and manufacturing efforts contribute to Ameripill's profits. There is a basic conflict between its emphasis on sales and our need to sell and manage this factory too." Grant adds, "I've had a number of conversations with Cassells about the incentive scheme. I am not sure that they realize the significance of the problems created by the incentive scheme. For example, the pressure to keep our inventories down and improve our ROA causes us to schedule many short manufacturing runs. As a result, we'll never get our unit costs close to the Hague numbers."

Phillips, now more agitated, states, "I do know, expanding manufacturing to include Smoothkare will not help our earnings, will create more manufacturing problems, and will increase our operating costs—all bad news for us, particularly for our IFPS results. Our asset base will increase, inventories will grow, and we'll need more people to handle the manufacturing. I heard that Germany paid The Hague about 8,500,000 pounds for Smoothkare this year. They use cost plus 20 percent for a transfer price, I think. We would have to use the same transfer price that The Hague used because Bartow guaranteed that price to the German subsidiary for a five-year period. Our manufacturing costs would be at least 15 percent higher than The Hague's if past comparisons hold."

Germany

Hans Drossel, controller of the German subsidiary, schedules lunch with Dr. Joachim Boch, the general manager. Both have been active in building a sales force in the former East German portion of the new Germany. This effort has fortunately begun to at least cover the out-of-pocket costs of building this new staff. Now near the end of 1992, the tentative financial results show strong potential. Boch says, "I didn't think our eastern sector strategy would pay off as fast as it has. It was risky, with only Roget's informal okay, but I think it's working." Drossel looks at the numbers and adds, "You know, it's the only way to get the growth we need to meet the financial goals we have in our 1993 budget. Right now the eastern German sales forecast is 2,000,000 marks, and the potential could be two or three times that if we had a strong generic drug product line. We just don't have the product lines to get a bigger market share. I think we'll have some explaining to do in our annual financial review when Cassells' people arrive from Bartow."

After looking at the product line sales days, Drossel comments, "Our ability to price Smoothkare just under our main competitor really helped sales and our responsibility earnings. I hope we can get another cost reduction from The Hague plant in 1993." Boch nods his head affirmatively.

Boch then asks Drossel about rumors that Bartow had made a formal decision to enter the former East Bloc markets. 'You know, I think our proposal about the eastern markets must have gotten lost in the mail. Roget says it's being studied by the financial guys—but, come on, isn't an eight months' study a little ridiculous? Not only that, but in the meantime, several really profitable small pharmaceutical firms have been gobbled up by the big Swiss drug companies. Where are *our* people?" Drossel responds, "We seem to be preoccupied with bottom-line results while the Swiss seem to be looking for market share first and let the profits develop later."

Required:

(1) Estimate the impact on in-country IFPS goals of:
    (a) United Kingdom: Expanding current manufacturing capacity by acquiring the Worsley plant.
    (b) Germany: Acquiring of Koblenz Chemie Co.
    (c) France: Withdrawing Saincoeur from the French market.

(2) Discuss potential strategic reactions of the general managers in the United Kingdom, Germany, and France to questions (1a), (b), and (c), respectively.

(3) Discuss the strengths and weaknesses of Ameripill's IFPS plan.

(4) Make specific recommendations for changing the IFPS plan. Support your recommendations by citing specific case examples.

References

Bescos, Pierre-Laurent, and Carla Mendoza. "ABC in France." *Management Accounting*, April 1995, pp. 33–41.

Brausch, John M. "Beyond ABC: Target Costing for Profit Enhancement." *Management Accounting*, November 1994, pp. 45–49.

Carlson, Neil F. "Global Risk Management." *Strategic Finance*, August 1999, pp. 34–37.

Cooper, Robert, and Robert W. Kaplan. *The Design of Cost Management Systems: Text, Cases, and Readings.* Englewood Cliffs, N.J.: Prentice Hall, 1991.

Cooper, Robin, and Regine Slagmulder. "Supply Chain Management for Lean Enterprises: Interorganizational Cost Management." *Strategic Finance*, April 1999, pp. 15–16.

Crane, D., K. Froot, S. Mason, A. Perold, R. Merton, Z. Bodie, E. Sirri, and P. Tufano. *The Global Financial System: A Functional Perspective.* Boston, MA.: Harvard Business School Press, 1995.

Damitio, James W., Gary W. Hayes, and Philip L. Kintzele. "Integrating ABC and ABM At Dow Chemical." *Management Accounting Quarterly*, Winter 2000, pp. 22–26.

Deloitte Research. *Making Customer Loyalty Real: Lesson from Leading Manufacturers.* New York: Deloitte Research, 1999.

Drucker, Peter F. "The Emerging Theory of Manufacturing." *Harvard Business Review*, May–June 1990, pp. 94–102.

Eiteman, David K., Arthur I. Stonehill, and Michael H. Moffett. *Multinational Business Finance*, 8th ed. Reading, MA: Addison-Wesley Publishing Company, Inc., 1998.

Financial Accounting Standards Board. *Statement of Financial Accounting Standards No. 133,* "Accounting for Derivative Instruments and for Hedging Activities." Norwalk, CT: Financial Accounting Standards Board, 1998.

_____. *Statement of Financial Accounting Standards No. 138,* "Accounting for Certain Derivative Instruments and Certain Hedging Activities." Norwalk, CT: Financial Accounting Standards Board, 2000.

Gange, Margaret L., and Richard Discenza. "New Product Costing Japanese Style." *CPA Journal*, May 1992, pp. 68–71.

Gersten, Alan. "Eastern Exposure: Companies Speak Candidly About What It's Like to Manage Risk in Asia." *Journal of Accountancy*, August 1999, pp. 53–58.

Harry, Mikel, and Richard Schroeder. *Six Sigma*. New York: Doubleday/ Currency, 2000.

Hobdy, Terrence, Jeff Thomson, and Paul Sharman. "Activity-Based Management at AT&T." *Management Accounting*, April 1994, pp. 35–39.

Horngren, Charles T., George Foster, and Srikant M. Datar. *Cost Accounting: A Managerial Emphasis*, 10th ed. Upper Saddle River, N.J.: Prentice Hall, 2000.

Igual De Montijo, Claire M. "Converting to a Central Financial Database." *Management Accounting*, September 1995, pp. 64–67.

Ihlwan, Moon, Pete Engardio, Irene Kunii, and Roger Crockette. "Samsung: The Making of a Superstar." *Business Week*, 20 December 1999, pp. 137–140.

International Accounting Standards Committee. "Financial Instruments: Recognition and Measurement." *International Accounting Standard 39*. London: International Accounting Standards Committee, 1999.

International Federation of Accountants. *Preparing Organizations to Manage the Future*. New York: International Federation of Accountants, 1997.

Kaiser, Thomas G. "Strategic Risk Financing." *Strategic Finance*, July 2000, pp. 34–38.

Kaplan, Robert S., ed. *Measures for Manufacturing Excellence*. Boston, MA: Harvard Business School Press, 1990.

Lebas, Michel. "Managerial Accounting in France." *The European Accounting Review*, vol. 3, no. 3 (1994), pp. 471–487.

Mandel, Michael J. "The New Economy." *Business Week*, 31 January 2000, pp. 73–77.

McCarthy, Ed. "Derivatives Revisited." *Journal of Accountancy*, May 2000, pp. 35–43.

Nair, Mohan. "Activity-Based Costing: Who's Using It and Why?" *Management Accounting Quarterly*, Spring 2000, pp. 29–33.

Organization for Economic Cooperation and Development. *A New Economy? The Changing Role of Innovation and Information Technology in Growth*. Paris: Organization for Economic Cooperation and Development, 2000.

PricewaterhouseCoopers. *Global Top Decision Makers Study on Business Process Outsourcing: Europe*. New York: PricewaterhouseCoopers, 1999.

_____. *A Guide to Accounting for Derivative Instruments and Hedging Activities: Understanding & Implementing Statement of Financial Standards No. 133*. New York: PricewaterhouseCoopers, 1998.

_____. *The New Standard on Accounting for Derivative Instruments and Hedging Activities (FAS 133): An Executive Summary*. New York: PricewaterhouseCoopers, 1998.

Rupp, Alan. "ABC: A Pilot Approach." *Management Accounting*, January 1995, pp. 50–55.

Sack, Robert J., James R. Boarsman, Robert S. Fell, Jack L. Krogstad, Spencer J. Martin, and Marcia S. Niles. "Mountaintop Issues: From the Perspective of the SEC." *Accounting Horizons*, March 1995, pp. 30–32.

Serwer, Andrew E. "Michael Dell Turns the PC World Inside Out." *Fortune*, 8 September 1997, pp. 38–44.

Shapiro, Alan C. *Multinational Financial Management*, 5th ed. Upper Saddle River, N.J.: Prentice Hall, 1996.

Sparks, Debra. "Partners." *Business Week*, 25 October 1999, pp. 106–112.

"The Power of Smart Pricing." *Business Week*, 10 April 2000, pp. 160–161.

Turney, Peter B.B. *Common Cents: The ABC Performance Breakthrough*. Portland, OR: Cost Technology, 1992.

Winograd, Barry N., and Robert H. Herz. "Derivatives: What's an Auditor to Do?" *Journal of Accountancy*, June 1995, pp. 75–80.

chapter

10

Transfer Pricing and International Taxation

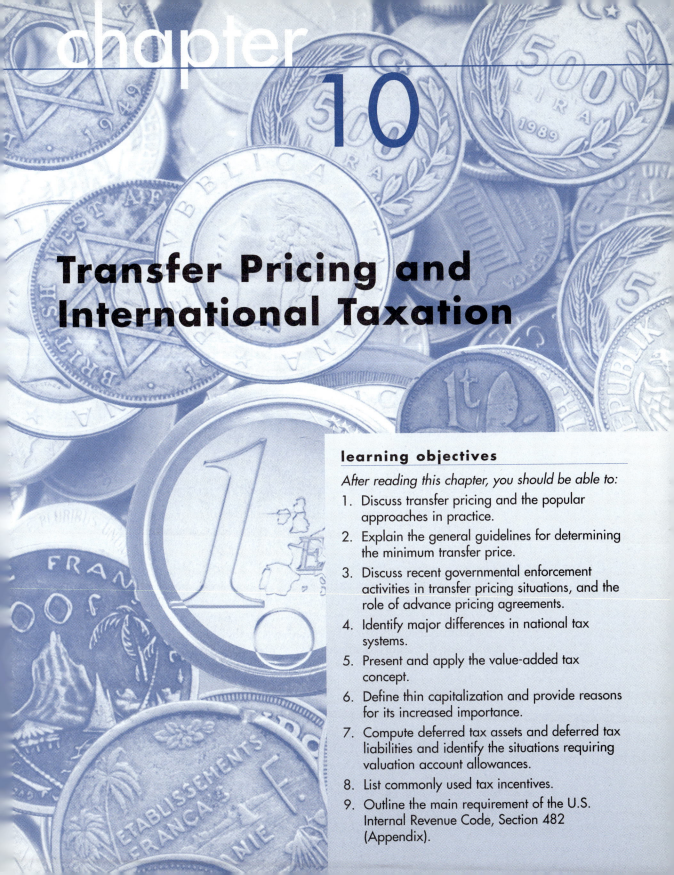

learning objectives

After reading this chapter, you should be able to:

1. Discuss transfer pricing and the popular approaches in practice.

2. Explain the general guidelines for determining the minimum transfer price.

3. Discuss recent governmental enforcement activities in transfer pricing situations, and the role of advance pricing agreements.

4. Identify major differences in national tax systems.

5. Present and apply the value-added tax concept.

6. Define thin capitalization and provide reasons for its increased importance.

7. Compute deferred tax assets and deferred tax liabilities and identify the situations requiring valuation account allowances.

8. List commonly used tax incentives.

9. Outline the main requirement of the U.S. Internal Revenue Code, Section 482 (Appendix).

Transfer Pricing

A **transfer price** is what one segment of a company charges another segment of the *same company* for the transfer of a good or a service. The segments may be subsidiaries, departments, branches, or any other part of the overall multinational organization. Conceptually, transfer pricing within a company results from the corporate decentralization strategy. The objective is evaluating the performance of each autonomous (decentralized) segment. The transfer of goods and services is common among subsidiaries of multinational corporations. Setting transfer prices among international subsidiaries or between the parent company and its international subsidiaries raises issues that are not present in the situations involving domestic intracompany transfers.

Transfer pricing and international taxation are interrelated: Both affect a multinational corporation's management decisions regarding the size, type, location, and the degree of autonomy of operations in different countries. Transfer pricing decisions are influenced both by the taxation systems and tax rates of the countries of international operations. Since goods and services transferred across national boundaries could be priced with the objective to minimize overall tax payments by shifting income to low income tax rate nations, tax authorities and legislatures in most countries are increasingly paying closer attention to multinational companies' transfer pricing practices. The U.S., for example, specifies the acceptable transfer pricing methods. The U.S. Internal Revenue Code empowers tax authorities to intervene if unacceptable transfer pricing methods are being used by a multinational corporation.

Objectives of International Transfer Pricing

The transfer pricing system adopted by a multinational corporation should ideally strike a balance between what potentially could be conflicting sets of objectives. A good system addresses the following (sometimes conflicting) objectives:

- *The achievement of strategic goals.* This means that the overall organization's interest should guide the subsidiary decisions, including transfer pricing decisions. In reality, foreign subsidiary management actions may not always be in harmony with the multinational's goals. It is especially true when any actions different from the ones taken by the subsidiary management may jeopardize the reported subsidiary performance. A transfer price resulting in higher *overall* taxes may be a direct consequence of a local manager's self-interest-based decision to report the highest possible profit for the subsidiary.

- *Freedom for local management to make decisions affecting their performance.* Decision-making freedom is enhanced where foreign subsidiaries are separate legal *and* economic units within the same multinational corporate family. Often this conflicts with what is in the best interest of the multinational enterprise. No interference, to support and maintain the independence of subsidiaries, could result in setting transfer prices at levels not in harmony with corporate goals. Subsidiary A may refuse to sell a product to Subsidiary

B at a price lower than the market price even though the lower price would make a contribution to overall corporate profit.

The transfer pricing objectives and the influence of local conditions outlined in Exhibit 10.2 demonstrate the complexity of determining the "right" transfer price.

Conflicting conditions may exist, thereby making it difficult to set a transfer price advantageous both to the subsidiary and to the company as a whole.

- A foreign country may have lower corporate tax rates and lower tariffs *and* duties on imports. The first condition supports lower transfer prices, while the latter supports higher transfer prices. If the foreign subsidiary is a joint venture with the foreign government and the local market is competitive, a transfer price higher than market price may alienate the foreign government. Alternately, the foreign government may prefer local sourcing of labor and materials.

- A foreign country with a balance of payments deficit tends to limit imports and restrict the outflow of hard currencies. These conditions may further complicate a multinational's investment strategy. A short-term investment strategy generally favors high transfer prices for goods and services sold to a foreign subsidiary and a quick repatriation of funds to the parent company.

- A foreign country may have a relatively high inflation rate *and* a stable political system and favorable business conditions. Again, the first condition supports higher transfer prices, while the latter support lower prices for the goods and services transferred to the subsidiary.

Results of a recent survey on managements' priorities in transfer pricing are shown in Exhibit 10.1.

exhibit 10.1 **Priorities In Transfer Pricing**

	Main Priority	Important but Not Main Priority	Not Very Important	Not Important at All
Maximizing Operating Performance	35	38	20	7
Documentation in Preparation for Audit	40	33	19	8
Optimizing Tax Arrangements	23	45	25	7
Financial Efficiencies	25	45	22	8
Performance Incentives	12	27	39	22

Source: Ernst & Young, *2000 Global Survey on Transfer Pricing*, 2000.

Over a period of time, conditions in a given country change in response to shifts in environmental factors. For example, the policies that discouraged foreign investments in the republics of the former Soviet Union have been mostly revoked. They are being replaced with policies favorable toward foreign investment.

Transfer Pricing Issues for Multinationals

Multinational corporations encounter all of the issues facing domestic companies in the design of a transfer pricing system. Since international subsidiaries are separate legal *and* economic entities, additional factors require consideration.

- *Government regulations and restrictions differ widely among countries.* Regulations governing the conduct of specific lines of business are common in many countries. Restrictions may be placed on commodities exported or imported. For example, a thorny trade issue between Japan and the U.S. for many decades has been the exclusion of other countries from the Japanese rice market. Other regulations may also cover the workforce, employee benefits, employment of foreign nationals, and ownership of land.

- *Tax rates applied to corporate income as well as allowable deductions differ significantly from one country to another.* Rates could be as low as 5 percent in one country and as high as 40 percent in another. For example, at present, rates are 40 percent and 18 percent in Slovakia and Hungary, respectively. In addition, there are likely to be taxes imposed by a country's various government levels, e.g., provinces, states, or cities.

- *Tariffs and duties are imposed on imports (and sometimes on exports) in most countries.* This directly affects sourcing and plant location decisions. Such trade barriers drive up the price of many imported products for consumers.

- *Many countries, especially developing nations, restrict outflows of hard currencies.* Some countries have multiple exchange rates that are unfavorable for transferring hard currencies out of the country. Such foreign exchange controls restrict currency movements and limit the availability of capital for business activities.

- *Different inflation rates among nations affect transfer price determination.* Fear of local currency devaluation because of higher inflation rates triggers a rush to convert local currency into the parent company's currency, or some other stable currency.

The previous factors may lead to overpricing or underpricing goods and services transferred across national boundaries. Exhibit 10.2 shows the local conditions under which the parent company (or one of its domestic subsidiaries) may be inclined to charge either higher or lower transfer prices to a foreign subsidiary. The conditions in the parent company's country would be reversed if goods were transferred to the parent company from a foreign subsidiary.

exhibit 10.2 Local Conditions for Overpricing or Underpricing Transfers from a Parent to a Foreign Subsidiary

Overpricing Conditions	Underpricing Conditions
Higher corporate tax rate	Lower corporate tax rate
Lower tariffs on imports	Higher tariffs on imports
High inflation rate	Low inflation rate
High political and economic risk	Low political and economic risk
Need to transfer capital out of foreign country	Need to keep capital locally for future investment
Short-term investment strategy in the foreign country	Long-term investment strategy in the foreign country
Local market share secure and satisfactory	Competitive position in local markets needs improvement

Transfer Pricing Approaches of Multinationals

Assume that Division A and Division B are segments of the same multinational corporation. When Division A sells a product or service to Division B, it would like to receive the highest possible price from Division B. Division B, on the other hand, would like to pay the lowest price. Managers of both divisions are very interested in the transfer price since the reported operating performance of each division is directly affected by transfer pricing. Multinational corporations use a variety of transfer pricing approaches. The common approaches include market-based, cost-based, and negotiated.

Market-based transfer pricing assumes the existence of an outside market price for the product (or service) that is being transferred from one segment to another segment of the corporation. The actual market price is often adjusted downward to reflect cost savings from selling internally. There are two practical problems encountered in using market-based transfer prices: Either the market may not be competitive or the product (or service) being transferred internally may not be identical to those sold in the competitive market.

Cost-based transfer pricing uses some type of cost as the base in setting a transfer price. The lowest cost-based transfer price equals incremental costs to the selling segment. Incremental costs of the selling segment are the costs that have to be incurred solely to produce goods (or services) for the buying segment. Other common cost-based transfer prices include variable costs plus markup, full absorption costs, and full absorption costs plus markup. Full absorption costs include both variable and fixed indirect production costs. It is desirable to use standard costs rather than actual costs of the selling segment in cost-based transfer prices. Using standard costs avoids passing inefficiencies of the selling segment to the buying segment, thus motivating the selling segment to control its costs.

Negotiated transfer pricing requires the managers of selling and buying segments to negotiate a mutually acceptable transfer price. It becomes necessary when there is no outside market for the product being transferred internally. Obviously, when no outside market exists, no market price would be available. Another situation requiring the negotiation of a transfer price involves the availability of idle capacity in the selling division. When the selling division has some unused capacity after meeting outside demand, it would benefit from transferring the product to another sister segment at any price above its incremental cost. How much above the incremental cost? This is where negotiation comes into the picture.

A General Guideline

There is no *one* method that can be applied to determine transfer pricing for optimal decisions. The reasons being that market conditions, the goal of transfer pricing, goal congruence, segment performance evaluation, and segment autonomy in a decentralized multinational organization must all be considered *simultaneously*. The correct transfer price depends on the purpose on hand.[1] The following general guideline is a helpful first step for most situations in setting a *minimum* transfer price:[2]

$$\text{Minimum transfer price} = \frac{\text{Incremental costs}}{\text{per unit}} + \frac{\text{Opportunity costs per unit to the}}{\text{selling segment}}$$

Incremental costs were discussed earlier. **Opportunity costs per unit** are the contribution margin per unit sacrificed by the selling segment due to the internal transfer of one unit of the good or service, rather than selling it in the external market.

If the selling segment is operating at full capacity, then:

$$\text{Opportunity costs per unit} = \text{Market price} - \text{Variable costs per unit}$$

Incremental costs are recorded in the accounting system, while opportunity costs are not recorded in the accounting system.

Idle capacity is the unused capacity of a selling segment that is not needed for producing products or services to meet demand from the external market. In case of idle capacity, the selling segment has no opportunity costs for internal transfers. The total demand from the external market has already been satisfied. Therefore, any unit of a product or service transferred internally would not result in the selling segment having to forego any contribution margin. The guideline still is valid and is equally applicable in situations involving idle capacity:

---

1 Charles T. Horngren, George Foster, and Srikant Datar. *Cost Accounting—A Managerial Emphasis.* 10th ed. Upper Saddle River, N.J.: Prentice Hall, 2000, pp. 801–803.

2 *Ibid.*, p. 803.

$$\text{Minimum transfer price} = \text{Incremental costs per unit} + \begin{array}{l}\text{Opportunity costs per unit}\\\text{to the selling segment}\end{array}$$

$$= \text{Incremental costs per unit} + 0$$

$$= \text{Incremental costs per unit}$$

In the case of idle capacity in a selling segment, any transfer price above the incremental costs per unit and below the outside selling price would be mutually beneficial to both the selling segment and the buying segment. This is the range within which they can negotiate a transfer price that is mutually acceptable, as Figure 10.1 shows.

Example

Caracas segment would like to buy 10,000 units of product C-21 from Gomez segment. The following data are available in Venezuelan bolivar (Bs):

Incremental costs per unit	Bs10,000
Selling price	Bs25,000

Gomez does not have any idle capacity.

$$\text{Minimum transfer price} = \text{Bs10,000} + (\text{Bs25,000} - \text{Bs10,000})$$

$$= \text{Bs10,000} + \text{Bs15,000}$$

$$= \text{Bs25,000}$$

Example

Use the same information as in the previous example, but now assume Gomez has idle capacity.

$$\text{Minimum transfer price} = \text{Bs10,000} + 0$$

$$= \text{Bs10,000}$$

Any transfer price above Bs10,000 and below Bs25,000 would benefit both Caracas and Gomez.

Recent Requirements and Enforcement Activities

International transfer pricing has become a subject of concern to many governments throughout the world. Many countries have introduced new transfer

figure 10.1   **Idle Capacity and Negotiation Range**

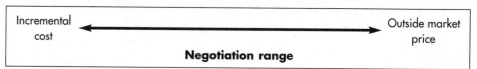

pricing rules and are vigorously imposing penalty regimes for transfer pricing arrangements as shown in Exhibit 10.3.

exhibit 10.3 Transfer Price—Recent Rules and Enforcement Actions

Country	
Denmark	The parliament passed transfer pricing laws, effective in 1999, providing authority to the tax authorities for making transfer pricing adjustments. The legislation also requires the parties under common control to apply prices and terms that would have been used between independent parties.[i]
U.K.	The law, applicable for periods ending on or after July 1, 1999, imposes documentation requirements and provides for imposition of penalties for the first time with respect to transfer pricing legislation. The law requires that transfer pricing should reflect the arm's length standard.[ii]
Australia	In 1999, the commissioner of taxation announced that the Australian Taxation Office (ATO) will start audits of 46 multinational companies with significant international related-party transactions. In addition, 60 enterprises would be subject to alternative compliance action. The commissioner especially expressed concern on the poor level of documentation found in reviews of the records of 190 companies to support that their transfer prices were in accordance with the arm's length standard. The announcement further stated that the ATO: • would continue to monitor taxpayers not selected for audit yet; • would launch another round of records reviews during the fiscal year; • would express written concerns to 160 additional companies about their transfer pricing practices.[iii]
Belgium	In June 1999, the Ministry of Finance issued the first transfer pricing guidelines in Belgium. The guidelines indicate that transfer pricing audits will normally be carried out where there are substantial differences between an enterprise's financial ratios and the industry standard ratios.[iv]
Hong Kong	Transfer pricing was formerly not a concern of the Hong Kong Inland Revenue Department (IRD). Since 1999, the IRD has been increasing its tax audits and is targeting companies involved in transactions with entities incorporated in tax-haven jurisdictions. The IRD will ask the companies to provide the substance of the overseas activities and look into the issue of profit allocation among companies within a group.[v]
South Africa	In 1999, the South African Revenue Service issued a due practice note. The practice note states that companies choosing to ignore proper transfer pricing arrangements could expose themselves to the risk of significant tax adjustments. When a multinational company applies different transfer pricing methods from country to country, or the application of methods differs significantly, a multinational company may be at risk for double taxation. The practice note emphasizes that documentation proving that transfer prices are consistent with the arm's length principle is of utmost importance. Due to the subjective nature of transfer pricing adjustments, the imposed penalties could prove to be extremely harsh.[vi]
Germany	Transfer pricing has become a major tax issue for multinational enterprises with operations in Germany. The tax authorities focus on transfer prices in almost every tax audit based on the assumption that multinational companies based in tax-credit system countries artificially shift profits

i   Deloitte Touche Tohmatsu, *World Tax News*, September 1998, p. 1.
ii *Ibid.*, January 1999, pp. 19–21.
iii *Ibid.*, September 1999, pp. 4–5.
iv *Ibid.*, pp. 5–6.
v   *Ibid.*, pp. 9–10.
vi *Ibid.*, pp. 21–22.

exhibit 10.3 *(continued)*

Country	
	abroad. The tax-credit system countries include the United States, Japan, and the United Kingdom.[vii]
	In 2000, the Federal Ministry of Finance published new guidelines replacing some of the rules on transfer pricing methods. The new principles tighten the documentation requirements for transfer pricing and include a detailed description of the methods to be used for determining transfer prices.[viii]
New Zealand	In early 2000, the Inland Revenue Department released transfer pricing draft guidelines dealing with transfer prices of services, intangible assets, and cost contribution arrangements.[ix]
Argentina	In October 1999, the Argentine Federal Revenue Board published rules on transfer pricing. The rules require that entities transacting business with related parties file an affidavit with the Federal Revenue Board declaring that the transfer prices are consistent with ordinary market practices between third parties. The transfer prices rules are applicable to not only the entities under common control but also when other specified relationships exist. For example, the rules stipulate that transactions with entities in low-tax jurisdiction are assumed to be between related parties unless proven otherwise. The transfer pricing rules also set out the criteria to determine whether the transfer prices between related parties are on an arm's length basis.[x]
	A new tax reform law became effective as of January 1, 2000. The law substantially amends the transfer pricing provision. Transactions between Argentine entities and the entities in low-tax jurisdictions are deemed to be related parties. The law requires filing of an affidavit twice a year containing detailed information on operations with such related parties.[xi]

vii *Ibid.,* March 2000, pp. 1–2.
viii *Ibid.,* May 2000, pp. 12–13.
ix   *Ibid.,* pp. 7–8.
x   *Ibid.,* January 2000, p. 13.
xi   *Ibid.,* May 2000, p. 10.

Transfer pricing policies affect the amount collected by governments from tariffs, duties, and corporate income taxes. The global economy inherently means increased and freer flow of goods and services across borders. The globalization of economy has made transfer pricing a major area for close governmental scrutiny in most countries. In 1999, Canada doubled its audit staff responsible for conducting transfer pricing audits.[3] Starting in the early 1990s, many countries have been vigorously enforcing their tax laws, regulations, and penalties relating to transfer prices, which is not surprising since transfer prices have a direct impact on the amount of governmental revenues in the global economy. Examples of the countries aggressively auditing transfer pricing policies and practices of multinational companies and enforcing related tax penalties include Australia, Brazil, Canada, China, France, Italy, Japan, Korea, the Netherlands, the U.K., and the U.S. In the U.S., for example, Section 482 of the Internal Revenue Code gives the government the right to prevent shifting of revenues or deductions

---

3 Steven Wrappe, Ken Milani, and Julie Joy. "The Transfer Price Is Right . . . Or Is It?" *Strategic Finance,* July 1999, p. 40.

among related taxpayers to exploit differences in tax rates between countries. Preference is given to market price—price based on *arm's length transactions* between unrelated entities. This requires the existence of a market for the same or similar products. Two other transfer pricing methods are allowed under the provisions of Section 482. The *resale price method* is based on the buyer's final resale price less the buyer's additional expenses and normal profit margin. The third method is the *cost-plus method*, regarded as the least desirable method. This method is based on the determination of the cost of production and distribution plus a normal profit margin for the seller. The text of Section 482 and its relevance to multinational transfer pricing are presented in more detail in Appendix 10A.

Advance Pricing Agreements

Advance pricing agreements are becoming increasingly popular both with companies and tax authorities. An **advance pricing agreement** between a company and tax authorities gives the company approval for using certain transfer pricing methods and the procedures for its application. Recent reports show that bilateral advance pricing agreements are gaining popularity. In a **bilateral advance pricing agreement** the multinational company receives the approval of proposed transfer pricing approaches from tax authorities of two countries. This requires the multinational company to submit applications to both countries' tax authorities approximately at the same time. Subsequently, the two countries' tax authorities coordinate and communicate with each other until the process is completed. Exhibit 10.4 presents some examples of recent developments in this area.

Advance pricing agreements are an effective way to avoid any potential transfer pricing adjustments and penalties in the future. They are a proactive, preventive measure found worthwhile by many multinational companies.

Recommended Transfer Pricing Strategy

Whenever possible, multinational corporations should use a market-based transfer price, i.e., the price used by uncontrolled entities or a derivative of a market price such as the resale price explained earlier in this chapter. A market-based pricing strategy is conceptually sound and also has the following practical advantages:

- *Legality.* Complies with pricing requirements imposed by governments throughout the world. This clears doubts about the multinational corporation's intention to assume fairly the tax and tariff burdens imposed by local governments.
- *Goal congruence.* Fully addresses the goal congruence issue. Market prices take into account the opportunity costs of selling internally instead of selling to outside parties.
- *Equitable treatment.* Ensures the equitable evaluation of performance of all subsidiaries involved. Both buyer and seller can readily accept the market forces behind market prices.

exhibit 10.4 Transfer Pricing—Advance Pricing Agreements

Country/Countries	
U.K.	Advance pricing agreements was incorporated in tax law in 1999. The procedure is available only for the situations when either reliable market prices are not available, or the presence of complex transfer pricing issues makes it difficult to determine the accurate application of transfer pricing methods.[i] In October 1999, the Inland Revenue published the procedures to be followed by companies when applying for bilateral advance pricing agreements. The procedures include the requirement that applications should be submitted to tax administrations of the two countries at approximately the same time. Moreover, the same information has to be provided to each tax administration.[ii]
Germany and the U.S.	The United States and Germany concluded their first bilateral advance pricing agreement for an undisclosed large U.S.-based multinational company in December 1998.[iii]
Japan and the U.S.	A bilateral agreement for Coca-Cola was reached in April 2000.
France	In September 1999, the tax administration introduced a procedure for advance price agreements for situations involving transfer pricing arrangements. The guidelines require that the application to the French authorities must set out the proposed transfer pricing method and include information supporting how it satisfies the arm's length principle.[iv]
Indonesia	The Ministry of Finance has announced proposals to introduce advance pricing agreements.[v]

i Deloitte Touche Tohmatsu, *World Tax News*, January 1999, pp. 3–5.
ii *Ibid.*, January 2000, p. 23.
iii *Ibid.*, January 1999, pp. 24–25.
iv *Ibid.*, January 2000, p. 15.
v *Ibid.*, July 2000, p. 13.

- *Simplicity.* A market price based on an arm's length transaction is simple to use and easy to understand.

Illustration: International Transfer Pricing, Taxes, and Tariffs

Let us illustrate how alternative transfer prices are computed and show the impact of different corporate tax rates and import tariffs resulting from changes in the transfer price. Best Shirt, Inc., a U.S. multinational corporation, owns two subsidiaries, one each in Malaysia and the U.S. The Malaysian subsidiary manufactures 100,000 shirts for sale to the U.S. subsidiary. The U.S. subsidiary resells the shirts for $14 each in the U.S. market. The Malaysian subsidiary's cost per shirt is as follows:

Production cost	$3.25
Variable cost (production and marketing)	3.50
Full production and marketing cost	4.05

Market-Based Transfer Pricing

The market price per shirt would be equal to the sales price in the local Malaysian market or the sales price to unrelated companies in the U.S. or in any other country. This sales price would be adjusted for any additional expenses necessary to sell to an unaffiliated party. Let us assume that a Canadian company offers to buy the shirts for $11.50 each. Estimated marketing expenses associated with the sale to the Canadian company are $3.50 per shirt. Given these conditions, the adjusted market price is $11.50 – $3.50 = $8.00 per shirt.

Cost-Based Transfer Pricing

Cost-based transfer prices would vary depending on the definition of "cost" used to determine the price and the amount of markup. We will look at three examples of cost-based prices.

- A price based on production cost plus 200 percent markup would be $3.25 + ($3.25 × 200%) = $9.75.
- A price based on variable production and marketing costs plus 150 percent markup would be $3.50 + ($3.50 × 150%) = $8.75.
- A price based on full production and marketing costs plus 100 percent markup would be $4.05 + ($4.05 × 100%) = $8.10.

Effect of Different Transfer Prices on Net Income of the Segments

The next two exhibits illustrate the effects of different prices on tariffs, income taxes, and net income for Best Shirt, Inc., the Malaysian subsidiary, and the U.S. subsidiary. For simplicity, the illustrations include only the amounts related to the manufacture and sale of 100,000 shirts under the cost structure shown previously.

Exhibit 10.5 shows summarized income statement data assuming a transfer price of $5 per shirt. The major income tax burden is in the U.S. where the corporate tax rate is 35 percent compared with 20 percent in Malaysia.

Exhibit 10.6 shows the data for the assumed transfer price of $8. This shifts taxable income to Malaysia, where the lower income tax rate more than offsets the increased U.S. tariffs. The net effect is a reduction in combined tariffs and taxes of $15,750 (from $234,000 to $218,250) with a corresponding $15,750 increase in net income.

Motivation

The Malaysian government would insist that the transfer price not be unrealistically low, since this would reduce its tax revenues. The U.S. government, to protect its revenues, will object to an overly high transfer price. The selling company will tend to prefer a high transfer price and the buying company will want the lowest possible transfer price.

What about the parent company? If we ignore constraints imposed by possible reactions of tax authorities and subsidiary management, then in this situation the parent would try to shift income to Malaysia to the point where no more tax

exhibit 10.5 Effect of Transfer Price of $5 per Shirt

Income Statement Data Best Shirt, Inc. and Subsidiaries	Malaysian Subsidiary	U.S. Subsidiary	Best Shirt, Inc.
Sales revenue	$500,000	$1,400,000	$1,400,000
Cost of goods sold	$325,000	$ 500,000	$ 325,000
Import tariffs (15%)	—	75,000	75,000
Cost of goods sold and import tariffs	$325,000	$ 575,000	$ 400,000
Gross profit	$175,000	$ 825,000	$1,000,000
Marketing and administrative expenses	80,000	425,000	505,000
Operating income	$ 95,000	$ 400,000	$ 495,000
Corporate income taxes (20% and 35%)	19,000	140,000	159,000
Net income	$ 76,000	$ 260,000	$ 336,000
Total taxes and tariffs	$ 19,000	$ 215,000	$ 234,000

exhibit 10.6 Effect of Transfer Price of $8 per Shirt

Income Statement Data Best Shirt, Inc. and Subsidiaries	Malaysian Subsidiary	U.S. Subsidiary	Best Shirt, Inc.
Sales revenue	$800,000	$1,400,000	$1,400,000
Cost of goods sold	$325,000	$ 800,000	$ 325,000
Import tariffs (15%)	—	120,000	120,000
Cost of goods sold and import tariffs	$325,000	$ 920,000	$ 445,000
Gross profit	$475,000	$ 480,000	$ 955,000
Marketing and administrative expenses	80,000	425,000	505,000
Operating income	$395,000	$ 55,000	$ 450,000
Corporate income taxes (20% and 35%)	79,000	19,250	98,250
Net income	$316,000	$ 35,750	$ 351,750
Total taxes and tariffs	$ 79,000	$ 139,250	$ 218,250

benefits would be available. The optimum transfer price would be the one that reduces taxable income of the U.S. subsidiary to zero.

International Taxation

Tax issues relevant to transfer pricing were discussed previously. Differences in tax rates and tax systems among nations affect transfer pricing. This section presents other selected taxation issues for multinational corporations. Different international tax regulations affect international investment decisions, legal form of the international operation, location, financing, and the flow of funds across national boundaries.

Different and often complex tax systems are perhaps the second most distinguishing aspect of multinational operations, after foreign currency. Foreign currency exchange rates frequently change, and so do corporate tax rates and tax systems. In England, for example, corporate tax rates are set annually as part of the national budget. Countries change their corporate tax rates and tax systems for a variety of reasons: to generate more revenues, to provide incentives for foreign investment, to eliminate tax loopholes, or to respond to new national and international developments.

There is universal agreement that a multinational corporation's income from domestic sources should be subject to the same tax that is levied on domestic companies' income. There is less agreement on whether and how to tax income earned from foreign sources. There is also less agreement on whether corporate taxes should be direct or indirect, and whether corporations should be taxed in the first place.

National Tax Systems

Environmental differences among nations account for many of the differences in national tax systems. Even in countries that share similar environmental factors, e.g., Western democracies, tax systems differ because of different national approaches to raising government revenues.

The Territorial and Worldwide Approaches

The **territorial approach**, used in Panama for example, taxes only domestic income. Foreign source income is not taxed in the countries using a territorial approach. The **worldwide approach**, used in the U.S., subjects both domestic source and foreign source income to taxes. The worldwide approach is more popular than the territorial approach and is receiving increasingly wider acceptance.

Classic and Integrated Systems

The **classic system** subjects income to taxes whenever income is received by a taxable entity. The **integrated system** attempts to eliminate double taxation by taxing corporate income differently depending on whether it is distributed to shareholders. Income retained internally is subjected to a higher tax rate. The classic approach is used in the U.S. while the integrated approach is used in Germany.

Allowable Deductions

Taxable income is the income amount on which tax is levied. Countries differ in allowing deduction of expenses from revenues to determine taxable income. Examples include the useful life allowed for computing depreciation, on depreciable assets, expensing versus capitalizing (recording initially as assets) treatment of research and development costs, and acceptable inventory costing methods.

Direct and Indirect Taxes

In the U.S., corporate tax is a direct tax on corporate income, while in many countries the value-added tax (VAT), an indirect tax, is the major source of government revenues from business organizations. The VAT is discussed later in this chapter.

These differences clearly influence how foreign source income is taxed. Exhibit 10.7 (page 392) presents a comparison of the tax treatment of foreign source income and foreign taxes in 28 countries.

Exhibit 10.8 (pages 393–394) shows the taxation of foreign business entities in the same 28 countries.

Foreign Tax Credit and Tax Treaties

A foreign tax credit is a means to avoid double taxation of foreign source income. In the U.S. credit is given for foreign income taxes paid by foreign subsidiaries of a U.S.-based parent company. For example, when a U.S.-based multinational company's subsidiary in Germany pays withholding taxes on dividends distributed to the parent company, its parent company in the U.S. is allowed a tax credit equal to the withholding tax paid in Germany.

The U.S. foreign tax credit (FTC) is a dollar-for-dollar reduction in the taxpayer's U.S. tax liability. Tax authorities limit the amount of the FTC allowed to prevent taxpayers from receiving credit against U.S. taxes levied on U.S. source income. The tax credit for any taxable year is limited to the *lesser* of actual foreign taxes paid or accrued and the U.S. taxes (before the FTC) on foreign source taxable income. The FTC limit is computed as follows:

$$\text{FTC limit} = \text{U.S. taxes before FTC} \times \frac{\text{Foreign source income}}{\text{Foreign source income} + \text{U.S. income}}$$

Many other countries, for example Japan and India, use similar procedures. The foreign tax credit allowed is the *lesser* of actual foreign taxes paid or accrued and taxes in the country, before foreign tax credit, on foreign source taxable income.

Example

A U.S. multinational corporation reported taxable income from an Irish subsidiary of $2,000,000 and U.S. income of $4,000,000. The company paid taxes of $800,000 to the government of Ireland. Its U.S. tax liability before FTC was

exhibit 10.7   Tax Treatment of Foreign Source Income and Foreign Taxes

Country	Taxation of Foreign-Source Income	Credit for Foreign Taxes Paid and Exemptions
Argentina	Yes	Tax credit available
Australia	Yes	Tax credit available
Austria	Yes	Credit for taxes on dividends, interest, and royalties only
Belgium	Yes	If taxed in another country, only 25% of foreign source income taxed
Brazil	Yes	Tax credit available
Chile	Yes	Tax credit available
China*	Yes	Tax credit available
Costa Rica	No	Not applicable
Czech Republic	Yes	None
France	Yes	Dividends exempted
Ghana	Yes	None
Hungary	Yes	None
India	Yes	Tax credit available
Indonesia	Yes	None
Italy	Yes	Tax credit available
Japan	Yes	Tax credit available
Malaysia	No with a few specified exceptions	Not applicable
Mexico	Yes	Tax credit available
Nigeria	Yes	None
Norway	Yes	Tax credit available
Panama	No	Not applicable
Philippines	Yes	Tax credit available
Singapore	Yes	Tax credit available
South Africa	No with a few specified exceptions (Yes, starting fiscal year 2001–2002)	Not applicable
South Korea	Yes	Tax credit available
Taiwan	Yes	Tax credit available
United States	Yes	Tax credit available
Venezuela	No	Not applicable

* For foreign investment enterprises. Foreign investment enterprises are approved as Chinese companies. Foreign interests in such enterprises must be more than 25%.

Sources: Deloitte Touche Tohmatsu. *Taxation in the Asia-Pacific Region,* 1999.
_____. *Taxation in Central and Eastern Europe,* 1999.
_____. *Taxation in Central and South America,* 1999.
_____. *Taxation in North America: The North American Free Trade Agreement,* 1999.
_____. *Taxation in Sub-Saharan Africa,* 1999.
_____. *Taxation in Western Europe,* 1999.

exhibit 10.8 **Taxation of Foreign Business Entities**

Country	Taxation of Foreign Entities
Argentina	Tax at the standard corporate tax rate is levied on Argentine source income and capital gains only. Argentine source dividends and gain on sale of shares, negotiable bonds, and government bonds not subject to tax.
Australia	Australian source income and capital gains taxed at the standard corporate tax rate. Special rules apply to interest, royalties, and dividends.
Austria	Standard corporate taxes on specific type of Austrian income and capital gains only. Withholding tax on dividends and royalties.
Belgium	Nonresident's tax on Belgian source income as well as withholding tax.
Brazil	Income arising in Brazil taxed at the standard corporate tax rate.
Chile	Standard corporate tax in Chilean source income.
China	The effective tax rate applicable to foreign investment enterprises is 33%.
Czech Republic	Czech source income taxed at the standard corporate tax rates.
France	Standard corporate taxes on income earned in France and capital gains on property owned in France.
Ghana	Income accrued in or derived from Ghana normally taxable at the standard tax rate for companies.
Hungary	Standard corporate tax on Hungarian source income. Interest paid by the Hungarian government and the National Bank of Hungary not taxed.
India	Income received, derived, or deemed to be received or derived is taxed at a rate different from domestic companies. The tax rates for foreign companies are higher than those for domestic companies.
Indonesia	Income from Indonesia is subject to tax at the standard tax rates.
Italy	Standard corporate taxes on income earned in Italy. Capital gains on assets used for businesses in Italy taxable. Dividend, interest, and royalty income from Italian sources subject only to withholding tax.
Japan	Only income earned from sources within Japan is subject to tax. The tax is levied at the standard corporate tax rates.
Malaysia	Income arising from business activities in Malaysia taxed at the standard corporate tax rate.
Mexico	Income from business activities in Mexico taxed at the standard corporate tax rate.
Nigeria	Income derived from Nigeria taxed at the standard corporate rate.
Norway	Norwegian source income subject to standard corporate tax.
Panama	Tax at standard corporate tax rate on the income derived from Panamanian sources.
Philippines	A *resident foreign corporation*, engaged in business activities in the Philippines, is taxed on its Philippine source income at the same rates that apply to domestic corporations. A *nonresident foreign corporation* is not engaged in business activities in the Philippines. It is taxed on its *gross* revenue from Philippine sources. No deductions are allowed.
Singapore	Taxed at standard corporate rate on income accruing in or derived from Singapore.

(continued)

exhibit 10.8 *(continued)*

Country	Taxation of Foreign Entities
South Africa	Taxed differently than domestic companies on the income arising from a source in South Africa.
South Korea	Tax at standard corporate tax rates on income derived in Korea.
Taiwan	Tax at standard corporate tax rate on Taiwanese source income.
United States	Generally subject to tax only on income from U.S. sources and from U.S. operations.
Venezuela	Tax at standard corporate tax rate on income derived from Venezuelan sources.

Sources: Deloitte Touche Tohmatsu. *Taxation in the Asia-Pacific Region,* 1999.
_____. *Taxation in Central and Eastern Europe,* 1999.
_____. *Taxation in Central and South America,* 1999.
_____. *Taxation in North America: The North American Free Trade Agreement,* 1999.
_____. *Taxation in Sub-Saharan Africa,* 1999.
_____. *Taxation in Western Europe,* 1999.

$2,100,000. The FTC claimed by the company is limited to $700,000 as the following computes:

$$\text{FTC limit} = \$2,100,000 \times \frac{\$2,000,000}{(\$2,000,000 + \$4,000,000)} = \$700,000$$

The global economy has prompted most countries to enter into tax treaties with other countries. The main objectives of tax treaties are avoidance of double taxation of income and reduction of obstacles to international trade and investments.

Value-Added Tax

Value-added tax (VAT) is a tax based on consumer spending. The governments in many countries rely very heavily on the value-added tax to generate revenue. There is a common misconception that VAT is mostly found in European countries. In reality, VAT is common in all regions of the world, as illustrated in Exhibit 10.9. The **VAT concept** is based on taxing each production activity or business activity that adds value to materials or goods purchased from other businesses. It is different from the sales tax, as the sales tax is levied only at the point of retail sale rather than at each of the production or marketing activities.

Example
A manufacturer sells a product to a wholesaler. The wholesaler distributes the product to retailers, who sell it to final customers. The value-added tax is levied on the difference between the sale price and purchase price at each transfer point.

exhibit 10.9 **Examples of Value-Added Tax In Different Regions**

Region	Country	Standard VAT Rate*
Asia-Pacific:	Australia	10.0
	China	17.0
	Indonesia	10.0
	Philippines	10.0
	New Zealand (GST)	12.5
	Singapore	3.0
	South Korea	10.0
	Taiwan (Business tax)	5.0
	Thailand: Until March 31, 2001	7.0
	From April 1, 2001	10.0
	Vietnam	10.0
Central and South America:	Argentina	21.0
	Chile	18.0
	Colombia	15.0
	Costa Rica	13.0
	Ecuador	10.0
	Guatemala	10.0
	Panama	5.0
	Peru	18.0
	Venezuela	15.5
Central and Eastern Europe:	Bulgaria	20.0
	Czech Republic	22.0
	Hungary	25.0
	Lithuania	18.0
	Poland	22.0
	Romania	22.0
	Russia	20.0
	Slovakia	23.0
	Yugoslavia (starting January 1, 2001)	20.0
North America:	Canada (GST)	7.0
	Mexico	15.0
Sub-Saharan Africa:	Cameroon	18.7
	Ghana	10.0
	Ivory Coast	20.0
	Kenya	16.0
	Nigeria	5.0
	South Africa	14.0
	Zambia	17.5

(continued)

exhibit 10.9 (continued)

Region	Country	Standard VAT Rate*
Western Europe:	Belgium	21.0
	Denmark	25.0
	France	20.6
	Germany	16.0
	Greece	18.0
	Italy	20.0
	Netherlands	17.5
	Portugal	17.0
	Spain	16.0
	Sweden	25.0
	Switzerland	6.5
	Turkey	15.0
	United Kingdom	17.5

Note: In some countries, VAT is called Goods and Services tax (GST) or Business tax.
*VAT rates on some items may be different.

The monetary unit of the country is the franc (F). Assume a value-added tax rate of 12 percent.

	Purchase Price	Sales Price	Amount Subject to VAT	VAT at 12% Rate
Manufacturer	F200*	F400	F200	F24
Wholesaler	F400	F500	F100	F12
Retailer	F500	F650	F150	F18
Total			F450	F54

*Purchase price for the raw materials.

Note: The total value added in all stages is $54. This amount added to the purchase price of $200 paid at the initial stage of manufacturing results in the selling price to the customer of $650. Total VAT, in the amount of $54, is equal to 12 percent of the total value added ($650 final selling price – $200 initial purchase price = $450). It is most common in European countries, and is also found in other countries, e.g., Australia and Canada. It generally does not affect tax expenses of the businesses because they charge VAT to their customers at the same rate at which they were charged the VAT. The customer that is unable to claim a refund of tax ultimately bears the burden of the tax.

Exhibit 10.10 illustrates a comprehensive situation involving a chain of suppliers. Each of the suppliers can recover VAT except the final consumer. It is assumed that all transactions are in the same country and are subject to VAT at a 10 percent rate. VAT rates vary from country to country. Certain transactions are exempt from VAT, including many international transactions. On some activities businesses cannot reclaim VAT. In such cases, those businesses are in the same position as the final customer in Exhibit 10.10.

Thin Capitalization

Thin capitalization is the set of taxation issues from the host government's perspective, arising from the perceived imbalance between debt capital and equity capital when a foreign investor is financing a business operation in the country. **Debt capital** is financing by borrowing, and **equity capital** refers to financing by share (stock) capital.

A multinational company makes an international investment either by starting a new operation or by acquiring an existing one. One of the decisions that has to be made is whether to finance the international operation by debt capital or by equity capital. The tax treatment of debt often differs from that of equity capital. Financing through interest-bearing debt generally provides tax benefits in the country where the international operation is located. Consequently, tax authorities in many countries are becoming increasingly concerned about the loss of tax revenue. They are closely scrutinizing debt financing.

exhibit 10.10   **Value-Added Tax Chain**

	Purchase Excluding VAT	Sale Excluding VAT	VAT at 10%		Payment to VAT Authority
(All Amounts In Euros)			Input	Output	
Materials supplier		500		50	50
Manufacturer	500	1,000	50	100	50
Wholesaler	1,000	1,600	100	160	60
Retailer	1,600	1,900	160	190	30
Final customer	1,900		190*		
					190**

*The amount paid by the final customer that the customer is unable to recover.
**The total amount received by the VAT authority from all sellers.

Exhibit 10.11 contains examples of some of the recent tax laws and regulations enacted to deal with investment financing situations with a high debt to equity ratio.

Tax laws of different countries differ in the area of thin capitalization. Some countries have no laws, while others do. It can be safely stated that the governments and their tax authorities are becoming increasingly concerned about thin capitalization.

A word of caution: The terms debt and equity are not defined uniformly worldwide. While confronted with the thin capitalization issues in a country, the first step is to have a clear understanding of how the two terms are defined and interpreted in that country.

Thin Capitalization Issues in International Taxation

The issues involving thin capitalization arise because most tax systems treat debt and equity differently. A clear example is the tax treatment of interest payments on debt versus dividend payments to shareholders. Different tax treatment accorded to debt capital compared with equity capital may influence some multinational corporations to misclassify equity capital as debt capital, or the other way around, to gain tax advantages.

When a company receives debt capital from a parent company or other affiliate and the borrower and the lender are located in different countries, the interest on the debt will generally be a deductible expense for income tax purposes provided the interest rate is the prevalent commercial rate.

In case of equity capital, the return on the capital is in the form of dividends. In most countries, dividend payments made to shareholders are not deductible for corporate income tax purposes. Dividend payments to the parent company,

exhibit 10.11   **Thin Capitalization—Recent Tax Requirements**

Country	New Requirements
Bulgaria	New laws, which became effective January 1, 1999, amended provisions relating to thin capitalization. The thin capitalization provisions are extended to apply to interest on installments under financial leasing contracts.[i]
Poland	Amendments to the corporate income tax law introduce thin capitalization provisions. Under the new provisions, which became effective January 1, 1999, interest on loans from shareholders and sister companies may be disallowed to the extent that the debt to equity ratio of a Polish company exceeds 3:1.[ii]
Denmark	Thin capitalization rules have been introduced that restrict the deductibility of interest expense on debt owed to foreign group companies and on debt guaranteed by group companies. The rules became effective January 1, 1999. If the debt to equity ratio exceeds 4:1, interest expense and capital losses are disallowed as a deduction for tax purposes with respect to the excess part of the controlled debt.[iii]

i   Deloitte Touche Tohmatsu. *World Tax News*, March 1999, p. 5.
ii *Ibid.*, January 1999, p. 16.
iii *Ibid.*, September 1998, pp. 1–2.

or an affiliate located in another country, are usually subject to a withholding tax at a rate higher than the applicable interest rate.

If a parent company decides to provide debt financing to a subsidiary in another country at the current commercial interest rate, the subsidiary's income taxes may be substantially reduced when compared with providing the funds as equity capital. Interest payments to a foreign parent company may be subject to interest withholding tax in a country. Such taxes are generally eliminated or drastically reduced if the two countries have a double tax treaty, the two countries in this case being where the parent company and the subsidiary are located.

So far, we have looked at the matter from the subsidiary perspective. Now let us look at it from the parent company's vantage point. Generally, it is to the advantage of the parent company to provide funds to the subsidiary as equity capital rather than debt capital. If equity capital is provided to the subsidiary company, the return on capital is commonly in the form of dividends. Such dividends are usually not taxable for the parent company. If funds are provided to the subsidiary as interest-bearing debt, interest received by the parent company is normally taxable for the parent company. Therefore, it can be concluded that the parent company is in a position opposite to the subsidiary company when tax effects of debt capital versus equity capital are considered.

Due to major differences in the tax treatments of debt and equity, many countries have included thin capitalization provisions in their tax laws. The thin capitalization provisions allow reclassifying debt to equity or equity to debt. They also allow reclassifying interest, and dividend income as the source of that income is determined to have been set up and classified incorrectly.

The countries with thin capitalization provisions in their tax laws focus primarily on those subsidiary companies that have classified funding from the parent company as debt, when in substance it is equity capital. The tax authorities deny interest deduction in such cases. The classic thin capitalization case is one in which the financing provided by the parent company represents a high ratio of debt to equity capital.[4]

Deferred Income Taxes

Accounting for deferred income taxes is an important topic worldwide. It is an important topic in professional examinations in most countries, including the CPA examination in China.[5] A **deferred income tax asset** represents future tax benefits because of the earnings that have already been taxed but have not been reported in the income statement yet. Such income is expected to be reported in the future. Therefore, the income taxes already paid on that income are, in

---

4 Deloitte Touche Tohmatsu. *Thin Capitalization*. New York: Deloitte Touche Tohmatsu, 1993, p. XIV.

5 An e-mail message from Professor Guangyou Liu, Zhongshan University, People's Republic of China, 3 August 2000.

essence, prepaid. These prepaid income taxes are termed as deferred income taxes. Like any prepaid expense, deferred income taxes are an asset. A **deferred income tax liability** is the expected future tax liability as a result of current or past periods' earnings that have already been reported in the financial statements but have not been taxed yet.

Temporary Timing Differences

The following example illustrates the impact of income taxes due to temporary timing differences.

Example

Goshi Javed SAOG is an Oman-based medical instrument manufacturing company. It uses the double declining balance method of depreciation for tax purposes and the straight-line method of depreciation for financial reporting purposes. The following depreciation data are for manufacturing equipment. The original cost was 550,000 Omani Rials (RO), estimated salvage value is RO40,000, and estimated useful life is five years.

	Double Decline Balance Method		Straight-line Method
Year	**Beginning Book Value**	**Balance Depreciation Expense**	**Depreciation Expense**
1	$550,000	40%* × RO550,000 = RO220,000	20%*** × RO510,000 = RO102,000
2	330,000	40% × RO330,000 = RO132,000	20% × RO510,000 = RO102,000
3	198,000	40% × RO198,000 = RO 79,200	20% × RO510,000 = RO102,000
4	118,800	40% × RO118,800 = RO 47,520	20% × RO510,000 = RO102,000
5	71,280	Plug** = RO 31,280	20% × RO510,000 = RO102,000
Total depreciation expense for 5 years		RO510,000	RO510,000

* 40% (Double of the straight-line rate) × Book value at beginning of the year.
** Plug to end up with a book value that equals the salvage value.
*** Straight-line rate for annual depreciation: 1/5 × 100 = 20%

Assume the corporate income tax rate is 25 percent.

	Differences in Depreciation Expense Between Two Methods	Deferred Income Tax Liability	
Year		**Increase (decrease)***	**Balance**
1	RO 118,000	RO 19,500	RO 29,500
2	RO 30,000	RO 7,500	RO 37,000
3	RO (22,800)	RO (5,700)	RO 31,300
4	RO (54,480)	RO(13,620)	RO 17,680
5	RO (70,720)	RO(17,680)	RO -0-

*Tax rate × difference in depreciation expense between two methods = deferred income tax liability.

In the previous example the deferred income tax liability arose in the years 1 and 2 because the depreciation expense amount for taxation was greater each year than the amount in the income statement. The situation reversed starting in year 3. Consequently, the balance of deferred income tax liability decreased each year during years 3, 4, and 5. At the end of year 5, the balance in the deferred income tax liability account was zero. Why? Because the *total* depreciation expense for the five-year period was RO510,000 for both the taxation purpose and the financial reporting purpose.

Had the straight-line method of depreciation for tax purposes and the double declining balance method for income tax purposes been used, there would have been a deferred income tax asset increase in years 1 and 2. During the last three years, the balance in the deferred income tax would have kept on decreasing until it became zero at the end of year 5.

The U.S. approach to deferred income taxes is called the asset-and-liability approach.[6] The **asset-and-liability approach** requires recognition of deferred tax liabilities or deferred tax assets for the income tax that will be levied or recovered on temporary timing differences between the taxable income amount and the pretax financial income amount. The previous example is consistent with the underlying concept of the asset-and-liability approach. Evidence indicates that the current trend is clearly toward worldwide adoption of the asset-and-liability approach.

International Accounting Standard 12 (Revised)

The International Accounting Standards Committee's *IAS 12* (revised in 1996) requires that deferred income taxes be included in the computation of income tax expense and that deferred taxes be reported on the balance sheet.[7] The guidelines in *International Accounting Standard 12* (Revised), for the most part, are consistent with U.S. standards.[8]

A notable difference between the *IAS 12* and the U.S. GAAP, in Statement 109, is that the *IAS 12* requires classification of all deferred tax assets and deferred tax liabilities as noncurrent in the balance sheet. U.S. GAAP requires the classification in the current and noncurrent sections of the balance sheet based on the classification of the related nontax asset or liability for financial reporting. This classification difference affects the calculation of balance sheet ratios and could result in noncomparability between enterprises using IASC standards and those applying U.S. GAAP.[9]

6 Financial Accounting Standards Board. "Accounting for Income Taxes." *Statement of Financial Accounting Standard 109*. Norwalk, Conn.: Financial Accounting Standards Board, 1992.

7 International Accounting Standards Committee. "Income Taxes." *International Accounting Standard 12*. London: International Accounting Standards Committee, 1996.

8 Financial Accounting Standards Board. *The IASC-U.S. Comparison Project. A Report on the Similarities and Differences Between IASC Standards and U.S. GAAP*. Norwalk, Conn.: Financial Accounting Standards Board, 1999, p. 195.

9 *Ibid.*, p. 157.

Asset-and-Liability Approach

As stated earlier, the asset-and-liability approach for deferred income taxes focuses on temporary timing differences between pretax income for financial reporting purposes and taxable income. The temporary timing differences result in
differences between the amount of income for financial reporting before income
taxes and the amount of taxable income. We will look at two situations:

- *The taxable income is less than the pretax financial reporting income.* Due to
  the nature of temporary timing differences, the taxable income in the future
  will be greater than the pretax income for financial reporting purposes. The
  income tax expected to be paid in the future on the difference between the
  two income amounts is recorded *now* as a deferred tax *liability.*

- *The taxable income is greater than the pretax financial reporting income.*
  Due to the nature of temporary timing differences, the taxable income in the
  future will be less than the pretax income for financial reporting purposes.
  The income tax reduction in the future is recorded *now* as a deferred income
  tax *asset.*

The following two examples illustrate the situations described earlier.

Example

Deferred income tax liability. Ramish Company reported pretax income of
$100,000 on the 2003 income statement. The income tax rate is 30 percent.

Included in the $100,000 amount is $20,000 income that will be taxed in the
future. The expected future tax on the $20,000 amount is $6,000 ($20,000 ×
30%) and is a *deferred income tax liability*. It is a deferred liability because it will
require a payment in the future. Ramish Company's taxable income is $80,000.
The journal entry to record this information for Ramish in 2003 is:

Income Tax Expense	30,000	
Income Taxes Payable		24,000
Deferred Income Tax Liability		6,000

Income taxes payable is a legal liability as the tax authorities expect to collect
$24,000 by the due date. Deferred income tax liability is not a legal liability.
However, since $20,000 of the income earned in 2003 will be taxed in the future,
deferred tax liability is recognized to ensure that all expenses associated with
2003 revenues are reported in the 2003 income statement, and all the liabilities
at the end of 2003 are reported on the balance sheet.

Example

Deferred income tax asset. In 2003, Levine Company had taxable income total-
ing $500,000. Levine Company offers rebates on its products. The company es-
timates that in 2004 rebates of $50,000 will be made on the goods sold in 2003.
The $50,000 estimated rebate claims are reported in the 2003 financial state-
ments. Assume that the tax authorities do not allow any tax deduction for rebates
until the rebates have actually been made. The income tax rate is 30 percent.

Income taxes payable is $150,000 ($500,000 × 30%). Levine Company can expect that the $50,000 rebates to be made in 2004 (on 2003 sales) will lower the 2004 tax payment by $15,000 ($50,000 × 30%). This $15,000 is a *deferred income tax asset*. It represents the expected benefit of a future tax deduction for an item already recorded and reported. In essence, Levine is prepaying income taxes this year for lower taxes in 2004. The journal entry to record the information for Levine for 2003 is as follows:

Income Tax Expense	135,000	
Deferred Income Tax Asset	15,000	
Income Taxes Payable		150,000

The income tax expense of $135,000 is the difference between the current taxes payable ($150,000) and the deferred tax benefit ($15,000).

Exhibit 10.12 displays deferred income tax assets and deferred income tax liabilities of some multinational companies. It should be noted that the amounts are impacted by the respective GAAP of each country: Under U.K. GAAP, for example, provision for deferred taxation is made when timing differences are expected to be reversed in the foreseeable future. U.S. GAAP, however, requires deferred tax provisions on a full liability basis on all temporary timing differences.

Permanent Differences

Some differences between financial accounting income and taxable income are permanent. **Permanent differences** are caused by certain types of revenues that

exhibit 10.12   **Deferred Income Tax Assets and Deferred Income Tax Liabilities**

	(Amounts in millions)		
Company	**Year**	**Deferred Income Tax Assets**	**Deferred Income Tax Liabilities**
Bayer	1998	DM754	DM1,534
Bestfoods	1999	$32	$7
BP Amoco	1999	£1,237	£6,082
DaimlerChrysler	1998	5,016	4,165
Delphi	1999	$3,001	$111
Dyno	1998	NKr420	NKr425
General Motors	1998	$17,780	$449
Honda	1999	¥358,879	¥215,498
ICI	1998	£180	£146
Orkla	1998	NKr143	NKr824
Renault	1998	F8,233	F1,284
Sony	1999	¥142,071	¥126,199

are exempted from taxation and certain types of expenses that are not deductible for tax purposes. Nontaxable revenues and nondeductible expenses, not included in determining taxable income, are included in determining income for financial reporting. Permanent differences are neither included in the computation of taxable income, nor do they affect current or future tax liability.

Example

This example shows the effect of permanent and temporary differences on the computation of income taxes. Assume that for the year ended December 31, 2002, Zaynab Corporation reported financial income before taxes of £500,000. The amounts include two permanent differences:

1. A nontaxable revenue of £50,000.
2. A nondeductible expense of £7,000.

Zaynab has one temporary difference: The depreciation expense for tax purposes is £30,000 higher than the amount in the profit and loss account. The corporate income tax rate is 30 percent for 2002. Income taxes payable for the year are computed as follows:

Pretax income from income statement		£500,000
Add (subtract) permanent differences:		
Nontaxable revenue	£(50,000)	
Nondeductible expense	7,000	(43,000)
Subtotal		£457,000
Deduct temporary difference:		
Excess of tax depreciation over reported depreciation		(30,000)
Taxable income		£427,000
Tax payable on 2002 taxable income		
£427,000 × 0.30		£128,100

The permanent differences are not included in taxable income. Permanent differences have no future tax effect. Temporary timing differences affect reported income and taxable income in different periods.

Valuation Allowance for Deferred Income Tax Assets

A deferred income tax asset is expected to provide future income tax benefits. The tax benefit is realized only when there is enough taxable income in the future. Accounting standards of many countries, including the U.S. and the U.K., require that the deferred income tax assets be reduced by using a valuation allowance if it is likely that some or all of the deferred income tax asset amount will not provide future tax benefit. The **allowance for deferred income tax assets** is a contra account to the deferred income tax assets account. When netted against the deferred income tax assets, it would reduce the asset to its expected realizable value in the future.

Example

Lopez SA sells a product that carries a one-year warranty against defects. During 2003, total revenue from the sale of the product was 750,000 pesos (Ps). Warranty expense on the product is expected to be 2 percent of the sales revenue. One-half of the warranty repairs are made during the year of sale and the remaining one-half during the next year. Lopez made the following adjusting entry at the end of 2003 to record the warranty expense on the sales made in 2003 for which repairs are expected to be made in 2004:

Warranty Expense	7,500	
Estimated Liability Under Warranties		7,500

Assume the taxation authorities allow the deduction of warranty expense when actual repair costs are incurred. The tax rate is 35 percent. Lopez SA's reported pretax income is Ps150,000, and its taxable income is Ps157,500. The entry for recording tax expense is as follows:

Income Tax Expense	52,500	
Deferred Income Tax Assets	2,625	
Income Tax Payable		55,125

Now assume that in early 2004, one of Lopez's competitors introduced a product in the market that makes Lopez's product obsolete. Lopez estimates that only 40 percent of the remaining warranty repair costs will have to be incurred, since 60 percent of the buyers are expected to replace Lopez's product with the modern product introduced by Lopez's competitor. This means that only 40 percent of the total warranty deduction of Ps7,500 is expected to be realized in 2004. Consequently, the expected realizable amount of the deferred income tax asset is Ps1,050 (Ps2,625 × 40%). The Ps1,575 difference (Ps2,625 − Ps1,050) is recorded as follows:

Estimated Liability Under Warranties	1,575	
Allowance for Deferred Income Tax Assets		1,575

In the valuation allowance area, exercise of judgment is necessary to determine the amount of deferred tax assets and related valuation allowance. All relevant information should be considered for determining whether deferred income tax assets will be fully realized. If it is determined that the deferred income tax assets will not be fully realized, then an entry needs to be made for the valuation allowance.

Exhibit 10.13 illustrates Honda Motor's deferred assets, valuation allowance, and deferred liabilities for the years 1998 and 1999. The "more likely than not" criterion mentioned in the exhibit means a greater than 50 percent chance.

exhibit 10.13   **Honda Motor Co., Ltd.—Deferred Tax Assets, Valuation Allowance, and Deferred Tax Liabilities**

	Yen (Millions)	
	1998	1999
Deferred tax assets:		
Inventory valuation	¥ 85,201	¥ 73,207
Allowance for dealers and customers	73,256	67,142
Foreign tax credit	—	20,804
Operating loss carryforwards	19,608	20,304
Minimum pension liabilities adjustment	76,790	88,401
Other	116,223	107,457
Total gross deferred tax assets	371,078	377,315
Less valuation allowance	16,466	18,436
Net deferred tax assets	354,612	358,879
Deferred tax liabilities:		
Inventory valuation	(16,385)	(16,580)
Depreciation and amortization, excluding lease transactions	(14,095)	(13,194)
Lease transactions	(114,433)	(111,263)
Undistributed earnings of subsidiaries and affiliates	(50,930)	(28,525)
Net unrealized gains on marketable equity securities	(21,135)	(21,630)
Other	(25,332)	(24,306)
Total gross deferred tax liabilities	(242,310)	(215,498)
Net deferred tax asset	¥ 112,302	¥ 143,381

The valuation allowance for deferred tax assets at March 31, 1997, was ¥17,086 million. The net change in the total valuation allowance for the years ended March 31, 1998 and 1999, was a decrease of ¥1,970 million ($16,342 thousand), respectively.

In assessing the realizability of deferred tax assets, management considers whether it is more likely than not that some portion or all of the deferred tax assets will not be realized. The ultimate realization of deferred tax assets is dependent upon the generation of future taxable income during the periods in which those temporary differences become deductible. Management considered the scheduled reversal of deferred tax liabilities, projected future taxable income, and tax planning strategies in making this assessment. Based upon the level of historical taxable income and projections for future taxable income over the periods that the deferred tax assets are deductible, management believes it is more likely than not that Honda will realize the benefits of these deductible differences, net of the existing valuation allowances at March 31, 1998 and 1999.

Source: Honda Motor Co., Ltd., *Annual Report 1999*, p. 39.

Tax Incentives

Countries compete to attract foreign investments and foreign capital. They also devise ways to encourage exports of goods and services. Tax incentives are among the most effective ways to attract foreign investment and to support exports. A common form of the former is a tax holiday. A **tax holiday** is the period of time during which a foreign investor is exempted from taxes. For the holiday, the investor fulfills certain conditions, such as investing in a specified industry, employing a certain number of native workers, or importing high technology machinery and equipment. The most common period for tax holidays is 10 years. Besides tax holidays, other types of tax incentives include:

- Tax holiday on income earned from research and development.
- Tax rebates.
- Income tax rate reduction for a specified number of years.
- Low tax rates.
- Advance rulings on tax issues by tax authorities.
- No capital gains tax.
- No tax on dividend income.
- Income tax deferral.
- Customs duties exemption on high technology machinery and equipment imported.
- Investment tax credits.
- Accelerated deductions.
- Bonus (extra) deductions.
- Exemptions from value-added tax, local tax, and other taxes.

Each of the tax incentives has been or is being used by different countries. A **tax credit** reduces the tax liability by an amount equal to the amount of the tax credit. Therefore, the tax benefit of a tax credit is always more than the tax benefit of a tax deduction.

Tax incentives to encourage exports take many forms. Countries may exempt exported goods from some taxes such as the value-added tax, or give favorable tax treatment to income earned from exporting goods and services. In the U.S., the foreign sales corporation (FSC) is a form of tax incentive designed to encourage exports by U.S.-based corporations. FSCs must meet certain conditions such as performing export functions outside the U.S. The income of an FSC is partially exempt from U.S. corporate income tax.

In some countries, special economic zones have been designated where export-oriented manufacturing firms are encouraged to start operations. There are more than 30 special economic zones in the Philippines where a registered enterprise can pay a flat tax at the rate of 5 percent of its gross income instead of all other national and local taxes.

Appendix

U.S. Internal Revenue Code—Section 482

Section 482 of the U.S. Internal Revenue Code states:

> *Section 482. Allocation of income and deductions among taxpayers.* In any case of two or more organizations, trades, or businesses (whether or not incorporated, whether or not organized in the United States, and whether or not affiliated) owned or controlled directly or indirectly by the same interests, the Secretary may distribute, apportion, or allocate gross income, deductions, credits, or allowances between or among such organizations, trades, or businesses, if he determines that such distribution, apportionment, or allocation is necessary in order to prevent evasion of taxes or clearly to reflect the income of any of such organizations, trades, or businesses. In the case of any transfer (or license) of intangible property (within the meaning of section 936(h)(3)(B)), the income with respect to such transfer or license shall be commensurate with the income attributable to the intangible.

Authority is given to the Secretary of the Treasury to prevent a shifting of income or deductions between related parties to take advantage of the differences in national tax rates. As it was explained in the transfer pricing section of the chapter, the intracompany transfer of goods and services across national boundaries may be overpriced or underpriced to avoid paying higher taxes.

U.S. tax regulations require that the pricing of intracompany transfers of goods and services be based on an "arm's length" price. The best example of an arm's length price is the market price used for the transfer of goods and services between unrelated parties. In essence, Section 482 is an attempt to ensure that intracompany transfers are priced as if the transfers were made between unrelated (uncontrolled) parties. In case of disagreement, Section 482 allows U.S. tax authorities to compute what the transfer price should be. The multinational corporation may dispute this computation by showing why it is unreasonable. Section 482 tax regulations state:

> The purpose of Section 482 is to place a controlled taxpayer on a tax parity with an uncontrolled taxpayer by determining, according to the standards of an uncontrolled taxpayer, the true taxable income from property and business of a controlled taxpayer.

Determination of transfer prices under Section 482 for the sale of tangible property can be done using one of three methods. These are the *comparable uncontrollable price* method, the *resale price* method, and the *cost-plus* method. The U.S. Internal Revenue Service prefers the first over the other two methods.

An arm's length price under the first method is the price determined from similar transactions between two parties where one or both are not members of the same corporate family. Similar transactions refer to the physical characteristics of the product being transacted. Adjustments are allowed in the price of uncontrolled transactions when reasonable differences exist and can be determined. For example, there can be differences in the shipping and insurance expense portion of the price for which an adjustment can be made. Infrequent or special sales are not considered comparable. The transfer price under this method is equal to the price paid in comparable uncontrolled transactions. The price is adjusted for any reasonable differences between the products or their transaction terms such as additional product packaging or price discount to maintain existing markets.

Comparable uncontrolled prices are not always available. In this case, the next preferred transfer pricing method is the resale price method. Under this method, the transfer price is determined by deducting from the resale price to an uncontrolled entity an appropriate markup and any reasonable expenses incurred by the reseller. For example, consider the case of Subsidiary A that sells a product to Subsidiary B, both subsidiaries controlled by the same parent company. Subsidiary B incurs additional expenses and resells the product to Company X, which is not controlled by the same parent company. The price for the product that Subsidiary A should charge is computed by using the resale price to Company X after deducting Subsidiary B markup and making other reasonable price adjustments for the additional expenses incurred by Subsidiary B.

Tax regulations allow the use of the resale price method when there are no comparable uncontrolled transactions, the resale is made within a reasonable period of time from the original transfer between controlled entities, and there are no significant product changes made by the reseller.

The third method, cost-plus, is the least preferred of the three methods. As the name implies, and as discussed in the transfer pricing section in the chapter, this method begins with the cost of producing the product. Product cost is determined according to acceptable cost accounting methods. A reasonable gross profit amount, based on a percentage of cost, is added to the cost to compute the transfer price. The gross profit percentage should be derived from transactions between uncontrolled parties.

U.S. tax authorities introduced new transfer pricing guidelines in 1988, allowing a corporation to apply for approval of its transfer prices. A multinational corporation would apply for an "Advanced Determination Ruling," or ADR, to get approval for a parent-subsidiary specific product pricing. The company is required to include justification and detailed financial information in support of the proposed price. The information is considered by tax authorities before an approval is granted. The main advantage is to have a transfer price that is approved in advance.

Note to Students

You have been presented with two major international managerial accounting topics: transfer pricing and international taxation issues. Both topics are technical and complex.

The following Internet addresses are very helpful in researching international tax topics.

International Tax Treaties: **http://www.danzigerfdi.com/dtas/
taxtreaty.htm**

Tax News International: **http://www.taxcast.com/f-knowledg.htm**

Foreign Tax Links: **http://vls.law.vill.edu/prof/maule/taxmaster/
taxfor.htm**

International Search Engine: **http://vls.law.vill.edu/prof/maule/
taxmaster/taxfor.htm#se**

The American Chamber of Commerce in Guangdong, China:
http://www.amcham.nu

Flinders University
International Tax Index: **http://commerce.flinders.edu.au/
internationaltax/**

Deloitte Touche Tohmatsu's Rate*Find* is a tax planning tool that draws on a firm's worldwide tax experience. It provides accurate and comprehensive information on 50 major trading nations. The software program provides tax rates and a detail of tax treaties entered into by the 50 countries. Rate*Find* is updated every six months. Rate*Find Lite* contains information on 15 countries. It is an evaluation version of Rate*Find* for demonstrating purposes. For information on Rate*Find* and Rate*Find Lite*, visit the Web site address: **http://tax. deloitte.com/**

Many issues related to transfer pricing and taxation have been debated in the news media for some time. Here are some examples:

- Debate as to whether "foreign" companies pay their "fair share" of U.S. corporate taxes.

- Discussion of reduction of import tariffs to encourage lower transfer pricing for imported goods, with higher corporate income tax collections to compensate for the lost government revenue from lower import duties.

- Consideration of possible benefits to consumers of tax and trade treaties.

Taxes are business expenses that are reflected in the selling prices of what you buy. Therefore, international tax policies have a direct monetary impact on you.

Chapter Summary

1. A transfer price is what a seller charges a buyer when both are members of the same corporate family.

2. Transfer pricing methods include market-based, cost-based, and negotiated.

3. Different transfer prices result in different reported operating income and reported performance for both the buying segment and the selling segment.

4. The market-based transfer price is the price charged by one entity to another unrelated entity based on an arm's length transaction. It is adjusted, when applicable, for savings resulting from intracompany transfers.

5. Many factors influence the choice of transfer pricing approaches employed by multinational corporations.

6. Taxation, tariffs, government regulations, and cash flow restrictions are among the factors considered in choosing a transfer pricing approach.

7. Market-based transfer prices have several advantages over cost-based transfer prices.

8. There are several possible cost-based transfer prices depending on the cost base used.

9. Cost-based prices are perceived as more objective and are typically based on cost information provided by the accounting system.

10. The tax system of a country is generally the product of its environments.

11. Tax systems differ depending on the taxation approach used by a country. Different approaches are based on concepts such as territorial, worldwide, classic, and integrated tax systems.

12. The foreign tax credit is designed to avoid double taxation of foreign source income.

13. The corporate income tax in most countries is based on the concept of worldwide income.

14. Globalization has made thin capitalization a major area of concern among governments and tax authorities.

15. The value-added tax is based on value added at each stage of production or business activity.

16. Deferred taxes are an important topic worldwide.

17. Many countries use tax incentives to attract foreign investment and to encourage exports.

Questions for Discussion

1. Explain what is meant by transfer pricing.

2. What are the objectives of a multinational transfer pricing system?

3. What factors are unique to the transfer pricing system of a multinational?

4. What is meant by market-based transfer pricing? Cost-based pricing?

5. How do tax laws and regulations affect multinational transfer pricing?

6. What is meant by a negotiated transfer price?

7. How does decentralization as a corporate goal influence the transfer pricing process?

8. Explain how transfer pricing affects the reported income of segments engaged in buying and selling of goods and services with each other.

9. Discuss how currency controls imposed by many developing nations impact the choice of transfer prices.

10. Discuss how tariffs imposed on imports affect the choice of transfer prices.

11. Explain what is meant by underpricing and the conditions that might lead to underpricing.

12. Explain what is meant by overpricing and the conditions that might lead to overpricing.

13. Why is the market-based transfer pricing method considered more desirable than other methods?

14. Why do countries tax corporate income?

15. Explain what is meant by:
   a. Territorial and worldwide approaches.
   b. Classic and integrated tax systems.

16. What is a tax credit?

17. Define value-added tax and differentiate it from sales tax.

18. What is thin capitalization?

19. How can the tax benefit of a deferred tax asset be realized?

20. How do deferred income taxes affect the amount of cash payments for income taxes?

21. What is meant by tax incentives?

22. What are the objectives for tax incentives?

23. (Appendix) State and explain transfer pricing methods allowed under Section 482 of the U.S. tax code.

Exercises/Problems

10-1 In each of the following cases, assume that North Division manufactures a product that can be sold either to customers in an external market or South Division of the same company. The company evaluates divisional managers on the basis of their division's profits.

	Case 1	Case 2
North Division:		
Capacity (in units)	50,000	50,000
Number of units sold in external market	50,000	40,000
Selling price in the external market	£150	£100
Incremental costs per unit	£100	£65
South Division:		
Number of product units needed	10,000	10,000

Required:

(1)   Refer to the data in case 1. If the managers are free to make buying and selling decisions, what will likely be the transfer price? Explain.

(2)   Refer to the data in case 2. If the managers are free to make buying and selling decisions, within what negotiation range will the transfer price fall? Explain.

10-2 The Canadian subsidiary of a Dutch multinational corporation sells one half of its output to local buyers and the other half to another subsidiary located in New York. The selling price of $40 per unit is the same for both buyers. Both subsidiaries operate as independent profit centers. It costs the Canadian subsidiary $36 to produce each unit, and 70 percent of the cost is variable. The U.S. subsidiary found out that it can buy the same product from a Brazilian supplier at $32 per unit.

Required:

Ignore the implication of any exchange rate changes, taxation, and tariffs.

(1)   Should the U.S. subsidiary be allowed to buy from outside? What action is best for the parent company assuming that the Canadian subsidiary has enough capacity to meet internal and external demand?

(2)   Would your answer in (1) be different if the Canadian subsidiary has no excess capacity, i.e., it can get enough orders from outside to utilize its full capacity?

(3)   What problems may arise if the parent company forces the Canadian subsidiary to lower its selling price for the U.S. subsidiary to match the $32 per-unit selling price of the Brazilian supplier?

10-3 URGlobal (URG) acquired a plant in Poland. The plant has been operating at 55 percent of capacity and efforts to bring it to 75 percent have not been successful. URG expects the plant to operate at 65 percent capacity during 2004. The price and cost per unit of one of its products, IMFRE, are:

Price	$1,350
Variable costs	$750*
Fixed costs	$150**

*50 percent direct labor
**Based on 65 percent capacity utilization, or 19,500 units

URG has another plant in Singapore that uses a component identical to IMFRE. The Singapore plant has been buying the component from an independent supplier at a cost of $950 per unit. However, the supplier has notified the Singapore plant's manager that the price of the component will be $1,000 per unit in the future. The Singapore plant manager thinks that she should be able to acquire IMFRE from Poland for $720, the incremental cost of producing one unit at the Polish plant. The Polish manager has refused, claiming that he must cover his cost ($870) and earn a reasonable profit. The vice-president for international business refuses to interfere and suggests the two managers meet to negotiate a price.

Required:

(1) What are the merits of each manager's arguments?

(2) What is the range of possible negotiated prices?

(3) Recommend a reasonable price. Support and document your answer.

(4) Assume now that the Polish manager cannot lay off workers due to local labor laws. What would be your answer to requirement (3) under this assumption?

10-4 Select the best available answer:

1. Which of the following may influence the determination of a transfer price?
   a. Taxation
   b. Tariffs
   c. Both of the above
   d. None of the above

2. A market-based transfer price for goods sold across national boundaries assumes that:
   a. A market-based price is available.
   b. A market-based price should not be adjusted for cost savings due to an internal transfer.
   c. Tax regulations are not relevant.
   d. Accurate product costs cannot be determined.

3. Subsidiary A sells goods to Subsidiary B. Subsidiary B is located in another country that has a lower tax rate. Given a high degree of centralization, this will tend to lead to:
   a. Overpricing.
   b. Underpricing.
   c. A transfer price determined by Subsidiary A.
   d. A transfer price determined by Subsidiary B.

4. The sale of goods by Subsidiary A to Subsidiary B when Subsidiary A is operating at full capacity requires that the transfer price should take into consideration:
   a. Opportunity cost to A.
   b. Opportunity cost to B.
   c. Opportunity cost to both A and B.
   d. Opportunity cost to neither A nor B.

10-5 Dela International, Inc. (DII) is a U.S.-based multinational company. DII plans to open a new branch in one of three locations in separate countries. Initial plans call for selling goods valued at $6,500,000 to the overseas branch. The International Business Operations Division has compiled the following information about the three countries:

	Country A	Country B	Country C
Estimated sales revenues	$14,200,000	$14,200,000	$14,200,000
Local costs and expenses:			
Variable costs (as percent of sales revenue)	12%	10%	14%
Fixed costs	$2,000,000	$2,500,000	$1,500,000
Import tariffs	6%	8%	10%
Local corporate tax rate	16%	10%	10%
Cash flow to DII (as percent of net income)	70%	60%	80%
Local taxes on distributed cash (as percent of distributed cash)	5%	5%	5%

Required:

(1) Prepare a projected income statement for each country.

(2) Compute the cash flow to DII from the proposed overseas branch in each country.

(3) The corporate tax rate in the U.S. is 35 percent. What would be DII's U.S. tax liability in each case before taking into account any foreign tax credit?

(4) Assuming that foreign taxes are creditable, compute the DII U.S. net tax liability after the foreign tax credit.

(5) Compute the taxes payable to each of the three countries being considered.

(6) The branch in which country would be most profitable?

10-6 Refer to the information in the previous problem. Assume that the value of goods of $6,500,000 is based on cost plus 20 percent markup on cost. Therefore, the assumed value of $6,500,000 is 120 percent of the cost.

Required:

Assume DII decides to transfer goods at cost rather than $6,500,000. Prepare a projected income statement for each country.

10-7 Patsburg International (PI) is a Netherlands-based multinational corporation. PI imports components for one of its products from Norway and processes them further to produce its popular bicycle model MT100. PI's marketing division sells the product to retail stores throughout Europe. PI provides you with the following financial information for its business in the Netherlands for 2003 in guilders (f.):

Cost of imported components	f. 5,620,000
Transfer price to marketing division	8,410,000
Sales to retailers	13,560,000

Assume that the value-added tax in the Netherlands is 17.5 percent.

Required:

(1) Compute the amount of value-added tax.

(2)   Assume that the value-added tax is abolished in favor of a 10 percent sales tax. Compute the amount of sales tax.

(3)   Compare the value-added tax approach with the sales tax approach.

10-8 The Philippines subsidiary of a Japanese multinational company would like to sell 500 units of its product X2-100 to a sister subsidiary in Thailand. The Philippines subsidiary has plenty of excess capacity to meet the Thailand subsidiary's needs for X2-100. The costs of production *per unit* are direct materials 10,000 pesos (P), direct labor P15,000, and variable overhead P5,000. Total fixed manufacturing overhead costs are P20,000,000. The price from another supplier to the subsidiary in Thailand is P70,000. The selling price of X2-100 is P80,000.

Required:

(1)   If the managers of the Philippines and Thailand subsidiaries get together to negotiate a transfer price, what is the range within which they could agree on a transfer price that would be mutually beneficial? Support your answer.

(2)   Assume the two managers cannot agree on a transfer price. The manager of the Thailand subsidiary buys from the outside supplier, and the Philippines facility consequently does not produce the 500 units. Determine the effect on the income of the Japanese company as a whole.

10-9 Rawat Company located in Port Louis, Mauritius, manufactures a variety of doors. It purchases its raw materials from local companies and sells its products to a wholesaler. The wholesaler distributes the products to retailers, who then sell to final customers. All of the following amounts are in Mauritian rupee (Rs).

	Purchase Price	Sales Price
Manufacturer	Rs100,000	Rs150,000
Wholesaler	Rs150,000	Rs200,000
Retailer	Rs200,000	Rs300,000

The value-added tax rate is 10 percent.

Required:

(1)   Compute the VAT collected by the tax authorities from the
      (a) Manufacturer.
      (b) Wholesaler.
      (c) Retailer.

(2)   What is the total amount of VAT collected by the tax authorities?

(3)   Who ultimately is taxed for the total amount of tax because that party is unable to recover it?

10-10 The following information pertains to the value-added tax chain. All amounts are in euros.

	Purchase Excluding VAT	Sale Excluding VAT	VAT at 15%		Payment to VAT Authority
			Input	Output	
Raw materials	—	—		60	—
Manufacturing	400	—	—	—	—
Wholesaling	—	—	—	150	—
Retailing	—	—	—	—	75
Consumer	—			—	—

Required:

Fill in the blanks.

10-11 Shaheen Inc. began operating on January 1, 2003. At the end of the first year of operations, Shaheen reported 250 million income before income taxes on its income statement. Shaheen's taxable income is 210 million. Analysis of the difference reveals that 30 million is a permanent difference and 10 million is a temporary difference. The tax rate is 30 percent.

Required:

Prepare the journal entry to record income taxes for 2003.

10-12 Kieso Instruments Ltd. includes a one-year warranty on its instrument sales. At the end of 2003, the warranty records reveal a temporary timing difference of $600,000 for warranty expenses. The book warranty expenses have exceeded the tax deductions allowed. Pretax income on the income statement is $10 million. The income tax rate for 2003 is 35 percent.

Required:

(1)   Make the journal entry for income taxes for 2003.

(2)   In 2004, it is determined that only 60% of the tax benefit from the temporary difference can be realized. Make the entry using a valuation allowance.

10-13 McCall Ltd. reported pretax income of £7,500,000 on its profit and loss account for 2003. The profit and loss account included £250,000 of entertainment expenses for customers, which are nondeductible for tax purposes. For financial reporting purposes, McCall reported bad debt expenses of £150,000. The amount of bad debt deductible for tax purposes was £135,000, which caused a temporary timing difference of £15,000. The tax rate is 35 percent.

Required:

Prepare the journal entry necessary to record income taxes for 2003.

10-14 Zahoor Manufacturing Corporation's taxable income is $1 million for the year 2003, its first year of operations. The temporary timing differences between financial reporting income and taxable income for 2003 follow.

Tax depreciation in excess of financial reporting depreciation	$100,000
Product warranty expense in excess of actual warranty claims (only actual warranty claims are tax deductible)	150,000
Installment sales revenue for financial reporting purposes in excess of taxable installment sales revenue	265,000

The corporate income tax rate is 30 percent.

Required:

Prepare the journal entry to record income taxes for 2003.

10-15 Nabila Microsystems reports taxable income of $500,000 for 2003, its first year of operations. The tax rate is 35 percent. Nabila has deducted $50,000 of expenses for financial reporting purposes that are temporary timing differences for tax purposes. Consequently, the pretax income on the income statement is $450,000.

Required:

(1)   Prepare the journal entry to record income taxes for 2003. Assume that there will be sufficient future income to realize any deductible amounts.

(2)   Repeat requirement (1) except assume that future taxable income will be sufficient to realize only 70 percent of the total $50,000.

Case

Vinings International Corporation

The electronic division of Vinings International Corporation, a diversified international company headquartered in Atlanta, sells switch-relay boards in the United States and several foreign countries. All divisions are treated as profit centers for performance evaluation purposes. The selling price for these kits is $40 in the United States, where the effective income tax rate is approximately 50 percent. Vinings International Corporation has a 60-percent-owned subsidiary in Chile, which buys substantial quantities of the switch-relay boards from the electronic division and sells them to local wholesalers at a price of 20,000 Chilean pesos per unit. The current exchange rate is 250 Chilean pesos to one U.S. dollar. The total cost of the boards delivered to the Chilean port is $30, of which $2 is transportation cost. Chilean tariffs on electronic division products are 40 percent on declared value. These duties are paid by the Chilean subsidiary and become part of its cost of inventory. The Chilean customs authorities will not permit the declared value to be less than $30; however, they have no set upper limit. The applicable income tax rate in Chile is 35 percent. There are no other restrictions or taxes affecting the transfer of funds from Chile to the United States.

Required:

What declared value would you recommend, as a representative of the:

(1) electronic division management?

(2) Chilean subsidiary management?

(3) Vinings International Corporation headquarters management?

Source: Adapted by Yezdi K. Bhada from Charles T. Horngren. *Cost Accounting: A Managerial Emphasis.* 5th ed. Englewood Cliffs, N.J.: Prentice-Hall, 1982, p. 658.

References

Crow, Stephen, and Eugene Sauls. "Setting the Right Transfer Price." *Management Accounting*. December 1994, pp. 41–47.

Deloitte Touche Tohmatsu. *Corporate and Withholding Tax Rates*. New York: Deloitte Touche Tohmatsu International, 1999.

_____. *Documentation Requirements in International Transfer Pricing*. New York: Deloitte Touche Tohmatsu International, 1995.

_____. *Executives Living Abroad—Guide to Tax Planning in 66 Jurisdictions*. Deloitte Touche Tohmatsu, 2000.

_____. *International Transfers of Technology: Licensing, Services, and Cost Sharing*. New York: Deloitte Touche Tohmatsu International, 1996.

_____. "IRS Issues Final Transfer Pricing Penalty Regulations." *Deloitte & Touche Review*, 19 February 1996, pp. 5–6.

_____. *Taxation in the Asia-Pacific Region*. New York: Deloitte Touche Tohmatsu International, 1999.

_____. *Taxation in Central and Eastern Europe*. New York: Deloitte Touche Tohmatsu International, 1999.

_____. *Taxation in Central and South America*. New York: Deloitte Touche Tohmatsu International, 1999.

_____. *Taxation in North America: The North American Free Trade Agreement*. New York: Deloitte Touche Tohmatsu International, 1998.

_____. *Taxation in Sub-Saharan Africa*. New York: Deloitte Touche Tohmatsu International, 1999.

_____. *Taxation in Western Europe*. New York: Deloitte Touche Tohmatsu International, 1999.

_____. *Thin Capitalization*. New York: Deloitte Touche Tohmatsu International, 1993.

_____. *Value Added Tax Refunds in Europe*. New York: Deloitte Touche Tohmatsu International, 1994.

Ernst & Young LLP. *1999 Transfer Pricing Global Survey*. Chicago: Ernst & Young, 1999.

_____. *2000 Transfer Pricing Global Survey*. Chicago: Ernst & Young, 2000.

Financial Accounting Standard Board. "Accounting for Income Taxes." *Statement of Financial Accounting Standard No. 109*. Norwalk, CT: Financial Accounting Standards Board, 1992.

_____. *The IASC-U.S. Comparison Project: A Report on the Similarities and Differences Between IASC Standards and U.S. GAAP*. 2nd ed. Norwalk, CT: Financial Accounting Standards Board, 1999.

Halperin, Robert, and Bin Srinidhi. "U.S. Income Tax Transfer Pricing Rules For Intangibles as Approximations of Arm's Length Pricing." *The Accounting Review*, vol. 71, no. 1 (1996), pp. 61–80.

International Accounting Standards Committee. "Income Taxes." *International Accounting Standard 12*. London: International Accounting Standards Committee, 1996.

Kelly, Jim. "Leading Companies Face Tougher Tax Line Over Transfer Pricing." *Financial Times*, 17 July 1995, pp. 1 and 14.

Organization for Economic Cooperation and Development. *Transfer Pricing Guidelines for Multinational Corporations*. Paris: Organization for Economic Cooperation and Development, 1995.

PricewaterhouseCoopers. *International Transfer Pricing 1998–1999*. Riverheads, IL. Commerce Clearing House, 1998.

Tomsett, Eric G., Martin McClintock, Otmar Thoemmes, and Reiner Imig. "International Planning Opportunities Through Commissionaire Arrangements." *World Tax News*, July 1995, pp. 1–4.

Wrappe, Steven C., Ken Milani, and Julie Joy. "The Transfer Pricing Is Right . . . Or Is It?" *Strategic Finance*, July 1999, pp. 39–43.

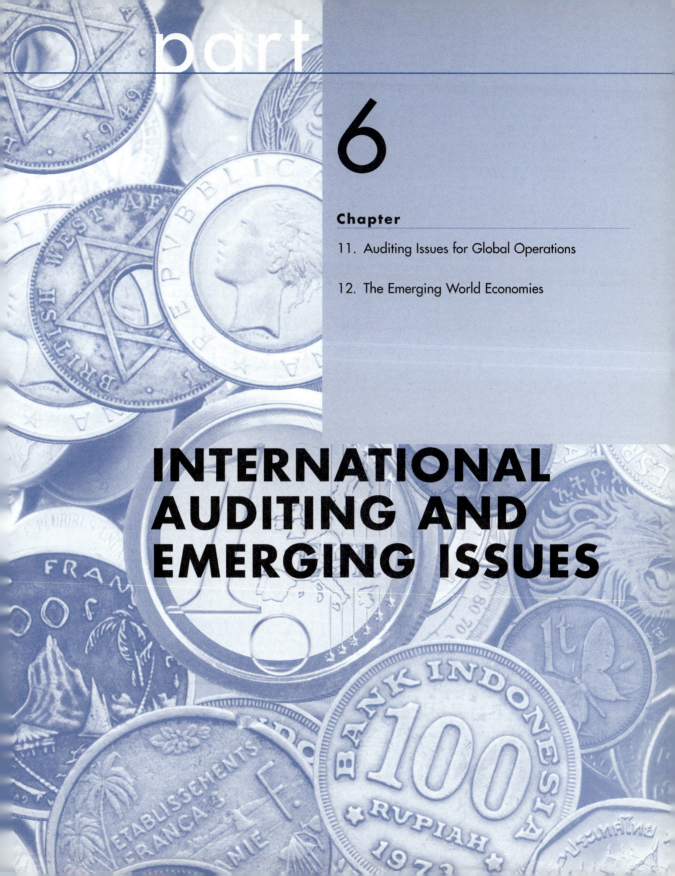

part

6

Chapter

INTERNATIONAL AUDITING AND EMERGING ISSUES

chapter

11

Auditing Issues for Global Operations

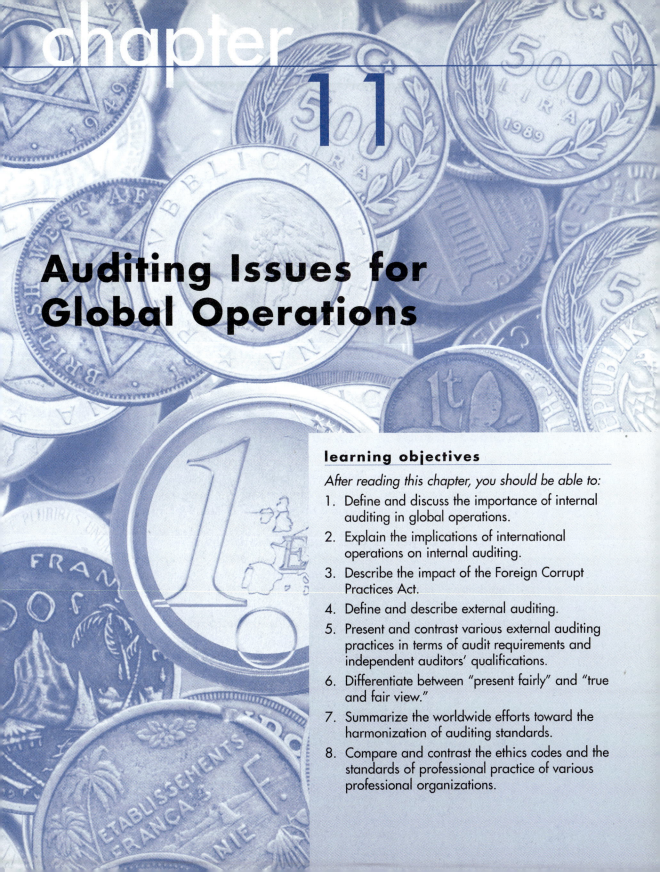

learning objectives

After reading this chapter, you should be able to:

1. Define and discuss the importance of internal auditing in global operations.

2. Explain the implications of international operations on internal auditing.

3. Describe the impact of the Foreign Corrupt Practices Act.

4. Define and describe external auditing.

5. Present and contrast various external auditing practices in terms of audit requirements and independent auditors' qualifications.

6. Differentiate between "present fairly" and "true and fair view."

7. Summarize the worldwide efforts toward the harmonization of auditing standards.

8. Compare and contrast the ethics codes and the standards of professional practice of various professional organizations.

Internal auditing and external auditing are two separate but related functions. The two audit functions share a common objective—to determine reliability of accounting information. In this chapter we first discuss the issues related to internal auditing and then the issues related to external auditing.

Internal Auditing

Internal auditing is an independent evaluation of the operations and internal control system of an organization to determine whether management's policies and prescribed procedures are being followed, and also whether the resources are safeguarded and used efficiently to achieve organizational objectives. The major objectives of internal auditing are to determine whether:

- Financial and operating information has reliability and integrity.
- Management and accounting controls are in place and are effective.
- Assets are safeguarded and used efficiently.

Internal auditing deals with the areas that are important to the management of a company: Accuracy of financial and operating reports, compliance with policies, and the safeguarding of assets and their efficient usage.

Global Trends in Internal Auditing

The importance of an internal audit function increases as operations of an organization become geographically dispersed. The practice of internal auditing is increasing worldwide. In many countries, internal auditing is required by law. Several factors have contributed to the enhanced status of internal auditing.

Board of Directors and Audit Committees

The role of boards of directors has been redefined during the last two decades. The boards are being held to much higher levels of accountability by stockholders and regulators. The trend toward electing board members from outside the organization, and also from other countries, has been gaining popularity. A recent study of 47 multinational companies in 16 countries confirms that the companies have increasingly been recruiting non-national members to their boards of directors. According to the study by The Conference Board, the percentage of companies with non-national directors increased from 37.8 percent in 1993 to 59.6 percent in 1998.[1] This indicates an increase of 21.8 percent (a rate of increase of 57.67 percent) during the five-year period as depicted in Figure 11.1.

---

1 The Conference Board. *Globalizing the Board of Directors: Trends and Strategies.* New York: The Conference Board, 1999.

figure 11.1   **Growth in Non-National Directors**

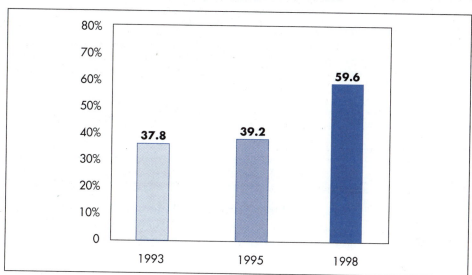

According to Deloitte and Touche:[2]

In addition to producing and selling goods and services in foreign markets, international companies must have a *global perspective* when considering corporate strategy and performance, acquisitions and divestitures, risk management, accounting and reporting systems and issues, legal requirements, ethical and civic responsibilities, and many other corporate issues. To achieve this perspective, senior management and boards of directors need to be culturally and nationally diverse [emphasis added].

The most important criterion for electing a member to Philips's Supervisor Board (Board of Directors) is the global perspective. This is evidenced by the statement in Exhibit 11.1.

These developments have shifted the balance of power from top operating executives to the board of directors. One outcome of the shift in power has been the widespread creation and use of audit committees. Typically, the audit committee consists of members of the board of directors, the majority of whom are usually from outside the organization. The internal auditors of the organization often report directly to the audit committee. It is interesting to note that in 1998, out of eight members of Philips's Supervisory Board, four were non-nationals. Three of the eight Supervisory Board members were members of the audit committee. Out of the three, one was non-national.[3]

2 Deloitte & Touche. "Globalizing the Board of Directors." *The Review*, 2 August 1999, p. 3.

3 Philips. *Annual Report 1998*, p. 68.

exhibit 11.1 **Philips Supervisory Board**

Profile of the Supervisory Board

The Supervisory Board will aim for an adequate spread of knowledge and experience among its members in relation to the global and multi-product character of the business of the Company. Consequently, the Board will aim for an adequate level of experience in financial, economic, social and legal aspects of international business and government and public administration. The Supervisory Board further aims to have available adequate experience within Philips by having one or two former Philips executives on the Supervisory Board. In the case of vacancies the Supervisory Board will ensure that when such persons are recommended for appointment, these various qualifications are reflected sufficiently.

Source: Philips, *Annual Report 1998*, p. 68.

An important factor contributing to the establishment of audit committees has been the Foreign Corrupt Practices Act (FCPA). The impact of the FCPA has been felt worldwide due to its broad scope and its penalty provisions. A later section of this chapter discusses the FCPA in detail. In the U.S., the New York Stock Exchange and the National Association of Securities Dealers Automated Quotations (NASDAQ) both require that all companies listed on those security markets have audit committees. The New York Stock Exchange mandates that the audit committees consist of non-management directors only, while NASDAQ requires that the majority be non-management directors. The Committee of Sponsoring Organizations (COSO) of the Treadway Commission in the U.K. considers an effective internal audit function to be important for the reliability and integrity of financial and operational information. COSO has also stated that an enlightened and proactive audit committee is a powerful agent for corporate self-regulation.

Technological Advances

Instantaneous electronic transfers and computerized information systems have raised new concerns about both asset security and data security. It makes the role of internal auditing significantly more important. The new technologies enable the internal auditor to perform audit tests and analyses faster and more economically.

Reliance of External Auditors on Internal Audit Reports

As discussed later in the chapter, for cost savings and avoidance of unnecessary duplication, it is common for external auditors to rely on internal audit reports. This further enhances the importance of the internal audit function.

International Operations

Conceptually, there is no difference between internal audits of domestic operations and internal audits of international operations. However, international operations add certain *practical* complexities that necessitate adaptations and adjustments.

- *Geographic distances.* Long geographic distances make it impossible to personally oversee operations through physical observation and visual inspection.

- *Local laws.* To ensure compliance with local laws, it is a prerequisite to be knowledgeable about them. Local laws apply to a multitude of operational areas: environmental protection, product safety, and working conditions, to name a few. In France, for example, a penal code that took effect in 1994 makes corporations, small companies, and nonprofit organizations accountable for endangering others. The code contains penalty provisions for "environmental terrorism," including willful pollution.

- *Business customs.* Business practices are different worldwide. In some countries (for example, Japan) banks typically do not return canceled checks. In other countries, confirmation of receivables and payables is not a customary practice.

- *National currencies.* With very few exceptions, most countries have their own national monetary unit. This requires that the internal auditors be familiar with the monetary unit of the country where an international operation is located.

- *Local records in the local language.* In most cases, local records are kept in the local language. This requires that either the internal auditor be proficient in the local language, or the records must be translated. Translation creates potential problems arising from differences in accounting terminology. Even when the language is the same, accounting terms may have different meanings. For example, the term turnover has an entirely different meaning in the U.K. than it does in the U.S.

- *Infrastructure.* The degree to which the infrastructure of a country is developed has a direct impact on the design of the internal control system and internal audit function.

- *Availability of internal auditors.* Lack of availability of well-trained, skilled internal auditors is a problem in many countries.

The previous factors often require top management to make decisions for balancing conflicting factors. Many tradeoffs required for making such decisions make them more complex than those made for domestic operations. Internal auditors can provide in-house consulting expertise in such a complex decision-making environment.

Policy Formulation in Different Cultures

Corporate policies have to be well thought-out and well articulated. This requires taking into account cultural differences, company goals, and business ethics. Some issues are easy to resolve, e.g., pork in company functions should not be served in Israel or in Muslim countries. Other issues are more complex and can be addressed only after careful analysis, synthesis, and then articulation in a corporate policy statement. *An important consideration to always keep in mind is that inherently an MNC's operations are not confined to one country. MNCs are corporate citizens of their base country as well as of the world.*

Some claim that cultural differences preclude applying one set of ethical standards worldwide. Research findings, however, indicate that despite cultural differences, standards of moral judgment do not vary significantly among countries.[4] Therefore, ethical considerations become critically important variables in the decision process to ensure a long-run approach, rather than short-run expediency.

A recent study by The Conference Board of 124 companies in 22 countries found that 78 percent of boards of directors are setting ethics standards. It is a significant jump from the comparable percentage of 21 percent in 1987 and 41 percent in 1991. Business leaders see the self-regulation through corporate ethics codes as a way to avoid litigation and fines. The study also revealed that ethics codes promote tolerance of diverse practices and local customs.[5]

In March 1996, the Organization of American States adopted the Inter-American Convention Against Corruption. Twenty-six countries signed the Convention, which became effective in March 1997. The Convention requires each signatory to enact laws making the bribery of governmental officials a crime. The Convention includes higher rules on ethics for government officials, and improved recording and disclosure systems. It also contains extradition agreements among the signatories.

In 1997, Canada developed an international code of ethics with the help of a number of multinational companies. The code is designed to make the companies engaged in international operations "ethically, socially, and environmentally responsible." It commits Canada-based companies to be conscientious about "human rights and social justice" while transacting business abroad.[6] The same year, the Institute of Management Accountants revised its standards of ethical conduct for management accountants. The revised ethic code specifies that its requirements are applicable both domestically and internationally.[7]

The World Bank has taken a strong position against corruption. It has impressed on the member countries and business organizations to develop codes of ethics to fight corruption. One of the recommended guidelines is to develop and implement effective internal control systems as preventive measures against corruption. The World Bank has also issued guidelines for imposing penalties if it is determined that a contract bidder or a potential borrower has engaged in corrupt practices or fraudulent activities.

---

4 Robert B. Sweeney. "Ethics in an International Environment." *Management Accounting,* February 1991, p. 27.

5 "Global Ethics Codes Gain Importance As A Tool To Avoid Litigation and Fines." *The Wall Street Journal,* 19 August 26, 1999, p. A1.

6 Nihal Kaneira. "Canada Sets Ethics for Companies." *Gulf News,* 9 September 1997, p. 26.

7 "IMA Revises SMA 1C, Standards of Ethical Conduct." *Management Accounting,* July 1997, p. 20.

Not all situations involving ethical dilemmas are easy to resolve. Nevertheless, proper focus does help: *Formulating corporate policy should focus on long-run results rather than short-term expediency.* The leadership and attitude of top management coupled with a proactive management style can go a long way toward cultivating a corporate culture in which constructive ideas are accepted, nourished, and given a chance to flourish. A multicriteria performance evaluation system that rewards performance in the areas of cultural sensitivity, innovation, ethical conduct, and a long-run perspective provides the incentives and motivates the managers and other employees to conduct themselves in a manner consistent with corporate policies.

Internal Auditing in the International Environment

As mentioned in an earlier section, international operations add certain practical complexities to the internal auditing function. Fortunately, some of those complexities are decreasing primarily due to three reasons.

1. *Business Practices.* The ever-increasing magnitude and importance of international business has resulted in a greater uniformity in business practices worldwide. Differences in business practices in different parts of the world are not as pronounced as they used to be. For example, written agreements are commonly accepted now in most of those countries where local customs previously dictated otherwise.

2. *Technology.* Advancements in technology such as the Internet and fax machines have alleviated many problems previously posed either by geographic distance or the lack of a well-developed infrastructure within a country. Communication systems are now very efficient and less costly than they were only a few years ago. A country's poor postal system, for example, does not pose as much of a problem now as it did a few years ago.

3. *Currencies.* Some currency-related issues have become relatively simple for a variety of reasons. Examples include adoption of a common currency by many countries (the euro); adoption of another country's currency as the national currency (U.S. dollar's adoption as the national currency in Ecuador and Panama); and stabilization of the national currencies in some countries (Brazil).

Structure of the Internal Audit Organization

The internal audit function is a management function. The management sets organizational policies and establishes a system of internal control that includes the internal audit function. One of the decisions involving the internal audit function is the structure of the internal auditing organization itself. *While selecting an organizational structure for the internal audit function, independence of the internal audit staff should be of paramount concern.* For this reason, internal auditors report directly to either the board of directors, a committee of the top corporate executives, or both in many organizations.

The benefits of any system should outweigh its costs. Even when costs of training a cadre of local professional staff appear to be exorbitant at first glance, the manager should take into account the resultant benefits from such training as well as the costs of an ill-trained internal audit staff that does not possess the necessary skills.

Standardizing the internal control reporting system, to the extent possible, and ensuring that users of the reports have the necessary training to understand and interpret the reports' contents can go a long way toward overcoming many potential problems posed by different languages, different business customs, different accounting principles, and different procedures. Even when detailed records are kept in the local language using local accounting procedures, standardized reports can be quite satisfactory. This can be accomplished with a skilled internal audit staff.

Forms of Internal Audit Organizations

An internal audit organization structure reflects management philosophy, the availability of a qualified staff, and the scope of international operations. We will describe six structures: Centralized structure, decentralized structure, and four hybrid structures.

1. *Centralized.* In this type of structure, there is only one central internal audit organization located at the parent company headquarters. The internal auditors travel to various parts of the world where operations are located to perform internal audits, and to perform other functions such as quality control, audit research, liaison with external auditors, training, and technical support.

2. *Decentralized.* Each international operation has its own internal audit organization. Consequently, internal auditors are on locations wherever international operations are located.

3. *Resident staff and regional reviewers.* Work of the resident internal auditors is reviewed by the regional reviewers to ensure uniformity. An independent review from the regional staff also enhances the degree of reliability of the reports.

4. *Regional staff.* The regional staff is responsible for performing internal audits in all of the operations within their region. This model has been gaining popularity among many multinationals.

5. *Resident staff and central reviewers.* The resident internal auditors located on site perform the audit work. Their work is periodically reviewed by the traveling members of the parent company's central internal audit staff.

6. *Resident staff and regional and central reviewers.* The resident staff conducts the internal audits. Regional reviewers, responsible for certain geographical areas, oversee their work to ensure compliance with the parent company policies. The central staff from headquarters makes periodic reviews to ensure reporting uniformity throughout all the regions.

Each of these six models has its strengths and weaknesses. Unless there are only a few small international operations, the centralized organization model would not be feasible. The decentralized model may not be economical, and generally it would not provide adequate reliability and uniformity. The four hybrid models require the parent company management to choose from combinations that require making tradeoffs. There is no one model that is most appropriate for all situations. However, certain guidelines may be helpful in making the choice:

- Because of a familiarity with the local language, culture, business customs, and contacts, the resident staff can usually get the job done more easily when cooperation from outsiders is needed. Confirmation of accounts receivable, for example, would be impossible without cooperation of outsiders (customers).

- Costs of travel to various international locations where operations are located would be substantial for the regional and central staff.

- Travel for performing an internal audit or conducting a review usually causes discomfort and fatigue. This may have an adverse effect on the performance of the traveling internal audit staff. A World Bank research study concluded that business travelers are much more likely to suffer stress-related psychological problems than colleagues who do not travel. The study found that rate was twice for those who made one overseas trip in a year and three times for those who made two or three trips during one year when compared with their colleagues who do not travel.[8] According to Dr. Rosekind, a consultant in California, jet lag can degrade decision-making abilities, communication, and memory between 30 percent and 75 percent.[9]

- Operating people at an international location may not be as trusting of someone who is not permanently at their location.

- The recommendation of a visiting auditor from central headquarters or from a regional office may not be as readily accepted by the local operating managers, again because of lack of trust.

- The local auditor can make recommendations to the local operating managers in a timely manner, thus making it possible for them to take corrective action without any delay.

All of the previous points are interrelated. Monetary costs are not the only relevant factor. Other factors such as stress, jet lag, etc., affect the quality of an internal audit. Quality is related to the knowledge, skill, and expertise of people performing an internal audit as well as their level of alertness. If jet lag or travel-related stress adversely affect an internal auditor's job performance, it should be of concern to the management. *Quality is necessary to achieve reliability and comparability.*

---

8 "Global Business Travelers Suffer More Mental Strain." *Gulf News*, 2 July 1997, p. 24.
9 Wendy Bounds. "A Cure for Jet Lag?" *The Wall Street Journal*, 7 April 2000, p. W16.

A local staff, with reviews by the regional and/or central staff, would be an appropriate structure in most situations. The regional or central staff can be assumed to possess a high level of expertise due to the size of the talent pool available to the parent company. The regional or central staffs' reviews are likely to have some or all of these advantages:

- Greater familiarity with parent company policies and more knowledge about top management's expectations of subsidiary operations because of frequent contacts with headquarters.

- Broad-based experience on different locations and settings that can be of valuable service to local operating managers. They may be able to quickly diagnose a problem and provide a satisfactory solution because of their encounters with similar problems on other locations. In addition, they can share information with local managers about innovations introduced in operations elsewhere.

- Involvement in internal audit reports of many operations can ensure a higher degree of reporting comparability.

- Freedom from undue influence of local operating managers and local controllers tends to make them more objective—thus enhancing the reliability of their reports. Culture plays an important role in the influence that local controllers and managers can have on internal auditors:[10]

> Boeing statistics offer one insight into how flying procedures work in the air. Its safety team has plotted accident rates for countries against various measurements of culture devised by social anthropologists. Two regions where accidents are more frequent than in America or Europe, and where pilot deviation from procedure scores highest as a cause of accidents, are Latin America and Asia. These regions also score high on an anthropological scale, known as the Hoffstede power-distance index, which measures the power relationship between two people as perceived by the weaker. Translated to the flight deck, that means that an Asian or a Latin American co-pilot is wonderfully obedient but less likely than his American or European counterpart to tell his boss that he is about to fly into a mountain—until it is too late. It is a high price to pay for deference.

Internal audit is an integral part of an internal control system. It provides feedback and may result in changing the goals of the parent company, or the expected level of performance from the international operation. It would be erroneous to assume, therefore, that the corrective action always takes place at the local level. It should also be noted that when the central or regional staff is involved in the internal audit, it is a common practice for them to report *both* to the central headquarters and the managers of local operations. By reporting to the local managers, they make it possible for the local managers to take corrective action

---

10 "Air Crashes—But Surely . . ." *The Economist*, 4 June 1994, pp. 86–87.

without any delay. It also fosters a more cooperative attitude on the part of the local managers toward the central or regional internal audit staff. Clearly, the central or regional staff needs to have excellent interpersonal skills, and should display sensitivity toward local managers to avoid conflicts.

Outsourcing

During the last decade, outsourcing certain internal audit activities or the whole internal audit function has been gaining acceptance. All of the Big Five actively market their internal audit services. The advantages cited for outsourcing include gaining specialized expertise, savings on costs, overcoming language barriers, and addressing regulatory and corporate governance concerns.[11]

Foreign Corrupt Practices Act

The **Foreign Corrupt Practices Act (FCPA)** was passed by the U.S. Congress in 1977 and revised in 1988. Although it is a U.S. law, due to its scope, its impact has been felt worldwide. The FCPA has implications both for internal audit and external audit. The act was passed as a result of the discovery by the U.S. Securities and Exchange Commission that hundreds of U.S.-based multinational companies had made illegal or questionable payments to foreign government officials and politicians amounting to hundreds of millions of dollars. These payments were either not recorded or were recorded improperly to conceal their nature.

The scope of the FCPA is quite broad. It makes it illegal for all U.S.-based firms, their affiliates, and agents to bribe government officials *both within the U.S. as well as outside the U.S.* Firms and executives can face criminal and civil prosecution if convicted of violation. The intent of the FCPA is to curb influence peddling. **Influence peddling** involves providing monetary or nonmonetary benefits to a person in a position of authority in exchange for an action by the person that benefits the company—an action that normally would not have been taken without the monetary or nonmonetary benefit. An example of influence peddling is to bribe a government official, who has the authority to award contracts, in exchange for receiving a contract. For example, in 1994 a federal grand jury indicted Lockheed Corporation and two of its executives for fraud and corruption involving a sale of three Lockheed C-130 transport planes to Egypt. U.S. federal authorities claimed that Lockheed illegally paid more than $1 million for securing a $79 million government contract for the company. In 1995, Lockheed pled guilty to violation of the FCPA. The company paid a total of $27.8 million in fines. The U.S. State Department also temporarily barred Lockheed from obtaining export licenses for its aeronautical division's products. A former Lockheed executive, who had been indicted, received an 18-month prison term.

---

11 Deloitte & Touche. "Major Changes Seen in Role of Internal Auditors." *Deloitte & Touche Review*, 5 February 1996, p. 3.

Accounting Implications

The accounting implications of the FCPA include the following provisions.

- *Recordkeeping provisions.* Books, records, and accounting should be accurate reflections of business transactions.
- *Internal control provisions.* All firms must develop and maintain a system of internal control to ensure that:
    - Transactions are executed with management authorization.
    - Transactions are recorded in a manner that permits preparation of financial statements in conformity with generally accepted accounting principles or other applicable standards.
    - Accountability of assets is maintained. Only authorized personnel have access to assets.
    - Recorded accountability of assets is regularly compared with existing assets. In case of discrepancies, appropriate action is taken.

In essence, the FCPA requires that all payments, including improper payments, must be recorded and disclosed. Firms and their executives can face criminal and civil prosecution for either of these violations:

- Company books are not kept properly.
- An adequate system of internal control is not developed and implemented.

Note that although the FCPA prohibits payments for influence peddling, it does not prohibit facilitating payments. **Facilitating payments** are payments made to influence an official to take an action that the official must take anyway. The objective for making a facilitating payment is solely for speeding up the process.

The FCPA applies to both domestic and foreign corporations that are registered under Section 12(b) of the Securities Act of 1934 or that are required to file reports under Section D of that act. Montedisson SpA, an Italy-based company, sold stock on the New York Stock Exchange. It registered its securities under Section 12(b) of the Securities Act of 1934. Montedisson was accused by the U.S. Department of Justice of concealing millions of dollars in payments to Italian politicians. The concealment materially affected the company's financial statements filed with the U.S. Securities and Exchange Commission. In late 1996, the U.S. Department of Justice filed a case against Montedisson for violating the FCPA.

The FCPA has been a major contributor to many recent actions that have upgraded the status of internal auditing. These include:

- Adoption of codes of ethical conduct by many companies and strengthening of pre-existing codes by others.
- Strengthening of internal control systems.
- Increasing the number of outside directors on the board.
- Formation of audit committees.

It is clear that the FCPA has had, and will continue to have, a worldwide impact.

Institute of Internal Auditors

The **Institute of Internal Auditors (IIA)**, established in 1941, is the most influential international organization in the development of internal auditing standards. Based in the U.S., the organization has 60,000 members in more than 100 countries. The IIA has taken a leadership role in the development of the internal auditing profession. IIA's general standard and Code of Ethics are contained in Appendixes 11A and 11B, respectively.

The IIA is the sponsoring organization for the certification program called Certified Internal Auditor (CIA). Besides passing the examination, the candidates must have two years of practical internal auditing experience before certification.

The IIA influences international auditing through participation in the United Nations' internal audit group, called the International Organization of Supreme Audit Institutions, as well as the International Federation of Accountants. The IIA is also involved in cooperative projects with several national and regional audit organizations. One of the regional organizations with which the IIA has a strong alliance is the **European Confederation of Institutes of Internal Auditing**. In November 1999, the IIA issued an exposure draft titled *Code of Ethics*. If promulgated, the exposure draft will revise the current code of ethics. The revised code of ethics requires adherence by all internal auditing professionals. Currently, only adherence is required from members of the IIA and certified internal auditors only. The stated purpose of the IIA's revised code of ethics is to promote an ethical culture in the global profession of internal auditing. Promoting an ethical framework is now the primary mission of the International Ethics Committee of the IIA.

Coordination of Internal Audits with External Audits

Coordination of the internal audit and external audit functions is desirable to ensure that the audit scope is adequate and there is minimal duplication of efforts. The Institute of Internal Auditors specifies that the director of internal auditing should coordinate internal and external audit work. This requires support of the board of directors to achieve effective coordination.[12] The International Federation of Accountants (IFAC) has also addressed the issue. The IFAC requires the external auditor to evaluate the internal audit function when it appears that internal auditing work is relevant to the external audit in specific areas. This assessment of the internal audit function will influence the decision about the extent of using internal auditing work.[13] The standard also contains guidance regarding the procedures that should be considered by the external auditor in evaluating and testing the work of an internal auditor for the purpose of using that work.[14]

---

12 Institute of Internal Auditors. *Codification of Standards for the Professional Practice of Internal Auditing.* Altamonte Springs, Fla.: The Institute of Internal Auditors, 1993, pp. 75–76.

13 International Federation of Accountants. *IFAC Handbook 1999: Technical Pronouncements.* New York: International Federation of Accountants, 1999, pp. 224–225.

14 *Ibid.*, pp. 226–227.

Even though external auditors cannot substitute the work of internal auditors for their own work, the scope of work for an external audit may be affected by internal auditing work. The extent to which this happens depends primarily on the assessment of external auditors regarding the competence and objectivity of internal auditors. All large international public accounting firms have policies on relations with a client's internal auditors. U.S. generally accepted auditing standards permit the external auditors to use the internal auditors for direct assistance on the external audit. In such cases, the U.S. auditing standards require the external auditors to assess the internal auditors' competency and objectivity. When internal auditors provide direct assistance in an external audit, external auditors should supervise and assess the internal auditors' work. The fee reduction for the external auditors is usually substantial when there is a highly regarded internal audit function. Additionally, the external audit may be completed in less time.[15]

Since the internal audit function is an important aspect of an internal control system, an understanding of the internal audit function by external auditors also contributes to their evaluation of the overall internal control system of the client company.

External Auditing

External audits are performed by public accountants. During the audit, external auditors perform the necessary audit procedures to the financial statements and supporting evidence to determine whether the financial statements are in conformity with generally accepted accounting standards. If the auditor's opinion states that the statements conform to the standards, it lends credibility to the representations contained in the financial statements. The external auditor's opinion is especially important for the parent company, investors, and creditors. The parent company can rely on the financial statements of international operations for preparing the consolidated financial statements and for internal decision making. The investors and creditors use financial statements audited by the external auditors to make their decisions. It is critical for a multinational company to make its audited financial statements available to regulatory agencies, investors, creditors, and security analysts for the purposes of listing its securities on international securities markets and for actively participating in international capital markets.

External Audit Objective

The basic objective of the external audit is the same in all countries—to determine if the financial statements are properly prepared. The external auditors audit financial statements and supporting evidence by applying the auditing stan-

---

15 Alvin A. Arens and James K. Loebbecke. *Auditing: An Integrated Approach*, 8th ed. Upper Saddle River, N.J.: Prentice-Hall, 2000, p. 794.

dards. *Though the objective is the same, external audits are performed differently in different countries since accounting standards as well as auditing standards differ from country to country.*

Accounting Standards

A prerequisite for conducting an external audit is that the external auditor must be knowledgeable of a country's accounting standards and also possess the expertise in their application. As we discussed in Chapter 1, accounting standards differ worldwide. Therefore, financial statements prepared in conformity with the accounting standards of one country are not comparable to financial statements prepared in accordance with the accounting standards of another country. For example, in some countries plant assets can be written-up subsequent to their acquisition, a practice that is not acceptable in other countries. The representations made by the financial statements in conformity with different accounting standards require different auditing standards and procedures.

Auditing Standards

The auditing standard-setting process differs from country to country. In some countries, auditing standards are set by the public accounting profession. In other countries, auditing standards are based on government requirements as mandated in the countries' laws and regulations. Then there are countries where both the public accounting profession and the government participate in the auditing standard-setting process.

In countries where statutory audit requirements exist, e.g., Germany, the purpose of the external audit is primarily to ensure that the financial records are kept and the financial statements are prepared according to legal requirements. In countries where the public accounting profession assumes the primary responsibility to set auditing standards, e.g., the United States, an external audit is conducted using generally accepted auditing standards. In such cases, auditing standards are set by the profession to determine whether the financial statements are in conformity with generally accepted accounting principles.

Regardless of who sets auditing standards, the standards and audit procedure requirements vary from country to country. For example, independent confirmation of accounts receivable and physical observation of inventory are required in some countries, while such requirements do not exist in other countries.

External Auditing in the International Environment

As we discussed in the last section, the objective of an external audit is the same throughout the world—to determine the conformity of financial statements to applicable accounting standards. As we noted earlier, accounting standards as well as auditing standards differ from country to country. These factors add extra dimensions to the audits conducted in an international setting.

For a multinational company with operations in many different parts of the world, it is not usually feasible to send external auditors from the base country to each of the locations of international operations for several reasons:

- Geographic distance makes travel costly and usually has an adverse effect on the performance of the auditor due to unfamiliar surroundings, fatigue, jet lag, and travel-related stress.

- Thorough knowledge of applicable accounting standards and the expertise in auditing standards of a country can only be acquired through training and practical experience in that country.

- In many countries, legal requirements have a direct and significant impact on the external audit. This requires an orientation that is different from the orientation in countries with few legal implications for an external audit.

- Business customs differ among countries. Familiarity with business customs of a country may be necessary to collect and test the supporting evidence for successfully completing the audit.

The previous points favor using an external auditor who practices in the country where an international operation is located. However, there is a need to have a coordination mechanism with the parent company. The quality of an external audit in an international setting depends heavily on the qualifications of an external auditor.

Qualifications

Education, experience, and certification requirements for external auditors vary in different parts of the world. For example, in some countries, an external auditor is not required to have any formal education and training in the audit function. This is especially the case in several countries with statutory audit requirements. Coordination is necessary to ensure that the qualifications of the external auditor are satisfactory to meet the parent company's needs for reliable information.

Fortunately, the problem is not as serious as it may appear. In this age of global capital markets, advanced communication systems, and sophisticated information technology, large as well as small multinational firms can rely on the expertise of public accounting firms that have the capability to perform external audits in all parts of the world. An obvious example is the "Big Five" accounting firms. The **Big Five** include Andersen, KPMG Peat Marwick, Deloitte Touche Tohmatsu, Ernst & Young, and PricewaterhouseCoopers. Each of these firms has offices throughout the world. In the countries where these firms do not have offices, they have "representative," "correspondent," or "associated" firms. The **representative, correspondent,** or **associated firms** are locally owned accounting firms. They have a common code of ethics and audit practice guidelines with the Big Five firms. This ensures a high degree of uniformity and mutual reliance. It would be erroneous, however, to assume that the Big Five are the only players in the international audit arena. Many small- and medium-size firms also have become involved in international auditing by having a correspondent relationship with local firms in other countries.

External Auditor's Report

The external auditor's report, often simply referred to as the auditor's report, communicates the results of the external audit. The format of the report is necessarily mandated by the nature of the audit. Since there are no worldwide uniform accounting and auditing standards, there is no worldwide uniform format of an auditor's report. In this section we will briefly discuss salient features of the standard format of an auditor's report in France, Germany, Japan, the Netherlands, and the U.S. Examples of these reports are presented in Exhibits 11.2 through 11.6.

The auditor's report for Renault, a France-based conglomerate, is presented in Exhibit 11.2. Examples of the auditor's report for two other well-known multinationals, Germany-based Volkswagen, and Japan-based Toyota, are contained in Exhibits 11.3 and 11.4 (pages 440 and 441). Volkswagen's report makes specific reference to the German commercial law and to professional standards.

The auditor's report for Philips Electronics N.V., in Exhibit 11.5 (page 442), states that financial statements comply with the Netherlands Civil Code and generally accepted accounting principles. Volkswagen and Philips are interesting examples for the reason that accounting standards promulgated by both the accounting profession and the government are applicable.

Finally, Exhibit 11.6 (page 443) displays the standard auditor's report in the U.S. The report states whether the financial statements are in accordance with generally accepted accounting principles. It is required that the title of the report

exhibit 11.2 **Auditor's Report: France**

Auditor's Report on the Consolidated Financial Statements
Year ended December 31, 1998

Pursuant to the mandate entrusted to us by your Annual Shareholders' Meeting, we have audited the accompanying consolidated financial statements of Renault for the fiscal year ended on December 31, 1998.

These consolidated financial statements have been approved by the Board of Directors. Our role is to express an opinion on these financial statements based on our audit.

We conducted our audit in accordance with professional standards. Those standards require that we plan and perform the audit so as to obtain a reasonable assurance that the annual accounts are free of material misstatement. An audit involves examining, on a test basis, evidence supporting the amounts and disclosures in the financial statements. It also involves assessing the accounting principles used and significant estimates made by management, as well as evaluating the overall presentation of the financial statements. We believe that our audit provides a reasonable basis for our opinion expressed below.

In our opinion, the consolidated financial statements give a true and fair view of the financial position and the assets and liabilities of the Group as at December 31, 1998, and results of its financial operations for the fiscal year then ended.

We have also verified the Group financial information provided in the Group management report.

We have no comments to make as to the fair presentation of this information nor its consistency with the consolidated financial statements.

Paris, March 16, 1999

The Auditors

DELOITTE TOUCHE TOHMATSU   ERNST & YOUNG, Audit

Olivier AZIERES   Dominique THOUVENIN

Source: Renault Group. *Annual Report 1998.* Paris, 1998, p. 48.

exhibit 11.3 Auditor's Report: Germany

Independent auditors' report

On conclusion of our audit, we are able to issue the following unqualified certification:

"We have audited the consolidated financial statements and the accompanying Group Management Report of VOLKSWAGEN AG, Wolfsburg, for the fiscal year ending December 31, 1998. The preparation of consolidated financial statements and a Group Management Report in accordance with German commercial law is the duty of the Board of Management of the Company. It is our duty, based on the audit conducted by us, to give an appraisal of the consolidated financial statements and the Group Management Report.

We conducted our audit of the financial statements in accordance with section 317 of the German Commercial Code, with due regard to the accounting principles laid down by the German Institute of Auditors (IDW). These stipulate that the audit shall be planned and executed in such a way that an assessment can be made, with sufficient certainty, as to whether the consolidated financial statements and the accompanying Group Management Report are free of significant defects. As part of the audit, the financial statements and the information presented in the Management Report are verified on the basis of random checks. The audit comprises an assessment of the individual companies' financial statements included in the consolidated financial statements, of the defined scope of consolidation, of the accounting and consolidation principles applied, and of significant estimates made by the Board of Management, as well as giving an appreciation of the overall presentation of the consolidated financial statements and Group Management Report. We are of the opinion that our audit forms an adequately sound basis for our appraisal.

Our audit gave rise to no objections.

In our view, with due regard to the generally accepted accounting principles, the consolidated financial statements give a true and fair view of the Group's assets, liabilities, financial position and profit or loss. The Group Management Report gives a generally accurate presentation of the position of the Group, and accurately sets out the risks of future developments."

Hanover, February 26, 1999

C&L Deutsche Revision
Aktiengesellschaft
Wirtschaftsprüfungsgesellschaft

Eichner   Dr. Heine
Wirtschaftsprüfer   Wirtschaftsprüfer

Source: Volkswagen AG. *Annual Report 1998.* Wolfsburg, Germany, 1999, p. 95.

---

includes the word *independent*. The standard report consists of three paragraphs covering introduction, scope, and opinion.[16]

- The *introduction* paragraph delineates the responsibilities for the financial statements between management and the external auditor. The auditor audits the financial statements, but they remain management's responsibility.

- The *scope* paragraph summarizes the essential aspects of an audit. It states that the audit was conducted in accordance with generally accepted auditing standards, and explicitly spells out an auditor's objective: to be reasonably satisfied that the financial statements have been prepared without material error.

---

16 *An Analysis of the New Auditor's Report.* New York: Touche Ross, 1988, pp. 2–3.

exhibit 11.4 Auditor's Report: Japan

REPORT OF INDEPENDENT PUBLIC ACCOUNTANTS

To the Board of Directors of Toyota Motor Corporation:

We have examined the consolidated balance sheets of Toyota Motor Corporation and its consolidated subsidiaries as of March 31, 1998 and 1997, and the related consolidated statements of income, shareholders' equity, and cash flows for each of the three fiscal years in the period ended March 31, 1998, expressed in yen. Our examinations were made in accordance with generally accepted auditing standards in Japan and, accordingly, included such tests of the accounting records and such other auditing procedures as we considered necessary in the circumstances. We did not examine the financial statements of certain consolidated subsidiaries for the fiscal years ended March 31, 1998, 1997, and 1996. Nor did we examine the financial statements of some affiliates, the investments in which are accounted for under the equity method of accounting for 1998, 1997, and 1996, or of one unconsolidated subsidiary, the investment in which is accounted for under the equity method of accounting for 1998. The statements of those consolidated subsidiaries and those affiliates and unconsolidated subsidiary were examined by other auditors whose reports have been furnished to us. Our opinion expressed here, inasmuch as it relates to the amounts included for those subsidiaries and affiliates, is based solely on the reports of the other auditors.

In our opinion, based on our examinations and the reports of other auditors, the aforementioned consolidated financial statements, expressed in yen, present fairly the financial position of Toyota Motor Corporation and its consolidated subsidiaries at March 31, 1998 and 1997, and the results of their operations and their cash flows for each of the three fiscal years in the period ended March 31, 1998, in conformity with generally accepted accounting principles in Japan, which have been applied on a consistent basis, except in regard to the changes in accounting procedures, with which we concur, described in Note 12 to the consolidated financial statements.

Our examinations also covered the translation of Japanese yen amounts into the United States dollar amounts included in the consolidated financial statements. In our opinion, that translation has been made in conformity with the basis stated in Note 1 to the consolidated financial statements. The United States dollar amounts are presented solely for the convenience of readers outside Japan.

Nagoya, Japan
June 25, 1998

Itoh Audit Corporation

Source: Toyota. *Annual Report 1998.* Nagoya, Japan, 1998, p. 45.

- The *opinion* paragraph indicates whether financial statements "present fairly in all material respects the financial position, results of operations, and cash flows in conformity with generally accepted accounting principles."

In contrast to the auditor's reports in Germany and France, the auditor's reports in Japan, the Netherlands, and the U.S. do not refer to the management report.

True and Fair View Versus Present Fairly

True and Fair View

The true and fair view (TFV) concept was briefly discussed in Chapter 6. The concept has been adopted in the *Fourth Directive* of the EU and in the corresponding commercial laws of the U.K., France, and Germany. Auditors' reports in Exhibit 11.2 (Renault) and Exhibit 11.3 (Volkswagen) specifically mention the term in the opinion paragraph. In spite of the common terminology, differences in its meaning exist from country to country. According to David Alexander,

exhibit 11.5 Auditor's Report: Netherlands

Auditors' report

Introduction

We have audited the 1998 financial statements of Koninklijke Philips electronics N.V. These financial statements are the responsibility of the Company's management. Our responsibility is to express an opinion on these financial statements based on our audit.

Scope

We conducted our audit in accordance with generally accepted auditing standards. Those standards require that we plan and perform the audit to obtain reasonable assurance about whether the financial statements are free of material misstatement. An audit includes examining, on a test basis, evidence supporting the amounts and disclosures in the financial statements. An audit also includes assessing the accounting principles used and significant estimates made by management, as well as evaluating the overall financial statement presentation. We believe that our audit provides a reasonable basis for our opinion.

Opinion

In our opinion, the financial statements present fairly, in all material respects, the financial position of the Company as of December 31, 1998 and of the results of its operations for the year then ended in accordance with accounting principles generally accepted in the Netherlands and comply with the financial reporting requirements included in part 9, Book 2 of the Netherlands Civil Code.

Eindhoven, February 9, 1999

KPMG Accountants N.V.

Source: Phillips Electronics. *Annual Report 1998.* Eindhoven, Netherlands, 1999, p. 134.

"countries are tending to interpret TFV in the context of national culture, national accounting tradition, and national GAAP."[17] It is interesting to note that there is no consensus on the operational definition of TFV. Alexander suggests, "In most situations TFV will work indirectly through influence on accounting and reporting regulation. This requires proper and sensible regulation prepared with rigour and intellectual honesty." He concludes, "The way forward, with TFV as with financial reporting as a whole, is through increasing conceptually based understanding of what financial statements are trying to do and how they can best do it, coupled with exploration and education of actions and attitudes across Europe and beyond."[18]

Present Fairly

The American Institute of Certified Public Accountants' Statement on Auditing Standards No. 69 explains the meaning of the phrase "present fairly" as used in the independent auditor's report. According to the standard, the independent auditor's judgment concerning the "fairness" of the overall presentation of financial statements should be applied *within the framework of generally accepted ac-*

---

17 David Alexander. "A European True and Fair View?" *The European Accounting Review,* 1, 1993, p. 59.

18 *Ibid.,* p. 75.

exhibit 11.6 Auditor's Report: United States

Report of Independent Auditors

To the Board of Directors of Unisys Corporation

We have audited the accompanying consolidated balance sheets of Unisys Corporation at December 31, 1999 and 1998, and the related consolidated statements of income, stockholders' equity and cash flows for each of the three years in the period ended December 31, 1999. These financial statements are the responsibility of Unisys Corporation's management. Our responsibility is to express an opinion on these financial statements based on our audits.

We conducted our audits in accordance with auditing standards generally accepted in the United States. Those standards require that we plan and perform the audit to obtain reasonable assurance about whether the financial statements are free of material misstatement. An audit includes examining, on a test basis, evidence supporting the amounts and disclosures in the financial statements. An audit also includes assessing the accounting principles used and significant estimates made by management, as well as evaluating the overall financial statement presentation. We believe that our audits provide a reasonable basis for our opinion.

In our opinion, the financial statements referred to above present fairly, in all material respects, the consolidated financial position of Unisys Corporation at December 31, 1999 and 1998, and the consolidated results of its operations and its cash flows for each of the three years in the period ended December 31, 1999, in conformity with accounting principles generally accepted in the United States.

As described in Note 5 to the consolidated financial statements, effective December 31, 1997, Unisys Corporation changed its method of accounting for the measurement of goodwill impairment.

Ernst & Young LLP

Philadelphia, Pennsylvania

January 18, 2000

Source: Unisys Corporation. *1999 Annual Report.* Philadelphia, Penn., 1999, p. 60.

---

counting principles. The auditor's opinion that financial statements present fairly an entity's financial position, results of operations, and cash flows in conformity with generally accepted accounting principles should be based on the auditor's judgment on the following issues:[19]

- The accounting principles selected and applied have general acceptance.

- The accounting principles are appropriate in the circumstances.

- The financial statements, including the related notes, are informative of matters that may affect their use, understanding, and interpretation.

- The information presented in the financial statements is classified and summarized in a reasonable manner.

- The financial statements reflect the underlying transactions and events in a manner that presents the financial position, results of operations, and cash flows within a range of acceptable limits.

---

19 American Institute of Certified Public Accountants. *Codification of Statements on Auditing Standards.* Chicago, Ill.: Commerce Clearing House, Inc., 1995, pp. 313–314.

The reporting standard further states that generally accepted accounting principles recognize the importance of reporting transactions and events in accordance with their substance. In other words, substance overrides form.

Exhibit 11.7, containing the auditors' report for U.K.-based ICI, is somewhat unusual. It has two opinion paragraphs, one for the U.K. and another for the U.S. It is noteworthy that for the U.K. opinion the term true and fair view is used; the U.S. opinion instead contains the term present fairly. Interestingly, the U.K. opinion paragraph refers to the Companies Act 1985, while the U.S. paragraph refers to the generally accepted accounting principles in the U.K. The following paragraph in the report contains the information that the U.K. GAAP differs in certain significant respects from the U.S. GAAP.

Independent Auditing Environment in Selected Countries

In this section, we will look at auditing practices in five countries and observe some notable trends.

Brazil

Public companies and financial institutions are required to publish financial statements audited by independent auditors registered with the Securities Commission. The required annual financial statements include a balance sheet, an income statement (profit and loss accounts), a statement of retained earnings, a statement of changes in financial position, a statement of sources and use of funds, and notes to the financial statements. The board of directors of a company selects independent auditors. The Corporate Law requires that the financial statements must be published within a specified time range before the general annual meeting of shareholders.

An independent auditor's qualifications in Brazil include membership in a professional organization in Brazil. This means meeting education and practical experience requirements for admission as a member of the professional organization.

Auditing standards in Brazil are set primarily by the Federal Council for Accounting. On a smaller scale, the Brazilian Institute of Accountants and the Securities Commission are also involved in the auditing standard-setting process. The Brazilian Institute of Accountants is a member of the International Federation of Accountants. Its auditing pronouncements generally conform to the IFAC guidelines.[20]

Germany

The German Commercial Code requires a statutory audit of the annual financial statements of all companies (except very small companies specified in the code). The financial statements required by law are the balance sheet, the income state-

---

20 Deloitte Touche Tohmatsu. *Brazil: International Tax and Business Guide.* New York: Deloitte Touche Tohmatsu International, 1997, pp. 45–49.

Exhibit 11.7 ICI Auditor's Report

**Auditor's report on the financial statements
to the Members of Imperial Chemical Industries PLC**

We have audited the financial statements on pages 48 to 100.

Respective responsibilities of Directors and Auditor

The Directors are responsible for preparing the Annual Report, including as described on page 45 the financial statements. Our responsibility to form an independent opinion on the financial statements, based on our audit, is described on page 45, together with our other associated responsibilities.

Basis of opinion

We conducted our audit in accordance with auditing standards generally accepted in the United Kingdom and in the United States. An audit includes examination, on a test basis, of evidence relevant to the amounts and disclosures in the financial statements. It also includes an assessment of the significant estimates and judgements made by the Directors in the preparation of the financial statements, and of whether the accounting policies are appropriate to the Group's circumstances, consistently applied and adequately disclosed.

We planned and performed our audit so as to obtain all the information and explanations which we considered necessary in order to provide us with sufficient evidence to give reasonable assurance that the financial statements are free from material misstatement, whether caused by fraud or other irregularity or error. In forming our opinion we also evaluated the overall presentation of information in the financial statements. We believe that our audit provides a reasonable basis for our opinion.

United Kingdom opinion

In our opinion the financial statements give a true and fair view of the state of affairs of the Company and the Group as at 31 December 1998 and of the profit of the Group for the year then ended and have been properly prepared in accordance with the Companies Act 1985.

United States opinion

In our opinion, the consolidated financial statements present fairly, in all material respects, the financial position of the Group at 31 December 1998 and 1997 and the results of its operations and cash flows for each of the years in the three-year period ended 31 December 1998, in conformity with generally accepted accounting principles in the United Kingdom.

Generally accepted accounting principles in the United Kingdom vary in certain significant respects from generally accepted accounting principles in the United States. Application of generally accepted accounting principles in the United States would have affected results of operations for each of the years in the three-year period ended 31 December 1998 and consolidated shareholders' equity at 31 December 1998 and 1997, to the extent summarised in note 43 to the consolidated financial statements.

KPMG Audit Plc
Chartered Accountants
Registered Auditor
London
10 February 1999

ment, and notes. All corporations listed on the stock exchange regardless of size are required to be audited. EU accounting and audit regulations are incorporated into German law.

Auditors are appointed by shareholders each year. The auditor conducting a statutory audit, whether an individual or a firm, must hold German professional qualifications. Statutory auditors must be independent of the client. They must not own shares in the companies they audit and may not be employees or members of the board of directors.

There are two professional organizations for auditors: the Chamber of Certified Public Accountants and the Institute of Public Accountants. Auditors are required by statutes to be members of the Chamber of Certified Public Accountants, which specifies duties and professional ethics requirements (to a large extent) of public accountants. The Institute of Public Accountants issues recommendations on audit standards within the legal framework. Compliance with the IFAC audit guidelines depends on whether they are incorporated in German audit standards.

The German Commercial Code requires the independent auditors to report whether the financial statements comply with legal provisions, give a *true and fair view* of financial position and results of operations, and are in conformity with required accounting standards that are incorporated in German law. Since German auditors are required to conduct a full-scope audit, an extensive information base of the audit client's operating environment and accounting system is accumulated.[21]

Japan

The Commercial Code requires stockholders of all corporations to elect statutory auditors. In addition, large corporations (discussed later) and corporations subject to the Securities and Exchange Law must appoint an independent auditor. The Commercial Code requires four basic financial statements: the balance sheet, income statement, business report, and proposal for appropriations of retained earnings. The business report covers a multitude of informational items such as a description of the business, important data for more than the past three years, names of directors and statutory auditors, names of major stockholders and their equity percentages, and names of major lenders, to name a few. The proposal for appropriations of retained earnings is prepared for approval by shareholders at the annual meeting. The appropriations proposed are for dividend payments and bonuses for directors and statutory auditors.

Statutory Auditors   There are no established professional qualifications for statutory auditors, and typically they are not professional accountants. The statutory auditor expresses an opinion as to whether the performance of the company's directors is in conformity with requirements of the Commercial Code. A statutory auditor may receive a portion of the corporation's profits as a bonus. Though usually not independent, the statutory auditor cannot be an employee or a director of the corporation.

Large Corporations   Large corporations (defined in terms of the size of share capital or total liabilities) must have a board of statutory auditors with at least three statutory auditors. Financial statements of every large corporation are sub-

21 Price Waterhouse. *Doing Business In Germany: Information Guide.* New York: Price Waterhouse, 1996, pp. 90–94.

ject to both an independent audit and a statutory audit. Statutory auditors of large corporations must report on the appropriateness of the financial statements and express an opinion on the independent auditor's report.

Independent Auditors   Independent auditors are either Japanese CPAs or an audit corporation. The Securities and Exchange Law and the Commercial Code have different requirements regarding the professional duties of independent auditors.

- The Securities and Exchange Law requires an independent auditor to express an opinion as to whether the financial statements are a fair representation of the financial position and results of operations of the company.

- The Commercial Code requires that the independent auditor express an opinion as to whether financial statements are in compliance with the Commercial Code and the company's articles of incorporation.

The appointment procedures prescribed for independent auditors differ between the Commercial Code and the Securities and Exchange Law.

- For Commercial Code purposes, the appointment is in two steps. First, the candidates for appointment are approved by the statutory auditors. Subsequently, shareholders appoint the independent auditors.

- Under the Securities and Exchange Law, the independent auditors are appointed by the board of directors. They are initially appointed for a one-year term but are eligible for automatic reappointment.

The independent auditors of a corporation submit their report on financial statements to the statutory auditors. The statutory auditors present their report to the board of directors. Guidelines for submission of reports from one level to the next include a specified time frame that varies according to the size of the corporation.

Auditing Profession   The Japanese Institute of Certified Public Accountants (JICPA) is the only professional accounting and auditing organization in Japan. Its Audit Committee is involved in establishing professional standards and standards for ethics. There are relatively few Certified Public Accountants in Japan when compared with other industrialized countries. This is attributable to rigorous examination standards and experience requirements.

Auditing standards are incorporated into Japanese law. Therefore, the degree of consistency of Japanese audit standards with the IFAC standards depends on the extent to which the IFAC standards are incorporated into laws. The financial statements subject to independent audit are the balance sheet and the income statement. The corporations that are subject to the Securities and Exchange Law, financial statements of the parent company, as well as the consolidated financial statements receive independent audit.[22]

22 Deloitte Touche Tohmatsu. *Japan: International Tax and Business Guide.* New York: Deloitte Touche Tohmatsu International, 1997, pp. 41–51.

The Japanese Institute of Certified Public Accountants and the Japan Federation of Economic Organizations are leading the efforts for formation of a private organization that will spearhead the development of Japanese accounting standards.

By establishing a private organization independent of the political sphere, The Japanese Institute of Certified Public Accountants and the Japan Federation of Economic Organizations aim to increase the transparency of the standard-setting process to boost international confidence in Japan's accounting standards.

The Finance Ministry has agreed in principle to transfer its authority in this area to the new entity. The new entity will be structured as a foundation that will draw members from the business community, the accounting profession, academia, and security dealers.

The Netherlands

Financial statements of all companies except qualifying small companies require statutory audit by independent auditors appointed by shareholders in a general meeting. The required financial statements are the balance sheet, the income statement, and notes to the financial statements. Large companies (according to the specified criteria) must also prepare a cash flow statement. The required annual financial statements are on two bases: a parent company only basis and the consolidated basis.

Legally, the only enforceable provisions dealing with accounting and auditing are those from the Civil Code. Therefore, both the EU Fourth Directive and EU Seventh Directive have been incorporated in the Civil Code. Though auditing rules come from the Civil Code, the auditing profession is self-regulated. Independent audits are performed by the registered accountants. Registered accountants must be members of the Royal Netherlands Institute of Registered Accountants. An auditor must be independent of the client company to be audited. This means not having any financial interest in the company.

In addition to an opinion on the financial statements, the independent auditor is required to ascertain whether the directors' report meets the legal requirements and is consistent with the financial statements. Independent auditors are also required to determine if all of the required disclosures have been made. The disclosure requirements in the Netherlands depend on the size of the company.

There is no explicit requirement for Dutch auditors to follow the IFAC guidelines. However, the Royal Netherlands Institute of Registered Accountants is a member of the IFAC and has issued statements on auditing practice that are largely based on IFAC guidelines. For all practical purposes, IFAC audit standards are complied with in the Netherlands.[23]

---

23 Deloitte Touche Tohmatsu. *Netherlands: International Tax and Business Guide.* New York: Deloitte Touche Tohmatsu International, 1998, pp. 58–59.

United States

Corporate laws of various states in the U.S. typically do not require appointment of an independent auditor. The Securities and Exchange Commission and the national securities exchanges, however, generally require audited financial statements for filing purposes. Independent auditors are usually appointed by the board of directors of nonpublic companies and by stockholders' approval for public companies.

Generally accepted auditing standards are issued by the Auditing Standards Board of the American Institute of Certified Public Accountants (AICPA) in the form of *Statements on Auditing Standards* (SASs). The generally accepted auditing standards, presented in Appendix 11C, provide a framework to the independent auditor. Independent auditors are required to comply with these 10 standards *and* all other SASs while performing an audit. Though the standards are formulated by the Auditing Standards Board, their requirements are often influenced directly by the Securities and Exchange Commission and court decisions, and indirectly by pressure from the U.S. Congress. In most material respects, the auditing standards are consistent with IFAC's International Standards on Auditing.

The AICPA *Code of Professional Conduct*, revised in 1999, is presented in Appendix 11D. It requires that certified public accountants must be independent (both in fact and in appearance) of their audit clients. They are required to possess integrity and objectivity. The Securities and Exchange Commission (SEC) has recently been aggressively campaigning that independent auditors should cease to provide most of the consulting services to their audit clients. Of the $30.6 billion revenue the Big Five earned in 1999, 70 percent came from non-audit services, including $14 billion from consulting services.[24] KPMG has filed for a $1 billion initial public offering of KPMG Consulting Inc. KPMG's ownership in KPMG Consulting is expected to be under 20 percent.[25] Ernst & Young has already sold its consulting business. The remaining two of the Big Five, Andersen and Deloitte & Touche, have expressed their vigorous disagreement to the SEC.[26]

Each state has its own board of accountancy to regulate the practice of public accounting within the state. All states have licensing requirements for the practice of public accounting. A public accountant can be licensed without being a member of the AICPA. In almost all states, only licensed certified public accountants (CPAs) can perform independent (external) audits. The annual financial statements filed with the SEC are required to be audited by, and the auditor's report is required to be signed by, licensed certified public accountants. All

---

24 Nanette Byrnes and Mike McNamee. "The SEC Vs. CPAs: Suddenly, It's Hardball." *Business Week*, 22 May 2000, p. 49.

25 Michael Schroeder. "SEC Calls For Rules To Curb Consulting by Auditing Firms." *The Wall Street Journal*, 28 June 2000, p. A4.

26 Raymond Hennessey. "Consulting Unit of KPMG Files $1 Billion IPO." *The Wall Street Journal*, 8 May 2000, p. C21.

state boards of accountancy are state governmental agencies. There is no federal agency that grants licenses to practice public accounting nationwide in the U.S.

Though specific requirements vary from state to state, generally all states require that an individual meet three requirements to become a licensed certified public accountant in the state:

- *Achieve a minimum level of higher education.* Most states require a baccalaureate degree with the equivalent of a major in accounting. Many states require education equivalent to a master's degree.

- *Pass the CPA examination.*

- *Obtain minimum acceptable professional experience.* States vary in their experience requirements—both in type and length. Most states require two to three years of experience in public accounting before a license to practice as a certified public accountant is granted.

Reciprocity among states—allowing a licensed CPA from another state to practice in the state without requiring him or her to obtain a license—depends on the laws of each state.

Independent auditors in the U.S. are required to consider "inherent risk" brought about by economic conditions while planning an audit. *The auditors should include global risks among the risk factors:*[27]

> In the past there has been a tendency to think of the U.S. economy when considering general economic conditions. Today, however, auditors must consider many global economic and financial aspects. Some clients will have operations in foreign countries, other clients will export products to foreign countries, and most clients will compete with goods and services from foreign countries. Thus, such factors as fluctuations in foreign exchange rates, restrictive international trade agreements, and political instability will create audit risks for many U.S. clients. Changes in foreign exchange rates may increase the cost of a client's exports, decrease the cost of competitors' imports, or create losses on repatriation of earnings from some foreign countries. Restrictive international trade agreements may restrict or impose tariffs on imports or exports. Political instability may jeopardize foreign markets. All of these factors create risks that should be considered when planning the audit. For example, the imposition of a tariff on a U.S. product may reduce the export sales of the product and increase the risk of excess inventory. The auditor may plan extended tests of the inventory valuation assertion in this case.

In their reports on financial statements, the U.S. auditors express an opinion as to whether the financial statements present fairly the corporation's financial position, results of operations, and cash flows in accordance with generally accepted accounting principles.

---

27 Donald H. Taylor and G. William Glezen. *Auditing: Integrated Concepts and Procedures*, 6th ed. New York: John Wiley & Sons, Inc., 1994, pp. 299–300.

Report on Financial Statements Prepared for Use in Other Countries   With the internationalization of business, auditors in the U.S. may be appointed to audit and report on financial statements of a U.S. entity that are prepared in conformity with accounting principles of another country, for use outside of the U.S.

If the financial statements (in conformity with generally accepted accounting principles of another country) are prepared for use *only* outside the U.S., the auditor may issue either one of the two forms of report.

1. A U.S.-style report modified to report on the accounting principles of another country.

2. The report form of the other country, whose accounting principles were used for preparation of the financial statements.

Opinions Based on Another Auditor's Report   An independent auditor may report on consolidated or combined financial statements, even if the auditor did not audit every entity in the consolidated or combined group. This happens when the principal auditor does not have an office in the country where the client has significant operations. Let us assume that the U.S.-based parent, Schoenen Company, has three subsidiaries: Sohail Company in Singapore, Younas Company in Pakistan, and Sajid Company in Abu Dhabi. Only Schoenen Company and Younas Company were audited by the principal auditor, while Sohail Company and Sajid Company were audited by local auditing firms. This is shown in Figure 11.2.

The principal auditor must decide whether to refer to other auditors' reports. If the principal auditor decides not to refer to other auditors' reports, there is no modification in the report on financial statements of the consolidated or combined entity. *In such cases, the principal auditor is assuming responsibility for the other auditors' work.*

If the principal auditor decides, instead, to refer to the reports of other auditors, the scope of the work done by the other auditors must be described in the

figure 11.2   Example of Parent and Affiliates Audited by Principal and Other Auditors

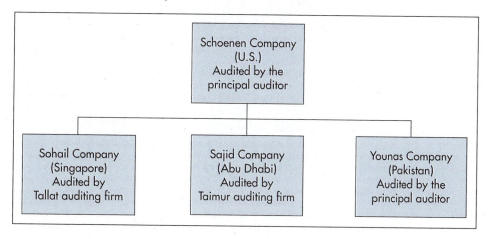

principal auditor's report. *By making reference to other auditors' reports, the principal auditor is indicating the degree of responsibility each auditor is assuming in the report.*

Note: The purpose of reference to other auditors' reports is only to clearly divide the extent of responsibility assumed by each auditor. Such a reference is not considered a qualified opinion.

Audit Considerations for the SEC   The SEC generally finds only unqualified opinions acceptable. Thus companies that file their financial statements with the SEC have the *de facto* requirement of resolving any issues regarding the acceptability of their financial statements.

A CPA firm that has been the auditor for an SEC registrant and either has resigned, has declined to stand for reelection, or has been dismissed is required to report that fact directly in writing to the former SEC client, with a simultaneous copy sent directly by the firm to the chief accountant of the SEC. This letter must be sent by the end of the fifth business day following the CPA firm's determination that the client-auditor relationship has ended.

Worldwide Harmonization of Auditing Standards

Worldwide harmonization of auditing standards is made difficult by the fact that generally accepted accounting principles are different worldwide. Required qualifications for independent auditors also differ in different parts of the world. Cultural issues related to harmonization have been addressed eloquently by Arthur R. Wyatt.[28]

> We must all come to understand that internationalization is not an effort to remake the professional accounting and auditing world in the image of any one culture. While it is clear that emerging standards in both accounting and auditing reflect the needs of those economies that rely on a diverse source of capital providers, those standards will, it is hoped, emerge as a blending of the best standards found in practice and a rejection of notions tried and found wanting. The fact that the standards that are emerging will require some adjustments to practices found in all societies should be of some comfort to those who fear the process is dominated by a single culture.

Despite all obstacles, there is a clear trend toward worldwide harmonization of auditing standards. *Internationalization of capital markets is the driving force behind this trend.*

There are many organizations attempting to harmonize auditing standards. Three of the most prominent players in this arena are the International Federa-

---

28 American Institute of Certified Public Accountants. "Global Perspectives." *Journal of Accountancy*, January 1993, p. 66.

tion of Accountants (IFAC), the International Organization of Securities Commissions (IOSCO), and the European Union.

International Federation of Accountants

The IFAC is a worldwide organization of national professional accounting organizations. As of August 2000, the IFAC had 153 member bodies in 113 countries representing two million accountants. Member organizations are recognized by law or by consensus in their countries. The IFAC was established in 1977 to promulgate international standards of auditing, ethics, education, and training. In January 1983, the IFAC and the IASC entered an agreement of "mutual commitments" for close cooperation and consultations with each other. Membership in the IFAC automatically includes membership in the IASC. The IFAC has seven standing technical committees, which are briefly described next.

International Auditing Practices

This committee has the responsibility for International Standards on Auditing and on related matters.

Education

The committee issues guidelines on, and standards for, education and training of professional accountants.

Ethics

The committee issues pronouncements on ethics and related issues. The outline of the IFAC's code of ethics is shown in Appendix 11E. The code requires that an auditor have integrity, objectivity, and independence. The independence criterion requires independence in fact and independence in appearance. It contains a confidentiality standard and prohibits disclosure of confidential information acquired during the course of performing professional services unless there is a legal or professional right or duty to disclose.

Financial and Management Accounting

Statements issued by this committee cover the application of accounting concepts for managerial decision making. The statements and studies deal with a variety of management accounting issues. For example, a study issued in October 1992 concluded that higher quality management can result from improvements in management accounting techniques such as just-in-time and executive information systems.[29]

Public Sector

The committee issues accounting and auditing guidelines for the public sector.

---

29 *Impact of Information Technology on the Accountancy Profession.* New York: International Federation of Accountants, October 1992.

Information Technology

This committee considers the impact of technology on the accounting profession.

Compliance

The objective of the committee is to ensure compliance of IFAC requirements by the member organizations.

Exhibits 11.8 and 11.9 contain two examples of actual independent audit reports. In each case, the report states that the audit was conducted in accordance with International Standards on Auditing.

International Organization of Securities Commissions

Membership of this influential organization consists of almost 150 securities regulatory bodies from around the world, including the U.S. Securities and Exchange Commission. The IOSCO is working with the IFAC and the IASC to harmonize international auditing and accounting standards that will meet the needs of global capital markets and the international business community.

exhibit 11.8 Independent Auditor's Report to the Members of The National Bank of Ras al-Khaimah (P.S.C.)

We have audited the accompanying balance sheet of The National Bank of Ras al-Khaimah (P.S.C.) at 31 December 1997 and the related statements of income and cash flows for the year then ended.

Respective responsibilities of directors and auditor

These financial statements are the responsibility of the Directors. Our responsibility is to express an opinion on these financial statements based on our audit.

Basis of opinion

We conducted our audit in accordance with International Standards on Auditing. Those Standards require that we plan and perform the audit to obtain reasonable assurance about whether the financial statements are free of material misstatement. An audit includes examining, on a test basis, evidence supporting the amounts and disclosures in the financial statements. An audit also includes assessing the accounting principles used and significant estimates made by management, as well as evaluating the overall financial statement presentation. We believe that our audit provides a reasonable basis for our opinion.

We obtained all the information and explanations which we considered necessary for the purpose of our audit.

Opinion

In our opinion, the financial statements present fairly, in all material respects, the financial position of The National Bank of Ras al-Khaimah (P.S.C.) at 31 December 1997 and the results of its operations and its cash flows for the year then ended in accordance with International Accounting Standards.

Also, in our opinion, proper books have been maintained by the Bank and the contents of the directors' report relating to the financial statements are in agreement with the books of account. No breach of the UAE Commercial Law of 1984 (as amended) or the Bank's Articles of Association has come to our attention that materially affects the Bank's business or financial position.

Coopers & Lybrand
Chartered Accountants
Dubai, 22 February 1998

exhibit 11.9 Schering AG Consolidated Financial Statements

Auditors' Report

We have audited the Consolidated Financial Statements of Schering Aktiengesellschaft as of December 31, 1998, including the Consolidated Cash Flow Statement. The preparation and the content of the Consolidated Financial Statements are the responsibility of the Company's Board of Executive Directors. Our responsibility is to express an opinion on the Consolidated Financial Statements based on our audit.

We conducted our audit in accordance with International Standards on Auditing as set down by the International Federation of Accountants (IFAC). Those Standards require that we plan and perform the audit of the Consolidated Financial Statements to obtain reasonable assurance about whether the Consolidated Financial Statements are free of material misstatement. An audit of Consolidated Financial Statements includes examining, on a test basis, evidence supporting the amounts and disclosures in the Consolidated Financial Statements. An audit also includes assessing the accounting principles and valuation methods used and significant estimates made by the Board of Executive Directors, as well as evaluating the overall Consolidated Financial Statement presentation. We believe that our audit provides a reasonable basis for our opinion.

In our opinion, the Consolidated Financial Statements including the Consolidated Cash Flow Statement give a true and fair view, in all material respects, of the assets, liabilities, and the financial position of the Group as of December 31, 1998, and of the results of its operations and its cash flows for the financial year and comply with the Standards of the International Accounting Standards Committee (IASC).

The Consolidated Financial Statements of Schering AG also comply with the German Commercial Code, so that we provide the following unqualified opinion:

"The Consolidated Financial Statements, which we have audited in accordance with professional standards, comply with German legal requirements. With due regard to generally accepted accounting principles, the Consolidated Financial Statements give a true and fair view of the assets, liabilities, financial position and the profit of the Group. The Management Report corresponds to the Consolidated Financial Statements."

Berlin, 2 March 1999

**BDO Deutsche Warentreuhand
Aktiengesellschaft**

Wirtschaftsprüfungsgesellschaft
Dyckerhoff   Schulz
Wirtschaftsprüfer   Wirtschaftsprüfer

Source: *Schering Annual Report 1998.* Berlin, Germany, 1999, p. 75.

A major part of IOSCO's efforts is to reduce obstacles to the free flow of capital in the global markets. At its October 1992 conference, the IOSCO approved a resolution to endorse IFAC's International Standards on Auditing (ISAs) as an acceptable basis for use in cross-border offerings and continuous reporting for foreign issuers. The IOSCO declared ISAs to be a comprehensive set of auditing standards, and audits conducted in accordance with them can be relied on by securities regulatory authorities for multinational reporting purposes. The IOSCO has recommended to its members that they take all steps necessary and appropriate in their respective jurisdictions to accept audits conducted in accordance with the IFAC's International Standards on Auditing.[30]

---

30 "IOSCO Endorses IFAC Auditing Standards." *Journal of Accountancy*, February 1993, p. 7.

European Union

The Eighth Directive of the European Union covers various aspects of the qualifications of statutory auditors. Adopted in 1984, the Eighth Directive deals with auditing financial statements of companies in the EU countries, and specifies that they be consistent with EU law. It also deals with statutory audits of consolidated statements. The Directive sets qualifications for the auditors and the firms conducting audits, including education and experience requirements. In addition, the Directive deals with ethical matters such as independence and includes sanction provisions for the cases when audits are not conducted as prescribed by the statute.

Other Organizations

There are many other international and regional organizations working toward the goal of greater harmonization of auditing standards. Those include the United Nations and the OECD. The United Nations Intergovernmental Working Group of Experts on International Standards of Accounting and Reporting, commonly referred to as ISAR, has submitted several recommendations to the IFAC for its consideration.

Appendix 11A

Standards for the Professional Practice of Internal Auditing

Independence   Internal auditors should be independent of the activities they audit.

Organizational status. The organizational status of the internal auditing department should be sufficient to permit the accomplishment of its audit responsibilities.

Objectivity. Internal auditors should be objective in performing audits.

Professional proficiency   Internal audits should be performed with proficiency and due professional care.

The internal auditing department

Supervision. The internal auditing department should provide assurance that internal audits are properly supervised.

Staffing. The internal auditing department should provide assurance that the technical proficiency and educational background of internal auditors are appropriate for the audits to be performed.

Knowledge, skills, and disciplines. The internal auditing department should possess or should obtain the knowledge, skills, and disciplines needed to carry out its audit responsibilities.

Supervision. The internal auditing department should provide assurance that internal audits are properly supervised.

The internal auditor

Compliance with standards of conduct. Internal auditors should comply with professional standards of conduct.

Knowledge, skills, and disciplines. Internal auditors should possess the knowledge, skills, and disciplines essential to the performance of internal audits.

Human relations and communications. Internal auditors should be skilled in dealing with people and in communicating effectively.

Continuing education. Internal auditors should maintain their technical competence through continuing education.

Scope of work The scope of internal auditing should encompass the examination and evaluation of the adequacy and effectiveness of the organization's system of internal control and the quality of performance in carrying out assigned responsibilities.

Reliability and integrity of information. Internal auditors should review the reliability and integrity of financial and operating information and the means used to identify, measure, classify, and report such information.

Compliance with policies, plans, procedures, laws, and regulations. Internal auditors should review the systems established to ensure compliance with those policies, plans, procedures, laws, and regulations that could have a significant impact on operations and reports and should determine whether the organization is in compliance.

Safeguarding assets. Internal auditors should review the means of safeguarding assets and, as appropriate, verify the existence of such assets.

Economical and efficient use of resources. Internal auditors should appraise the economy and efficiency with which resources are employed.

Accomplishment of established objectives and goals for operations or programs. Internal auditors should review operations or programs to ascertain whether results are consistent with established objectives and goals and whether the operations or programs are being carried out as planned.

Performance of audit work Audit work should include planning the audit, examining and evaluating information, communicating results, and following up.

Planning the audit. Internal auditors should plan each audit.

Examining and evaluating information. Internal auditors should collect, analyze, interpret, and document information to support audit results.

Communicating. Internal auditors should report the results of their audit work.

Following up. Internal auditors should follow up to ascertain that appropriate action is taken on reported audit findings.

Management of the internal auditing department The director of internal auditing should properly manage the internal auditing department.

Purpose, authority, and responsibility. The director of internal auditing should have a statement of purpose, authority, and responsibility for the internal auditing department.

Planning. The director of internal auditing should establish plans to carry out the responsibilities of the internal auditing department.

Policies and procedures. The director of internal auditing should provide written policies and procedures to guide the audit staff.

Personnel management and development. The director of internal auditing should establish a program for selecting and developing the human resources of the internal auditing department.

External auditors. The director of internal auditing should coordinate internal and external audit efforts.

Quality assurance. The director of internal auditing should establish and maintain a quality assurance program to evaluate the operations of the internal auditing department.

Source: *Codification of Standards for the Professional Practice of Internal Auditing.* Altamonte Springs, FL: Institute of Internal Auditors, 1993, pp. 5–8.

Appendix 11B

Internal Auditor Code of Ethics

Purpose

A distinguishing mark of a profession is acceptance by its members of responsibility to the interests of those it serves. Members of the Institute of Internal Auditors (Members) and Certified Internal Auditors (CIAs) must maintain high standards of conduct in order to effectively discharge this responsibility. The Institute of Internal Auditors (Institute) adopts this *Code of Ethics* for Members and CIAs.

Applicability

This Code of Ethics is applicable to all Members and CIAs. Membership in The Institute and acceptance of the "Certified Internal Auditor" designation are voluntary actions. By acceptance, Members and CIAs assume an obligation of self-discipline above and beyond the requirements of laws and regulations.

The standards of conduct set forth in this Code of Ethics provide basic principles in the practice of internal auditing. Members and CIAs should realize that their individual judgment is required in the application of these principles.

CIAs shall use the "Certified Internal Auditor" designation with discretion and in a dignified manner, fully aware of what the designation denotes. The designation shall also be used in a manner consistent with all statutory requirements.

Members who are judged by the Board of Directors in The Institute to be in violation of the standards of conduct of the Code of Ethics shall be subject to forfeiture of their membership in The Institute. CIAs who are similarly judged also shall be subject to forfeiture of the "Certified Internal Auditor" designation.

Standards of Conduct

- Members and CIAs shall exercise honesty, objectivity, and diligence in the performance of their duties and responsibilities.

- Members and CIAs shall exhibit loyalty in all matters pertaining to the affairs of their organization or to whomever they may be rendering a service. However, Members and CIAs shall not knowingly be a party to any illegal or improper activity.

- Members and CIAs shall not knowingly engage in acts or activities which are discreditable to the profession of internal auditing or to their organization.

- Members and CIAs shall refrain from entering into any activity which may be in conflict with the interest of their organization or which would prejudice their ability to carry out objectively their duties and responsibilities.

- Members and CIAs shall not accept anything of value from an employee, client, customer, supplier, or business associate of their organization which would impair or be presumed to impair their professional judgment.

- Members and CIAs shall undertake only those services which they can reasonably expect to complete with professional competence.

- Members and CIAs shall adopt suitable means to comply with the *Standards for the Professional Practice of Internal Auditing*.

- Members and CIAs shall be prudent in the use of information acquired in the course of their duties. They shall not use confidential information for any personal gain nor in any manner which would be contrary to law or detrimental to the welfare of their organization.

- Members and CIAs, when reporting on the results of their work, shall reveal all material facts known to them which, if not revealed, could either distort reports or operations under review or conceal unlawful practices.

- Members and CIAs shall continually strive for improvement in their proficiency, and in the effectiveness and quality of their service.

- Members and CIAs, in the practice of their profession, shall be ever mindful of the obligation to maintain the high standards of competence, morality, and dignity promulgated by The Institute. Members shall abide by the Bylaws and uphold the objectives of The Institute.

Source: *Codification of Standards for the Professional Practice of Internal Auditing.* Altamonte Springs, FL: Institute of Internal Auditors, 1993, pp. 93–95.

Appendix 11C

U.S. Generally Accepted Auditing Standards

General Standards

1. The audit is to be performed by a person or persons having adequate technical training and proficiency as an auditor.

2. In all matters relating to the assignment, an independence in mental attitude is to be maintained by the auditor or auditors.

3. Due professional care is to be exercised in the planning and performance of the audit and the preparation of the report.

Standards of Field Work

1. The work is to be adequately planned and assistants, if any, are to be properly supervised.

2. A sufficient understanding of internal control is to be obtained to plan the audit and to determine the nature, timing, and extent of tests to be performed.

3. Sufficient competent evidential matter is to be obtained through inspection, observation, inquiries, and confirmations to afford a reasonable basis for an opinion regarding the financial statements under audit.

Standards of Reporting

1. The report shall state whether the financial statements are presented in accordance with generally accepted accounting principles.

2. The report shall identify those circumstances in which such principles have not been consistently observed in the current period in relation to the preceding period.

3. Informative disclosures in the financial statements are to be regarded as reasonably adequate unless otherwise stated in the report.

4. The report shall either contain an expression of opinion regarding the financial statements, taken as a whole, or an assertion to the effect that an opinion cannot be expressed. When an overall opinion cannot be expressed, the reasons thereof should be stated. In all cases where an auditor's name is associated with financial statements, the report should contain a clear-cut indication of the character of the auditor's work, if any, and the degree of responsibility the auditor is taking.

Source: American Institute of Certified Public Accountants. *Codification of Statements on Auditing Standards.* Chicago: Commerce Clearing House, Inc., 1999.

Appendix 11D

The AICPA Code of Professional Conduct

Section 51—Preamble

.01 Membership in the American Institute of Certified Public Accountants is voluntary. By accepting membership, a certified public accountant assumes an obligation of self-discipline above and beyond the requirements of laws and regulations.

.02 These Principles of the Code of Professional Conduct of the American Institute of Certified Public Accountants express the profession's recognition of its responsibilities to the public, to clients, and to colleagues. They guide members in the performance of their professional responsibilities and express the basic tenets of ethical and professional conduct. The Principles call for an unswerving commitment to honorable behavior even at the sacrifice of personal advantage.

Section 52—Article I: Responsibilities

In carrying out their responsibilities as professionals, members should exercise sensitive professional and moral judgments in all their activities.

.01 As professionals, certified public accountants perform an essential role in society. Consistent with that role, members of the American Institute of Certified Public Accountants have responsibilities to all those who use their professional services. Members also have a continuing responsibility to cooperate with each other to improve the art of accounting, maintain the public's confidence, and carry out the profession's special responsibilities for self-governance. The collective efforts of all members are required to maintain and enhance the traditions of the profession.

Section 53—Article II: The Public Interest

Members should accept the obligation to act in a way that will serve the public interest, honor the public trust, and demonstrate commitment to professionalism.

.01 A distinguishing mark of a profession is acceptance of its responsibility to the public. The accounting profession's public consists of clients, credit grantors, governments, employers, investors, the business and financial community, and others who rely on the objectivity and integrity of certified public accountants to maintain the orderly functioning of commerce. This reliance imposes a public interest responsibility on certified public accountants. The public interest is defined as the collective well being of the community of people and institutions the profession serves.

.02 In discharging their professional responsibilities, members may encounter conflicting pressures from among each of those groups. In resolving those conflicts, members should act with integrity, guided by the precept that when members fulfill their responsibility to the public, clients' and employers' interests are best served.

.03 Those who rely on certified public accountants expect them to discharge their responsibilities with integrity, objectivity, due professional care, and a genuine interest in serving the public. They are expected to provide quality services, enter into fee arrangements, and offer a range of services—all in a manner that demonstrates a level of professionalism consistent with these Principles of the Code of Professional Conduct.

.04 All who accept membership in the American Institute of Certified Public Accountants commit themselves to honor the public trust. In return for the faith that the public reposes in them, members should seek continually to demonstrate their dedication to professional excellence.

Section 54—Article III: Integrity

To maintain and broaden public confidence, members should perform all professional responsibilities with the highest sense of integrity.

.01 Integrity is an element of character fundamental to professional recognition. It is the quality from which the public trust derives and the benchmark against which a member must ultimately test all decisions.

.02 Integrity requires a member to be, among other things, honest and candid within the constraints of client confidentiality. Service and the public trust should not be subordinated to personal gain and advantage. Integrity can accommodate the inadvertent error and the honest difference of opinion; it cannot accommodate deceit or subordination of principle.

.03 Integrity is measured in terms of what is right and just. In the absence of specific rules, standards, or guidance, or in the face of conflicting opinions, a member should test decisions and deeds by asking: "Am I doing what a person of integrity would do? Have I retained my integrity?" Integrity requires a member to observe both the form and the spirit of technical and ethical standards; circumvention of those standards constitutes subordination of judgment.

.04 Integrity also requires a member to observe the principles of objectivity and independence and of due care.

Section 55—Article IV: Objectivity and Independence

A member should maintain objectivity and be free of conflicts of interest in discharging professional responsibilities. A member in public practice should be independent in fact and appearance when providing auditing and other attestation services.

.01 Objectivity is a state of mind, a quality that lends value to a member's services. It is a distinguishing feature of the profession. The principle of objectivity imposes the obligation to be impartial, intellectually honest, and free of conflicts of interest. Independence precludes relationships that may appear to impair a member's objectivity in rendering attestation services.

.02 Members often serve multiple interests in many different capacities and must demonstrate their objectivity in varying circumstances. Members in public practice render attest, tax, and management advisory services. Other members prepare financial statements in the employment of others, perform internal auditing services, and serve in financial and management capacities in industry, education, and government. They also educate and train those who aspire to admission into the profession. Regardless of service or capacity, members should protect the integrity of their work, maintain objectivity, and avoid any subordination of their judgment.

.03 For a member in public practice, the maintenance of objectivity and independence requires a continuing assessment of client relationships and public responsibility. Such a member who provides auditing and other attestation services should be independent in fact and appearance. In providing all other services, a member should maintain objectivity and avoid conflicts of interest.

.04 Although members not in public practice cannot maintain the appearance of independence, they nevertheless have the responsibility to maintain objectivity in rendering professional services. Members employed by others to prepare financial statements or to perform auditing, tax, or consulting services are charged with the same responsibility for objectivity as members in public practice and must be scrupulous in their application of generally accepted accounting principles and candid in all their dealings with members in public practice.

Section 56—Article V: Due Care

A member should observe the profession's technical and ethical standards, strive continually to improve competence and the quality of services, and discharge professional responsibility to the best of the member's ability.

.01 The quest for excellence is the essence of due care. Due care requires a member to discharge professional responsibilities with competence and diligence. It imposes the obligation to perform professional services to the best of a member's ability with concern for the best interest of those for whom the services are performed and consistent with the profession's responsibility to the public.

.02 Competence is derived from a synthesis of education and experience. It begins with a mastery of the common body of knowledge required for designation as a certified public accountant. The maintenance of competence requires a commitment to learning and professional improvement that must continue throughout a member's professional life. It is a member's individual responsibility. In all engagements and in all responsibilities, each member should undertake to achieve a level of competence that will assure that the quality of the member's services meets the high level of professionalism required by these Principles.

.03 Competence represents the attainment and maintenance of a level of understanding and knowledge that enables a member to render services with facility and acumen. It also establishes the limitations of a member's capabilities by dictating that consultation or referral may be required when a professional engagement exceeds the personal competence of a member or a member's firm. Each member is responsible for assessing his or her own competence—of evaluating whether education, experience, and judgment are adequate for the responsibility to be assumed.

.04 Members should be diligent in discharging responsibilities to clients, employers, and the public. Diligence imposes the responsibility to render services promptly and carefully, to be thorough, and to observe applicable technical and ethical standards.

.05 Due care requires a member to plan and supervise adequately any professional activity for which he or she is responsible.

Section 57—Article VI: Scope and Nature of Services

A member in public practice should observe the Principles of the Code of Professional Conduct in determining the scope and nature of services to be provided.

.01 The public interest aspect of certified public accountants' services requires that such services be consistent with acceptable professional behavior for certified public accountants. Integrity requires that service and the public trust not be subordinated to personal gain and advantage. Objectivity and independence require that members be free from conflicts of interest in discharging professional responsibilities. Due care requires that services by provided with competence and diligence.

.02 Each of these Principles should be considered by members in determining whether or not to provide specific services in individual circumstances. In some instances, they may represent an overall constraint on the nonaudit services that might be offered to a specific client. No hard-and-fast rules can be developed to help members reach these judgments, but they must be satisfied that they are meeting the spirit of the Principles in this regard.

.03 In order to accomplish this, members should

- Practice in firms that have in place internal quality-control procedures to ensure that services are competently delivered and adequately supervised.

- Determine, in their individual judgments, whether the scope and nature of other services provided to an audit client would create a conflict of interest in the performance of the audit function for that client.

- Assess, in their individual judgments, whether an activity is consistent with their role as professionals (for example, is such activity a reasonable extension or variation of existing services offered by the member or others in the profession?).

Source: American Institute of Certified Public Accountants Web site http://www.aicpa.org.

Appendix 11E

Outline of IFAC's International Code of Ethics

The code was first issued in 1990 and has been revised several times. The latest revision was made in 1998, which mainly dealt with confidentiality and "low balling" (work accepted at a relatively low fee).

Part A: Applicable to All Professional Accountants

Section 1   Integrity and Objectivity
Section 2   Resolution of Ethical Conflicts
Section 3   Professional Competence
Section 4   Confidentiality
Section 5   Tax Practice
Section 6   Cross-Border Activities
Section 7   Publicity

Part B: Applicable to Professional Accountants in Public Practice

Section 8   Independence
Section 9   Professional Competence and Responsibilities Regarding the Use of Non-Accountants
Section 10   Fees and Commissions
Section 11   Activities Incompatible with the Practice of Public Accountancy
Section 12   Clients' Monies
Section 13   Relations with Other Professional Accountants in Public Practice
Section 14   Advertising and Solicitation

Part C: Applicable to Employed Professional Accountants

Section 15   Conflict of Loyalties
Section 16   Support for Professional Colleagues
Section 17   Professional Competence
Section 18   Presentation of Information

Note to Students

This chapter deals with internal and external auditing issues within the global context. As you have learned from the chapter, both audit functions have been, and will continue to be, influenced by environmental factors.

The public accounting profession is going through some fundamental changes in many countries. The impact is most noticeable on the Big Five in the United States. The situation is still very much in a state of flux.

Internal auditing career opportunities are now available to those employed by public accounting firms, in addition to traditional in-house internal auditing departments. As mentioned in the chapter, many companies are now outsourcing at least some internal auditing activities. Internal auditing is becoming increasingly attractive as a career because of global operations. This career option should not be overlooked by students.

The following Web site addresses can be very valuable in obtaining additional information on the topics covered in this chapter.

http://

American Institute of Certified Public Accountants (also to obtain information on the U.S. CPA examination): **http://www.aicpa.org**

Institute of Internal Auditors: **http://www.theiia.org**

Institute of Management Accountants: **http://www.imanet.org**

Japanese Institute of Certified Public Accountants: **http://www.jicpa.or.jp**

German Institute of Public Accountants: **http://www.wpk.de**

US Brazil Service & Information Network: **http://www.usbrazil.com/**

The World Bank Group: **http://www.worldbank.org**

U.S. National Association of State Boards of Accountancy: **http://www.nasba.org**

U.S. Securities and Exchange Commission: **http://www.sec.gov**

International Federation of Accountants: **http://www.ifac.org**

Canadian Institute of Chartered Accountants: **http://www.cica.ca**

List of CPA Firms: **http://www.cpafirms.com**

Universal Currency Converter (foreign exchange rate conversion): **http://www.xe.net/currency/**

U.S. Central Intelligence Agency (CIA) World Factbook: **http://www.odci.gov/cia/publications/factbook/index.html**

Institute for Global Ethics: **http://www.globalethics.org**

The references at the end of this chapter include many listings to further enrich your understanding of many topics discussed in the chapter. One of the listed items is especially recommended: *The Philosophy of Auditing* by Mautz and

Sharaf. This book is a classic and deals primarily with external auditing. It is concise, enjoyable to read, and intellectually exciting.

Chapter Summary

1. Internal auditing and external auditing share a common objective—to determine the reliability of accounting information.

2. The internal audit is performed to determine whether an organization's policies and procedures are being followed, and whether its assets are safeguarded and used efficiently.

3. Factors contributing to the enhancement of internal auditing include audit committees, technological advances, reliance of external auditors on internal audit reports, and international operations.

4. Policy formulation in different countries should take into account cultural differences, company goals, and business ethics.

5. Top management's attitude and its leadership are critical factors in the cultivation of a healthy corporate culture for the long-term survival of an organization.

6. Internal audit organizations can take various forms. While making a selection, the independence of internal auditors should be the uppermost consideration.

7. The Foreign Corrupt Practices Act, though a U.S. law, has worldwide impact.

8. The Institute of Internal Auditors is the most influential organization in the development of internal auditing standards.

9. The basic objective of the external audit is to determine if the financial statements are properly prepared.

10. External audits are performed differently in different countries because accounting and auditing standards differ among countries.

11. Many public accounting firms, especially the Big Five, provide external audit services throughout the world.

12. The "true and fair view" concept has been adopted in the EU Fourth Directive.

13. "Present fairly," as used in the U.S., requires an independent auditor to use judgment on several issues.

14. Many countries require statutory audits to determine whether the financial statements are in compliance with applicable laws.

15. Many countries have either successfully adopted the IFAC audit standards or have changed national auditing standards to make them consistent with the IFAC standards.

16. The IFAC, the IOSCO, and the EU are among the most prominent organizations attempting to harmonize auditing standards.

Questions for Discussion

1. "The scope of internal auditing is limited to determining the reliability of the financial statement." Do you agree? Explain.

2. What are the two main objectives of internal auditing?

3. Name and discuss at least three global trends in internal auditing.

4. Describe the impact of technological advances on internal auditing.

5. Identify and discuss at least four complexities brought on by international operations in the practice of internal auditing.

6. Discuss the role of ethics in policy formulation.

7. Can company management help set the "right tone" for corporate culture? Explain.

8. What are the two factors that have contributed toward alleviating or eliminating some of the complexities associated with internal auditing of international operations?

9. "The regional or central staff involved in the internal audit of local operations should report to both the central headquarters and the managers of local operations." Do you agree? Explain.

10. Does the FCPA apply to the corporations operating within the U.S. only?

11. Identify and describe the two accounting implications of the FCPA.

12. Is the scope of an external audit affected by the work of internal auditors?

13. State the main reason why external audits are performed differently in different countries.

14. Why is it important to coordinate an external audit of an international operation with the parent company's external auditor?

15. "The true and fair view concept has a common meaning in all the countries where it is applied." Do you agree? Explain.

16. What are the three general requirements to be licensed as a Certified Public Accountant in the U.S.?

17. Name the two most important organizations concerned with the harmonization of auditing standards worldwide.

18. "The scope of the activities of the IFAC is limited to international auditing standards." Do you agree? Explain.

19. (Appendixes) The independence of an independent auditor differs from that of an internal auditor. How?

Exercises/Problems

11-1 The chapter lists six forms of internal audit organization for a multinational operation.

Required:

Describe each of these six forms and provide comments regarding the relative strengths and weaknesses of each.

11-2 In addition to the high level of expertise, four other reasons are provided for the involvement of a regional or central staff in internal auditing of international operations.

Required:

List those reasons in their order of importance (as determined by you), starting with the most important. Give reasons why you chose that listing order.

11-3 The FCPA makes a distinction between two types of payments: Influence peddling, and facilitating.

Required:

Describe each type of payment and give at least two examples of each type.

11-4 Review the auditor's reports shown in Exhibits 11.2 through 11.6.

Required:

Prepare an analysis to compare the reports contained in the five exhibits.

11-5 Prepare a matrix analysis of the external auditing in the five countries discussed in the chapter. The analysis should include, at the minimum, the following:

    a. Scope: What types of companies are required to be audited?

    b. The type of audit(s) required, e.g., independent, statutory, etc.

    c. Qualifications of different types of auditors.

    d. Procedures for appointment of auditors.

    e. Source(s) of generally accepted auditing standards.

    f. National auditing standards' consistency with the IFAC standards: Identical, similar, etc.

11-6 Refer to the previous problem. Make interpretive and evaluative statements based on your analysis for the previous problem.

11-7 Aliya International is a multinational company based in the U.S. It has five subsidiaries, which are listed here with their location:

Subsidiary	Location	Local Independent Auditors?
Rashid Ltd.	London, U.K.	Yes
Diljeet Co.	Jullunder, India	Yes
Amir Co.	Islamabad, Pakistan	Yes
Epstein Corp.	Los Angeles, U.S.	No*
Rabin Co.	Toronto, Canada	No*

*Epstein Corp. and Rabin Co. are audited by the same auditing firm that audits the parent company, Aliya International.

Describe the report options available to the principal auditor of the parent company for expressing an opinion on consolidated financial statements. Specifically include a mention of the responsibility assumed by the principal auditor in each option.

11-8   Reread the quote from Arthur R. Wyatt in the chapter.

Do you agree with Mr. Wyatt's assertions relating to harmonization? Is it possible to reconcile differing needs of different economies with harmonization? Is it possible to harmonize standards without diluting the cultural imprints on the auditing standards of a country? Discuss these issues. Feel free to raise and discuss additional issues relevant to harmonization.

11-9   Select a publication from the references listed at the end of the chapter. Critique the publication in 200 to 300 words.

11-10 Write a 200- to 300-word report on the International Federation of Accountants.

Case 1

Trouble in Paradise—Big Five Stop Making Music Together

For decades the largest of the U.S. public accounting firms always took a united public stand. They used to be a cohesive and, often, a formidable force against any threat to their common interest. This tradition was broken recently. The U.S. Securities and Exchange Commission has raised serious objections against the continuation of providing consulting services by the Big Five (and other auditors) to their audit clients. The articles written by partners from two of the Big Five took opposing positions on the issue.

In an article, James Copeland, CEO of Deloitte & Touche LLP and Deloitte Touche Tohmatsu, wrote:[31]

> The SEC posits that America's accountants have an "independence" problem because companies that perform audits for publicly traded companies also provide non-audit consulting services for some of the same clients. Yet just last month, a panel initiated at the urging of the SEC, and including former SEC commissioners, concluded that the auditing profession is sound. "The Panel is not aware of any instances of non-audit services having caused or contributed to an audit failure or the action loss of auditor independence." In fact, the panel found that in about a quarter of the relevant audits it reviewed, consulting services enhanced audit quality.

---

31 James E. Copeland, Jr. "Accounting Ain't Broke, So Don't Fix It." *The Wall Street Journal*, 25 July 2000.

. . . Yet the proposed rule would lead to the sale of consulting units by the largest professional services firms (it already has in some cases). The irony is that we would then need to contract with "pure" consulting firms to employ their expertise—quite possibly rehiring the same experts to work on the same audits, for the same clients, but without the same degree of oversight. There would be no effective mechanism to monitor and maintain the independence of contractors participating in audit teams, and these contracted experts are less likely to adhere to the same independence rules as partners in public accounting firms. It's hard to imagine public confidence in audits being strengthened under such a scenario.

. . . In short, what the SEC proposes is nothing less than a fundamental restructuring of a profession that for more than a century has provided financial markets and the U.S. economy with the assurances needed for the efficient capital flows that support prosperity.

Scott Hartz, global managing partner for management consulting services at PricewaterhouseCoopers, stated his position in another article:[32]

Meanwhile, the consulting industry has been forced to reinvent itself to meet the demands of the new "e" world. Over the past decade, the Big Five have grown into two very different businesses under one roof—audit and consulting. One side is focused on financial market integrity and investor protection; the other on helping companies succeed by guiding them through complex business transformations. For one, objectivity and independence are crucial; for the other, having a direct interest in clients' success—such as joint product development, alliances and equity participation ("skin in the game")—is critical.

The SEC has recognized the shift and has understandably considered action. But even without the attention of the SEC, it's clear that the current arrangement of consulting businesses within accounting firms can't continue. In February, PricewaterhouseCoopers announced it would split its auditing and consulting businesses.

How can the current model possibly accommodate two businesses with such diverse and conflicting missions? The New Economy has caused a major shift in what and how companies are buying. Meeting these new demands requires a vigorous response.

Required:

(1) What are the major issues raised by Mr. Copeland and Mr. Hartz to augment their respective positions?

(2) Do you see any ethical conflict when auditors provide consulting services to their audit clients? Provide reasons for your answer.

---

32 Scott Hartz. "Audit and Advice Should Split." *The Wall Street Journal*, 15 August 2000, p. A26.

Case 2

The Politics of Mutual Recognition

Daimler-Benz (now DaimlerChrysler) was the first Germany-based multinational to file with the U.S. Securities and Exchange Commission for a listing on the New York Stock Exchange. This occurred in 1993. The reconciliation of Daimler-Benz's income between the U.S. and German GAAP resulted in some interesting numbers. Under German GAAP, Daimler reported income of DM602 million for the year ended December 31, 1993. That income turned into a loss of DM1.839 billion under U.S. GAAP. *The principal differences were that the items under U.S. GAAP were charged against current period income, but under German GAAP had been made to reserves (appropriated against retained earnings) in prior periods.*

The annual congress of the Fédération des Experts Comptables Européens, held in September 1993 in Copenhagen, had a panel discussion. The question posed was "What is the future of mutual recognition of financial statements and is comparability really necessary?" The panelists included Walter Schuetze, Chief Accountant of the SEC; Dr. Herbert Biener, from the German Justice Ministry; and David Cairns, Secretary General of the International Accounting Standards Committee.

Their three different viewpoints were reported in the *European Accounting Review*.[33]

Mr. Schuetze argued:[34]

> I believe that it is, in large part, the SEC's commitment to a financial reporting system with the objective of providing full disclosure to investors that has made the U.S. securities markets attractive for global as well as domestic capital formation. Such transparency must, in my personal view, be a primary ingredient in any standards that are to receive worldwide recognition.

Dr. Biener stated:[35]

> Financial reporting is not an end in itself, but is intended to provide information that is useful in making business and economic decisions and for making choices among alternative uses of scarce resources in the conduct of business and economic activities. In the FASB Statement of Concepts, it is clearly stated that investor-owned business enterprises are the most important category in the USA and that investor-owners are usually more interested in returns from dividends and market-price appreciation of their securities than in active participation in directing corporate affairs. It is obvious that this interest has first priority in devel-

---

33 "The Politics of Mutual Recognition." *European Accounting Review*, vol. 3, no. 2 (1994), pp. 329–352.

34 *Ibid.*, p. 334.

35 *Ibid.*, pp. 339–340.

oping accounting standards in the USA. This may not be so in Continental Europe, where the protection of creditors, shareholders, employees and the enterprise itself seems to have priority. If Continental Europe is not faced with the problem of changing fundamental accounting standards towards Anglo-American objectives, the positive and negative effects on the whole economy and on all interested parties, especially on the decision-making process of managers, shareholders, investors, bankers and other lenders, employees, governments, including tax authorities, and last but not least on the strength of enterprises, should be examined and discussed before any political decisions are made.

Mr. Cairns stated:[36]

International Accounting Standards are developed through an international due process that involves accountants, financial analysts and other users of financial statements, the business community, stock exchanges, regulatory authorities and other interested organizations from around the world. National standard-setting bodies are increasingly involved in that process. International Accounting Standards deal with most of the topics that are important internationally in the presentation of general purpose financial statements.

Required:

Discuss the three viewpoints. Which one is the most acceptable to you? Provide reasons to support your preference.

Case 3

Lustra S.p.A. (Copyright © by the President and Fellows of Harvard College.)[37]

Peter Scala, president of Lustra S.p.A., Naples, Italy, quietly reflected on the contents to a letter he had sent the day before to his company's U.S. certified public accountant (Exhibit 11.16) in response to an earlier letter from the firm's U.S. certified public accountant (Exhibit 11.15). Scala's letter detailed his reaction to a significant accounting controversy that had arisen during the company's preparation for a planned U.S. issuance of its common stock. Of immediate concern to Peter Scala was what strategy he should adopt in reply to the auditor's anticipated response to his letter.

---

36 *Ibid.*, p. 349.

37 Professor David F. Hawkins prepared this case as the basis for class discussion rather than to illustrate either effective or ineffective handling of an administrative situation. Adapted from case materials prepared by D.P. Frolin and J.F. Smith.

Background

Lustra was a distributor and retailer of fashion eyewear. The firm had been founded in 1965 by the late John Scala in Naples, Italy. In 1977, the company went public with an offering of common stock on the Milan Exchange. In 1982, Peter replaced his father as president. In 1987, Lustra opened two retail outlets in New York. From 1965 to 1989, sales and profits had grown steadily each year. Year 1989 proved to be Lustra's best year with profits after tax of over $3.0 million, as shown in Exhibit 11.10.[38]

Financing Activities

Since 1977, Lustra had twice sought significant external financing in Italy to fund the company's expansion. Exhibit 11.11 details the company's capital structure and common stock prices for 1988 and 1989.

In September 1985, a common stock issue with warrants added 200,000 common shares to Lustra's equity base. The warrants, issued one for each common share acquired, permitted the purchase of one additional share of common stock for $10 cash until September 2000.

In June 1989, the company issued subordinated convertible debentures with a face value of $7.2 million, a 9-1/8% coupon rate of interest, and a life of 25 years. Each debenture was convertible after June 1991 into Lustra common stock at a conversion price of $20 per share. Thus, each $1,000 debenture was equivalent to 50 shares of common stock.

The relatively small size of the debenture issue resulted in somewhat limited distribution of the initial offering in a very thin and inactive secondary market. The debentures were offered and sold out on June 29 and the first trade in the over-the-counter secondary market occurred on July 5, as per Exhibit 11.12.

In order to finance the expansion of Lustra's U.S. business, Peter Scala planned to sell Lustra stock in the United States.

exhibit 11.10   Lustra S.p.A.—Financial Information

	1988	1989
Net sales (millions)	$102.3	$108.6
Gross margin (millions)	52.4	53.4
Profit after tax (millions)	3.00	3.05
Earnings per share*	3.00	3.05

*Computations for Italian reporting purposes. Net income divided by average number of common shares outstanding.

---

38 All financial data have been restated to their U.S. dollar equivalent.

exhibit 11.11   Partial Capital Structure and Common Stock Prices

	1988	1989
Common shares outstanding	1,000,000	1,000,000
Warrants outstanding	200,000	200,000
Exercise price $10, expiration date September 2000. Common shares reserved for exercise	200,000	200,000
Convertible debentures 9-1/8%. Face value outstanding maturity date, 2014, conversion price $20.	0	$7,200,000
Common shares reserved for conversion	0	360,000

Common stock price—Milan Exchange*

	1988	1989	Close	Average
First quarter	6-5/8	6-3/4	12-1/4	10
Second quarter	7	7-7/8	17	15-1/4
Third quarter	8-1/8	8-3/4	14-1/2	17-5/8
Fourth quarter	9-7/8	5-5/8	9-3/4	12-1/8
Year	8	13-3/4		

*The stock traded below $10 prior to 1988.

exhibit 11.12   9-1/8% Convertible Debentures

Date	Event	Price	Average Italian Aa Equivalent Corporate Bond Yield
June 29	Issue priced and marked	98	14.25%
July 5	First trade secondary market	97	14.50%

1989 Annual Report

During preparations for the planned U.S. underwriting, Peter Scala was informed by his independent auditors, Peat, Waterhouse & Co., that the 1989 earnings per share computations that he had prepared for Italian financial statement purposes and shown in Exhibit 11.10 were not acceptable under *Accounting Principles Board (APB) Opinion No. 15*. The senior official in charge of the audit indicated that Lustra S.p.A. had failed to include as common stock equivalents the convertible debentures issued in 1989 and the outstanding common stock warrants issued in 1985. The requirements to treat both as common stock equivalents was explained as follows:

- 9-1/8% Convertible Debentures: The effective yield, based on its market price, was less than two-thirds of the then-average Italian equivalent of the Aa corporate bond yield. Thus, the convertible qualifies as a common stock equivalent and must be counted in primary and fully diluted earnings per share on an "as if" converted basis.

- Common Stock Warrants: The market price of the common stock during the year exceeded the exercise price of the warrant, hence, they are dilutive and must be counted as outstanding during the year in the primary and fully diluted earnings per share figures using the "treasury stock" method of calculation.

The audit senior proposed that the earnings per share figures shown in Exhibit 11.13 be published with the financial statements. Supporting calculations for the treasury stock method appear in Exhibit 11.14.

exhibit 11.13   U.S. Auditor's Calculation of Earnings per Share

	Primary Earnings per Share	
	1988	1989
Profit after tax (000s omitted)	$3,000	$ 3,050
Add back after-tax interest savings on convertible debentures (tax rate = 46%)	0	177
Profit after tax (adjusted)	$3,000	$ 3,227
Common shares outstanding (000s omitted)	1,000	1,000
Adjustments:		
Add conversion of debentures	0	180
Add exercise of warrants	0	47.6
Common shares outstanding (adjusted)	1,000	1,227.6
Primary earnings per share	**$ 3.00**	**$ 2.63**

	Fully Diluted Earnings per Share	
	1988	1989
Profit after tax (adjusted; 000s omitted)	$3,000	$ 3,277
Common shares outstanding (000s omitted)	1,000	1,227.6
Add additional shares outstanding upon exercise of warrants based on closing (not average) prices	0	12.6
Common shares outstanding (adjusted)	1,000	1,240.2
Fully diluted earnings per share	**$ 3.00**	**$ 2.60**

exhibit 11.14 **Adjustment to Common Shares Outstanding for Warrants, Using the Treasury Stock Method**

For primary EPS: Using average common stock price.

1988—Antidilutive, no adjustment.

1989—   **(000s omitted)**

Quarter	Exercise	Purchase	Increment
1	200	200	0
2	200	131.1	68.9
3	200	113.5	86.5
4	200	164.9	35.1
Total			190.5
Average			47.6

For fully diluted EPS: Using higher of average or closing quarterly common stock price.

1988—Antidilutive, no adjustment.

1989—   **(000s omitted)**

Quarter	Exercise	Purchase	Increment
1	200	163.3	36.7
2	200	117.6	82.4
3	200	113.5	86.5
4	200	164.9	35.1
Total			240.7
Average			60.2

Additional shares over primary (60.2 − 43.6) = 12.6

Peter Scala's reaction to the audit senior's proposal was initially one of bewilderment, soon replaced by anger. The U.S. rules seem to make no sense.

Peter Scala and his controller discussed the matter at length with Donna Christiansen, audit partner responsible for the Lustra audit. The result was a stalemate—Christiansen maintained that her hands were tied by *APB Opinion No. 15*, and Scala insisted that the rules were arbitrary and unfair and that he would have difficulty abiding by them. The meeting ended on strained terms. In the days following, Scala had several telephone conversations with Ms. Christiansen and with Mr. Mark DuMond, the partner-in-charge of the New York office of Peat, Waterhouse & Co. Three days later, Peter Scala received a letter from Mr. DuMond stating the position that Peat, Waterhouse & Co. intended to maintain in this matter. This letter appears as Exhibit 11.15. On the following day, Peter Scala drafted a reply to Mr. DuMond. This reply is shown in Exhibit 11.16.

Required:

(1) If you were Ms. Christiansen, how would you explain the rationale supporting *APB Opinion No. 15*?

(2) Should Lustra adopt *APB Opinion No. 15* for Italian reporting purposes?

(3) Does it really matter what earnings per share figure Lustra reports? For instance, will the security market be influenced by this figure?

exhibit 11.15   **Auditor's Position Letter to Client**

June 6, 1990

Mr. Peter Scala, President
Lustra S.p.A.
Lustra Building, Via Saicar 551
Naples, Italy

Dear Peter:

This letter is written in follow-up to the telephone conversations that you had with Ms. Donna Christiansen and me earlier today concerning the computation of earnings per common share for the year ended December 31, 1989, for inclusion in your Security and Exchange filing in connection with your forthcoming public offering in the United States.

After giving careful consideration to all factors pertinent to the computation of earnings per common share as outlined in *APB Opinion No. 15*, it is the unanimous opinion of the National Accounting and Auditing Policy Committee of our firm that Lustra's convertible debentures (even though issued in Italy) and the company's warrants must properly be included as common stock equivalents in this computation. The Committee also noted that, even if the convertible debentures were not counted as common stock equivalents, thereby included in the primary earnings per share calculations, they would always be counted as converted in the fully diluted earnings per share calculation. Thus, in any case, the decline in earnings per share from 1988 to 1989 would be published on the face of the income statement.

It is our official position that if the earnings per common share included in the financial statements are not computed in accordance with *APB Opinion No. 15*, we will be unable to issue an unqualified opinion and must indicate that the computation is not within generally accepted accounting principles.

Sincerely,

Mark DuMond
Partner
Peat, Waterhouse & Company

/pbh

exhibit 11.16 **Client's Response to Auditor's Position Letter**

June 9, 1990

Mr. Mark DuMond, Partner
Peat, Waterhouse & Co.
One Lander Street
New York, NY 10021

Dear Mark:

I am very disappointed in the position you and your firm seem to have adopted on Lustra's per-share calculation.

In my opinion, the rules in question are arbitrary at best and they are unfair to Lustra because they present a distorted picture of the current year's operations. I have always believed that it was our obligation to present true and fair financial statements to our shareholders. Consequently, when we have found Italian accounting practices unsatisfactory, we have turned to the International Accounting Standards for our accounting guidance. There is no comparable accounting standard in effect in Italy or in the International Accounting Standards to *APB Opinion No. 15*. I now find it distressing to be forced to issue what I consider to be misleading statements in order to comply with your country's listing requirements.

With regard to the convertible debentures, I believe, inherent in the argument that these securities should be deemed converted to common shares for earnings per share computations is the assumption that conversion is imminent (or at least highly probable) in the foreseeable future. In point of fact, the rational investor will not convert to common shares until such time as the market price of the common exceeds the conversion price of $20 per share. Given the current market price of 9-1/4 and the downward price trend, it would appear that the probability of conversion in the foreseeable future is, in fact, nil. Further, if Lustra's earnings per share are computed as prescribed by *APB Opinion No. 15*, the resulting decrease in earnings per share will likely further depress the market price, thereby even further lessening the probability of conversion.

It is interesting to note that, if what you have identified to be the Italian equivalent of the average Aa corporate bond yield at the issue date of the convertible debenture issue has been slightly lower, your position would reverse; or, if Lustra's debenture interest rate had been slightly higher, your position would reverse. Furthermore, if you would have bothered to check the record, you would also see that, against the average Aa corporate bond yield for the full year, the convertible debenture issue would more than meet the corporate bond yield test and be excluded from the common stock equivalent category.

1989 was a year of interest rate turmoil. Interest rates changed numerous times. Under such conditions it hardly seems appropriate for the accounting treatment for a 25-year debenture to depend on the average interest rate in effect on a particular day, or even during a particular week.

Furthermore, when we sold the convertible debenture, we did not anticipate that one day we would seek financing in U.S. markets. If we had, I can assure you that we would have priced the convertible issue to remove it from the primary-earnings-per-share category. Now, after the fact, to impose this U.S. accounting rule on us is unfair.

Concerning the warrants, again inherent in the argument that the warrant should be deemed exercised for earnings per share computations is the assumption that actual exercise is imminent (or at least highly probable) in the foreseeable future. In point of fact, the rational investor will never exercise a warrant until it expires. Lustra's warrants expire in 2000, nearly ten years hence. The fact that the market price of our common shares exceeded the warrant exercise price at various times during 1989 means absolutely nothing regarding the probability of exercise by the holder of the warrant; its only effect is to change the price of the warrant in the marketplace. We realize that the earnings per share impact of the warrants is relatively insignificant this year. The problem is in the future as our share price rises and the earnings per share impact becomes more significant.

(continued)

exhibit 11.16   *(continued)*

I am also troubled by the fact that the financial statements we issue to our Italian investors will henceforth show different earnings than those reported to our U.S. investors. This discrepancy will cause confusion that, I believe, will not help our stock price in either country.* Also, your lower 1989 earnings per share figures will make it more difficult for us to sell securities in the U.S. After all, who wants to invest in an IPO when the earnings are already sliding down? Maybe we will have to abandon our U.S. financing plan.

I have come to the conclusion that—as you say in America—"the bottom line" is this: in order to go ahead with our U.S. equity issue, we must conform to U.S. GAAP, including *APB Opinion No. 15*. Frankly, I am hesitant to go forward with the U.S. underwriting. Selling shares following a decline in earnings per share is not likely to enhance their value. Before our final decision on whether to proceed with the U.S. underwriting, please check the rules once again to see if it is truly necessary to report the figures you propose.

In the meantime, I hope you will assist me to understand the reasoning behind *APB Opinion No. 15* so that I can in turn help my board to understand why we must now report different earnings per share to our Italian and U.S. investors. Perhaps, when I understand *APB Opinion No. 15* better, Lustra may even want to use it for our Italian reports; but I am not prepared to do so at this time.

Very truly yours,

Peter Scala
President, Lustra S.p.A.

*For U.S. listing purposes, Lustra S.p.A. had to adopt U.S. GAAP for financial statements issued to U.S. investors. Because of the nature of the business, the fact that it had grown without acquisitions, and Peter Scala's insistence on high-quality accounting practices, the net income the company reported for U.S. and Italian listing purposes was essentially the same.

References

Accounting Standards Committee. "Legal Opinion on 'True and Fair.'" *Accountancy*, November 1983.

Alexander, David. "A European True and Fair View?" *The European Accounting Review*, vol. 2, no. 1 (1993), pp. 59–80.

Barlas, Stehen (ed.). "More Auditor Proposals From SEC." *Strategic Finance*, July 2000, pp. 27–28.

Barroso, Manuel. "The Globetrotting Auditor." *Internal Auditor*, August 1995, pp. 22–23.

Bell, Timothy, Frank Marrs, Ira Solomon, and Howard Thomas. *Auditing Organizations Through A Strategic-Systems Lens*. New York: KPMG Peat Marwick, 1997.

Busse van Colbe, W. "A True and Fair View: A German Perspective." *EEC Harmonisation: Implementation and Impact of the Fourth Directive*, edited by Gray, S.J., and A.G. Coenenberg. North Holland: Elseview, 1984, pp. 121–128.

Byrnes, Nanette. "The SEC vs. CPAs: Suddenly It's Hardball." *Business Week*, 22 May 2000, p. 49.

Chastney, J.G. *True and Fair View: History, Meaning and the Impact of the Fourth Directive*. London: Institute of Chartered Accountants in England and Wales, 1975.

Commission of the European Communities. *The Accounting Harmonisation in the EC: Problems of Applying the 4th Directive on the Annual Accounts of Limited Companies*. Luxembourg: Office for Official Publications of the EC, 1990.

Deloitte Touche Tohmatsu. *Brazil: International Tax and Business Guide*. New York: Deloitte Touche Tohmatsu International, 1997.

_____. *Internal Audit in Leading Financial Institutions: A Worldwide Study of the Changing Landscape*. New York: Deloitte Touche Tohmatsu International, 1995.

_____. *Japan: International Tax and Business Guide*. New York: Deloitte Touche Tohmatsu International, 1997.

_____. *Netherlands: International Tax and Business Guide*. New York: Deloitte Touche Tohmatsu International, 1998.

Fritsch, Peter. "Brazil's Big Gamble On Fraga Pays Off in a Rapid Recovery." *The Wall Street Journal*, 2 June 2000, pp. A1 and A8.

Frost, Carol A., and Kurt P. Ramin. "International Auditing Differences." *Journal of Accountancy*, April 1996, pp. 62–68.

Hill, Robert, and M. Zafar Iqbal. "Auditing Standards: Reflective or Prospective." *The Woman CPA*, January 1983, pp. 14–18.

"IMA Revises SMA 1C, Standards of Ethical Conduct," *Management Accounting*, July 1997, pp. 20–21.

Institute of Internal Auditors. *Codification of Standards for the Professional Practice of Internal Auditing*. Altamonte Springs, Fla.: The Institute of Internal Auditors, 1993.

Institute of Management Accountants. "SEC's Levitt Wants New Rules for Auditors." *Strategic Finance*, June 2000, pp. 101–102.

_____. "Statements on Management Accounting: Objectives of Management Accounting." *Statement No. 1C*. Montvale, N.J.: The Institute of Management Accountants, 1997.

International Federation of Accountants. *The Accountancy Profession and the Fight Against Corruption*. New York: International Federation of Accountants, 1999.

_____. *Auditors' Legal Liability in the Global Marketplace: A Case for Limitation*. New York: International Federation of Accountants, 1995.

_____. *Codifying Power and Control: Ethical Codes in Action*. New York: International Federation of Accountants, May 1999.

_____. "German Auditing Standards Compared With ISAs." *IFAC Quarterly*, April 1998, pp. 15–17.

_____. *IFAC Handbook 1999: Technical Pronouncements*. New York: International Federation of Accountants, 1999.

_____. *Statement of Policy of IFAC Council, Assuring the Quality of Audit and Related Services*. New York: International Federation of Accountants, July 1992.

"Investing in Brazil: Trouble in Paradise." *The Economist*, 3 June 2000, pp. 63–64.

Kelly, Jim. "World Bank Warns Big Five Over Global Audit Standards." *Financial Times*, 19 October 1998, p. 1.

Koliver, Olivio. "The Accountancy Profession in Brazil—Panorama and Challenges." *IFAC Quarterly*, July 1996, pp. 1–3.

Lavelle, Louis. "Cozying Up To The Ref." *Business Week*, 31 July 2000, pp. 85–86.

McLean, Bethany. "Hocus-Pocus: How IBM Grew 27% a Year." *Fortune*, 26 June 2000, pp. 165–168.

McNamee, Mike, and Paula Swyer. "How Good Is Levitt's Endgame?" *Business Week*, 13 March 2000, pp. 130–134.

Maijoor, S.J. *The Economics of Accounting Regulation: Effects of Dutch Accounting Regulation for Public Accountants and Firms*. Maastricht: Datawyse, 1991.

Mautz, R.K., and Hussein A. Sharaf. *The Philosophy of Auditing*. Sarasota, Fla.: American Accounting Association, 1961.

Moore, Pamela L. "This Scandal Changes Everything: Breaches of Auditor Independence at PWC Could Lead To An Overhaul of the Big Five." *Business Week*, 28 February 2000, pp. 140–143.

PricewaterhouseCoopers. *Audit Committees: Best Practices for Protecting Shareholder Interests*. New York: PricewaterhouseCoopers, 1999.

_____. *Audit Committees Update 1999*. New York: PricewaterhouseCoopers 1999.

Price Waterhouse. *Doing Business In Germany: Information Guide*. New York: Price Waterhouse, 1996, and 1 January 1997 supplement.

Roussey, Robert, and Kenneth Gilmour. "Adopting ISAs: An Opportunity and a Responsibility." *IFAC Quarterly*, April 1997, pp. 8–9.

Schilder, Arnold. "Auditor Independence." *De Accountant*, October 1994, pp. 80–83.

Sears, Brian. "Multinational Auditing." *Internal Auditor*, October 1994, pp. 28–31.

Smith, Gerald P. "Horses of Another Color." *Internal Auditor*, August 1995, pp. 18–21.

Takahashe, Zen-ichiro. "Issues Facing the Japanese Profession." *IFAC Quarterly*, April 1998, pp. 9–10.

Tie, Robert. "SEC Renews Push for More Oversight of Auditors." *Journal of Accountancy*, July 2000, pp. 16–17.

Turner, Lynn E., and Joseph H. Godwin. "Auditing, Earnings Management, and International Accounting Issues at the Securities and Exchange Commission." *Accounting Horizons*, September 1999, pp. 281–297.

Van Lieshouta, Menno P. "Internal Audit in The Netherlands: Between Financial and Operational." *De Accountant*, October 1994, pp. 87–90.

Zeff, Stephen A. "International Accounting Principles and Auditing Standards." *The European Accounting Review*, 1993, pp. 403–410.

_____, F. vander Wel, and K. Camfferman. *Company Financial Reporting: A Historical and Comparative Study of Dutch Regulatory Process*. Amsterdam: North Holland, 1992.

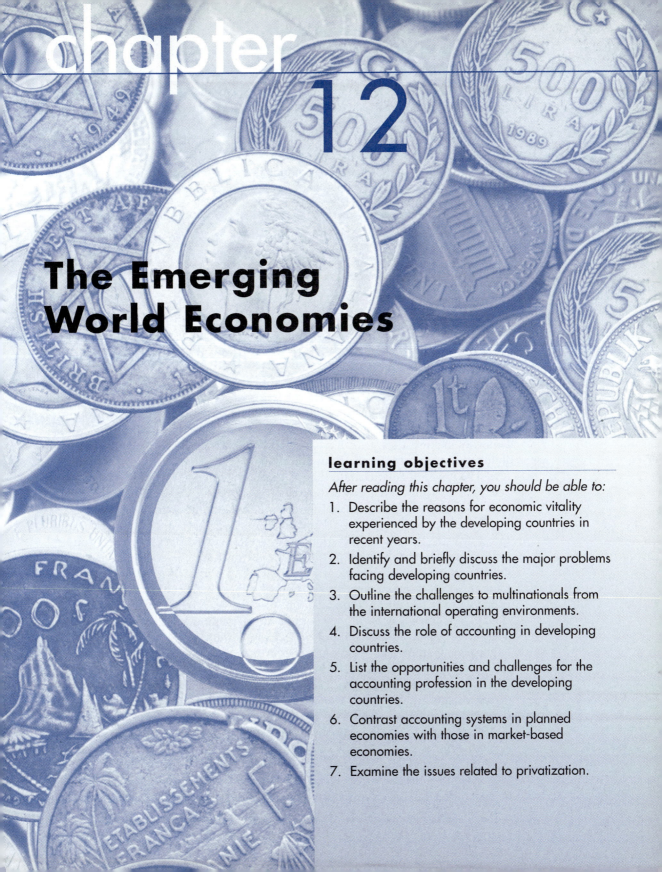

chapter

12

The Emerging World Economies

learning objectives

After reading this chapter, you should be able to:

1. Describe the reasons for economic vitality experienced by the developing countries in recent years.

2. Identify and briefly discuss the major problems facing developing countries.

3. Outline the challenges to multinationals from the international operating environments.

4. Discuss the role of accounting in developing countries.

5. List the opportunities and challenges for the accounting profession in the developing countries.

6. Contrast accounting systems in planned economies with those in market-based economies.

7. Examine the issues related to privatization.

Economic development of many Third World countries in Asia and Latin America has resulted in the emergence of many countries as economic powers. Over three billion people in the world are participants in the free markets today, 15 years ago the number was only one billion. This is a development of historic proportion.

Literacy levels, economic development, technology, and infrastructure development vary widely among the developing countries. Nevertheless, they share many common socio-economic problems. The accounting profession can make important contributions to facilitate their economic growth as discussed in later parts of this chapter.

Economic Progress and Potential

The eighteenth century Scottish political economist Adam Smith stated: "If a foreign country can supply us with a commodity cheaper than we ourselves can make it, better buy it off them with some part of our own industry." Were he alive today, Adam Smith would be very pleased. His theory is receiving increasingly wide acceptance all over the world—regardless of national, geographic, and, often, political boundaries.

The movement from socialistic to free market economies is nowhere more evident than in Asia: China and India are among the converts. The two countries have a combined population of well over 2 billion—one-third of humanity. Other countries making a fast transformation to a free market system include Thailand, Indonesia, Malaysia, Czech Republic, Poland, Hungary, and Oman to name a few. The governments in many Latin American countries also have recently accelerated their movement toward a free market system. Especially notable among such countries are Chile, Argentina, Peru, Brazil, and Mexico.

The developing countries are inviting foreign investors for both direct and indirect investments. **Direct investment** means establishing operations in a country; **indirect investment** involves buying equity or debt securities originating from a country as investments. Brazil attracted over $31 billion of foreign direct investment in 1999. In many developing countries, there has been a drastic shift in attitude toward foreign investments. Until recent years, the presence of multinational companies was often viewed with suspicion and sometimes with distrust. They were perceived as a symbol of Western dominance. Now most developing countries apparently have concluded that they can achieve economic prosperity only through integration with the global economy—not by economic isolation from the rest of the world. This is evidenced by the fact that China attracted more direct foreign investment in 1999 than any other single country. It was not too long ago when China had sealed itself off from rest of the world.

Southeast Asia has a large population of low-wage and well-educated workers. India has become a major source of high-technology workers for the industrialized countries, e.g., the U.S. The economic growth in developing countries has brought economic prosperity, thus creasing a sizable middle class—a major consideration for direct investors from abroad. Many products now manufactured in Asia are not just for export but also to meet domestic demand from the newly created middle class. It has also motivated many of the richest Southeast Asian countries to invest in the region.[1]

Privatization and Economic Reforms

There are two major driving forces behind this new economic momentum in Third World countries: privatization of state-owned enterprises and introduction of economic reforms. **Privatization** entails the transfer of enterprise ownership from the state to the private sector. Privatization has resulted in the private ownership of enterprises that were previously owned by governments. Global markets are transforming those enterprises into efficient and competitive entities. Voluntary, and sometimes imposed, economic reforms have contributed to the removal of many restrictive policies on trade and investments, such as currency-flow restrictions, high tariffs, import quotas, and percentage limits on equity ownership by foreign investors. *The push for privatization and economic reforms has come from three major sources: the World Bank, the international monetary fund, and the World Trade Organization.*

Thanks to privatization and economic reforms, the outcome has been a surge in trade between the developing countries and industrialized countries, and among the developing countries themselves. Investment funds can flow relatively easily to different parts of the globe in search of high returns. The opportunities in developing countries can play an important role in the investment decisions, since the returns that can be earned in many developing countries more than offset the higher level of risks.

Emerging Asian markets especially favored for indirect investment by foreign investors include Taiwan, Thailand, Malaysia, Singapore, Hong Kong, and South Korea. Developing countries have achieved varying levels of industrialization and technological advancement. *Some East Asian countries are currently at the point where they are soon expected to make the transition to fully industrialized, high-technology status.* In fact, one of the Four Tigers of Asia, Singapore, became Southeast Asia's first developed economy on January 1, 1996. Singapore is an exporter of high-technology products. Both India and Singapore are exporting their technology expertise. Taiwan manufactures entire personal computers as well as key parts for some of the largest computer companies in the world, such as Apple and Compaq. Samsung, based in South Korea, is the largest manufacturer of monitors in the world.

East and Central European, Asian, and Latin American markets are becoming vital to many companies based in the U.S., Japan, and Western Europe. Corporations such as Coca-Cola, Siemens, Hitachi, ABB Asea Brown Boveri, Mitsubishi, Alcatel-Alsthom, and General Electric are focusing on high-growth countries. It is necessary for their own long-term growth since developing countries

---

1 "SE Asian Dragons' Economies Still Spark." *San Francisco Chronicle*, 3 January 1995, p. D6.

have billions of consumers with an increasingly significant purchasing power. The importance of global operations intensifies as corporate size grows. *Not only is size no obstacle to international expansion, but early entry into the global markets may be a clear sign of success.*[2]

Regulatory Controls on Security Trading

A strong regulatory framework for security markets is a prerequisite to building investor confidence. In recent years, the governments in several developing countries have taken active steps to regulate security trading. For example, the government of India empowered the Securities and Exchange Board of India to control the country's 21 security exchanges. Malaysia and Thailand have established securities commissions, while Indonesia has privatized its stock exchanges.

Infrastructure as a Competitive Weapon

As mentioned earlier, individual developing countries are at different stages of industrial and technological development. Some are still heavily reliant on their competitive advantages of cheap labor, agriculture, and natural resources, while others are progressing to join the league of industrialized, high-technology countries.

Many of the developing countries that are dependent on their competitive advantage of low-cost labor, export of agricultural products, or vast natural resources recognize that these advantages will disappear in the future. They are striving to become more industrialized to prepare for the future. A recent example of such a country is Saudi Arabia. The development of infrastructure has become a top priority to achieve this goal for several reasons:

- To produce high-quality goods and services that can withstand competitive pressures in global markets.
- To attract foreign investments that, in the absence of essential infrastructure, would not be made.
- To meet the existing need for infrastructure from the growth already achieved.

Saudi Arabia is actively seeking investment from abroad to diversify its oil-dependent economy. The same is true of most other countries in the Middle East region, e.g., UAE, Oman, Bahrain, and Kuwait to name a few. The urgency to develop the infrastructure, therefore, comes from the plans to develop a future competitive ability, to attract foreign investments, and to meet already existing needs.

The **Association of Southeast Asian Nations (ASEAN)** is the most important trading bloc in Southeast Asia. The 10 member countries include Brunei, Cambodia, Indonesia, Laos, Malaysia, Myanmar, the Philippines, Singapore, Thailand, and Vietnam. The ASEAN member countries plan to establish a free-trade

---

2 "Weighing Strategic Options," *Deloitte & Touche Review*, 18 April 1994, p. 2.

zone by 2003. This will be accomplished by reducing tariffs to a maximum of 5 percent by January 2003, by six of the member countries. The other four, for example Vietnam, have until January 2006 to make the tariff cuts. The tariff reduction process was started in 1993. Japan has been making direct investments of billions of dollars in ASEAN member countries since 1990.

Technology Transfer and Development of Human Capital

A natural outcome of the participation by many American, Japanese, and Western European companies in the infrastructure development is the transfers of some types of advanced technologies to developing countries. The developing countries also benefit in the form of a cadre of skilled technocrats, managers, machinists, and technicians. This human capital development is a direct outcome of hands-on involvement in the complex infrastructure projects. Many developing countries have sizable pools of highly educated individuals, some with advanced degrees from the universities in the U.S. and Europe. Practical experience through involvement in complex projects can provide them with the opportunities to apply the concepts they already know.

When companies from industrialized countries compete for infrastructure development contracts, adopting the following strategies can provide a competitive advantage:[3]

- Willingness to transfer advanced technology at low prices.
- Forming long-term alliances through the continual transfer of newer technologies, instead of concentrating on one-time sales.
- Willingness to develop human capital by sharing knowledge and expertise.
- Providing financing at a price the Asians consider reasonable.
- Avoiding the perception of making excessive profits.

Japanese companies have generally been found to be more reluctant to transfer advanced technology than companies from the U.S., France, and Germany.

Problems and Challenges

Though many developing countries have made impressive progress in economic growth and industrial development in recent years, growth and industrialization have also intensified many serious problems, such as environmental pollution and natural resources' depletion. Unless these problems are resolved, economic gains made may be endangered. In this section, we will look at some of the major problems and challenges facing developing countries. This is necessary to help us later focus on the role of accounting in finding solutions to many of these problems.

---

3 William J. Holstein. "Building the New Asia." *Business Week*, 28 November 1994, pp. 65–68.

Population Growth

High population growth rates continue to exacerbate the already existing over-population problem in developing countries. Developing countries include three of the four most populous nations in the world.

Country	Population
China	1,300 million
India	1,000 million
Indonesia	210 million

The world population is estimated at 6 billion people, and Southeast Asia accounts for over 60 percent of this number. India and China together account for approximately 40 percent of the world's population. The population growth rate has been brought under some control in several countries, notably in Bangladesh, China, Indonesia, Hong Kong, South Korea, Singapore, Taiwan, and Thailand. Family planning programs have helped reduce the average number of children born per woman in developing countries from 6.0 in the late 1960s to around 3.5 currently. The fertility rate in China is currently below the population replacement level of 2.1 children per woman. The population growth rates, however, remain high in many other developing countries especially those where traditional cultural values prize large families or religious beliefs discourage family planning.

Overpopulation is acknowledged to be the major cause of environmental pollution and the depletion of natural resources. Overpopulation also burdens the economy of a developing country and makes it difficult to provide food, education, housing, health care, and employment for a population that is continuously increasing. Child labor—putting young children to work at a very early age—is a sad byproduct of overpopulation in many countries.

Environmental Pollution

Population growth and industrial development have fueled the problem of environmental pollution and natural resource depletion. Deforestation, air and water pollution, toxic waste, and loss of farmland due to urban sprawl are just a few examples. Automobiles are a major source of air pollution in most developing countries. Smog is so thick over Benxi, a city of one million in northeastern China, that the city does not appear on satellite maps.

Environmental negligence has often been fostered by the desire for rapid industrialization regardless of environmental costs. Chile typifies this dilemma. The Chilean capital city, Santiago, has a serious smog problem attributable to a fleet of 10,000 outmoded diesel buses. The extremely poor air quality has forced the government to declare pre-emergency or emergency air conditions many times, advising children to stay home from school and avoid exercise for part or all of the day. The smog problem is even worse in Mexico City. In most cities in Pakistan, traffic constables wear nose masks to filter out polluted air while breathing, and many people do the same. In many big cities in developing countries, it takes only a few hours for a clean set of clothes to become visibly dirty from pollutants in the atmosphere.

Corruption

Corruption has been, and still is, a serious threat to the economic and social health of most, if not all, developing countries. The impact of corruption is far more serious in countries that already suffer from acute poverty among masses.[4] *Diversion of scarce national economic resources from the public economic development projects causes misallocation of resources in the countries that can least afford it.* Widespread corruption is so prevalent in some countries that it has almost become a part of national culture.[5] In many developing countries former heads of government and heads of state have been convicted of corruption, and in some cases hundreds of millions of dollars have been recovered from their bank accounts in other countries.[6] In 1999, a constitutional assembly in Venezuela declared a judicial emergency because of a pending accusation of corruption or other irregularities against half of the country's 4,700 judges.[7]

In most cases, the acceptance of bribes by government officials is attributed to their low salaries. This, of course, provides an explanation but not a justification. Even the United Nations has not received immunity from this problem. In some countries where UNICEF (the U.N. children's fund) has developmental programs, it had to pay "salary supplements" to government officials as an incentive to carry out programs. Auditors for the UNICEF warned in 1994 that "while the payment of salary supplements may ensure the achievement of immediate program objectives and lead to more successful policy execution, in the long run it will endanger the sustainability of development effort and erode national capacity building."[8] A subtler form of corruption, nepotism, is also widespread in many developing countries. **Nepotism** means that relatives of those in power are able to easily obtain business licenses, lucrative government contracts, real estate deals, high-level government jobs, and other forms of patronage.

Many countries, such as South Korea, China, Indonesia, and recently Nigeria, have started concerted efforts to crack down on corrupt practices. However, such efforts often face tough resistance. In several cultures, bribe payments have come to be regarded as harmless tips or donations, thus making them socially quasi-acceptable. Examples of rampant corruption easily can be found in

---

4 "China Auditors Say Billions of Dollars Lost to Corruption." *The Wall Street Journal*, 18 August 1999, p. A12.

5 Greg Myre. "Bribery and Corruption Are a National Legacy in Nigeria." *The Tribune*, 27 August 2000, p. A5.

6 *Ibid.*

7 "Judicial Emergency Declared in Venezuela." *San Francisco Chronicle*, 20 August 1999, p. D3.

8 "U.N. Relief Agency Warns Against Bribes, Payments." *San Francisco Chronicle*, 25 December 1994, p. C13.

many developing countries. Fortunately, the problem is now receiving worldwide attention at various levels and from various sources. The IFAC and the World Bank are among the organizations actively addressing the corruption problem.

Political Instability and Civil Unrest

Many developing countries suffer from political instability and civil unrest to varying degrees. Specific causes of political instability and social disorder vary from country to country. The common factors contributing to the problem are ethnic and religious conflicts, regional disputes, political feuds, and governmental corruption and incompetence. *The root causes, according to knowledgeable observers, are economic deprivation and systematic discrimination based on social stratification.*

Why are political stability and social order important? Today more and more economists believe that it is politics, policies, and institutions that help or hurt economic growth.[9]

> . . . burgeoning bureaucracies and interest groups in both developing and industrialized nations can throw sand in the economic gears and lead to political paralysis or instability. And political instability is one surefire predictor of poor economic performance, says Harvard University economist Alberto Alesina . . . In developing countries, the accompanying uncertainty reduces investment and encourages capital flight, while among industrialized nations, instability leads to poor policy choices. "If a government is unlikely to be reelected, it has an incentive to follow particularly shortsighted policies," argues Alesina.

According to Moeen Qureshi, a former vice president of the World Bank, "It is futile to expect a sustained flow of foreign capital if peaceful conditions do not exist."[10]

Other Problems

Other major problems facing developing countries are:

- High rates of inflation.
- Unstable national currencies.
- Heavy national debts and deficit spending.
- Politicization of the decision-making process for development projects.

It is difficult to isolate these problems; they are all interrelated. For example, heavy government deficit spending contributes to a high rate of inflation, which

---

9 Karen Pennar, Geri Smith, Rose Brady, Dave Lindorff, and John Rossant. "Is Democracy Bad for Growth?" *Business Week*, 7 June 1993, pp. 85–86.

10 Vasantha Arora. "Ex-Pak PM Concerned Over Law and Order." *India-West*, 16 December 1994, p. 26.

in turn often contributes to currency instability. Currency instability often leads to the exodus of foreign capital. When foreign investors withdraw, a government's ability to pay its debts and to finance operations is adversely affected. Inability of a government to pay its debts when they are due for payment creates a *major* financial crisis. This phenomenon occurred in Mexico in December 1994 and in many Asian countries in mid-1997 as a result of foreign investors' lack of confidence. These crises were not contained within the affected countries only but were felt worldwide.

Though inflation is not as serious a problem as it was a few years ago, double-digit and sometimes triple-digit inflation rates still persist in many developing countries. Poland, for example, has a low double-digit inflation rate. It is necessary to curb high inflation to achieve sustained fast economic growth, but it is very difficult for developing economies to bring down inflation to low single digits. This phenomenon is known as the Balassa-Samuelson effect. According to the **Balassa-Samuelson Theory**, it is difficult to get rid of inflation in a fast-growing economy. It can be brought down to manageable, single-digit levels, but to further decrease it to low single digits is extremely difficult. According to W. Groenenberg, an economist with Salomon Smith Barney in London, "So far, [East Europeans] have done the easy part, which was to get inflation down to single digits. The hard part is going to be getting inflation down below 5 percent."[11] Many developing countries also need to curtail their heavy government deficit spending, which often leads to high inflation rates. For dozens of developing countries, heavy debt is having a crippling effect on economic growth and is keeping away investments from abroad.

The politicization of development projects often results in less than optimal decisions. A highly politicized decision-making process often leads to project delays, waste of resources, and loss of quality. Some analysts believe this to be the main reason for problems with infrastructure projects in some countries.

Operating Environments' Challenges to Multinationals

Multinational companies operating in developing countries have tremendous opportunities to grow due to those countries' growth economies. With the opportunities come the challenges related to the operating environments in the developing countries. To succeed, companies must be aware of the existing and potential problems in a country and formulate the strategies to cope with them *before* starting operations in the country.

Trade and Remittance Restrictions

Many countries have strict business regulations, sometimes directed primarily at multinational companies. Egypt and India have labor policies covering the employment of local citizens. It can cause major problems for a company that needs

---

11 Paul Hofheinz. "Inflation Hiccup Threatens East Europe." *The Wall Street Journal*, 30 August 2000, p. A22.

to restructure its operations for sound business and economic reasons. Many foreign contractors and managers complain that the regulations give virtually permanent protection to the local workers they hire. Some countries have stiff rules restricting capital remittances by foreigners. Many countries are continuing their protectionist policies through high import tariffs, and importing many products is either restricted or prohibited. A few countries have strict exit policies that make it difficult for a multinational company to curtail its operations in an orderly and efficient manner.

Bureaucratic Hurdles

Governmental red tape and bureaucratic obstacles, both in government and in other institutions, often frustrate managers of multinational companies. It may take months, or even years, to get a decision after submission of an application for approval of a project. Even after its approval, there is no guarantee that the project can be completed as planned. The world's largest energy company, Exxon-Mobil, decided to scrap its $50 million investment in Bangladesh following "bureaucratic wrangles."[12]

Workforce

Lack of a skilled workforce in adequate supply is a problem in many countries. In some cases, the education system appears to be insensitive to the actual needs of the labor market. In other cases, the quality of education is inferior.

Inadequate Legal and Financial Systems and Infrastructure

A comprehensive legal system provides protection to investors and creditors, and a banking system facilitates transactions. Both are critical for transnational companies to conduct business. Lack of legal and financial systems and infrastructure creates significant obstacles and further compounds the problem. In 1997, Hewlett-Packard Co. abandoned its plans to locate a $400 million inkjet printer plant in India. According to a company official, "India does not have the infrastructure to support the plant."[13] Indonesia's senior economics minister recently stated that the country is not stable enough to appeal to foreign investors. "If I were a foreign investor, I wouldn't come to Indonesia," he said. "The law enforcement is not there, but not only that, the whole thing is so confusing. How can you come here?"[14] Several other countries, for example, Cambodia and Laos, also suffer from inadequate legal and banking systems and poor infrastructure.

In spite of the problems related to operating environments most analysts believe that there is tremendous opportunity at the present and immense potential in the future in developing countries.

---

12 David Chazan. "Exxon-Mobil To Pull Out of Bangladesh." *Financial Times*, 17 July 2000, p. 4.

13 "HP Abandons India Project." *Gulf News*, 9 August 1997, p. 21.

14 "Indonesia Minister Won't Seek Investors." *The Wall Street Journal*, 12 May 2000, p. A14.

Role of Accounting

Economic reforms and economic growth in developing countries have brought the role of accounting to the limelight. Accountants have a vital role to play in this dynamic economic environment. Accounting systems record and report the transactions involving transfer of goods, services, and financial resources. It is necessary to meet the information needs of—among others—multinational enterprises, global capital markets, and international investors. In addition, accounting provides useful information to corporate managers and technocrats for policy formulation and decision making. *Ultimately, accounting plays a pivotal role in resource allocation decisions. It is a powerful role that accounting plays in the world economy.*

Accounting Profession

Accounting practices in a country are heavily influenced by its culture. *When there is a drastic change in the political or economic system of the country, it is bound to change the objectives of financial reporting.* In developing countries, such as China, the movement toward a market-oriented economy has necessitated a revision of the financial reporting system. *This revision in accounting and disclosure standards is considered essential for the success of economic reforms.*[15] In countries with centrally planned economies, the traditional accounting focus was on the stewardship concept. Their transition to a market-based economy makes the financial and operating information of primary importance. This major shift in the financial reporting objectives requires reorientation on the part of the accountants in those countries. Developing countries have taken active steps to address these issues. For example, Deloitte Touche Tohmatsu International has assisted the development of continuing professional education for the Chinese Institute of Certified Public Accountants. Also, Western accounting firms have entered into joint ventures for conducting audits with Chinese accounting firms. An important reason cited for such joint ventures is that it will help upgrade accounting standards in China. The upgrading is expected to eventually help attract foreign financial capital.[16] The strategy has apparently been successful, since China attracted more foreign direct investment in 1999 than any other developing country. Dozens of developing countries are adopting IASC's *International Accounting Standards.* This is so because many developing countries are seeking to list their securities in other countries and also to attract foreign investors to their own security markets.

---

15 Gary M. Winkle, H. Fenwick Huss, and Chen Xi-Zhu. "Accounting Standards in the People's Republic of China: Responding to Economic Reforms." *Accounting Horizons*, September 1994, p. 48.

16 "Andersen, Peat Both Open Chinese Joint Ventures." *Accounting Today*, 11 May 1992, p. 44.

Accounting Education

Accounting educators in the developing countries that have adopted economic reforms and privatization policies face two major challenges: the challenge of restructuring accounting curricula to reflect the impact of these changes and the challenge of restructuring the curricula to adapt to advances in information technology. It is absolutely essential to meet these challenges for maintaining the relevancy and currency of their accounting programs. The accountant's role is critical to the successful implementation and execution of economic reforms.

Specific Opportunities and Challenges

We now focus on some of the specific opportunities and challenges in the developing countries for the accounting profession.

- The strategic decisions involving infrastructure projects are of critical importance to the developing countries since they have a direct effect on their future competitive ability. The speed and quality of decision making (along with the existence of a competitive private sector) are important factors.[17] *The countries that allow decisions to be made by qualified technocrats or nonpartisan consortiums, rather than by politicians, are making faster progress.* Accountants possess the requisite analytical skills to be able to provide technical support to the civilian authorities. Cost-benefit analysis, project cost estimation, and post-completion control systems development are just a few of the examples.

- The management of infrastructure projects is a challenge for the companies working on the projects. Those companies' accountants can make important contributions by developing systems for project management and project control.

- Corruption is acknowledged to be a major problem in many developing countries. As stated earlier, corruption causes misallocation of economic resources. Corruption is undesirable and unacceptable anywhere, anytime. However, the effects of corruption are decidedly far more harmful on the developing economies since these countries can least afford misallocation of their scarce resources. Accountants can help alleviate this problem by designing and developing strong internal control systems to detect fraud and waste. Internal auditing has a natural and important role in the efforts to curb corrupt practices.[18] Regular internal audits in themselves are a deterrent to corrupt and wasteful practices.

---

17 William J. Holstein. "Building the New Asia." *Business Week*, 28 November 1994, pp. 63–67.

18 Institute of Internal Auditors. *Codification of Standards for the Professional Practice of Internal Auditing.* Altamonte Springs, Fla.: Institute of Internal Auditors, 1993, p. 31.

- The lack of data accuracy is common in developing countries. As has been observed, "It takes accurate numbers to institute free-market reforms."[19] Internal auditors, by reviewing the reliability and integrity of financial and operating information, can help achieve accuracy of the data critical to the successful implementation of economic reforms.

- A common problem among the developing countries is that policy formulation is not necessarily followed by policy implementation. Internal audits can help determine whether economic plans are actually being implemented.

- All cultures have values regarding what is "good" or acceptable. A review of the cross-cultural literature suggests that there are international differences in perceptions of what constitutes ethical behavior. Several researchers have found cross-national differences in ethical reasoning in a business context.[20] The value system of a country could possibly be in direct conflict with corporate policies. Through their adherence to carefully crafted codes of professional ethics developed for worldwide application (e.g., the Institute of Management Accountant's *Standards of Ethical Conduct for Practitioners of Management Accounting and Financial Management*), accountants are knowledgeable about professional ethics. They can be helpful to their organizations in developing ethical guidelines that are useful to the operating managers in diverse cultural settings.

  Apart from culturally based ethical dilemmas, the operating management of an organization can benefit from the contributions by management accountants in the ethics area in general. Accountants can design incentive systems that reward ethical behavior of employees. The management accountant is in a unique position to encourage ethical conduct within the company both by quantifying and reporting losses from litigation and punitive government actions such as fines and other types of penalties. Management accountants can be helpful in preparing or revising policies and mission statements that reflect management's commitment to responsible and ethical behavior.[21] Internal auditors, through their periodic audits, can determine if the organization's established ethical policies are being followed.

- Cost accounting clearly has a major role. Estimating costs of proposed infrastructure projects was mentioned earlier. Another example is the cost-benefit analysis to determine whether a state enterprise is achieving its economic and social objectives. Findings of such analyses can help in the decision as to whether a particular public enterprise should be privatized. Besides cost accounting, internal auditing also has a role in such a decision-

19 Christopher Farrell, Joyce Barnathan, and Elisabeth Malkin. "Statistics Can't Be Damn Lies Any Longer." *Business Week*, 7 November 1994, p. 118.

20 Jeffrey R. Cohen, Laurie W. Pant, and David J. Sharp. "Culture-Based Ethical Conflicts Confronting Multinational Accounting Firms." *Accounting Horizons*, September 1993, p. 2.

21 Debra R. Meyer. "More on Whistleblowing." *Management Accounting*, June 1993, p. 26.

making process. It is commonly acknowledged that the public sector tends to be inefficient. Internal audits can be conducted to see if there is efficient use of resources by public sector entities.

- The governmental accounting area in developing countries is full of potential opportunities for accountants. For example, accountants can help in developing a regulatory framework for securities trading. Some of the dubious practices in emerging markets have included illegal share sales, share price manipulation, and insider trading. Enactment of a strong regulatory framework helps bolster investor confidence. A lack of regulatory controls has resulted in securities scandals in many developing countries. Another area in dire need of attention by governmental accountants is the developing of systems for regular reporting on the economic and operational performance of public sector enterprises. Accountants can make significant and original contributions in this area.

- Development of financial accounting and reporting standards is necessary for the development of financial infrastructure. The need in this area is far from being satisfied. Investors need meaningful and informative financial reports for decision making. The development of financial reporting requirements for security registration and for periodic reporting by listed companies helps meet investors' needs for making informed decisions.

- Tax accounting in developing countries has been identified by many as another area of great opportunity for accountants. Many developing countries need to streamline and improve their taxation and tax-collection systems. In addition, investors and companies doing business in these countries need information about applicable tax laws and regulations for tax planning, tax law compliance, and decision making. Tax accountants can make valuable contributions in those areas.

- Environmental accounting deserves greater attention in the developing countries because of environmental costs associated with rapid growth, and infrastructure development. The environmental impact of economic growth is already being felt in all developing countries. Rapid infrastructure development can only intensify the environmental impact. Accounting practitioners, as well as accounting researchers, have an excellent opportunity to make significant contributions in environmental accounting. For researchers, the developing countries provide a laboratory setting to test hypotheses in the environmental accounting area and to identify accounting and reporting issues relating to environmental costs and liabilities. There has been increasing interest for environmental information by financial statement users. Some of the important issues requiring attention in the environmental accounting area are:

  - Identification of environmental costs.
  - Environmental liabilities and their recognition and measurement.
  - Disclosure of environmental costs and liabilities.

- Environmental contingent liabilities.
- Disclosure of environmental accounting policies.
- Disclosure of future environmental expenditures.
- Cost analysis in areas such as energy and waste.
- Cost-benefit analysis of environmental reclamation programs.

- In the area for the development of business codes within the legal framework, such as investment and banking codes, accountants have the technical expertise to support those responsible for developing such a code. As mentioned earlier, in many developing countries, a lack of a comprehensive legal framework and an absence of a full-service established banking system are among major obstacles to attract trade and investments.

Clearly, accountants are not mere spectators in the global economy. They are active participants. Their skills, expertise, and talents are needed by all players in the global economy—governments, investors, capital market regulators, and companies. Accountants have exciting opportunities to make important professional contributions that will help the efficient allocation of resources in emerging economies.

Socialist Accounting

With the disintegration of the USSR and the reunification of Germany, the countries of the former Eastern bloc are moving toward a free market economy. The speed of movement varies among the countries. The transition to a market economy necessarily requires a high degree of privatization.

Accounting has a key role in the transition from a centrally planned economy to a market-based economy. Accounting, as the language of business, is crucial to a business enterprise. The effectiveness of privatization programs is dependent to a great extent on the application of market-driven accounting concepts—especially the managerial accounting concepts originating from customer focus.

Choosing representative examples of transformations to capitalism in the former Eastern bloc countries is not an easy task. Wars and economic collapse have devastated several countries in the region. Wars in the former Yugoslavia (Bosnia-Herzegovina and parts of Croatia); economic ruin in Bulgaria and Romania; ethnic conflicts in Armenia, Azerbaijan, Georgia, Moldova, and Tajikistan—all have made economic progress difficult.

Financial Accounting Systems

Certain commonalties exist between accounting systems in a free market environment and socialist accounting. They include double-entry recording (in most cases), calculation of profit for self-supporting enterprises, periodic reporting of financial results, and use of the historical cost basis. However, under a non-market-based system the state has complete control over the volume and flow of goods and services. Prices of goods and services are set by the governmental central planning authorities, rather than by market forces.

Since entrepreneurial activity was minimal in the former Eastern bloc and public (state) ownership of enterprises was the rule, it is understandable why accounting systems were based on macroeconomics principles. In fact, there is a distinct similarity between accounting for not-for-profit organizations, such as public universities and socialist accounting systems. In essence, it was a fund-based accounting system. In such an accounting system, the main objective is to ensure that resources are used for the prescribed purposes. In socialist accounting, the main classifications of a balance sheet are as shown in Exhibit 12.1.

Working capital in a socialist entity consists of current assets only. Budgetary accounts are integrated with actual accounts to determine whether working capital exceeds or is under the budgeted amount. A socialist system accounting is necessarily inflexible and detailed. There is an account for each and every item because subsidiary ledgers are *not* used.

The distribution of profit is another area of difference between a socialist enterprise and a capitalist entity. Profits are used to pay for productive assets, bank interest charges, and reserves. Any residual profit goes into the state budget. A simplified version of such distribution appears in Exhibit 12.2.

Cost Accounting Systems

Cost accounting systems in socialist countries are also different from those in capitalist countries. The objective of the former systems is to provide information for calculating national income. Since no market system exists to set prices of goods and services, the void is filled by standardized costs. Cost standards, however, are imposed by governmental authorities rather than developed internally.

The intent of this overview is to develop an appreciation of the problems in making the transition from a centrally planned economy to a market-based economy. It requires an entirely new orientation. Concepts such as profit, easily understood in free market economies, are alien to socialist economies.

exhibit 12.1 **Sample Socialist Balance Sheet**

A Socialist Enterprise Balance Sheet December 31, 20xx			
Active		**Passive**	
Fixed and noncirculating assets	x	Sources of own and equivalent capital	x
Normal circulating means	x	Bank credits	x
Cash, settlements and other assets	x	Other liabilities	x
Balance	xx	Balance	xx

exhibit 12.2 **Sample Socialist Distribution of Profit Statement**

A Socialist Enterprise Distribution of Profit For the Year Ended December 31, 20xx	
Profit distribution:	
For productive assets	xx
Bank interest charges	xx
Other (reserves)	xx
Macroeconomics measures (economic stimulation funds, i.e., state budget)	xx
Total	xxx

Privatization

A prerequisite to privatization is a national legal framework. A national legal framework is the foundation for a commercial code. Examples of the matters covered in a commercial code include property ownership and transfer, payment to creditors, bankruptcy, and employee rights. The purpose of these laws is to facilitate business-operating activities under a market-based economy. Investors from other countries are often invited and encouraged to participate in the ownership of enterprises. In certain cases, the maximum percentage owned by investors from other countries might be restricted. Restrictions may be made as to who may be a member of the board of directors. Important to the survival of a newly privatized enterprise acquired by a multinational company are the infrastructure, licenses, and foreign exchange allotments. Negotiations with the government must be undertaken before acquisition to ensure that these matters are handled efficiently.

In the countries changing from a centrally planned economy to a market-based economy, legal structures—taken for granted in market-based economies—must be developed. Constitutional changes are often required, such as amendments for allowing private ownership of property. Accounting and reporting problems to be addressed while changing to a market-based economy include:

- Transition period.
- Inflation.
- Valuation.
- Disclosure.
- Training of accounting personnel.

Transition Period

Since there is no history of the enterprise performance under a market-based economy, it is difficult to predict future performance. In most cases, there are no meaningful financial statements and certainly no marketing expertise. One of the first important tasks is to develop accounting principles and auditing standards. As mentioned earlier, centrally planned economies use a fund accounting system. The focus of fund accounting is providing public services from appropriations. The mindset has to change so that financial reporting now, instead, encompasses a profit orientation.

Although the inclination may be to duplicate accounting standards and auditing rules of other countries, they may not be well suited to the country due to different environmental factors. A conscientious effort must be made to ensure that newly established accounting and reporting rules do not create confusion because of high complexity, or lend themselves to misinterpretation, misapplication, or manipulation.

The two essential elements for a successful transition to the market-based accounting system are:

1. Adoption of a set of comprehensive accounting and auditing standards.
2. Development of an accounting profession.

An accounting conceptual framework is a prerequisite to determine the objectives of financial reporting and an identification of the principal users of financial statements. Ideally, an independent accounting body should be set up to develop the accounting standards. The development of an accounting profession is needed for the development and continuous improvement of accounting theory and practice.

The accounting data used in a centrally planned economy are not oriented toward providing information on performance. Unrealistic depreciation rates, the lack of responsibility centers, the emphasis on production volume rather than on profitability, and the lack of accountability all make the accounting data meaningless for decision making. Concepts such as discounted cash flow and return of investment for making investment decisions are largely foreign to accounting and financial personnel in centrally planned economies.

Inflation

Inflation has been a problem in different parts of the world at different times. The inflation topic was discussed in Chapter 3 and also in an earlier section of this chapter. Prior to the switch to a market-based economy, inflation issues were not a major concern for Eastern bloc countries. In a market-based economy, when the purchasing power of the monetary unit drastically decreases through inflation, the financial reporting implications require attention.

Valuation

Valuation of the assets in formerly planned economies is often difficult. The fixed assets are the most difficult for valuation purposes. For land, buildings, and equipment there are no established market values. In such cases, net profit may be a guide in estimating market value.

Example
Assume the following situation (amounts in Russian ruble):

Net profit	R12,000,000
Current assets	R50,000,000
Rate of return on current assets	10 percent
Rate of return on fixed assets	20 percent
Return on current assets	R5,000,000 (10% × R50,000,000)
Return on fixed assets	R7,000,000 (R12,000,000 total − R5,000,000 on current assets)
Cost assigned to fixed assets	R35,000,000 (R7,000,000 ÷ 20%)

Other valuation issues concern receivables and inventories. In the case of receivables, an analysis must be made to determine estimated losses from uncollectible accounts. A provision for bad debts then must be made. Computation of net realizable values of inventories (estimated selling prices less costs of completion and disposal) may lead to a write-down of inventories.

To comply with market-driven accounting standards, the classification of liabilities must be changed. The usual classifications of liabilities, including trade payables, accruals, taxes payable, and long-term debt, must be presented in the balance sheet. Items such as pension obligations and other estimated liabilities and loss contingencies are also important elements of the liabilities section of the balance sheet.

Disclosure

In offering capital stock and other securities for sale to the public in a market-based economy, it is necessary to disclose information needed by the users to make an informed judgment. Figure 12.1 shows the main steps in a public offering.

Potential investors need information on the risks and rewards surrounding a security issue. In a market-based economy, it is required to supply audited financial statements of the entity to the users. Users assume that the audited financial statements are a fair presentation of the financial position, and the results of operations of an enterprise in conformity with generally accepted accounting prin-

figure 12.1   Main Steps in a Public Offering

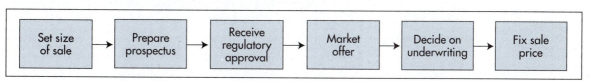

ciples. The prospectus includes the issuer's past history, comparative audited financial information as well as pro forma information. This information is deemed essential to investors in formulating opinions about expected future returns and associated risks of the investment. No such system of disclosure exists in centrally planned economies because security offerings to the public are not made.

Training of Accounting Personnel

Under socialist accounting systems, the accounting function is limited mostly to bookkeeping. Transformation to a market-based economy requires that accounting personnel be retrained so that they acquire the knowledge in accounting theory to understand the underlying accounting assumptions and concepts such as accounting entity, periodicity, going concern, matching, full disclosure, and revenue recognition. The attendant conventions of conservatism and materiality are also important to comprehend.

Accounting must be viewed as an information system providing relevant and timely information for decision making. This requires a completely new orientation for the accountants of former Eastern bloc countries.

Besides the accounting assumptions and conventions previously mentioned, the importance of an internal control system and its components also must be understood. The internal audit function (related to the internal control system) is a new phenomenon for accountants in formerly centrally planned economies. The fundamentals of a market-based economy need to be taught to make market-driven accounting meaningful to the trainees. This requires that the instructor be knowledgeable in accounting systems both in a centrally planned economy as well as in a free market-based economy.

Financial Statement Practices and Trends

Exhibit 12.3 summarizes the status of GAAP in 18 former Eastern bloc countries.

Concluding Remarks

Political, economic, legal, and social systems in the emerging markets in the former Eastern bloc are in a state of transition. It appears that the Czech Republic, Poland, Hungary, Slovakia, and Slovenia are progressing faster than other countries in the region. The situation in the former Eastern bloc countries has not stabilized as quickly as many had expected and hoped for, after the demise of communism. Students should keep abreast of the developments in order to appreciate changes in the region, the individual countries of the region, and their role in the global economy.

exhibit 12.3 **Accounting Standards in the Former Eastern Bloc**

Country	Membership		Security Exchanges Requiring IASs	Source of Financial Reporting Standards
	IASC	IFAC		
Armenia	Yes	No	—	IASs
Azerbaijan	No	No	—	Modified Soviet-era accounting standards
Belarus	No	No	—	Modified Soviet-era accounting standards
Czech Republic	Yes	Yes	Prague: Required	Czech accounting standards; IASs required from publicly listed companies; EU accounting directives
Estonia	Yes	No	Tallinn: Required	Estonian standards, same as IASs
Georgia	Yes	Yes	—	IASs
Hungary	Yes	Yes	Budapest: Required only from foreign listed multinationals, and companies with international operations. Other companies *may* use IASs.	Hungarian GAAP; IASs; EU accounting directives
Kazakhstan	Yes	Yes	Kazakhstan: Required only from "A-listed" companies	Soviet-era standards modified by the Ministry of Finance
Kyrgyzstan	Yes	Yes	—	Kyrgyzstani standards
Latvia	Yes	No	Riga: Required only from "Official Trading List" companies	IASs *recommended*
Lithuania	Yes	No	National: Required only from "Official Trading List" companies	Either Lithuanian standards or IASs *and* EU accounting directives
Moldova	Yes	Yes	—	National standards conform to the IASs
Poland	Yes	Yes	Warsaw: Foreign listed companies *may* use IASs	Polish standards. IASs only if no Polish standard exists on the matter
Russia	Yes	No	—	IASs acceptable for consolidated statement; Otherwise modified Soviet-era standards
Tadzhikistan	No	No	—	Modified Soviet-era standards
Turkmenistan	Yes	No	—	Modified Soviet-era standards
Ukraine	Yes	No	Ukraine: Foreign listed companies *may* use IASs or Ukranian standards	Ukranian GAAP that Soviet-era standards modified by the Ministry of Finance
Uzbekistan	Yes	Yes	—	National GAAP that is IASs-based

Sources: http://www.iasc.org.uk/
David Alexander and Simon Archer (eds.). *European Accounting Guide,* 4th ed. New York: Aspen Publishers, Inc., 2001.

Note to Students

As you study this chapter, you realize that developing countries provide exciting opportunities for accounting professionals. They can make significant contributions to facilitate the economic development of these countries.

To keep abreast of the developments in this dynamic area of emerging economies, the following periodicals are especially valuable: *The Asian Wall Street Journal Weekly*, *The Economist*, *Far Eastern Economic Review* (published in Hong Kong), *Gulf News* (published in the United Arab Emirates), Beijing's *Economic Daily*, *Business Week*, *Fortune*, and *Financial Times*.

The following Web site addresses are valuable sources of information on the developing countries, organizations, regions, etc.:

http://

Inside China Today: **http://www.insidechina.com/china.html**

India: **http://www.webhead.com/wwwvl/india/**

Association of Southeast Asian Nations: **http://www.asean.or.id/**

Central Asian Post: **http://www.bishkek.su/cap/**

China News Digest International: **http://www.cnd.org/**

Africa News Online: **http://www.africanews.org**

Latin America: **http://lanic.utexas.edu/las.html**

Latin Chamber of Commerce USA: **http://www.camacol.org**

Central Europe Online: **http://www.centraleurope.com/**

Central and Eastern Europe Business Information Center: **http://www.mac.doc.gov/eebic/ceebic.html**

Russian Information Services: **http://alice.ibpm.serpukhov.su/friends/commerce/rispubs/**

International Monetary Fund: **http://www.imf.org**

Corruption Perceptions Index: **http://www.transparency.de/**

Please grasp the important idea that the developing countries go through an evolutionary process. They usually start out as sources of cheap labor and evolve into industrialized countries. Taiwan, Singapore, and South Korea appear to have almost completed this evolutionary process.

http://

To learn how accounting is developing in the former Soviet republics, the IASC Web site is an excellent source: **http://www.iasc.org.uk/**

Annual reports of companies based in other countries contain a wealth of information about the accounting standards of the country.

Chapter Summary

1. The most drastic shift from centrally planned economies to free-market economies has occurred in Asia.

2. Developing countries are inviting both direct and indirect investments from abroad.

3. Northern Asia and India are economically vibrant regions.

4. Privatization and economic reforms are the two major driving forces behind the economic growth and development in the Third World countries.

5. Markets in the developing countries are becoming increasingly important to business enterprises in developed countries as well as developing countries.

6. Governments in many developing countries have recently introduced securities markets regulations.

7. Infrastructure development should be a high priority for many reasons.

8. As a byproduct of infrastructure development, developing countries are acquiring high technology and human capital.

9. Developing countries share many common problems that threaten erosion of past gains and potential future growth. Those problems include population growth, environmental pollution, corruption, and political instability and civil unrest.

10. Challenges are accompanied by opportunities for multinational companies in developing countries.

11. The accounting profession and accounting education have an important role in emerging economies of the world.

12. A wide array of opportunities exists for accountants in numerous areas such as internal auditing, cost accounting, financial accounting, governmental accounting, taxation accounting, and ethics.

13. Environmental accounting is a fertile area for accounting practitioners and accounting researchers for making significant contributions.

14. The countries of the former Eastern bloc are presently in a state of transition. With the disintegration of the Soviet regime and the reunification of Germany, the transition to a market economy requires that infrastructures such as stock exchanges, banks, commercial laws, and accounting and legal framework be established.

15. The chapter provides an overview of socialist accounting. It also addresses the issue of privatization, together with the legal and accounting facets of such a move from a state-controlled economy to a market economy.

16. Accounting problems in former Eastern bloc countries involve the issues of transitioning, inflation, valuation, and disclosure to meet new challenges in the accounting function.

17. Noticeable progress has been made in countries such as Hungary, Poland, and the Czech Republic and some others.

18. To reach the goal of providing accounting information for a market-based economy, the three critical elements are a set of comprehensive accounting standards, development of an accounting profession, and training of accounting personnel.

Questions for Discussion

1. Name the continent that has had the most visible shift to free-market economies.

2. Name three countries in Asia making progress to a free-market system.

3. Name two countries in Latin America that are moving toward a market-oriented system.

4. Describe the shift in attitude in many developing countries regarding investment by multinational companies.

5. Name the two major driving forces for economic momentum in developing countries.

6. Describe the impact of privatization on previously wholly state-owned enterprises.

7. Give three examples of economic reforms.

8. What forces have provided the impetus for privatization and economic reforms?

9. Why are the markets in developing countries becoming increasingly important to companies in industrialized countries and developing countries?

10. Is the small size of a company an obstacle to international expansion? Explain.

11. Why is infrastructure development considered to be so important by many for developing countries?

12. How will educated individuals in developing countries benefit from their active involvement in infrastructure development projects?

13. Name two problems that are intensified by growth and industrialization.

14. What is the major cause of environmental pollution, global warming, and the depletion of natural resources?

15. Why does corruption have a significantly more harmful impact on a developing country?

16. What is nepotism?

17. What are the root causes of political instability and social disorder?

18. Name three of the factors that contribute to political instability and social unrest.

19. What are the consequences of political instability in developing countries?

20. List some of the challenges facing developing countries.

21. What is the role of accounting in emerging economies?

22. How are financial reporting and disclosure affected by a shift from a socialistic system to a market-oriented system?

23. How can accountants be helpful in the strategic decisions made for infrastructure projects?

24. What accounting area is a natural for designing and implementing control systems to curb corruption?

25. What kinds of opportunities exist in developing countries for governmental accountants?

26. What is the main objective of accounting in a state-controlled system?

27. How are prices set in a centrally planned economy?

28. Why is a legal framework important for moving toward a market-based economy?

29. What is the overall objective of accounting in a market-based economy?

30. What is the main problem in making the transition from a centrally planned economy to a market-based economy?

31. "Valuation of assets can be a problem in the process of privatization." Explain.

32. Contrast the accounting information needs in a centrally planned economy versus a market-driven economy.

33. List the main steps of a public offering.

34. Why do potential investors need audited financial statements?

35. Why do accountants in the former Eastern bloc need to be retrained?

Exercises/Problems

12-1 Many developing countries consider the development of infrastructure critical for continued growth.

Required:

(1) Describe what is meant by infrastructure. Give specific reasons why infrastructure development is considered a necessity by many developing countries.

(2) Discuss the role of decision making in infrastructure development.

12-2 The chapter describes the strategies companies should adopt to gain competitive advantage in obtaining infrastructure development contracts.

Required:

(1) Describe and critique those strategies.

(2) Explain if those strategies will work in the countries that have a high degree of political instability and social unrest.

12-3 Select an Asian country that has had political instability during the last 3–5 years. Research the impact of political instability on the country's economic development. Prepare a two-page report of your research findings.

12-4 Complete the requirements in Problem 12-3 for an African country.

12-5 Complete the requirements in Problem 12-3 for a Latin American country.

12-6 In a report of approximately one to two pages, describe how internal auditing can contribute in many different ways in developing countries. Focus especially on accounting and other internal controls.

12-7 Describe the role of cost accounting in facilitating the economic growth of a developing country in a report of approximately one to two pages.

12-8 If a multinational enterprise is operating in a country, it should respect the country's cultural values and not attempt to impose the values of a foreign culture, i.e., the base country of the multinational. Do you agree? Disagree? Provide reasons to support your answer.

12-9 The following remarks were made by Pehr Gyllenhammar, chairman of Volvo, as the keynote speaker at the 14th World Congress of Accountants in Washington, D.C.:

The world economy in the 1990s is operating with an entirely different set of systems than those of the 1950s and 1960s. But there was in those days, whether you liked it or not, someone clearly in charge of the systems. There was a responsibility for stability, and the United States assumed that responsibility. In today's multipolar world, there is no clear leadership. No one has the power or the means to assume responsibility for managing the new systems. And we don't seem to be able to do it collectively.

So the global economy of the 1990s is leaderless—and we have plenty of recent and current evidence of this—while at the same time there is a lengthening agenda of issues requiring leadership. The risk is that we will be driven by accident and not by design. So what we will call the 1990s—the no-navigation 1990s? And what lessons can be learned from where we are now and how we got here?

Lesson number one is that international leadership is indispensable but is now in short supply. Vulgar election and cheap-shot referendum campaigns will not help. A leaderless global economy is likely to be highly accident-prone, putting at stake our institutions and our stability.

Lesson number two is to focus on fundamentals, the very simple things that were so often seemingly forgotten in the 1980s. Soul-searching for subtleties is not the task at this point. Productivity is still the source of wealth creation, certainly not inflated asset values and financial engineering. Leverage is not good when it gets out of hand, that is, when it stretches the balance sheets.

Lesson number three is, don't believe the market can solve everything. It was only a couple of years ago when we were told there would never again be a shortage of capital; now banks hardly lend money. And in today's economic climate we should not rely on the market's returning to "normal."

Required:

Comment on the previous statements by Mr. Gyllenhammar.

12-10 Following are excerpts from an article "Is Democracy Bad for Growth?"
published in *Business Week* (7 June 1993, p. 84).

But that freedom of choice is hardly a prerequisite for economic growth.
On the contrary, it often seems to hinder it. India has languished under
democratic leadership, while Chile and South Korea, both dictatorships
until recently, are success stories. Today, capitalism thrives without democracy, as the rapid growth charted by China's communist leaders amply
demonstrates.

Nor does democracy ensure growth for the world's leading industrialized nations. Many are mired in recession or sluggish recovery, and democratic governments from Italy to Japan have been damaged by scandal
and aren't delivering growth. Just a few years after the fall of the Berlin
Wall and communism's failure in Eastern Europe, democracy's weaknesses
seem glaring.

Just what is the relationship between democracy and growth? John F.
Helliwell, an economist at the University of British Columbia, compared
economic results for nearly 100 nations from 1960 to 1985 and concluded
that there was a slight downdraft for democracies compared with non-
democracies or authoritarian regimes. His findings confirm the view that
over the near term, authoritarian governments, especially those that offer
citizens "economic rights" such as the protection of private property, can
achieve strong results.

Required:

Comment on the previous statement. Provide reasons to support your statements.

12-11 The chapter mentions several challenges (problems) that make it more difficult to take advantage of the opportunities in developing countries.
These include legal, workforce, banking, and infrastructure problems,
among others. Take one or more of these problems and discuss how a
multinational might structure and conduct its operations to profit despite
the obstacles. Hint: There is no "correct" answer for this problem, but
some answers are certainly more thoughtful than others.

12-12 Research the current state of the accounting profession and prepare a report not exceeding 500 words for one or more of the following. Be prepared to discuss your findings in class.

(1) A Latin American country.
(2) An Asian country.
(3) An African country.

12-13 Research the current state of accounting education and prepare a report
not exceeding 500 words for one or more of the following. Be prepared to
discuss your finding in class.

(1) A Latin American country.
(2) An Asian country.
(3) An African country.

12-14 Select the best available answer:

1. Which of the following is *not* a distinguishing characteristic of an enterprise in a centrally planned economy in contrast to a business enterprise in a market economy?
   a. Accounting systems are based on macroeconomics principles.
   b. A defined ownership cannot be sold or transferred.
   c. Cost accounting systems are less important.
   d. The profit motive is absent.

2. The financial reporting objectives of enterprises in a centrally planned economy are:
   a. the same as the objectives of financial reporting by business enterprises.
   b. to ensure that resources are used for the intended purpose.
   c. set forth in the International Accounting Standards.
   d. to assist governments to be publicly accountable in a socialist society.

3. The accounting system used by an enterprise in a centrally planned economy must make it possible to:
   a. prepare a consolidated accrual basis statement for the unit.
   b. prepare financial statements as required by the EU Fourth Directive.
   c. present fairly the financial position of the enterprise and results of its operation.
   d. present the financial position of the funds.

4. A controlled economy reporting enterprise:
   a. publishes financial information the administration wants to provide to the public.
   b. consolidates all financial data and publishes consolidated financial statements.
   c. has an account for every item since subsidiary ledgers are not used.
   d. publishes a comprehensive annual financial report.

5. Which country was the first to open a stock exchange in the Eastern bloc?
   a. Russia
   b. The Czech Republic
   c. Hungary
   d. Poland

6. In moving from a controlled economy to a market-based economy, the most difficult area with respect to valuation is:
   a. receivables.
   b. payables.
   c. tangible fixed assets (property, plant, and equipment).
   d. cash.

7. In a market-based economy, it is not necessary to have:
   a. an accounting profession.
   b. generally accepted accounting principles.
   c. trained accounting personnel.
   d. a national accounting board.

12-15 You are provided with the following data for an enterprise in Russia:

Net profit	R50 million
Current assets	R220 million
Rate of return on current assets	11 percent
Rate of return on fixed assets	15 percent

Required:

Determine the cost assigned to fixed assets.

Case 1

Corruption—An Effective Equalizer of the Free Market System? And Don't Forget Mutual Pleasure!

In its August 21, 1995 issue, *Fortune* published an article on corruption in Asia, accompanied by a chart titled "Asia Corrupt-O-Meter."[22] The article stated that American companies seeking business in Asia face a dilemma: Huge, attractive emerging markets (with billions of consumers) are also the most corrupt in Asia. The article was based on a report by the Hong Kong-based firm, Political & Economic Risk Consultancy Ltd. The firm has been analyzing corruption and political stability for more than a decade. According to the consulting firm, paying off government officials to gain business can add 5 percent to operating costs in China.

The article stated that what bothers business executives most is their inability to take legal recourse against "squeeze tactics." The suggested solution by the consultancy firm was to learn how the system works in each place, and cultivate local leaders without giving them questionable payments. The author of the *Fortune* article was less than fully convinced by this approach. "Easier said than done," he stated, "particularly when competitors show up with briefcases full of cash."[23]

Political & Economic Risk Consultancy Ltd. compiled the corruption rating by surveying both its own analysts and 95 corporate managers from North

---

22 Louis Kraar. "How Corrupt is Asia?" *Fortune*, 21 August 1995, p. 26.
23 *Ibid.*

America, Europe, and Australia. For comparison, the 95 managers rated corruption in their countries at an average of 2.12 on a scale of 1 (least corrupt) to 10 (most corrupt). Singapore was rated at 1.19 and Japan at 1.97. According to Kenneth Sawka, an analyst at the Futures Group (a U.S. firm that advises companies on strategies), Asia is not the most corrupt region for business. He stated that corruption, for example, is far more pervasive and brash in Russia than in China. Following publication of the article, some interesting viewpoints were expressed by readers who wrote letters to the *Fortune* editor. The managing director of a firm in Thailand wrote:[24]

> The practice not only reflects the mutual consent of the giver and taker but also implies mutual pleasure, and should be called anything but "corruption." Giving money for favors is embedded in human nature. It spreads the wealth around and acts as an effective equalizer of the free-market system. The strongest and the biggest do not always win over the little guys with this system. And what is wrong with that?
>
> Perhaps a more appropriate title for the table you labeled "Asia Corrupt-O-Meter" would be "Business Opportunity Cost Index," or "In-Country Wealth Distribution Program Cost Index." You should also rank all the countries in the world. I bet the U.S. would be in the top five.

A reader in the U.S. wrote:[25]

> Why do we insist on preaching morality? Payoffs are against American law. That law restricts our investing in the rest of the world. To us it may be a perception of corruption; to others it is a business expense. What I call blatant corruption is the boondoggles, lobbies, etc., right on our home ground. They are causing more harm to our economy than foreign payoffs.

A letter from a Ph.D. candidate in economics from China, studying at a U.S. university, appeared in the next issue of *Fortune*:[26]

> Basically, paying bribes is just a redistribution of wealth among different economic agents within the system. It makes more sense to view corruption in China as a way to privatize the state-owned economy.
>
> For example, a businessman friend from Korea gave a Chinese customs officer two gold necklaces and got a whole container of goods entered without paying one penny of customs tax. Because the two necklaces cost much less than the customs tax he should pay, his operating cost is actually lower.
>
> The real problem for an American businessman in China could be how to find the right person to bribe. But the cost of this learning process

24 *Fortune*, 18 September 1995, p. 14.

25 *Ibid.*

26 *Fortune*, 2 October 1995, p. 29.

should not add 5 percent to operating costs if you are reasonably smart. And I've been amazed at how smart those foreign business people I met in Beijing are, and how fast they learn.

Required:

(1) Comment on the methodology used by Political & Economic Risk Consultancy Ltd. to analyze and rate countries on a corruption scale.

(2) Can bribes be viewed just as an expense of doing business? Why or why not?

(3) One of the readers stated that domestic lobbying in the U.S. does more harm to the U.S. economy than foreign payoffs. Do you agree? Give reasons for your position.

(4) The readers who wrote letters to the editor of *Fortune* made provocative comments regarding the "benefits" of paying bribes. List those claimed benefits and critique each one.

(5) What is your opinion of the solution proposed by the firm to avoid paying bribes? Do you think this would be an effective approach? Give reasons.

(6) Can you think of an approach that would be more effective?

Case 2

Privatization Russian Style

Following are excerpts from a recent article from The Wall Street Journal.[27]

. . . Mr. Yeltsin had signed a privatization law in mid-1991, creating a state agency to oversee the unloading of state assets: the State Property Committee, known by its Russian initials, GKI. But little happened until—on the eve of the Soviet collapse—Mr. Gaidar appointed as head of the GKI a youthful politician from St. Petersburg, Anatoly Chubais.

. . . To help decide strategy, Mr. Chubais and his advisers compared plans for case-by-case privatization, such as Poland's, and mass privatization, such as the Czech Republic's. They debated how the models would translate to Russia. At that time, production in Russia was centrally controlled by ministries or subministries, each running an entire industry. These organizations might not easily give up their authority. Reporting to the ministries were legions of so-called red directors, the apparatchiks spread across Russia who ran the actual factories, mines, oil fields and other state assets.

Mr. Chubais and his team concluded that in tackling this network, finesse would matter less than speed and scale. The only chance to re-

---

27 Claudia Rosett and Steve Liesman. "Starting From Scratch: Much Has Gone Wrong With Russia's Privatization Efforts. But a Lot More Has Gone Right." *The Wall Street Journal*, 2 October 1995, pp. R14–R15.

form Russia's economy and shore up the nation's new democracy was to start by quickly breaking the Soviet chains of central command.

In this divide-and-conquer strategy, the reformers aimed to entice the red directors into supporting privatization by offering them stakes in the enterprises they were already managing for the state. The industrial ministries, stripped of their assets, would be left to wither.

. . . A further aim was to create a broad base of property owners who would be opposed to reversing the changes. Matters such as raising revenue for the state and fine-tuning the distribution of state assets were secondary. For midsize and large enterprises, the GKI planners adopted a mass privatization strategy to be carried out largely by voucher auction, more like the high-speed Czech model than the deliberate Polish approach. The first step was for thousands of state enterprises to be "corporatized," or transformed into shareholding companies, with some portion of their shares slated for auction.

. . . To win over managers and workers of state businesses, as well as regional politicians, the GKI added a typically Russian touch of complexity: Each enterprise was allowed to choose from a menu of privatization plans.

In varying degrees, the plans allotted packets of shares—in many cases controlling stakes—to company insiders in exchange for cash or vouchers, or sometimes as straight giveaways. Another portion of the business would be auctioned to voucher holders generally. And in many cases a slice was reserved for the state—often for the regional GKI—to sell later for cash or so-called investment tenders, commitments to make substantial investments in companies in exchange for blocks of shares. When managers and workers could choose to keep a controlling interest in their privatized business, they usually did so.

Russian privatizers acknowledge that this tilt toward insider ownership was far from ideal for Russia's economy. Studies in recent years, including at least one on Russia, suggest that new owners and managers are more likely than old insiders to efficiently restructure a company. And restructuring of privatized businesses in Russia has indeed proved slow.

From a political standpoint, however, this approach offered incentives for both businesses and regional governments to go along with privatization in the first place.

. . . Since then, Russia has moved to the less systematic, more cumbersome process of selling net more businesses, and remaining state stakes in companies, for investment tenders. Instead of spreading a company's shares among tens of thousands of little shareholders, as with vouchers, investment tenders allow big investors to put up the money needed for restructuring companies in exchange for big stakes.

But because investment-tender deals are generally decided on a case-by-case basis, not in an open auction, the opportunity for shady dealing is greater.

. . . Russian reformers are still grappling with some mighty hand-overs of central planning. One basic problem is the lack of property law—something privatizers in developed democracies can usually take for granted. Here, ambiguous property rights have deterred much-needed investment.

Russia's stock market, after an initial rally in 1994, went into a long slump from which it has only recently begun to recover. The slide was brought on when foreign investors discovered they couldn't be sure of owning stock they had paid for; company insiders could simply strike their names off the shareholder registers, most of which the companies themselves ran. As outlandish as it seems, there was no practical legal re-course. Only in the past few months has Russia begun crafting securities regulations to protect shareholders.

. . . Some shortcomings of Russia's initial blitz to create private prop-erty are also now making themselves felt. The special deals offered as in-ducements to insiders gave a big share of the pie to the old communist elite.

The resulting drag on restructuring means many ordinary Russians—those who didn't buy bread stores, but still work the nickel mines—have yet to feel big benefits from privatization. Meanwhile, they are resentfully watching the new nomenklatura enjoying the new perquisites of private ownership.

The greatest weakness of the program, says the World Bank's Mr. Blitzer, is that "The distribution of wealth which emerged was so un-equal."

Required:

(1) Distinguish between the Polish and Czech privatization models.

(2) Discuss the strategy adopted by GKI to implement privatization. What were its strengths? Shortcomings?

(3) Referring to (2), what would you have done differently if you were in Mr. Chubais's position?

(4) Comment on the importance of a legal framework for economic develop-ment.

(5) According to Mr. Blitzer of the World Bank, the greatest weakness of the Russian privatization program was that "the distribution of wealth which emerged was so unequal." Identify the reasons for this outcome of the pro-gram. What, if anything, could have been done differently to avoid this?

References

Aguilar, Linda M., and Mike A. Singer. "Big Emerging Markets and U.S. Trade." *Economic Perspectives*, July/August 1995, pp. 2–13.

Alexander, David, and Simon Archer. *European Accounting Guide*, 4th ed. New York: Aspen Publishers, Inc., 2001.

Allen, Michael. "Pro and Con." *The Wall Street Journal*, 2 October 1995, pp. R27–28.

_____. "What Is Privatization, Anyway?" *The Wall Street Journal*, 2 October 1995, p. R4.

_____, and Jeanne Whalen. "Ukraine Corruption Probe Finds Huge Funds Transfer." *The Wall Street Journal*, 19 November 1999, pp. A16, A18.

Arora, Vasantha. "Communist Basu Turns Realist for Dollars." *India-West*, 30 June 1995.

Barrett, Amy. "It's a Small (Business) World." *Business Week*, 17 April 1995, pp. 96–101.

Baydoun, N., and R. Willett. "Cultural Relevance of Western Accounting Systems to Developing Countries." *ABACUS*, March 1995, pp. 67–92.

Becker, Gary S. "Rule No. 1 in Switching to Capitalism: Move Fast." *Business Week*, 29 May 1995, p. 18.

Behar, Richard. "Russia: Capitalism in a Cold Climate." *Fortune*, 12 June 2000, pp. 194–216.

Clifford, Mark L. "Taiwan: The Hazards for Chen Aren't Just across the Straits." *Business Week*, 29 May 2000, p. 66.

Cohen, Jeffrey R., Laurie W. Pant, and David J. Sharp. "Culture-Based Ethical Conflicts Confronting Multinational Accounting Firms." *Accounting Horizons*, September 1993, pp. 1–13.

Coleman, Linda Jane, and Elizabeth Beaulieu. "Marketing in Russia: A Problem or Opportunity?" *Journal of East-West Business*, vol. 4 (4), 1999, pp. 69–80.

Danziger, Elizabeth. "Overnight to India." *Journal of Accountancy*, June 2000, pp. 57–59.

Dawson, Margaret. "Two Tigers Sharpen Up Their Markets." *Business Week*, 24 October 1994, pp. 50–51.

Deloitte Touche Tohmatsu. *Taxation in Central and Eastern Europe: International Tax and Business Guide*. New York: Deloitte Touche Tohmatsu International, 1999.

Eddy, Kester. "Big Changes on the Hungarian Road to Capitalism." *Financial Times*, 3 August 2000, p. 5.

_____. "Central and Eastern Europe: East Has Cultural Lessons for the West." *Financial Times*, 24 April 2000, p. 14.

"Emerging Economies: Let the Good Times Roll." *The Economist*, 15 April 2000, pp. 76–78.

Ernst & Young. *Doing Business in Hungary. International Business Series*. New York: Ernst & Young International, 1996.

_____. *Doing Business in Russia. International Business Series*. New York: Ernst & Young International, 1998.

Fairlamb, David, Dawn Smith, and Christopher Condon. "How Far, How Fast? Is Central Europe Ready to Join the EU?" *Business Week*, 8 November 1999, pp. 64–66.

"GE's Brave New World." *Business Week*, 8 November 1993, pp. 64–70.

Glasgall, William, Dave Lindorff, Drusilla Menaker, Ian Katz, Elisabeth Malkin, and Bill Javetski. "Global Investing." *Business Week*, 11 September 1995, pp. 68–78.

Gray, R.H. *Accounting for the Environment*. London: Paul Chapman Publishing Ltd., 1993.

_____, and K.J. Bebbington. "Accounting Environment and Sustainability." *Business Strategy and the Environment*, Summer (Part 2), 1993, pp. 1–11.

Hurt, Harry III. "It's Time to Get Real About Mexico." *Fortune*, 4 September 1995, pp. 98–106.

"India Plans End to Protectionism." *Gulf News* (United Arab Emirates), 26 August 1995, p. 21.

Katz, Ian. "It's Tougher to Do Business in Brazil. That's Good." *Business Week*, 15 November 1999, p. 62.

Kemp, Peter, and David Alexander. "Accountancy and Financial Infrastructure in Central and Eastern European Countries." *IFAC Quarterly*, April 1997, pp. 4–5.

KPMG Peat Marwick. *International Survey of Environmental Reporting*. London: KPMG National Environment Unit, 1993.

Kraar, Louis. "Indonesia: The Corrupt Archipelago." *Fortune*, 24 July 2000, pp. 200–204.

Kripalani, Manjeet, and Mark L. Clifford. "Electronics: India Wired." *Business Week*, 6 March 2000, pp. 82–91.

Macve, R., and A. Carey, eds. *Business, Accountancy and the Environment: A Policy and Research Agenda*. London: Institute of Chartered Accountants in England and Wales, 1992.

Madhavmohan, V.K. "Reforms Must Address Disparity in Incomes." *India-West*, 7 April 1995, pp. 4–6.

Maltby, J. "Review of 'Environmental Auditing and the Role of the Accounting Profession.'" *Accounting and Business Research*, Winter 1993.

Mankiw, N. Gregory. "Ukraine: How Not To Run An Economy." *Fortune*, 12 June 2000, pp. 46–58.

Matthews, M.R. *Socially Responsible Accounting*. London: Chapman and Hall, 1993.

Miller, Karen Lowry. "The Worst Is Finally Over in Eastern Germany." *Business Week*, 19 June 1995, p. 54.

Moore, Jonathan, and Bruce Einhorn. "Asia: A Business-To-Business E-Boom." *Business Week*, 25 October 1999, p. 62.

Moshavi, Sharon, Pete Engardio, Shekhar Hattangadi, and Dave Lindorff. "India Shakes Off Its Shackles." *Business Week*, 30 January 1995, pp. 48–49.

Multinational Investments in Emerging Markets. New York: Ernst & Young, 1994.

Nakarmi, Laxmi, Joan Warner, and Margaret Dawson. "Two Tigers Sharpen Up Their Markets." *Business Week*, 24 October 1994, pp. 50–51.

Neff, Robert, Michael Shari, Joyce Barnathan, Margaret Dawson, and Edith Updike. "Japan's New Identity." *Business Week*, 10 April 1995, pp. 108–114.

Nowak, Jan, and Josef Pöschl. "An Assessment of Progress in Transition, Economic Performance, and Market Attractiveness of CEFTA Countries." *Journal of East-West Business*, vol. 4 (4), 1999, pp. 27–48.

Owen, D., ed. *Green Reporting*. London: Chapman and Hall, 1992.

Palmer, Brian. "What the Chinese Want." *Fortune*, 11 October 1999, pp. 229–234.

Power, Christopher, Rose Brady, Joyce Barnathan, and Karen Lowry Miller. "Second Thoughts on Going Global." *Business Week*, 13 March 1995, pp. 48–49.

PricewaterhouseCoopers. *Doing Business and Investing in the Czech Republic: Information Guide*. New York: PricewaterhouseCoopers, 1999.

_____. *Doing Business and Investing in Poland: Information Guide*. New York: PricewaterhouseCoopers, 2000.

Riahi-Belkaoui, Ahmed. *Accounting in the Developing Countries*. London: Quorum Books, 1994.

Roberts, Dexter. "China's Wealth Gap." *Business Week*, 15 May 2000, pp. 172–180.

Rohwer, Jim. "Asia's Economy: A Precarious Balancing Act." *Fortune*, 26 June 2000, pp. 210–218.

Rosett, Claudia, and Steve Liesman. "Starting from Scratch." *The Wall Street Journal*, 2 October 1995, pp. R14–R15.

Rossant, John. "Europe Ten Years Later . . ." *Business Week*, 8 November 1999, pp. 57–61.

Sachs, Jeffrey D. "Life after Communism." *The Wall Street Journal*, 17 November 1999, p. A22.

Salter, S.B., and F. Niswander. "Cultural Influence on the Development of Accounting Systems Internationally: A Test of Gray's [1988] Theory." *Journal of International Business Studies*, vol. 26, no. 2 (1995), pp. 379–397.

Saudagaran, S.M., and G.C. Biddle. "Foreign Listing Location: A Study of MNCs and Stock Exchanges in Eight Countries." *Journal of International Business Studies*, vol. 26, no. 2, pp. 319–341.

Sherry, Gerald, and Russell Vinning. "Accounting for Perestroika." *Management Accounting*, April 1995, pp. 42–46.

Starobin, Paul, and Sabrina Tavernise. "Russia: Will Putin Crack Down?" *Business Week*, 3 April 2000, pp. 54–56.

Stead, W.E., and J.G. Stead. *Management for a Small Planet*. Newbury Park, Calif.: Sage, 1992.

Suzman, Mark. "Deal With Corruption or Risk Losing Aid, US Tells Moscow." *Financial Times*, 17 September 1999, p. 1.

United Nations Conference on Trade and Development, Programme on Transnational Corporations. *Accounting, Valuation, and Privatization*. New York: United Nations, 1993.

Wallace, R., S. Olesegun, John M. Samuels, and Richard J. Briston. *Research in Third World Accounting: A Research Annual*, vol. 1. London: Jai Press Ltd., 1990.

Warner, Melanie. "The Indians of Silicon Valley." *Fortune*, 15 May 2000, pp. 356–372.

Whalen, Jeanne. "BP Amoco Loses Stake in Russian Oil to Small Rival." *The Wall Street Journal*, 29 November 1999, pp. A20.

_____, and Bhushan Bahree. "How Siberian Oil Field Turned into a Minefield: BP Amoco Learns Bruising Lessons on Investing in Russia." *The Wall Street Journal*, 9 February 2000, p. A21.

Winkle, Gary M., H. Fenwick Huss, and Chen Xi-Zhu. "Accounting Standards in the People's Republic of China: Responding to Economic Reforms." *Accounting Horizons*, September 1994, pp. 48–57.

Glossary

A

accounting exposures The transaction and translation risk exposures.

accounting principles *See* Accounting standards.

Accounting Principles Board Opinion No. 15 A standard issued by the Accounting Principles Board in the U.S. that outlines all the factors pertinent to the computation of earnings per common share.

accounting standards The rules that govern the measuring and recording of economic activities and the reporting of accounting information to external users.

accrual accounting rate of return (AARR) method A capital budgeting method that reports accounting income using the accrual basis.

activity-based costing (ABC) An approach to costing that focuses on activities as the fundamental cost objects. It uses the cost of these activities as the basis for assigning costs to other cost objects such as products, services, or customers. It provides more accurate allocation of indirect costs than traditional methods.

activity-based management (ABM) A discipline that focuses on the management of activities for improving the value received by the customer and the profit achieved by providing this value.

activity ratios *See* Efficiency ratios.

advance pricing agreement An agreement between a company and tax authorities that gives the company approval for using certain transfer pricing methods and the procedures for its application.

advanced determination ruling (ADR) A transfer pricing guideline in the U.S. that allows a company to get approval for a parent-subsidiary specific product pricing.

allowances for deferred income tax assets A contra account to the deferred income tax assets account.

American Institute of Certified Public Accountants (AICPA) An organization that issues the gener-

ally accepted auditing standards in the form of Statements on Auditing Standards in the United States.

arbitrage An activity done to take advantage of rate discrepancies by buying the currency in the low-cost markets and selling in the high-cost markets.

Asia-Pacific Economic Cooperation (APEC) An organization committed to the trade and investment concept of open regionalism. Its 20-member countries include Australia, Brunei, Canada, Chile, China (including Hong Kong), Indonesia, Japan, Korea, Malaysia, Mexico, New Zealand, Papua New Guinea, Peru, Philippines, Russia, Singapore, Chinese Taipei, Thailand, U.S.A., and Vietnam.

asset-and-liability approach The recognition of deferred tax liabilities or deferred tax assets for the income tax that will be levied or recovered on temporary timing differences between the taxable income amount and the pretax financial income amount.

associated firms. *See* Representative firms.

Association of Southeast Asian Nations (ASEAN) The most important trading bloc in Southeast Asia. The member countries include Brunei, Cambodia, Indonesia, Laos, Malaysia, Myanmar, the Philippines, Singapore, Thailand, and Vietnam. The member countries plan to establish a free-trade area by 2003.

auditor's report A report that communicates the results of the external audit, and the format of the report is necessarily mandated by the nature of the audit. Since there are no worldwide uniform accounting and auditing standards, there is no worldwide uniform format of an auditor's report.

B

balance of payments deficit When a country's cumulative imports exceed its cumulative exports.

balance of payments surplus When a country's cumulative exports exceed its cumulative imports.

balance sheet recognition Information presented within the balance sheet.

Balassa-Samuelson Theory A theory that states inflation is difficult to get rid of in a fast-growing economy.

Big Five Public accounting firms that have the capability to perform external audits in different parts of the world. The Big Five accounting firms include Andersen, KPMG Peat Marwick, Deloitte Touche Tohmatsu, Ernst & Young, and PricewaterhouseCoopers.

Bilan Social (social report) A required report in France. It contains mainly employee-related information covering topics such as pay structure, hiring policies, health and safety conditions, training, and industrial relations.

bilateral advance pricing agreement When the multinational company receives the approval of proposed transfer pricing approaches from tax authorities of two countries.

budget The translation of corporate plans into financial terms.

business report A report that covers many of the matters typically found in the Management Discussion and Analysis part of companies' annual reports in North America.

C

capital budgeting The process of identifying, evaluating, and planning long-term investment decisions.

capital lease A lease treated as a purchase of property by the lessee.

capital structure ratios *See* Coverage ratios.

centralized internal audit model In this type of organization, there is only one central internal audit organization that is located at the headquarters of the parent company. The internal auditors travel to various parts of the world where operations are located to perform internal audit, and to perform other functions such as quality control, audit research, liaison with external auditors, training, and technical support.

centralized multinational organizations Organizations that retain to a great extent the authority to make decisions at parent company headquarters.

certified internal auditor (CIA) A certification program sponsored by the Institute of Internal Auditors consisting of an examination and a mandatory two years of practical experience in internal auditing before certification.

certified public accountant (CPA) The professional designation for public accountants and independent (external) auditors in the United States and some other countries.

classic system A national tax system that subjects income to taxes when income is received by the taxable entity.

collectivism The feeling that interests of the organization should have top priority.

comarketing agreement Two or more companies who share the risks and rewards of long-term marketing programs.

consistency principle A requirement that accounting methods be used consistently from one period to the next unless conditions have changed that make it appropriate to switch to another method to provide more useful information.

consolidated financial statements The statements prepared by the parent company that essentially portray the financial position and results of operations of the parent and its subsidiaries as though they were one economic unit.

constant dollar accounting *See* Constant monetary unit restatement.

constant monetary unit restatement A general term for restating historical cost basis financial statements for changes in general purchasing power of the monetary unit.

control system A system that compares the actual performance (results) with planned performance (goals) so that management may take appropriate action as necessary.

convenience translation Translation of currency using the year-end exchange rates.

conversion value The equivalent amount of another currency at a given exchange rate.

copromotion agreement A product that is promoted jointly by two companies under the same brand name and marketing plan. Generally the manufacturing company handles receivables, inventory, and so on and pays a commission to the copromotor. Compensation is almost always based on the product sales level.

correspondent firms *See* Representative firms.

cost-based transfer pricing The price one segment of a company charges another segment of the same company for the transfer of a good or a service based on some type of cost. Examples include variable manufacturing costs, full manufacturing (absorption) costs, and full product costs.

cost center A responsibility center in which a manager is accountable for costs only.

cost driver Any factor that causes a change in the cost of an activity.

cost object Any customer, product, service, project, or other work unit for which a separate cost measurement is desired.

coverage ratios Ratios that measure the degree of protection for long-term creditors and investors.

cross-currency swap An agreement by two parties to exchange their liabilities or assets in different currencies.

currency options contract A contract giving one of the parties the right to decide in the future whether an exchange will actually take place at a certain price.

currency swap An agreement to exchange two different currencies at an agreed exchange rate.

current cost accounting *See* Current value accounting.

current exchange rate The exchange rate on the balance sheet date.

current-noncurrent method A translation method in which balance sheet items classified as "current" are translated at the current exchange rate on the balance sheet date, and items classified as "noncurrent" are translated at appropriate historical rates.

current purchasing power accounting *See* Constant monetary unit restatement.

current rate method A translation method that translates all assets and all liabilities at the current exchange rate—the rate on the balance sheet date. Paid-in capital accounts are translated at the applicable historical rates, dividends at the exchange rate on the date of declaration and on the income statement, and all revenue and expense items at the weighted average exchange rate for the period.

current value accounting Valuation systems designed to show the effects of changes in prices of individual items on financial statements.

customer-centric companies Companies that set explicit targets for retaining customers and make extraordinary efforts to exceed their customer loyalty goals.

D

debt capital Capital that is financed by borrowing.

decentralized internal audit model In this type of organization, the internal auditors are on locations throughout the world, wherever international operations are located. Each international operation has its own internal audit organization.

decentralized multinational organizations Organizations that give managements of the subsidiaries considerable independence of action.

deferred income tax asset The future tax benefits from earnings that have already been taxed but have not been reported in the income statement yet.

deferred income tax liability The future tax liability that results from current or past periods' earnings that have already been reported in the financial statements but have not been taxed yet.

derivative A contract whose market value fluctuates in direct proportion to fluctuations in the market value of a commodity or a financial instrument or a foreign currency.

direct-financing lease. A lease where the lessor provides financing only, and assumes financial risks but does not assume inventory risk.

direct investment Establishing operations in a country.

disclosure Financial statements.

downsizing The elimination of jobs due to reengineering.

E

earnings flexibility *See* Income smoothing.

economic exposure A condition that results from the impact of changes in exchange rates on future cash flows.

economic risk The uncertainty surrounding key elements of the investment process.

efficiency ratios Ratios that measure how effectively the enterprise is using the assets employed.

The Eighth Directive The EU Eighth Directive deals with auditing of financial statements of companies in EU countries, and specifies that they be consistent with EU law. It also sets qualifications for auditors and the firms conducting audits, including education and experience requirements. In addition, the Directive deals with ethical matters such as independence, and includes sanctions for cases in which audits are not conducted as prescribed by statute.

environment-specific An accounting system designed to provide information for making decisions in a given environment. Five major environmental influences on accounting consist of the economic system, political system, legal system, educational system, and religion.

equity capital Capital that is financed by shares (stocks).

equity method A method in which income of a subsidiary is recognized by the parent company according to ownership percentage. The investment in the subsidiary account balance is adjusted accordingly.

equity reserves A general term to describe many different types of reserves that serve different purposes.

European Confederation of Institutes of Internal Auditing This organization, comprised of 17 internal audit organizations representing 18 European nations plus Israel, helps in the development of internal auditing standards.

European Union (EU) A single trading block currently linking 15 European nations into a single market in order to eliminate tariff and custom restrictions. The 15 nations include Austria, Belgium, Denmark, Finland, France, Germany, Great Britain, Greece, Ireland, Italy, Luxembourg, Netherlands, Portugal, Spain, and Sweden.

European Union directives Rules issued by the European Union. These are binding on member countries.

exchange rate The amount of one currency needed to obtain one unit of another currency.

exit measurement *See* Output price measurement.

expense liability reserves An equity reserve used to achieve income smoothing or to show a steady growth in income from year to year.

external failure costs The costs of a defective product after it is shipped to the customer.

F

facilitating payments Payments made to influence an official to take an action that the official must take anyway.

factors of production A firm's inputs, such as costs for labor, materials, machines, and buildings that are necessary for bringing the good to the market.

femininity The quality of life, nurturing, and relationships.

finance lease *See* Capital lease.

financial accounting A component of an organization's internal accounting system that provides information primarily for users outside the organization.

Financial Accounting Standards Board (FASB) The main body responsible for promulgating accounting standards in the United States.

financial ratio analysis An evaluation of financial performance and financial position between two or more firms.

financial reporting disclosures The information presented in financial statements. Such disclosures may be either within the statements or in the accompanying notes.

financial statement analysis The conversion of the data in financial statements into useful information.

fixed rate currency Currency with a fixed rate of exchange within narrow limits against a major currency, such as the U.S. dollar or the British pound.

floating rate currency Currency whose exchange rate is determined by market forces.

footnote disclosure Information contained in a note accompanying the financial statements.

Foreign Corrupt Practices Act (FCPA) An act passed by the U.S. Congress in 1977 and revised in 1988 intended to curb influence peddling.

foreign currency forward contract An agreement with a currency trader, e.g., a bank, to deliver in the future one currency for another at an agreed-upon "forward" exchange rate.

foreign currency transactions Transactions denominated in a currency other than the reporting currency of the entity.

foreign currency translation A conversion of amounts in accounts of international subsidiaries (recorded in a foreign currency) to the currency used for consolidated financial statements.

foreign exchange risk management The management of the risk of loss from currency exchange rate movements on transactions, translation, or remeasurement involving foreign currency.

forward exchange contract An agreement to buy (or sell) a foreign currency in the future at a fixed rate called a forward rate.

forward rate The fixed future rate used in a forward exchange contract.

The Fourth Directive The EU Fourth Directive contains comprehensive accounting rules relevant to corporate accounting. It covers financial statements, their contents, methods of presentation, valuation methods, and disclosure of information.

free market economic system An economic concept used to denote the economic system of a country unimpeded by government restrictions, and ideally subject to the laws of supply and demand of the market.

functional currency The currency of the primary environment in which the international subsidiary operates.

G

gearing adjustment A gearing adjustment equals the average borrowing divided by average operating assets multiplied by total current value adjustments for cost of goods sold, depreciation, etc. It shows the benefit (or disadvantage) to shareholders from debt financing during a period of changing prices. The amount of gearing adjustment is added (deducted) to current cost income.

general price index An index used to estimate the amount of inflation or deflation in an economy.

general price-level accounting *See* Constant monetary unit restatement.

general reserve An equity reserve that normally serves the same purpose as an appropriation of retained earnings, i.e., it temporarily restricts the maximum amount that can be declared for dividends.

generally accepted accounting principles (GAAP) Accounting principals in the U.S. that are recognized by a standard-setting body or by authoritative support.

global International or worldwide.

global capital markets Capital markets in a global economy that attract investors and investees from throughout the world.

going concern concept The accounting concept that an economic entity will continue in operation for the foreseeable future.

goodwill The amount paid by the buyer of a business for above-normal profits.

H

harmonization Keeping the differences among national accounting standards to a minimum. Alternative accounting rules or practices may exist in different countries as long as they are "in harmony" with one another and can be reconciled.

hedging Measures taken to protect against risks associated with foreign exchange fluctuations.

high power distance culture A state in which a person at a higher position in the organizational hierarchy makes the decision and the employees at the lower levels simply follow the instructions.

historical cost convention A method of accounting using data in terms of the units of currency in which a transaction originally took place.

I

idle capacity The unused capacity of a selling segment that is not needed for producing products or services to meet demand from the external market.

imperfect market A market where factors of production are somewhat immobile.

imperfect market theory A firm engages in international trade to gain access to factors of production.

income leveling *See* Income smoothing.

income smoothing Use of reserves to transfer income between periods.

indirect investment Buying equity or debt securities originating from a country as investments.

individualism The trait in which the employee attaches higher importance to personal and family interests than to the organization.

inflation accounting. Accounting to cope with changing price levels.

influence peddling Providing monetary or nonmonetary benefits to a person in a position of authority in exchange for an action by that person that benefits the company—normally an action that would not have been taken without the monetary or nonmonetary benefit.

input price measurement A current value is assigned to an item on the basis of its replacement cost.

Institute of Internal Auditors (IIA) The most influential international organization in the development of internal auditing standards. It was established in 1941.

integrated international operation A foreign operation whose economic activities have a direct impact on the reporting (parent) entity.

integrated system A national tax system that attempts to eliminate double taxation by taxing corporate income differently depending on whether it is distributed to shareholders.

internal auditing An objective evaluation of operations and control systems of an organization to determine whether its policies and procedures are being followed, and also whether its resources are safeguarded and used efficiently to achieve organizational objectives.

internal failure costs The costs incurred when a defective product is detected before it is shipped to customers.

international *See* Global.

international accounting Accounting for international transactions, comparisons of accounting principles in different countries, harmonization of diverse accounting standards worldwide, and accounting information for the management and control of global operations.

International Accounting Standard (IAS) An accounted rule developed by the International Accounting Standards Committee in order to harmonize accounting standards worldwide.

international corporation A company that exports its products overseas.

International Federation of Accountants (IFAC) An organization engaged in efforts to harmonize auditing standards worldwide.

International Organization of Securities Commission (IOSCO) A private organization of securities market regulators that promotes the integration of securities markets worldwide. Currently, it is working with the IASC to develop a core set of accounting standards by 1999 that will be acceptable for listing in securities markets worldwide.

International Standards on Auditing (ISA) A comprehensive set of auditing standards issued by the International Federation of Accountants. Audits conducted in accordance with these standards can be relied on by securities regulatory authorities for multinational reporting purposes.

intervention An action taken by the central bank of a country to influence the exchange rate of its currency in the market.

investment center A responsibility center where the manager is responsible for costs, revenues, profits, and investment in assets.

J

just-in-time A production system in which materials are purchased and goods are produced when needed to meet actual customer demand.

K

kaizen A budgeting approach that projects costs on the basis of continuous improvements rather than current practices and methods.

L

labor productivity A measure of the relationship between workers' hours and the actual output produced.

large power distance culture The culture where a person at a higher position in the organizational hierarchy makes the decisions, and the employees at the lower levels simply follow the instructions.

lease A contract between a lessor and a lessee that gives the lessee the right to use specific property owned by the lessor, for a given time period, in exchange for cash or other consideration—typically a commitment to make future cash payments.

leverage ratios *See* Coverage ratios.

licensing program Proprietary information, such as patent rights or expertise, that is licensed by the owner (licenser) to another party (licensee). Compensation paid to the licenser usually includes license issuance fees, milestone payments, and/or royalties.

liquidity ratios Ratios that measure the enterprise's short-run ability to pay its maturing obligations.

long-term orientation The adaptation of traditions to meet current needs.

low power distance culture A state in which employees perceive few power differences and follow a superior's instructions only when either they agree or feel threatened.

M

managed earnings *See* Income smoothing.

managerial accounting (or management accounting) A component of an organization's internal accounting system that provides financial and nonfinancial information used by managers and others within the organization for use in planning, controlling, and decision making.

market-based transfer pricing The price one segment of a company charges another segment of the same company for the transfer of a good or a service based on its current market price.

masculinity The relative importance of the qualities associated with men such as assertiveness and materialism.

master operating budget A plan for achieving the corporate goals for a period of time (normally one year).

materiality concept This concept, requiring use of professional judgment, describes information that must be included or disclosed to prevent financial statements from misleading their users.

measurement Recording economic transactions in the accounting system.

monetary items All assets and liabilities expressed in fixed amounts of currency.

monetary-nonmonetary method A translation method that restates monetary items on the balance sheet at the current exchange rate on the balance sheet date and nonmonetary items at their historical exchange rates.

multinational corporation (MNC) A company that considers the globe as a single marketplace.

multinational enterprise (MNE) *See* Multinational corporation.

N

negative exposure A condition that exists when a foreign subsidiary has more current liabilities than current assets.

negotiated transfer pricing A system that requires managers of selling and buying divisions to negotiate a mutually acceptable transfer price.

nepotism Relatives of those in power tend to easily obtain business licenses, lucrative government contracts, real estate deals, etc.

net present value (NPV) The difference between the initial investment and the net present value of expected future net cash inflows.

net realizable value The disposal value of an item less the related disposal costs.

new economy High productivity and low inflation.

nonmonetary item An item that does not represent a claim to, or for, a specified number of monetary units.

nonroutine reports Reports prepared for the purpose of providing information to managers to assist them in formulating policies, preparing strategic plans, and preparing tactical (operational) plans.

North American Free Trade Agreement (NAFTA) A trade agreement among Canada, Mexico, and the U.S. with the objective of creating a single market with no trade barriers.

O

one-transaction approach An approach used to translate foreign currency where the transaction is not considered to be completed until the final settlement. Any transaction gain or loss will be reflected on the settlement date in an adjustment to the value of the resource acquired.

open regionalism The use of declarations instead of treaties to combine an informal regional trading strategy with a commitment to global openness.

operating leases A lease where the lessor retains most of the risks and rewards of ownership; commonly referred to as rentals.

operational plans Nonroutine plans that are designed to implement strategic plans.

opportunity costs per unit The contribution margin per unit sacrificed by the selling segment due to the internal transfer of one unit of the good or service, rather than selling it in the external market.

Organization for Economic Cooperation and Development (OECD) An organization that promotes worldwide economic development in general, and economic growth and stability of its member countries in particular. Its work focuses primarily on providing financial accounting and reporting guidelines to multinational corporations for disclosures to host countries.

output price measurement The current value of an item equals its net realizable value.

P

parent The company acquiring the stock of a subsidiary.

parent/subsidiary relationship A combination of companies where control of other companies, known as subsidiaries, is achieved by a company, known as the parent, through acquisition of voting stock.

participatory design approach The design of the information system where all users must be actively involved.

payback period (PBP) method A capital budgeting method that measures the time it will take to recoup, in the form of net cash inflows, the net dollars invested in a project.

performance report A routine report that compares actual performance against budgetary goals.

permanent differences Differences that are caused by certain types of revenues that are exempted from taxation and certain types of expenses that are not deductible for tax purposes.

political risk The actions and activities of foreign (host) governments directed at multinational corporations.

pooling of interests method An accounting method used for a business combination where the acquired entity's assets and equities are combined at book value. No goodwill is created in a pooling of interests.

portfolio approach A method used to manage economic exposure of a company by offsetting negative exposure in one country with positive exposure in another.

positive exposure A condition that exists when a foreign subsidiary has more current assets than current liabilities.

power distance The extent of inequality between superiors and subordinates.

privatization The transfer of property from the state to individuals and private enterprises.

product cycle theory A firm's progression from its domestic markets to international markets with exports being the entry point in international trade.

productivity The output per hour of workers' time.

profit center A responsibility center where the manager is responsible for both revenues and costs.

profitability ratios Ratios that measure the degree of success or failure of an enterprise or division for a given period of time.

proposal for appropriation of retained earnings A report prepared for approval at the stockholders' meeting for dividend payments and bonus payments to members of the board of directors and statutory auditors.

prudence concept The concept that provision be made for all known liabilities and losses whether the amount is known with certainty or not.

purchase method An accounting method used for a business combination where the acquired entity's assets and equities are combined at fair market value. Goodwill is created to the extent that cost exceeds the fair market value of the identifiable assets of the unit acquired.

purchasing power gain A gain that arises from holding monetary items during times when the general purchasing power of the monetary unit changes.

purchasing power loss A loss that arises from holding monetary items during times when the general purchasing power of the monetary unit changes.

R

realized gains Gains that are actually incurred.

realized losses Losses that are actually incurred.

reengineering The configuration of the internal processes, products, and employees so that essential operating activities are performed effectively and efficiently. All non-essential activities and tasks are eliminated, thereby reducing costs.

regional audit staff internal audit model In this type of organization, the regional staff is responsible for performing audits in all of the operations in the region. This model has recently been gaining popularity among many multinationals.

regular reports Reports that assist managers in planning activities and controlling operations.

rental A type of lease in which the lessor retains not only legal title, but most of the risks and rewards of ownership.

replacement cost The total cost to acquire another item that would perform the functions identical to those performed by an existing item.

representative firms Locally owned accounting firms that have agreements with a Big Five or some other accounting firm. The agreement covers areas such as standards of performance and standards of conduct.

research and development costs The direct and indirect outlays for exploring potential new products and developing new products.

research collaboration Two or more companies that participate in a defined research program and benefit from the results. Research costs can be funded entirely by one of the parties, shared equally by the parties, or shared according to some other agreed-upon proportion.

resident staff and central reviewers internal audit model In this type of organization, the resident internal auditors located on site perform the audit work. Their work is periodically reviewed by the traveling members of the parent company's central internal audit staff.

resident staff and regional and central reviewers internal auditing model In this type of organization, the resident staff conducts the internal audits. Regional reviewers, responsible for certain geographical areas, oversee their work to ensure compliance with the parent company policies. The central staff from headquarters makes periodic reviews to ensure reporting uniformity throughout all the regions.

resident staff and regional reviewers internal audit model In this type of organization, the work of the resident internal auditors is reviewed by the regional reviewers to ensure uniformity. Independent review from regional staff also enhances the degree of reliability of the reports.

residual income (RI) RI expresses performance in the form of a profit amount that is left after the cost of invested capital has been subtracted.

return on assets (ROA) ROA equals net income divided by total assets.

return on investment (ROI) ROI incorporates the investment base and profits to assess performance.

revaluation reserve An equity reserve used to value fixed assets at an appraised value or a replacement value. This is done by upward adjustment of the asset and correspondingly recording an equal amount in a revaluation reserve.

revenue center A responsibility center in which a manager is accountable for revenues only.

rightsizing *See* Downsizing.

risk management The identification of threats and the design of an approach to their containment.

routine reporting Reports that enable managers to plan activities and control operations.

Rules of Professional Conduct A section in the American Institute of Certified Public Accountants' Code of Professional Conduct that contains rules that govern the performance of professional services and identify both acceptable and unacceptable behavior.

S

sales-type lease In the U.S., a type of capital lease where a dealer's or manufacturer's profit or loss is a basic part of the transaction for the lessor.

secondary statement approach A complete set of financial statements including accompanying notes prepared according to the accounting standards of another country. Independent auditors express an opinion on secondary statements using the auditing standards of that country.

selective restatements Partial restatements of companies' reports used to help resolve the problems created by diversity in accounting standards throughout the world.

self-sustaining international operation A foreign operation whose activities generally have no direct impact on the reporting entity's operations.

settlement date The date when payment of funds is made on the maturity of a foreign exchange contract.

The Seventh Directive The EU Seventh Directive addresses consolidated financial statement issues.

short-term orientation Values that respect tradition, personal stability, quick results from the efforts made, and concern with appearances.

six sigma quality 3.4 defects per million units processed.

small power distance culture A culture where employees perceive few power differences and follow a superior's instructions only when they either agree or feel threatened.

solvency ratios *See* Liquidity ratios.

special reports Reports that help managers formulate policies, prepare strategic plans, and prepare operational plans.

specific price index An index that shows the price changes for a specific good or service over time.

spot rate The rate quoted for current currency transactions.

stakeholders The users of financial reports.

standardization Full comparability of accounting information.

Statement of Financial Accounting Standards No. 52 A U.S. foreign currency standard issued by the Financial Accounting Standards Board acknowledging that the functional currency of an entity is the currency of the primary environment in which the entity operates.

Statements on Auditing Standards (SAS) Standards issued by the American Institute of Certified Public Accountants in the U.S. concerning generally accepted auditing standards.

statutory merger One company acquires the net assets of another company or companies.

statutory (legal) reserve An equity reserve required by several countries to provide additional protection to creditors.

strategic alliance A firm's collaboration with companies in other countries to share rights and responsibilities as well as revenues and expenses as defined in a written agreement. Some common types of strategic alliances include research collaboration, a licensing program, and a copromotion deal.

strategic plan A plan that integrates an organization's major goals, policies, and action sequences into a cohesive whole.

strategic planning The process of deciding on the goals of the organization and the strategies for attaining these goals.

subsidiary The company whose voting stock is acquired by a parent company to exercise control over it.

T

target costing A costing method that sets cost targets for new products based on market price.

tax credit The reduction of a tax liability by an amount equal to the amount of the tax credit.

tax holiday The period of time during which a foreign investor is exempted from taxes.

taxable income The income amount on which tax is levied.

temporal method A currency translation method in which translation is viewed as a restatement of the financial statements. The foreign currency amounts are translated at the exchange rates in effect at the dates when those items were measured in the foreign currency.

territorial approach A national tax system that only taxes domestic income.

theory of comparative advantage Each country should produce only those goods and services that it can produce with relative efficiency.

thin capitalization The set of taxation issues from a host government's perspective, arising from the perceived imbalance between debt capital and equity capital when a foreign investor is financing a business operation in the country.

trading blocs Free trade zones created by member countries through mutual agreements.

transaction risk exposure A condition that is caused by the changes in the exchange rate between the transaction date and the settlement date.

transfer price The price one segment of a company charges another segment of the same company for the transfer of a good or a service.

transnational corporation (TNC) The term favored by the United Nations as an alternative to the term *multinational corporation*.

trend analysis A financial analysis that provides intrafirm as well as interfirm comparisons for two or more periods or dates.

true and fair view A British concept of what financial statements ought to convey and an important feature of the Fourth Directive. The implementation of this concept means that companies may be required to disclose additional or different information. Each country determines, based on its own circumstances, how its corporations should comply with the true and fair view concept.

turnover ratios *See* Efficiency ratios.

two-transaction approach An approach used to translate foreign currency where any gains or losses are separately recorded as gains or losses from exchange rate exchanges.

U

uncertainty acceptance The extent to which uncertainty is considered a normal part of life; feeling comfortable with ambiguity and unfamiliar risks.

uncertainty avoidance The extent to which uncertainty is avoided in a culture.

United Nations (UN) An organization representing governments of all countries in the world.

universal *See* Global.

unrealized (holding) gains Gains that are not yet actually incurred, for example, as a result of a foreign currency translation.

unrealized (holding) losses Losses that are not yet actually incurred, for example, as a result of a foreign currency translation.

V

value added Value added equals total revenue minus the cost of goods, materials, and services purchased externally.

value-added activities Activities that customers perceive as increasing the utility (usefulness) of the products or services they purchase.

value added statements Primarily used in European countries for the purpose of showing, in financial terms, the contributions made by many participating groups in the creation of wealth in a company.

value-added tax (VAT) A tax based on consumer spending.

variance The difference between actual performance and planned performance.

VAT concept A concept based on taxing each production activity or business activity that adds value to materials or goods purchased from other businesses.

W

worldwide approach A national tax system that subjects both domestic source and foreign source income to taxes.

Subject Index

Web Index